David J. Hoewes
Concordia College

STUDY GUIDE

Modern Economics

Jan Hogendorn

 PRENTICE HALL, Upper Saddle River, NJ 07458

Project Editor: *Joseph F. Tomasso*
Acquisitions Editor: *Leah Jewell*
Associate Editor: *Teresa Cohan*
Manufacturing Buyer: *Vincent Scelta*

 © 1995 by Prentice Hall, Inc.
A Simon & Schuster Company
Upper Saddle River, NJ 07458

All rights reserved. No part of this book may be
reproduced, in any form or by any means,
without permission in writing from the publisher.

Printed in the United States of America

10 9 8 7 6 5 4 3 2 1

ISBN 0-13-150590-4

Prentice-Hall International (UK) Limited, *London*
Prentice-Hall of Australia Pty. Limited, *Sydney*
Prentice-Hall Canada Inc., *Toronto*
Prentice-Hall Hispanoamericana, S.A., *Mexico*
Prentice-Hall of India Private Limited, *New Delhi*
Prentice-Hall of Japan, Inc., *Tokyo*
Simon & Schuster Asia Pte. Ltd., *Singapore*
Editora Prentice-Hall do Brasil, Ltda., *Rio de Janiero*

To Chris, Kim, and Sean

who are always seeking out new adventures

To Cheryl

whose indomitable spirit provides encouragement for others

and for her optimism

Table of Contents

PREFACE V

ACKNOWLEDGEMENTS VII

Part 1 — Introduction

Chapter 1	What is Economics?	1
Chapter 2	The Market System	25

Part 2 — Microeconomics

Chapter 3	Demand and Supply I: The Concept of Demnad	41
Chapter 4	Demand and Supply II: The Concept of Supply, the Market Mechanism	71
Chapter 5	When Government Intervenes	109
Chapter Six	Revenues and Costs of the Firm: and the Case of Perfect Competition	129
Chapter 7	Imperfect Markets I: Why They Exist and the Case of Monopoly	155
Chapter 8	Imperfect Markets II: Monopolistic Competition and Oligopoly	175
Chapter 9	Controlling Market Power Government Regulation and Antitrust Law	195
Chapter 10	Externalities: When Private and Social Costs and Benefits Diverge	215
Chapter 11	Factor Productivity and Income	245
Chapter 12	Wages, Rent, Interest, and Profit	267
Chapter 13	Income Distribution and Poverty	285

Part 3 — Macroeconomics

Chapter 14	An Introduction to Macroeconomics	299
Chapter 15	Measuring Economic Performance	313
Chapter 16	How the Level of Output is Determined: The Concept of Macroeconomic Equilibrium	337
Chapter 17	Pursuing the Fixed-Price (Keynesian) Analysis	361
Chapter 18	A Contemporary Model of Aggregate Supply and Aggregate Demand	389
Chapter 19	Money and the Banking System	407
Chapter 20	The Tools of Monetary Policy	431
Chapter 21	The Conduct of Monetary Policy	447
Chapter 22	Fiscal Policy: Taxation and Spending	461
Chapter 23	Deficits and Debt in a Modern Economy	479
Chapter 24	The Long Run: Stagflation and Long Term Unemployment	497
Chapter 25	Macroeconomic Innovation	517
Chapter 26	Economic Growth in Market Economies	531

Contents

Part 4 ■ International Economic Experience

Chapter 27   International Trade 547
Chapter 28   International Finance 569
Chapter 29   Reforming the Command Economies 591
Chapter 30   Economic Development of the LDCs 601

Preface

As the author of your text, Jan Hogendorn, mentions in his preface, his goal was to write a shorter, more condensed principles text, one which would not overwhelm beginning economics students -- a worthy and admirable goal. I have found it difficult to write a shorter study guide since there are so many questions and exercises that I think are essential in providing a good solid foundation in economic analysis. In spite of the length of this study guide, there are still many useful problems and questions which were excluded. As with everything, difficult choices had to be made, and priorities examined and reexamined.

Over the many years that I have taught principles of economics classes, I have found that the only effective way to learn economics is to do economics. It is not enough to just sit and listen to your instructor or to read your text. There is very little memorization involved in learning economics -- the emphasis is on comprehension. Students invariably ask me how many hours they should set aside for studying economics, and I can't answer that question. You have to work at it until there is an understanding of the material, and an ability to apply the economic concepts to new and different situations. For some, the time involved may not be all that long; for others, it could be considerable. Hopefully, you will find the study guide a useful, and user-friendly source of help as you begin your exploration of what I think is an exciting and relevant discipline.

I think the way to get the most out of the study guide is to read the text, and then attempt as many of the self examination exercises as you can. After you have checked your answers, you will have a much better idea of what topics and concepts need additional work and study.

Each chapter in the study guide has several components:

(1) A short overview of the chapter designed to help give you a feel for the chapter's main concepts. Reading the study guide's overview along with the objectives at the front of each chapter in the text as well as the summaries at the end of each of the text chapters should provide you with an excellent overview.

(2) A set of learning objectives follows which are more detailed than the ones listed in your text. Again, after reading both sets of objectives you should have a good basis for what you should learn in the chapter.

(3) The first task under the self-evaluation section is to select the most appropriate term for a series of statements. Each chapter of your text ends with definitions of key words which will be helpful in completing this part of the study guide.

(4) A problems section follows the list of terms. These problems are designed to illustrate a particular concept or help you understand how the concept can be used. I have tried to develop a set of problems that you will find both interesting and challenging. A number of these problems, particularly those related to the theory of the firm, the Keynesian model, and those problems that ask you to plot data of some kind, can be more efficiently solved using a spreadsheet program.

(5) A series of true/false questions follows the problems. As you know from other classes you have taken, true/false questions always seem to be a bit ambiguous, so each one is commented on in some depth in the answers section.

(6) No study guide would be complete without multiple-choice questions, and they comprise the last part of the self-examination part of each study guide chapter. My questions tend to be longer and probably more difficult than you might see in other study guides, and they will provide a test of your knowledge on a variety of economic concepts and theories.

(7) Following the multiple-choice questions, answers are provided for each of the self-examination sections.

(8) Each chapter ends with a brief summary of the chapter. Typically, although not always, the summary discusses some broader aspects of the economic concepts contained in the chapter.

Economics is perceived by many students as being a relatively difficult subject area. Both the text and the study guide are designed to help you gain an understanding of the basic concepts of economics in a shorter, more compact format than that found in many of the basic principles books. This should help you focus on the core of important concepts that we expect beginning economics students to grasp, with less potentially confusing detail and a bit less breadth of topics. One of the most important determinants of your success in the principles class will be the amount of time that you can devote to the study of economics. It requires a serious commitment of time and effort on your part to not only attend class, read the text, but in addition, complete the exercises in the study guide.

My time in the classroom has also taught me the value of student feedback. Perceptions differ considerably depending upon which side of the podium you are on. Please feel free to contact me at the Department of Business and Economics, Concordia College, Moorhead, Minnesota, 56562, about any aspect of the study guide. My e-mail address is moewes@gloria.cord.edu.

Acknowledgements

I was first informed about Jan Hogendorn's principles of economics textbook and the need for a study guide to accompany his text by Paul Nockleby. He provided the leadership and expertise to get the original Mayfield Publishing project going. Without him, I would not have been involved in writing the study guide. He has continued to provide counsel, and offer his publishing expertise to me as the project has continued. I am also indebted to Jan Hogendorn for his support in the early stages of this project. He also provided some valuable feedback on initial drafts of the study guide as did several other reviewers.

Students from my principles of economics classes have provided me with feedback on various chapters of the text, and there is simply no substitute for that kind of input.

Finally, I want to thank my family for their encouragement throughout this project. Writing the study guide has taken up much of my time for the last four years, and there have been many forgone family activities and projects. Now that this project is over, some of the things which have been postponed can be undertaken.

Chapter 1
What is Economics?

Overview of the Chapter

This chapter sets the stage for the entire book. Economics is defined in terms of making choices in an environment of scarcity and constraints and society's goal (and each individual's as well) is to try and attain the best or optimal alternative from those that are attainable at the time. Society's resource base (its set of factors of production) is classified into four basic categories: labor, land, physical and human capital, and entrepreneurship. A set of priorities (some kind of ranking system) is a necessity for choosing among the various alternatives that can be chosen. The study of economics can be broken down into two major categories -- macroeconomics and microeconomics. The former examines the performance and problems associated with the entire economic system, while the latter analyzes the individual decision-making units that make up the economy.

An initial economic model (the production possibilities model) is introduced which provides some useful insights into how societies answer the important economic question of "what bundle of goods and services should be produced." As simple and abstract as the model is, it will give you a better understanding of such important economic concepts as economic scarcity, opportunity cost, economic efficiency, and economic growth -- concepts that are fundamental to understanding what the discipline of economics is all about.

The concept of an economic model is developed. Economic models are used to explain and predict phenomena, and four desirable criteria are presented which can be used to evaluate economic models. The concept of *ceteris paribus* is introduced -- which allows economists to assume that all the other factors which affect a variable or situation being studied are held constant so we can focus on just one variable without having to be concerned about other factors also changing. Without the assumption of *ceteris paribus*, economists would have difficulty in analyzing complex real world events and determining cause and effect.

The role of values in economic theory and analysis is also discussed. It is vitally important that you be able to recognize the difference between positive economic theory (value free) and normative economic theory which specifies what should be done. All of these concepts will be utilized in later chapters, so it is especially important for you to have a good grasp of these basic, foundation concepts.

The appendix at the end of the chapter explains how graphs are plotted and discusses the slope of a line and how to measure, calculate, and intrepret it.

Learning Objectives

After completing this chapter, you should be sure that you are able to:

- identify and discuss the five basic questions of economics that every society must address.

- explain the difference between the following terms:
  - micro and macro economics
  - positive and normative economics
  - productive efficiency and inefficiency
  - consumption and capital goods

- understand the concept of opportunity cost and how it differs from the concept of monetary cost.

- understand the importance of the assumption of *ceteris paribus* in analyzing real world events and phenomena.

- specify the various ways of evaluating the validity of an economic model.

- understand the production possibilities model, the assumptions behind the model, the economic rationale for its concave shape, and the factors which result in the production possibilities frontier shifting either inwards or outwards.

- show how a production possibilities model can illustrate the following:
  - economic growth
  - efficient and inefficient production outcomes
  - the concept of opportunity cost

- understand why economic theory is necessarily abstract and generalized.

Self Evaluation

List of Terms

Capital Goods
Ceteris Paribus
Consumption Goods
Economic Growth
Economic Model
Economic Theory
Economics
Efficiency
Empirical

Entrepreneurship
Factors of Production (Factor resources)
Inventories
Microeconomics
Macroeconomics
Normative Economics
Opportunity Cost
Positive Economics
Production Possibilities Model
Technology

For the statements below, fill in the term from the list above which provides the best fit.

1.) Economic goods and services are scarce because the _Factors of Prod_ are scarce relative to society's wants and needs.

2.) ✓ Statements which are presumed to be value free are defined as _Positive_ statements.

3.) ✓ The sacrifice or trade-off that one must make when selecting a particular action or alternative is known as an _opportunity cost_.

4.) Economists use the term _Factors of Prod_ [Technology] to describe the specific ways and methods that the various factors of production are combined in the production process.

5.) When a person makes a decision about various alternatives, subject to various constraints, he or she is dealing with _economics_.

6.) In order to isolate and determine the effect of one variable on another, one must make the assumption of _Ceteris Paribus_ for all the other relevant variables.

7.) Analysis of the decision-making units in the economy (i.e., consumers and firms) is known as _MicroEco_.

8.) To test the validity or real world correspondence of an economic theory, the theory's outcomes must be compared with _Empirical_ data.

9.) The relationship between factor inputs and the output of economic goods and services involves the concept of _Economic Theory_ [efficiency].

10.) The inclusion of value judgements or opinions necessarily makes a statement into one which is characteristic of _Normative_.

11.) Goods which are used to produce other goods are known as _Capital goods_.

12.) The economic model that analyzes the alternative bundles that society can produce is known as the _Prod Poss Model_.

13.) The difference between the amount of total sales and the amount of production is defined as a firm's _Inventories_.

14.) Goods and services which are consumed and in that process provide utility to households are known as _Consumption goods_.

15.) When studying the performance of the economy as a whole, one engages in the study of _Macroeconomics_.

16.) A set of speculative hypotheses about real world phenomena (events) is known as _economic theory_ and somewhat interchangeably as an _economic model_.

3

17.) An increase in an economy's productive capacity involves the process of _____.

18.) The managerial activities of innovation, managing resources, and risk taking are generally referred to as ___entrapenurial___.

Problems

The Production Possibilities Curve

You are given the following "menu" of possible production bundles for a hypothetical economy:

Production Bundles

	A	B	C	D	E	F
Fast Food Burgers (FFBs)	50	40	30	20	10	0
Video Tape Recorders (VCRs)	0	10	18	24	28	30

Assumptions:
a. only two goods: FFBs and VCR
b. only two factors of production: labor (L) and capital (K)
c. the factors of production are fixed in amount
d. the two goods differ in their factor intensity (i.e., they use different proportions of labor and capital). In this case, assume that the FFBs are labor intensive (i.e., the most cost efficient method of production utilizes a relatively large amount of labor and relatively small amounts of capital) and that the VCRs are capital intensive (requiring relatively sophisticated technologies and capital to produce them.)
e. more of each good is preferred to less (each good is perceived to have positive utility)

On the basis of the production possibilities schedule above, plot this society's production possibilities curve on the graph which follows.

Figure 1-1

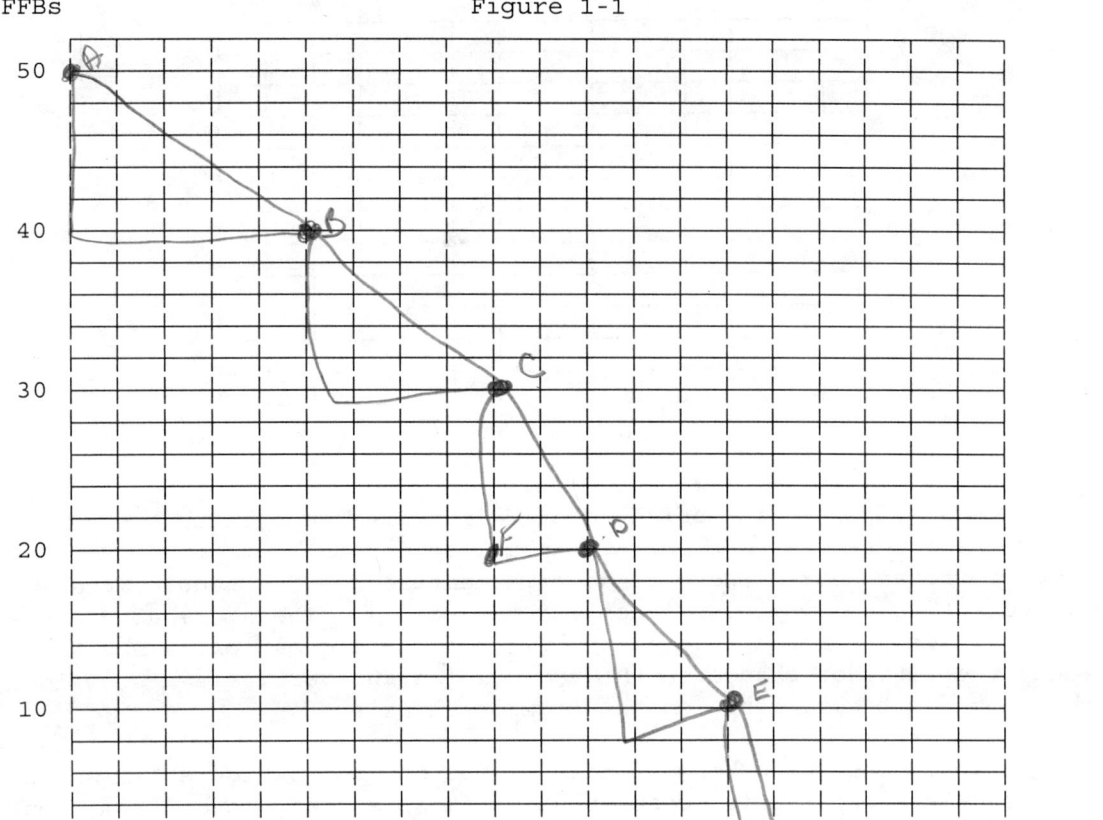

- Point F represents a bundle containing 20 FFBs and 18 VCRs.

Plot that point and briefly describe why society might be located at that particular point.

Not running at peak efficiency

Instead of thinking of the production possibilities curve as a smooth curve, it can also be thought of as a series of steps -- a decrease in one good and an increase in the other good -- as shown in the following example:

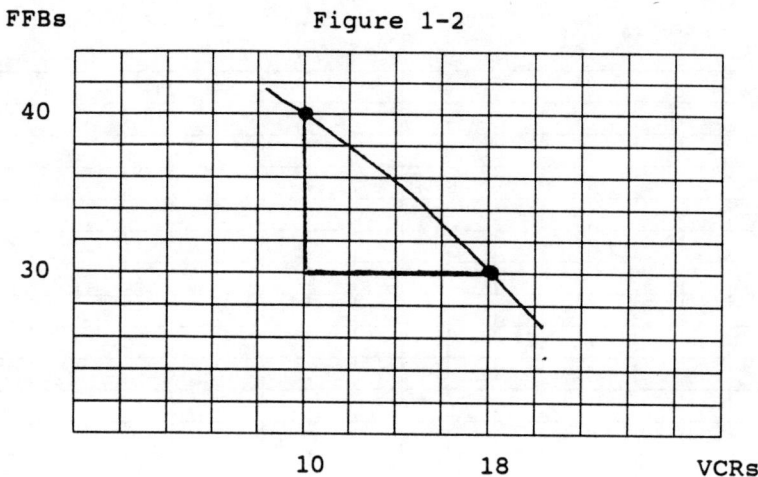

Figure 1-2

The reason that it is useful to draw in these steps is that they emphasize the trade-offs that society is making in moving from one point on the pp curve to another. Those trade-offs measure the opportunity cost associated with the movement between the two points. The steps also measure the slope of the curve between the two points in question, since they represent the ratio of change in the variable on the vertical axis divided by the change in the variable on the horizontal axis.

- Draw in the steps between each of the points in Figure 1-1 and then show the opportunity costs that exist as society moves from complete specialization in one good to complete specialization in the other good.

Fast Food Burgers (FFBs)	Video Tape Recorders (VCRs)	Opportunity Costs The Extra Cost of VCRs in Terms of Units of FFBs
50	0	
40	10	1 FFBs per VCR
30	18	1.20 FFBs per VCR
20	24	1.67 FFBs per VCR
10	28	2.50 FFBs per VCR
0	30	5.00 FFBs per VCR

- Briefly explain why the opportunity cost of VCRs (in terms of the number of FFBs that have to be sacrificed) increases as more VCRs are produced.

_____

_____

_____

Distinguishing Between Positive and Normative Statements

Indicate how you would classify the following statements, using a **P** for statements you think are positive in nature and a **N** for those you think are normative.

1.) __N__ Taxes should be increased to reduce the budget deficit.

2.) __P__ An increase in the rate of taxation will reduce people's incentives to work.

3.) __N__ To prevent a tax increase, government spending should be cut.

4.) __P__ The standard of living for the middle class has slowly increased in the past ten years.

5.) __N__ Government deficits are irresponsible.

6.) __N__ Income taxes are fairer than property taxes.

7.) __P__ An increase in the minimum wage will reduce the incidence of poverty by 3%.

8.) __P__ A decrease in the value of the dollar stimulates the sale of U.S. products in foreign countries.

9.) __P__ People on fixed incomes suffer reduction in their ability to buy during inflation.

10.) __N__ The minimum wage should be increased to help those in poverty.

11.) __P__ Increases in oil prices will result in both higher unemployment and higher inflation.

Distinguishing Between Macroeconomic and Microeconomic Statements

Indicate how you would classify the following statements, write the term **Micro** in front of those statements you think are associated with microeconomics and the term **Macro** for those you think are associated with macroeconomics.

1.) __Macro__ Unemployment rose this month to 6.8%.

2.) __Micro__ The auto industry laid off 45,000 workers last month.

3.) __Macro__ Because of the recession, new entrants to the labor force are finding it difficult to find jobs.

4.) __Macro__ The decreasing value of the dollar on foreign exchange markets has caused exports to increase at a faster rate than imports.

5.) _____ As a result of increased concern about fats and cholesterol, consumer expenditures shift from red meat to chicken, turkey, and fish.

6.) _____ Congress enacts a price ceiling on credit card interest rates.

7.) _____ The Soviets buy more U.S. wheat.

8.) _____ As a consequence of increased consumer spending, the rate of inflation increases.

9.) _____ As a result of competition from Japanese automobile imports, an American automobile producer installs the latest computerized manufacturing processes.

True/False Statements

Indicate whether you think the statements below are true or false. These questions are designed to make you think about the concepts presented in the text. There may not be any easy clear-cut answers. Some thoughts about the answers are presented at the end of the chapter.

1.) T   It is possible for a point inside the production possibilities curve to be preferred over a point on the production possibilities curve.

2.) F   An economic model tells us how some aspect of the economy ought to perform.

3.) T   With respect to the production possibilities model, there are some instances in which the output of both goods can be increased without sacrificing any of either good.

4.) T   Economic theory can provide a basis for determining whether or not society ought to legalize gambling.

5.) F   The statement "The minimum wage should be increased in order to provide a minimum standard of living for unskilled workers" is an example of a positive economic statement.

6.) T   The production possibilities curve is convex with respect to the origin because of the fact that as a society produces more of one good, it must necessarily produce less of another.

7.) F   A theory which is based on the assumption that firms maximize profits is no longer useful if it can be shown that firms make decisions which are not consistent with strict profit maximization (i.e., a firm spends more on its office space than it has to in order to provide a "pleasant" working environment for its workers).

8.) __F__ Economic theory is so abstract and removed from everyday situations that it is difficult to apply the theory to normal, daily events and problems that face individuals.

9.) __T__ The more the production techniques and factor mixes of the two goods differ from one another, the more concave the production possibilities curve will be.

Multiple-Choice Questions

Select the "best" answer from the alternatives provided.

1.) Which of the following will result in a movement along an existing production possibilities curve?
   a. an increase in productive efficiency
   b. an increase in one of the factors of production
   c. one of the two goods becomes more preferred by society ✓
   d. a decrease in unemployment

2.) Which of the following will result in an outward shift in the production possibilities curve?
   a. an increase in productive efficiency
   b. society's labor force increases
   c. a change in society's preferences for the two commodities
   d. using more capital and less labor in the production process

3.) If there were two goods x and y and the production possibilities curve were a straight line instead of being a concave curve, that would indicate that
   a. society had equal preferences for x and y.
   b. in this special case, there are no trade-offs between x and y.
   c. the resources and methods of producing x and y were the same. ✓
   d. production of x requires only one of the factors of production, and the production of y utilizes only the other factor.

4.) A point inside a society's production possibilities curve may be due to
   a. society not wanting one or the other of the two goods
   b. decreasing costs of production.
   c. a decrease in demand.
   d. diminishing returns in the production of the two goods.
   e. some kind of production inefficiency such as poor management or workers employed in tasks that they are not skilled at.

5.) The assumption of *ceteris paribus* in economic analysis
   a. is necessary so that the effects of one variable on another variable can be examined.
   b. means that every possible variable that might affect the variable being studied is held constant.
   c. means that some of the less important or significant variables are held constant while allowing the more important or significant variables to vary so that their effect can be analyzed.
   d. means that the larger macro variables are held constant while allowing the smaller micro variables to vary.
   e. means that the smaller micro variables are held constant while allowing the larger macro variables to vary.

6.) In one of his State of the Union addresses, President Bush stated: (1) the capital gains tax should be reduced to stimulate risk taking and new investment spending and (2) an increase in the tax credit for children and dependents would stimulate additional consumption spending.
   a. Both statements are positive economic statements.
   b. Both statements are normative economic statements.
   c. Statement (1) is a positive economic statement, and statement (2) is a normative economic statement.
   d. Statement (1) is a normative economic statement, and statement (2) is a positive economic statement.

7.) In one of his State of the Union addresses, the president stated: (1) that the tax on yachts should be recinded and (2) the income tax withholding tables would be revised to give people more take-home pay
   a. Both statements are macroeconomic statements.
   b. Both statements are microeconomic statements.
   c. Statement (1) is a microeconomic statement, and statement (2) is a macroeconomic statement.
   d. Statement (1) is a macroeconomic statement, and statement (2) is a microeconomic statement

8.) There are two goods in a society, with capital goods represented on the vertical axis and consumption goods represented on the horizontal axis of a normal, concave shaped production possibilities curve (ppc). Refer to the figure below for each of statements listed below.

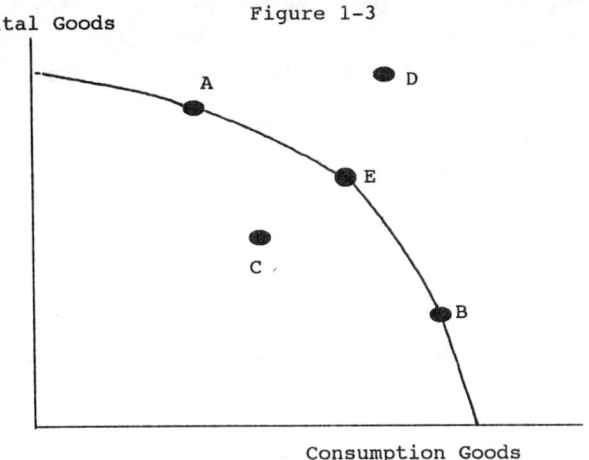

Figure 1-3

a. At point C, this economy will not experience any economic growth at all.
b. Point A will yield less current consumption but more future consumption.
c. Point B will have more current consumption and, because of the high consumption levels, will grow faster in the future.
d. Point E, being near the approximate midpoint of the ppc, is the best choice for both present and future consumption.
e. Point D will not be attainable from point A, since it involves more of both goods which is an impossibility.

9.) Economic models
a. are difficult to apply to specific situations because they are so abstract.
b. indicate how an economy "ought" to perform.
c. are useless when the *ceteris paribus* assumption is violated.
d. can be thought of as if ... then ... statements.
e. can almost never be tested, since every event is unique.

10.) If a country produces either current consumption goods or capital goods, then
a. the more consumption goods it produces, the faster it will grow in the future, all other things remaining the same.
b. the more capital goods it produces, the faster it will grow in the future, all other things remaining the same.
c. the current bundle produced has no impact on the future growth rate.
d. none of the above.

11.) Which of the following statements is true regarding the production possibilities model?
   a. An increase in productive efficiency will shift the curve to the right.
   b. A straight line production possibilities curve means that consumers like the two goods equally well.
   c. The best production point on a production possibilities curve is typically near the center, since opportunity costs for the two goods rise as the endpoints are approached.
   d. Better management techniques can move society from a point within the production possibilities curve to one closer to the production possibility curve.
   e. None of the above.

12.) The assumption of *ceteris paribus*:
   a. requires that nothing change during the period of analysis in question.
   b. allows economists to isolate the effect of one variable on another variable even though other relevant variables are changing.
   c. is such an unrealistic assumption that it is rarely very useful.
   d. none of the above.

13.) The opportunity cost of attending your economics class
   a. equals the tuition paid for the class.
   b. equals the tuition paid for the class plus additional expenses for books, etc.
   c. equals the tuition paid for the class plus the income you could have earned while you were attending class even if you didn't have a job.
   d. equals the tuition paid for the class plus any additional expenses plus any foregone income plus the benefits of other activities you could have engaged in had you not been in class.

14.) The production possibilities curve has a concave, "bowed-in" shape because
   a. the production of one good means less resources for the other good.
   b. as more of one good is produced, consumers value it less and less and production tapers off.
   c. production efficiency is dramatically decreased as the endpoints are approached and production amounts taper off towards the endpoints.
   d. factor inputs for the two goods are not equally substitutable and transferring resources from one good to the other involves increasing marginal costs.
   e. none of the above.

Discussion Questions

1.) Why is it necessary for economic theory to simplify the real world? Isn't detail needed to give a theory realism?

2.) Is it possible to "prove" economic theories and laws? What would provide acceptable evidence that the "Law of Demand -- the higher the price, the smaller the amount demanded and the lower the price, the larger the amount demanded" is a valid statement?

3.) Can you think of any choices, alternatives, situations or actions in which there are no opportunity costs (i.e., nothing has to be sacrificed or traded-off)?

4.) Is it possible for economic models to be valid if they have unrealistic assumptions? if a model's results are not testable? Is an abstract model like the production possibilities model testable?

5.) Suppose that, in the future, technological advances make it possible for every inhabitant of the planet to have every commodity that they would like to have -- completely eliminating the scarcity of goods and services. Would economics play any role at all in such a bizarre world?

Answers and Solutions to Problems and Exercises

Completing Statements from the List of Terms

1.) factors of production
2.) positive economics
3.) opportunity cost
4.) technology
5.) economics
6.) *ceteris paribus*
7.) microeconomics
8.) empirical
9.) efficiency
10.) normative economics
11.) capital goods
12.) production possibilities model
13.) inventories
14.) consumption goods
15.) macroeconomics
16.) economic theory and economic model
17.) economic growth
18.) entrepreneurship

Problems

Production Possibilities Model

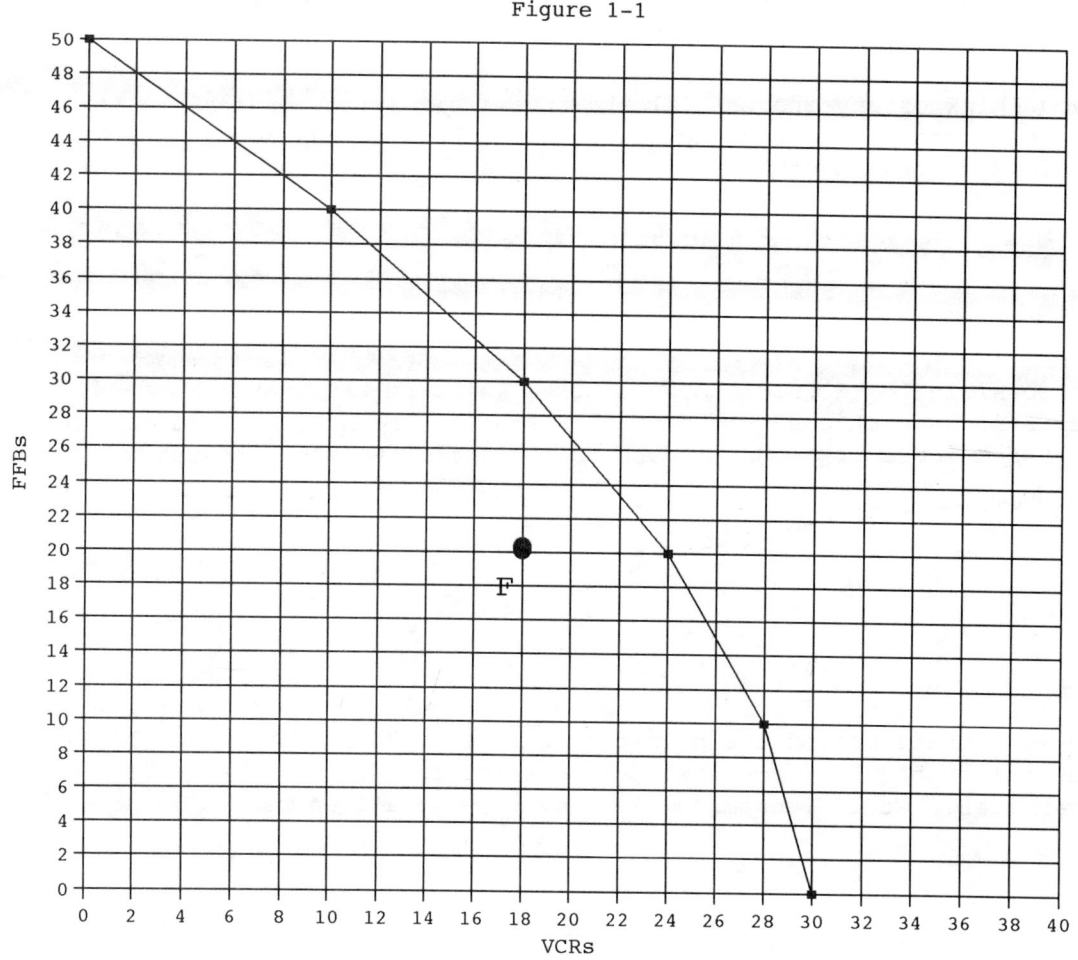

Figure 1-1

Point F is inside the production possibilities curve and, therefore, represents an inefficient outcome. Perhaps individual workers are not employed in those jobs that they do best or management is inept or there exists some unemployment in this society.

As society moves down its pp curve, the opportunity cost of VCRs is:

1   FFB per VCR
1.25   FFB per VCR
1.67   FFB per VCR
2.5   FFB per VCR
5   FFB per VCR

As society increases the number of VCRs it produces, the opportunity cost of VCRs increases, because the factors of production do not substitute perfectly for one another. Fast food burgers utilize labor extensively, while VCRs are more capital intensive. Thus, increasingly less suitable resources are being put into VCR production and, not surprisingly, the returns (VCR output) diminish as that process continues.

Distinguishing Between Positive and Normative Statements

1.) **Normative** There are other ways to reduce the deficit, so this statement reflects a specific value judgement about the way in which the deficit should be reduced.

2.) **Positive**

3.) **Normative**

4.) **Positive**

5.) **Normative** Obviously, a strong opinion is expressed here!

6.) **Normative**

7.) **Positive**

8.) **Positive**

9.) **Positive**

10.) **Normative** An expression of the best way that should be used to eliminate poverty.

11.) **Positive** A prediction of specific outcomes that is testable against actual real world data.

Distinguishing Between Macroeconomic and Microeconomic Statements

1.) **Macroeconomics**

2.) **Microeconomics** Statement refers to a specific industry. It should be kept in mind that macroeconomic forces may well have caused this result.

3.) **Macroeconomics** The level of unemployment is a fundamental macroeconomic concept.

4.) **Macroeconomics**

5.) **Microeconomics**

6.) **Microeconomics** A specific market, the credit card market, is affected.

7.) **Microeconomics** Again, a change in a specific market.

8.) **Macroeconomics** The rate of inflation is the rate of change of the overall price level, a macroeconomic concept.

9.) **Microeconomics** A change in production techniques for a product is a classic microeconomic topic.

True/False Statements

1.) **True.** Since points on the production possibilities frontier are production efficient points, such points would always be preferred to points inside the frontier which are production inefficient. However, preferences also have to be taken into account, and there might be a circumstance in which society would prefer an inefficiently produced bundle (inside the frontier) which contained more of a preferred good than an efficiently produced bundle (on the frontier) which had less of the preferred good. The answer to the statement is that it is possible, but almost always points on the production possibilities curve are preferred to those inside the curve.

2.) **False.** The word "ought" is the critical one in this statement. Typically, "ought" has a normative sense, telling us how the economy should perform, what it ought to be doing. In that context, the statement is false, because the purpose of economic models is to explain or predict various kinds of economic phenomena, not to tell us what should be happening.

3.) **True.** When moving from an inefficient point inside the production possibilities curve to a point on the curve itself. This is the only exception to the rule that every action has a positive opportunity cost associated with it. Once on the pp curve, more of one good can be obtained only at the expense of having less of the other good.

4.) **False.** Economic theory can provide insights into the various costs and benefits of a legalized gambling measure, but ultimately this issue will be decided on the basis of society's values. If society determines that the economic benefits are important to its overall well-being, then it may well decide to legalize gambling. On the other hand, if members of society see this issue as one involving society's morality and gambling is perceived as being wrong, then gambling would not be allowed.

5.) **False**. The statement is advocating a particular course of action that society should take -- it is telling society what should be done, and that involves subjective values. Normative statements contain value judgements (opinions), while positive statements are expected to be free of values.

6.) **False**. This statement indicates why the production possibilities curve has a negative slope (more of one good implies less of the other good), but convexity is dependent upon the law of increasing costs. As society moves towards specialization in either of the two goods, the resources involved in the production of that good become increasingly less suitable and the marginal oppportunity cost of producing additional units of that good increase. The term "imperfect factor substitution" explains why a production possibilities curve has a convex shape.

7.) **False**. Generally speaking, it is important for theoretical assumptions to be realistic, however, in this case, if firms "act as if they maximize profits," a theory which assumes that firms solely maximize profits will still yield accurate predictions.

8.) **False**. Economic theory is not effective or valid if it cannot explain specific events or phenomena. Theory is abstract in order to identify and isolate the critical and significant factors which affect the situation being examined. Such abstractness is necessary to reduce the confusion that exists in the real world where literally thousands of factors (forces) are changing. But because economic theory is abstract, it is also very general and therefore applicable to a wide variety of situations and events.

9.) **True**. If the production possibilities curve were a straight line, then factor inputs could substitute perfectly for one another in the production of the two goods. Therefore, it stands to reason that the less substitutability that exists, the greater the concavity of the curve.

Multiple-Choice

1.) c   2.) b   3.) c   4.) e   5.) a   6.) d

7.) c   8.) b   9.) d   10.) b   11.) d   12.) b

13.) d   14.) d

Discussion Questions

1.) Since there are so many different events occurring, it is easy to "get lost" in the facts and data. One needs a framework for determining what factors are important and what are not. A theory is realistic when it is able to predict events correctly in a wide variety of settings. Theories which attempt to be realistic by including numerous specific details have no generality and can be used in only a small number of similar situations.

2.) Proof is difficult in the social sciences because of the large number of potential factors involved in establishing cause and effect relationships. It is always possible that new data will come along and invalidate a theory. Actual real world data can be used to confirm or support theoretical results and, of course, theoretical predictions which are at odds with reality mean that the theory must be reexamined. Empirical data can be used to reject theories or in cases where the predictions are valid, the data have failed to reject the theoretical hypothesis. But "failed to reject" is a much weaker concept than proof.

In a situation where all other factors have remained constant, say in a very short period of time, a decrease in consumption after a price increase would tend to support the theory.

3.) In terms of the production possibilities model, such a case occurs only if society moves from a point inside the pp curve, in a northeasterly direction, to a point on the curve. If society increases its efficiency, then it is possible to have more of both goods.

4.) There is some controversy in the economics discipline about whether or not economic assumptions must necessarily be "realistic." In the final analysis, business firms may not maximize profits to the maximum extent possible, but as long as they "act as if they do," then a theory which assumes profit maximization will yield satisfactory explanations and predictions of firms' behavior.

A very abstract model like the production possibilities model is not really testable in any meaningful way, yet the model is a very useful way of thinking about costs, economic efficiency, and economic growth.

5.) Even in a world characterized by complete abundance, there are still scarce resources: time and information. Since economics is concerned with selecting optimum alternatives within a set of constraints, one could argue that economics would still be a relevant discipline. People would still have to decide what to consume and would be willing to pay to receive better information about the commodities that they consume.

Summary

Although Chapter 1 is relatively brief, it provides a superb introduction to several important economic concepts -- opportunity cost, economic efficiency, micro and macro economics, positive and normative economic theory, and economic growth. The production possibilities model serves as an excellent vehicle to illustrate several of these concepts. And as your text shows, in spite of the model's simplicity, it is possible to use it to provide insights into a number of interesting policy situations for society as a whole, such as shifts in defense and civilian spending patterns and investment and economic growth outcomes.

Every society, no matter how it is structured, must somehow address the five main questions of economics. The production possibilities model furnishes us with perspectives about each of the questions except for question three, the distribution question. In the next chapter, we'll examine in more detail exactly how the market system as well as several other economic systems addresses all five questions.

Finally, the role of values and political ideology can't be understated in terms of developing economic policy in response to specific economic problems. Even if there is agreement about an economic problem and the factors that are affecting it, there may be substantial disagreement about what an optimal policy response might be. Although the author of your text has worked very hard to present you with an unbiased and accurate set of economic principles, undoubtedly there are other economists who would present topics and policies and theory in a different way, with a different set of biases and viewpoints. In a perfect world, economists would provide an understanding of what makes things happen and then each of you will apply your own set of values in deciding what ought to be done to address specific problems.

Chapter 1 -- Appendix

Overview of the Appendix

Graphs play an especially important role in the study of economics, since they help us to gain insights into economic relationships which are often complex and sometimes obscure. Concepts and theories which are difficult to understand on first reading often become much clearer if you have access to a graph illustrating the concept. Thus, it is essential that you have an understanding of the concept of slope and rates of change and know how to plot curves and relationships between variables.

Learning Objectives

After completing this chapter appendix, you should be sure that you are able to:

- understand the x-y coordinate system
- plot or fit a line to set of data points
- measure the slope of a line
- identify negative and positive slopes, increasing or decreasing slopes

Problems

Plotting Graphs from Sets of Data

Plot each of the x-y relationships shown below on Figure 1-4.

Data Set A		Data Set B		Data Set C	
y	x	y	x	y	x
5	0	5	0	5	0
7	1	3	1	6	1
9	2	1	2	9	2
11	3	-1	3	14	3
13	4	-3	4	21	4
15	5	-5	5	30	5
17	6	-7	6	41	6

What is the slope of each line?

Data Set A +2
Data Set B -2
Data Set C +2x

Can you determine the equation for each set of data?

Data Set A $y = 5 + 2x$
Data Set B $y = 5 - 2x$
Data Set C $y = 5 + x^2$

20

Variable Y   Figure 1-4

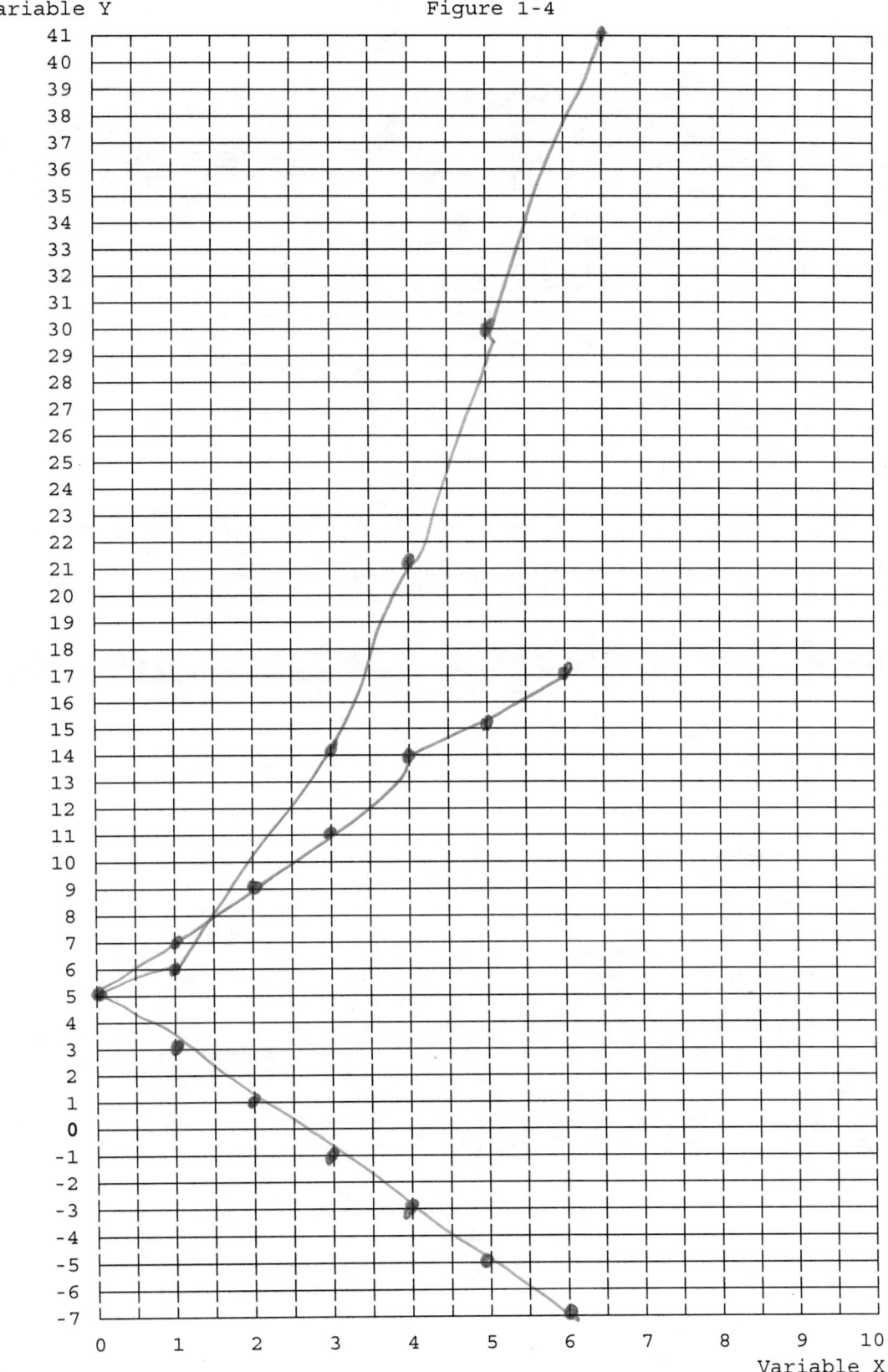

21

Answers and Solutions to Problems and Exercises

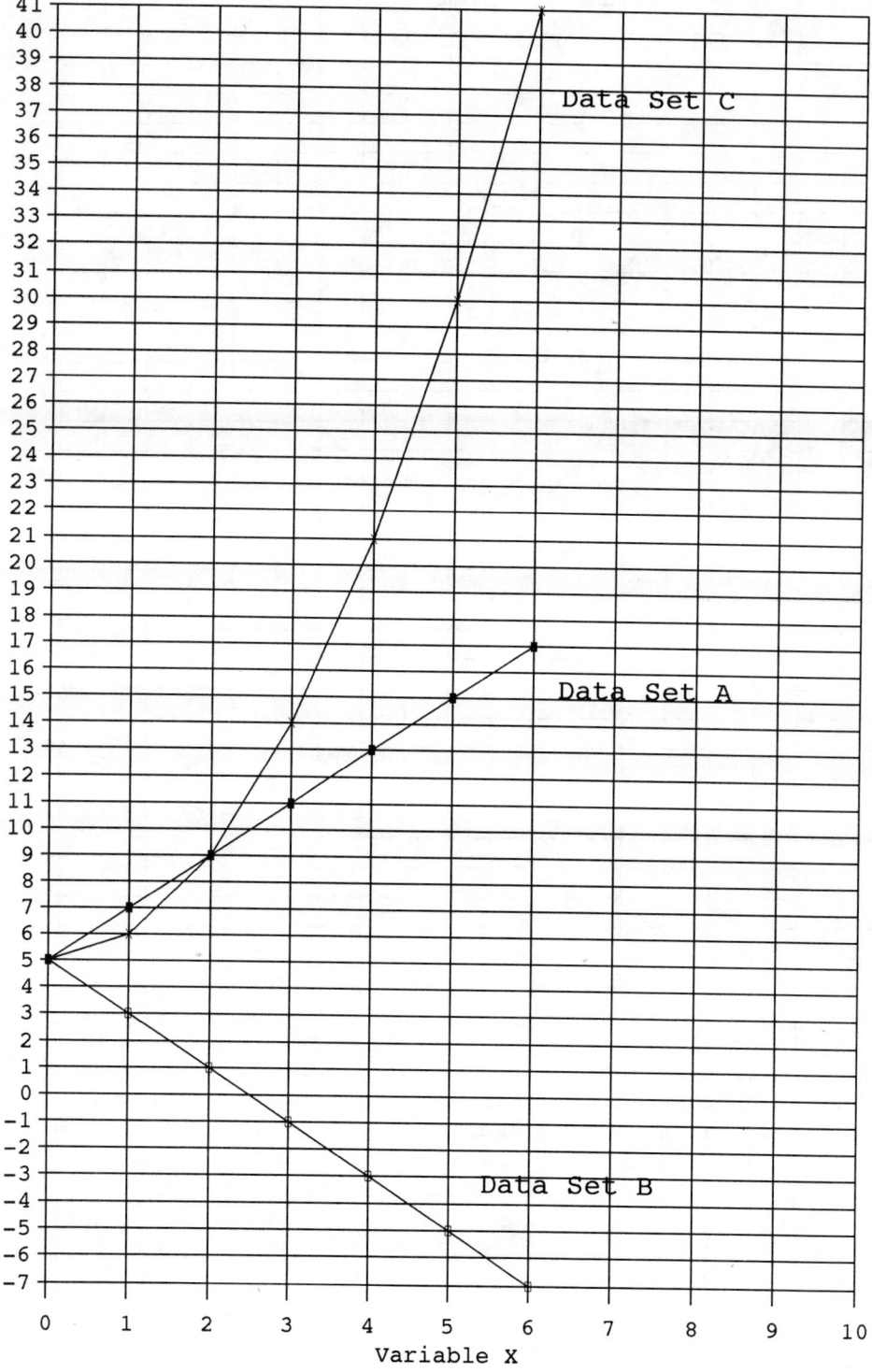

Figure 1-4

Data Set A **+2**

Data Set B **-2**

Data Set C **+2x** [slope varies and is dependent upon the x-value]

Data Set A **y = 5 + 2x**

Data Set B **y = 5 - 2x**

Data Set C **y = +5 + x^2**

Chapter 2
The Market System

Overview of the Chapter

This chapter provides a broad overview of the major economic systems -- traditional, market, and command, with an emphasis upon the market system and how it emerged. After a brief discussion of the characteristics of traditional societies and their historical setting, some of the structural features that characterize such societies are described. It is especially important to see these societies in their proper context and to be able to recognize the consequences that result from certain kinds of economies.

Economic systems have different sets of advantages and disadvantages associated with them. Traditional systems respect established ways of dealing with their economic problems and tend to be relatively stable. Although many of these traditional economies were able to generate "surpluses" over and above what was needed for subsistence, because of the non-economic orientation of the society, economic growth was seldom achieved. Any surpluses that were achieved were typically invested in projects which did little to enhance their future production possibilities.

There were certain precursors that were necessary for the development of a market system -- an independent labor force, the breakup of the feudal system (in Europe), well-defined property rights, and the ability to enforce contracts. The market system resulted in a major revolution in the fundamental characteristics of society and its economic structure. Self interest became the dominant motivation, and production decisions were now determined by profitability. Can a system which is characterized by the the pursuit of self interest and the maximization of profits yield results which also promote society's overall welfare? An interesting question.

Adam Smith answered that question when he created the image of the "invisible hand." Individual producers, interested only in their own self interest, are guided as if by an "invisible hand" to promote the public interest. The goods and services that society wants will be the most profitable for the producers, and by giving consumers their preferred bundle, the overall welfare of society will be maximized as will be producer profits. In a market economy, the goods and services that are supplied on the market will be the ones that are the most profitable.

A market's results are determined through the interaction of the forces of demand and supply. If a market is functioning effectively, then the market price will reflect the economic scarcity of a commodity, generating valuable economic signals for both buyers and sellers. Specific preferences (wants) and their intensity have an effect on market price as does the overall cost of production.

The market price will tend to move towards an equilibrium price -- a price which will tend to persist. If the actual market price is below its equilibrium price, there will be a shortage, and competition among buyers will drive the price back up towards its equilibrium level. If, on the other hand, the actual market price is higher than the equilibrium price, suppliers will put too much of the commodity on the market, and a surplus will result. Competition among sellers to get rid of the surplus will cause the market price to fall back towards its equilibrium level.

Marxism arose largely as a result of the "excesses" associated with early market economies and the industrial revolution -- entire families having to work six days a week under often hazardous conditions just to earn subsistence wages. Marx argued that workers had nothing to lose by instituting an economic system in which there was no private ownership of capital. The means of production were to be owned and managed by the workers and society as a whole.

Extensive centralized planning was implemented in the USSR, and prices no longer provided accurate information about the economic scarcity of either factors of production nor of final goods and services. After a difficult transition period, command economies were able to achieve impressive rates of growth, due in part to their unhindered ability to allocate resources to the investment sector and away from the consumer sector. But eventually, the lack of incentives within the system, the lack of meaningful information about resource prices and consumer wants, and the lack of coordination among the various sectors of the economy led to the command system's downfall, at least as practiced in the USSR and Eastern Europe.

Learning Objectives

After completing this chapter, you should be sure that you are able to:

- discuss the major differences between the three major kinds of economic systems -- traditional, market, and command.

- identify the characteristics associated with traditional economies as well as some of the problems associated with this kind of economic structure.

- identify the factors which facilitated the transition in Europe from a traditional economy to an emerging market economy.

- discuss how the market system answers the five basic economic questions that every society must address.

- discuss the role of profits in the market system and how they are calculated and determined.

- understand demand and supply curves and how they interact together to determine the market's equilibrium price.

- define a market shortage and surplus and the role each plays in achieving an equilibrium price.

- explain how an economic system like the market system that is based on maximizing behavior and the pursuit of maximum profits by producers promotes the public interest.

- describe the historical setting of the Soviet command economy and some of its major characteristics.

Applications

Since factor resources are unable to meet the virtually unlimited wants of societies, they are forced to deal with the issue of scarcity. That is the essence of the third economic question which addresses the problem of allocating or distributing output. If it is not possible to have all of the goods and services that society would like to have, how can society allocate the output that it does have, in such a way as to maximize the total welfare of society as a whole?

Because scarcity exists, the achievement of maximum efficiency in production is of critical importance if society is to acquire as many goods and services as possible in order to maximize its well-being. Fortunately, the price system provides a set of economic signals which assist firms in selecting the most efficient method of production. For a given amount of factor inputs, maximum production efficiency will be achieved when total output is at a maximum or alternatively, for a given level of output, the amount of factor inputs is minimized. When dealing with several inputs of varying cost, those definitions become impractical. However, if instead of focusing on the amounts of the inputs, the focus is changed to the total cost (TC) of production, maximum efficiency of production can be thought of as the "least cost" method of production. Any change which reduces costs thus represents a movement towards greater efficiency and also greater profitability. Total profits (TP_r) are equal to the difference between total revenues (TR) and total costs (TC):

$$TP_r = TR - TC$$

where: $TR = Q_p \times P_p$

$TC = (Q_L \times P_L) + (Q_K \times P_K) + (Q_N \times P_N) + (Q_E \times P_E)$
(Q_L and P_L) -- Quantity and Price of the labor (L) input
(Q_K and P_K) -- Quantity and Price of the capital (K) input
(Q_N and P_N) -- Quantity and Price of the land (N) input
(Q_E and P_E) -- Quantity and Price of the entrepreneurial services (E) input

An increase in production efficiency will affect total profitability in either of two ways:

(1) ↑ TP_r = TR - TC ↓ [as a result of greater efficiency, total costs of production are reduced, total output and revenues are unaffected]

(2) ↑ TP_r = ↑ TR - TC [more output results from increased efficiency, increasing total revenue, total costs are unaffected]

If the methods of production, factor prices, the price of output are specified, then it is possible to calculate TP_r, TR, and TC, and thereby determine the most efficent production method.

Price of a unit of labor: $ 350
Price of a unit of capital: $ 700
Price of a unit of land: $ 300
Price of entrepreneurial services: $ 500

Price of Output = $ 80/unit

	Methods of Production (All yielding 500 units of output)		
	I	II	III
Units of Labor	56	46	37
Units of Capital	9	12	15
Units of Land	8	10	16
Units of Entrepreneurial Services	3	5	7
Total Cost (TC)	$ 29,800	$ 30,000	$ 31,750
Total Revenue (TR)	$ 40,000	$ 40,000	$ 40,000
Total Profit (TP_r)	$ 10,200	$ 10,000	$ 8,250

On the basis of the information above, it can be seen that production method I is the least cost method and therefore the most efficient in production and that method is also the most profitable for the firm.

If any of the factor prices should change, suppose the price of labor increases from $ 350 per unit to $ 500 per unit, the impact of that price change can be seen on the cost associated with each of the methods of production and a determination can be made about whether to change methods. In this case, after re-calculating its costs, the firm should switch to production method II to keep its costs as low as possible. Note, however, that because of the substantial increase in the cost of labor, the firm's profitability declined considerably -- decreasing from $10,200 using method I to $3,100 with the newly adopted method II. After the increase in labor cost, even method III became more profitable than the previous optimum, method I. As the price of the labor input increases, firms will respond by using less labor intensive methods of production. Since labor's productivity (in terms of output) has not changed, that factor has become less cost efficient for the firms and they adapt by using methods of production which use more capital and/or more natural resources and/or entrepreneurial services.

The revised total cost and total profit data are shown below:

	I	II	III
Total Cost (TC)	$38,200	$36,900	$37,300
Total Revenue (TR)	$40,000	$40,000	$40,000
Total Profit (TP$_r$)	$1,800	$3,100	$2,700

Self Evaluation

List of Terms

Barter
Command Economy
Debt Financing
Demand
Diminishing Returns
Economies of Scale
Equilibrium
Equity Financing
Gains from Trade
Invisible Hand
Just Price

Market
Market System
Maximizing Principle
Principle of Comparative Advantage
Shortage
Supply
Surplus
Total Cost
Total Profit
Total Revenue
Traditional Economy

For the statements below, fill in the term from the list above which provides the best fit.

1.) Adam Smith indicated that even though producers were interested in maximizing their total profits, they would be guided as if by an _invisible hand_ to promote the public interest.

2.) An economic system in which decisions are made by an centralized planning agency: _Command Economy_

3.) As additional units of a variable input are added to fixed amounts of the other factors, the concept of _Diminishing_ means that eventually the increase in total output associated with an additional unit of the variable input will fall.

4.) The output price times the quantity of output equals _Total Revenue_

5.) Both parties to a transaction can receive _Gains of Trade_ by specializing in those commodities in which they have a comparative cost advantage and trading for those commodities in which they have a comparative cost disadvantage.

6.) A _Market_ is a setting where buyers and sellers can engage in transactions for a specific commodity.

7.) A _____ society is one in which economic factors play a relatively minor role.

8.) The _____ for a commodity is closely related to an individual's preferences and intensity of wants/desires.

9.) A _____ system is one in which commodities are traded for one another with little or no use of a commonly accepted currency.

10.) The _____ suggests that individuals evaluate the various options and alternatives open to them and select the one which makes them best off.

11.) _____ can be thought of as the sum of all the factor costs incurred by a firm.

12.) If the average cost per unit decreases when all inputs are proportionally increased, then _____ are present.

13.) _____ refers to the various amounts of a commodity that a producer will offer for sale over a range of possible prices.

14.) The difference between total revenues and total costs is called _____.

15.) A transactions price which would not allow any excess profit and which would tend to perpetuate the status quo was known as a _____.

16.) An economic system in which the price and output of goods and services as well as the major economic questions such as the allocation of resources and distribution are answered through the interaction of buyers and sellers is known as the _____.

17.) The _____ states that overall welfare will be maximized if different countries specialize in and export those commodities in which they have a comparative cost advantage and import those commodities in which they have a comparative cost disadvantage.

18.) If the market price is below its equilibrium level, a _____ will result.

19.) The development of banking institutions and broader, more accessible credit markets facilitated _____ for newly emerging businesses, giving them access to greater credit and financial resources than they could raise on their own.

20.) If the market price is above its equilibrium level, a _____ will result.

21.) _____ for markets represents a position of stability, and that position will tend to persist until some factor which affects either demand or supply changes.

22.) The emergence of _____ greatly increased the ability of corporations to raise funds from large numbers of small private investors.

Problems

Determining the Least Cost Method of Production

You are given the following set of factor prices, price of output, and methods of production. From that information, determine which method of production is the most efficient for the firm and the profits associated with each method.

Price of a unit of labor: $ 300
Price of a unit of capital: $ 700
Price of a unit of land: $ 600
Price of entrepreneurial services: $ 450

Price of Output = $ 200/unit

Methods of Production
(All yielding 1000 units of output)

	I	II	III	IV
Units of Labor	285 85,500	250 75,000	186 55,800	160 48,000
Units of Capital	58 40,600	62 43,400	74 51,800	80 56,000
Units of Land	74 44,400 / 22,200 / 14,800	83 49,800 / 16,600	106 63,600 / 21,200	121 72,600 / 24,200
Units of Entrepreneurial Services	16 7200	18 8100	22 9900	25 11,250
Total Revenue (TR)	$ 200,000	$ 200,000	$	$
Total Cost (TC)	$ 199,500	$ 176,300	$ 181,100	$ 187,850
Total Profit (TP$_r$)	$ 44,500	$ 23,700	$	$

The most profitable, least cost method of production is ___II___

Assume that the price of land (natural resources) decreases from $600 to $200. Recalculate total costs (TC), total revenue (TR), and total profit (TP$_r$) to see if the firm would change its optimum method of production.

	I	II	III	IV
Total Revenue (TR)	$ 200,	$	$	$
Total Cost (TC)	$ 148,100	$	$	$
Total Profit (TP$_r$)	$	$	$	$

After the change in the cost of land, the most profitable, least cost method of production is now _____.

True/False Statements

Indicate whether you think the statements below are true or false. These questions are designed to make you think about the concepts presented in the text. There may not be any easy clear-cut answers. Some thoughts about the answers are presented at the end of the chapter.

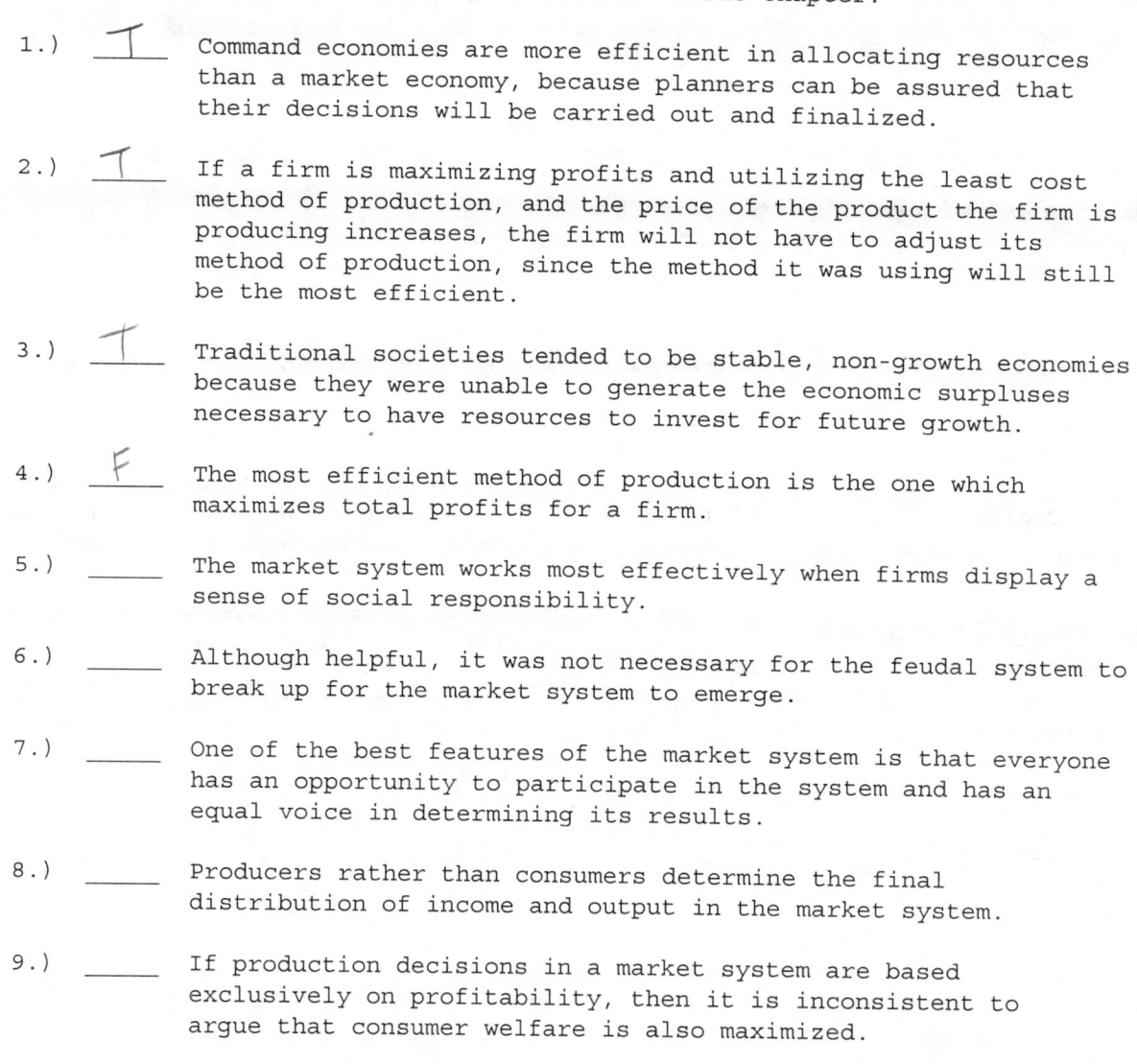

1.) __T__ Command economies are more efficient in allocating resources than a market economy, because planners can be assured that their decisions will be carried out and finalized.

2.) __T__ If a firm is maximizing profits and utilizing the least cost method of production, and the price of the product the firm is producing increases, the firm will not have to adjust its method of production, since the method it was using will still be the most efficient.

3.) __T__ Traditional societies tended to be stable, non-growth economies because they were unable to generate the economic surpluses necessary to have resources to invest for future growth.

4.) __F__ The most efficient method of production is the one which maximizes total profits for a firm.

5.) _____ The market system works most effectively when firms display a sense of social responsibility.

6.) _____ Although helpful, it was not necessary for the feudal system to break up for the market system to emerge.

7.) _____ One of the best features of the market system is that everyone has an opportunity to participate in the system and has an equal voice in determining its results.

8.) _____ Producers rather than consumers determine the final distribution of income and output in the market system.

9.) _____ If production decisions in a market system are based exclusively on profitability, then it is inconsistent to argue that consumer welfare is also maximized.

Multiple-Choice Questions

Select the "best" answer from the alternatives provided.

1.) The law of diminishing returns indicates that
   a. total output will fall as additional workers are added.
   b. total output will increase by smaller and smaller increments as additional workers are added.
   c. if all factors of production are doubled, output will increase but not double.
   d. as workers are paid higher wages, their productivity increases at a decreasing rate.

2.) If a plant or factory can realize economies of scale, then
   a. as additional workers are added, its costs of production will fall.
   b. if all factors of production are changed by the same proportion, total output will increase by the same proportion.
   c. if all factors of production are increased by 25%, total output will increase by more than 25%.
   d. the firm will achieve greater efficiencies and lower costs of production as its size increases.
   e. both c and d.

3.) Is it possible for an economic system based on profits and self interest to also promote the public interest and maximize the overall welfare of society?
   a. No, because production undertaken for strictly for profit will not be the most preferred production bundle for society.
   b. Yes, because in the final analysis, consumer and producer interests are similiar and coincide -- they are both essentially after the same thing.
   c. Yes, because businesses will maximize their profits by producing the bundle of goods and services that society wants.
   d. No, because firms can maximize profits only by taking advantage of consumers.

4.) The law of comparative advantage suggests that
   a. each country should be able to export something to other countries.
   b. if every country specialized in those commodities in which they have a comparative cost advantage and imported those commodities in which they have a comparative cost disadvantage, total world welfare would be enhanced.
   c. international trade results mainly from differences in preferences among the various countries.
   d. trade is possible only if production costs differ among the various countries.
   e. alternatives (a) and (b)
   f. alternatives (b) and (d)

5.) Traditional non-market economies which had non-economic goals
   a. didn't have to deal with the five basic questions of economics.
   b. achieved roughly the same results as a market economy using time tested, customary methods.
   c. had to address the five basic questions in one way or another.
   d. tended to be rigid, subsistence societies.
   e. alternatives (c) and (d)

6.) Command economies
   a. don't have to deal with the five basic questions of economics.
   b. answer the five basic economic questions through a central planning agency.
   c. typically have difficulty achieving any signficant economic growth.
   d. can emulate the market process through careful economic planning.
   e. can often generate high rates of investment by restricting resources devoted to consumption purposes.
   f. alternatives (b) and (e)

7.) When a market achieves a position of equilibrium
   a. excess demand = excess supply.
   b. the market price cannot change.
   c. everyone is getting as much as they want of the commodity.
   d. firms will earn the maximum amount of profits.
   e. the amount supplied will just equal the amount demanded.

8.) In the period preceding the emergence of the market system
   a. the concept of a just price contributed to the economic stability so necessary for the establishment of the market system.
   b. a significant number of feudal estates started small-scale manufacturing operations which formed the economy's industrial base.
   c. the lack of trade and transportation effectively stimulated local town economies.
   d. the emergence of a free labor force was a significant factor in the development of the market system.

Discussion Questions

1.) Why do you think that traditional economies were not particularly interested in economic growth? Did they lack the necessary prerequisites for growth?

2.) How did Adam Smith use the concept and imagery of the "invisible hand" to answer the question, "Can a society in which each person seeks his own selfish ends serve to enhance the general welfare?" Is the "invisible hand" concept still a relevant one in today's society? Can you think of any exceptions (i.e., where the pursuit of self interest has not resulted in promoting the public interest or general welfare)?

3.) What do you think were the main factors that contributed to the fall of the planned command economies in the Eastern Bloc? What problems will these societies face when they try to change over to more market-oriented economic systems? Should such change be gradual or as rapid as possible?

4.) How does the price system help a firm achieve maximum efficiency in production? Discuss the role of factor prices and profits.

5.) If an industry is characterized by significant economies of scale, then as firms become larger, they also become more efficient (i.e., their average cost of production falls as they increase output). Based on what you know about firms and how they operate, how can they become more efficient by becoming larger? Can they become inefficient by becoming too large?

Answers and Solutions to Problems and Exercises

Completing Statements from the List of Terms

1.) Invisible Hand
2.) Command Economy
3.) Diminishing Returns
4.) Total Revenue
5.) Gains from Trade
6.) Market
7.) Traditional Economy
8.) Demand
9.) Barter
10.) Maximizing Principle
11.) Total Cost
12.) Economies of Scale
13.) Supply
14.) Total Profit
15.) Just Price
16.) Market System
17.) Principle of Comparative Advantage
18.) Shortage
19.) Debt Financing
20.) Surplus
21.) Equilibrium
22.) Equity Financing

Problems

Determining the Least Cost Method of Production

	I	II	III	IV
Total Revenue (TR)	$ 200,000	$ 200,000	$ 200,000	$ 200,000
Total Cost (TC)	$ 177,700	$ 176,300	$ 181,100	$ 187,850
Total Profit (TP_r)	$ 22,300	$ 23,700	$ 18,900	$ 12,150
		Most Efficient		

In response to the change in the price of land to $200:

	I	II	III	IV
Total Revenue (TR)	$ 200,000	$ 200,000	$ 200,000	$ 200,000
Total Cost (TC)	$ 148,100	$ 143,100	$ 138,700	$ 139,450
Total Profit (TP_r)	$ 51,900	$ 56,900	$ 61,300	$ 60,550
			Most Efficient	

The most efficient method of production changes to Method III which utilizes a larger amount of land in the production process. A decrease in the price of a factor of production gives cost-conscious firms an incentive to utilize more of that factor and less of some other factors. Total profits also increases as a result of the cost decrease in the land.

True/False Statements

1.) **False.** Recent history has shown how difficult it has been for centralized planning agencies to generate enough information to be able to make the millions of decisions that are associated with the functioning of an economy. The trend has been towards decentralization, allowing those involved in the various sectors of the economy to make pricing and allocation decisions.

2.) **True.** Changes in revenues do not affect the costs of production. If a firm was using the most efficient, least cost method of production before the price change, that method will still be the most efficient.

3.) **False.** Traditional societies tend to be stable, non-growth-oriented societies because of their lack of technological change and preference for using time tested methods of production. Many of these societies were able to generate substantial surpluses, but they were not invested in projects or endeavors that increased their capacity to produce.

4.) **True.** For a given total revenue, the most efficient method of production will be the least cost method of production and that method will, in turn, maximize the difference between total revenues and total costs.

5.) **False.** If firms are operating in a very competitive environment, then owners/entrepreneurs will find it very difficult to address social issues on their own, since any response they make will typically increase their costs, putting them at a cost disadvantage. If a single firm decides to clean up its pollution but no other firms do so, then eventually this firm will be faced with exit from the industry.

6.) **False.** It's hard to say how history would have turned out if events had been different, but it was extremely important to break the institutional ties between the feudal lords (landholders) and the serfs. Monetization of feudal obligations was a step towards a more market-oriented economy, and releasing serfs from their ties to the manor was necessary to have a autonomous, independent labor force, free to work at different firms.

7.) **False** Although everyone has an opportunity to participate in and determine the outcomes of a market society, individuals with more income have more influence on output decisions than low income individuals. Purchases can be looked upon as signals to the producers about what to produce, and some individuals cast a larger shadow than others.

8.) **False.** Consumers affect the distribution of income through their purchases of goods and services. Purchase of a particular product provides income for firms, workers, and owners of factors that are associated with the product. Your decision to attend the university or college you are currently attending directly affects the income and employment of faculty, staff, and administrators of the institution.

9.) **False.** Adam Smith argued to the contrary. By responding to consumer wants and preferences, firms will maximize their profits. Maximum welfare is obtained when society obtains its most preferred bundle of goods and services.

Multiple-Choice

1.) b   2.) e   3.) c   4.) f   5.) e   6.) f

7.) e   8.) d

Discussion Questions

1.) Given the overall non-economic orientation of such societies, there was simply not much concern for increasing their production capacities. One absolute necessity for achieving economic growth is the existence of a surplus of some kind that can be invested or used for future-oriented purposes. If a society consumes all of its output, then growth is not possible. Saving is necessary to release the resources required for investment. Traditional societies were able to generate surpluses, but such surpluses were not used for capital formation. Rather, the surpluses were used for religious or other purposes.

2.) Smith's phrase -- "the invisible hand" -- is still referred to today and remains quite popular, a testament to the power of the image that he developed. The main point that he was trying to make was that the producers of goods and services, pursuing the maximum possible level of profits, are promoting the public welfare without being aware of it. They are not producing commodities because society needs them, but rather because there are profits to be earned in producing the production bundle that society prefers the most. By giving consumers what they want, producers maximize their profits and produce the bundle which maximizes overall welfare. The concept remains valid today, although there are problems just as there were in Smith's time about whether or not certain sectors of the economy should be guided exclusively by profit considerations. There are instances, such as situations where there are large social costs (costs associated with a transaction which are imposed on society at large without society's permission or knowledge) and the maximizing of self interest results in an overall decrease in society's welfare.

3.) Books could be written about the factors which caused the fall of these command economies. The rigidity of centrally planned economies would have to be a leading factor -- the failure of planning agencies in adjusting to changes and their inability to anticipate all of the direct/indirect effects associated with a change.

The lack of incentives within these systems clearly played an important role. If workers are not rewarded adequately for their efforts and see no incentive to work hard and efficiently, and if there are no incentives for managers of factories to maximize output nor any incentives to produce what consumers or other buyers really want to have, then profound difficulties are bound to develop.

Changing over to a market system will be fraught with difficulties. How will state-owned or -operated firms know what market price to charge? What will happen if another state-owned bread company charges a different price? What will happen if prices increase much more rapidly than the incomes? Expectations about future prices are a critical factor and directly affect suppliers' willingness to offer goods and services to the market.

Regarding the rate of change, too rapid a pace and it will be difficult for society to adjust and too slow a pace will mean that the necessary changes are not being made at a rate sufficient to address the problems associated with the old centrally planned system.

4.) Inefficient firms will have higher costs of production and over time, the less efficient firms will not be able to compete effectively with their more efficient counterparts. Ultimately, the less efficient firms would be forced to exit. Profitability is a broad measure of efficiency.

Factor prices provide firms with important information about the relative scarcity of the different factors of production. Comparing factor prices with their productivity allows firms to select that combination of factors which will maximize their production efficiency and productivity.

5.) There are a number of factors that are associated with the scale or size of a firm and their costs of production. Larger firms may be more efficient because they have more flexibility in combining factors (being able to match machines with different capacities), being able to have their workers do specialized tasks which they can become very skilled at, being able to order larger quantities of materials, and being able to spread out the costs of a very expensive machine over a larger number of units (spreading the fixed costs or overhead costs of production). It is possible for firms to become so large that communications among different levels of management and operating areas becomes increasingly more difficult and complex, thus raising costs.

Summary

Chapter 2 has provided you with a brief historical orientation about the market system, discussing some of the factors which either delayed or assisted its development. With the technological changes occurring in the communications sector, it is possible that the market system will evolve into something quite different from what we have today. The success of home shopping channels on cable television and the bidding for time allotments for television networks on communications satellites remind us of how much our concepts of a market have changed in the last few years.

Adam Smith's justification of an economic system based on profit and self interest continues to be relevant and provides a foundation for those who support market-oriented approaches as opposed to policies which involve greater governmental intervention. His justification emphasizes "consumer sovereignty" -- the inherent power of consumers in a market-based system. Even though consumers as a group are disorganized and fragmented compared to some special interests in our society, we should not lose track of their importance.

Another meaningful concept revolves around the market system and the economic signals that it sends to firms so that they can maximize their profits. Maximum economic efficiency is obtained when a firm utilizes the least cost method of production. For a given level of total revenue (TR), minimizing the firm's costs of production generates the largest amount of total profit (TP_r). Thus, any cost saving that the firm can implement will enhance economic efficiency. Instead of the term economic efficiency being a somewhat vague theoretical term, it now becomes something specific with a definite operational context -- **anything that reduces costs increases economic efficiency.**

The concepts of demand and supply are very briefly introduced, and for the first time there is a discussion of the term equilibrium. Equilibrium is defined as a condition of stability -- the market will stay at its equilibrium position until some economic factor changes. If a market works the way it is supposed to, then the market will always be moving towards its equilibrium price and quantity. If equilibrium is not attained, then there will be a shortage or surplus in the market and the market will be allocatively inefficient, and the overall welfare of society will be less than it otherwise would have been.

The chapter concludes with a brief listing of the functions of government in a market system. Questions about the proper role of government continue to loom large in ongoing debate about public policy. While there are many things that the market does well, there are also some areas in which it doesn't perform nearly as well. In those areas of the economy, we must decide whether a good should be produced in the private or public sector.

Chapter 3
Demand and Supply I:
The Concept of Demand

Overview of the Chapter

Chapter 3 begins our in-depth exploration of the market, discussing the concepts of demand and elasticity. Demand can be thought of as the various amounts that an individual is willing and able to purchase over the range of possible commodity prices. The term demand, as used in an economic context, represents effective demand -- to be included in a particular market, an individual must be able to purchase the commodity.

The Law of Diminishing Marginal Utility provides a rationale for the inverse relationship that exists between the commodity's market price and its quantity demanded. That law hypothesizes that as more of a commodity is consumed, the marginal or extra utility associated with an additional unit of the commodity declines at some point. Since a consumer receives less extra satisfaction from each successive unit consumed (i.e., marginal utility declines), price must decline if consumption is to increase, because buyers will be willing to pay less and less for additional units.

A number of economic factors, other than the price of the commodity itself, also affect the demand for a commodity. The demand for a commodity increases if for each and every price, there is a larger quantity demanded than before. Or, alternatively, demand is said to have increased if, for each and every quantity, buyers are willing to pay a higher price than before. It is important that you understand how changes in each of the demand determinants affect the demand for a commodity.

Students often find it difficult to distinguish between a shift in a demand curve and a movement along a demand curve. If the price of the commodity itself changes, the demand curve itself will remain unchanged and there will be a change in quantity demanded -- a movement along an existing demand curve. Other demand factors will cause the demand curve to shift. **A change in the commodity's own price does not result in a change in demand but rather a change in quantity demanded.** If demand changes because of a change in any of the main demand determinants other than the price of the commodity itself, then the market equilibrium price will also change.

The demand curve is dependent upon the *ceteris paribus* assumption -- that the other demand determinants (except price) being held constant. In reality, these other factors are constantly changing but the assumption is needed to conceptually isolate the specific relationship between the price of the commodity and quantity demanded. Otherwise it would be impossible to isolate the effect of price on quantity demanded.

Only a few exceptions to the Law of Demand have been found. The most legitimate case is known as a Giffin good. The circumstances surrounding a Giffin good are decidedly unique: it is found in situations where a single commodity (such as potatoes or some other staple) constitutes a significant percentage of people's total caloric intake. If the price of the staple decreases, purchasing power is released for buying other commodities, and less of the staple is purchased. If the price of the staple increases, more is purchased, since consumers can't afford other diet components.

Other possible exceptions involve goods where there is some misperception a good's quality. Buyers assume that lower prices imply lower quality as well, thus they may purchase less of a commodity as its price goes down. In the so-called "lemon" case, buyers perceive higher risks with lower prices -- often due to inadequate information. Cases of conspicuous consumption represent the opposite case, where buyers want to impress others and a commodity's so-called snob appeal increases as its price increases, thus the quantity demanded increases as its price increases.

Elasticity is an interesting and useful characteristic of demand. Elasticity measures the responsiveness that exists between two variables. Although we are aware that price and quantity demanded are inversely related, there is no way of knowing the degree of responsiveness that exists between the two variables. Does a small change in price result in a small or large change in quantity demanded? The price elasticity of demand provides a way to measure this important demand characteristic. The elasticity of income measures the responsiveness of quantity demanded to changes in income, an especially useful concept in dynamic and growing markets. The cross elasticity of demand can be used to determine the degree of substitutability or complementarity that exists between two goods.

Learning Objectives

After completing this chapter, you should be sure that you are able to:

- understand the concept of demand and the underlying relationship that exists between an individual's demand for a commodity and his/her preferences as illustrated by their marginal utility schedule.

- explain the process by which consumers obtain the bundle of goods and services which yields the greatest amount of satisfaction -- the so-called maximizing rule.

- understand the importance of the *ceteris paribus* assumption in deriving a demand curve.

- identify the set of factors which are the main determinants of demand and be able to discuss how changes in these determinants affect the demand for commodities.

- understand the difference between a change in demand and a change in quantity demanded.

- graph a demand curve and illustrate increases and decreases in demand.

- explain the phenomena of Veblen and Giffin goods and why they constitute rare exceptions to the Law of Demand.

- explain the concept of demand and income elasticity as well as cross elasticity. You should also be able to calculate these elasticity coefficients, using the total revenue method in the case in demand elasticity and by calculating actual percentage changes for all three elasticity types.

- explain the three elasticity categories: elastic, inelastic, and unitary elastic. You should be aware of the factors which affect the elasticity of commodities.

Applications

Application #1

Elasticity coefficients are extremely useful in gaining an understanding of consumer behavior and in predicting how consumers will respond to certain changes. We might start off by asking **how could a firm obtain price elasticity data about a commodity it is selling?** One way would be to have a sale for a short period of time during which it would be have to be assumed that everything else that affected the consumption of the commodity was unchanged. That may well be a reasonable assumption for a period of a week or two if competitors' prices remain unchanged. By changing the commodity's market price and noting how much quantity demanded changes, an estimate of elasticity could be derived.

For example: an appliance firm decreases the price of its washing machines from $490 to $445 for a one-week special sale. Sales of the appliance increase to 36/week, an increase of four from the previous year's weekly average of 32/week. **What is the estimated price elasticity of demand for washing machines sold by this firm?**

Calculations:
$$\epsilon_d = \frac{\%\, \Delta Q_d}{\%\, \Delta P} = \frac{\Delta Q_d / \text{average } Q_d}{\Delta P / \text{average } P} = \frac{4/34}{45/467.5} = \frac{0.11765}{0.09626} = 1.22$$

Based on your elasticity calculations, the firm's demand for washing machines is price elastic -- the quantity demanded will change in a more than proportional fashion for a given price change (at least in the price range between $490 and $445). In this specific case, the price changed by 9.626%, and in response the quantity demanded changed by 11.765%.

A second relevant question would be: **how could a firm utilize elasticity information?** In the case above, the demand for washing machines is slightly elastic, and the firm could generate more total revenues by lowering the price of the machines. When demand is elastic, a price increase of a given amount would result in a more than proportional decrease in the quantity demanded. This provides the firm with some useful insights into an appropriate pricing strategy, one which should help the firm achieve its goal of profit maximization.

Application #2

The Clinton Administration pushed through a deficit reduction program, part of which included an increase of 4.3 cents in the gasoline tax. **Public Policy Question: How much will the gasoline tax affect the consumption of gasoline?** To calculate the impact of the new tax on the price of gasoline, one needs to know the price elasticity of demand for gasoline (approximately 0.2) and the current price of gasoline (approximately $1.20 per gallon). For purposes of this example, we will assume that the price of gasoline increases by the amount of the tax. In actuality, the new price could rise either more or less than the amount of the tax increase.

Calculations:
$$\epsilon_d = \frac{\% \Delta Q_d}{\% \Delta P} = \frac{\Delta Q_d / \text{average } Q_d}{\Delta P / \text{average } P}$$

$$0.2 = \frac{(x) \% \Delta Q_d}{4.3/122.15} = \frac{(x) \% \Delta Q_d}{0.0352 = 3.52\%}$$

$$(x) \% \Delta Q_d = 0.2 (0.0352) = 0.00704 \quad (0.704\%)$$

The equation above has one unknown, the percentage change in quantity demanded, which can be solved easily by multiplying the elasticity coefficient by the percentage change in price (0.0352). The estimated change in quantity demanded turns out to be 0.00704 (0.704%). We can see from our calculations that the tax is not going to have a major impact on the consumption of gasoline. Using data from <u>The Statistical Abstract of the United States: 1992</u>, we can obtain a "ballpark" estimate of the actual effect of the tax on gasoline consumption.

According to the <u>Statistical Abstract</u>, in 1988, households owned 147.5 million vehicles which they drove 1,511 billion miles, consuming 82.4 billion gallons of gasoline in the process. If the quantity demanded for gasoline decreased by 0.704% as a result of the tax, gasoline consumption would be expected to decrease to a level of 81.82 billion gallons -- a decrease of 0.58 billion gallons. If gasoline consumption after the tax was indeed 81.82 billion gallons, our tax revenue forecast would be that the tax would raise 81.82 times 4.3 cents/gallon for a total tax revenue increase of about $3.52 billion dollars, an amount that will not appreciably reduce the Federal deficit.

Obviously the accuracy of our forecast will depend upon the appropriateness of the assumptions that were used in the analysis. A recent report indicated that the Clinton Administration expected to raise about $23 billion from the gas tax over the five year period of the deficit reduction plan. If one makes allowance for the fact that gasoline consumption undoubtedly increased from 1988, the latest year for which data were available, the estimate derived above is not all that far off the mark.

An interesting secondary effect of the tax increase is that the tax will reduce carbon emissions associated with gasoline consumption. It is estimated that the combustion of one gallon of gasoline generates about twenty pounds of carbon dioxide. Thus, a decrease in gasoline consumption of 0.58 billion gallons would also have the effect of reducing carbon dioxide emissions by 11.6 billion pounds (5.8 million tons).

Self Evaluation

List of Terms

Complementary Goods
Ceteris Paribus
Change in Demand
Conspicuous Consumption
Cross Elasticity of Demand
Demand
Demand Curve
Diminishing Marginal Utility
Elastic
Elasticity
Engel Curve
Equilibrium Quantity
Giffin Good

Income Effect
Income Elasticity
Inelastic
Inferior Good
Lemon Goods
Marginal Utility
Normal Good
Price Elasticity of Demand
Quantity Demanded
Substitution Effect
Substitute Goods
Unitary Elastic
Veblen Good

For the statements below, fill in the term from the list above which provides the best fit.

1.) __Marginal Utility__ implies that individuals obtain more satisfaction from the second unit of consumption than the third unit and value the third unit more than the fourth.

2.) If, in response to a price change of a certain percentage, consumers respond in a less than proportional fashion, demand is a said to be __Inelastic__.

3.) A good which stresses it's high price and exclusiveness is likely to be a __Veblen Good__.

4.) __Elasticity__ is a measure of the responsiveness that exists between two economic variables.

5.) Goods whose use goes hand in hand with each other are known as __Complementary__.

6.) If consumers are willing to pay more or less for each quantity demanded or buy more or less at each market price, then a __Change in Demand__ has occurred.

7.) The __Equilibrium__ indicates the level of production and sales that the market is always headed towards.

8.) The __Demand__ is the amount purchased at a specific market price.

45

9.) One reason that consumers buy more of a commodity as its price decreases is that a price decrease increases, to some small extent, effective consumer income. The effect is called the _____.

10.) An _____ plots how the consumption of a good changes as total income changes.

11.) If more of a good is purchased as consumers' incomes increase, then it must be a _____.

12.) The Law of Demand as well as the Law of Supply is valid only when we make the assumption of _____.

13.) A _____ plots the relationship that exists between market price and quantity demanded.

14.) If the price of a commodity increases by 10% and consumers respond by decreasing their consumption proportionally, demand is said to be _____.

15.) The rare exception to the Law of Demand, where price and quantity demanded are positively and directly related to one another, is known as a _____.

16.) Buying luxury items simply to impress your neighbors is an example of _____.

17.) The relationship that exists between income changes and subsequent changes in the quantity demanded for a commodity is captured by the _____.

18.) Demand is _____ when consumers respond to a price change by changing their consumption in a more than proportional fashion.

19.) The _____ means that consumers will always buy more of a commodity when its price decreases relative to its potential substitutes.

20.) When consumers buy less of a commodity when their incomes rise, that commodity is referred to as an _____.

21.) The _____ is a measure which tells us something about the sensitivity of the quantity demanded to changes in market price.

22.) One way to determine whether or not commodities are substitutes or complements for one another or how effective substitutes they are, is to calculate the _____ between the two commodities.

23.) _____ is an economic concept which reflects the preferences and the intensity of those preferences for the buyers of a commodity.

24.) The demand curve for _____ may not have a typical downward slope because of the perceived risk associated with buying such items.

25.) A major determinant of demand is the price of _____.

26.) The extra amount of satisfaction obtained from consuming an additional unit of a commodity is called _____.

Problems

The Demand Curve and Changes in Demand

In the table below, indicate the effect of the event described on the left and show how it can be depicted on a demand and supply graph. All of the events shown below have an effect only on demand. The first one has been completed as an example.

Market Involved	Event	Effect on Demand	Graph
1. New CDs	Stores start to sell used CDs	Less demand for new CDs / shifts left	*(example graph)*
2. Personal computers	Prices decrease	Qnt demanded increases / shifts down	
3. Milk	Consumers react adversely to milk produced with BST (Bovine Growth Hormone which enhances milk production)	Demand decreases	
4. Fur coats	Animal rights groups change consumers' attitudes towards this product	less demand	
5. Personal computers	Consumers expect significant price decreases in the future	move demand / shifts up	
6. Grocery products in small town	Increase in population	more demand / shifts out right	
7. Chicken	Price of beef increases	more demand / shifts right	
8. Large screen TVs	Latest recession decreases total personal income	less demand / shifts left	

47

Market Involved	Event	Effect on Demand	Graph
9. Household cable TV	The cost of television sets decreases	Increase	
10. CD players	The price of CDs decreases because of technological changes and economies of scale	Increase	
11. Satellite dishes	The FCC decides it is no longer illegal to pick up private satellite signals	Increase	
12. Natural gas	Global warming increases winter temperatures by 2.5 degrees F.		
13. Private brand tuna	Per capita incomes increase as the economic recovery kicks in		
14. Automobiles	New oil discoveries in the Middle East lower the price of energy		
15. U.S. clothing	The latest "Buy American" campaign succeeds		

Elasticity Problems

Using the information provided in each case below, calculate the apppropriate elasticity coefficient. Be sure to interpret in terms of the problem, the meaning of each coefficient.

1.) The price of a commodity increases from $10 to $15, and as a result the Q_d changes from 2000 units per month to 1300 units per month.

Elasticity coefficient: $\frac{\% \Delta Q}{\% \Delta P} = \frac{700/1650}{5/12.5} = \frac{.42}{.40} = 1.05$

Interpretation: Elastic for ever 1% change in price 1.05% change in Q

2.) The price of a commodity decreases from $200 to $180, and as a result the Q_d increases from 400 units per day to 475 units per day.

Elasticity coefficient: $\frac{75/437.5}{20/190} = \frac{.17}{.11} = 1.55$

Interpretation: Elastic for every 1% change in price 1.5% change in Q

3.) The price of a commodity increases from $2.40 to $2.60, and as a result the Q_d decreases from 60 units per day to 44 units per day.

Elasticity coefficient: $\dfrac{16/52}{.20/2.50} \rightarrow \dfrac{.31}{.08} = 3.88$

Interpretation: very Elastic –

4.) The price of a commodity increases from $6.00 to $6.60, and as a result the Q_d changes from 12,800 units per year to 12,000 units per year.

Elasticity coefficient: $\dfrac{.60/6.30}{800/12400} = \dfrac{.10}{.06} = 1.67$

Interpretation:

5.) At the latest OPEC (the Organization of Petroleum Exporting Countries) meeting, the foreign ministers decide to limit the daily output of petroleum. As a result, the price of petroleum rises from $19.20 to $20 per barrel. Petroleum consumption in the United States changes from 8.5 million barrels per day (mbd) to 8.4 mbd. What is the price elasticity of demand for petroleum in the United States?

Elasticity coefficient: $\dfrac{.80/19.60}{.10/8.45} = \dfrac{.04}{.01} = 4.0$

Interpretation:

6.) The price of pencils rises from 40 cents to 50 cents. Total pencil sales at your college's bookstore decline from 12,600 to 12,000. What is the elasticity of demand for pencils at your college?

Elasticity coefficient: $\dfrac{.10/.45}{600/12300} = \dfrac{.22}{.05} = 4.44$

Interpretation:

7.) The price of movies decreases at your local theatre from $4 to $3. Attendance (made up mostly of college students) increases from 750 per month to 1000 a month.

Elasticity coefficient:

Interpretation:

8.) Last year, per capita income in the United States increased from $17,000 per person to $18,200. During the same time period, the consumption of beef fell from 110 pounds per person to 104 pounds per person. Assume for this problem, all other factors which affect the consumption of beef did not change.

Elasticity coefficient:

Interpretation:

9.) The price of a gallon of gas rises from $1.20 to $1.40, and as a result the Q_d of large cars changes from 1.8 million units per year to 1.6 million units per year.

Elasticity coefficient:

Interpretation:

Calculating Elasticity Coefficients

Referring to the demand schedule for bicycles shown in the following table, calculate total revenue and the elasticity of demand for each of the price/quantity combinations contained in the table. Spaces are provided between the line for your elasticity coefficients, reflecting the fact that your calculations are based on price and quantity data from two different lines of the table.

Table 3-1

Price P	Quantity Demanded Q_d (in millions)	Total Revenue TR = P × Q_d (in billions of $)	Elasticity of Demand E_d
$220	0	0	
$200	6	1200	20
$180	12	2160	5.6
$160	18	2880	
$140	24	3360	
$120	30	3600	
$100	36	3600	
$80	42	3360	
$60	48	2880	
$40	54	2160	
$20	60	1200	
$0	66	0	

Handwritten calculations in margin:
ΔQ = 6/3 = 2.0
20/210 = .10
6/9 = .67
20/170 = .12

Plot the above demand curve on the top graph (Figure 3-1) on the next page. Draw a bracket illustrating that part of the demand curve which is elastic, unitary elastic, and inelastic. On the graph below, plot your total revenue data.

After examining the two graphs, what conclusions can you draw about the relationship of the elasticity of demand along a straight line demand curve and total revenue?

_____

What can be said about the elasticity of demand as one moves along a straight line demand curve?

_____

_____

The Demand for Bicycles
Figure 3-1

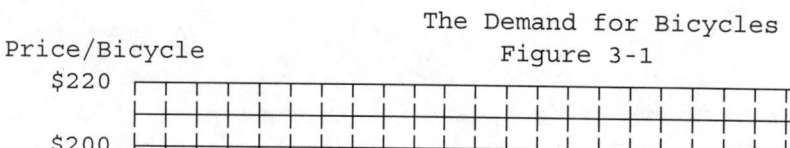

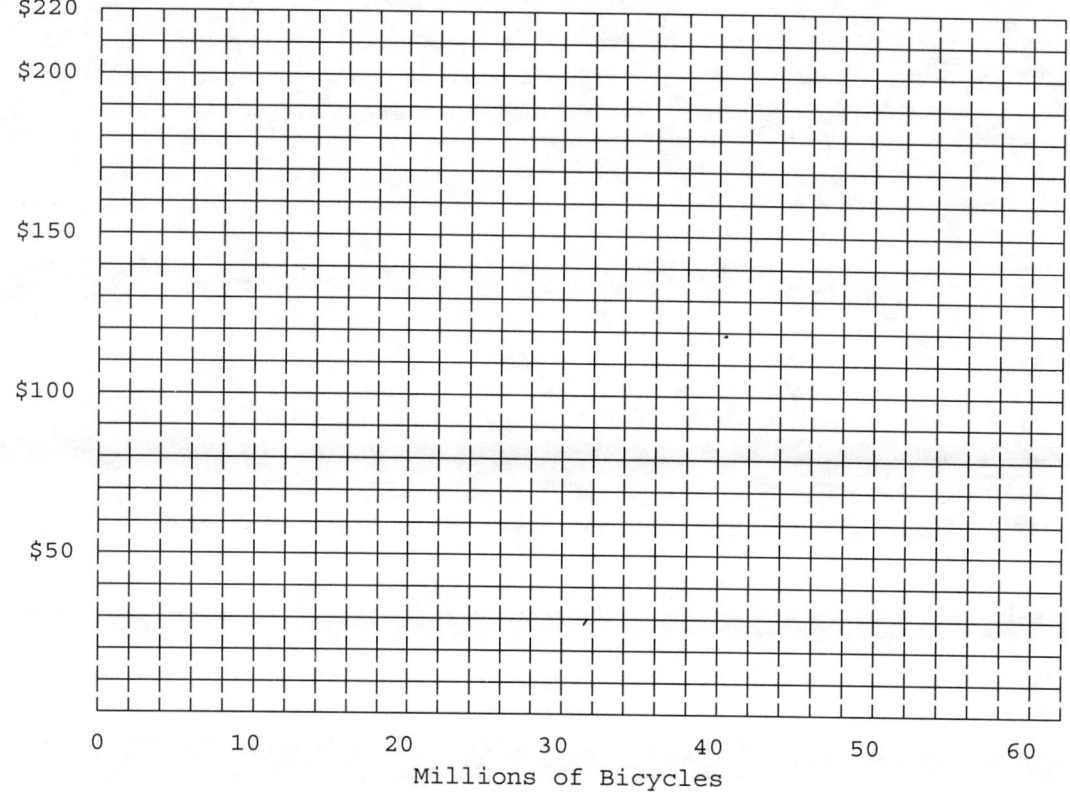

Price/Bicycle (y-axis, $0 to $220)
Millions of Bicycles (x-axis, 0 to 60)

Total Revenue (in billions of $) Figure 3-2

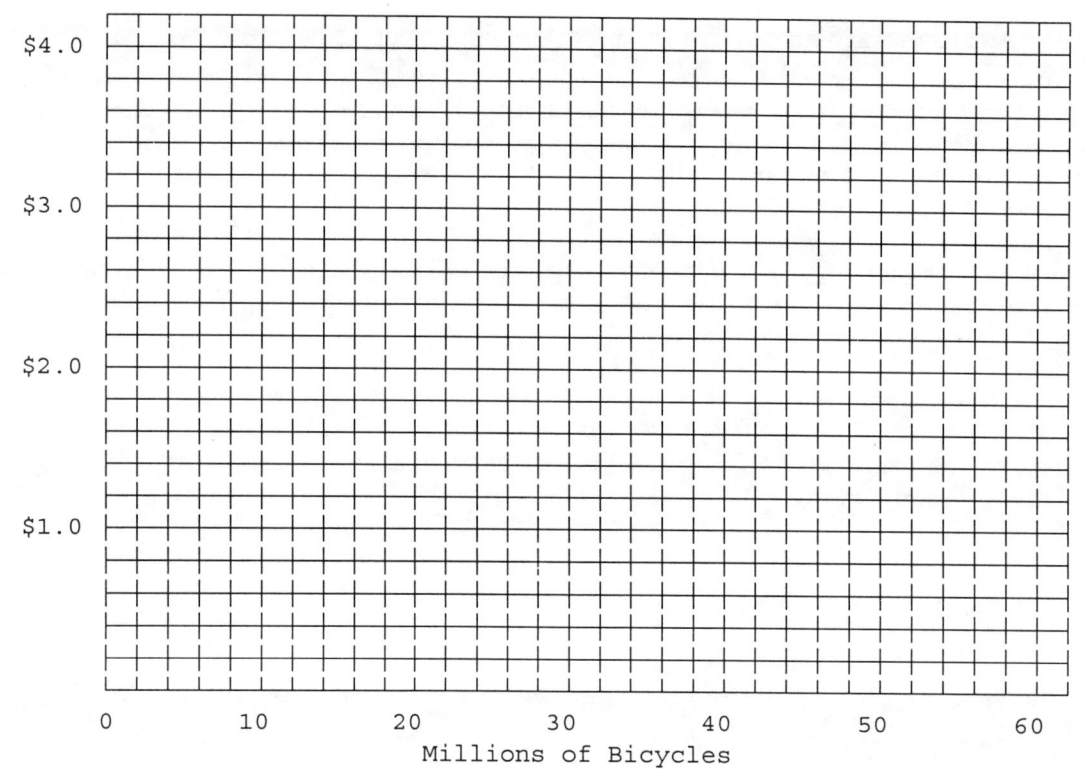

Millions of Bicycles (x-axis, 0 to 60); y-axis $0 to $4.0

Interpret, in terms of the bicycle market, the meaning of your calculated elasticity coefficient for the segment of the demand curve from $140 - $120:

_____

the segment of the demand curve from $80 - $60:

_____

True/False Statements

Indicate whether you think the statements below are true or false. These questions are designed to make you think about the concepts presented in the text. There may not be any easy clear-cut answers. Some thoughts about the answers are presented at the end of the chapter.

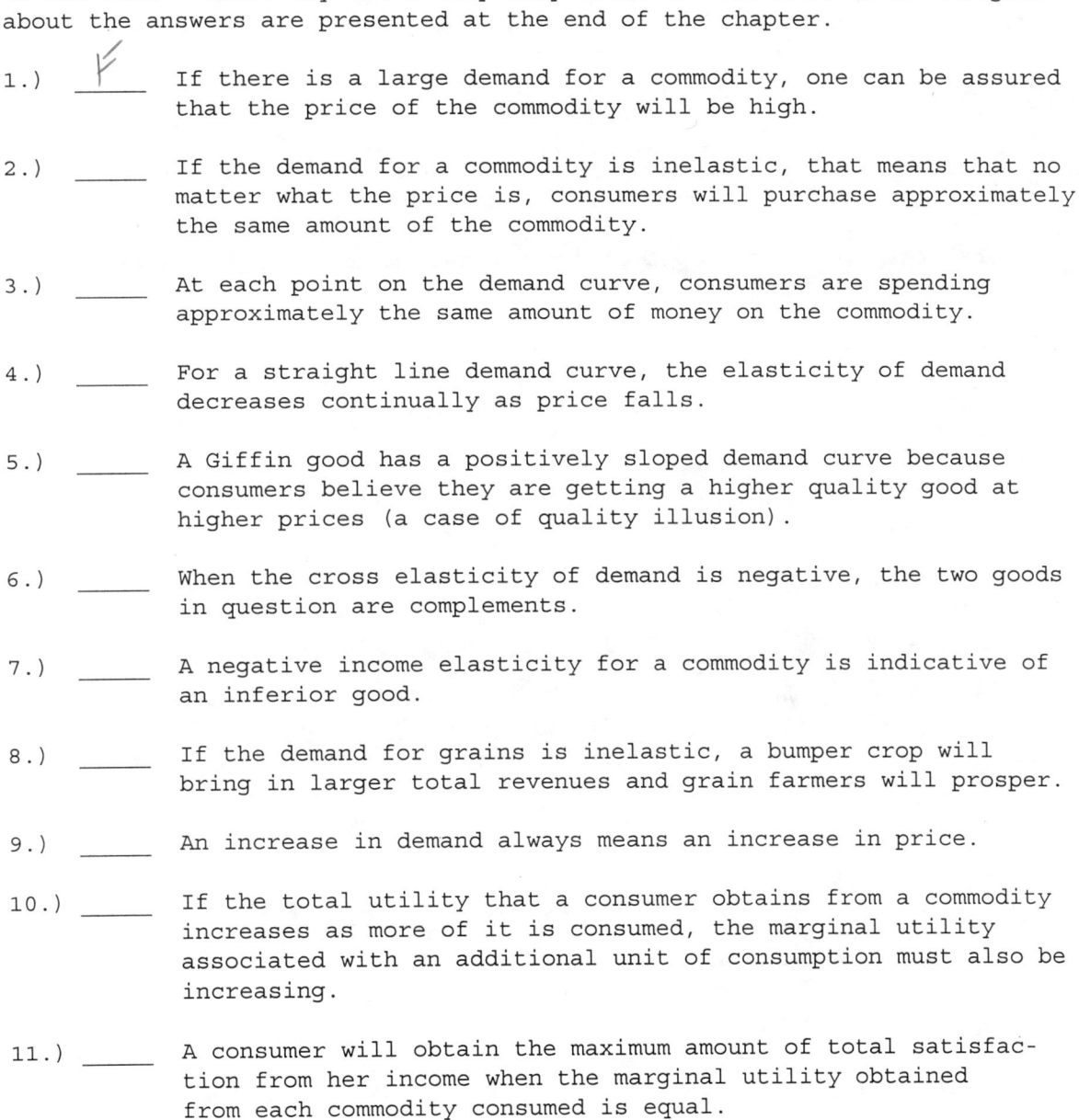

1.) __F__ If there is a large demand for a commodity, one can be assured that the price of the commodity will be high.

2.) _____ If the demand for a commodity is inelastic, that means that no matter what the price is, consumers will purchase approximately the same amount of the commodity.

3.) _____ At each point on the demand curve, consumers are spending approximately the same amount of money on the commodity.

4.) _____ For a straight line demand curve, the elasticity of demand decreases continually as price falls.

5.) _____ A Giffin good has a positively sloped demand curve because consumers believe they are getting a higher quality good at higher prices (a case of quality illusion).

6.) _____ When the cross elasticity of demand is negative, the two goods in question are complements.

7.) _____ A negative income elasticity for a commodity is indicative of an inferior good.

8.) _____ If the demand for grains is inelastic, a bumper crop will bring in larger total revenues and grain farmers will prosper.

9.) _____ An increase in demand always means an increase in price.

10.) _____ If the total utility that a consumer obtains from a commodity increases as more of it is consumed, the marginal utility associated with an additional unit of consumption must also be increasing.

11.) _____ A consumer will obtain the maximum amount of total satisfaction from her income when the marginal utility obtained from each commodity consumed is equal.

Multiple-Choice Questions

Select the "best" answer from the alternatives provided:

1.) If, over a period of time, we observe that the quantity demanded of commodity has increased while at the same time, its price increased
   a. this would be a legitimate exception to the law of demand.
   b. this is an impossible situation which violates the law of demand.
   c. this situation most likely occurred because the supply of the commodity decreased.
   d. this could have occurred if consumer income increased during the period of time.

2.) Analyze the following statement: **"Imposing taxes doesn't really affect the price of an item. With the imposition of a tax, the commodity's price rises temporarily, but the price rise decreases the demand for the item and that, in turn, causes the price to go back down again, leaving the price unchanged from before."**
   a. This economic analysis is basically correct.
   b. The analysis is incorrect, confusing the term demand with quantity demanded.
   c. The analysis is incorrect, since taxes don't increase prices even temporarily.
   d. The analysis is incorrect, since changes in demand don't affect the price of a commodity.

3.) A commodity is more likely to have an inelastic demand if
   a. it is a luxury good that people don't really need.
   b. there are not very many good substitutes for the commodity.
   c. the price of the commodity is very high.
   d. the commodity is normally used in conjunction with another product.
   e. the commodity represents a significant portion of consumers' total income.

4.) The difference between a "change in demand" and a "change in quantity demanded"
   a. depends on whether or not the supply curve shifts or not.
   b. is that a "change in demand" means that a shift in the demand curve has occurred, while a "change in quantity demanded" refers to a movement along an existing demand curve.
   c. refers to the magnitude of the shifts in the demand curve and the price change.
   d. is a distinction without meaning, since the terms can be used interchangeably.

5.) Suppose you are able to identify two different points on a commodity's demand curve with prices $22 and $18 and quantities 110 and 130 units. The commodity's elasticity of demand between those two points is:
   a. 1.00   b. 0.83   c. 1.20   d. 0.69
   e. Unable to calculate

6.) Which of the following will cause the demand for wheat to increase?
   a. a decrease in the cost of producing wheat
   b. an increase in the price of bread
   c. a decrease in the price of wheat
   d. a decrease in the price of bread
   e. a decrease in the supply of wheat

7.) If the elasticity of demand for a commodity is 0.75, then
   a. expenditures on the commodity will rise by 0.75 % for each 1 % decrease in price.
   b. the quantity demanded of the commodity will remain roughly the same for a price change, since demand is inelastic.
   c. for every change in price of 1 unit, the quantity demanded will change by 0.75 unit.
   d. for every 1 % change in price, quantity demanded will change by 0.75 %.

8.) When the demand for a commodity changes
   a. the elasticity of demand changes in the same direction.
   b. there has been a movement along the existing demand curve.
   c. the quantity demanded will change proportionally with each price change.
   d. the demand curve has shifted either to the left or right.
   e. none of the above.

9.) If the price of complementary good X decreases, then the demand for good Y will
   a. shift to the right.
   b. shift to the left.
   c. remain unchanged; there will be a movement along the demand curve of good Y
   d. become more elastic.
   e. become more inelastic.

10.) When a seller set the product price at $10, total revenues amounted to $120,000. When the price was reduced to $8, total expenditures changed to $128,000. Based on this information
   a. the demand for the commodity is inelastic.
   b. the demand for the commodity is elastic.
   c. the demand for the commodity is unitary elastic.
   d. it is not possible to determine elasticity from this information.

11.) Suppose that a demand schedule for a product has a downward slope and that the price of the product increases from $4.50 to $5.00. Which of the following will result?
   a. Consumer tastes for this product will increase.
   b. The demand for the product will increase.
   c. The supply of the product will decrease.
   d. Quantity demanded of the product will increase.
   e. Quantity demanded of the product will decrease.

12.) When deriving a demand curve for a commodity, we make the assumption of *ceteris paribus* which means that all except the following are held constant:
   a. consumer tastes
   b. consumer income
   c. price and quantity demanded
   d. the price of substitute goods
   e. the number of consumers in the market

13.) Suppose that the price of product G increases from $10 to $20 and, in response, quantity demanded declines from 100 to 80. Using the price elasticity formula, the elasticity of demand is
   a. .25.   b. .33.   c. .67.   d. 1.35.   e. 1.97.

14.) If the demand for product X shifts to the left as the price of product Y increases, then
   a. X and Y are complementary goods.
   b. X and Y are substitute goods.
   c. X and Y are unrelated goods.
   d. the income of consumers of Y has increased.
   e. product X is price elastic.

15.) If the demand for a commodity decreases, one possible cause for that would be
   a. consumer expectations of future price increases.
   b. a decrease in the price of a substitute commodity.
   c. a new use for the commodity.
   d. a decrease in consumer income and the commodity in question is an inferior good.
   e. an increase in the price of a complementary commodity.

16.) If the elasticity of income of a commodity is greater than +1.0
   a. the commodity in question is an inferior good.
   b. the commodity in question is a normal good but income inelastic.
   c. the commodity in question is a normal good but income elastic.
   d. the commodity in question is a normal good, but nothing can be said concerning whether it's elastic or inelastic.

17.) A Giffin good will exist when
   a. consumers spend a large percentage of their income on the good.
   b. consumers buy more of the commodity at higher prices than at lower prices.
   c. a good has an income elasticity of zero.
   d. consumers are forced to buy more of the commodity than they would really prefer.
   e. both a and b

18.) If the cross elasticity of demand between two commodities equals -2.6
   a. the two commodities are strong substitutes for one another.
   b. the two commodities are weak substitutes for one another.
   c. The two commodities are weak complements for one another.
   d. the two commodities are strong complements for one another.

19.) Which of the following would be the most likely to categorized as a Veblen good?
   a. a popular novel that everyone is reading
   b. the latest diet pill, guaranteed to take those pounds off
   c. a Jaguar sports car
   d. L. L. Bean hunting boots
   e. both c and d

20.) Abby Jones is currently consuming 5 CDs and 8 pizzas a month while she attends school at Northland University, majoring in economics (of course!). The CDs cost $8 each, while the pizzas run $10 apiece. Her marginal utility for the last CD she bought was 48 units of utility, while she obtained 50 units of utility from the last pizza consumed. If Abby wants to maximize her overall utility from her limited income
   a. Abby should consume more pizzas and less CDs.
   b. Abby should consume more CDs and less pizzas.
   c. Abby should consume more of both goods.
   d. Abby should not change her current consumption pattern.

Discussion Questions

1.) What is the difference between the concept of overall scarcity and a shortage?

2.) Assume you had control of a budget of a local municipality with the following expenditure categories:
   Education $4   Million
   Roads $10 Million
   Parks $0.5 Million
   Police and Fire $2.7 Million

   Explain how you could use the rule for attaining optimum satisfaction for consumers (see pages 55 and 56 in Hogendorn's text) for allocating your municipal budget in an optimum fashion. What would your optimizing rule be?

3.) If we lived in a world where everything was free, use the rule for obtaining an optimal combination of purchases for consumers to explain how much of each available commodity we would consume?

4.) A change in price results in a change in the quantity demanded of a commodity, while a change in demand causes a change in the price of the commodity. Please explain.

5.) A recent TV newscast reported on a story about a dairy farmer killing several of his dairy cows to get the public's attention about the plight of dairy farmers. Using the concept of the price elasticity of demand, explain the economic point the farmer was trying to make. What must dairy farmers be assuming about the price elasticity of milk?

6.) Briefly explain why you would expect the demand for gasoline to be more inelastic than the demand for a major oil company's brand of gasoline.

7.) The demand for most agricultural products is inelastic. Why do you think that is the case? Suppose that the demand for Columbian Coffee in the United States is price inelastic. Would Columbian coffee growers be pleased or disheartened by freezing weather which destroyed about one third of their total coffee harvest? Do you think the demand for Columbian coffee is income elastic or inelastic? If you were exporting a product to the United States, would you prefer that your product be income elastic or income inelastic?

8.) Use the concept of the cross elasticity of demand between cameras and film to explain why a firm like Kodak which makes both products might want to offer some good quality, low cost cameras (perhaps even lowering their profit margin or selling the camera at cost)?

9.) There have been quite a number of consumer-oriented articles which have pointed out to consumers that there is little difference among various brands of aspirin. How would you explain how several firms are able to sell their brand of aspirin at quite high prices compared to the generic brands of aspirin (which the articles suggest are about the same as the "name" brands).

Answers and Solutions to Problems and Exercises

Completing Statements from the List of Terms

1.)	Diminishing Marginal Utility	14.)	Unitary Elastic
2.)	Inelastic	15.)	Giffin Good
3.)	Veblen Good	16.)	Conspicuous Consumption
4.)	Elasticity	17.)	Income Elasticity
5.)	Complementary Goods	18.)	Elastic
6.)	Change in Demand	19.)	Substitution Effect
7.)	Equilibrium Quantity	20.)	Inferior Good
8.)	Quantity Demanded	21.)	Price Elasticity of Demand
9.)	Income Effect	22.)	Cross Elasticity of Demand
10.)	Engel Curve	23.)	Demand
11.)	Normal Good	24.)	Lemon Goods
12.)	*Ceteris Paribus*	25.)	Substitute Goods
13.)	Demand Curve	26.)	Marginal Utility

The Demand Curve and Changes in Demand

Market Involved	Event	Effect on Demand	Graph
1. Music CDs	Stores start to sell used CDs	Less demand for new CDs	
2. Personal computers	Prices decrease	Decrease in quantity demanded No shift in demand Movement along an existing demand curve	
3. Milk	Consumers react adversely to milk produced with BST (Bovine Growth Hormone which enhances milk production)	Decrease in demand Preferences have changed	
4. Fur coats	Animal rights groups change consumers' attitudes towards this product	Decrease in demand Preferences have changed	

Market Involved	Event	Effect on Demand	Graph
5. Personal computers	Consumers expect significant price decreases in the future	Decrease in current demand as consumers postpone purchases	D'←D
6. Grocery products in small town	Increase in population	Increase in demand Larger number of buyers	D→D'
7. Chicken	Price of beef increases	Increase in demand Chicken becomes a cheaper substitute	D→D'
8. Large screen TVs	Latest recession decreases total personal income	Decrease in demand Less ability to purchase the TVs	D'←D
9. Household cable TV	The cost of HBO and The Disney Channel increases	Decrease in demand Price of complementary good increases	D'←D
10. CD players	The price of CDs decreases because of technological changes and economies of scale	Increase in demand Price of complementary good decreases	D→D'
11. Satellite dishes	The FCC decides it is no longer illegal to pick up private satellite signals	Increase in demand Commodity becomes more useful	D→D'
12. Natural gas	Global warming decreases winter temperatures by 2.5 degrees F.	Decrease in demand Less need for the commodity	D'←D
13. Private brand tuna	Per capita incomes increase as the economic recovery kicks in	Assuming this is an inferior good, decrease in demand	D'←D
14. Automobiles	New oil discoveries in the Middle East lower the price of energy	Increase in demand Decrease in the price of complementary good	D→D'
15. U.S. clothing	The latest "Buy American" campaign succeeds	Increase in demand Change in preferences	D→D'

Elasticity Problems

1.) Elasticity coefficient: 1.0606

   Interpretation: slightly elastic demand. For every 1% change in price, quantity demanded will change by 1.06%.

2.) Elasticity coefficient: 1.628

   Interpretation: elastic. For every 1% change in price, quantity demanded will change by 1.628%.

3.) Elasticity coefficient: 3.846

   Interpretation: very elastic and responsive demand. For every 1 % change in price, quantity demanded will change by 3.846%.

4.) Elasticity coefficient: 0.677

   Interpretation: inelastic demand. For every 1% change in price, quantity demanded will change by 0.677%.

5.) Elasticity coefficient: 0.28994

   Interpretation: very inelastic and unresponsive demand. For every 1% change in price, quantity demanded will change by 0.28994%.

6.) Elasticity coefficient: 0.2195

   Interpretation: very inelastic demand because of the small expenditure involved. For every 1% change in price, quantity demanded changes by 0.2195%.

7.) Elasticity coefficient: 1.0

   Interpretation: unitary elastic, since the amount spent on movies remains the same. For every 1% change in price, quantity demanded changes by 1%.

8.) Elasticity coefficient: - 0.8692   (Income elasticity)

   Interpretation: slightly income inelastic. For every 1% change in consumer income, quantity demanded changes by 0.8692% Inferior good.

9.) Elasticity coefficient: - 0.765   Cross elasticity of demand

   Interpretation: since the cross elasticity coefficient is negative, the two commodities are complementary to one another, although not all that responsive to price changes. For every 1% change in the price of gasoline, the quantity demanded of large cars changes by 0.765% in the opposite direction of the price change.

Calculating Elasticity Coefficients

Table 3-1

Price P	Quantity Demanded Q_d (in millions)	Total Revenue TR = P X Q_d (in billions of $)	Elasticity of Demand E_d
$220	0	$ 0	
			21.00
$200	6	$ 1.2 B	
			6.33
$180	12	$ 2.16 B	
			3.40
$160	18	$ 2.88 B	
			2.14
$140	24	$ 3.36 B	
			1.44
$120	30	$ 3.60 B	
			1.00
$100	36	$ 3.60 B	
			0.69
$80	42	$ 3.36 B	
			0.47
$60	48	$ 2.88 B	
			0.29
$40	54	$ 2.16 B	
			0.16
$20	60	$ 1.2 B	
			0.05
$0	66	$ 0	

After examining the two graphs, what conclusions can you draw about the relationship of the elasticity of demand along a straight line demand curve and total revenue? **Total revenue rises when demand is elastic, falls when it is inelastic, and is at a peak when elasticity is unitary elastic.**

What can be said about the elasticity of demand as one moves along a straight line demand curve? **The price elasticity of demand continuously declines from infinity to zero as one moves down a straight line demand curve.**

Interpret, in terms of the bicycle market, the meaning of your calculated elasticity coefficient: the segment of the demand curve from $140 - $120: ϵ_D = **1.44   Since the elasticity coefficient is greater than one, that segment of the demand curve is elastic -- for every 1% change in price, the quantity demanded changes by 1.44%.**

the segment of the demand curve from $80 - $60: ϵ_D = **0.47   Since the elasticity coefficient is less than one, that segment of the demand curve is inelastic -- for every 1% change in price, the quantity demanded changes by 0.47%.**

Figure 3-3
The Demand for Bicycles

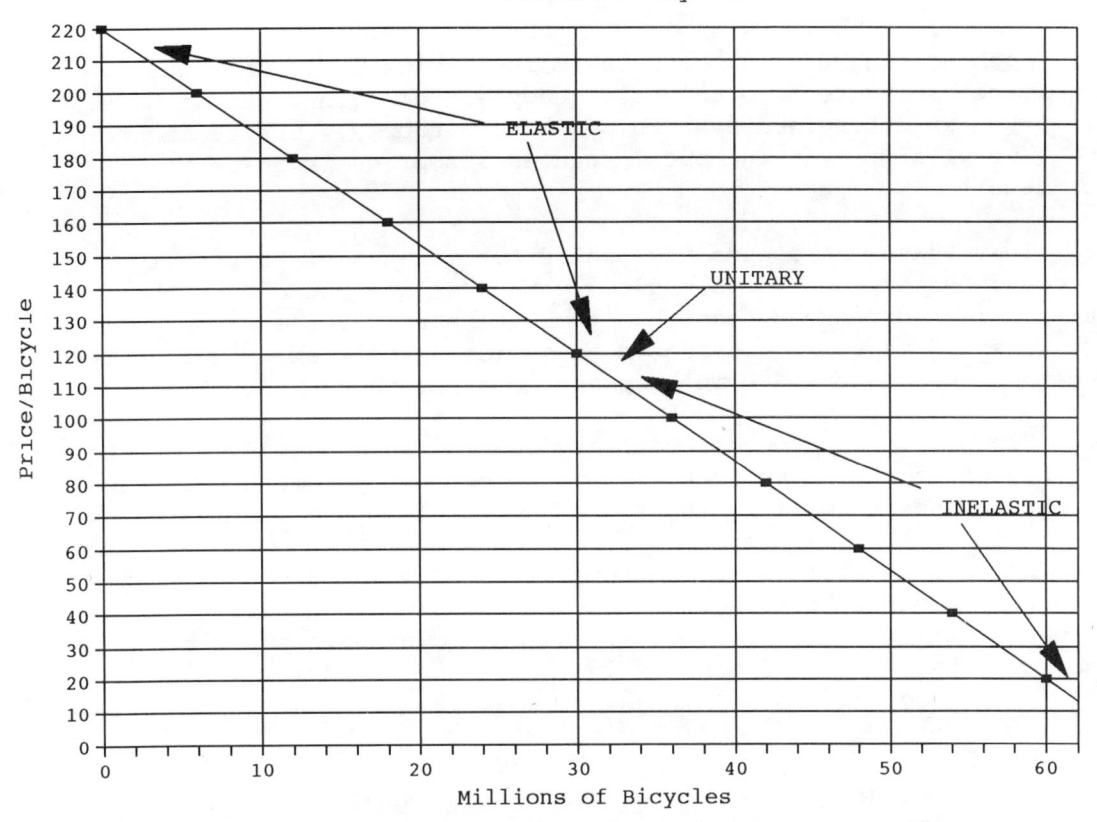

Figure 3-4
Total Revenue

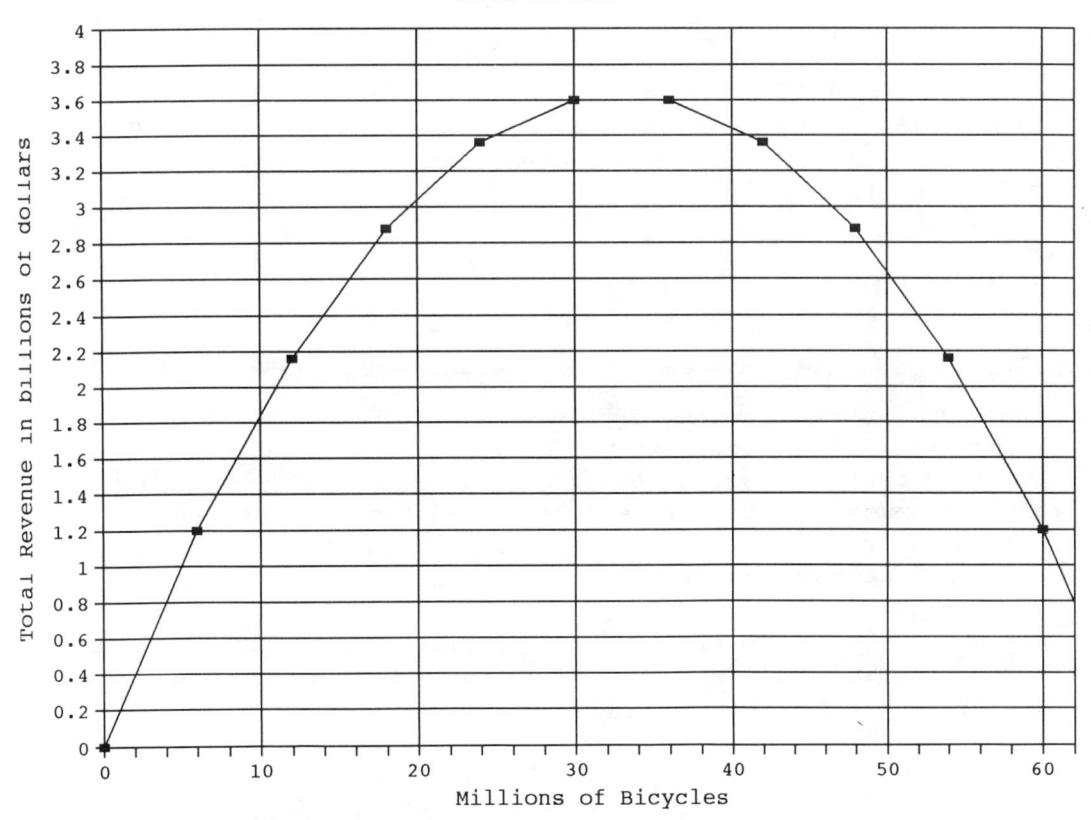

True/False Statements

1.) **False.** Nothing can be said about the market price until the other blade of the "scissors," in this case supply, comes into the picture. Market price is determined by both demand and supply. The demand for water is very large, yet in most instances its price is quite low, if not free.

2.) **False.** This statement sounds reasonable but is actually true only when demand is completely inelastic. Demand is inelastic when the quantity demanded changes less than proportionately for a given price change. Demand is still considered to be inelastic even when quantity demanded changes by 9.9% in response to a 10% change in price.

3.) **False.** Wrong! Total expenditures vary considerably depending on the elasticity of demand. Expenditures on the commodity remain constant only when demand is unitary elastic.

4.) **True.** The upper portion of the straight line demand curve is elastic (with high elasticity coefficients), the midpoint is unitary elastic with an elasticity coefficient of 1, and the lower portion of the demand curve below the midpoint is inelastic with elasticity coefficients ranging from less than one to zero.

5.) **False.** The positive sloped demand curve associated with a Giffin good is believed to occur because of the good's dominance in low income households. When the price rises, they have to give up some of the other diet items they had been consuming and buy even more of the Giffin good. When the price falls, it releases sufficient purchasing power so that households can afford to buy other goods. Potatoes are one possible example.

6.) **True.** This would occur when an increase in the price of one good results in a decrease in demand for another good. In terms of the equation for the cross elasticity of demand, a plus divided by a negative.

7.) **True.** By definition, an inferior good is one where less is purchased as income increases -- a situation which yields a negative income elasticity.

8.) **False.** If demand remains relatively constant, a good harvest will decrease the price of the agricultural commodity, and if the demand for that commodity is inelastic, lower prices are associated with lower total revenues, not higher revenues. The increase in the quantity sold associated with the larger harvest is more than offset by the resulting decrease in price.

9.) **False.** If supply is completely elastic (completely horizontal), then an increase in demand will result in an increase only in the equilibrium quantity. A unique case perhaps.

10.) **False.** The Law of Diminishing Marginal Utility indicates that each additional unit consumed will yield less extra satisfaction than the previous unit consumed. If that law holds, total utility will rise, but at a decreasing rate.

11.) **False.** Consumer equilibrium will occur when the **marginal utility per dollar** for each commodity consumed is the same. The equilibrium condition has to be put on a per dollar basis to take into account the different prices of the commodities.

Multiple-Choice

1.) d   2.) b   3.) b   4.) b   5.) b   6.) d

7.) d   8.) d   9.) a   10.) b   11.) e   12.) c

13.) b   14.) a   15.) e   16.) c   17.) e   18.) d

19.) c   20.) c

Discussion Questions

1.) Scarcity is a general economic condition which occurs because the demand for goods and services exceeds what is freely available. Our wants and demands are larger than what can be provided at a zero price. A shortage is caused by the market price being too low for equilibrium and can be solved by raising the market price to its equilibrium market clearing price. Scarcity will always be with us, while shortages can be corrected by allowing the market price to move towards its point of equilibrium.

2.) Consumers can achieve the maximum amount of satisfaction or utility from their scarce income by allocating their purchases of goods and services in such a way that the marginal utility per dollar is approximately the same for each of the goods and services purchased. In a similar fashion, we should allocate our scarce municipal budget funds in such a way that the perceived benefits from spending an extra (or marginal) dollar in each of the expenditure categories is approximately the same. Using this reasoning, the budget would be optimal when the extra benefits obtained from spending an additional dollar on education is roughly equal to the extra benefits that would be generated from spending an extra dollar on roads or parks or police and fire services.

3.) If every commodity were free, then consumption should proceed up to the point where the marginal utility of each commodity consumed is zero. That point will occur sooner for some commodities than others.

4.) The first phrase refers to a movement along an existing demand curve, while the second phrase refers to a shift in the entire demand curve.

5.) If the demand for milk is inelastic (which is what this dairy farmer apparently believes), then the high productivity of dairy farmers leads to a large supply of milk which in turn keeps the price of milk low. If the demand for milk is inelastic (not responsive to price changes), then dairy farmers would be better off with higher milk prices since their total revenue would be larger. This situation will worsen as efficiency is further increased through the use of bovine growth hormone (BST).

6.) The major oil company's brand of gasoline has many more effective substitutes than does the commodity gasoline.

7.) For most agricultural products, the quantity demanded for these products does not increase significantly as the price decreases, perhaps because the marginal utility of additional units of the product falls rather rapidly. The demand for coffee is likely to be inelastic with coffee drinkers not responding proportionately to price changes. If demand is inelastic, a freeze would raise the price of the coffee, and the growers would be pleased since total revenue would be larger. Definitely income elastic because then you would share in the growth of the U.S. market. For non-gourmet coffee, the demand is probably income inelastic which doesn't bode well for the growers' export prospects.

8.) Since there is a high degree of complementarity between the two products, firms may well want to get as many cameras as possible into the hands of the public so that film sales will be vigorous.

9.) The brand name producers use advertising to try and convince consumers that there is a difference between their product and all other products. Such advertising changes consumer preferences, shifting the demand curve to the right and making it more inelastic. Once consumers have been convinced of that difference, a higher price can be charged.

Summary

One of the more important concepts to be gained from an introductory economics course is a working knowledge of how consumers allocate their scarce income in such a way that they get the maximum utility possible from their consumption purchases. Although the process may still seem a bit strange and complicated, all that it requires is that a consumer do the very best that he/she can. It is assumed that consumers are rational and always pick the item that they think will make them best off. In more technical terms, this means that consumers always select the commodity that yields the largest marginal utility (most extra satisfaction) per dollar. In a larger context, with a full array of goods and services, this maximizing process ultimately means that at the margin (the last few dollars spent by a consumer) each of the goods and services consumed will yield appproximately the same marginal utility per dollar. If that is not the case, the consumer would be better off by consuming those goods which have the largest satisfaction per dollar.

This maximizing principle, sometimes referred to as the equi-marginal rule (literally equal at the margin), is applicable and useful in a wide variety of situations. For example, using the perspectives gained from this maximizing rule, the student association's budget at your college or university could be analyzed. Would an extra $1,000 have more impact if spent on campus-wide student entertainment than it would on the homecoming festivities or perhaps the football cheerleaders? The maximizing rule reminds us that if student association budget funds have been allocated in an optimal fashion, then the last dollar spent should yield approximately the same extra benefits in all budget areas.

Appendix on Indifference Curves

Overview

The appendix to Chapter 3 presents an alternative method of analyzing demand and the demand curve. Indifference curve analysis is a more theoretical method than the one presented in the regular text -- a method that is preferred, since it requires less information of the consumer. Indifference curve analysis requires only that consumers be able to rank different bundles (i.e., be able to indicate only whether one bundle is preferred over another bundle or whether the two bundles are equally preferable).

Problem

Deriving a Demand Curve Using Indifference Curves

Assume we are analyzing the behavior of a consumer who can consume two goods -- CDs and Pizza. The price of a CD is $10 and the price of a pizza is $5. Listed below are three different schedules, each of which is made up of various combinations of CDs and pizza, which yield the same amount of satisfaction to the consumer. Our task will be to determine what bundle of CDs and pizzas will result in the highest level of satisfaction, constrained, of course, by the level of income.

Indifference Schedule I 100 units of satisfaction		Indifference Schedule II 120 units of satisfaction		Indifference Schedule III 135 units of satisfaction	
CDs	Pizzas	CDs	Pizzas	CDs	Pizzas
12	1	12	3	12	5
9	2	10	4	10	6
7.5	3	8	5	8	7
5	5	6	6	6	8
3	7	5	7	5	9
2	10	4	8	4	13
1	15	3.5	10	3.5	18
0.5	20	3	13		
		2	20		

Plot the three indifference schedules on the graph below. Initially the consumer has an income of $80. Plot the budget restraint line associated with that level of income -- consisting of all combinations of the two goods that can be purchased with $80. The end points of the budget restraint line will reflect the amount of each good that can be purchased for that level of income -- in this case 8 CDs or 16 pizzas for the $80.

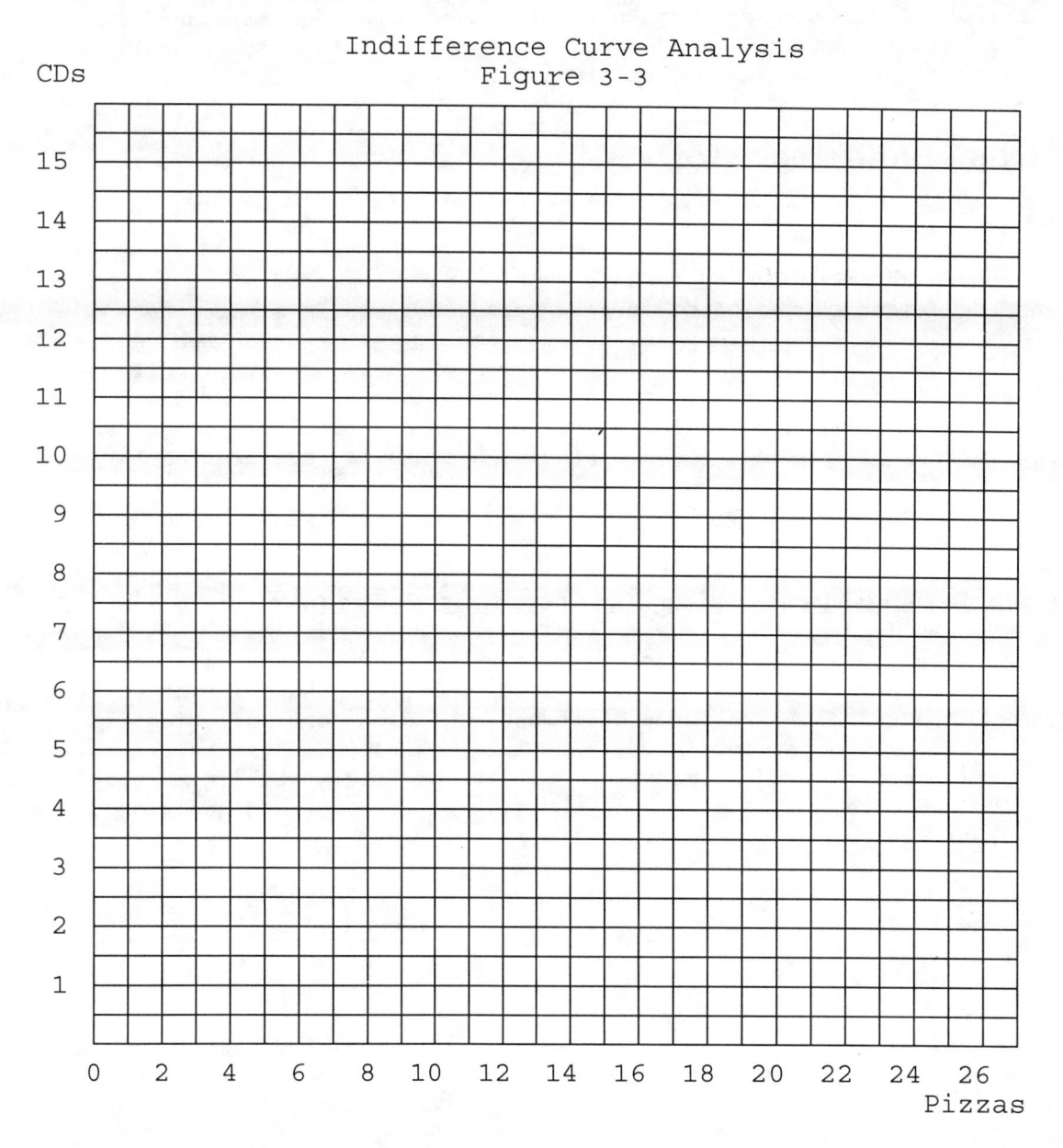

Indifference Curve Analysis
Figure 3-3

CDs

(graph with y-axis CDs labeled 1-15 and x-axis Pizzas labeled 0-26)

Pizzas

Given an income of $80 and the three indifference schedules above, what combination of CDs and pizzas yields the greatest amount of satisfaction for this consumer? _____ CDs _____ Pizzas

By changing the price of pizzas (by adjusting the x-intercept of the budget restraint line), we can determine the points on the consumer's demand curve. Please note that total income remains constant at $80 for these changes.

In the figure above, draw in a new budget restraint line with a y-axis intercept of 8 (the same as before with the price of CDs at $10) and a new x-axis intercept of 24 (this would correspond to a pizza price of $80/24 = $3.33) and another budget restraint line with an x-axis intercept of 12 (corresponding to a pizza price of $80/12 = $6.67).

After you have determined the points of tangency for the three budget restraint lines, you have enough information to fill in the table below regarding the quantity demanded for pizzas.

Price of Pizza	Quantity Demanded
$6.67	_____
$5.00	_____
$3.33	_____

The income and substitution effects of a price change can be isolated and identified using indifference curves and budget restraint lines. Referring back to the price decrease in pizzas from $5 to $3.33, part of the increase in the quantity demanded is due to the income effect of the price change, and part is due to the substitution effect. To separate the two different effects, a new budget restraint line has to be drawn which is tangent to the new, higher indifference curve that is parallel to the initial, higher priced budget restraint line. The income effect is represented by the change in quantity demanded that occurs in moving to the new higher indifference curve, and the substitution effect is represented by the change in quantity demanded that occurs along the new higher indifference curve.

By drawing a series of parallel budget restraint lines corresponding to different levels of income, it is also possible to plot the change in quantity demanded that occurs as consumer income changes.

Answers and Solutions to Problems and Exercises

Deriving a Demand Curve Using Indifference Curves

Figure 3-3
Indifference Curves for CDs and Pizzas

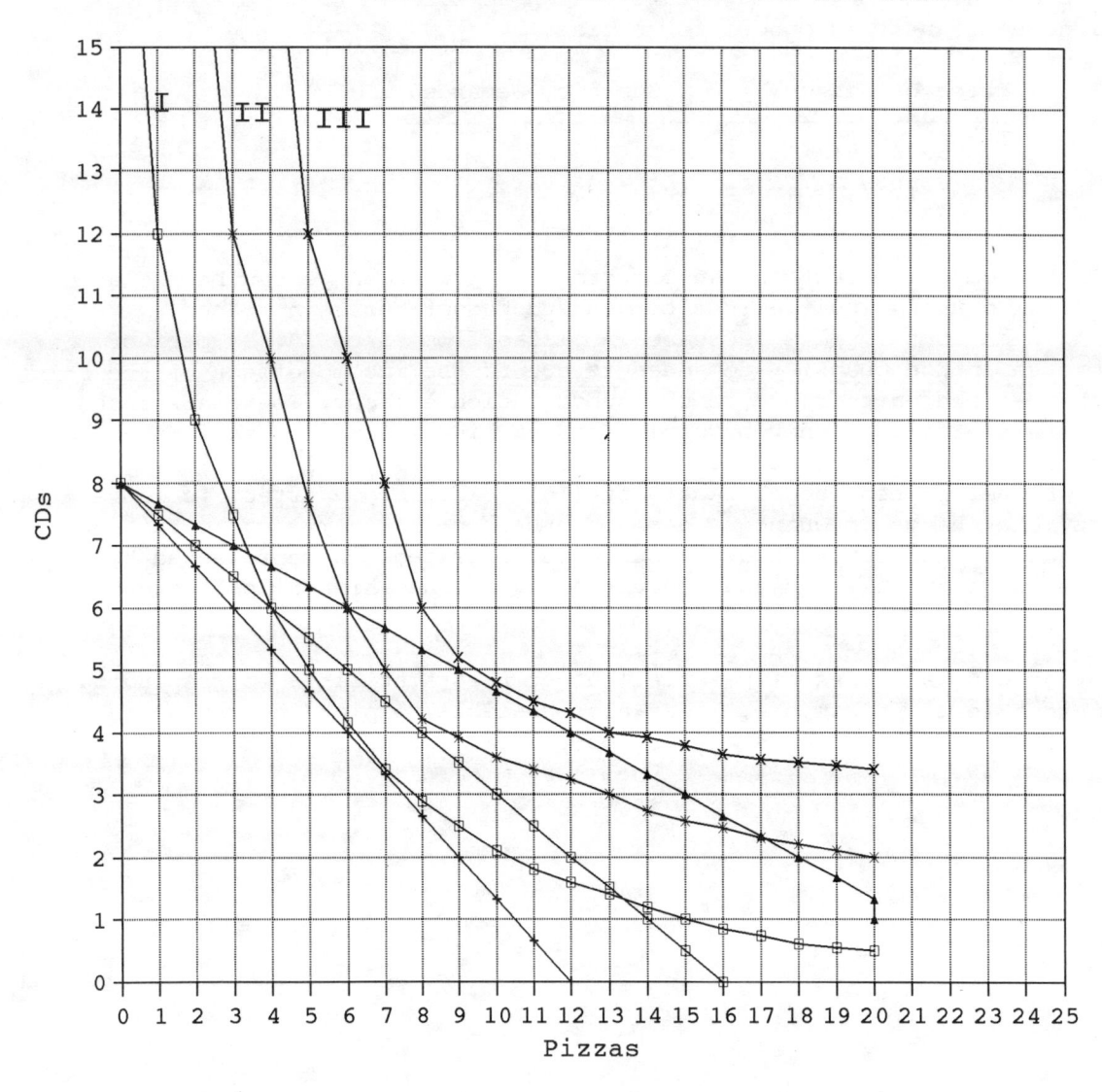

Given an income of $80 and the three indifference schedules above, what combination of CDs and pizzas yields the greatest amount of satisfaction for this consumer?   **4 CDs and 8 Pizzas**

Price of Pizza	Quantity Demanded
$6.67	7
$5.00	8
$3.33	9

Chapter 4
Demand and Supply II:
The Concept of Supply, the Market Mechanism

Overview of the Chapter

This chapter examines supply and the factors that cause the market supply to change. The elasticity of supply is added to the other three elasticity measures which were covered in Chapter 3. The market model is examined in greater detail, and the terms consumer surplus and producer surplus are introduced to facilitate a discussion about allocative efficiency and the deadweight losses to society that occur when markets are not permitted to attain allocative efficiency.

The supply curve is based on the various amounts that sellers are willing and able to produce over the range of all possible prices that they might receive for the commodity in question. Supply will change whenever a change occurs in one of the "supply shifters" -- the set of factors which also affect the supply of a commodity.

A supply curve, sloping upward and to the right, reflects the positive relationship that exists between the price of the commodity and the various quanitities supplied to the market (Q_s). The supply curve is also based on the assumption of *ceteris paribus* -- all other factors that affect the market supply being held constant. In a larger context, the supply curve rises because of the law of increasing marginal costs -- as more of any commodity is produced, resources must necessarily be bid away from other competing uses, thus raising the cost of producing additional units.

The elasticity of supply indicates how responsive producers are to changes in the price of a commodity -- for a given price change, do producers respond in a more than proportional manner or in a less than proportional manner?

The market represents a way of resolving the basic conflict that exists between consumers whose welfare is enhanced by low prices and producers whose goal of profit maximization is furthered by selling at as high a price as possible. Ultimately a price will be reached where the market clears -- where the amount supplied to the market by producers will just equal the amount buyers are willing to purchase. That price will be stable, a point of equilibrium since there will be neither a shortage nor a surplus of the commodity.

If the market price happens to be above its equilibrium price, then producers will offer more to the market than consumers will want to purchase -- <u>a condition of excess supply</u>. The excess supply results in larger inventories which may have significant costs associated with them. In response to these inventory costs, firms will compete the price down towards the equilibrium price where the market will clear, i.e., where there is no inventory accumulation. Thus, competition among sellers is the behavorial mechanism that assures that the market price will be either at its point of equilibrium or moving towards it. At prices below the equilibrium price, a shortage results and the competition among buyers will bid up the price until it reaches its equilibrium level.

Changes in demand or supply or both affect the equilibrium market price and output, and it is extremely important that you have a thorough understanding of what causes the demand and supply curves to shift, in what direction they shift, and how the shift(s) affects the equilibrium position of the market. When you have gained some familiarity with the market model, then you're ready to start applying the model to real world situations where you will find that the demand and supply model is extremely useful in explaining how the world works.

Your text defines <u>allocative inefficiency</u> in a simple but direct fashion: <u>an outcome or intervention is allocatively inefficient when the overall benefits to society are less than what they would be when compared to the efficient market outcome.</u> When markets are allowed to function without interference and an equilibrium outcome is attained, overall benefits are maximized. There is no other outcome that results in as large a sum of consumers' and producers' surpluses.

The chapter ends with a discussion of tax incidence -- who actually pays a tax that is imposed on a commodity. The tax burden depends upon the elasticity of the demand and supply schedules. Perhaps the most important lesson to be learned is that just because a tax is imposed upon a specific group does not mean that that group necessarily pays the tax. Several different applications of the market model are presented to give you an initial basis about how the model can be used in a real world setting. The effects of both buyers' and sellers' boycotts are briefly analyzed

Learning Objectives

After completing this chapter, you should be sure that you are able to:

- identify the set of factors which are the main determinants of supply and how changes in these determinants affect the supply of a commodity.

- understand the importance of the *ceteris paribus* assumption in deriving supply curves.

- understand the difference between a change in supply and a change in quantity supplied.

- understand how demand and supply interact with one another in determining an equilibrium price and quantity, how the market responds to shortages and surpluses.

- graph demand and supply curves, noting the equilibrium price and quantity. You should also know how to show surpluses and shortages on a demand and supply graph.

- explain the concept of the elasticity of supply. You should also be able to calculate the elasticity of supply coefficients.

- illustrate how the market model (demand and supply) can be applied to a wide variety of real world situations/events.

- understand the difference between allocative efficiency and allocative inefficiency and the different ways to visualize allocative inefficiency.

- understand the concepts of consumer and producer surplus, how they are measured, and their economic importance.

- understand how interference with free-market equilibrium (a price support or price ceiling) results in outcomes that are allocatively inefficient.

- define the concept of tax incidence (how the tax burden is shared) and show the effect that different demand and supply elasticities have on tax incidence. You should also be able to show how elasticities affect the sharing of a subsidy between buyer and seller.

Applications

The elasticity of supply is an important determinant of market performance, dictating whether or not changes in demand lead to higher prices or larger outputs. For example, suppose that an energy crisis, similar to what occurred in the mid and late 70s, causes the prices of home heating fuels to increase significantly. An increase in price will normally lead to a smaller quantity demanded, but it also motivates individuals to search for less expensive substitute commodities. Solar energy would become a more attractive option as fuel oil becomes more and more expensive as it did during those previous crises. The demand for solar panels would shift to the right as shown in the diagram below.

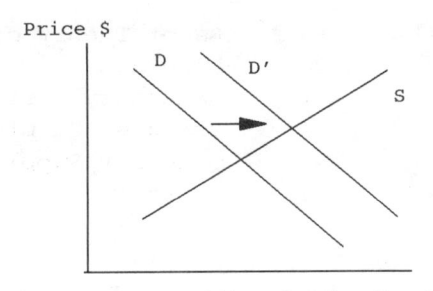

The elasticity of supply plays an important role here. If the supply of solar panels is very elastic, suggesting that producers in the industry are quite responsive to price changes and that the resources used in the industry are non-specialized and widely available, then the increase in demand will lead to an increase in the equilibrium quantity of solar panels, with some increase in the price of the units. (Refer the following diagram on the left).

If, on the other hand, the supply of solar panels is inelastic, suggesting that the producers in the industry are not very responsive to price changes and that the resources utilized in the production of solar panels are specialized and not widely available, the market outcome is quite different. In this case, an increase in demand will result mainly in an increase in price, with relatively small increases in the quantity of solar panels sold. (Refer to the following diagram on the right).

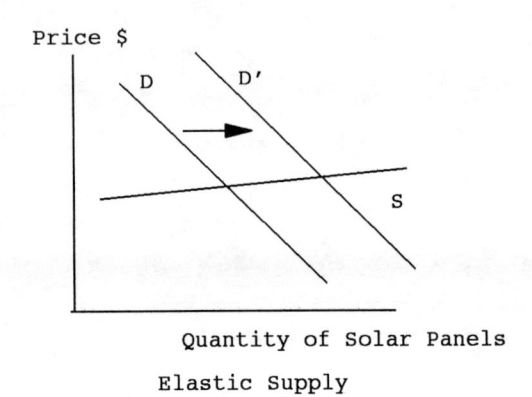

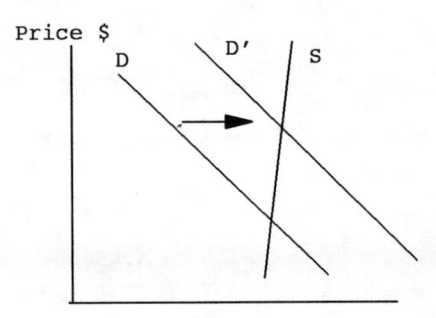

From a public policy standpoint, it is obvious what the preferred outcome would be. In the one instance, larger quantities of solar panels are sold and installed, allowing homeowners and consumers some degree of relief against the higher energy prices. In the other instance, only a small increase occurs in the number of solar panels installed, the increase in demand resulting mainly in an increase in price for the units -- at least in the short run.

Self Evaluation

List of Terms

Allocative Inefficiency
Backward Bending Supply Curve
Change in Supply
Consumer Boycott
Consumer Surplus
Deadweight Loss
Elasticity of Supply
Embargo
Equilibrium

Labor Theory of Value
Long Run
Momentary Period
Producer Surplus
Quantity Supplied
Shortage
Short Run
Supply
Surplus

For the statements below, fill in the term from the list above which provides the best fit.

1.) Occasionally, less labor is offered to the market when wages rise above a certain level, providing evidence of a _____.

2.) The _____ is that period of time in which the firm can adjust or modify some of the factors of production but not all, permitting some change in the quantity supplied.

3.) The _____ measures the responsiveness that exists between the price of a commodity and the quantity supplied to the market.

4.) The period of time during which the quantity supplied can not be adjusted is labeled the _____.

5.) At the point of _____, the quantity supplied equals the quantity demanded.

6.) That period of time necessary to adjust all factors of production (thus permitting complete adjustment of quantity supplied) is known as the _____.

7.) Price ceilings and price supports prevent the attainment of equilibrium and result in _____ because society's welfare with those programs in place is less than what would be the case if the market was allowed to achieve equilibrium.

8.) Because of the intensity of their preferences or their income or both, some consumers are willing to pay more for a commodity than its current market price. The difference between what they would have been willing to pay and the market price is labeled _____.

9.) The difference between the price that suppliers would have been willing to offer their output to the market and the actual market price is called _____.

10.) When the market is not allowed to reach its equilibrium point where allocative efficiency is maximized, society incurs a _____.

11.) The _____ of a commodity refers to the various quantities of a good or service a seller is willing and able to offer to the market over the range of possible prices.

12.) An _____ is one way a country can inflict economic damage on another without resorting to military action.

13.) If suppliers are willing to offer more or less to the market at the same market price or must have a higher or lower price for each quantity supplied, then a _____ has occurred.

14.) If the market price is not allowed to reach its equilibrium level because of a price ceiling, a _____ will result.

15.) The specific amount offered to the market at a given market price is known as the _____.

16.) Initially the _____ was used to resolve the questions that early economists had concerning the value and price of commodities.

17.) If the current price of a commodity is above its equilibrium price, then a _____ will result.

18.) A _____ needs to be publicized, organized, and sustained over a period of time in order to be effective.

Problems

The Supply Curve and Changes in Supply

In the table below, indicate the effect of the event described on the left and show how it can be depicted on a demand and supply graph. All of the events shown below have an effect only on supply. The first one has been completed as an example.

Market Involved	Event	Effect on Supply	Graph
1. Milk	Department of Agriculture allows the hormone BST which enhances milk production supplied by dairy producers	Change in technology, supply shifts to the right	P| ___ Q_d
2. Potatoes	Harvest forecast predicts low prices because of the intentions of many farmers to plant more potato acreage	Quantity increases	
3. Wheat	Cold and wet growing season and early frost	Supply decreases	
4. Plastics	The price of petroleum, an essential raw material, decreases by $3/barrel	increases	
5. Personal computers	Some firms leave the industry as competition heats up	decreases	
6. Barley	The price of wheat increases	decreases	

(Wheat and barley can be grown with the same set of resources)

7. Steel	Government imposes stiff new pollution regulations on steel mills designed to decrease toxic emissions	Down	
8. Cigarettes	Excise tax on cigarettes is increased to help pay for universal health insurance coverage	no change	

76

Market Involved	Event	Effect on Supply	Graph
9. Poultry	Firms in this industry decide not to push their workers so hard and to give them more time off to be with their families		
10. Western ski resorts	Record settlement of $7 million to family riding on faulty ski gondola which fell to the ground	decrease	
11. Fast food	The minimum wage is increased to $5.50		
12. AIDS Drug	Controversial AIDS drug is legalized after pressure from AIDS interest groups	increase	
13. Athletic shoes	Athletic shoe prices increase in response to spectacular ad campaign featuring Nikki the gorilla	increase / no shift	
14. Automobiles	Government requires air bags for all passengers	decrease	

Determining Equilibrium Price and Quantity

You are given the following demand and supply schedules for a standard ten-speed touring bicycle:

Table 4-1
(in millions of bicycles)

Price P	Quantity Demanded Q_d	Quantity Supplied Q_s	Excess Supply (Surplus) ($Q_s - Q_d$)	Excess Demand (Shortage) ($Q_d - Q_s$)
$220	0	40	40	-40
$200	6	36	30	-30
$180	12	32	20	-20
$160	18	28	10	-10
$140	24	24	0	0
$120	30	20	-10	10
$100	36	16	-20	20
$80	42	12	-30	30
$60	48	8	-40	40
$40	54	4	-50	50
$20	60	0	-60	60
$0	66	0	-66	66

Plot the demand and supply curves for this market on the graph below.

Figure 4-1

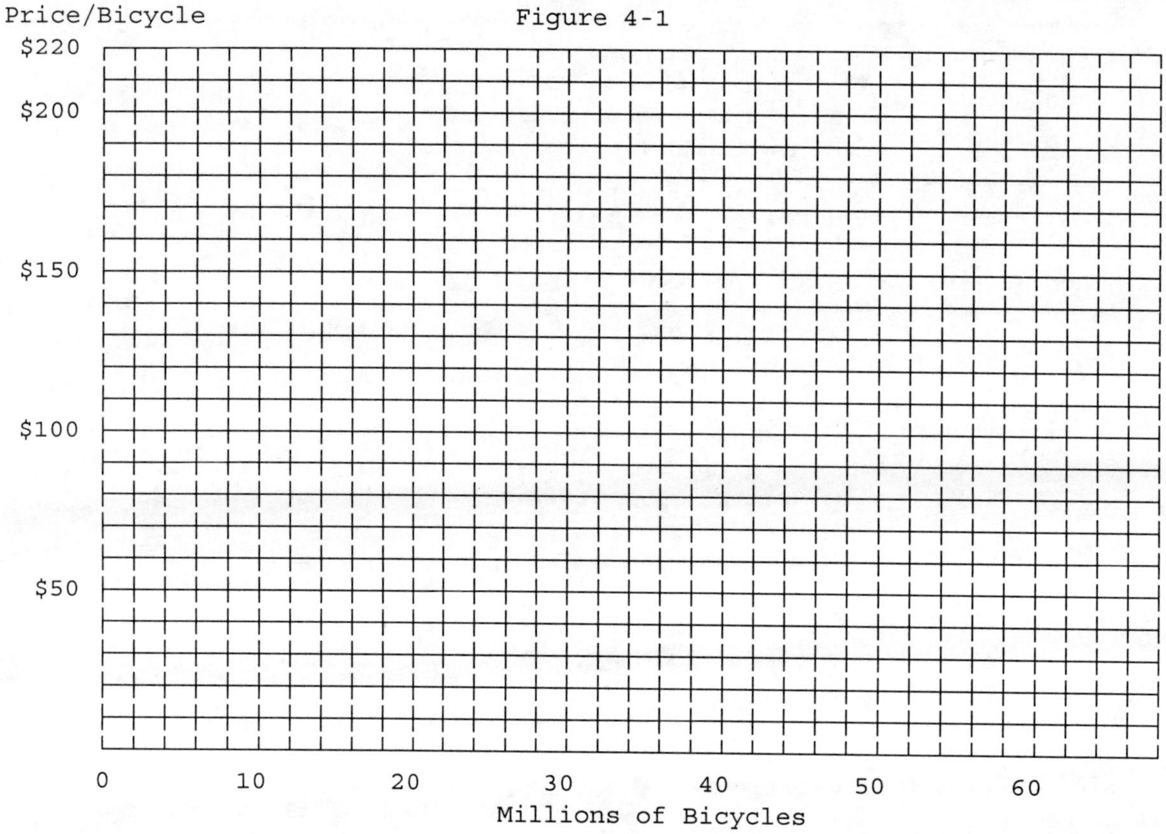
Price/Bicycle
$220
$200
$150
$100
$50
0
10
20
30
40
50
60
Millions of Bicycles

Answer the following questions on the basis of the information above:

The equilibrium price for this market is: ____________

The equilibrium quantity for this market is: ____________

Briefly explain what happens in this market at a price of $180:

____

____

Briefly explain what happens in this market at a price of $80:

____

____

Briefly explain what happens in this market at a price of $140:

____

____

Refer to the bicycle market on the preceding page for determining what effect each of the following events will have upon the equilbrium price and quantity of bicycles. Also indicate whether the event would increase or decrease the demand/supply of bicycles or have no effect on that market. Use the following notation: I -- Increase   D -- Decrease   U -- Unchanged   A -- Ambiguous, unable to determine without more information

Change in Demand	Change in Supply	Change in Equilibrium Price	Change in Equilibrium Quantity	
				1.) The price of electricity increases and that, in turn, results in an increase in the price of aluminum used in bicycle frames.
				2.) Consumers, including those who purchase bicycles, are widely anticipating a prolonged series of price increases for most goods.
				3.) Domestic bicycle producers convince Congress to impose an additional 15% tariff on imported bicycles.
				4.) Cities and counties build more bicycle paths.
				5.) The price of gasoline increases due to higher exploration and production costs.
				6.) Shortages of skilled workers result in increased wages for many types of workers used in the production of bicycles.
				7.) Television ratings for the Tour de France decrease dramatically indicating less interest in cycling for all age groups.
				8.) The price of bicycles increases.
				9.) Bicycle firms expect that bicycles will be selling for up to 10% more within six months.
				10.) Because of exceptional profitability in the bicycle industry, a number of new firms enter the industry.

Change in Demand	Change in Supply	Change in Equilibrium Price	Change in Equilibrium Quantity	
				11.) Bicycle firms can also produce childrens' tricycles with the same set of productive inputs. Demographers predict a decrease in the number of children over the next 10 years.
				12.) A mandatory bicycle helmet law is passed.
				13.) Real household income rises by over 4%.
				14.) Many bicycle firms adopt an advanced, more costly new frame technology.
				15.) Property taxes for bicycle firms decrease.

Calculating Elasticity Coefficients

Referring once again to the supply schedule for bicycles referred to above, calculate the elasticity of supply for each of the price and quantity combinations contained in the table on the next page. Spaces between the lines are provided for your elasticity coefficients, reflecting the fact that your calculations are based on price and quantity data from two different lines of the table.

Table 4-2

Price P	Quantity Supplied Q_S (in millions)	Elasticity of Supply E_S
$220	40	1.10
$200	36	
$180	32	
$160	28	
$140	24	
$120	20	
$100	16	
$80	12	
$60	8	
$40	4	
$20	0	

Handwritten work beside table: 20/210 ÷ -4/38 = .10/.10 ≈ $1.10; .12; .11

What can be said about the elasticity of supply as one moves along a straight line supply curve?

_____

_____

Interpret, in terms of the bicycle market, the meaning of your calculated elasticity coefficient for the segment of the supply curve from $140 - $120:

_____

the segment of the supply curve from $80 - $60:

_____

Examining the Effects of Intervention in the Market: Revisiting the Bicycle Market

Return to the hypothetical demand and supply schedules shown above for a standard ten-speed touring bicycle.

81

Table 4-1

(in millions of bicycles)

Price P	Quantity Demanded Q_d	Quantity Supplied Q_s
$220	0	40
$200	6	36
$180	12	32
$160	18	28
$140	24	24
$120	30	20
$100	36	16
$80	42	12
$60	48	8
$40	54	4
$20	60	0
$0	66	0

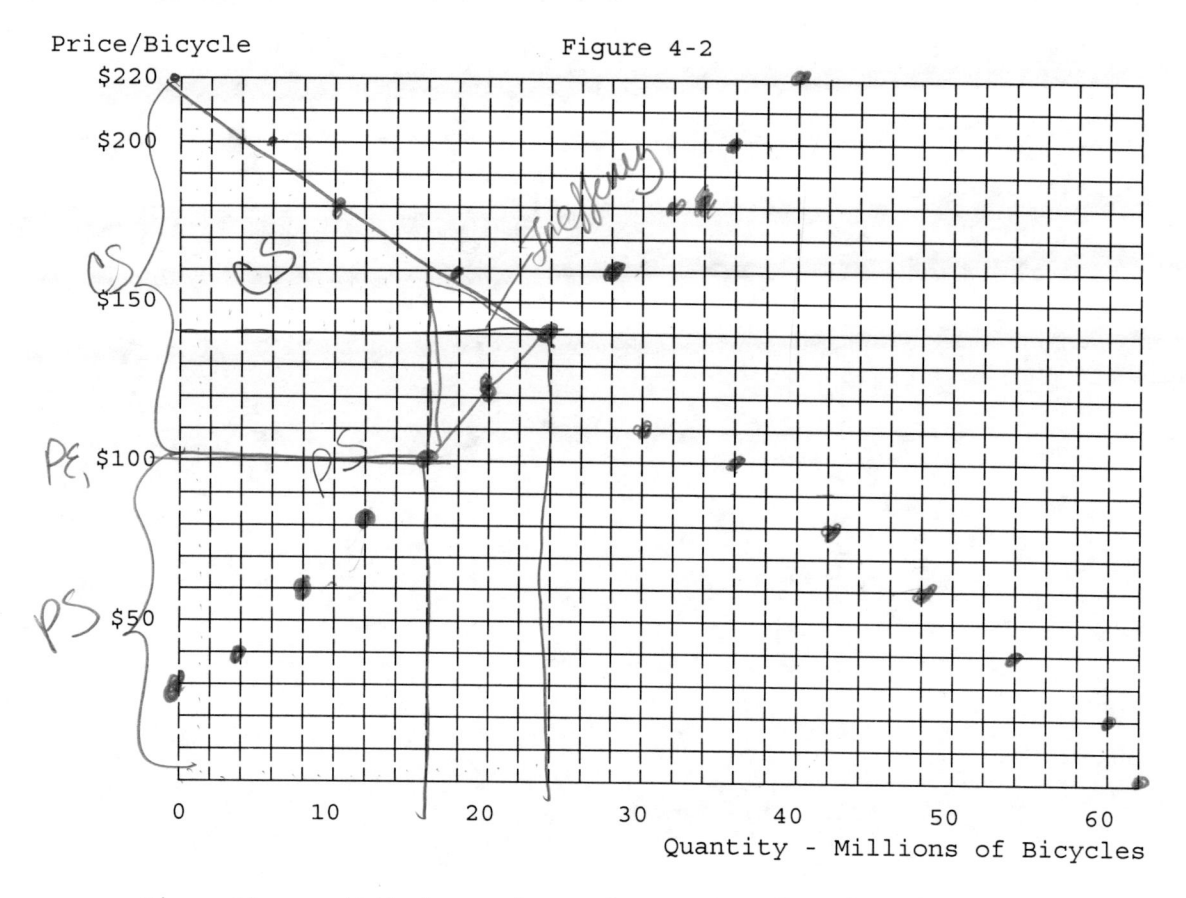

Figure 4-2

Given the equilibrium price and quantity for the bicycle market, lightly shade in the area in your demand and supply diagram that depicts the amount of consumers' surplus for this market, labeling it **CS**.

In terms of this problem and the bicycle market, explain exactly what consumers' surplus refers to:

the number of bikes the consumer would buy at the price above equilibrium

Estimate the value of consumers' surplus: (CS) = $ _4300_

Note: there are several ways to make a "rough" estimate of the value of consumers' surplus. One way is to calculate the monetary value of one square in the market diagram and then count how many squares are included in the relevant area. Using that method:

CS = ($ value of one square) X (number of squares in the CS area)

Another method can be used if the areas to be measured are depicted as triangles or squares or rectangles. Thus, if the CS area is clearly a triangle, then the area of the triangle can be determined by taking half of the product of the height of the triangle times its base. Even if the area to be measured is not a strictly defined triangle or rectangle, it is often possible to define a triangle or rectangle which represents most of the area, and the other remaining areas can be estimated using the first method described above.

Given the equilibrium price and quantity for the bicycle market, lightly shade in the area in your demand and supply diagram that depicts the amount of producers' surplus for this market, labeling it **PS**.

In terms of this problem and the bicycle market, explain exactly what producers' surplus refers to:

what producers are willing to produce below equil price

In the same way as you did for consumers' surplus, estimate the value of producers' surplus: (PS) = $ _1680_

Total surplus is defined as the total of consumers' and producers' surplus. In the case of the bicycle market,

total surplus = CS + PS = $ _2110_

The amount of total surplus which you just calculated will be used, as your text suggests, as a benchmark for analyzing the allocative inefficiency associated with market interventions of various kinds.

Suppose that, in its wisdom, Congress specifies a **price ceiling of $100** on ten speed-touring bicycles.

Recalculate consumers' surplus (CS) and producers' surplus (PS) after the price ceiling of $100 has been put in place.

Consumers' surplus (CS) with the price ceiling: $ _____

Producers' surplus (PS) with the price ceiling: $ _____

Total surplus (CS + PS) with the price ceiling: $ _____

Net change in total surplus from the equilibrium market position: $ _____

Estimate the amount of society's deadweight loss resulting from this piece of legislation: $ _____

Suppose that after intensive, high powered lobbying from the Ten Speed Touring Bicycle Manufacturers Association (TSTBMA), Congress, in its wisdom, passes a law that guarantees a **support price of $180** for ten-speed touring bikes.

Recalculate consumers' surplus (CS) and producers' surplus (PS) after the price support of $180 has been put in place.

Consumers' surplus (CS) with the price support: $ _____

Producers' surplus (PS) with the price support: $ _____

Total surplus (CS + PS) with the price support: $ _____

Net change in total surplus from the equilibrium market position: $ _____

Estimate the amount of society's deadweight loss resulting from this piece of legislation: $ _____

From the perspective of market surpluses/shortages, what is the effect of:
    the price ceiling of $100: _____

    the price support of $180: _____

Why are markets inefficient and resources mis-allocated if either a surplus or a shortage is present?

_____

_____

A third way to look at market efficiency is in terms of an equality between the price that buyers are willing to pay for a given quanity of a commodity (the demand price) and the price that sellers must have to offer that quantity to the market (the supply price). Whenever a price ceiling or a price support is imposed on a market, there will be either a shortage or a surplus, making it difficult to determine what the actual market quantity will be, since there will be a different Q_D and Q_S.

One rule that you may find useful states that **"the short side of the market always dominates."** By that it is meant that when there is a shortage (the actual market price is below its equilibrium price), the relevant quantity is the quantity supplied Q_S, because that will be the amount that is actually produced and put on the market. The fact that the quantity demanded Q_D is larger makes no difference. Similarly, if there is a support price and a surplus (the actual price being above its equilibrium price), the relevant quantity will be the quantity demanded Q_D, because that will be the actual amount that will be sold or taken off the market. In this case, the larger quantity supplied Q_S is irrelevant.

When the bicycle market is allowed to attain its equilibrium position, what are buyers willing to pay for the equilibrium quantity? $ _____

what price must sellers have in order to offer the equilibrium quantity to the market? $ _____

When a price ceiling of $100 is imposed on the bicycle market:
what are buyers willing to pay for the relevant market quantity?
$ _____

what price must sellers have in order to offer the relevant quantity to the market? $ _____

When a price support of $180 is imposed on the bicycle market:

what are buyers willing to pay for the relevant market quantity?
$ _____

what price must sellers have in order to offer the relevant quantity to the market? $ _____

Government Intervention in the Bread Market

The government imposes a price ceiling of $0.90 on the market for bread, after a study indicates that many impoverished people can no longer afford to pay the current equilibrium price which averages $1.30. Economic research by leading economists indicates that at the equilibrium price, 20 million loaves of bread are sold, and at the ceiling price of $0.90, the quantity demanded will be about 36 million, while suppliers would be expected to supply about 12 million loaves of bread at that price.

Illustrate the situation above by drawing in the appropriate demand and supply diagrams in the figure on the following page.

Price/Bread   Figure 4-3

$1.90

$1.50

$1.00

$0.50

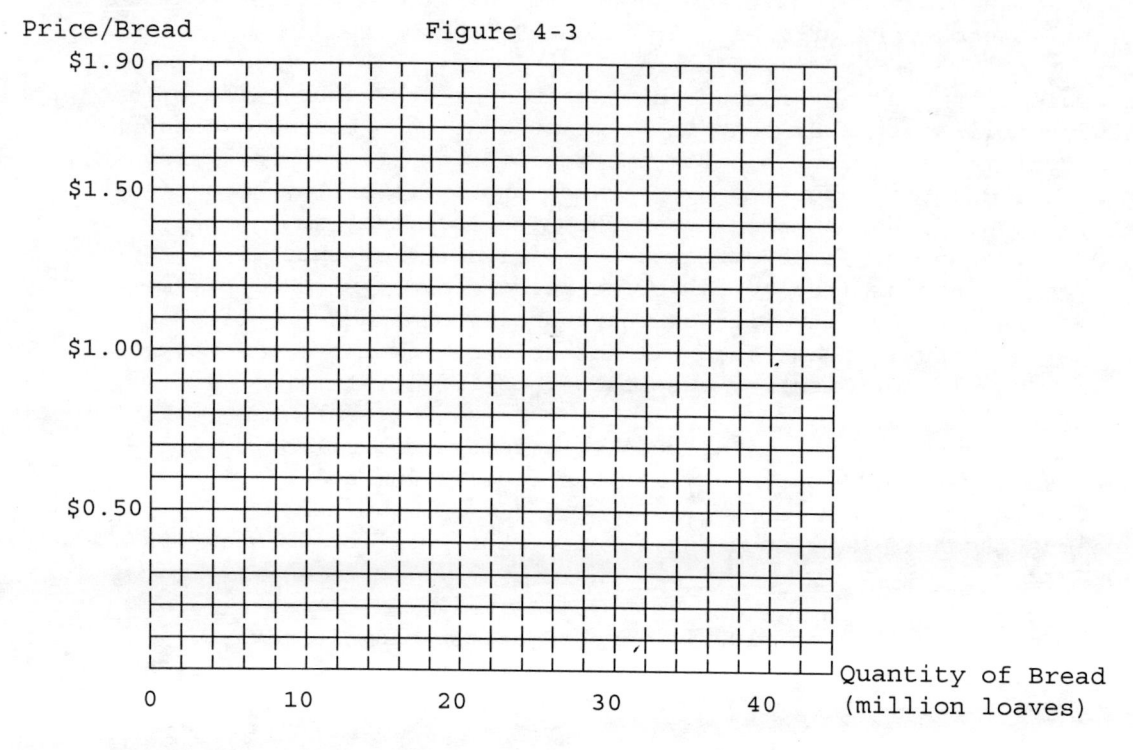

0   10   20   30   40   Quantity of Bread (million loaves)

Label the ceiling price and the shortage or surplus that results on your graph above.

Calculate the elasticity of demand and the elasticity of supply for bread given the information above.

ϵ_D =

ϵ_S =

Define consumers' surplus (in terms of this problem):

Define producers' surplus (in terms of this problem):

Neatly show the changes in consumers' and producers' surplus that occur because of the price ceiling.

Show the deadweight welfare loss associated with the price ceiling.

Comment on whether the price ceiling is appropriate public policy (please reread the beginning statement of the problem).

86

If the problem is that some people cannot afford bread, what should be done? (i.e., what is effective economic policy?)

_____

_____

Analyzing the Impact of a Tax on a Commodity

The market for cigarettes is shown below. Answer the following questions on the basis of the information provided in Figure 4-4.

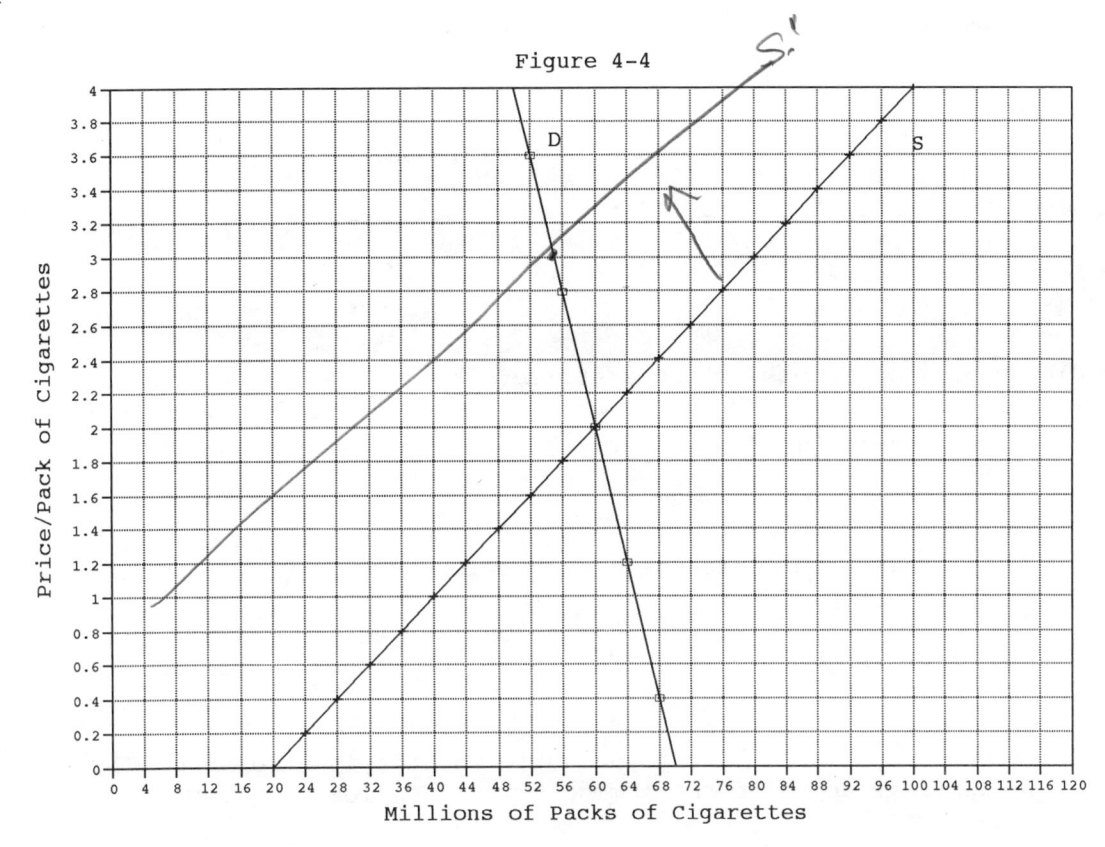

Figure 4-4

[Graph: Price/Pack of Cigarettes vs Millions of Packs of Cigarettes, with curves D, S, and S' drawn]

How much are consumers spending on cigarettes when the market price is at its equilibrium point: 120 million

What are the total receipts received by cigarette firms when the market is in equilibrium at $2.00/pack?

Suppose that legislation is passed which imposes a tax of $1/pack on cigarettes in an attempt to address the large social costs associated with cigarette smoking. Show the effect of the tax on cigarettes on the diagram above. Label the new supply curve S'

What will be the new equilibrium price and quantity after the tax?

How much will consumers spend on cigarettes after the tax?

How much tax revenue will be collected?

What is the actual tax incidence (burden):
for consumers: for producers:

Why would tax authorities prefer to tax commodities with an inelastic demand rather than those which have an elastic demand?

True/False Statements

Indicate whether you think the statements below are true or false. These questions are designed to make you think about the concepts presented in the text. There may not be any easy clear-cut answers. Some thoughts about the answers are presented at the end of the chapter.

1.) _____ When supply is completely inelastic, then the supply curve completely determines the market price.

2.) _____ The market supply curve is based on the ability of the most efficient suppliers to produce over the range of relevant market price.

3.) _____ Supply is usually highly inelastic when it is hard to produce additional units of the commodity in question.

4.) _____ When the demand for a product increases, the profit that can be made by producing it generally increases and, other things being equal, more resources will be devoted to its production.

5.) _____ When supply is highly elastic, an increase in demand results mainly in a higher price for the commodity.

6.) _____ Supply is generally more elastic when a longer time period is considered.

7.) _____ Lower market prices always increase consumers' surplus.

8.) _____ If the supply of labor in a particular country had a backward bending supply curve, then an increase in wages might not necessarily result in more labor (or hours) being offered to the market.

9.) _____ The short run is the period of time it takes a firm to make a production decision.

10.) _____ In the long run, all factors of production can be adjusted in an optimum fashion.

11.) _____ Price ceilings basically help consumers by preventing profit maximizing firms from charging excessive prices.

12.) _____ If the demand for a normal good increases because household income has increased, the supply curve will also increase as producers respond by offering more to the market.

13.) _____ Supply will more be elastic if the factor resources involved producing a commodity are non-specialized and widely available.

14.) _____ If demand is perfectly elastic, suppliers will keep all of a subsidy, passing none of it along to consumers.

15.) _____ Consumer boycotts are an effective way to inflict economic harm on producers, sending them an "economic message."

16.) _____ In a free enterprise, private market economy every citizen has an equal voice in determining what is produced.

17.) _____ In a free enterprise, private market economy, profits determine what will be produced.

18.) _____ When a market has attained its equilibrium position where $Q_d = Q_s$, we can safely say that everyone who wants that commodity is getting as much as he/she wants.

Multiple-Choice Questions

Select the "best" answer from the alternatives provided.

1.) When the government imposes a price ceiling on a particular market
   a. consumers are protected against excessively high market prices, and total consumer welfare increases.
   b. producers view this as unfair and as a result decrease supply to the market.
   c. the good continues to be rationed in much the same way as before.
   d. this action is allocatively inefficient since total welfare declines.

2.) As you are undoubtedly aware, frisbees are a popular recreational item, and plastic comprises a signficant portion of total production costs. Assume that the frisbee market is in equilibrium and suddenly because of increases in the world price of petroleum, the price of plastic increases considerably. Based on your knowledge of demand and supply, the increase in the price of plastic will cause
   a. the demand for plastic to increase as suppliers compete with one another to obtain adequate supplies of plastic.
   b. the demand for frisbees to decrease as they become more expensive.
   c. the supply of frisbees to decrease because of increased costs of production.
   d. the supply of frisbees to increase as suppliers supply more to the market in an attempt to offset higher plastic costs.

3.) In response to an increase in the support price of milk from $1.25 to $1.45, milk suppliers increase production from 20 million pounds to 24 million pounds. Based on that information, the elasticity of supply for milk is
   a. 1.25.
   b. 1.208.
   c. 1.227.
   d. not able to be calculated, since the example involves price supports which are a non-equilibrium situation.

4.) If producers must obtain higher prices than previously in order to produce various levels of output, one can say that there has occurred
   a. an increase in supply.
   b. a decrease in supply.
   c. an increase quantity supplied.
   d. a decrease in demand.

5.) In a market, you observe that after a specific event has occurred, the equilibrium market price decreases and that the equilibrium quantity also decreases. Given your knowledge of demand and supply, what do you think most likely happened?
   a. A small decrease in demand and a large increase in supply.
   b. A decrease in supply.
   c. A decrease in demand.
   d. An increase in supply.
   e. None of the above -- events like this simply do not occur.

6.) What is the most likely market outcome when a change in production technology occurs at the same time as an increase in the price of a substitute good?
   a. Q_e will decrease, and P_e will increase.
   b. P_e decrease, and Q_e will decrease.
   c. Q_e will increase, but the effect on P_e depends on the magnitude of the shifts.
   d. P_e will increase, but the effect on Q_e depends on the magnitude of the shifts.
   e. These are offsetting changes, and P_e and Q_e will not change.

7.) If the demand for a commodity decreases and, at the same time, the supply of that commodity increases, what can be said about the new equilibrium price and quantity?
   a. ↓P_e and ↑Q_e
   b. ↓P_e and ↓Q_e
   c. ↓P_e and unable to determine the direction of change in Q_e
   d. ↑P_e and ↑Q_e
   e. unable to determine the direction of change in either P_e or Q_e

8.) Which of the following would cause the supply curve to shift to the right?
   a. Consumer preferences for the commodity increase dramatically.
   b. The imposition of an excise tax on the commodity.
   c. The expectation that the price of this commodity will be less expensive in the future than it is now.
   d. An increase in the price of the commodity.
   e. None of the above.

9.) Supply would be more elastic
   a. the more firms there are in the industry.
   b. the more specialized the resources used to produce the commodity.
   c. the higher the price of the commodity.
   d. the longer the period of time firms have to adjust to new circumstances.
   e. none of the above.

10.) If the demand for a commodity is highly inelastic,
   a. a change in supply will have little if any effect on equilibrium price.
   b. then the supply curve is likely to be highly inelastic also.
   c. a change in supply will result in a relatively large change in the equilibrium price.
   d. then changes in demand will result in a relatively large change in the equilibrium price.
   e. none of the above

11.) Price ceilings result in market outcomes that are allocatively inefficient, because
   a. at the ceiling price, consumers value an additional unit of the commodity more than the marginal cost of producing an additional unit of the commodity.
   b. the resulting surplus means too many units have been produced.
   c. the resulting shortage means that the commodity would not be rationed in an economically efficient manner.
   d. both a and c.
   e. none of the above.

12.) When the market reaches a position of equilibrium,
   a. the equilibrium price and quantity will not change from that time on.
   b. the actual price and quantity may change but will always return to their equilibrium levels.
   c. everyone who wants the commodity will be able to obtain it.
   d. both consumers and producers are satisfied with the equilibrium price.
   e. none of the above.

13.) When the supply curve is characterized as "backward bending,"
   a. the supply curve shifts to the left when the market price rises above a certain level.
   b. it is not possible to achieve a position of equilibrium.
   c. the demand curve is also very likely to be backward bending as well.
   d. quantity supplied (Q_s) declines when the market price rises above a certain level.
   e. none of the above.

14.) Which of the following circumstances would be associated with a backward bending supply curve?
   a. the labor supply for an especially dangerous occupation, like high rise construction.
   b. an industry which has only a few large firms.
   c. the labor supply of teenaged workers after the minimum wage has been increased.
   d. the labor supply of workers whose main goal is to accumulate a pre-determined amount of money.
   e. none of the above.

15.) If the equilibrium market price increases and the equilibrium quantity decreases,
   a. demand and supply must have both decreased.
   b. demand remained constant and supply decreased.
   c. demand increased and supply decreased.
   d. demand decreased and supply remained constant.
   e. unable to determine.

16.) If the demand for cigarettes or liquor is highly inelastic and the supply of those commodities is fairly elastic, then the economic effect of placing a tax on either of these commodities will be that
   a. the tax burden of consumers/suppliers will be determined by the IRS.
   b. most of the tax burden will fall on suppliers of the commodity.
   c. the tax burden will be split 50-50 between consumers and suppliers.
   d. the consumption of the commodity will decrease dramatically in an effort to avoid paying the tax.
   e. most of the tax burden will fall on consumers of the commodity.

Discussion Questions

1.) As you are aware, the market system is a rationing and distribution system, determining who gets what. Exactly how does the market system (the forces of demand and supply) answer the distribution question?

2.) Consumer welfare is increased through lower prices which allow greater consumption. Are consumers helped by government programs which lower prices below their market equilibrium level?

How would you explain to someone who has never had any economics why a price ceiling that lowers commodity prices (which everyone wants) is not in the public's best interests?

3.) It has been suggested that many concerts (especially rock concerts) are not priced correctly. What evidence would tend to support that view? Why do you think performing artists (and their agents) would charge a price that is less than the market clearing equilibrium price?

4.) The term scalping is applied to situations where someone resells a ticket that they have purchased at the box office to someone who is willing to pay a higher price for the ticket. What can be said about the markets and the ticket pricing policy for those events where scalping occurs? How does scalping (assuming it is done without coercion of any kind) affect allocative efficiency and society's overall welfare? Why do you think scalping is illegal in some areas?

5.) Why are governmental taxing agencies at both the state and federal levels interested in taxing commodities which have an inelastic demand?

6.) Should taxes and subsidies be used by government as appropriate social/economic policy to discourage and encourage the use and consumption of selected commodities because of perceived "morality issues" associated with the commodities? For example, if liquor is perceived as "bad" for society as a whole, should it be taxed in an attempt to reduce its consumption.

Answers and Solutions to Problems and Exercises

Completing Statements from the List of Terms

1.) Backward Bending Supply Curve
2.) Short Run
3.) Elasticity of Supply
4.) Momentary Period
5.) Equilibrium
6.) Long Run
7.) Allocative Inefficiency
8.) Consumer Surplus
9.) Producer Surplus
10.) Deadweight Loss
11.) Supply
12.) Embargo
13.) Change in Supply
14.) Shortage
15.) Quantity Supplied
16.) Labor Theory of Value
17.) Surplus
18.) Consumer Boycott

Problems

The Supply Curve and Changes in Supply

Market Involved	Event	Effect on Supply	Graph
1. Milk	Department of Agriculture allows the hormone BST which enhances milk production supplied by dairy producers	Change in technology, supply shifts to the right	S → S'
2. Potatoes	Harvest forecast predicts low prices because of the intentions of many farmers to plant more potato acreage	Expectations change, current supply is decreased	S' ← S
3. Wheat	Cold and wet growing season and early frost	Shift to the left as less is available to be put on the market	S' ← S
4. Plastics	The price of petroleum, an essential raw material, decreases by $3/barrel	Increase in the cost of factor resources, decrease in supply	S → S'
5. Personal computers	Some firms leave the industry as competition heats up	Decrease in supply	S' ← S
6. Barley	The price of wheat increases	Decrease in the supply of barley as farmers switch to wheat in expectation of higher profits	S' ← S
7. Steel	Government imposes stiff new pollution regulations on steel mills designed to decrease toxic emissions	Increase in costs results in decrease in supply	S → S'
8. Cigarettes	Excise tax on cigarettes is increased to help pay for universal health insurance coverage	Tax is looked upon as an increase in production costs and supply will decrease	S → S'
9. Poultry	Firms in this industry decide not to push their workers so hard and to give them more time off to be with their families	Change in firms' goals, in this instance decreasing supply	S' ← S
10. Western ski resorts	Record settlement of $7 million to family riding on faulty ski gondola which fell to the the ground	Litigation costs are just like any other costs. Increase in costs results in decrease in supply	S → S'

Market Involved	Event	Effect on Supply	Graph
11. Fast food	The minimum wage is increased to $5.50	Higher labor costs decrease supply	
12. AIDS Drug	Controversial AIDS drug is legalized after pressure from AIDS interest groups	Change in legal status. Legal supply now appears on the market (increase in supply)	
13. Athletic shoes	Athletic shoe prices increase in response to spectacular ad campaign featuring Nikki the gorilla	No shift in supply since the commodity's own price does not change supply	
14. Automobiles	Government requires air bags for all passengers	Increase in costs of production, decrease in supply	

Determining Equilibrium Price and Quantity

Table 4-1
(in millions of bicycles)

Price P	Quantity Demanded Q_d	Quantity Supplied Q_s	Excess Supply (Surplus) ($Q_s - Q_d$)	Excess Demand (Shortage) ($Q_d - Q_s$)
$220	0	40	40	
$200	6	36	30	
$180	12	32	20	
$160	18	28	10	
$140	24	24	0	0
$120	30	20		10
$100	36	16		20
$80	42	12		30
$60	48	8		40
$40	54	4		50
$20	60	0		60

Answer the following questions on the basis of the information above:
The equilibrium price for this market is: **$140**
The equilibrium quantity for this market is: **24 million units**

Figure 4-1
The Bicycle Market

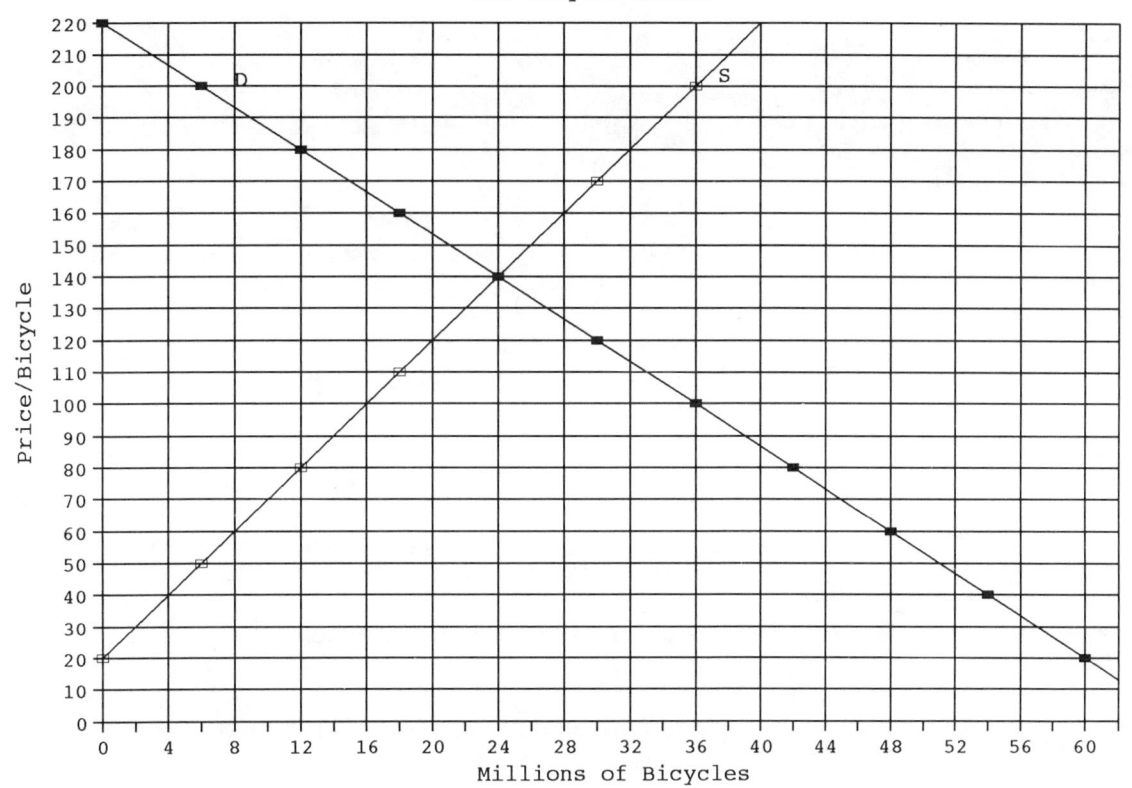

[Graph showing demand curve D sloping down from (0, 220) to (60, 20) and supply curve S sloping up from (0, 20) to approximately (60, 220), intersecting at (24, 140). X-axis: Millions of Bicycles (0 to 60). Y-axis: Price/Bicycle (0 to 220).]

Briefly explain what happens in this market at a price of $180: **An excess supply or surplus of 20 million units occurs at this price. Quantity demanded equals 12 million units, while the quantity supplied equals 32 million units. The price will fall towards the equilibrium price as long as the surplus is greater than zero.**

Briefly explain what happens in this market at a price of $80: **An excess demand or shortage of 30 million units occurs at this price. Quantity demanded equals 42 million units, while the quantity supplied equals 12 million units. The price will rise towards the equilibrium price as long as the shortage is greater than zero.**

Briefly explain what happens in this market at a price of $140: **At this price, the market clears in the sense that the amount demanded by buyers (Q_d) 24 million just equals the amount that suppliers offer to the market (Q_s) 24 million. There is no shortage or surplus, and market price will remain at its equilibrium level until some factor changes.**

Briefly explain why the price and quantity indicated above represent an equilibrium position for this particular market: **See the answer above.**

Change in Demand	Change in Supply	Change in Equilibrium Price	Change in Equilibrium Quantity		
U	D	I	D	1.)	The price of electricity increases and that, in turn, results in an increase in the price of aluminum used in bicycle frames.
I	U	I	I	2.)	Consumers, including those who purchase bicycles, are widely anticipating a prolonged series of price increases for most goods.
U	D	I	D	3.)	Domestic bicycle producers convince Congress to impose an additional 15% tariff on imported bicycles.
I	U	I	I	4.)	Cities and counties build more bicycle paths.
I	D	I	A	5.)	The price of gasoline increases due to higher exploration and production costs.
U	D	I	D	6.)	Shortages of skilled workers result in increased wages for many types of workers used in the production of bicycles.
D	U	D	D	7.)	Television ratings for the Tour de France decrease dramatically indicating less interest in cycling for all age groups.
U	U	A	A	8.)	The price of bicycles increases.
U	D	I	D	9.)	Bicycle firms expect that bicycles will be selling for up to 10% more within six months.
U	I	D	I	10.)	Because of exceptional profitability in the bicycle industry, a number of new firms enter the industry.
U	I	D	I	11.)	Bicycle firms can also produce childrens' tricycles with the same set of productive inputs. Demographers predict a decrease in the number of children over the next 10 years.
D	U	D	D	12.)	A mandatory bicycle helmet law is passed.
I	U	I	I	13.)	Real household income rises by over 4%.
U	I	D	I	14.)	Many bicycle firms adopt an advanced, more costly, new frame technology.
U	I	D	I	15.)	Property taxes for bicycle firms decrease.

Calculating Elasticity Coefficients

Price P	Quantity Supplied Q_s (in millions)	Elasticity of Supply E_s
$220	40	
		1.105
$200	36	
		1.118
$180	32	
		1.133
$160	28	
		1.154
$140	24	
		1.083
$120	20	
		1.22
$100	16	
		1.286
$80	12	
		1.00
$60	8	
		1.667
$40	4	
		3.00
$20	0	

What can be said about the elasticity of supply as one moves along a straight line supply curve? **No general trend. The intercept of the supply curve determines the overall elasticity category.**

Interpret, in terms of the bicycle market, the meaning of your calculated elasticity coefficient: the segment of the supply curve from $140 - $120: **The elasticity of supply equals 1.083 (slightly elastic) -- for every 1% change in price, quantity supplied changes by 1.083%.**

the segment of the supply curve from $80 - $60: **The elasticity of supply equals 1.00 (unitary elastic) -- for every 1% change in price, quantity supplied changes by 1.0%.**

Examining the Effects of Intervention in the Market - Revisiting the Bicycle Market

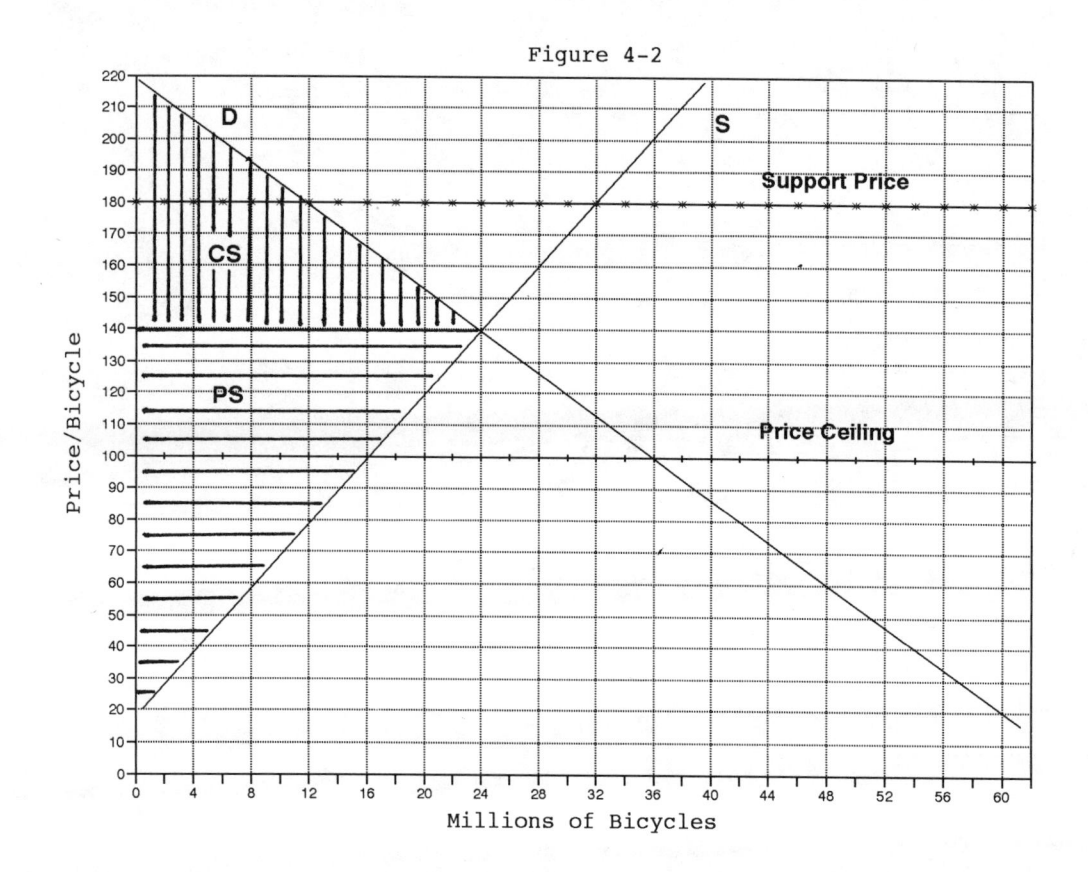

Figure 4-2

   In terms of this problem and the bicycle market, explain exactly what consumers' surplus refers to: **Consumers' surplus is the difference between the price that buyers would have been willing to pay for the bicycles and what they actually had to pay -- the actual market price ($140).**

   Estimate the value of consumers' surplus: (CS) = **$ 960 million**

   In terms of this problem and the bicycle market, explain exactly what producers' surplus refers to: **Producers' surplus is the difference between the actual market price and the price that producers would have been willing to accept**

   In the same way as you did for consumers' surplus, estimate the value of producers' surplus: **(PS) = $ 1440 million**

   Total surplus is defined as the total of consumers' and producers' surplus. In the case of the bicycle market, **total surplus = CS + PS = $2400 million**

Consumers' surplus (CS) with the price ceiling: **$ 1480 million**

Producers' surplus (PS) with the price ceiling: **$ 640 million**

Total surplus (CS + PS) with the price ceiling: **$ 2120 million**

Net change in total surplus from the equilibrium market position: **$ -280 million**

Estimate the amount of society's deadweight loss resulting from this piece of legislation: **- $ 270 million**

Consumers' surplus (CS) with the price support: **$ 240 million**

Producers' surplus (PS) with the price support: **$ 1560 million**

Total surplus (CS + PS) with the price support: **$ 1800 million**

Net change in total surplus from the equilibrium market position: **$ -600 million**

Estimate the amount of society's deadweight loss resulting from this piece of legislation: **- $ 600 million**

From the perspective of surpluses/shortages, what is the effect of:

    the price ceiling of $100: **shortage of 20 million**

    the price support of $180: **surplus of 20 million**

Why are markets inefficient and resources mis-allocated if either a surplus or a shortage is present? **Basically because shortages or surpluses will be resolved in a non-economic, non-efficient fashion. In the case of a shortage, ability to pay will no longer be the criterion to decide who gets the commodity, since the shortage can be allocated in a number of non-economic ways: first come, first served, randomly, equally, etc. None of these methods are economically efficient. The same kind of argument applies to how a surplus would be allocated among a fewer number of buyers.**

When the bicycle market is allowed to attain its equilibrium position, what are buyers willing to pay for the equilibrium quantity? **$ 140**

what price must sellers have in order to offer the equilibrium quantity to the market?   **$ 140**

When a price ceiling of $100 is imposed on the bicycle market:

What are buyers willing to pay for the relevant market quantity? **$ 167**

What price must sellers have in order to offer the relevant quantity to the market?   **$ 100**

When a price support of $180 is imposed on the bicycle market:

What are buyers willing to pay for the relevant market quantity?
$180

What price must sellers have in order to offer the relevant quantity to the market? $ 80

Government Intervention in the Bread Market

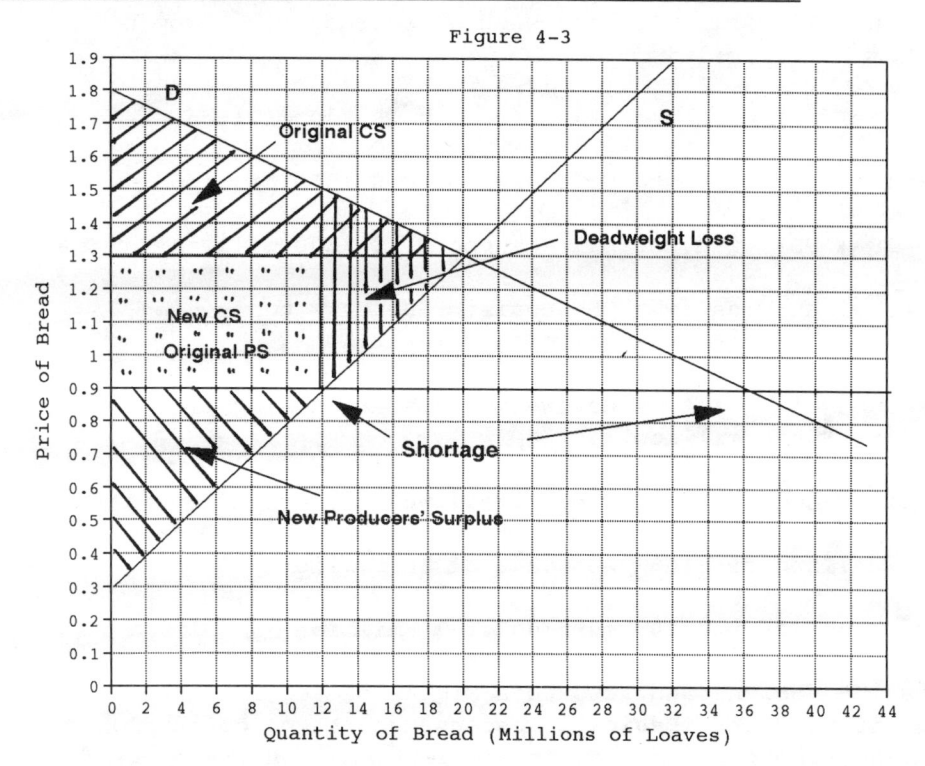

Figure 4-3

Calculate the elasticity of demand and the elasticity of supply for bread given the information above.

ϵ_D = (16/28)/(0.40/1.10) = 1.571
ϵ_S = (8/16)/((0.40/1.10) = 1.375

Define consumers' surplus in terms of this problem:
The difference between what those consumers whose preferences are represented on the portion of the demand curve above the equilibrium price would have been willing to pay for bread and the actual market price they have to pay.

Define producers' surplus in terms of this problem:
The difference between what the suppliers of bread on that portion of the supply curve below the equilibrium price would have been willing to offer their bread to the market, and the market price they actually received.

Comment on whether the price ceiling is good public policy
The price ceiling results in a shortage with less bread actually available than was available without the price ceiling. Bread is cheaper and easier to purchase, but there is less of it on the market! The resulting shortage will be resolved (rationed) in a non-economic fashion which will necessarily be allocatively inefficient.

At the twelve million output level, consumers are willing to pay considerably more for the bread than the governmentally-imposed ceiling price, and that is another aspect of allocative inefficiency.

If the problem is that some people cannot afford bread, what should be done? (i.e., what is effective economic policy?) **One solution might be to do more in the way of income redistribution via the tax system, taking a larger portion of income away from higher income taxpayers and channeling that income directly to lower income individuals and households. There may also be something that the government can do in the way of stimulating the supply of bread to try and reduce the market price. The problem with the ceiling price proposal is that it ignores the supply side of the market -- suppliers respond to it by decreasing their quantity supplied.**

Analyzing the Impact of a Tax on a Commodity

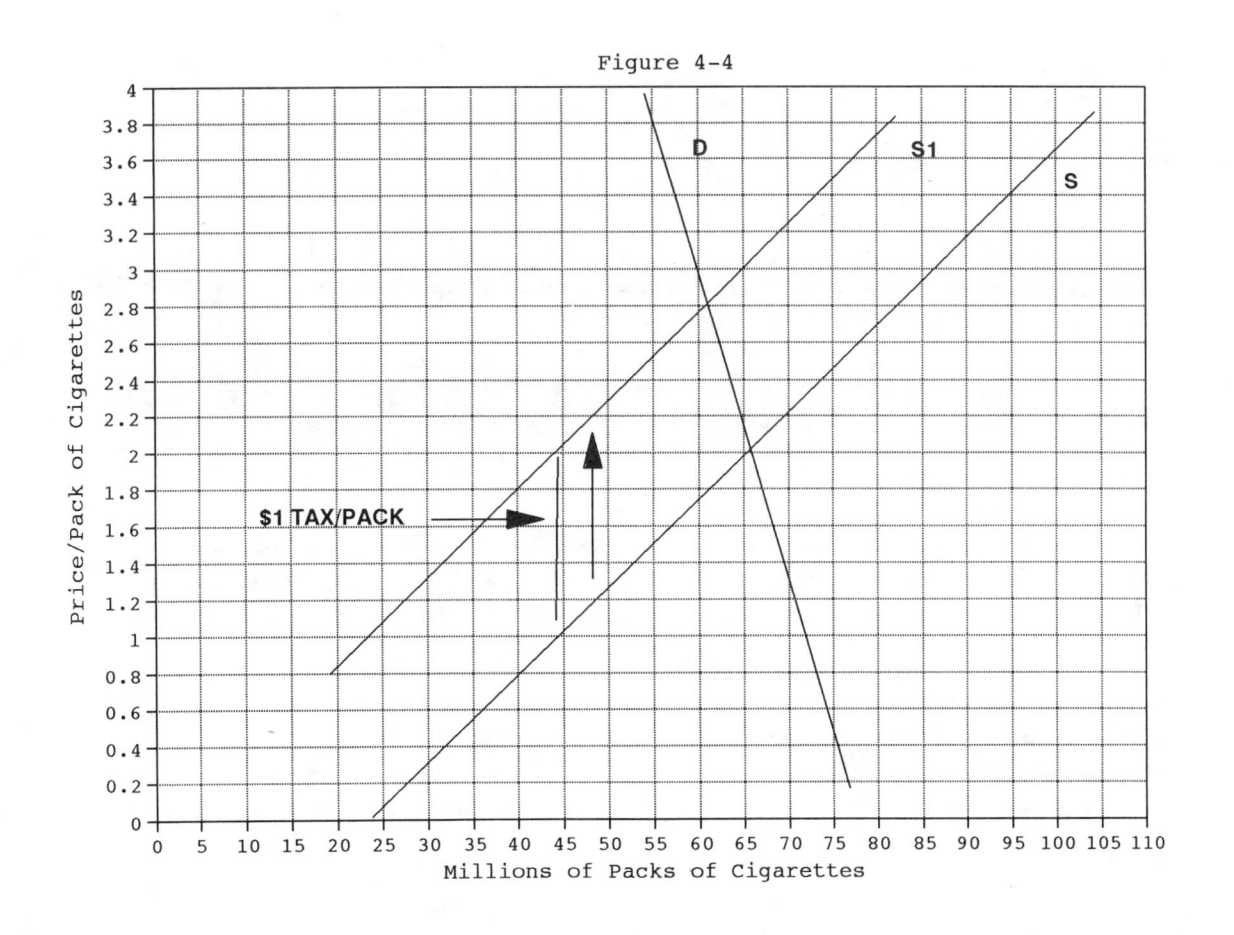

Figure 4-4

How much are consumers spending on cigarettes when the market price is at its equilibrium point: **$120 million**

What are the total receipts received by cigarette firms when the market is in equilibrium at $2.00/pack? **$120 million**

What will be the new equilibrium price and quantity after the tax? **Approximately $2.80 per pack with an equilibrium quantity of 56 million**

How much will consumers spend on cigarettes after the tax? **$156.8 million**

How much tax revenue will be collected? **$56 million**

What is the actual tax incidence (burden):
for consumers: **$0.80/pack**   for producers: **$0.20/pack**

Why would tax authorities prefer to tax commodities with an inelastic demand rather than those which have an elastic demand? **Taxing commodities with inelastic demand curves helps maximize total tax revenues since the quantity demanded decreases less than proportionately. Imposition of a tax on an elastic commodity would result in more than proportional decreases in consumption and therefore less tax revenue.**

True/False Statements

1.) **False.** When supply is completely inelastic, the position of the demand curve determines the market equilibrium price.

2.) **False.** The **market** supply curve is a summation of all producers, efficient and inefficient.

3.) **True.** Since it is difficult to produce additional units of the commodity, suppliers will be limited in how responsive they can be to a change in price.

4.) **True.** Production decisions are based on profit possibilities, and an increase in profits will attract other firms to an industry. Output will be increased, and more resources will be used in the production of the commodity.

5.) **True.** When supply is inelastic, suppliers are unresponsive to a price change and the quantity supplied to the market will not change significantly. Consequently, the market equilibrium price will absorb most of the change. A diagram helps considerably here.

6.) **True.** In very short time periods, firms often have difficulty in increasing their production levels in response to a price change, resulting in an inelastic supply curve. Over time, production levels can be changed, making for a more responsive and elastic supply curve.

7.) **True.** Since consumer surplus is defined as the difference between the price that the consumer would have been willing to pay and the actual price paid, the lower the market price (the price paid), the larger consumer surplus will be.

8.) **True.** After a certain point on the supply curve, higher prices will induce a smaller quantity supplied of labor rather than more.

9.) **False.** The momentary period is defined as the minimum period of time necessary to make some kind of decision within the firm. The short run is a period of time in which some of the factors of production can be changed but not all, typically labor.

10.) **True.** In the long run, all the factors of production can be adjusted. When everything can be adjusted, the final result should be optimal.

11.) **False.** Price ceilings keep the price below what it would otherwise be if the market were allowed to function in a normal fashion. But a ceiling price results in a shortage, so even though the price is lower than it would be at equilibrium, not all buyers can obtain the commodity. Your text shows that when price ceilings are imposed, the sum of producers' and consumers' surplus is less than what they would be if the market were allowed to attain its equilibrium position. Thus, overall welfare is less than it would otherwise be.

12.) **False.** As the demand increases and shifts to the right, it moves along an existing supply curve. There will be an increase in quantity supplied as the price rises, but there is no shift in the supply curve itself, since none of the supply shifters have changed. You have to make sure you know the difference between a change in quantity supplied and a change in supply.

13.) **True.** In such a case, firms should have no difficulty in expanding their output in response to an increase in price.

14.) **True.** Market price remains unchanged after the subsidy because of the perfectly elastic nature of the demand curve.

15.) **Maybe.** Consumer boycotts can be effective if consumers are organized in an effective fashion. But that is difficult to achieve, since each individual consumer has very little impact and therefore has no real incentive to participate since his/her participation really doesn't make a difference.

16.) **False.** In a market economy, people vote for their preferred bundles through their expenditures, thus one dollar equals one vote. The more dollars one has spent, the more influence that a person will have on what will be produced. Since incomes are not distributed equally, the statement is false.

17.) **True.** The goal of firms is typically to maximize profits, so production decisions will be based on profitability considerations.

18.) **False.** It merely means that the market is at its equilibrium market clearing price where there will be no shortages or surpluses.

Multiple-Choice

1.) d   2.) c   3.) c   4.) b   5.) c   6.) c

7.) c   8.) c   9.) d   10.) c   11.) d   12.) b

13.) d   14.) d   15.) d   16.) e

Discussion Questions

1.) The market system provides a means for determining which consumers obtain a specific commodity and what producers supply the commodity. Referring to a demand and supply diagram, the market "rations out" consumers who have entered the market at prices below the market clearing equilibrium price. If the equilibrium price of bread is $1.25/loaf, then those consumers whose preferences or income prevent them from purchasing bread at that price will be rationed out. On the supply side of the market, those who producers enter the market at prices above the equilibrium price are rationed out. If a producer cannot produce a loaf of bread for less than $1.45/loaf, then that producer will be rationed out of the market.

2.) Since consumers have income constraints which prevent them from purchasing as much as they would like of various commodities, their welfare is enhanced by lower prices which allows their income to go further, thus increasing their total satisfaction. But, the supply of a commodity must be considered -- lower prices result in smaller quantities supplied to the market. Consumers are not helped if the prices of items are low but it is difficult to obtain any of them because the quantity demanded exceeds the quantity supplied. Certainly those consumers who are able to obtain the cheaper items are helped, but what about consumers as an entire group?

Because of the limited supply available to consumers, they are willing to pay more for an additional unit of the commodity than it costs the producers to produce the item -- another sign of allocative inefficiency.

3.) Popular concerts are often sold out in hours, suggesting that the ticket price was below its equilibrium price. A recent Garth Brooks concert for 25,000 people was sold out in less than four hours and when a second concert was added, it was sold out just as quickly. Economic efficiency would require that a concert should be composed of those people who were willing to pay the most to attend the concert. One reason for forgoing short-run profits would be to maximize long-term profits. Another reason may be that performing groups feel that the hoopla surrounding fans' efforts to obtain scarce tickets (camping out for a week at the ticket outlet) enhances a group's popularity.

4.) Scalping is evidence of market failure in that some people are willing to pay more for a ticket than the stated price. Again, an event has been priced at a below equilibrium price. A scalping transaction would increase overall welfare, since both the seller and buyer would not have participated in the transaction had they not felt better off -- a plus plus situation. It appears to be a victimless crime if it occurs without coercion of any kind. Scalping implies that the original seller retains the property rights to the ticket even after the ticket has been sold -- an interesting and controversial perspective.

5.) For the most part, the goal of tax agencies is to raise as much money as possible. Therefore, it would be unwise to tax commodities which have an elastic demand, since the decrease in supply that would be associated with the tax could decrease the consumption of the commodity in a significant fashion. Another reason is that when demand is elastic, suppliers typically end up paying most of a tax and the usual legislative intent (not always) is for consumers to pay the tax.

6.) Your answer to this question probably depends on your perspective on the appropriate role of government. Liberals are more willing to implement taxes on commodities like these, since they view such situations as areas where government intervention can play a positive role -- reducing the consumption of a commodity which has identifiable and measureable costs for society as a whole. Conservatives, on the other hand, probably see this as something that government should stay out of. We should stay away from such efforts at "social engineering."

Summary

Chapter 4 puts the finishing touches on the market model -- demand and supply analysis. After completing this chapter, you should be able to put your new found knowledge to good use analyzing a wide variety of real world situations and problems. Applying the concepts of demand and supply can, in many instances, provide useful insights about the impact of changes in economic variables. Just a few current examples: efforts to control rising healthcare costs through legislated price ceilings are likely to result in shortages, an alternative, less efficient way of rationing, and will mis-allocate scarce resources; consumer boycotts of brands of tuna can be effective in signaling producers that alternative methods of harvesting tuna (which do not result in widespread dolphin deaths) should be used; the proposed increases in cigarette taxes will be borne mainly by the smokers themselves, since the demand for cigarettes is inelastic; and the demand for relatively unskilled workers in the United States will decrease as U.S.

firms move south to take advantage of the cost savings associated with hiring Mexican workers willing to work for much less than their American counterparts.

Even the strongest advocates of the market system sometimes end up advocating governmental intervention in one way or another to assist specific sectors of the economy. Your text does an excellent job explaining how such intervention reduces allocative efficiency, creating deadweight losses which makes society as a whole worse off. Public choice theory provides some interesting explanations about such legislation and how it gets passed into law. Even though consumers are frequently harmed by such intervention, the effect on any one consumer is small, perhaps not even noticed, and concerted action by consumer groups is infrequent.

Economic analysis of the impact of taxes and subsidies clearly identifies the responsiveness of buyers and sellers to price changes as the dominant factor in determining who actually pays a tax or receives a subsidy. With BTU taxes, gasoline taxes, and cigarette and other sin taxes receiving widespread attention as potential revenue enhancers, an understanding of tax incidence is quite useful in following the congressional debates.

Chapter 5
When Government Intervenes

Overview of the Chapter

Chapter 5 presents a number of interesting examples of the results of market intervention and the resulting impact on allocative efficiency and society's welfare. Many of the issues examined are discussed and debated in the public arena, so there is no doubt about their relevance. When the government intervenes in the market process by imposing price ceilings (to protect consumers) or instituting price supports (to assist suppliers), the resulting outcome is allocatively inefficient.

Using a price ceiling as an example, there are three different ways to view the misallocation of resources: (1) the price ceiling results in a shortage which will be resolved in a non-economic fashion -- those willing to pay the most may not obtain the commodity; (2) because of the price ceiling, consumers will be willing to pay more for the amount of the commodity available than the market price as represented by the ceiling price; (3) the sum of consumers' surplus plus producers' surplus will be less than what that sum would have been at the equilibrium price.

Price controls are the first issue examined. Typically, some kind of emergency situation is involved before price controls are put into effect. Although the price controls may have the public's support, they have undesirable effects on economic efficiency which impair their overall effectiveness. In many instances, black markets develop to overcome shortages of the commodity and a demand and supply framework is devised for illustrating how such markets function. When formal rationing mechanisms are utilized, it is instructive to compare the outcomes that occur with a black market as opposed to a white market which allows the legal trading of ration allotments. White markets more closely approximate the outcomes of an efficient market, since individuals can approximate their orignal consumption patterns through their white market transactions.

Rent controls and taxicab regulation provide excellent insights about the effects of direct governmental intervention into specific economic sectors. In the former case, the intervention is justified on the grounds of assisting low income renters and in the latter case, the intervention is rationalized by the need to regulate the number of taxicabs. Rent control is an excellent example of well-intentioned legislation that ends up harming the group that the legislation was designed to protect. The price ceiling on rents results in a shortage of low income dwelling units, and ultimately the rental situation will get worse as owners of rent controlled units shift their housing resources to other, more profitable uses. When economic policies ignore the role of economic incentives, those policies are not likely to be very effective, and rent controls are a case in point. Minimum wage legislation suffers from very similar faults. When society specifies that employers must pay a certain group of workers a prescribed minimum wage without increasing the workers' productivity, we shouldn't be surprised to see that unemployment increases.

Two other major issues, income on the farm sector and health care, are examined in this chapter. Public policies designed to enhance overall farm income can be categorized as follows: (1) price supports; (2) deficiency payments; and (3) output and input restrictions. Each method is discussed and analyzed in terms of its effect on price, output, total revenue, and total taxpayer cost. Price supports are characterized by surpluses which must be stored or disposed of in some way. Deficiency payments do not generate surpluses but typically cost more because farmers produce more under the program, and the market price of the commodity decreases at the same time. Crop restriction programs are the best known of the output restriction programs. Since the least productive land is taken out of production, the effect on output is typically less than anticipated.

For these farm programs, the level of government assistance is dependent upon the level of production or the size of the farming operation. Thus, even though the programs were designed to help the smaller, less efficient farmer, least able to withstand unfavorable market prices or adverse weather conditions, the larger farms receive the most income assistance. Direct income subsidies which would make up the difference between a prescribed minimum level of income and actual farm income based on free market prices would be a much more efficient way to handle the problem than the current programs that are now in place.

Most countries are facing a health care crisis as they attempt to provide cost efficient, quality health care to their citizens. Although the health care sector is subject to the same kind of economic restraints as any other sector of the economy, when it comes to their own health care, almost everyone would agree that economic costs should not be a consideration with respect to their own treatment. Third party health care insurance has inadvertently contributed to the health care crisis by creating the illusion that the costs of providing health care services are low or nonexistent, greatly diminishing any economic incentives on the part of providers to be cost efficient. While competition between suppliers usually results in lower prices and greater efficiency, competition among health care providers may result in the unnecessary duplication of costly equipment and services.

Learning Objectives

After completing this chapter, you should be sure that you are able to:

- demonstrate familiarity with the examples of government intervention discussed in the text, including price ceilings, price support programs, black markets, official rationing programs, rent controls, the regulation of taxicabs, the health care sector, agricultural programs, and minimum wage legislation.

- understand the rationale for price controls during wars and other emergency situations and the economic effects (both positive and negative) of such controls.

- understand the basis for black markets and how they differ from official forms of rationing and white market schemes.

- explain and diagram the specific effects of rent control on the housing market.

- distinguish among the various public policies that have been developed to enhance farm incomes and compare their different economic effects.

- apply the market model to analyze the effects of minimum wage legislation.

- discuss the major features of the current health care system, identify the main causes of high cost health care in the United States, and evaluate possible solutions.

Self Evaluation

List of Terms

Black Market
Deficiency Payments
Price Supports
Quotas

Rationing
Subsidies
Theory of Public Choice
Ticket Scalping
White Market

For the statements below, fill in the term from the list above which provides the best fit.

1.) _____ are one way that the government can assist farmers by guaranteeing a specific market price.

2.) The price system is a distribution system or method of _____ based on consumer incomes and preferences and market prices.

3.) Market supply can be increased through direct government _____.

4.) Although sometimes illegal, _____ enhances allocative efficiency by redistributing output towards those who are willing to pay the most.

5.) One way that has been used to raise farm incomes involves the use of _____ to restrict the production of various commodities.

6.) Prices on the _____ are almost always higher than prices in regular markets because of the illegality of participating in this market.

7.) When the market price for farm commodities falls below the targeted price, farmers receive _____ equal to the difference between the two prices.

8.) The _____ provides many useful insights about why legislation gets passed that helps small special interest groups at the expense of the public at large.

9.) Although point rationing programs may be necessary in times of a national emergency, allowing people to participate in a _____ increases the economic efficiency of such rationing schemes.

Problems

Price Supports for Potatoes

The current equilibrium market price for potatoes is $4.00 per hundred weight bag. In response to intense lobbying by the American Potato Growers Association (APGA), the Congress passes legislation providing a price support for potatoes of $5.00/bag. The intent of the legislation is to enhance the income of potato growers to provide continuity of supply.

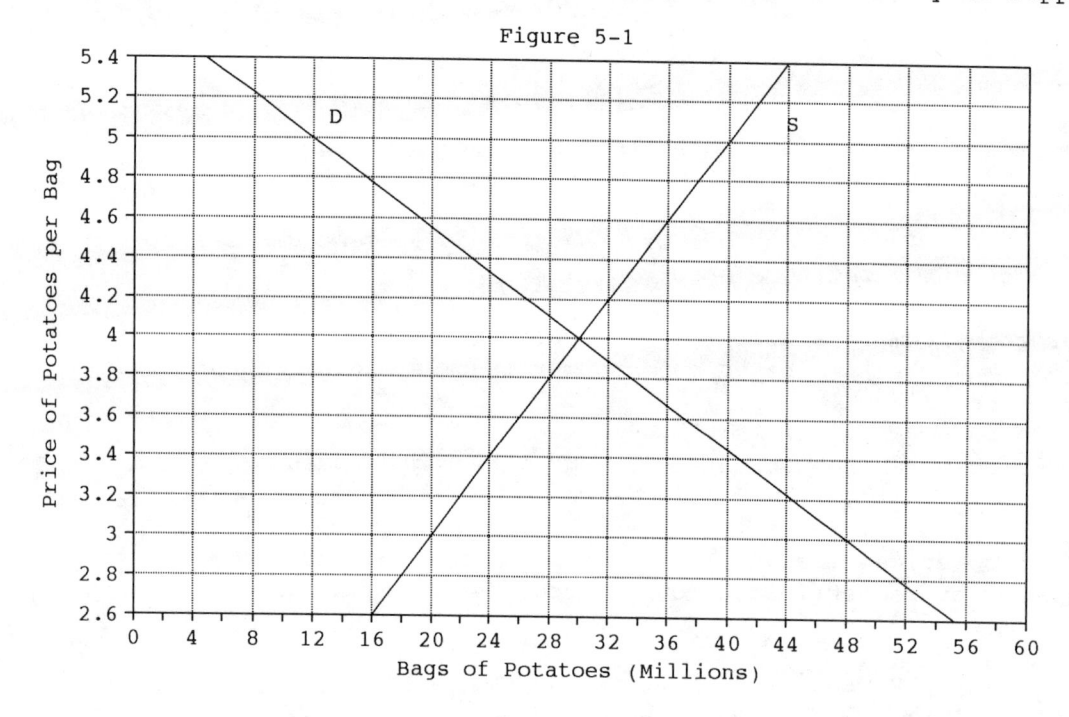

Figure 5-1

Given the demand and supply diagram above, answer the following questions:

How much are consumers spending on potatoes when the market price is at its equilibrium point:

What are the total receipts received by potato growers when the market is in equilibrium at $4.00?

Show the effect of the price support program on the diagram above:

How much will consumers spend on potatoes after the price support program is implemented?

What will be the potato growers' total receipts after the price support program has been implemented?

What is the cost of the price support program to taxpayers?

The Economic Effects of Minimum Wage Legislation

The figure below depicts the labor market for unskilled workers in the fast food sector of the economy.

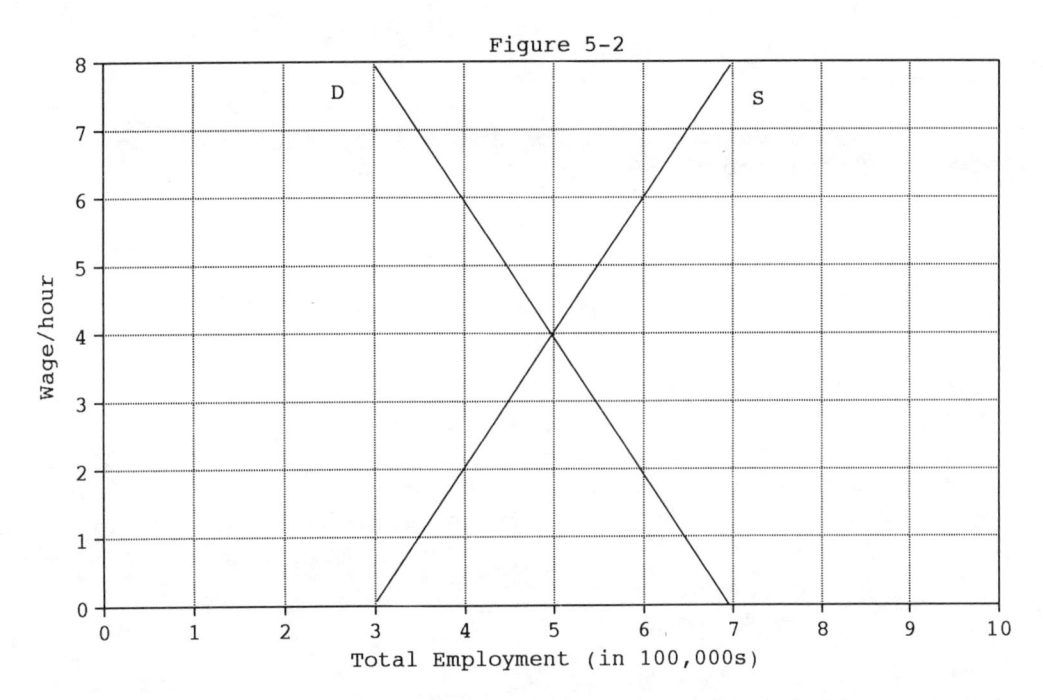

Figure 5-2

Suppose the government passes minimum wage legislation requiring fast food employers to pay their employees a minimum of $6 per hour. Indicate above how that legislation can be shown on the figure above.

How many workers were employed before the minimum wage was implemented?

How much will total employment change?

How many workers will be unemployed after the minimum wage legislation is passed?

Based on the information about the unskilled labor market shown on the preceding page, see if you can determine how much of the unemployment is due to unsuccessful new entrants coming into the labor force as a result of the higher minimum wage and how much of the the unemployment is due to existing job holders losing their job due to the higher legislated wage.

Number of unsuccessful new entrants: _____

Number of existing job holders losing their jobs: _____

Before the minimum wage legislation passed, what was the total wage income of fast food workers? (Assuming a 40 hour workweek and 48 weeks of employment per year, total wage income would equal: (wage/hour) X (40 hours/week) X (48 weeks))

After the minimum wage legislation was passed, what was the total income of fast food workers?

How does the elasticity of demand for labor and the elasticity of the supply of labor affect the amount of unemployment caused by the minimum wage?

Deficiency Payments to Farmers

The following figure illustrates the market for natural spray millet which is marketed as a premium food treat for caged birds. In an attempt to encourage small grain farmers to diversify their production, the government sets a target price of $6.00 per pound for spray millet.

Figure 5-3

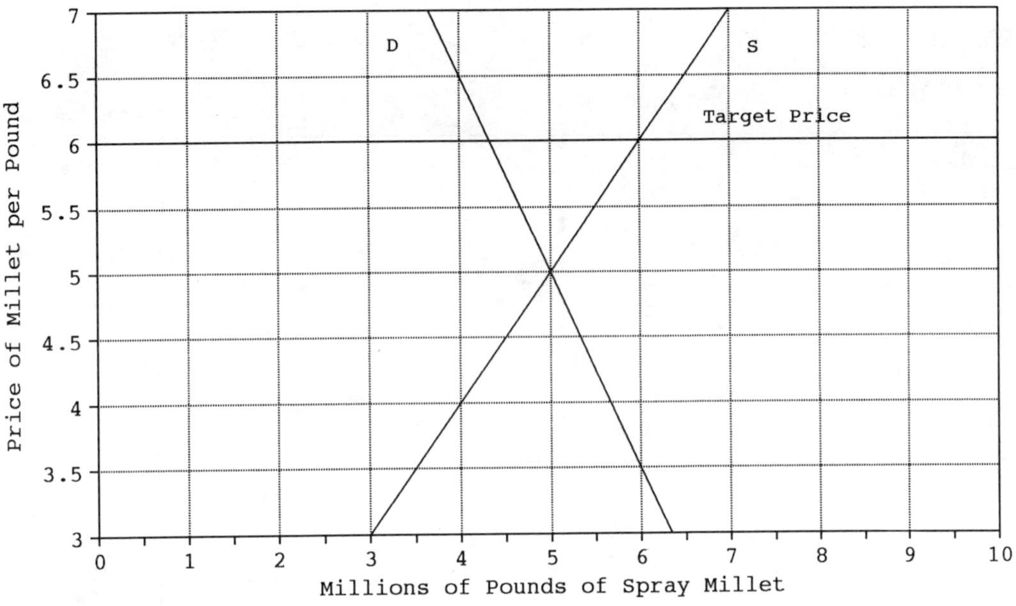

Given a target price of $6/pound, what would be the total cost of government deficiency payments to millet growers?

Given the same target price of $6, what would be the total cost of government deficiency payments?

Compare total farm income from growing spray millet under the deficiency program, with the price support program, and without any governmental programs at all.

	Total Farm Income	Cost of Government Program
Deficiency Payment Program	________	________
Price Support Program	________	________
Free Market	________	________

Crop Restriction Programs

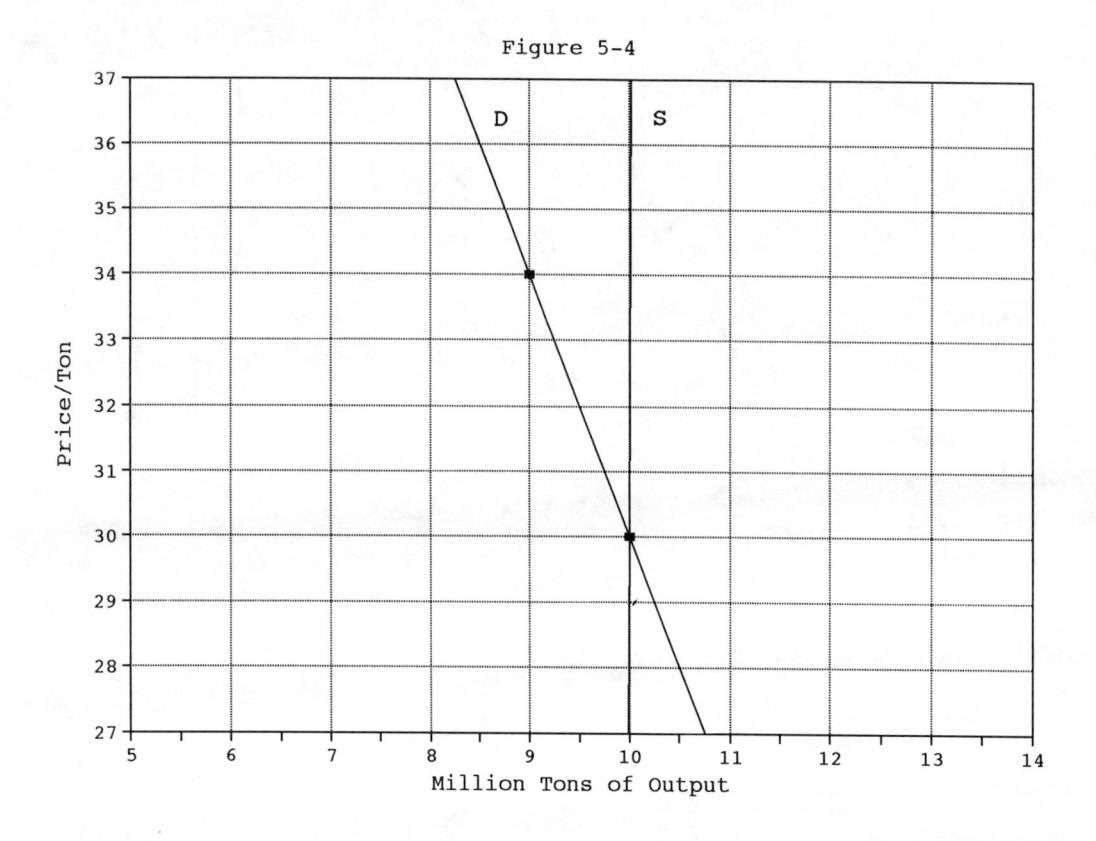

Figure 5-4

[Graph showing Price/Ton vs Million Tons of Output, with demand curve D sloping downward and vertical supply curve S at 10 million tons, intersecting at P=$30, Q=10 million tons. Point marked on D at approximately (9, $34).]

Assume that there are 2,000 farms that always plant 100 acres of their farmland in a particular commodity -- their supply is completely inelastic. Current yields are 50 tons per acre. A crop restriction program is being proposed to help the growers of this commodity, but an agricultural subcommittee would first like to have some information on the total cost of the program. The diagram above with demand and supply curves D_1 and S_{1p} represents the current market status for this commodity -- with an equilibrium price P_e = $30 and an equilibrium quantity Q_e = 10 million tons.

What are grower receipts at the current market price? $ _____

How much would the supply of the commodity have to be reduced to obtain a target commodity price of $34/ton? _____ Draw in the new supply curve on the diagram above.

How many acres per farm would have to be taken out of production? _____

Assume the government is willing to pay $1,000 per acre. How large would the cash payments from the government be to growers?

How much would the crop restriction program cost consumers of the commodity? _____

True/False Statements

Indicate whether you think the statements below are true or false. These questions are designed to make you think about the concepts presented in the text. There may not be any easy clear-cut answers. Some thoughts about the answers are presented at the end of the chapter.

1.) _____ White markets are more economically efficient than black markets.

2.) _____ Less low income housing will be available under a community, wide rent control program than without such a program.

3.) _____ Guaranteed price support programs are generally more costly than agricultural programs involving deficiency payments, since there is no costly surplus to buy up and store with deficiency price programs.

4.) _____ Farm programs designed to raise the income of farmers almost always help smaller family farms more than the larger farm units.

5.) _____ Price controls are necessary and in the best interests of the public at large to prevent price gouging during catastrophes and emergency situations.

6.) _____ Local government control of taxis through the issuance of licenses (or taxi medallions) is necessary to ensure that taxis are available to the public without significant waiting time.

7.) _____ Government minimum wage programs result in increased unemployment among the least skilled workers.

8.) _____ Because of private third party health care insurance, both patients and health care professionals act as if costs are not an important consideration.

Multiple Choice-Questions

Select the "best" answer from the alternatives provided.

1.) Because of an unusual situation, the supply of a basic commodity has decreased significantly. In response, the government has imposed a price control on the commodity to prevent its price from reaching record levels. A black market in the commodity soon develops. In comparing the government controlled market and the black market
   a. a shortage would develop in both the government controlled market and the black market.
   b. both the government controlled market and the black market would be in equilibrium, but the black market price would be above the government controlled price.
   c. the government controlled market would have a shortage, and the black market would be in equilibrium at price above the government controlled price.
   d. the government controlled market would have a surplus, and the black market would be in equilibrium at price above the government controlled price.
   e. the government controlled market would have a shortage, and the black market would be in equilibrium at price below the government controlled price.

2.) When the government imposes a price ceiling on a particular market
   a. consumers are protected against excessively high market prices, thus increasing society's overall welfare.
   b. producers view this as unfair and, as a result, the supply curve shifts to the left.
   c. the good continues to be rationed in much the same way as before.
   d. this action is allocatively inefficient, and the total welfare of society declines.
   e. a surplus eventually develops after suppliers have had a chance to respond to the price ceiling.

3.) When the government guarantees a price support level in a particular market
   a. suppliers are assured of receiving a specific price, thus increasing society's overall welfare
   b. consumers view this as unfair and, as a result, the demand curve shifts to the left.
   c. this action is allocatively inefficient, and the total welfare of society declines.
   d. a shortage eventually develops after consumers have had a chance to respond to the price support.

4.) When Berkeley, California, imposes rent control laws on its housing market to protect low income renters
   a. economists would generally agree that this is good policy, since it lowers the price of an essential good such as housing.
   b. such legislation would result in a surplus of housing units on the market.
   c. such legislation would result in a shortage of housing units on the market.
   d. such legislation would result in the demand for housing shifting to the right.
   e. such legislation encourages the building of new housing units to meet the increased demand and that not only helps the housing sector and renters but it also stimulates the entire economy.

5.) In discussing the economics of the health care situation in the United States, it should be noted that
   a. third party insurance helps foster the idea that health care is actually a free good, greatly increasing the quantity demanded.
   b. most people have a highly inelastic demand for health care since health care is something one simply has to have.
   c. health care is not subject to the kind of rationing that normally characterizes economic goods and services.
   d. the United States spends about the same share of its total output on health care as other developed countries.

6.) When the government institutes a guaranteed price support program to aid farmers
   a. a shortage develops which must be resolved by the Department of Agriculture.
   b. a surplus develops which must either be stored, sold, or given away.
   c. those farmers with the largest output will receive the largest payments.
   d. equal payments will be made to all farmers.
   e. both (b) and (c)

7.) A government legislated minimum wage program
   a. increases the total income and wages going to all unskilled workers.
   b. increases the supply of unskilled, poor workers.
   c. decreases the demand for unskilled workers by employers.
   d. may result in some upward pressure on prices in certain sectors of the economy.

8.) The citizens of Gotham City recently voted for a law to control what they consider to be excessive prices for using taxis and poor service (i.e., rude drivers, unsafe and dirty taxis, excessive waiting times). From now on, the Gotham City government will require each taxi to have a Gotham City Medallion (with the image of a spotlight and a highlighted caped, bat-like figure) to operate legally in the city. It is estimated that before the legislation was passed there were 2,100 taxicabs operating in the city. The city, under some pressure from the larger taxi firms, plans to issue 1,500 medallions. From our economic perspective, we would expect
   a. taxicab service to be greatly improved with shorter waiting times.
   b. the price of taxicab services to remain about the same.
   c. total expenditures for taxicab services to rise if demand is elastic.
   d. a windfall gain to accrue to those able to obtain the medallions.

9.) During a national emergency, a price ceiling is imposed on gasoline as shown in the figure below:

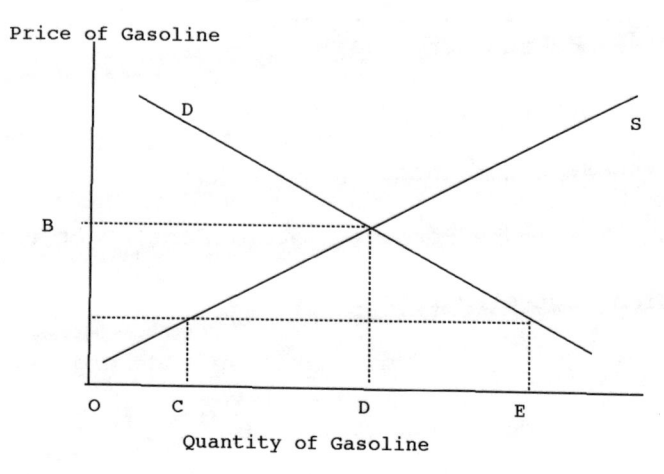

The amount of gasoline which will have to be rationed to gasoline consumers is:
a. OA
b. OE
c. OD
d. OC
e. CE

Discussion Questions

1.) Consumer welfare is increased through lower prices which allow greater consumption. Are consumers helped by government programs which lower prices below their market equilibrium level?

How would you explain to someone who has never had any economics why a price ceiling that lowers commodity prices (which everyone wants) is not in the public's best interests?

2.) If you were an economic advisor and the nation was facing a severe restriction of imported petroleum, why might you advocate a "white market" rationing system as opposed to a more traditional system of official rationing in which rationing coupons are distributed equally to the general population and the reselling of rationing coupons is made illegal?

3.) It has been said that rent controls have resulted in substantial decreases in the amount of low income housing that is available. How can it be that a well intentioned program like this can have such disastrous results?

4.) Articles on ticket scalping always seem to materialize when a popular musical group comes to your city, or other larger than life events like the Super Bowl, NCAA championships, or the latest Barbra Streisand concert take place. In most areas of the United States, ticket scalping is against the law. Why do you think that is the case? As an economist, how would you respond to a reporter's question asking you what you think about ticket scalping?

Answers and Solutions to Problems and Exercises

Completing Statements from the List of Terms

1.) Price Supports
2.) Rationing
3.) Subsidies
4.) Ticket Scalping
5.) Quotas
6.) Black Market
7.) Deficiency Payments
8.) Theory of Public Choice
9.) White Market

A Problem on Price Supports for Potatoes

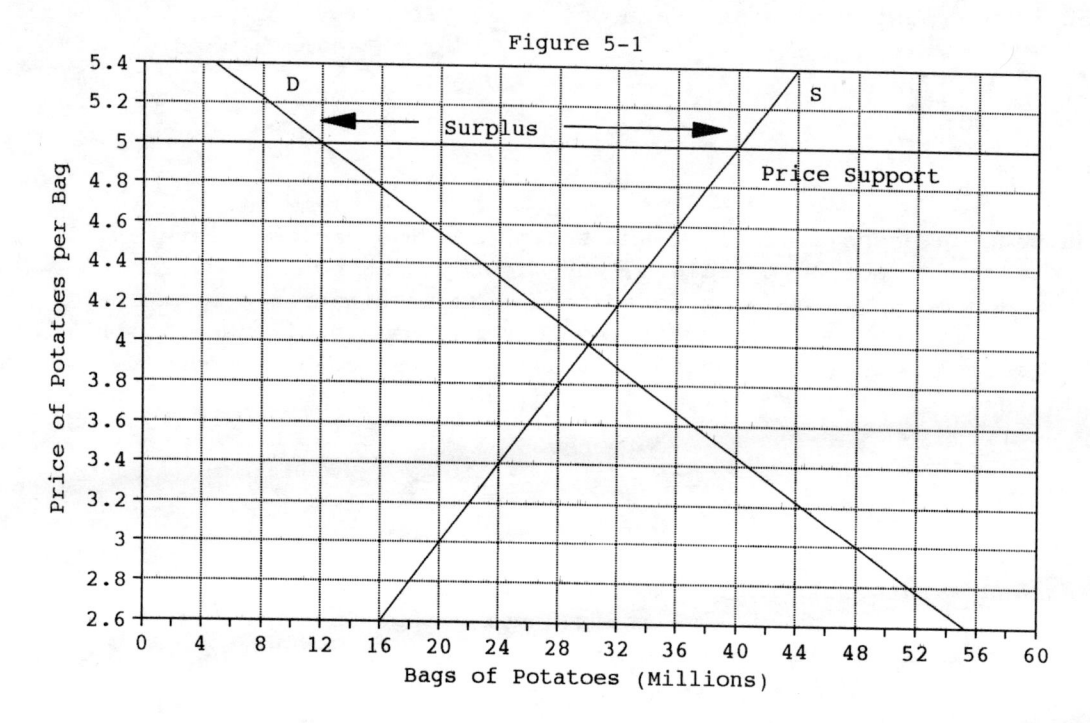

Figure 5-1

[Graph: Price of Potatoes per Bag (y-axis, 2.6 to 5.4) vs. Bags of Potatoes (Millions) (x-axis, 0 to 60), showing Demand curve D, Supply curve S, with a Price Support line at $5 indicating a Surplus between demand and supply at that price.]

How much are consumers spending on potatoes when the market price is at its equilibrium point: **$120 million**

What are the total receipts received by potato growers when the market is in equilibrium at $4.00? **$120 million**

How much will consumers spend on potatoes after the price support program is implemented? **$60 million**

What will be the potato growers' total receipts after the price support program is implemented? **$200 million**

What is the cost of the price support program to taxpayers?
$140 million = 28 million units times $5/unit

The Economic Effects of Minimum Wage Legislation

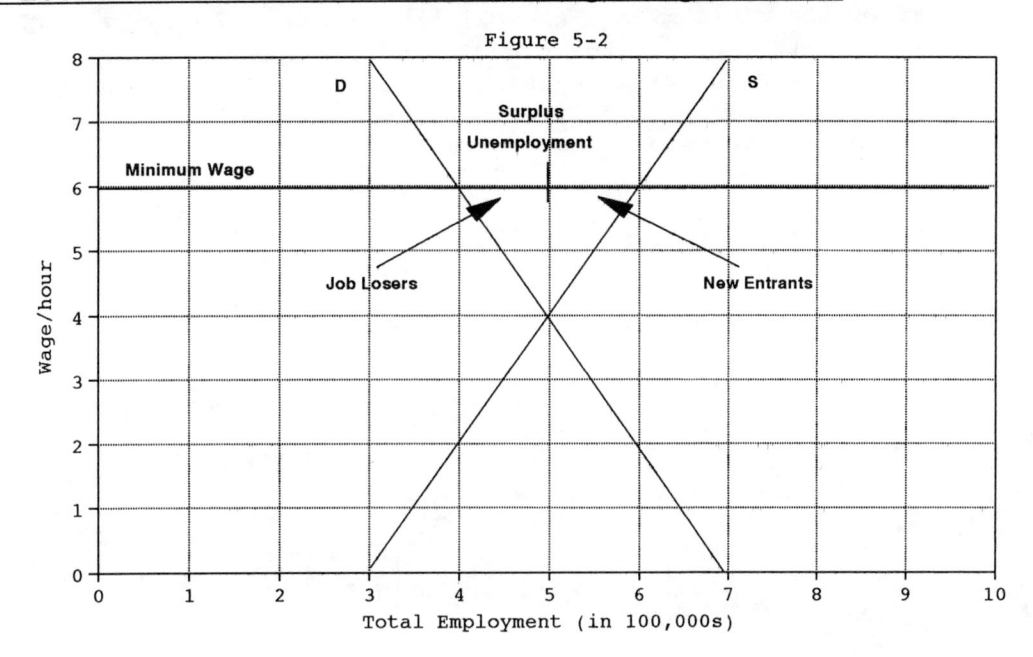

Figure 5-2

[Graph: Wage/hour (y-axis, 0-8) vs Total Employment in 100,000s (x-axis, 0-10). Demand curve D and Supply curve S intersect at (5, 4). Horizontal Minimum Wage line at $6, creating Surplus/Unemployment between employment levels 4 and 6. Arrows indicate Job Losers and New Entrants.]

How many workers were employed before the minimum wage was implemented? **500,000**

How much will total employment change? **100,000**

How many workers will be unemployed after the minimum wage legislation is passed? **200,000**

Number of unsuccessful new entrants: **100,000** **The number of people who entered the labor force as a result of the higher minimum wage was obtained by moving up the labor supply curve to the new minimum wage of $6.**

Number of existing job holders losing their jobs: **100,000 Total employment decreased from 500,000 to 400,000 (moving up the demand for labor curve).**

Before the minimum wage legislation passed, what was the total wage income of fast food workers?
$4/hour X 40 hours/week X 48 weeks = $7,680 per worker

$7,680 per worker X 500,000 workers = $3.84 billion

After the minimum wage legislation was passed, what was the total income of fast food workers?
$6/hour X 40 hours/week X 48 weeks = $11,520 per worker

$11,520 per worker X 400,000 workers = $4.608 billion

How does the elasticity of demand for labor and the elasticity of the supply of labor affect the amount of unemployment caused by the minimum wage? **Demand and supply elasticities determine the amount of unemployment that will result from the minimum wage as well as the impact on total wage income. The more inelastic the demand, the greater the increase in total wage income. But since minimum wage legislation is primarily directed towards unskilled workers, it is more likely that the demand and supply elasticities would be elastic rather than inelastic.**

Deficiency Payments to Farmers

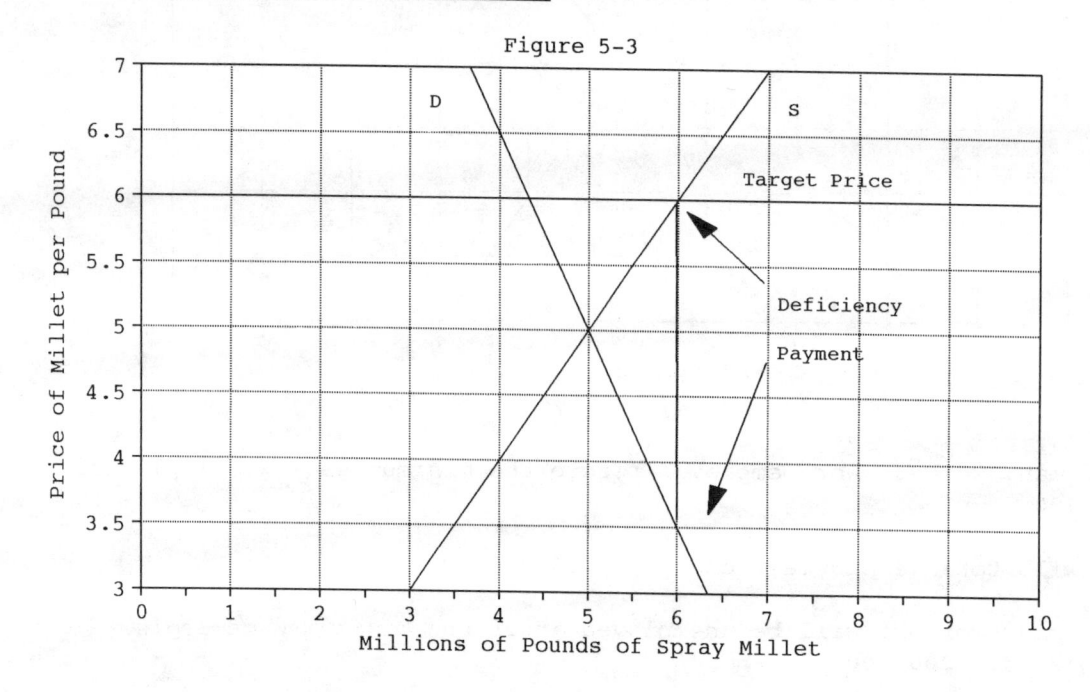

Figure 5-3

[Graph: Price of Millet per Pound (y-axis, 3 to 7) vs. Millions of Pounds of Spray Millet (x-axis, 0 to 10). Shows Demand (D) and Supply (S) curves intersecting at approximately (5, 5). A horizontal line at $6 marks the Target Price, with an arrow indicating the Deficiency Payment.]

Given a target price of $6/pound, what would be the total cost of government deficiency payments to millet growers?
$2.50/pound deficiency payment X 6 million pounds = $15 million

Given the same target price of $6, what would be the total cost of government deficiency payments?
$6/pound support price X 1.5 million pounds = $7.5 million

Compare total farm income from growing spray millet under the deficiency program, with the price support program, and without any governmental programs at all.

	Total Farm Income	Cost of Government Program
Deficiency Payment Program	$36 M	$ 15 M
Price Support Program	$36 M	$ 7.5 M
Free Market	$25 M	$ 0 M

Crop Restriction Programs

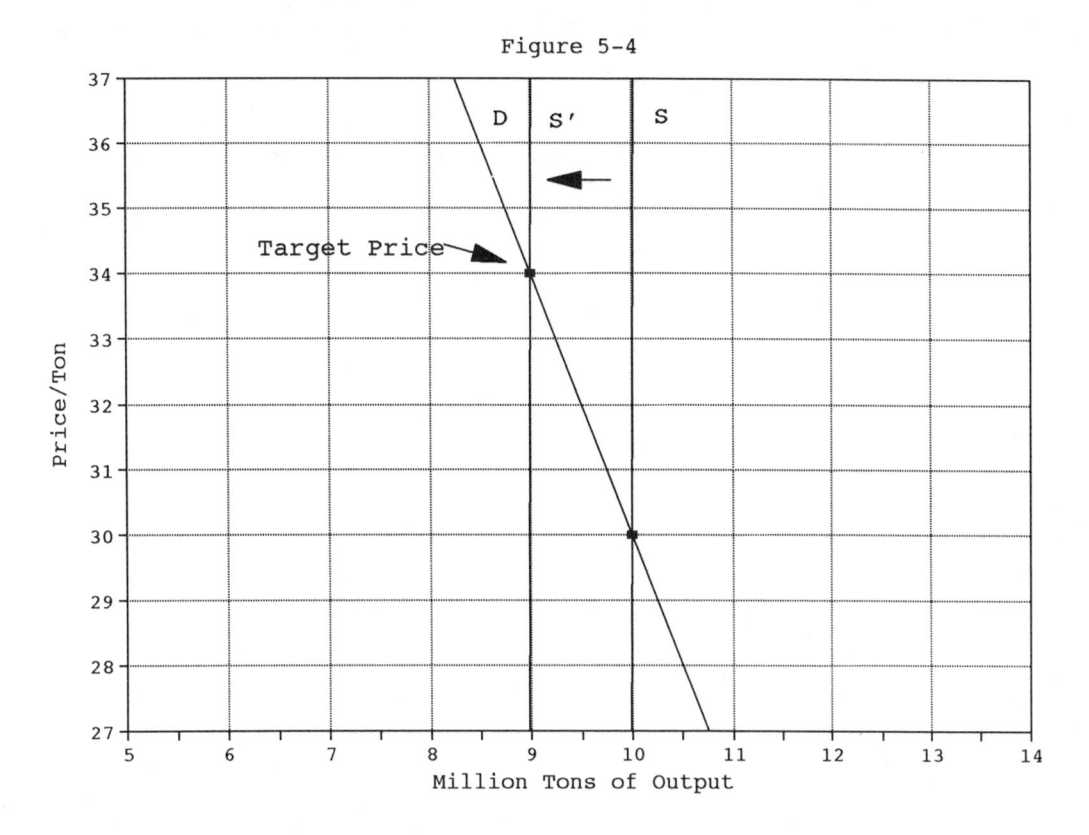

Figure 5-4

[Graph: Price/Ton (y-axis, 27-37) vs Million Tons of Output (x-axis, 5-14). Shows demand curve D, supply curves S (at 10) and S' (at 9), with Target Price marked at $34 where S' meets D, and market equilibrium at $30 where S meets D.]

What are grower receipts at the current market price?
$30/ton X 10 million tons = $300 million

How much would the supply of the commodity have to be reduced to obtain a target commodity price of $34/ton? **1 million tons**

How many acres per farm would have to be taken out of production? **10 acres**

How large would the cash payments from the government be to growers? **10 acres/farm X $1,000/acre X 2,000 farms = $20 million**

How much would the crop restriction program cost consumers of the commodity? **Total expenditures increase from $300 million to $306 million for a net increase of $6 million.**

True/False Statements

1.) **True.** White markets allow trading of rationing coupons among different individuals, so output tends to be allocated more efficiently than it would be with systems that don't allow trading. Because of their illegality, black markets distort both demand and supply to some degree.

2.) **True.** Because the controlled rent price will be below its free market equilibrium value, a shortage of low income housing will occur. Over time, the supply of that kind of housing will shift to the left as landlords shift resources to areas of greater economic return.

3.) **False.** Programs with deficiency payments are typically more expensive, because output will rise and the actual market price will fall, creating a larger difference between the guaranteed price and the market price. The difference between those two prices will be larger, the greater the inelasticity of both supply and demand.

4.) **False.** For all three of the basic types of programs used to raise farm incomes (price supports, deficiency payments, and output restrictions), the more production a farmer has, the larger the size of the check from Washington. This is a bit ironic, since the programs were initially intended to keep the small family farmer on the farm.

5.) **Maybe.** No one wants to see people getting ripped off at a time of personal and community crisis, so, in that sense, fixing prices is perhaps the only humanitarian thing to do. However, what must be kept in mind is that price fixing of any kind distorts the market, making the outcome allocatively inefficient. From an economic point of view, scarce, post-crisis resources should go where they are needed the most in an emergency, not to those who can wait in line the longest. Government controlled ice should go to the grocery store that has $15,000 worth of meat on the verge of spoiling, not to someone who wants to keep sandwiches and soft drinks cold. Not to be forgotten is that fact that high prices encourage additional supply. There may be many more chain saws coming into a devastated area if the price is not controlled than if it is.

6.) **False.** Allowing complete freedom of entry is the way to accomplish that goal. Once the medallions have been issued, there will always be political pressure not to issue any more, since that increases the value of the medallion to the existing holders.

7.) **True.** The minimum wage legislation raises the wage that must be paid to a group of workers, but their productivity remains unchanged. The decision to hire is based on a comparison of the wage paid and the value of the productivity of the potential employee. Unfortunately, some workers will not longer be worth the increased wage that must be paid. Some firms have a fixed amount that can be paid out for wages. If wages increase, then less people can be employed or the same number of people can be employed for a smaller number of hours.

8.) **True.** Since third party insurance significantly reduces the actual out-of-pocket cost to patients, their demand for services is greatly increased. If there is no significant out-of-pocket cost, why shouldn't every possible test and treatment be explored? Since health care providers have been reasonably sure of being reimbursed for the medical procedures and tests they prescribe, they are also under no pressure to be cost conscious.

Multiple-Choice

1.) c   2.) d   3.) c   4.) c   5.) a   6.) e

7.) d   8.) d   9.) d

Discussion Questions

1.) Not necessarily in this instance, since lower prices result in shortages. The problem with shortages is that they are resolved in non-economic ways such as first come, first served, in a random fashion, equally, etc. These methods are not economically efficient. The price ceiling will also decrease the total of producers' surplus and consumers' surplus meaning that total surplus and welfare has declined. There is an unrecoverable deadweight loss in welare. In situations like this, supply has to be taken into account. Lower priced commodities aren't necessarily in consumers' best interest, if there are none or very few available.

2.) A white market is more economically efficient, since it allows a redistribution of rationing coupons more in accordance with individual needs and preferences. There is simply no way that a predetermined, government controlled rationing system can be allocated in an economically efficient and equitable fashion. The white market approach comes much closer to obtaining the results of a free market.

3.) Programs like rent control change the incentives and rates of return on housing to owners and landlords. When faced with a controlled rate of return that is less than the expected market rate of return, suppliers of low income housing will either try to increase their return through under-the-table schemes such as outrageous key deposits or will transfer their resources to other areas which have a higher rate of return. It is more than a little ironic that such programs have tended to increase the supply of housing not subject to the rent control legislation. The moral of all this is that society can not arbitrarily decrease the price or return going to providers of a commodity without having some impact on the provision of that commodity.

4.) Ticket scalping appears to be a victimless crime as long as the transaction is voluntary and there is no coercion involved. Such transactions are positive sum games in which both parties perceive themselves to be better off (the buyer wouldn't have bought the item if she had not thought they were better off buying than not buying, and the seller would not have sold unless she were made better off) and as a result overall welfare is increased. The ticket sellers are concerned about buyers buying up blocks of tickets and reselling them at a higher price and that's the basis for the law.

Summary

Although many people think of the free market system when describing the U.S. economy, there is a substantial amount of government involvment and intervention in the economy which influences the outcomes of the market. The extent of government involvement in the workings of the market system is, of course, the subject of continuing debate between political conservatives who ardently believe that the market is the best way to allocate resources and that it performs best with a minimum of regulations and those of a more liberal persuasion who are just as resolute in their belief that government intervention can play a positive role.

On some issues, such as the minimum wage, there is a clear-cut division between liberal and conservative viewpoints, with conservatives seeing it as an unwarranted intervention in the labor market and liberals championing the legislation as a help to the unskilled working class. On other issues, such as farm programs, the split between liberals and conservatives is sometimes not so clear. But as the olding saying goes -- politics can indeed make for strange bedfellows.

One of the major points of this chapter is that governmental intervention always results in gains and losses to certain groups in society (i.e., those who gain from the intervention and those who are made worse off). Obviously, different people will evaluate the magnitude and extent of those gains/losses in quite different ways. Minimum wage legislation helps one group of employees who end up with higher wages than they would have received through the market, and it harms that group of workers that ends up unemployed or working less hours because of the legislation. Agricultural price supports greatly benefit larger producers while harming consumers and taxpayers. Since such intervention can result in economic impacts in the billions of dollars, a basic knowledge of markets and the effects of government intervention is an important part of being economically literate.

Chapter 6
Revenues and Costs of the Firm: and the Case of Perfect Competition

Overview of the Chapter

Now that you have a basic understanding of the demand and supply model, you're ready to learn about the theory of the firm. It's important to understand why firms make the decisions that they do and how those decisions affect market supply. The market structure that the firms compete in affects their behavior and determines the kinds of questions that they must address. Since perfectly competitive firms have no market power and are price takers, economic analysis of the behavior of firms is simplified, since the only major decision they have to make is how much to produce. So our task is somewhat easier if we begin with perfect competition.

Even though there are no sectors of the economy that satisfy the rigorous requirements of perfect competition, the perfectly competitive market structure is frequently used as a benchmark to compare actual market outcomes against the normative outcomes of a perfectly competitive market. So it is of fundamental importance to have an understanding of what those outcomes are and how they are obtained.

Economists look at costs differently than accountants, and you must be aware of those differences. First of all, to an economist, full costs are made up of both explicit and implicit costs. Accountants must necessarily limit themselves to agreed-upon measurable explicit costs. They define profits as the difference between total revenues and total explicit costs, while economists calculate profits by substracting full costs (explicit plus implicit) from revenues. The other major difference involves the concept of normal or nominal profits. Economists believe that the entrepreneur (owner/manager) has to be compensated for his/her managerial skills and the risk they are incurring or the firm will shut down and the commodity won't be offered to the market. Thus, this minimum or normal profit can be looked upon as a necessary cost of production that must be paid, just like any other business cost.

One of the outcomes of a perfectly competitive market that is particularly beneficial from society's point of view is that the market price equals average total cost of production. When that outcome is obtained, it means that consumers are not being exploited, since the price they are paying is the same as the average cost of production. But, it is important to realize that the average cost of production, as defined here, includes a normal profit, which is just enough to stay in business.

Most of our analysis will involve the short run, a period of time where some of the factors of production can be adjusted but not all of them. Typically, we assume that labor can be adjusted but the firm's capital can't be changed within this period of time. The long-run is a sufficiently long period of time so that all factors of production can be adjusted and therefore, the long-run can be viewed as optimal since everything should be able to be changed. You should be aware of the differences between short-run and long-run cost curves and short-run and long-run equilibrium.

The real substance of this chapter involves the firm's cost and revenue curves. It is vitally important that you know how to calculate and graph the various cost and revenue curves. You should have a good grasp of their shape, the rationale for their shape, how they interact with each other, and what factors affect the curves. Of particular importance is the firm's shut-down point which indicates at what point the firm should continue to produce, even with losses, or whether it should shut down. In every case, the firm should continue to produce in the short run as long as its revenues cover its variable, out-of-pocket costs.

Learning Objectives

After completing this chapter, you should be sure that you are able to:

- identify the requirements necessary to have a purely competitive market.

- distinguish between firms which are price takers and price makers.

- distinguish between accounting costs and economic costs.

- understand the role and significance of "normal" profits.

- understand the distinction made between the short run and the long-run.

- calculate and plot total fixed costs, total variable costs, total costs, average fixed costs, average variable costs, average total costs, and marginal costs.

- calculate and plot total revenue, average revenue, and marginal revenue.

- calculate and plot total profit and average profit.

- understand the relationship that exists between average total costs and average variable costs and the marginal cost curve.

- understand the relationship between short-run average total cost curves for different sized plants and the long-run average total cost curve envelope.

- understand why a firm's marginal cost curve above the minimum average variable cost curve represents its short-run supply curve.

- understand how firms maximize profits in the short-run and the adjustment process that takes place over time and how super-normal profits are eliminated.

- describe how efficiency in production is maximized under perfect competition and why perfectly competitive outcomes are frequently used as a benchmark against which actual market outcomes can be compared.

Self Evaluation

List of Terms

Accounting Profit
Average Fixed Costs
Average Total Costs
Average Variable Costs
Diseconomies of Scale
Division of Labor
Economic Profit
Economies of Scale
Fixed Costs
Implicit Wage
In-Plant Economies
Long-Run Average Costs

Marginal Costs
Marginal Revenue
Normal Profits
Perfect Competition
Price Maker
Price Taker
Shut-Down Point
Short-Run
Super-Normal Profits
Total Costs
Variable Costs

For the statements below, fill in the term from the list above which provides the best fit.

1.) The sum of average fixed cost per unit and average variable cost per unit equals _____.

2.) Subtracting total explicit costs from total revenues provides an estimate of a firm's _____.

3.) _____ increase with the level of production.

4.) Although it is unlikely any sector of the economy satisfies all of the requirements of _____, it is used as performance benchmark by economists.

5.) A purely competitive firm is also known as a _____, since it has no market power whatsoever.

6.) To estimate the economic return associated with being an owner/manager of a firm, entrepreneurs should subtract the _____ that they could have earned from their actual earnings.

7.) If average total costs decrease signficantly as industry output increases, it is likely that production is subject to _____.

8.) Whenever average revenue/unit exceeds a firm's average total cost of production at the profit maximization point, the firm will earn _____.

9.) The extra costs associated with producing an extra unit or batch of production units are called _____.

10.) _____ decline continuously as a firm's output increases.

11.) The envelope curve of all possible short-run average total cost curves (for various plant sizes) depicts _____.

12.) A firm's _____ is defined in terms of the minimum point of its average variable cost curve.

13.) The minimal rate of return or profit that a firm or an owner/manager must have to stay in business is known as _____.

14.) To determine _____, one must divide total variable costs by the quantity of units produced.

15.) Some costs of the firm do not vary with output and are labeled as _____.

16.) _____ are the sum of total fixed costs and total variable costs.

17.) If average total costs increase signficantly as industry output increases, it is likely that production is subject to _____.

18.) In contrast to purely competitive firms, a monopoly can be described as a _____.

19.) The difference between total revenues and the sum of explicit and implicit costs is a firm's _____.

20.) The _____ is a period of time in which some of the factors of production can be changed but not all.

21.) The _____ suggests that total output can increase significantly when workers are assigned specialized tasks instead of doing a variety of tasks.

22.) If a firm can limit the number of product variations or different models that it produces, it can achieve _____.

23.) The extra revenue associated with the production of an extra unit of output or a batch of production units is called _____.

Problems

Farming -- As Close to Perfect Competition As It Gets

Ms. Sawyer, who owns a 500 acre wheat farm in the upper midwest, attempts to run her farm as economically efficient as possible. According to her calculations, her costs for the last production year were $95,000 total fixed costs and $45,000 total variable costs. Her production yield last year averaged 60 bushels of wheat per acre, and the price of wheat averaged out to $4.50 per bushel. Had she not owned and operated the farm herself, she estimates that she could have earned $25,000 in interest income from the money she had invested in the farm, and had she worked for someone else instead of managing her farm, she could have earned $12,000/year in wages.

Based on the information above, calculate the following:

Total Revenue	$ 135,000
Total Accounting Cost	$ 140,000
Total Economic Cost	$ 177,000
Total Accounting Profit	$ -5,000
Total Economic Profit	$ -42,000

Based on your calculations, what would you advise Ms. Sawyer to do?

If the price of wheat increased to $5 per bushel, her accounting profits would change to: $ 10,000, and her economic profit would equal: $ 27,000.

What price of wheat would result in a decision to get out of farming? (Base your decision on accounting costs.) $ 1.50 /bushel

Lately, Ms. Sawyer has been thinking about changing over to organic farming. If she were to do that, she would be able to command a small price premium (organic wheat sells for $5/bushel). Her yield per acre would decrease to 50 bushels per acre, and her total variable costs (primarily chemical costs) would decrease to $26,000 (assume the same level of fixed costs).

The Organic Farming Scenario

Total Revenue	$ 125,000
Total Accounting Cost	$ 121,000
Total Economic Cost	$ 158,000
Total Accounting Profit	$ 4,000
Total Economic Profit	$ -33,000

Based on your calculations, what would you advise Ms. Sawyer to do? Should she convert to organic farming?

Widgets Unlimited

Suppose that you are given the following information concerning the total costs of the **Widgets Unlimited** firm which manufactures very expensive, high quality "widgets" and sells them in a perfectly competitive market.

Output (per day)	Total Cost ($/day)	MC
0	$ 400	400
1	500	100
2	700	200
3	1,000	300
4	1,500	500
5	2,200	700
6	3,000	800
7	4,000	1000
8	5,500	1500

Assume for purposes of this exercise that the firm can produce only whole widgets and not fractions of widgets.

If the price of a widget is $600, how many widgets should the firm produce? __4__ units   MC=500 less than MR=600

What would be the total profit/loss at that level of production? $ __900.00__   TR=4×600=2400   TC=1500 so 2400−1500=900 profit   R−C=P

How much are the fixed costs for this firm? $ __400__

If fixed costs decreased by $200, indicate the effect of that change upon the following: the profit maximizing level of production _____ units
total profits/losses $ __200__

Returning to the original fixed costs, calculate the following at an an output level of 7 units:

__57.14__ AFC   _____ AVC   _____ ATC   __1000__ MC   _____ Aπ/unit

FC=400/7=57.14

What is the lowest market price (in $/widget) that the firm could accept and still continue to produce without shutting down? $ _____

What is the most economically efficient level of output for this firm? _____ units

Recalling your basic knowledge of demand/supply, plot the firm's supply curve on the following figure. Remember, a supply curve indicates how much of a commodity a particular firm will offer to the market at the various market prices.

Price/Widget   Figure 6-1

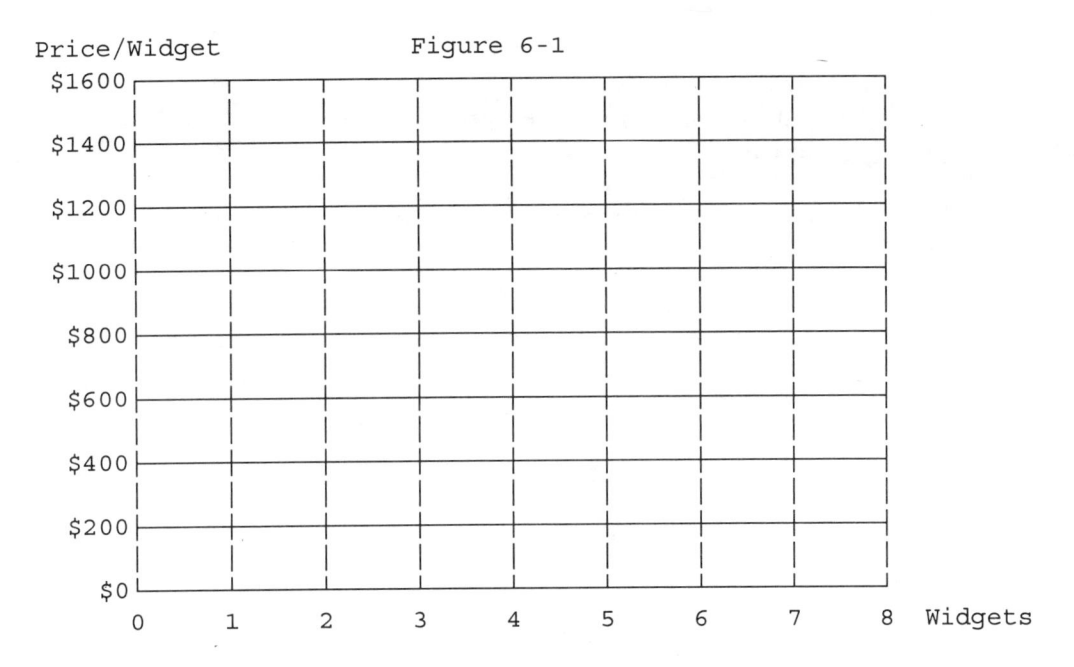

[Blank graph: y-axis labeled from $0 to $1600 in $200 increments; x-axis labeled 0 to 8 Widgets]

Calculating Cost and Revenue Curves

You are given the information about total cost for a purely competitive firm which is selling a product which has a **market price of $20**. Fill in the columns below:

Level of Output Q	Total Cost TC	Total Fixed Cost TFC	Total Variable Cost TVC	PXQ Total Revenue TR	TR − TC Total Profit Tπ	TFC/Q Average Fixed Cost AFC	TVC/Q Average Variable Cost AVC	TC/Q Average Total Cost ATC	TR/Q Average Revenue AR	AR − ATC Tπ/Q Average Marginal Profit Aπ	ΔTC/ΔQ Marginal Cost MC	ΔTR/ΔQ Marginal Revenue MR	MR − MC Marginal Profit Mπ
0	$300	300	—	0	−300	—	—	—					
10	400	300	100	200	−200	30	10	40	20	−20	10.0		
20	480	300	180	400	−80	15	9	24	20	−4	6.0		
30	500	300	200	600	100	10	6.66	16.68	20	3.32	4.0		
40	560	300	260	800	260	7.5	6.5	14	20	6	6.0		
50	650	300	350	1000	350	6.0	7.0	13	20	7			
60	840	300	540	1200	540	5.0	9.0	14	20	6			
70	1100	300	800	1400	800	4.29	11.4	15.71	20	4.29			
80	1500	300	1200	1600	1200	3.75	15.0	18.75	20	1.25			
90	2100	300	1800	1800	1900	3.3	20.0	23.33	20	−3.33			
100	2900	300	2600	2000	2600	3.0	26.0	29	20	−9			

135

At what level of output should the firm produce in order to maximize total profits? _____ units

Briefly explain why producing up to the point where MC = MR or equivalently MC = P maximizes profits.

_____

_____

Plot total revenue (TR), total fixed costs (TFC), total variable costs (TVC), total costs (TC), and total profit (Tπ) on the figure below.

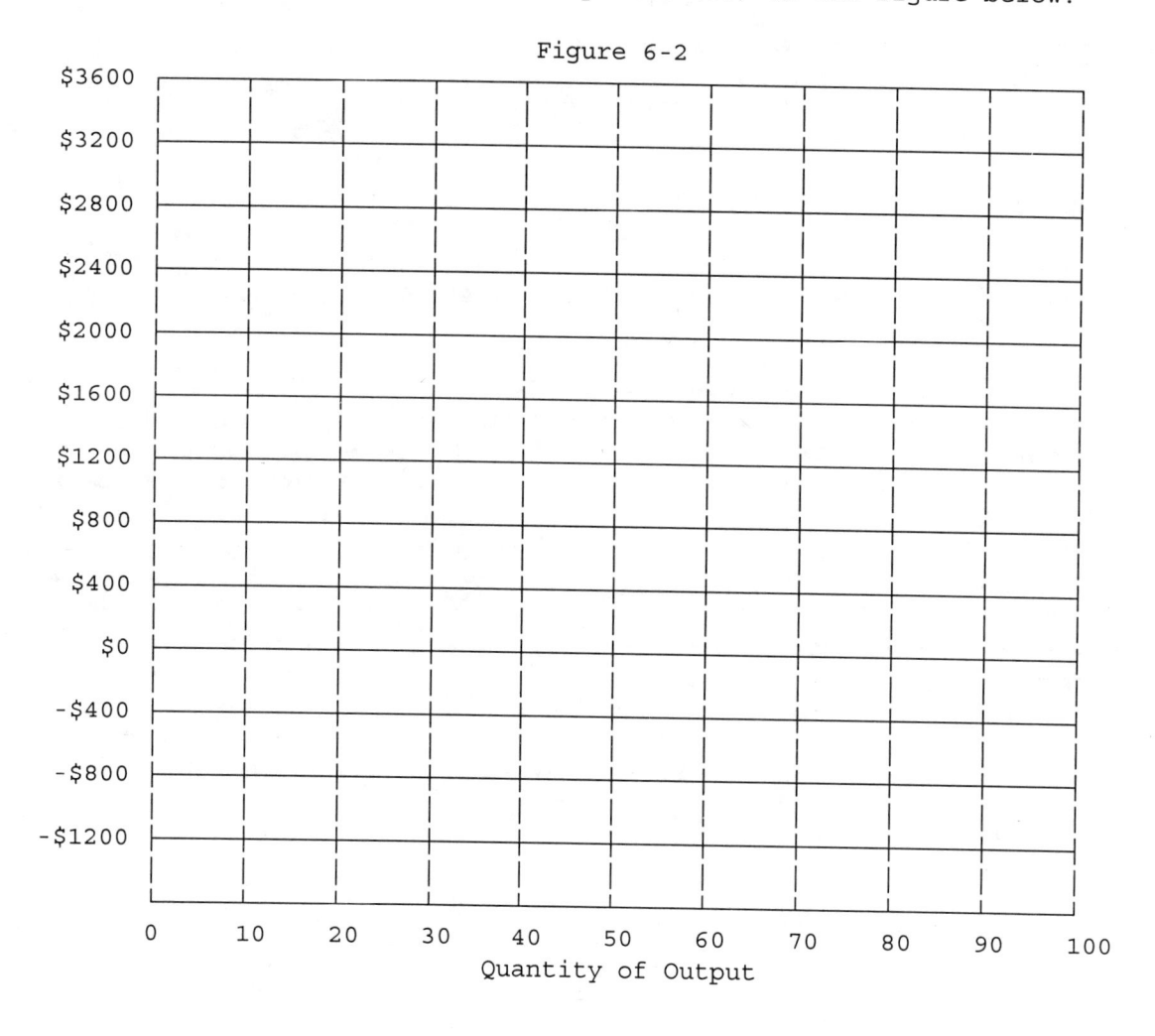

Figure 6-2

Plot average fixed costs (AFC), average variable costs (AVC), average total costs (ATC), average revenue (AR), marginal revenue (MR), price (P), and marginal costs (MC) on the figure below. Also indicate on your graph the shut-down point for the firm. Note: you may want to use colored pencils to help distinguish the different curves. This is a very busy graph!

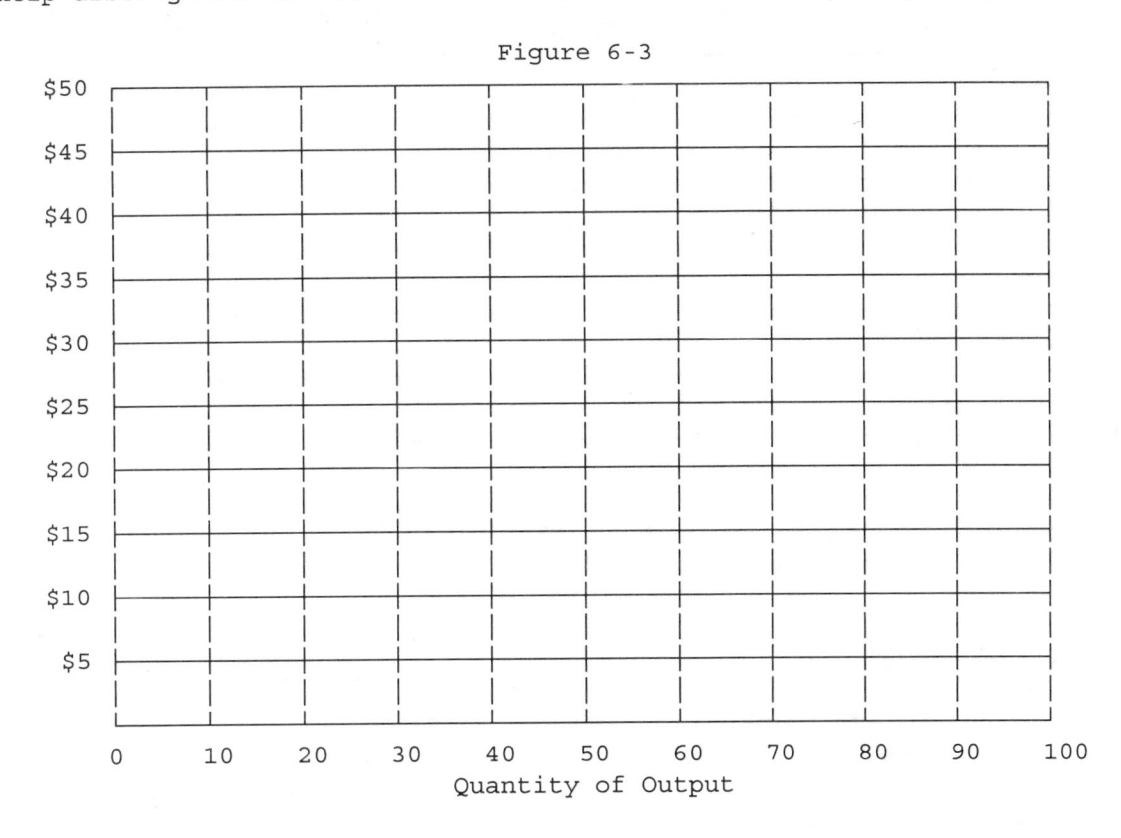

Figure 6-3

Plot average total costs (ATC), average revenue (AR), marginal revenue (MR), and marginal costs (MC) on the following figure. Indicate on your graph the average profit per unit and shade in lightly the total profit rectangle.

What will be the long-run equilibrium price for this industry -- assuming that all of the firms in the industry are exactly like the one above? $ _____

How does long-run equilibrium differ from short-run equilibrium?

_____

_____

137

Figure 6-4

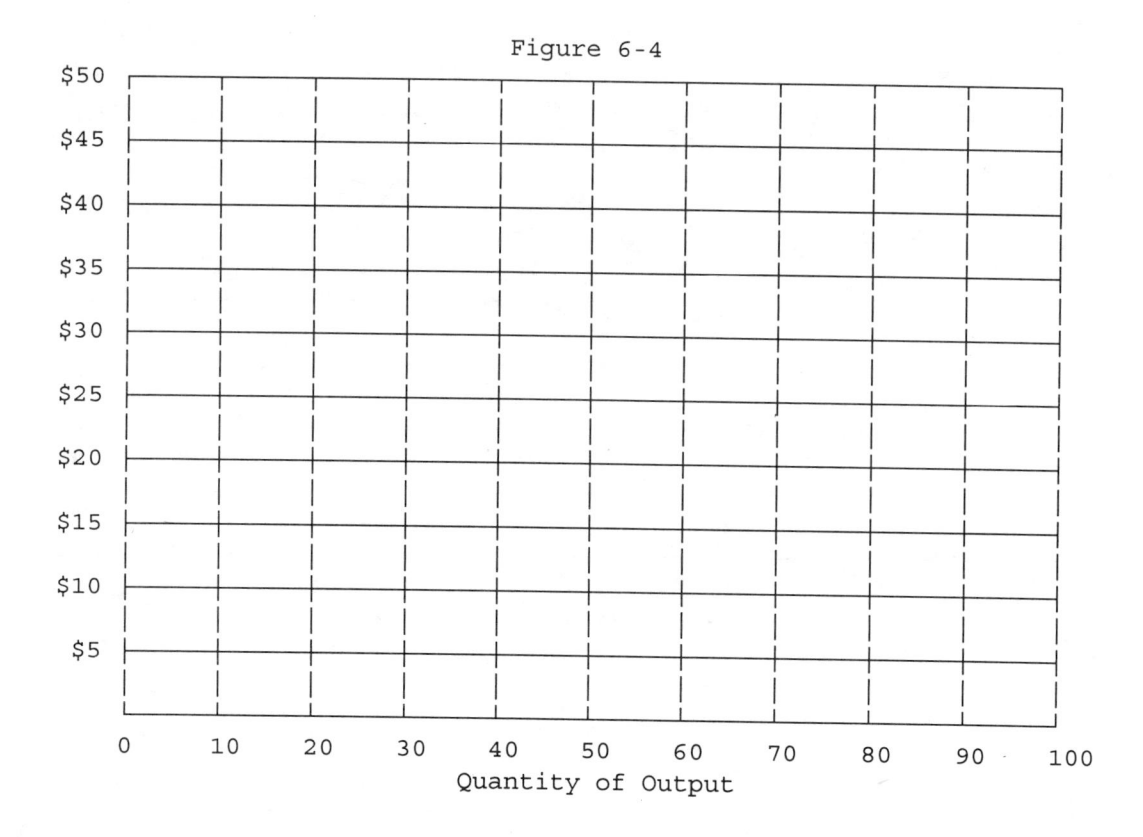

(blank graph: Y-axis labeled in $5 increments from $5 to $50; X-axis labeled "Quantity of Output" from 0 to 100 in increments of 10)

True/False Statements

Indicate whether you think the statements below are true or false. These questions are designed to make you think about the concepts presented in the text. There may not be any easy clear-cut answers. Some thoughts about the answers are presented at the end of the chapter.

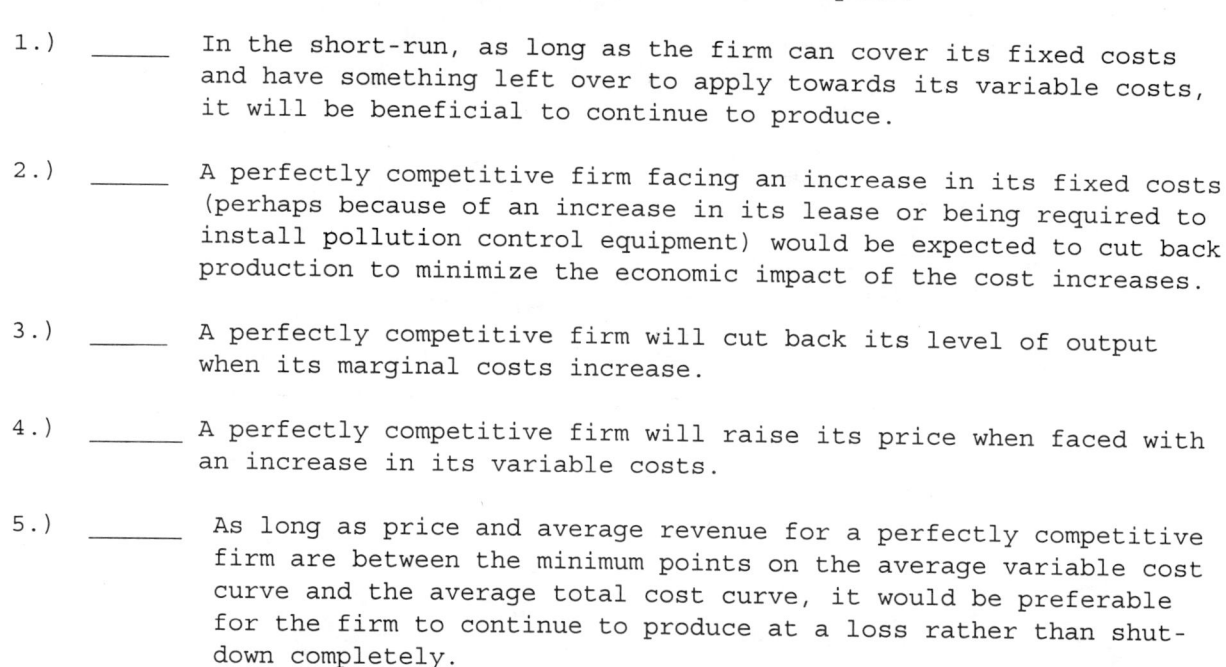

1.) _____ In the short-run, as long as the firm can cover its fixed costs and have something left over to apply towards its variable costs, it will be beneficial to continue to produce.

2.) _____ A perfectly competitive firm facing an increase in its fixed costs (perhaps because of an increase in its lease or being required to install pollution control equipment) would be expected to cut back production to minimize the economic impact of the cost increases.

3.) _____ A perfectly competitive firm will cut back its level of output when its marginal costs increase.

4.) _____ A perfectly competitive firm will raise its price when faced with an increase in its variable costs.

5.) _____ As long as price and average revenue for a perfectly competitive firm are between the minimum points on the average variable cost curve and the average total cost curve, it would be preferable for the firm to continue to produce at a loss rather than shut-down completely.

6.) _____ Economic costs are always larger than accounting costs.

7.) _____ If the MC of the last unit produced is less than the market price, firms should increase production until the MC and price are equal.

8.) _____ If the entry of new firms into an industry raises the cost of factors of production for all firms in the industry, the long-run supply curve will be upward sloping.

Multiple-Choice Questions

Select the "best" answer from the alternatives provided.

1.) If marginal cost is rising but less than average total costs, then
   a. average total costs must also be rising.
   b. average total costs must be declining.
   c. average total costs have bottomed out and are rising.
   d. nothing can be said about what is happening to average total costs.

2.) Average fixed costs
   a. fall to some minimum point then rise after that.
   b. decline continuously as output increases.
   c. are equal to average total costs minus average variable costs.
   d. both b and c.

3.) If market price exceeds average total costs at the profit maximizing level of output, then
   a. the firm is earning normal profits.
   b. the firm is earning super-normal profits.
   c. the firm may be earning super-normal profits, depending upon the other cost curves.
   d. new firms will enter the industry.
   e. b and d.

4.) If a perfectly competitive firm produces up to the point where MC = P, then
   a. the firm is making a profit.
   b. the firm is producing at its most efficient point on its average total cost curve
   c. the firm is covering its variable costs and making a contribution towards its fixed costs.
   d. new firms will be attracted to this industry.
   e. none of the above.

5.) Assume a perfectly competitive firm is involved in the production of a product whose market price is $30. The firm's current level of output equals 500 units, and total costs are $12,000, with $4,000 being fixed costs and $8,000 being variable costs. The next batch of 100 units of output will raise total costs to $16,000. Should the firm go ahead and produce that last batch of 100 units?
a. Yes, because the firm will make a profit of $2,000.
b. Yes, because the firm will better utilize it capacity and lower average fixed costs by spreading the overhead over a larger number of units.
c. No, the marginal costs per unit of the last batch are greater than the market price.
d. No, because the last batch of production units raises the average total cost curve.

Use the information below to answer the next 5 questions.

A perfectly competitive firm's costs are given below:

Output	Total Costs
0	$50
1	$60
2	$66
3	$69
4	$76
5	$85
6	$96
7	$112
8	$136

6.) Average fixed costs when five units are produced equal:
a. $10   b. $35   c. $17   d. $7
e. Unable to determine

7.) Average variable costs when production equals 7 units:
a. $112   b. $8.86   c. $16   d. $62
e. Unable to determine

8.) The marginal costs associated with producing the 4th unit are:
a. $19   b. $26   c. $6.50   d. $7
e. Unable to determine

9.) If the current market price is $12, this firm should produce:
a. 5 units   b. 6 units   c. 7 units   d. 8 units
e. Unable to determine

10.) At a price of $12, the firm's total profits will be:
a. - $50   b. - $25   c. - $28   d. - $24
e. Unable to determine

11.) The effect of increased energy costs on a perfectly competitive firm will be that
   a. average fixed costs, marginal costs, average variable costs, and average total costs will all increase.
   b. average fixed costs, marginal costs, average variable costs, and average total costs will all decrease.
   c. marginal costs, average variable costs, and average total costs will all increase.
   d. some cost curves will increase, some will decrease, but it is difficult to know which ones will do what without more information.

12.) If a perfectly competitive firm experiences an increase in its variable costs, it will
   a. increase output to decrease average fixed costs in an attempt to offset the increased variable costs.
   b. maintain its profit margin by increasing price and passing the cost increases on to consumers.
   c. try to cut back on costs in other areas which weren't affected to maintain roughly the same level of production and profitability.
   d. decrease output and accept a decrease in total profits.
   e. none of the above.

13.) A firm is producing in a perfectly competitive environment. The market price is currently $25, and the firm is producing 2000 units at an average total cost (ATC) of $20. If the firm decides to produce a batch of ten more units, its ATC will increase from $20 to $20.10. Should the firm produce that last batch of ten units?
   a. Yes, since the price exceeds the average total cost of producing the ten extra units.
   b. No, production of that batch will decrease overall profits by $151.
   c. Yes, since total profits will rise by $49.
   d. Not enough information has been provided to make a decision.

Use the information below to answer the next 5 questions.

Market Price = $12

Output	Total Cost	Total Fixed Costs	Total Variable Costs	Average Total Costs	Marginal Costs
0	$100	$100	$0	-	-
10	$180	$100	$80	$18	$8
20	$230	$100	$130	$12	$5
30	$250	$100	$150	$8	$2
40	$290	$100	$190	$7	$4
50	$370	$100	$270	$7	$8
60	$500	$100	$400	$8	$13
70	$650	$100	$550	$9	$15
80	$900	$100	$800	$11	$25

14.) What would be the profit maximizing level of output for a perfectly competitive firm facing the market price and cost data above?
   a. 0 units   b. 50 units   c. 40 units   d. 60 units
   e. Unable to determine

15.) Given the information above, what would be the maximum amount of profits that a perfectly competitive firm could earn?
   a. -$100   b. $220   c. $190   d. $230   e. Unable to determine

16.) If the market price were to fall to $6, what would be the new profit maximizing level of output?
   a. 0 units   b. 30 units   c. 40 units   d. 50 units
   e. Unable to determine

17.) At the new lower price of $6, total profits would change to:
   a. -$100   b. -$50   c. -$70   d. $40   e. Unable to determine

18.) Returning to the initial case where market price was $12, if total fixed costs changed from $100 to $200,
   a. total profits would decrease by some proportion of the $100 change in fixed costs.
   b. production would increase to offset the increase in costs.
   c. production would decrease as the firm adjusted to the higher level of costs.
   d. production would remain unchanged.
   e. none of the above.

Use the information below to answer the next 5 questions.

Price = $55

Output	Average Fixed Costs	Average Variable Costs	Average Total Costs	Marginal Costs
0	-	-	-	-
5	$100	$20	$120	$20
10	$50	$18	$68	$16
15	$33	$17	$50	$14
20	$25	$18	$43	$20
25	$20	$20	$40	$30
30	$17	$23	$40	$40
35	$14	$29	$43	$60
40	$13	$38	$50	$100

19.) What would be the profit maximizing level of output for a perfectly competitive firm facing the market price and cost data above?
a.   0 units   b.   25 units   c. 30 units   d.   35 units
e.   Unable to determine

20.) Given the information above, what would be the maximum amount of profits that a perfectly competitive firm could earn?
a. $450   b. $375   c. $425   d. $250   e.   Unable to determine

21.) If the market price were to fall to $15, what would be the new profit maximizing level of output?
a.   0 units   b.   10 units   c. 15 units   d.   20 units
e.   Unable to determine

22.) At the new lower price of $15, total profits would change to:
a. -$525   b. -$500   c. -$530   d. -$550   e.   Unable to determine

Discussion Questions

1.) Explain why a perfectly competitive firm does not expand its sales without limit if its horizontal demand curve means that it can sell as much as it wants to at the current market price.

2.) The perfect competition model is of little practical use, since there are no sectors of the real world economy which come close to satisfying the requirements of perfect competition (i.e., there are no real world counterparts to perfect competition). If the above statement is valid, then why should we study the perfectly competitive model?

3.) Economists tell us that it is possible to have situations in which a firm or an individual earns an accounting (and taxable) profit which when viewed from the economic perspective are actually economic losses. Is this beyond the realm of possibility -- another game that economists play with us -- or is it economic wisdom of the highest order?

4.) Can you think of a situation where a perfectly competitive firm would ever produce on the right hand side (the increasing part!) of its average total cost curve? Remember, for a firm to do so would imply that it goes beyond the most efficient production point within the firm.

5.) Your text mentions that the firm's marginal cost curve is also its short-run supply curve. How would you explain the basis for that statement?

6.) Suppose that a new law results in an increase in total fixed costs for firms in a perfectly competitive industry. Industry representatives respond that the new law will result in substantial layoffs as firms cut back production in response to higher costs. The news media ask for your opinion on the economic impact of the new legislation. Your comments, please.

7.) If firms are earning super-normal profits in the short-run, the market outcome is not allocatively efficient. Briefly comment.

Answers and Solutions to Problems and Exercises

Completing Statements from the List of Terms

1.) Average Total Costs
2.) Accounting Profit
3.) Variable Costs
4.) Perfect Competition
5.) Price Taker
6.) Implicit Wage
7.) Economies of Scale
8.) Super-Normal Profits
9.) Marginal Costs
10.) Average Fixed Costs
11.) Long-Run Average Costs
12.) Shut-Down Point
13.) Normal Profits
14.) Average Variable Costs
15.) Fixed Costs
16.) Total Costs
17.) Diseconomies of Scale
18.) Price Maker
19.) Economic Profit
20.) Short-Run
21.) Division of Labor
22.) In-Plant Economies
23.) Marginal Revenue

Problems

Farming -- As Close to Perfect Competition As It Gets

Total Revenue	$ 135,000
Total Accounting Cost	$ 140,000
Total Economic Cost	$ 177,000
Total Accounting Profit	- $ 5,000
Total Economic Profit	- $ 42,000

Based on your calculations, what would you advise Ms. Sawyer to do? **Continue to produce in the short run even though she is experiencing losses. In the long run, something will have to change -- either the price of wheat will have to increase, or her costs will have to decrease. A firm cannot sustain losses in the long run.**

If the price of wheat increased to $5 per bushel, her accounting profits would change to: **$ 10,000**, and her economic profit would equal **- $ 27,000**

What price of wheat would result in a decision to get out of farming? (Base your decision on accounting costs.) **$ 1.50/bushel** At that point, total revenues equal total variable costs. At a price less than that, revenues would not cover variable costs and Ms. Sawyer's losses would exceed her total fixed costs. Whenever that happens, the firm should shut down.

The Organic Farming Scenario

Total Revenue	$ 125,000
Total Accounting Cost	$ 121,000
Total Economic Cost	$ 158,000
Total Accounting Profit	$ 4,000
Total Economic Profit	- $ 33,000

Based on your calculations, what would you advise Ms. Sawyer to do? Should she convert to organic farming? **Yes -- her accounting profit would move from a loss to a gain, while her economic profit would be less of a loss.**

Widgets Unlimited

If the price of a widget is $600, how many widgets should the firm produce?
4 units at that output level, MC = MR

What would be their total profit/loss at that level of production?
Tπ = $900   TR = $2,400   TC = $1,500

If fixed costs decreased by $200, indicate the effect of that change upon the following: profit maximizing level of production   **No change**
          total profits/losses   **Increase of $200**

Returning to the original fixed costs, calculate the following at an an output level of 7 units:

$57.14 AFC $514.29 AVC $571.43 ATC $1,000 MC $28.57 A$\pi$/unit

What is the lowest market price (in $/widget) that the firm could accept and still continue to produce without shutting down?
$100 = minimum average variable cost

What is the most economically efficient level of output for this firm?
3 units @ $333.33/unit = minimum point on ATC curve

Plot the firm's MC curve (the firm's short-run supply curve).

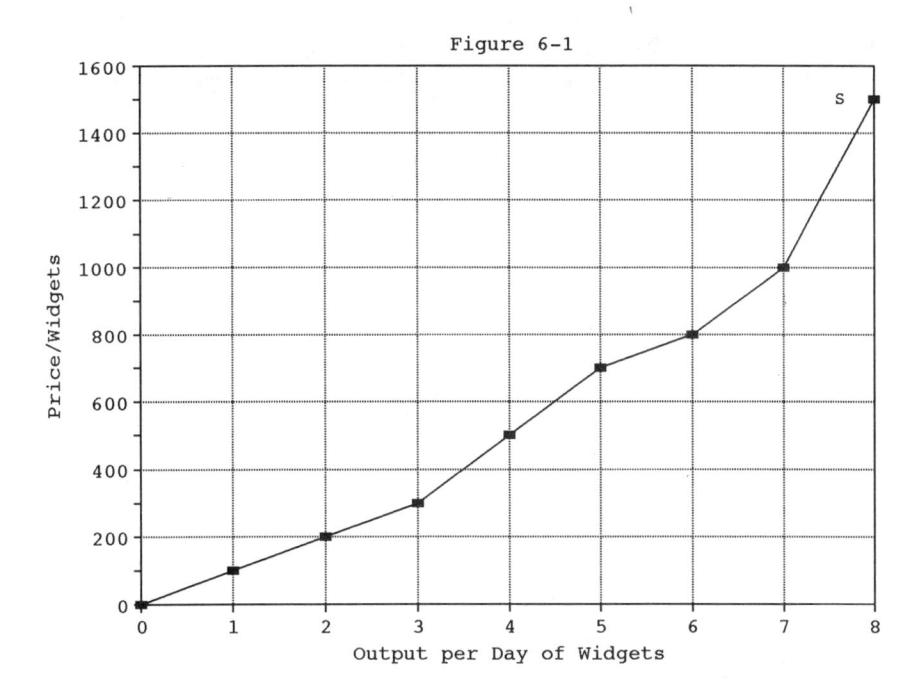

Figure 6-1

Calculating Cost and Revenue Curves

Level of Output Q	Total Cost TC	Total Fixed Cost TFC	Total Variable Cost TVC	PXQ Total Revenue TR	TR - TC Total Profit Tπ	TFC/Q Average Fixed Cost AFC	TVC/Q Average Variable Cost AVC	TC/Q Average Total Cost ATC	TR/Q Average Revenue AR	AR - ATC Tπ/Q Average Profit Aπ	ΔTC/ΔQ Marginal Cost MC	ΔTR/ΔQ Marginal Revenue MR	MR - MC Marginal Profit Mπ
0	300	300	0	0	-300	-	-	-	-	-	-	-	-
10	400	300	100	200	-200	30.0	10.0	40.0	20.0	-20.0	10.0	20.0	10.0
20	460	300	160	400	-60	15.0	8.0	23.0	20.0	-3.0	6.0	20.0	14.0
30	500	300	200	600	100	10.0	6.7	16.7	20.0	3.3	4.0	20.0	16.0
40	560	300	260	800	240	7.5	6.5	14.0	20.0	6.0	6.0	20.0	14.0
50	650	300	350	1000	350	6.0	7.0	13.0	20.0	7.0	9.0	20.0	11.0
60	840	300	540	1200	360	5.0	9.0	14.0	20.0	6.0	19.0	20.0	1.0
70	1100	300	800	1400	300	4.3	11.4	15.7	20.0	4.3	26.0	20.0	-6.0
80	1500	300	1200	1600	100	3.8	15.0	18.8	20.0	1.3	40.0	20.0	-20.0
90	2100	300	1800	1800	-300	3.3	20.0	23.3	20.0	-3.3	60.0	20.0	-40.0
100	2900	300	2600	2000	-900	3.0	26.0	29.0	20.0	-9.0	80.0	20.0	-60.0

What output should the firm produce in order to maximize total profits?
60 units of output

Explain why producing up to the point where MC = MR or equivalently MC = P maximizes profits. **Assume that a firm doesn't produce up to the point where MC = MR. If it is producing at a point where MR > MC, then the extra revenue associated with selling one more unit or batch of output is larger than the extra cost of producing that unit or batch. Obviously, a firm would want to**

147

expand production as long as this inequality holds. Take the opposite situation: MC > MR. In that case, the extra cost of producing a marginal unit will exceed the extra revenue it will bring in and profits would be diminished by producing that unit. A firm would cut back production when that inequality held.

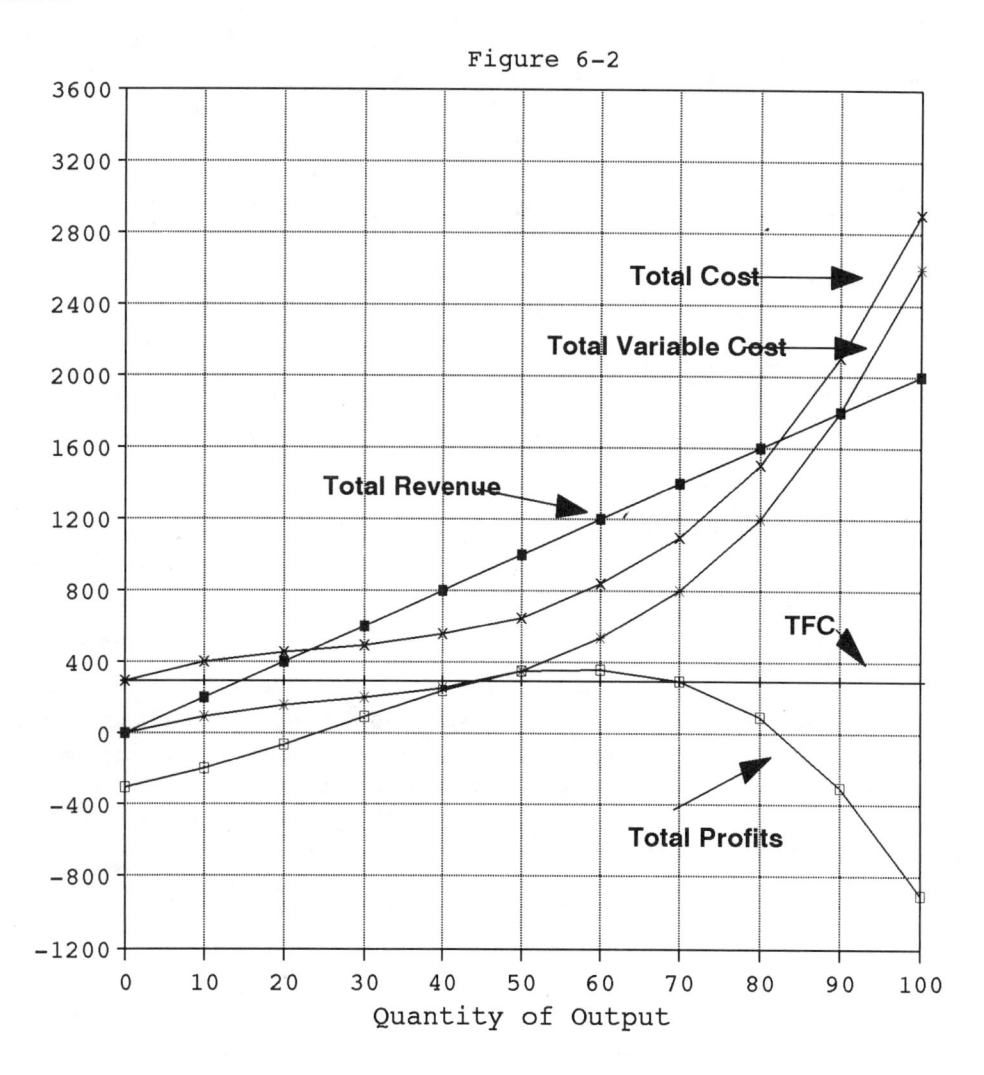

Figure 6-2

Figure 6-3

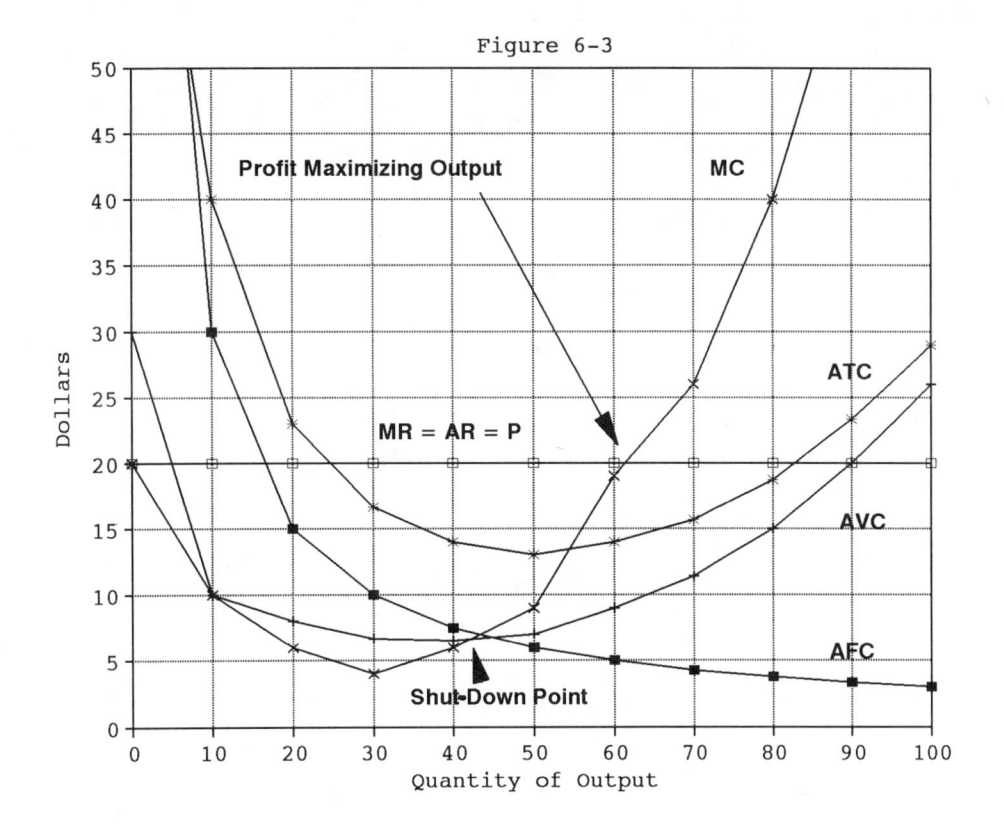

[Graph showing cost curves: MC, ATC, AVC, AFC, and horizontal line MR = AR = P at $20. Profit Maximizing Output indicated where MC intersects MR around Q=60. Shut-Down Point labeled near Q=40 at the minimum of AVC.]

What will be the long-run equilibrium price for this industry -- assuming that all of the firms in the industry are exactly like the one above? **$13**

How does long-run equilibrium differ from short-run equilibrium? **In the short run, the firm attempts to maximize profits by producing up to the point where MC = MR. At that level of production, the firm may be making a profit, incurring a loss, or breaking even. In the long run, the industry itself is stable, with no exit or entry of firms, and that occurs only when each firm is making a normal profit.**

Figure 6-4

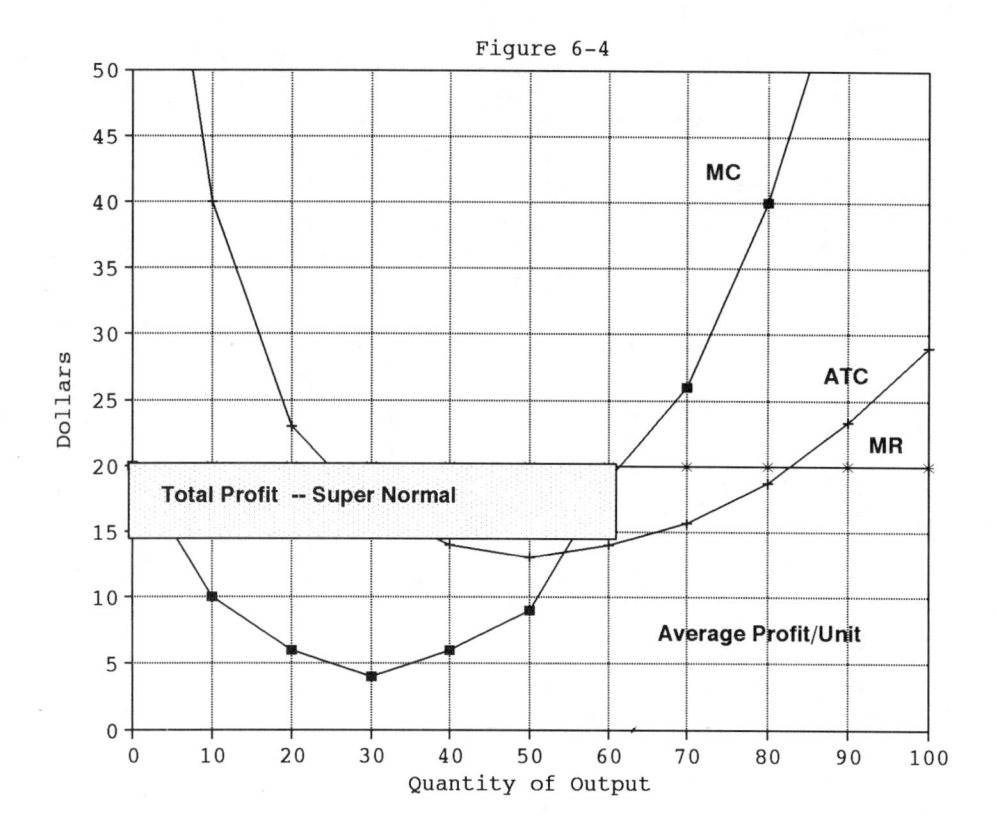

[Graph showing MC, ATC, and MR curves with Quantity of Output on x-axis (0-100) and Dollars on y-axis (0-50). Shaded rectangle labeled "Total Profit -- Super Normal" between approximately $15 and $20 from quantity 0 to ~60. "Average Profit/Unit" labeled below MR line.]

True/False Statements

1.) **False.** The rule has always been that the variable costs must be covered. If total revenues exceed total variable costs, then a contribution can be made to total fixed costs which must be paid whether or not production takes place. Fixed costs are sunk costs and do not affect marginal decisions.

2.) **False.** Similar reasoning as above. Changes in fixed costs affect the overall profitability of a firm but cannot affect the production decision which is determined on the basis of comparing the price of the output with marginal cost.

3.) **True.** When price remains the same and marginal cost increases, some previously profitable units of production now become unprofitable, since their extra cost exceeds the price or extra revenue brought in from the item.

4.) **False.** Perfectly competitive firms have no market power and can't raise their prices even if they wanted to.

5.) **True.** As long as the price exceeds minimum average variable cost, variable costs will be covered and a contribution can be made to fixed costs.

6.) **True.** Accounting costs are based solely on measurable, explicit costs while economic costs are based not only on explicit costs but also implicit opportunity costs.

7.) **True.** The firm should increase production until the marginal cost (MC) of the last unit produced just equals the market price.

8.) **True.** The average total cost curves for all firms in the industry will shift upward as entry occurs and that, in turn, means that additional output will be forthcoming only at higher costs.

Multiple-Choice

1.) b   2.) d   3.) e   4.) e   5.) c   6.) a

7.) b   8.) d   9.) b   10.) d   11.) c   12.) d

13.) b   14.) b   15.) d   16.) c   17.) b   18.) d

19.) c   20.) a   21.) a   22.) b

Discussion Questions

1.) While it is true that a perfectly competitive firm can sell as much as it wants at the existing market price, rising marginal and average total costs will effectively put a limit on the amount of production.

2.) The perfectly competitive model provides a conceptual framework, a way of thinking about the interaction that exists between many competitive firms and the industry made up by the firms. Purely competitive outcomes can be used as a standard of comparison to see how "real world" industries stack up against the theoretical counterpart. We know that after all adjustment has been completed, the market price will equal the average total cost of production and that production will take place at the minimum of the firm's most efficient short-run plant size. These socially optimum outcomes can be compared against actual market results to evaluate the real world industry.

3.) Sounds like true economic wisdom! Economists include implicit costs as part of full costs. Thus, whenever anyone decides upon a particular alternative or path of action, a relevant cost of that decision involves what the individual had to give up in order to do what he/she did.

For example, if you owned and managed a restaurant franchise and managed to earn a profit of $25,000, that might turn out to be an economic loss based on what other returns are being given up in order for you to own and manage the franchise. If you could have earned $18,000 in interest on the funds you have invested in the franchise, and you could have worked as an employee for another firm and earned $20,000, then the economic profit of the franchise is actually -$13,000 (the return on the franchise is $13,000 smaller than could have been earned with the investment funds and labor).

4.) If the price is sufficiently high, then it will pay the firm to increase output, even producing units which may be considerably more costly.

5.) To be more specific, the firm's short-run supply curve is that portion of its marginal cost curve which lies above the minimum point of its average variable cost curve. The basis for the statement is that the intersection of the market price (the average revenue AR curve) and the marginal cost curve indicates the profit maximizing level of output for the firm. Thus, the MC curve yields the same information as a supply curve -- relating various prices and resulting outputs.

6.) Economic analysis would suggest that changes in fixed costs should not affect the profit maximizing level of output since fixed costs do not affect variable and marginal costs. Changes in fixed costs will, of course, have an effect on total profits.

7.) This is an interesting concept. Since we normally assume that the market in which the price is determined is in equilibrium, that would suggest that the outcome is allocatively efficient. Yet, at the level of the firm, price exceeds the average total cost of production, and that is not consistent with allocative efficiency. Thus, it is not allocatively efficient.

Summary

Economists look at the world differently than other people, and nowhere is that difference more apparent than in the area of how costs are defined. Since it is absolutely necessary that entreprenuers (owners) be able to earn some minimal or normal profit when they supply a commodity to the market, what everyone else considers to be a profit is defined by economists to be a cost.

Secondly, implicit costs, which are notoriously difficult to measure, play an important role in the economist's scheme of things. The importance of that way of thinking becomes apparent when an individual is considering different alternatives. Even though an individual may be earning a substantial income (as determined by accountants and the IRS) through the ownership and management of his own business, from the economist's viewpoint that individual may be experiencing an economic loss if the return from current activities is not as great as what might be earned in some other activities.

The economic viewpoint is focused on what else the individual might be doing with this productive factors, and if he is not engaged in the activity with the highest return, it is defined as a loss in terms of that activity. That provides a useful perspective for evaluating our efforts.

As your text notes, there are no real world sectors of the economy which satisfy the strict requirements of the perfectly competitive model. However, that is not as restrictive as it may appear, since many industries and sectors of the economy appear to behave **"as if"** they were perfectly competitive -- even though they are not perfectly competitive, the perfectly competitive model is useful in predicting what will happen when a change occurs. With that in mind, the model provides an simple but helpful framework for analyzing changes in firms' environment, and what effects such changes will have on both the firm and the industry. If a new wage settlement is reached which is expected to raise firms' costs or if the demand for a specific product suddenly increases, broad predictions can be made about what is likely to happen to total output, profits, market price, and entry/exit into the industry.

The outcomes of the perfect competition model are worth striving for and can be used as a standard against which outcomes in various markets can be compared and evaluated. From a consumer standpoint and from an allocative efficiency standpoint, it is important to try to find out if the market price equals the perceived minimum average cost of production (P = min AC). Obviously other considerations may come into play here, but a working knowledge of the competitive model and its market outcomes is essential before any judgement can be made about any specific industry or sector.

Chapter 7
Imperfect Markets I:
Why They Exist and the Case of Monopoly

Overview of The Chapter

Almost all, if not all, of the economy operates under conditions of imperfect competition; thus, the perfect competition model is of limited relevance in explaining imperfectly competitive phenomena and situations. Market imperfections can arise because of the costs associated with obtaining accurate information, significant transactions costs, economies of scale, control of essential raw materials and resources, patents, and copyrights, barriers to entry, and even superior management skills.

You can visualize the spectrum of market structures as running from perfect competition with its many sellers having no power whatsoever to the other extreme of monopoly in which there is only one firm with considerable market power. Simplifying the task of analyzing the behavior of firms in different market structures is the fact that firms' cost curves and their relationship with each other are the same regardless of market structure. The major difference lies on the revenue side, with marginal revenue (MR) no longer being the same as average revenue (AR). As it turns out, MR for a monopolist has twice the slope of its related AR curve and bisects the horizontal axis midway between the origin and the point where the AR line cuts the horizontal axis. Other than that signficant difference, the method of analysis remains exactly the same.

Monopolists maximize profits by producing up to the point where MR just equals the MC of the last unit of production. As long as MR is greater than MC, total profits can be enhanced by increasing production, and if MC is greater than MR, then total profit will be increased by decreasing production. Once the profit maximizing level of production has been determined, the market demand curve is brought into play to find out how much consumers are willing to pay for that level of production. Total profit can be illustrated by drawing a rectangle whose width represents the quantity of production and whose height depicts the average profit per unit (the difference between the price and the average total cost).

Compared to a perfectly competitive outcome, the monopoly outcome is characterized by lower output and higher market prices. Typically, there will be significant barriers to entry, so any super-normal profits that are earned will not be competed away. Because the monopolist produces on the declining segment of its average total cost curve, the monopoly outcome is allocatively inefficient, since at the profit maximizing level of output, consumers are willing to pay more for the level of output than it costs the monopoly to produce those units.

Finally, this chapter deals briefly with price discrimination and the conditions necessary for discrimination to be effective. A firm engages in price discrimination in an attempt to extract as much consumers' surplus from the market as possible (i.e., to charge more to those willing to pay a high price and a lower price to those whose demand is more responsive to price increases and the absolute price). Price discrimination will be effective only if different segments of the market have different elasticities, if the firm is able to distinguish and segregate consumers on the basis of those elasticity differences, and finally if resale of the differently priced output among the different segments of the market is not possible or else budding entrepreneurs will take advantage of the price differences in the market.

Learning Objectives

After completing this chapter, you should be sure that you are able to:

- distinguish between perfect and imperfect competition.

- identify the major causes of market imperfections in today's economy.

- explain why the marginal revenue curve falls below the average revenue curve for an imperfectly competititive firm.

- understand how a monopoly determines its profit maximizing level of production and how the market price is set in a monopoly situation.

- illustrate graphically the profit maximizing level of production, the determiniation of the market price, and the total profit rectangle.

- list the disadvantages and economic consequences of monopoly market outcomes.

- show graphically the deadweight efficiency loss associated with monopoly market outcomes.

- explain why firms may want to engage in price discrimination and identify the conditions that must hold for price discrimination to be effective.

Self Evaluation

List of Terms

Deadweight Loss
Imperfect Competition
Imperfect Information
Marginal Revenue
Monopoly

Natural Monopolies
Patents/Copyrights
Price Discrimination
Rent Seeking Activities
Transactions Costs
X-Inefficiency

For the statements below, fill in the term from the list above which provides the best fit.

1.) Many monopolists engage in _____ in order to maintain or increase their monopoly profits.

2.) A _____ represents a situation in which the firm is the same as the industry.

3.) Giving retired people a discount on their restaurant meals is an example of _____.

4.) Since the price a monopolist charges is higher than the marginal cost of production, the market results are allocatively inefficient and result in a _____ to society as a whole.

5.) Economic sectors where significant economies of scale exist, allowing adequate profitability for only one firm, are sometimes referred to as _____.

6.) Since every price decrease involves both a loss and a gain in revenue, _____ is always less than average revenue for a monopolist.

7.) Whenever firms face a downward sloping demand curve, we are dealing with a situation of _____.

8.) If a monopolist delayed installing newer, more economically efficient capital in order to maximize the returns associated with its current capital stock, that would be an example of _____.

9.) _____ are an example where governmental policy enhances a firm's market power, allowing it to charge higher prices.

10.) One reason that firms are able to differentiate their products and charge different prices for essentially the same product involves _____.

11.) One rationale for obtaining more market power and greater influence over market price involves _____.

Problems

Calculating Cost and Revenue Curves for the Monopolist

You are given the following information about a monopolist's demand curve and its costs. Fill in the columns below: (Note that the costs are the same as the cost problem for pure competition in Chapter 6.)

Table 7-1

Quantity Q	Price P	Total Revenue TR	Total Cost TC	Total Fixed Cost TFC	Total Variable Cost TVC	Total Profit Tπ	Average Revenue AR	Marginal Cost MC	Marginal Revenue MR	Marginal Profit Mπ
0	$50		$ 300							
10	45		400							
20	40		480							
30	35		500							
40	30		560							
50	25		650							
60	20		840							
70	15		1100							
80	10		1500							
90	5		2100							
100	0		2900							

Table 7-1 Continued

Quantity Q	Average Fixed Cost AFC	Average Variable Cost AVC	Average Total Cost ATC	Average Revenue AR	Average Profit Aπ
0					
10					
20					
30					
40					
50					
60					
70					
80					
90					
100					

What output should this monopolist produce in order to maximize total profits? _____ units

What price will be its profit maximizing price? $ _____

How much total profit/loss will it earn? $ _____

Why would a monopolist, like the one above, want to produce at a level where average total costs are not a minimum (i.e., production takes place at a place other than the minimum point on the ATC).

_____

_____

Plot average fixed costs (AFC), average variable costs (AVC), average total costs (ATC), average revenue (AR), marginal revenue (MR), price (P), and marginal costs (MC) on the following figure. Also indicate on your graph the shut-down point for the firm. Note: you may want to use colored pencils to help distinguish the different curves. Another very busy graph!

Figure 7-1

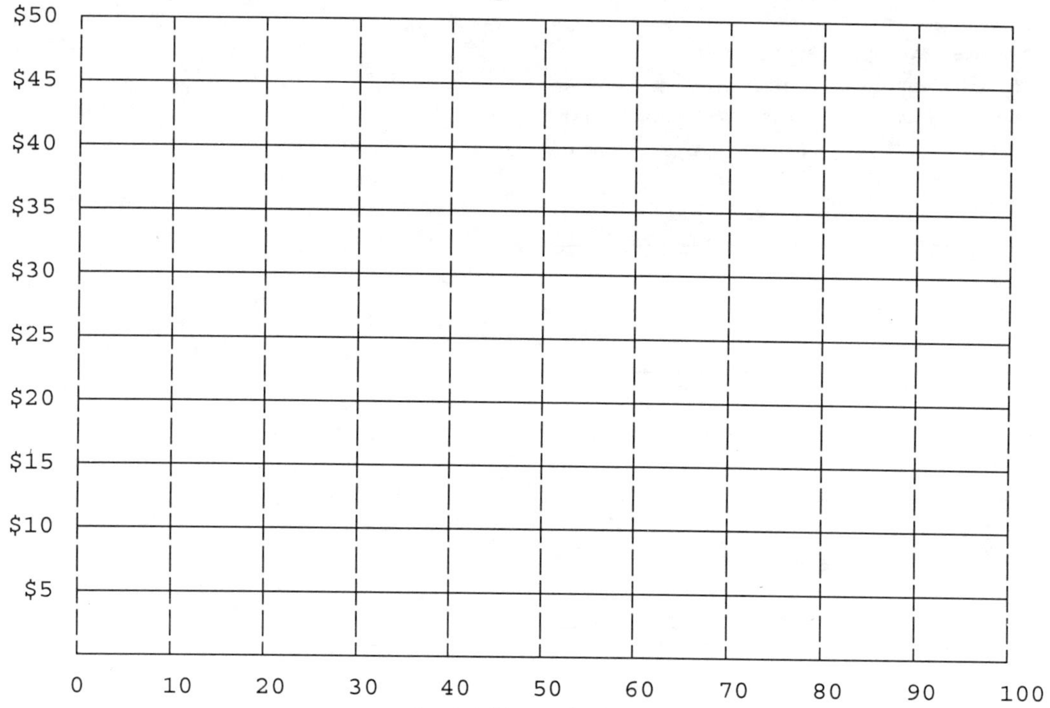

Plot average total costs (ATC), average revenue (AR), marginal revenue (MR), and marginal costs (MC) on the figure below. Indicate on your graph the average profit per unit and shade in lightly the total profit rectangle.

Figure 7-2

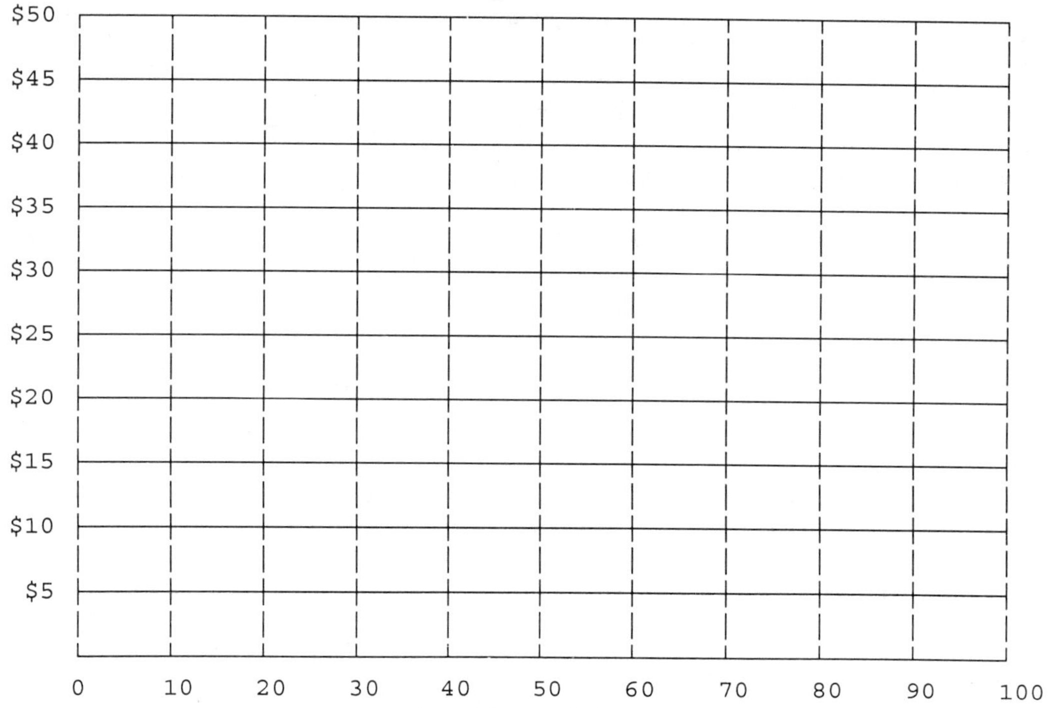

Determining the Profit Maximizing Level of Output and Price, Total Profits, and the Deadweight Efficiency Loss

You are given the following demand and cost curves for a monopoly.

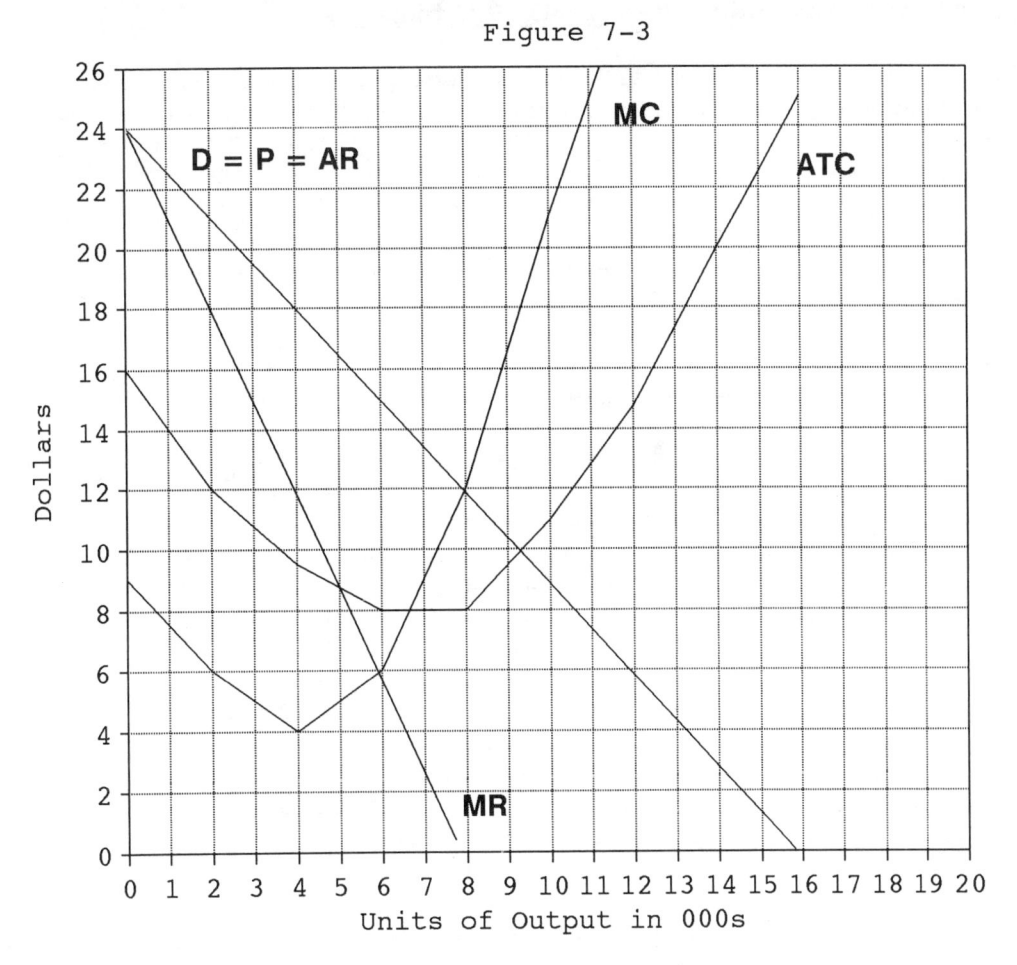

Figure 7-3

Illustrate on the graph above, the profit maximizing level of output, label it Q_{pm}. Label the price that the monopoly will charge P. Explain how that price is determined.

Using the information contained in the graph, estimate as closely as you can the following:

TR = $ _____
TC = $ _____
Tπ = $ _____
Average Profit/unit (AR - ATC) = $ _____
Estimated Deadweight Efficiency Loss = $ _____

Estimate the variables above by determining the dollar value of each square and counting the number of squares associated with the variable in question.

161

Lightly shade in the total profit rectangle for this monopolist.
Darkly shade in the total deadweight efficiency loss associated with the monopolist's profit maximizing price and quantity.

Do Monopolists Always Earn Super-Normal Profits?

Because they can have total control over product price, monopolists are always able to generate pure economic profits because they can charge the highest price consumers will pay. True or False? Explain. Illustrate your answer on the graph below containing the demand curve (AR), MR, ATC, and MC cost curves.

Figure 7-4

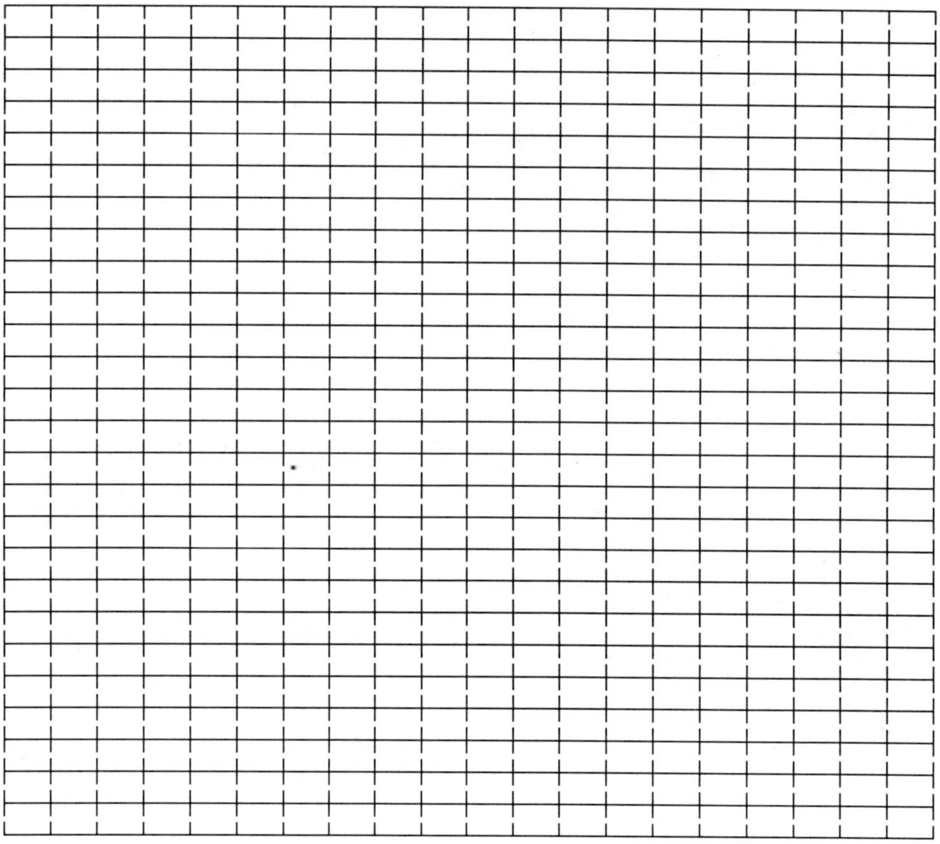

_____

_____

_____

True/False Statements

Indicate whether you think the statements below are true or false. These questions are designed to make you think about the concepts presented in the text. There may not be any easy clear-cut answers. Some thoughts about the answers are presented at the end of the chapter.

1.) ____ In order to maximize total profits, a monopolist should produce up to the point where MC = MR.

2.) ____ Since monopolies have virtually no competition, they can use their market power to set whatever price they wish.

3.) ____ Because of their unique market structure, monopolies do not have to worry about incurring losses.

4.) ____ Price discrimination is effective among different groups of consumers only if those groups have different elasticities of demand.

5.) ____ Compared to a perfectly competitive situation, monopolists always charge higher prices and offer smaller amounts of production to the market.

6.) ____ In a monopolistic situation, average revenue is always twice as large as marginal revenue.

7.) ____ Natural monopolies are likely to exist in those sectors of the economy characterized by having large amounts of fixed costs.

8.) ____ It is conceivable for a monopolist to have an elastic demand curve for its product.

9.) ____ Monopolists are less efficient than perfectly competitive firms.

Multiple-Choice Questions

Select the "best" answer from the alternatives provided.

1.) You are given information about two points on a monopolist's demand curve: at $9, thirty units will be demanded and at $8, thirty one units will be demanded. What is the marginal revenue associated with the 31st unit?
   a. $8   b. $0   c. -$22   d. $248   e. $270

You are given the following information about the demand curve facing a monopolist and several cost curves. On the basis of that information, determine what the profit maximizing level of production will be for the monopolist.

Quantity	Price	Total Cost of Production
0	$20	$10
1	$18	$20
2	$16	$25
3	$14	$28
4	$12	$32
5	$10	$38
6	$ 8	$46
7	$ 6	$56
8	$ 4	$70
9	$ 2	$90
10	$ 0	$120

2.) The marginal revenue associated with selling the 5th unit of output is:
    a. $3   b. $48   c. $50   d. $2   e. unable to determine

3.) The marginal cost associated with producing the 3rd unit of output is:
    a. $3   b. $25   c. $5   d. $9.33   e. unable to determine

4.) What is the profit maximizing level of output for this monopolist?
    a. 2 units   b. 3 units   c. 4 units   d. 5 units
    e. unable to determine from the information provided

5.) What is the maximum total profit the monopolist can earn given the data above?
    a. $14   b. $16   c. $12   d. $7   e. unable to determine

6.) To protect consumers, the government imposes a price ceiling of $6 for this product. The monopolist's response to this price ceiling should be
    a. to get in touch immediately with the monopolist's regulatory committee.
    b. to close down all operations.
    c. to continue to produce at the $6 price and hope that the price ceiling will be rescinded.
    d. increase total advertising expenditures to shift the demand curve to the right.

Use the information provided below to answer the next 4 questions.

Price	Quantity	Total Cost	Total Fixed Costs	Total Variable Costs	Average Fixed Costs	Average Variable Costs	Average Total Costs	Marginal Costs
$100	0	$1,200	$1,200	$0	-	-	-	-
$90	10	$1,400	$1,200	$200	$120	$20	$140	$20
$80	20	$1,550	$1,200	$350	$60	$18	$78	$15
$70	30	$1,625	$1,200	$425	$40	$14	$54	$8
$60	40	$1,750	$1,200	$550	$30	$14	$44	$13
$50	50	$1,950	$1,200	$750	$24	$15	$39	$20
$40	60	$2,200	$1,200	$1,000	$20	$17	$37	$25
$30	70	$2,700	$1,200	$1,500	$17	$21	$39	$50
$20	80	$3,400	$1,200	$2,200	$15	$28	$43	$70
$10	90	$4,300	$1,200	$3,100	$13	$34	$48	$90
$0	100	$5,400	$1,200	$4,200	$12	$42	$54	$110

7.) What would be the profit maximizing level of output for a monopoly facing the market price and cost data above
   a. 0 units   b. 30 units   c. 40 units   d. 50 units
   e. unable to determine

8.) Given the information above, what would be the maximum amount of profits that the monopoly could earn?
   a. $475   b. $650   c. $550   d. $200   e. unable to determine

9.) What is the marginal revenue per unit associated with increasing sales and production from 50 to 60 units of output:
   a. $10   b. -$100   c. -$10   d. $1   e. unable to determine

10.) At the profit maximizing level of output (see Question 7), marginal revenue and marginal cost are equal to (respectively)
   a. $10, $20   b. $50, $8   c. -$10, $25   d. $30, $13
   e. unable to determine

Use the information provided below to answer the next 5 questions.

Price	Quantity	Average Fixed Costs	Average Variable Costs	Average Total Costs
$50	0	-	-	-
$45	25	60.00	3.00	63.00
$40	50	30.00	4.00	34.00
$35	75	20.00	5.33	25.33
$30	100	15.00	7.00	22.00
$25	125	12.00	8.80	20.80
$20	150	10.00	11.33	21.33
$15	175	8.57	14.29	22.86
$10	200	7.50	17.50	25.00
$5	225	6.67	20.89	27.56
$0	250	6.00	24.00	30.00

11.) Total fixed costs in the example above are:
a. $0   b. $1000   c. $1500   d. $1200
e. unable to determine

12.) The marginal cost (MC) per unit when production is increased from 175 units to 200 units is: a. $25   b. $23   c. $32   d. $40
e. unable to determine

13.) The marginal revenue (MR) per unit when sales are increased from 25 units to 50 units is: a. $35   b. $2000   c. $87.5
d. $875   e. unable to determine

14.) The profit maximizing level of output for this monopolist would be:
a. 50 units   b. 75 units   c. 100 units   d. 125 units
e. unable to determine

15,) The maximum amount of profit the monopolist would earn would be:
a. $300   b. $725   c. $800   d. $525
e. unable to determine

Discussion Questions

1.) Now that you have a better theoretical understanding of perfect competition and monopoly, how would you compare the two different market outcomes?

2.) Given that perfect competition is often used as a benchmark of market performance, can you think of any situations in which a monopoly would be preferable to having a perfectly competitive industry?

3.) Your text mentions airline and movie tickets as examples of situations in which price discrimination is effective. Can you come up with some other situations not mentioned in the text where you think price discrimination would be effective?

4.) What do economies of scale have to do with "natural" monopolies?

5.) What can government do in terms of public policy to mitigate market imperfections which can lead to monopoly?

Answers and Solutions to Problems and Exercises

Completing Statements from the List of Terms

1.)	Rent Seeking Activities		6.)	Marginal Revenue
2.)	Monopoly		7.)	Imperfect Competition
3.)	Price Discrimination		8.)	X-Inefficiency
4.)	Deadweight Loss		9.)	Patents/Copyrights
5.)	Natural Monopolies		10.)	Imperfect Information
			11.)	Transactions Costs

Problems

Calculating Cost and Revenue Curves for the Monopolist

Table 7-1

Quantity Q	Price P	Total Revenue TR	Total Cost TC	Total Fixed Cost TFC	Total Variable Cost TVC	Total Profit Tπ	Average Revenue AR	Marginal Cost MC	Marginal Revenue MR	Marginal Profit Mπ
0	$50	$ 0	$ 300	$300	$ 0	-$ 300	$50	-	-	-
10	45	450	400	300	100	50	45	$10	$45	$35
20	40	800	480	300	160	340	40	6	35	29
30	35	1050	500	300	200	550	35	4	25	21
40	30	1200	560	300	260	640	30	6	15	9
50	25	1250	650	300	350	600	25	9	5	- 4
60	20	1200	840	300	540	360	20	19	- 5	- 24
70	15	1050	1100	300	800	- 50	15	26	- 15	- 41
80	10	800	1500	300	1200	- 700	10	40	- 25	- 65
90	5	450	2100	300	1800	- 1650	5	60	- 35	- 95
100	0	0	2900	300	2600	- 2900	0	80	- 45	- 125

Quantity Q	Average Fixed Cost AFC	Average Variable Cost AVC	Average Total Cost ATC	Average Revenue AR	Average Profit Aπ
0	-	-	-	-	-
10	$ 30	$ 10	$ 40	$45	$ 5
20	15	8	23	40	17
30	10	6.7	16.7	35	18.3
40	7.5	6.5	14	30	16
50	6	7	13	25	12
60	5	9	14	20	6
70	4.3	11.4	15.7	15	- 0.7
80	3.8	15	18.8	10	- 8.8
90	3.3	20	23.3	5	- 18.3
100	3	26	29	0	- 29

What output should this monopolist produce in order to maximize total profits? **40**   What price will be its profit maximizing price? **$30**
How much total profit/loss will it earn? **$640**

Why would a monopolist, like the one above, want to produce at a level where average total costs are not a minimum (i.e., production takes place at a place other than the minimum point on the ATC). **Although efficient production is very important, the monopolist must be careful not to produce too much, since the price must be lowered as production is increased. The most profitable level of production occurs when MC = MR, not when ATC is minimized.**

168

Figure 7-1

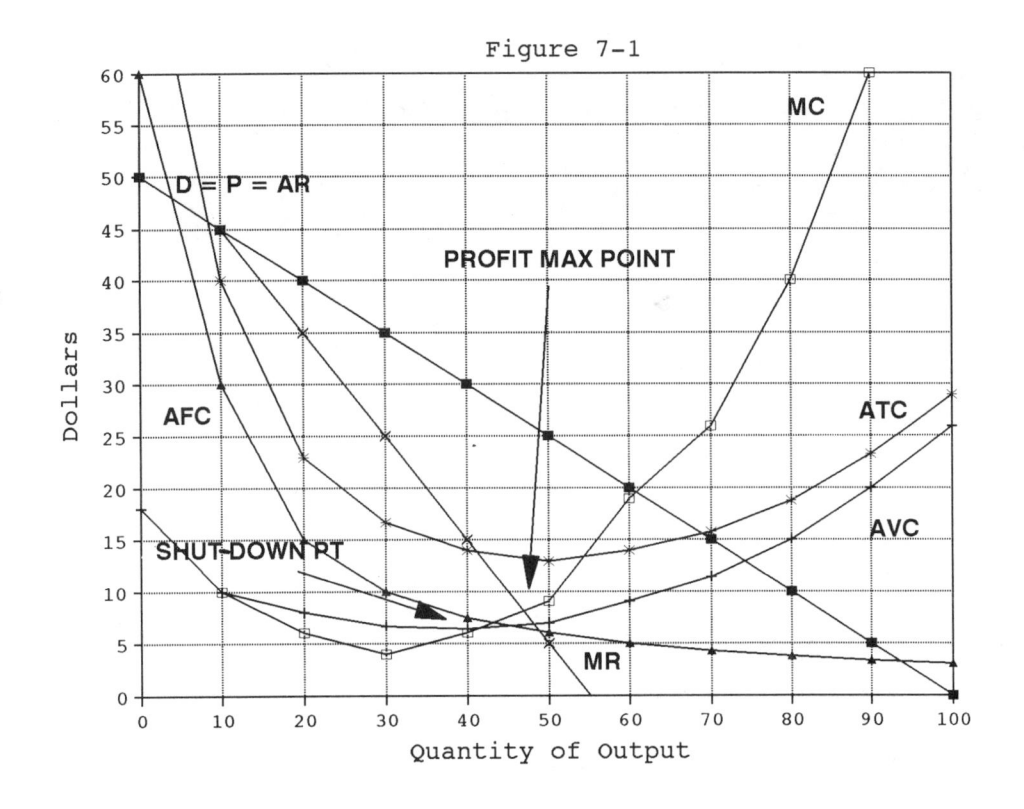

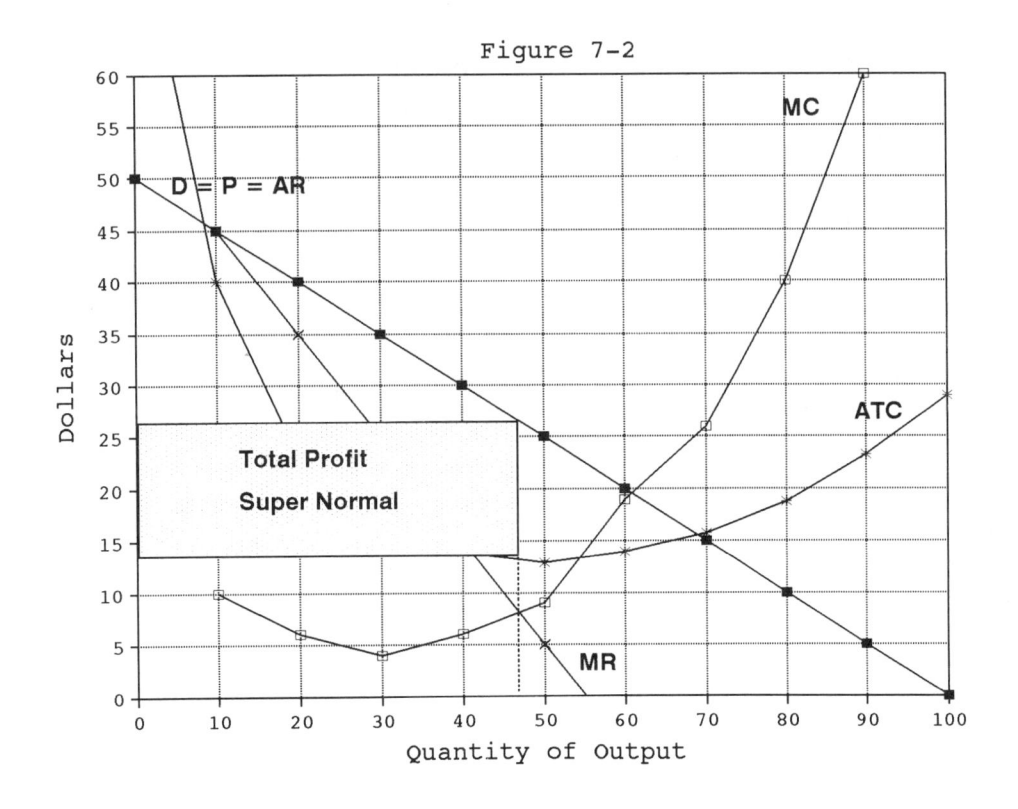

Figure 7-2

Determining the Profit Maximizing Level of Output and Price, Total Profits, and the Deadweight Efficiency Loss

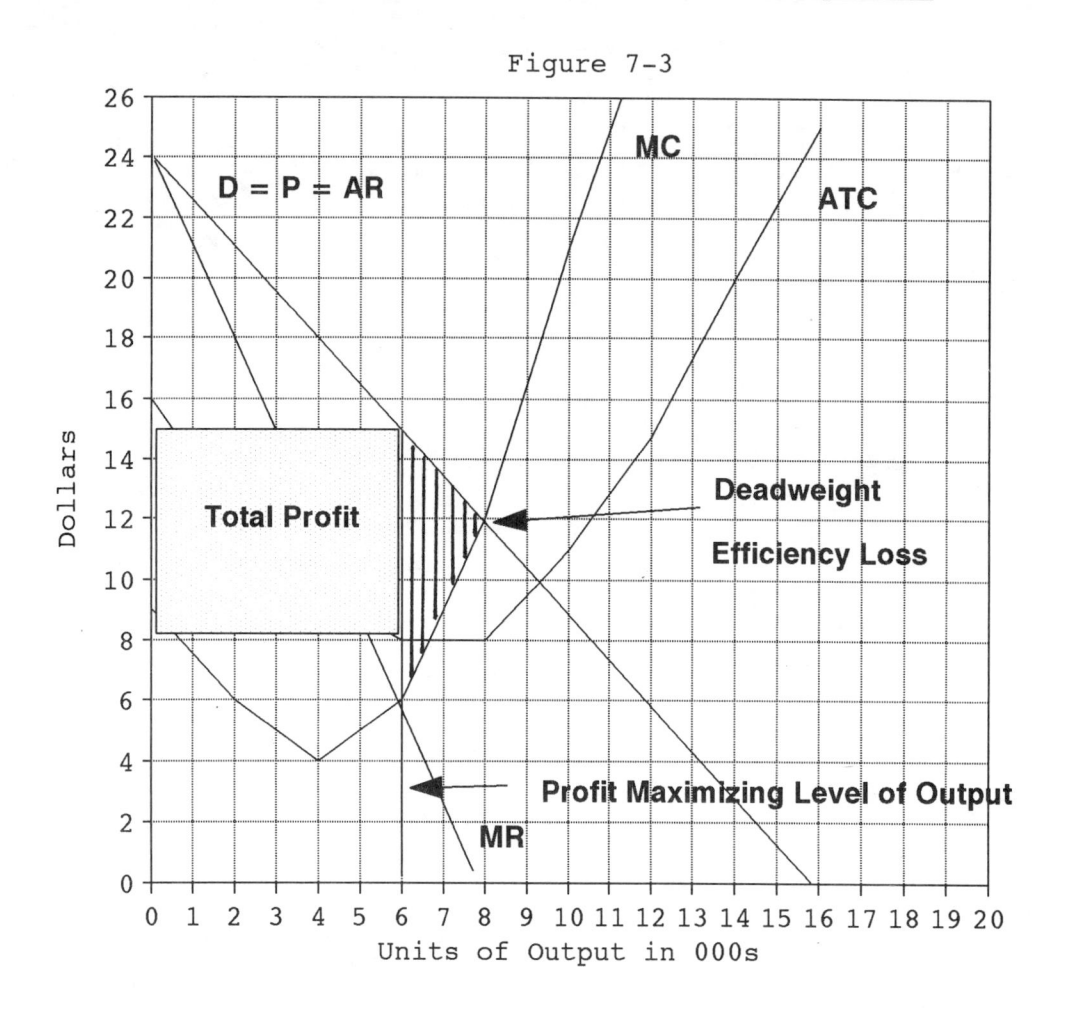

Figure 7-3

Illustrate on the graph above, the profit maximizing level of output, label it Q_{pm}. Label the price that the monopoly will charge P. Explain how that price is determined. **The monopolistic firm produces up to the point where MC = MR. Once the profit maximizing quantity is determined, the profit maximizing price is found by using the demand curve to determine the price that is associated with the profit maximizing quantity. In this case, the profit maximizing price = $15/unit and the profit maximizing quantity = 6,000 units.**

Using the information contained in the graph, estimate as closely as you can the following:
TR = $15/unit X 6,000 units = $90,000
TC = $8/unit ATC X 6,000 units = $48,000
Tπ = $7 average profit/unit X 6,000 units = $42,000
Average Profit/unit (AR - ATC) = $15 AR/unit - $8 ATC/unit = $7 profit/unit
Estimated Deadweight Efficiency Loss = approximately $10,000

Do Monopolists Always Earn Super-Normal Profits?

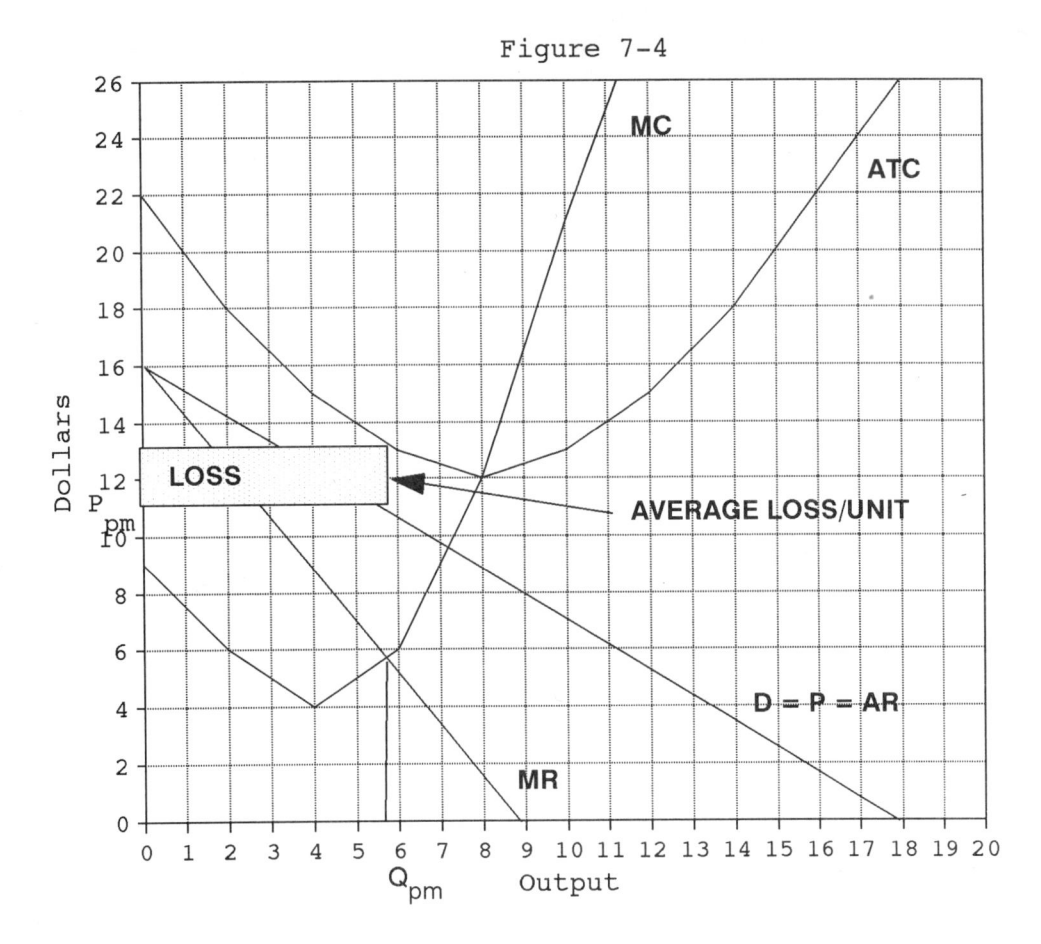

Figure 7-4

[Graph showing Dollars vs Output with MC, ATC, D=P=AR, and MR curves. A shaded "LOSS" rectangle is shown with an arrow labeled "AVERAGE LOSS/UNIT". The monopolist's price P_{pm} is around 10-11 and quantity Q_{pm} is around 6.]

False. Overall profitability depends upon the relationship that exists between average total costs and price or the position of the demand curve relative to the ATC curve. If the demand curve for the product lies everywhere below the ATC curve, then no profit will be generated. The diagram above illustrates that situation.

True/False Statements

1.) **True.** As long as the extra revenue associated with selling an additional unit of production (the monopolist's marginal revenue (MR)) is larger than the extra cost of producing an additional unit (the monopolist's marginal cost), then total profits will be increased by continuing to produce. If MC exceeds MR, then the monopolist will cut back production and profits will rise.

2.) **False.** Most people think that monopolists can set whatever price they wish, however they are constrained by the market and consumers' willingness to pay for the product just like all other firms. The theory of the firm assumes that the monopolist will maximize its profits by producing at the point where MC = MR. Once the level of production is decided upon, the demand curve basically determines the price that the monopolist will charge.

3.) **False.** Again, the answer to this depends upon consumer demand. If the monopolist's average total cost curve lies above the demand curve, then the monopolist will simply not be able to charge a price which covers its average cost of production and a loss will result.

4.) **True.** Price discrimination allows the firm to take advantage of differences in the market. The price discriminating firm will try to charge a higher price for those whose demand is inelastic and charge a lower price to those who are more sensitive to price. If there are no differences in elasticities among market components, then it obviously doesn't make any sense to charge different prices.

5.) **True.** Since the MR curve for a monopolist always lies to the left of its average revenue curve (the firm's demand curve), the profit maximizing level of production will always be less than what would occur under perfect competition. For a given market demand curve, a smaller quantity supplied will result in a higher market price.

6.) **False.** The MR curve has a slope that is twice that of its associated AR curve but that does not mean that AR is twice is large as MR. Keep in mind that when MR crosses the horizontal axis (MR = 0), AR is positive. That characteristic alone makes the statement false.

7.) **True.** In many instances these sectors have large fixed costs tied up with their distribution systems (i.e., natural gas, electricity, cable television). Average fixed costs can be reduced significantly by increasing the number of customers served by the distribution system. Consider what would happen to average total cost if there were eight different natural gas companies serving a community. While there would be more competitive pressures, ATCs would be quite high.

8.) **False.** An elastic demand curve for a product would imply that there are effective substitutes for the product, and that would severely curtail any monopolistic tendencies.

9.) **True, but ....** Competitive pressures to reduce costs would certainly be less in a monopoly setting. However, monopolists are able to achieve significant economies of scale which allow them to reduce the average total cost of production as the scale of output increases. Perfectly competitive firms cannot achieve significant economies of scale.

Multiple-Choice

1.) c   2.) d   3.) a   4.) c   5.) b   6.) b

7.) c   8.) b   9.) c   10.) d   11.) c   12.) d

13.) a   14.) c   15.) d

Discussion Questions

1.) Perfect competition results in lower prices and larger quantities than a comparable industry with a monopoly. Super-normal profits are temporarily possible under perfect competition but will be competed away as new firms enter the industry and existing firms expand production. Monopolistic barriers allow super-normal profits to exist for an extended period of time. Probably more product innovation would take place under perfect competition than under monopoly.

2.) Yes, in those economic sectors that are subject to significant economies of scale. In that situation, society would not want a perfectly competitive market structure in which a large number of firms supplied the product, producing with very high cost, relatively small-sized plants. Typically, these sectors are characterized by large fixed costs (such as distribution systems -- natural gas pipelines), and per unit costs fall rapidly as those costs are spread out over a large number of customers.

3.) Senior and student discounts are widespread examples.

4.) Refer to the answer to discussion question 1.

5.) Vigorous anti-trust action against vertical and horizontal mergers that decrease competition may be effective.

Summary

Just as it is useful to understand the perfect competition model, it is also necessary to have an awareness of the opposite end of the competitive spectrum. Since free market, uncontrolled monopolies are hard to find, most of our exposure to monopolies involves regulated monopolies or government-owned monopolies like the post office or the local/regional utility company. Government efforts to regulate monopolies are discussed in a later chapter.

Although the advantages of perfect competition have been stressed, it is important to keep in mind that, under certain circumstances, society may be better off under a monopoly (or should we say under a regulated monopoly?) than it would be under perfect competition. In spite of the considerable market power that monopolies possess, the level of consumer demand still plays an important role -- even monopolies can't sustain themselves if there is insufficient demand. However, boycotting a monopolist's product may be difficult if it is a necessity with few effective substitutes. From a public policy standpoint, fear of potential entrants may be effective in convincing monopolists to not charge as much as they possibly can.

Price discrimination, on the other hand, appears to be a fairly widespread phenomenon -- airline, utilities, theatres, coupons for grocery and related items, and lodging establishments. By charging different prices to different segments of the market, firms are attempting to extract as much consumers' surplus from their customers as possible. Many utility companies have a different price for the first 500 or 1000 kilowatts than for the second. Senior citizen discounts are everywhere. In each case, firms are trying to charge a higher price to those who have higher incomes or an inelastic demand, while charging a lower price to the more responsive segment of the market (price elastic).

Chapter 8
Imperfect Markets II:
Monopolistic Competition and Oligopoly

Overview of the Chapter

The two previous chapters have analyzed the two extremes of market structure -- perfect competition and monopoly. Chapter 8 focuses on the two intermediate market structures -- monopolistic competition and oligopoly. Both of these market structures are characterized by imperfectly competitive conditions, downward sloping demand curves for the firms' products, product differentiation, and in the case of oligopoly, taking into account competitors' actions. However, their cost curves have the same basic shapes, and the profit maximization rule still holds.

The monopolistic competitive model is characterized by product differentiation among competing firms but maintains the assumption of relatively easy entry and exit (similar to perfect competition) into and out of the industry. This competitive model is most applicable to industries that have large numbers of firms, each of which differentiates its product slightly from its competitors. Each firm has a monopoly on its product but there are many good substitutes for it.

In the long run, entry and exit of firms will take place if supernormal profits are generated or losses sustained. Each firm's demand curve and market share will shift accordingly until a tangency equilibrium position is attained by all the firms. At the point of tangency, the firm's demand curve will be tangent to its average total cost curve (ATC), and therefore the firm will earn only a normal profit. Since the monopolistically competitive firm has a downward sloping demand curve, the long-run tangency position will involve a higher price and a lower quantity than would be the case for a perfectly competitive firm, and the firm will no longer produce at its minimum, most efficient point on the average total cost curve.

Oligopolistic industries are typically difficult to model, because products may or may not be differentiated, because barriers to entry may be quite high or relatively easy, because the number of firms may vary considerably, and because oligolistic industries may or may not be subject to the leadership of a dominant firm, market outcomes may differ significantly within the oligopolistic category.

Several models have been proposed to explain the tendency in some oligopolistic markets towards price stability. One explanation has been called the "kinked demand model" and hypothesizes that prices are stable because of a discontinuity (kink) in the firm's demand curve. Because of the kink, there are two marginal revenue (MR) curves, and a gap between the two MR curves exists at the current price and output. Another explanation is based upon a flat MC and AC curve in the relevant output range, and, in this case, the demand curve could shift to the right and the firm would not change its price since the MC curve is flat at that point.

Economies of scale provide significant economic incentives for firms to become larger, and even the largest markets may support only a few firms. Unfortunately, from the standpoint of economic efficiency and industry competitiveness, many firms are larger than the minimum efficient scale of production. Fewer competitors also leads to greater likelihood of collusion and/or some form of price leadership within the industry. Oligopolistic firms have the ability to produce at low cost because of their production efficiencies but they also have the market power to set prices above their average cost and that causes a dilemma for society. Barriers to entry, limit pricing, predatory pricing, and the deliberate maintaining of excess capacity have all enhanced and perpetuated super-normal profits on the part of oligopolistic firms.

This chapter also analyzes two of the most important kinds of non-price competition -- quality change and advertising. The addition of these two competitive dimensions to the competitive pricing decision makes management's task of profit maximization more difficult and complex. Not only must a firm determine the most profitable price and quantity combination, but it must also decide what represents the optimum amount of quality control, research and development, product innovation, and advertising.

Economic theory provides a useful conceptual framework for analyzing these important microeconomic issues: in each case, the firm should proceed with the specific activity up until the point where the marginal benefits associated with the activity are just equal to its perceived marginal costs (the standard profit maximization rule).

Unfortunately, decisions about optimums in these areas may not be quite as simple as the profit maximization rule suggests because of the many difficulties in measuring the effects on consumers and profitability of those activities. Both quality change and advertising have short-run and long-run effects that need to be taken into account. Since these decisions are being made in an imperfectly competitive environment, the actions/reactions of the firm's competitors represent an important factor to be considered. Even if a firm feels that it has optimized everywhere it can, its decisions may no longer be optimum if a competitor initiates a different strategy.

Learning Objectives

After completing this chapter, you should be sure that you are able to:

- distinguish between perfect competitive, monopolistically competitive, oligopolistic, and monopolistic market structures.

- understand why a monopolistically competitive industry achieves a tangency solution where price equals average total cost in the long run.

- understand why the long-run equilibrium price would be higher and equilibrium output smaller than it would be for a perfectly competitive industry.

- understand concentration ratios and how they can be used to identify oligopolistic industries.

- understand what makes markets "contestable" and how the contestability affects antitrust decisions.

- understand how the kinked demand curve and saucer-shaped cost curves can be used to explain the price stability that often exists in oligopolistic markets.

- define the term cartel and explain the economic rationale for their formation.

- can explain why collusion is more likely to occur in oligopolistic industries than in other industries with different market structures.

- understand why oligopolistic firms are often fearful of direct price competition and why some form of price leadership often develops.

- recognize how barriers to entry, limit pricing, predatory pricing, and excess capacity work to maintain super-normal profits in oligopolistic industries.

- discuss the pros and cons of the oligopolistic market structure for society as a whole.

- understand why firms are motivated to bring out new and better products and how quality change functions as a competitive strategy.

- understand the trade-off that may exist between product differentiation and economies of scale.

- contrast and discuss the advantages and disadvantages of quality change.

- explain how firms might decide on the optimal amount of quality change and advertising.

- explain the relationship that exists between advertising expenditures, economies of scale, and a firm's cost curves.

- understand the impact on the theory of the firm of different maximization principles (other than profit maximization). You should be sure that you understand the concepts of mark-up pricing, sales maximization, and satisficing behavior and how they differ from the traditional profit maximization model.

Applications

Game Theory

Game theory represents an interesting way to analyze that strategies that oligopolists can utilize against each other. One strategy that a firm might implement would be to select that strategic option which minimizes the maximum gain that an opposing firm could achieve. Alternatively, a firm could choose options that would minimize the damage that another firm could inflict upon it.

Take, for example, the following hypothetical strategy and payoff matrix for firms A and B. In this case, the firms' options are limited to either raising or lowering their price from the current price. The payoff matrix illustrates the effect of a specific strategy on the profits and market share of each firm.

		Firm A's Strategies	
		lower price	raise price
Firm B's Strategies	lower price	A's profits ↓ A's market share unchg. B's profits ↓ B's market share unchg.	A's profits ↓ A's market share ↓ B's profits ↑ B's market share ↑
	raise price	A's profits ↑ A's market share ↑ B's profits ↓ B's market share ↑	A's profits ↑ A's market share unchg. B's profits ↑ B's market share unchg.

The payoff matrix above is consistent with the behavioral assumptions that are associated with the so-called "kinked demand curve" oligopoly model discussed in your text. If a firm raises its price, while other competing firms do not follow, that firm rapidly loses profits and market-share. If, on the other hand, a firm decrease its price, the other firms will be forced to follow or they will lose profits and marketshare.

In terms of payoffs, the upper left cell represents the worst possible case, direct price competition leading to lower profits all around. The lower right cell is the best possible outcome since profits for both firms increase. However, given a structural change in the market such as a change in costs, the firms may have to respond in a simultaneous fashion, not knowing how the other firm is going to respond until after they have also responded to the change. Which option will the opposing firm select? The strategic game becomes much more interesting. Will the opposing firm behave in a cooperative fashion, selecting the strategic option that is best for everyone or will it attempt to gain a competitive advantage? With more competitive dimensions and more than two firms, the strategic game becomes more interesting and complex.

Self Evaluation

List of Terms

Barriers to Entry
Cartel
Collusion
Competitive Advertising
Concentration Ratios
Contestable Markets
Dominant Firm
Duopoly
Game Theory
Informative Advertising
Interdependence
Kinked Demand Curve

Limit Price
Mark-Up Pricing
Monopolistic Competition
Non-price Competition
Oligopoly
Predatory Pricing
Price Leadership
Product Differentiation
Sales Maximization
Satisficing Behavior
Takeovers
Tangency Solution

For the statements below, fill in the term from the list above which provides the best fit.

1.) Whenever the number of competitors is small enough that they take into account each others' actions, the possibility of _____ must be considered.

2.) The _____ is one explanation for the relative stability in prices that was observed in certain oligopolistic industries.

3.) Some oligopolistic industries have a single firm which provides _____ for the entire industry.

4.) _____ is a oligopolistic model which attempts to apply probabilities and rational strategies to the interaction that exists among oligopolistic firms.

5.) _____ are assumed to produce better economic performance, no matter what the number of firms in the industry, because of the fear of entry of new firms.

6.) In contrast to perfectly competitive firms which react only to overall market conditions, oligopolistic firms are typically characterized as having considerable _____ among firms.

7.) _____ describes an industry with relatively few competitors, barriers to entry, and interdependent pricing and output strategies.

8.) A group of firms that coordinates their pricing and output decisions in order to maximize their joint profits is known as a _____.

9.) One way to measure potential industry competitiveness is to calculate industry specific _____.

10.) Similar to the long-run equilibrium position of perfectly competitive industries, long-run equilibrium under monopolistic competition is also characterized by a _____.

11.) In an effort to keep potential competitors from entering a market, oligopolistic firms may choose to set a _____ which is too low for a new firm to earn any profits.

12.) Historically, several oligopolistic industries have allowed a _____ to determine policies for all firms.

13.) _____ describes an industry with substitutable but differentiated products, many sellers, and relatively easy entry.

14.) Whenever _____ exists, a firm's demand curve will be downward sloping.

15.) A market with only two firms competing against each other is called a _____.

16.) Oligopolistic firms have often been accused of _____ policies as a strategy to eliminate their competition.

17.) Oligopolies and monopolies are able to maintain super-normal profits because of significant _____.

18.) Because of their small numbers, oligopolistic firms may engage in _____ so as to not decrease all firms' profits.

19.) Many firms rely on _____ policies based on their "feel" of the market to simplify their pricing.

20.) Both friendly and unfriendly _____ have increased in number in the last ten years because of the perception that many firms and their component parts were not being as efficiently managed as they could be.

21.) In many instances, _____ is a more reasonable assumption than profit maximization, especially if management salaries are tied to the level of sales.

22.) _____ doesn't provide any meaningful product information but attempts to bring new customers into the market or attract consumers from competing firms.

23.) For larger firms, attempts to maximize profits may be too time consuming or complicated to do on a regular basis and they may instead resort to what has been called _____.

24.) _____ plays an important role in educating consumers about product features and characteristics.

Problems

The Kinked Demand Curve

An oligopolistic firm is currently selling its product for $16 with monthly sales of 2,000 units. If the firm raises its price unilaterally and its competitors do not follow, the firm will sell 500 fewer units per month for each $1 price increase. If the firm lowers its price, it can expect that all of its competitors will follow and the firm's sales will sell an additional 250 units per month for each $1 it decreases its price.

On the following graph, indicate the current price and monthly sales. From that point, draw in the firm's demand curve if it raises its price above the current price of $16. Label that curve AR1. You will also need to draw in the marginal revenue curve that is associated with AR1, labeling it MR1. Keep in mind that a marginal revenue curve has twice the slope (i.e., it falls twice as fast) of the demand curve it is associated with. For each of these curves, draw only that segment from the origin to the current sales quantity of 2,000 units.

Do the same for the the firm's demand curve if it lowers its price below the current price of $16. Label that curve AR2 and draw in its marginal revenue curve as well (labeling it MR2). For each of these curves, draw only that segment from the current sales quantity of 2,000 units to 6,000 units.

Figure 8-1

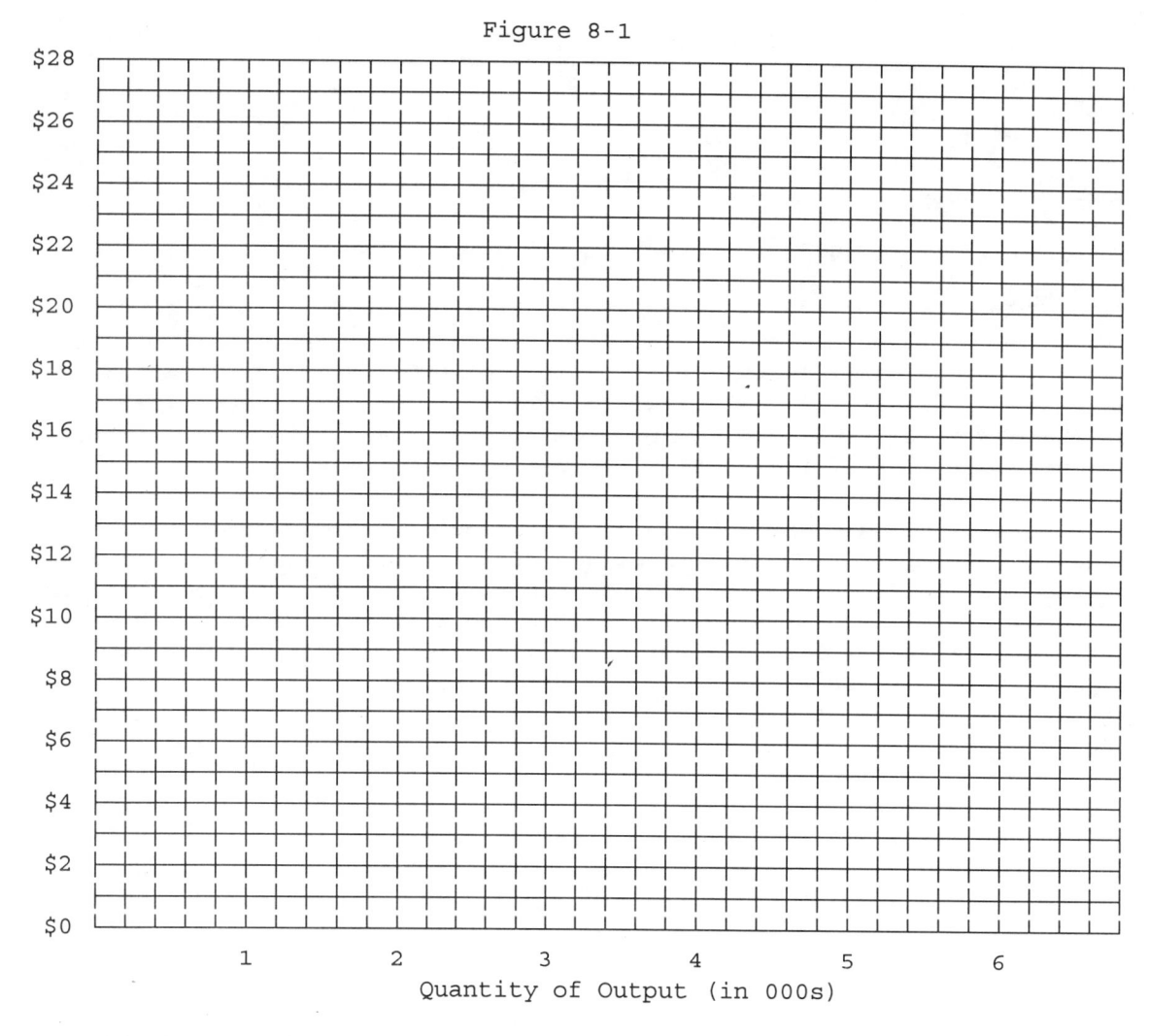

[Blank graph: y-axis labeled from $0 to $28 in $2 increments; x-axis labeled "Quantity of Output (in 000s)" from 1 to 6]

Briefly explain why the "kink" in the firm's demand curve occurs.

_____
_____
_____

Briefly explain why the marginal revenue curves are discontinuous at the currrent price and output levels.

_____
_____

Based on your diagram above, how much could the marginal costs (MC) of production change without the firm changing its price and output levels?

_____

182

How can the "kinked demand" curve model explain the apparent price stability that exists is some oligopolistic industries?

_____

_____

True/False Statements

Indicate whether you think the statements below are true or false. These questions are designed to make you think about the concepts presented in the text. There may not be any easy clear-cut answers. Some thoughts about the answers are presented at the end of the chapter.

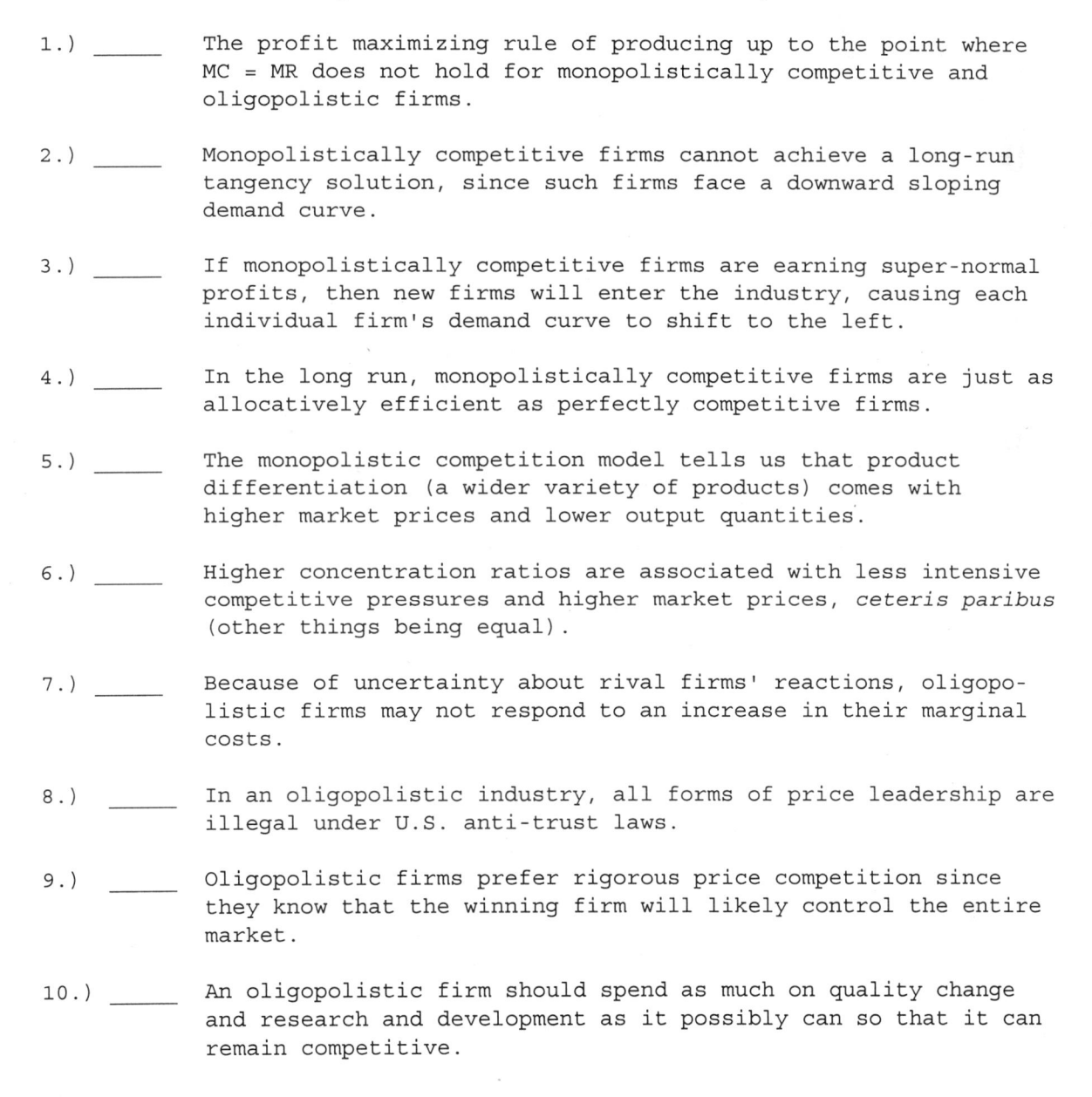

1.) _____ The profit maximizing rule of producing up to the point where MC = MR does not hold for monopolistically competitive and oligopolistic firms.

2.) _____ Monopolistically competitive firms cannot achieve a long-run tangency solution, since such firms face a downward sloping demand curve.

3.) _____ If monopolistically competitive firms are earning super-normal profits, then new firms will enter the industry, causing each individual firm's demand curve to shift to the left.

4.) _____ In the long run, monopolistically competitive firms are just as allocatively efficient as perfectly competitive firms.

5.) _____ The monopolistic competition model tells us that product differentiation (a wider variety of products) comes with higher market prices and lower output quantities.

6.) _____ Higher concentration ratios are associated with less intensive competitive pressures and higher market prices, *ceteris paribus* (other things being equal).

7.) _____ Because of uncertainty about rival firms' reactions, oligopolistic firms may not respond to an increase in their marginal costs.

8.) _____ In an oligopolistic industry, all forms of price leadership are illegal under U.S. anti-trust laws.

9.) _____ Oligopolistic firms prefer rigorous price competition since they know that the winning firm will likely control the entire market.

10.) _____ An oligopolistic firm should spend as much on quality change and research and development as it possibly can so that it can remain competitive.

11.) _____ Oligopolistic firms are more likely to go out of business if they don't strictly maximize profits.

12.) _____ Advertising expenditures increases firms' costs, thus causing the equilibrium market price to increase.

Multiple-Choice Questions

Select the "best" answer from the alternatives provided:

1.) According to the "kinked demand" theory,
   a. competing firms will follow either price increases or decreases.
   b. competing firms will not follow either price increases or decreases.
   c. competing firms will follow a price increase but not a price decrease.
   d. competing firms will not follow a price increase but will follow a price decrease.

2.) The optimum amount an imperfectly competitive firm should spend on quality change and research and development expenditures
   a. is basically determined by its financial condition and the amount of funds available for these activities.
   b. is determined by how much competitors are spending on these activities.
   c. occurs at the point where the estimated marginal benefits from those activities just equals the extra cost of the activities.
   d. can't be discussed in an economic framework, since the effects of the activities are so ambiguous and can't be quantified.

3.) When a monopolistically competitive firm is in short-run equilibrium,
   a. it is producing at the point where MC = MR.
   b. it is producing at the point where its average cost curve is at its minimum point.
   c. it is producing at the point where TR = TC (just breaking even).
   d. any of the above just so long as it is not incurring a loss.

4.) When monopolistically competitive firms are earning super-normal profits in the short-run,
   a. entry of new firms will occur, driving up costs for all firms and gradually eliminating the super-normal profits.
   b. existing firms will compete more intensively with each other, driving prices and profits back down.
   c. entry of new firms will occur, shifting each firm's demand curve to the left until it is just tangent with the firm's average cost curve.
   d. the super-normal profits may continue indefinitely because of barriers to entry.
   e. monopolistically competitive firms never earn super-normal profits, so it is not a problem.

5.) Comparing final market outcomes between perfect competition and monopolistic competition:
   a. market price and output are essentially the same for both market structures.
   b. market price is higher and output lower under monopolistic competition.
   c. market price is higher and output lower under perfect competition.
   d. market price is higher, but output is also higher under monopolistic competition.
   e. there are so many structural differences between the two market structures, comparisons like this can't be made.

6.) One theory which attempts to explain oligopolistic behavior is the "kinked demand" curve theory. According to that theory,
   a. firms will not follow price increases but will follow price decreases.
   b. oligopolistic competitors may not respond to increases in their variable costs, since their MC curves intersect their MR curves where there is a gap in the MR.
   c. prices have a tendency to remain stable in spite of small up and down fluctuations in variable costs.
   d. all of the above.

7.) Price leadership in an oligopolistic industry
   a. must be accomplished through the dominant firm in the industry.
   b. is illegal under U.S. antitrust laws if it can be shown it was accomplished through explicit agreements and/or actions.
   c. is inconsistent with the goal of profit maximization.
   d. is successful only if all firms in the industry are satisfied with the price leader's decisions.

8.) The difference between perfect competition and monopolistic competition is that while
   a. perfect competition has relatively costless entry and exit, monopolistic competition does not.
   b. perfectly competitive firms have homogeneous products, while monopolistically competitive firms have differentiated products.
   c. perfect competition has many buyers and sellers, while monopolistic competition has smaller numbers of buyers and sellers.
   d. perfectly competitive firms cannot earn super-normal profits, while monopolistically competitive firms can.
   e. is largely academic -- most people would not be able to tell the difference between the two market structures.

9.) Predatory pricing
   a. is no different than regular pricing competition.
   b. is where prices are set at levels below average cost.
   c. refers to a situation in which at least two competitors conspire together to set prices without the knowledge or permission of other firms in the industry.
   d. is intended to force competing firms out of business or keep them from entering new markets or developing new products.
   e. both (b) and (d)

10.) When imperfectly competitive firms (firms with downward sloping demand curves) advertise
   a. it raises their average cost curves and ultimately will result in higher market prices because of increased costs.
   b. it increases the amount of competition between firms, raises consumer awareness about different alternatives, and ultimately lowers prices.
   c. it increases the total market for the product, increasing demand and profits for all firms.
   d. it doesn't appear to affect the market outcome at all.

11.) When comparing perfectly competitive market outcomes with oligopolistic market outcomes,
   a. oligopolistic market structures would tend to be preferred in those sectors where significant economies of scale exist.
   b. perfectly competitive market structures would exhibit more direct price competition than would oligopolistic markets.
   c. perfectly competitive market structures would have greater product differentiation because of the larger number of firms.
   d. both types of market structure would eventually achieve long-run equilibrium positions with no super-normal profits.
   e. both (a) and (b)

12.) With respect to advertising expenditures, which of the following statements is most valid?
   a. Advertising expenses increase a firm's costs and result in higher prices.
   b. Successful advertising campaigns often result in a dramatic increase in total demand for a product.
   c. Most firms carefully equate the marginal cost of advertising with its expected marginal benefits, just as economic theory suggests.
   d. Because of the uncertainties associated with advertising, many firms use rules of thumb (advertising expenditures being set at a certain percentage of sales or profits) to determine their advertising expenditures, contrary to what economic theory suggests.

13.) Regarding price leadership within an oligopolistic industry,
   a. studies suggest that almost always, price leadership is associated with the largest, most profitable firm in the industry.
   b. in order to be successful, price leadership must necessarily maximize total profits for each of the firms in an industry.
   c. the courts have generally allowed price leadership to exist as long as consumers are not harmed, even if there is a formal, written agreement among the industry's firms.
   d. in an industry with several, equally powerful firms, a smaller firm whose judgement is trusted by others in the industry may become the price leader.

Discussion Questions

1.) How can society decide whether or not if it is better to have more competitive markets (with larger number of firms) or fewer and larger firms which are more efficient because of economies of scale?

2.) Monopolistically competitive firms will necessarily produce at a point which is to the left of the minimum point on their average total cost curve in long-run equilibrium in contrast to the perfectly competitive long-run equilibrium position which lies at the bottom of its average total cost curve. Doesn't that mean that the monopolistically competitive market structure is not as optimal (less allocatively efficient) as perfect competition?

3.) Within the perfectly competitive model, firms have no reason to advertise since each firm is producing the same homogenous product. With imperfectly competitive market structures, however, a firm's own advertising as well as its competitors may be prove to be an important factor in determining the ultimate viability of the firm. From a societal point of view, how should we evaluate the role of advertising with respect to allocative efficiency and market performance?

4.) Why do you think oligopolistic firms tend to prefer non-price competition rather than direct head-to-head price competition?

5.) If the market price of the firms in an oligopolistic industry are all about the same, is this evidence of direct price collusion?

6.) Should government anti-trust authorities prosecute firms that set prices below their average cost of production? Is predatory price competition any different than regular, run-of-the-mill price competition?

Answers and Solutions to Problems and Exercises

Completing Statements from the List of Terms

1.) Collusion
2.) Kinked Demand Curve
3.) Price Leadership
4.) Game Theory
5.) Contestable Markets
6.) Interdependence
7.) Oligopoly
8.) Cartel
9.) Concentration Ratios
10.) Tangency Solution
11.) Limit Price
12.) Dominant Firm
13.) Monopolistic Competition
14.) Product Differentiation
15.) Duopoly
16.) Predatory Pricing
17.) Barriers to Entry
18.) Non-price Competition
19.) Mark-Up Pricing
20.) Takeovers
21.) Sales Maximization
22.) Competitive Advertising
23.) Satisficing Behavior
24.) Informative Advertising

Problems

The Kinked Demand Curve

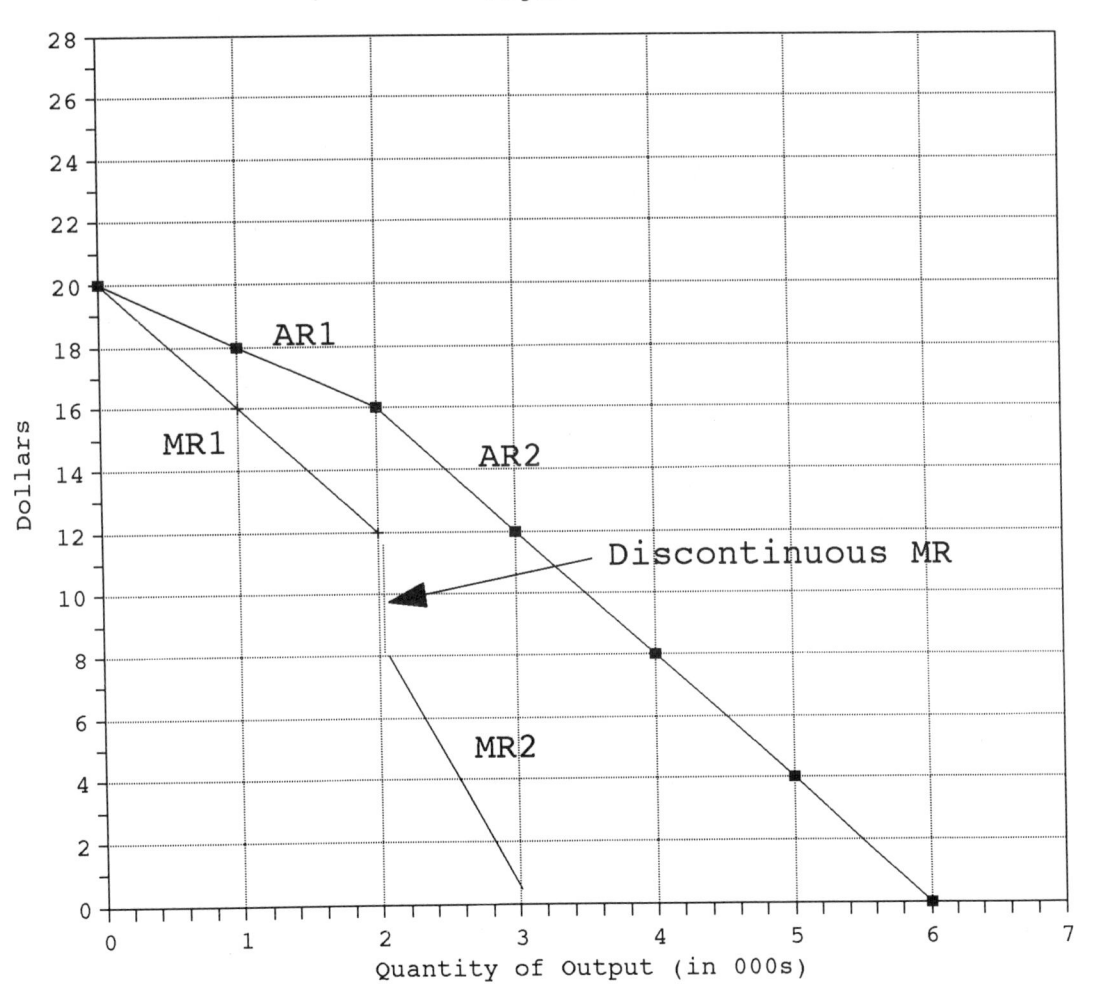

Figure 8-1

Briefly explain why the "kink" in the firm's demand curve occurs. **The firm has a different elasticity of demand (and essentially) a different demand curve both above and below its current price -- very elastic above current price and less elastic below current price.**

Briefly explain why the marginal revenue curves are discontinuous at the currrent price and output levels. **The two different demand curves have two different marginal revenue curves, and at the current price there is a discontinuity between the two marginal revenue curves. There is no way to know which marginal revenue curve is the appropriate one at the current price level.**

Based on your diagram above, how much could the marginal costs (MC) of production change without the firm changing its price and output levels? **Between $8 and approximately $12.50**

How can the "kinked demand" curve model explain the apparent price stability that exists is some oligopolistic industries? **If we assume that profit maximizing firms equate their marginal revenue and marginal cost curves, then at the point of discontinuity, marginal costs could change and the firm would not respond, since marginal revenue is ambiguous at the point. Thus, costs could change, and there would be no reaction.**

True/False Statements

1.) **False.** The profit maximizing rule is based on logic and holds for all firms, regardless of market structure. If MR is greater than MC, then the firm should continue to produce; if MC exceeds MR, then it should cut back on production.

2.) **False.** In the long run, after all adjustments have been made, a tangency solution is arrived at in monopolistic competition. However, since the firm's demand curve is downward sloping, the tangency occurs at a point to the left of the firm's minimum average cost curve. As with perfect competition, when the demand curve is just tangent to the average cost curve, then P = AC and no super-normal profits are earned.

3. **True.** This is the adjustment process by which excess profits are competed away, returning each firm to the point where P = AC.

4.) **False.** When monopolistically competitive firms are in long-run equilibrium, P = AC, but AC is not at its minimum point and at the point of long-run equilibrium, P > MC, which means that the market price is greater than the cost of producing an additional unit of the product and that, by definition, is not allocatively efficient.

5.) **True.** Because each firm's demand curve is downward sloping, the long-run equilibrium solution occurs to the left of the firm's minimum AC at a higher average cost per unit, and the quantity of production would be less for that same reason.

6.) **Generally True.** We would expect less competitive pressures and consequently higher market prices with fewer firms in industries that are more concentrated.

7.) **True.** Individual firms may be afraid that their rivals will not follow them if they pass along the cost increase in the form of a higher price.

8.) **False.** Only tangible and explicit agreements to coordinate prices and policies are deemed illegal. Tacit or implied price leadership may occur in situations where other firms have found out over time that it is in their best interests to follow the policies of a specific firm.

9.) **False.** When there are only a small number of competitors, direct price competition is often felt to be mutually destructive and self-defeating. If one firm lowers its price, other firms necessarily have to follow or risk losing market share. The result is that all firms end up charging a lower price than before with reduced profitability.

10.) **False.** Like anything else, the costs and benefits of the activity have to be carefully weighed and evaluated before deciding upon an optimal amount of spending. Similar to our profit maximization rule, the optimal amount spent by the firm should be determined by comparing the extra benefits of those activities with their extra cost. Spending should proceed up to the point where the extra benefits of quality change and R & D just equal their extra costs.

11.) **False.** Certainly in a purely competitive or monopolistically competitive industry, the statement would be considered to be true. In an oligopolistic setting, we are less certain of the answer. If none of the firms in an industry are strict profit maximizers, then failure to maximize profits may not pose a serious risk to the firm. Furthermore, the barriers to entry that are present in oligopolies may tend to prevent outside firms from entering the industry and taking advantage of the situation.

12.) **False.** Although advertising does indeed boost costs, there are situations in which the additional competitive pressures created by advertising result in lower rather than higher market prices. Your text provides an example of one of these cases.

Multiple-Choice

1.) d   2.) c   3.) a   4.) c   5.) b   6.) d

7.) b   8.) b   9.) e   10.) b   11.) e   12.) d

13.) d

Discussion Questions

1.) This issue poses an extremely difficult problem for our society. When significant economies of scale exist in an industry, it is not in society's interest to have many small, high cost firms comprising the industry. Yet having only a few very large firms in an industry that compete mainly with each other in non-price formats may result in excessively high prices. A number of studies have shown that many large firms have plants that are well beyond the point of minimum efficient scale. That means that they are larger than they really have to be in order to take advantage of the economies of scale. If society could somehow have firms with plants near the minimum efficient scale, then there would be room in the industry for more competitors.

2.) Another difficult question! Perfect competition ensures that firms will be at or near the most efficient points on their average cost curves. Monopolistic competition, because of the firms' downward sloping demand curve, will have higher market prices and lower output quantities. However, production differentiation surely produces many benefits for our consumer-oriented society. Would we prefer low cost, efficiently produced clothing that was the same for everyone or would we prefer to pay higher prices for having many different product variations that allow consumers to express their individuality and unique tastes? My guess is that we would much prefer the latter situation.

To add to the difficulty of this question, many critics have argued that much of the product differentiation that takes place in the market place is without substance. Can that be justified?

3.) Through advertising, producers can influence consumer preferences and demand -- negating the principal of consumer sovereignty. Profits can be enhanced if consumers can be persuaded to buy the products that the producers think they should buy and that's not always in the best interests of consumers. Auto makers in the 1970s seemed to have been able to convince consumers that cars that would resist low speed collisions without major damage would not be stylish and attractive.

In those situations where advertising conveys information about products and prices, there are tangible benefits that accrue to society. In other situations, such as in the beer industry, where advertising is largely uninformative and in response to other firms' advertising, it is difficult to see very many benefits.

4.) When there are a relatively small number of firms in an industry, firms can easily see that direct price competition is mutually destructive, resulting in lower prices and profitability. Local gasoline wars provide a graphic example of the impact of what happens when firms start to lower their prices. Because of the adverse effects associated with price competition, firms typically compete on the basis of non-price characteristics such as service and quality.

5.) Under perfect competition, one would expect prices to be the same for all firms. Without other collaborating evidence, the mere fact that prices are the same does not mean that collusion has taken place. There may be significant competitive disadvantages associated with having prices that are higher than those of other firms, so one shouldn't be too surprised that prices are about the same in an imperfectly competitive environment.

6.) Pricing below cost is considered to be unfair, even though it obviously helps consumers. In terms of public anti-trust policy, one concern is that larger firms with many outlets will lower prices below cost in a specific area in order to put local competitors out of business, afterwards increasing prices with newly acquired monopoly power. In such a scenario, the long term impacts of predatory pricing could adversely impact consumers. In other contexts, the impact of predatory pricing is more difficult to identify. Is it predatory pricing if a department store has a sale (at below cost) of an item that it can't sell at regular prices?

Summary

While the monopolistic competition model could be used to characterize a number of industries thirty to forty years ago, many of them have evolved into oligopolistic industries as the industries have become much more concentrated. At the present time, it would apply to a relatively small portion of the economy.

With the interdependencies that exist in oligopolistic industries, it continues to be a difficult task to come up with a general behaviorial model that provides credible predictions all of the time. Modeling has become even more challenging with the development of theories which do not assume profit maximization, but rather a different, possibly conflicting, set of goals for managers. Since oligopolistic industries constitute such a significant portion of American industry, it is vitally important from a public policy standpoint to have an accepted and reliable conceptual framework for analyzing and predicting oligopolistic behavior.

From society's point of view, quality change and advertising have a complicated set of pluses and minuses associated with them. To the extent that both types of expenditures result in higher product prices than would otherwise be the case, consumers are harmed. J. K. Galbraith has argued that advertising adversely affects the allocation of society's resources between the public and private sectors by making private goods seem more desirable. Public goods like police protection, education, and clean air and water, on the other hand, which address a variety of important societal problems, may lack widespread support, since there is no widespread advertising to convince people that public programs should be supported.

Appendix

The assumption of profit maximization is a central part of the theory of the firm, and although firms may not maximize profits to the nth degree with every decision that they make, the assumption yields good predictions in most instances. With the separation of owners from managers in the modern corporation, it is entirely possible that the managers' objectives may differ significantly from that of the owners (to maximize profits). If, for instance, managers are more interested in maximizing total revenues (perhaps because their compensation scheme is based on that variable), then it may be difficult to predict how a firm will react to a change in its economic environment using a model which assumes profit maximization instead of revenue maximization. Another possibility involves satisficing behavior on the part of managers. Instead of maximizing total profits, managers are assumed to generate returns on stockholders' equity which are satisfactory to them (the stockholders) but are not necessarily the maximum possible return.

Given the size and complexity of modern corporations and the difficulty in responding to each and every competitive change made by a firm's competitors, a number of economists have argued that firms are more likely to make daily decisions on the basis of simple, easy to implement rules of thumb. The requirements of profit maximization do not require firms to actually measure and evaluate the marginal costs and revenues of every single decision that they make, just that they attempt to do the best they can according to the information they have available. In a pragmatic sense, it may not be in firms' best interests to be constantly adjusting prices and competitive strategy -- too much uncertainty may be created in consumers' minds, and that may be ultimately self-defeating. It is important to keep in mind that the simplifying use of rules of thumb yields an entirely different set of predictions about how firms respond and interact with one another.

Chapter 9
Controlling Market Power

Overview of the Chapter

As we learned in Chapter 7, certain sectors of the economy naturally lend themselves to the establishment of a single monopoly firm, because of the existence of significant economies of scale. Society faces a very real dilemma in those situations -- costs of production can be significantly lowered if the monopoly's fixed costs can be spread out over as large a number of customers as possible; however, an unregulated monopoly has sufficient market power and barriers to entry such that it can set prices that generate large super-normal profits. Society has generally been unwilling to allow firms to exercise so much market power and has regulated the rates that the public utilities can charge.

There are several ways in which natural monopolies can be regulated by the government in order to achieve more favorable market outcomes. The first method, average cost pricing, forces the monopoly to price at the point where its demand curve intersects its average cost curve (P = AR = AC), allowing it to earn a normal or so-called fair rate of return. The monopoly would end up producing units whose marginal cost (MC) exceeds their marginal revenue (MR).

Marginal cost pricing forces the monopoly to price at the point where its demand curve intersects its marginal cost curve (MC). That involves an even lower price, more output, and depending on the specific location of the demand curve, a possible net loss for the monopoly. The economic rationale for the marginal cost regulatory approach is that it eliminates the allocative inefficiency associated with the unregulated monopoly and the average cost regulatory approach. The market price that consumers pay just equals the marginal cost of producing the last unit, so in that sense there is no exploitation of consumers.

Both methods are not without some serious drawbacks. Essentially, both regulatory methods set the market price on the basis of costs, and as a result there is little if any incentive for public utilities to be as cost efficient as they would be in a competitive situation. On the contrary, they have substantial incentive to increase their cost base as much as possible so that total profit will be as large as possible. Another problematic area has been the influence the public utilities have on their regulatory agencies.

Antitrust legislation was first passed at the federal level in 1890 in response to abuses of power and restraints of trade initiated by the large trusts. The Sherman Antitrust Act attempted to control conspiracies and restraints of trade but had little effect initially, because there was no effective enforcement power and there was considerable legal maneuvering about what the term commerce meant and what constituted illegal behavior. Subsequently, the Clayton Act tightened up several areas of anti-trust policy -- notably tied contracts, certain forms of price discrimination, the purchase of shares in competing companies, and interlocking directorates among competing firms.

Over time, the courts have moved to a position that excessive market power was illegal in and of itself even in the absence of explicit anti-competitive acts. More recently, service contract tie-ins (an important dimension of many capital purchases) have also been found to be in restraint of trade. The stance of the Justice Department towards vertical mergers, which were once monitored fairly closely and opposed when there were found to be significant competitive impacts, has changed to a tacit acceptance of the economic advantages that can be gained from such mergers.

Conglomerate mergers, because of their uncertain competitive impacts, have generallly been allowed to take place unopposed. The issue of conglomerate mergers raises an important question for society about the concentration of corporate power and its impact on society as a whole and the overall legislative and regulatory environment of corporations.

As trade barriers become less restrictive, competition from firms based outside a particular country may have a significant effect on the domestic competitive environment. A country's anti-trust policy may end having less influence on competitive behavior than its foreign trade policy. It is important to note that a number of countries are more lenient towards cooperative behavior among competing firms, behavior that would violate U.S. anti-trust laws. The more restrictive legal environment could conceivably put U.S. firms at a competitive disadvantage, since they face more obstacles in establishing joint research or joint production agreements with competing firms. Anti-trust policy in Europe has historically been more lenient than in the United States.

Japanese anti-trust policy has been closer to the European experience than to the U.S. experience, with cooperative behavior and larger, more efficient firms encouraged. Initially, after the Second World War, the Japanese approach was characterized by active governmental involvement with the Ministry of Trade and Industry (MITI) picking winners/losers and developing policies (mainly in the form of protecting domestic markets) which would assist newly emerging infant industries. Japanese firms tend to have much closer relationships with their suppliers -- the Keiretsu. With that system in place, they have been able to closely monitor the quality of parts, develop just-in-time manufacturing processes, and enhance product development.

Learning Objectives

After completing this chapter, you should be sure that you are able to:

- describe average cost and marginal cost methods of regulating public utilities, their rationales, and their advantages and disadvantages.

- identify the major components of the Sherman Antitrust Act of 1890 and the Clayton Act of 1914.

- distinguish among vertical, horizontal, and conglomerate mergers.

- list some of the fundamental differences between European, Japanese, and American anti-trust policies towards businesses.

- explain the rationale for concentration ratios and the Herfindahl indices of market concentration.

Self Evaluation

List of Terms

Average Cost Pricing
Clayton Act of 1914
Concentration Ratios
Conglomerate Merger
Deregulation
Herfindahl Index

Horizontal Merger
Keiretsu
Marginal Cost Pricing
Rule of Reason
Sherman Antitrust Act of 1890
Vertical Merger

For the statements below, fill in the term from the list above which provides the best fit.

1.) Earliest antitrust legislation tried to outlaw attempts to restrain trade among competitors: _____.

2.) _____ attempts to regulate the price of a monopoly so that it can earn only a normal profit.

3.) An empirically based measure of the competitiveness, the _____ is used by the Justice Department to assist them in deciding whether or not to contest a merger.

4.) Legal belief that size in and of itself was not sufficient to show violation of antitrust legislation: _____.

5.) _____ attempts to regulate the price of a monopoly so that the market price is equal the incremental cost of the last unit of production.

6.) A _____ joins firms which operate at different stages in the production process.

7.) The vertically integrated relationships that exist between Japanese manufacturers and their suppliers are known as _____.

8.) The rationale for _____ is that free market forces and competition enhance efficiency and result in better outcomes than would be the case with government regulation.

9.) _____ are based on the percent of sales or total market share accounted for by the top four or eight firms in an industry.

10.) The _____ attempted to make U.S. antitrust legislation more effective by closing some of the original loopholes in the Sherman Antitrust Act.

11.) A merger between the "Best in the West" Pet Store and the "Northland" Dog and Cat Emporium would be an example of a _____.

12.) A merger between firms with unrelated product lines is called a _____.

Problems

Average and Marginal Cost Pricing of Utilities

You are given the following demand curve and cost curves for a monopoly.

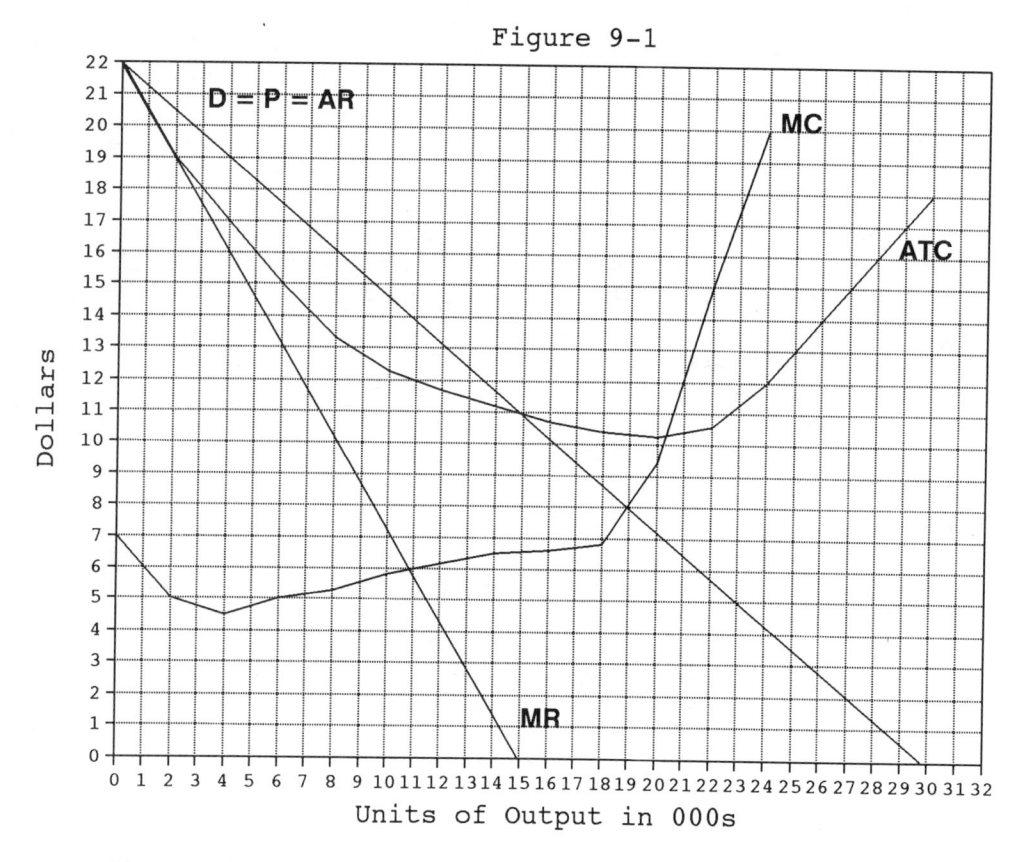

Figure 9-1

Indicate the profit maximizing level of production and price for this monopoly based on the information contained in the graph above.

Briefly explain why this monopoly should be regulated instead of being allowed to maximize its profits:

___

Indicate the price and level of production that would occur under average cost pricing for this monopolist.

___

Provide a rationale for an average cost pricing policy for this monopolist:

___

Indicate the price and level of production that would occur under marginal cost pricing for this monopolist.

___

Provide a rationale for a marginal cost pricing policy for this monopolist:

___

Roughly estimate (by counting the squares) the amount of profit/loss this monopolist would earn when allowed to maximize its profits.

___

Roughly estimate (by counting the squares) the amount of profit/loss this monopolist would earn under an average cost pricing scheme.

___

Roughly estimate (by counting the squares) the amount of profit/loss this monopolist would earn under a marginal cost pricing scheme.

___

Estimating Allocative Inefficiency

Referring to the same demand and set of cost curves used in the previous exercise, graph and compare the amount of allocative inefficiency (by counting the squares) for a profit maximizing monopolist, a monopoly subject to average cost pricing, and a monopoly subject to marginal cost pricing.

Figure 9-2

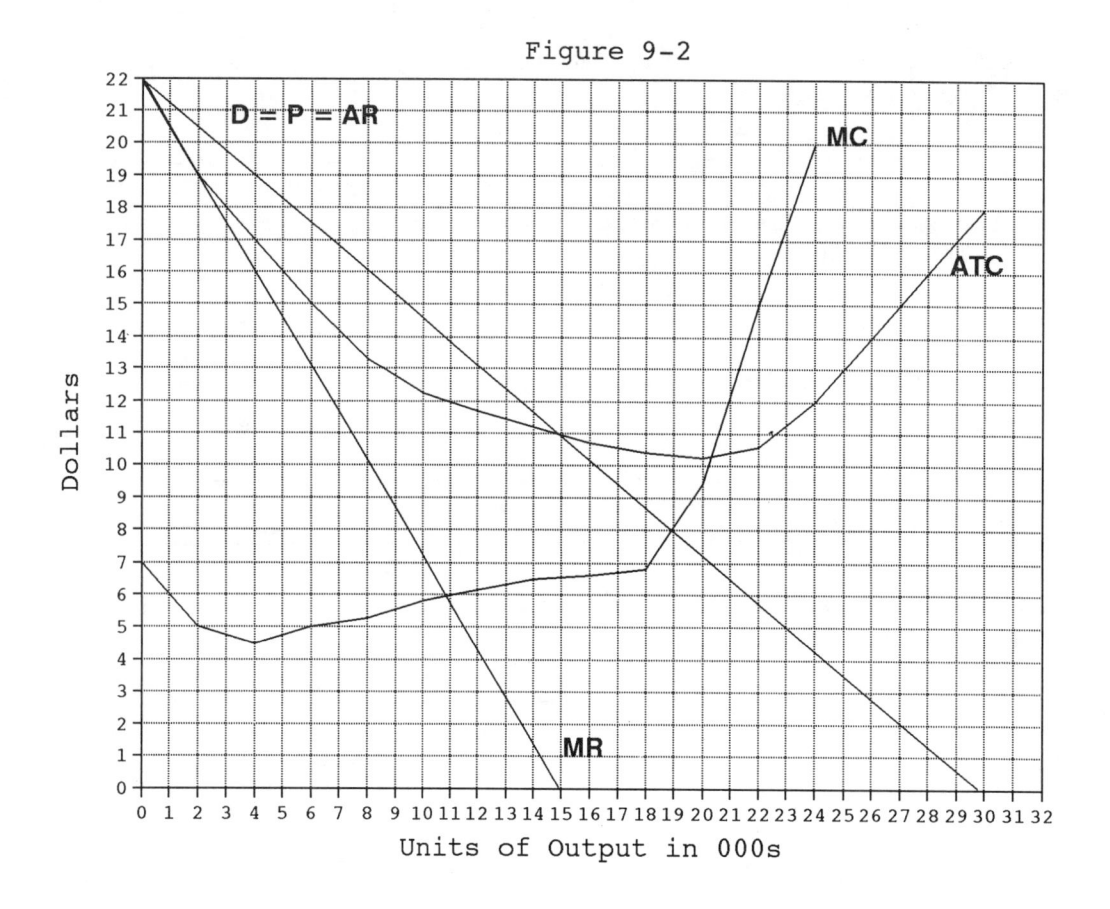

[Graph showing D=P=AR, MR, MC, and ATC curves with Dollars on y-axis (0-22) and Units of Output in 000s on x-axis (0-32)]

Calculating the Herfindahl Index

Most of the time and attention that we have devoted to the study of markets and their performance has focused on purely competitive markets. One of the reasons for that emphasis is that purely competitive market results represent an economic benchmark against which actual economic performance can be compared. Thus, even though there are no markets or sectors of the economy which satisfy the fairly rigid requirements associated with pure competition, it is useful to have an idea of what this theoretical construct is all about. Purely competitive markets result in equilibrium conditions in which the market price equals the average cost of production (at its lowest point if the industry is at long-run equilibrium): Price = Minimum Average Cost

Yet in the "real" world, there are market imperfections which result in imperfect competition. There are significant barriers to entry which allow super-normal economic profits to exist for extended periods of time. Some economic sectors exhibit substantial economies of scale which means that per unit costs decrease as the level of output increases. As a result of such economies, competing firms tend to be larger and a given sized market will support fewer firms.

Is there a way to determine how competitive markets are in the "real" world? That's a difficult task, and there have been a variety of approaches which have addressed themselves to what economists call "the concentration problem." The Herfindahl index estimates the degree of market concentration occuring in a specific market by squaring each individual firm's market share and summing those squared market shares for the entire range of producers.

$$H = s_i^2 + s_i^2 + s_i^2 + \ldots + s_i^2$$

where H = Herfindahl index of market concentration
s_i = percentage market share of the ith firm

The Herfindahl index ranges from a high of 10000 (for a monopoly: $100^2 = = 10000$) to a low of 0 (very large number of firms each with very small, insignificant market shares).

To illustrate how the Herfindahl index could be applied, let's calculate the Herfindahl index for a market which has the following market-share distribution:

Firm	Percent of Industry Sales
firm 1	29%
firm 2	22%
firm 3	20%
firm 4	12%
firm 5	5%
firm 6	3%
firm 7	3%
firm 8	2%
firm 9	2%
firm 10	1%
firm 11	1%

$$H = 29^2 + 22^2 + 20^2 + 12^2 + 5^2 + 3^2 + 3^2 + 2^2 + 2^2 + 1^2 + 1^2$$

$$= 841 + 484 + 400 + 144 + 25 + 9 + 9 + 4 + 4 + 1 + 1 = \mathbf{1922}$$

It would also be possible to calculate concentration ratios from the data provided above. The concentration ratio for the largest four firms equals 83 percent, while the concentration ratio for the largest eight firms equals 96 percent. In the sixties, the Justice Department used the rule of thumb of "75-10-2" to determine whether a proposed merger in a specific industry would be opposed in the courts. As your text points out, the rule meant that the Justice Department would oppose a merger if the four-firm concentration ratio was 75 percent or more, and a firm with 10 percent or more of the market was attempting to merge with any other firm which had more than two percent of the market.

Using the market data above as an example, according to the "75-10-2" rule, the Justice Department would have objected to a proposed merger between firms 1 and 7, but would have allowed a merger between firms 1 and 9. In a similar fashion, a merger between firms 5 and 7 would have been allowed under the guidelines, but a merger between firms 4 and 7 would have been opposed.

After the Herfindahl index of market concentration was developed, the Justice Department's rule changed to the following: small chance of challenge for industries where H < 1000. If H lies between 1000 and 1800, mergers would be opposed if the proposed merger would raise H by more than 100. For those industries with Herfindahl indices over 1800, the Justice Department would take a keen interest in merger proceedings in which H would rise by more than 50.

Let's examine our hypothetical market data again to see what antitrust actions would be taken based on the Herfindahl index. Using the Herfindahl index, the three of the four mergers listed above (between firms 1 and 7, between firms 1 and 9, and between firms 4 and 7) would be opposed. Only the merger between firms 5 and 7 would not have been challenged by the Justice Department. Using the older concentration ratio rule, the merger between firms 1 and 9 would have been allowed, but it would not have been allowed under the Herfindahl index rules.

Suppose we have an industry or product market with the following annual sales. (The distribution of sales shown below approximates the sales pattern of a very popular product which shall remain nameless. Much of their advertising is oriented towards young adults.)

Firm	Annual Industry Sales (in millions of $)	Percent Market Share	Percent Market Share Squared
firm 1	$2,700		
firm 2	$2,023		
firm 3	$ 362		
firm 4	$ 355		
firm 5	$ 194		
firm 6	$ 107		
firm 7	$ 94		
firm 8	$ 40		
firm 9	$ 34		
firm 10	$ 18		
firm 11	$ 17		
firm 12	$ 15		

Calculate market shares for the firms shown above.

Calculate the Herfindahl index for this market.

_____

_____

Using the Department of Justice guidelines mentioned above, indicate whether or not the Justice Department would allow the following mergers:

Proposed Merger	Post Merger Herfindahl Index	Change in Herfindahl Index	Justice Department Action
firm 1 with firm 2?			allowed or contested?
firm 1 with firm 4?			allowed or contested?
firm 3 with firm 4?			allowed or contested?
firm 3 with firm 5?			allowed or contested?

True/False Statements

Indicate whether you think the statements below are true or false. These questions are designed to make you think about the concepts presented in the text. There may not be any easy clear-cut answers. Some thoughts about the answers are presented at the end of the chapter.

1.) _____ Average cost pricing of utilities guarantees that utilities will earn a "fair" rate of return.

2.) _____ A public utility that has its rates regulated according to an average cost policy will have to set its price below the unregulated profit maximizing price.

3.) _____ Average cost regulating policies result in the same degree of economic efficiency that would occur in an unregulated market.

4.) _____ Marginal cost pricing policies result in greater economic efficiency than average cost pricing policies.

5.) _____ Marginal cost pricing policies may require public utilities to produce at a loss.

6.) _____ The Sherman Antitrust Act of 1890 outlawed all monopolies.

7.) _____ The Clayton Act of 1914 modified the Sherman Antitrust Act by making mere size itself illegal.

8.) _____ Under the Justice Department's "75-10-2" rule for mergers/takeovers, a merger of a firm with an 12% marketshare to another firm with a 4% marketshare in an industry with a concentration ratio of 80% would not be allowed.

9.) _____ Current antitrust policy is more concerned with horizontal mergers than vertical mergers.

10.) _____ It is relatively easy to determine whether or not a conglomerate merger will adversely affect the degree of competitiveness in a particular market.

11.) _____ Japanese anti-trust policies allow for a much greater degree of cooperation and interaction among competing firms than is possible in the United States.

12.) _____ An industry with the four largest firms each having 20 percent of the market could conceivably have the same concentration ratio as an industry which has one firm that has 62 percent of the market and the other three largest firms having six percent each.

Multiple-Choice Questions

Select the "best" answer from the alternatives provided:

Refer to the following graph to answer the next two questions.

$ |
  |
  |
  |
  |
  |
  |
  |
  |
  |_____
                                      Quantity of Output

1.) Assume the graph above describes a public utility's demand and cost curves. If it is decided to regulate the utilty by an average cost pricing scheme,
   a. the utility would charge price P_1 and produce output Q_1.
   b. the utility would charge price P_2 and produce output Q_2.
   c. the utility would charge price P_3 and produce output Q_3.
   d. the utility would charge price P_4 and produce output Q_4.

2.) If it were decided to regulate the utility by a marginal cost pricing scheme,
   a. the utility would charge price P_1 and produce output Q_1.
   b. the utility would charge price P_2 and produce output Q_2.
   c. the utility would charge price P_3 and produce output Q_3.
   d. the utility would charge price P_4 and produce output Q_4.

3.) Under the rule of reason of 1920,
   a. certain anti-competitive activities were deemed acceptable as long as they were "reasonable".
   b. it was difficult to win antitrust cases against large firms with monopoly power unless they resorted to obvious anti-competitive activities.
   c. the Justice Department negotiated a "reasonable" solution with the firm or firms being prosecuted.
   d. the existence of monopoly power was held to be illegal whether or not it was used.

4.) If General Motors were to merge with Ford Motor Company, under what legislation would the merger would be opposed by the Justice Department?
   a. The Sherman Antitrust Act.
   b. The Clayton Act of 1914.
   c. The Celler-Kefauver Act.
   d. None of the above, the merger would be allowed since it increase efficiency.

5.) Concerning the concentration ratios and the Herfindahl index which have both been used in an attempt to gauge the impact of mergers:
   a. Concentration ratios are more heavily influenced by the market shares of the largest firms, while the Herfindahl index is based upon the market shares of all firms.
   b. While the two indices may differ from one another, they never differ in terms of whether or not mergers should be allowed.
   c. The two indices differ from one another, and they can differ in terms of whether or not mergers should be allowed.
   d. both (a) and (c)

6.) Regarding average cost pricing,
   a. it is an optimal pricing policy, because consumers pay the same as the average cost of production and the utility earns only a normal profit.
   b. it is an optimal pricing policy, since it is more allocatively efficient than marginal cost pricing which sometimes results in a loss for the utility.
   c. it is allocatively efficient, since market price = average total cost.
   d. it is allocatively inefficient, since market price is greater than the cost of producing an additional unit of output.

7.) If a monopoly is operating on the upward portion of its average cost curve,
   a. marginal cost pricing will result in a profit.
   b. marginal cost pricing will result in a loss.
   c. average cost pricing will result in a loss.
   d. the monopoly should be closed down since it is inefficient.

8.) If foreign trade becomes a more important component of a domestic market,
   a. even more vigorous enforcement of antitrust legislation is needed.
   b. the foreign firms are exempt from U.S. antitrust laws.
   c. the domestic market may become more competitive and less likely to be the subject of antitrust actions.
   d. enforcement of antitrust legislation is not usually affected.

9.) Marginal cost pricing of a monopoly,
   a. is more allocatively efficient than average cost pricing.
   b. forces the monopoly to produce at the minimum point of its average cost curve.
   c. always allows a profit to be earned by the monopoly.
   d. always results in more output being produced than would be the case for average cost pricing.

10.) An example of a conglomerate merger would be
   a. a large department store chain buying out a small locally-owned department store.
   b. a nationwide retailer purchasing some of its supplier firms.
   c. an entertainment firm merging with a publishing firm.
   d. a large foreign corporation purchasing a domestic firm.
   e. none of the above.

11.) The Sherman Antitrust Act of 1890
   a. specified that monopolies *per se* were illegal.
   b. outlawed mergers between two competing firms.
   c. set an absolute size limit on firms.
   d. made interlocking directorates among competing firms illegal.
   e. could be used only in cases where firms engaged in explicit actions such as price fixing.

Discussion Questions

1.) Can you think of any examples in which mergers would enhance the competitiveness of a market?

2.) Should mere size be an antitrust offense (i.e., should firms be broken up after they have reach a certain size, say $5 or $10 billion in total sales)?

3.) Why would you expect a utility that is regulated under average cost pricing or "fair rate of return" price to lack incentives to control or lower its costs? Is there any solution to that problem?

4.) Although the term "market" is used extensively throughout your text, and most people have a good intuitive sense of what a market is, why might it be difficult to actually define a real world market? What implications would that have for antitrust policy?

5.) Why should society be careful about deregulating the airline industry, allowing airlines to compete against one another on their routes?

6.) An argument can be made that American firms should be allowed to form alliances with each other in order to compete against foreign firms which are often subject to much more lenient antitrust laws. Should we modify our antitrust laws to take this into account?

Answers and Solutions to Problems and Exercises

Completing Statements from the List of Terms

1.) Sherman Antitrust Act of 1890
2.) Average Cost Pricing
3.) Herfindahl Index
4.) Rule of Reason
5.) Marginal Cost Pricing
6.) Vertical Merger
7.) Keiretsu
8.) Deregulation
9.) Concentration Ratios
10.) Clayton Act of 1914
11.) Horizontal Merger
12.) Conglomerate Merger

Problems

Average and Marginal Cost Pricing of Utilities

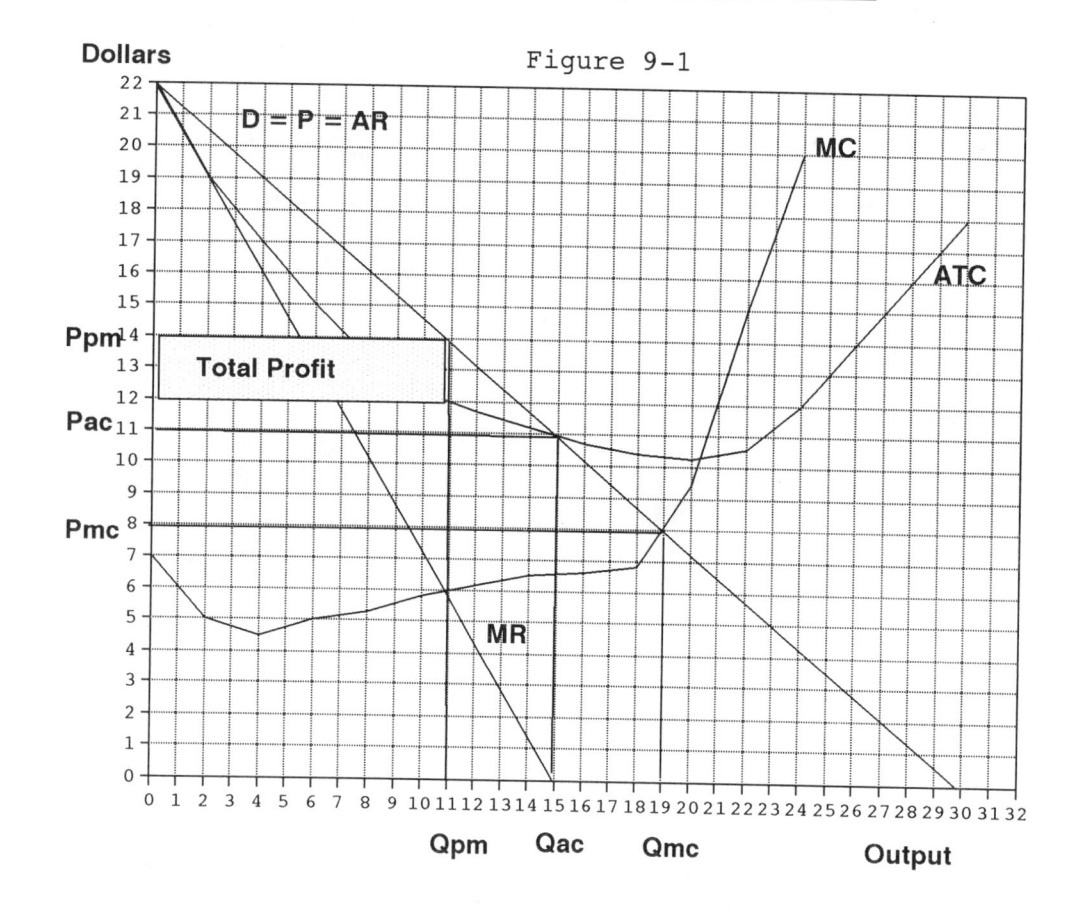

Figure 9-1

Indicate the profit maximizing level of production and price for this monopoly based on the information contained in the graph above.
P = $14 and Q = 11,000 units

Briefly explain why this monopoly should be regulated instead of being allowed to maximize its profits: **With few, if any, substitutes available to consumers, the monopoly would have sufficient market power to keep the market price at a high level with correspondingly large profits.**

Such a situation is allocatively inefficient and puts consumers at a considerable disadvantage.

Indicate the price and level of production that would occur under average cost pricing for this monopolist. **P = $11 and Q = 15,000 units**

Provide a rationale for an average cost pricing policy for this monopolist: **It would force the monopolist to the point where P = ATC and, at that point, only a normal profit would be earned.**

Indicate the price and level of production that would occur under marginal cost pricing for this monopolist. **P = $8 and Q = 19,000 units**

Provide a rationale for a marginal cost pricing policy for this monopolist: **If market price = marginal cost, the market outcome will be allocatively efficient. The price that consumers are willing to pay for the last unit just equals the marginal cost of producing the last unit.**

Roughly estimate the amount of profit/loss for the three different cases:
Profits under profit maximization = $ 22,000
Profits under average cost pricing = $ 0 just the normal profit included in the average cost curve
Profits under marginal cost pricing = − $ 38,000

Estimating Allocative Inefficiency

Figure 9-2

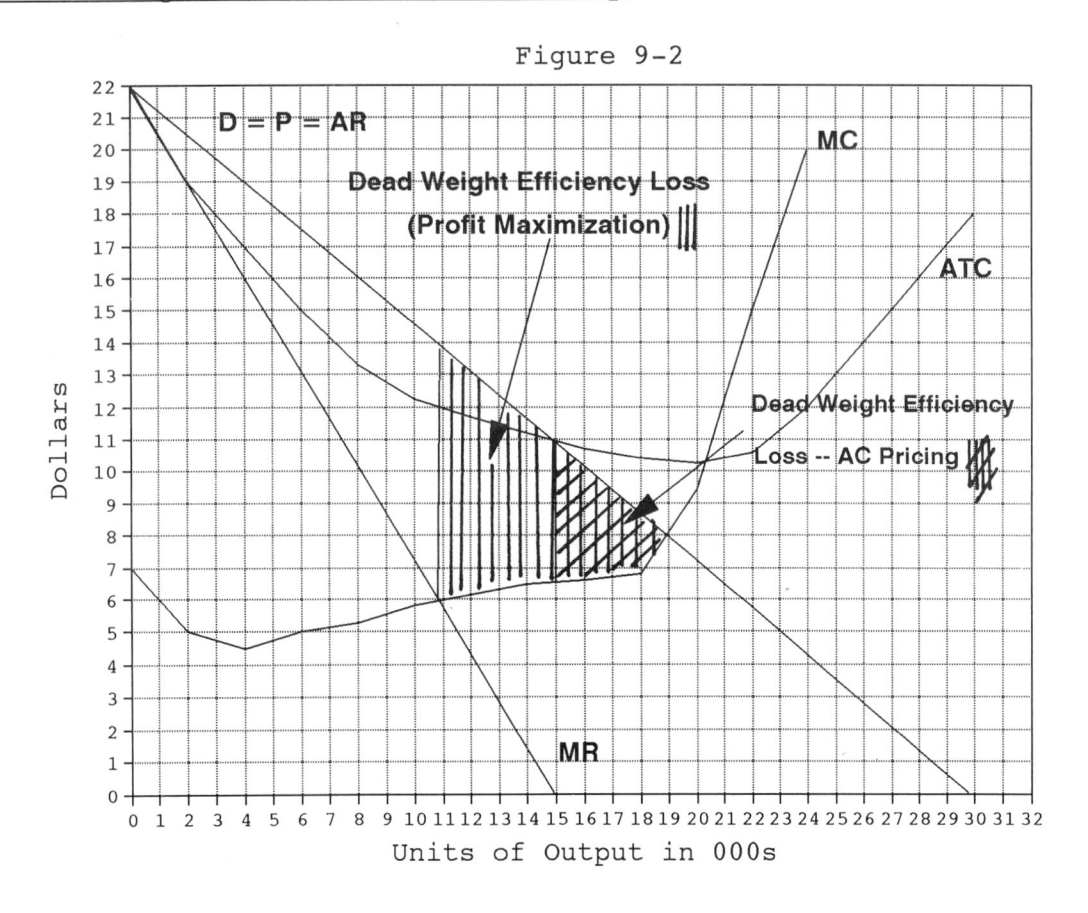

Allocative Inefficiency estimates:
    Profit Maximization = approximately $ 32,400
    Average Cost Pricing = $ 8,700
    Marginal Cost Pricing = $ 0

Calculating the Herfindahl Index

Firm	Annual Industry Sales (in millions of $)	Percent Market Share	Percent Market Share Squared
firm 1	$2,700	45.31	2052.96
firm 2	$2,023	33.95	1152.51
firm 3	$ 362	6.08	36.90
firm 4	$ 355	5.957	35.49
firm 5	$ 194	3.256	10.599
firm 6	$ 107	1.796	3.224
firm 7	$ 94	1.577	2.488
firm 8	$ 40	0.671	0.451
firm 9	$ 34	0.571	0.326
firm 10	$ 18	0.302	0.091
firm 11	$ 17	0.285	0.081
firm 12	$ 15	0.252	0.063
	$5,959	100.00	3295.19

Calculate the Herfindahl index for this market. **H = 3295.19**

Proposed Merger	Post Merger Herfindahl Index	Change in Herfindahl Index	Justice Department Action
firm 1 with firm 2?	6371.59	3076.4	contested
firm 1 with firm 4?	3835.04	539.85	contested
firm 3 with firm 4?	3367.57	72.38	contested
firm 3 with firm 5?	3334.74	39.55	allowed

True/False Statements

1.) **True.** At least the regulated monopoly will earn what its regulatory commission thinks a normal profit rate is for similar types of businesses.

2.) **True.** The public utility has to increase its level of output and lower its price to reach the point where its demand curve intersects its average cost curve. It would be expected that the regulated rate set by the public utility would be lower, otherwise there wouldn't be a rationale for price regulation.

3.) **False.** Since the regulated price is not equal to marginal cost, it is not allocatively efficient.

4.) **True.** Since the price consumers pay is equal to the cost of producing the last unit of production, allocative efficiency is attained.

5.) **True.** As long as the public utility is producing in the output range where average costs are falling, this would always be true. If, on the other hand, output is subject to increasing average costs (beyond the minimum point of the AC curve), then the statement is not true.

6.) **False.** It made efforts to restrain trade illegal. It was not until the late 1930s and early 1940s that the courts held that monopoly power was illegal *per se*.

7.) **False.** It attempted to address some of the loopholes that existed in the Sherman Antitrust Act and broke some new ground in outlawing interlocking directorates, excluding trade unions from the provisions of the Sherman Act, and made corporate officials personally responsible for their acts.

8.) **True.** In an industry with that overall concentration ratio, any firm with a marketshare over 10 % could not merge with any firm having more than 2 % marketshare.

9.) **True.** The competitive implications are more evident for horizontal mergers than they are for vertical mergers. Vertical integration may be necessary for U.S. firms to compete successfully with Japanese and other foreign firms.

10.) **False.** Since conglomerate mergers are by definition mergers in different product lines, it is much more difficult to determine the competitive impact of mergers.

11.) **True.** Cooperation among firms is encouraged by the Japanese government and its policies. Much of their orientation is towards making firms effective world-wide competitors rather than achieving domestically competitive industries.

12.) **True.** If the concentration ratios are based on the percent of the market controlled by the largest four firms, then the two industries would have the same calculated concentration ratio. Unfortunately, the competitive dynamics of the two industries would, in all likelihood, be quite different. Thus, any fixed rule like the 75-10-2 rule discussed in your text would lead to a flawed antitrust policy because of ambiguities introduced by the basic measuring unit -- the concentration ratio.

Multiple-Choice

1.) c   2.) d   3.) b   4.) c   5.) d   6.) d

7.) a   8.) c   9.) a   10.) c   11.) e

Discussion Questions

1.) One example would be a market in which there are several large and dominant firms with a number of smaller firms. Mergers between the smaller firms might enhance the competitiveness of the larger, combined firm. The merger between Northwest Airlines and Republic Airlines was supported by some people on the grounds that a larger Northwest Airlines would be better able to compete with the larger airlines such as American, United, and Delta Airlines, even though competition in several markets was eliminated.

2.) The size of a firm, in and of itself, is not necessarily indicative of whether or not it has monopoly power. A $5 billion dollar auto producer would not be a particularly large player in the domestic United States market nor would it be a dominant firm in nation-wide retailing. On the other hand, a much smaller firm might be able to act like a monopoly in a relatively isolated area of the country.

3.) Essentially average cost pricing allows utilities to recoup their costs plus an estimated "normal" rate of return. Under those circumstances, the lack of competitive pressures to control costs may result in higher costs and less overall efficiency. Your text mentions price-cap regulation which provides incentives to keep costs below the costs used in determining the price ceiling for the utility. What is needed is a scheme which allows utilities to keep part of any cost savings that result.

4.) Many markets are made up of components that are linked together with varying degrees of substitution. The market of automobiles provides an illustration: there is a considerable degree of substitution and competition between small cars with medium cars under $25,000 and possibly with sports cars under $25,000. There is probably not much competition between small cars and large cars over $25,000 or with luxury cars. Are motorcycles part of the auto market, since there may some degree of competition between them and small cars? What about bicycles? You see the point?

Since Justice Department guidelines are often based on market share, it becomes difficult to determine whether or not antitrust action should be initiated if it is difficult to implement the guidelines.

5.) Many felt that lower prices and competitive pressures might lead to less maintenance on airframes and less overall safety for passengers. While that appears not to have happened very frequently, there were some reports that airlines that were in financial difficulty had not kept up with required maintenance. It certainly is a legitimate concern in terms of public policy.

6.) There are some situations in which our regulatory environment is going to put domestic firms at a disadvantage. Bribery is accepted as a normal way of doing business in some areas of the world, but, it is illegal in the United States. There has not been a lot of pressure to change that provision in our legal system. Firms have set up alliances with foreign firms, but such agreements need to be carefully monitored. The text has already identified the many advantages of competition for society, and actions which move us towards less competition should be carefully examined.

Summary

The issue of corporate influence and power is an extremely important one for society today. Mergers and take-overs are occurring at a rapid pace and while the motivation for many of these actions is increased efficiency and the avoidance of duplicate functions (i.e., a merger between two banks with the closure of one of the bank's mortgage processing department, funneling all of the combined mortgages into the remaining bank's mortgage department), there are often competitiveness issues that are either ignored or downplayed.

Even as domestic industries become more concentrated and possibly less competitive, the growing presence of foreign competition often provides a competitive counterbalance to domestic firms. Since international markets are often very competitive, foreign imports have the potential to exert real restraint on the prices of domestic firms. This would tend be true even if competitive conditions in the exporters' own domestic markets were not very competitive.

Deregulation has had a significant impact on some key sectors of the United States economy. There is evidence that passengers on the main airline trunk routes realized significant savings as a result of deregulation, although residents of rural areas have not fared as well as airline fares increased in many of those less-traveled markets. For those economic sectors that are still regulated, average cost pricing is used extensively, but, as your text mentions, there are some innovative guidelines that have been introduced in an effort to give regulated utilities additional incentives to reduce costs and become more efficient.

Further modification of pricing policies may be needed to give consumers more accurate signals about the true cost of their consumption. Electricity consumers who use appliances during the peak periods of the day impose more costs on the system than those who use electricity during off-peak periods. For certain types of energy, there are questions about whether or not the average total cost is declining or increasing for the relevant range of consumption. It would be a significant change if consumers were charged more as they consumed more instead of receiving quantity discounts.

Chapter 10
Externalities:
When Private and Social Costs and Benefits Diverge

Overview of the Chapter

Frequently, market transactions result in costs or benefits that affect third parties (i.e., society at large) without their knowledge or their permission. We call these external effects externalities. Negative externalities (commonly referred to as social costs) are the most common kind of externality, and they are associated with both consumption and production activities. Positive externalities (also known as social benefits) are less common and similar to negative externalities; they are associated with both consumption and production activities.

Externalities are not exclusive characteristics of market systems. With the breakup of the former Soviet Union, we are now much more aware of the extent of environmental degradation that can occur in a command economy. Apparently, the state government simply did not have the resources required to install the necessary pollution control equipment and minimized both their start-up and ongoing maintenance costs by spending as little as possible in the way of pollution control equipment.

The last decade has been characterized by a growing awareness of the global dimensions of the negative externalities associated with increasing levels of economic activity on the planet -- ozone depletion, global warming, toxic waste disposal, and pollution of the oceans. A major obstacle in addressing and alleviating large scale externalities is the problem of the free rider. Does a small country like Norway, which has provided leadership on a number of global environmental issues, have any real incentive, other than its own resolve, to embark upon a program of stabilizing carbon dioxide emissions when much larger countries like the United States are not pursuing similar policies? Norway would bear the domestic costs of such a program but would have virtually no impact on overall global emissions.

Typically, negative externalities occur in those areas where property rights are ambiguous. Since no one seems to have an inherent property right to "clean" air, the atmosphere becomes polluted as both firms and individuals use it as a low cost disposal sink to reduce their real consumption and production costs.

The traditional demand and supply graphs that you have studied so far are based on the private costs of suppliers and the private benefits of buyers. When the negative externalities associated with the production of a commodity are incorporated into demand and supply analysis, the new supply curve, representing the full costs of production (private and social), will lie to the left of the original supply curve which was based only on private costs. In that case, the equilibrium quantity will be lower than before, and the equilibrium price will be higher.

With respect to negative externalities and the demand for commodities, the private benefits associated with the original demand curve will be decreased by the existence of the negative externalities, and the new revised demand curve will lie to the left of the original. In the case of positive externalities, original demand and supply curves based only on private costs and benefits will shift to the right in both cases.

What then is appropriate public policy for dealing with commodities and economic sectors that have significant externalities associated with their activities? One solution for negative externalities is to tax the production or consumption of affected commodities. In a sense, a tax internalizes the social costs associated with the commodity and allows suppliers and/or consumers to take the social costs into account. Such an approach would result in an economically efficient response to the externality as opposed to a non-market regulatory approach. In a similar fashion, positive externalities, in which benefits to society as a whole exceed private benefits, should be subsidized to encourage their production/consumption. The more of these activities, the more benefits that are generated and the better off society will be.

An important question revolves around the issue of what is an optimum amount of pollution. As with many economic decisions, comparing the marginal costs and benefits of changes in cleanup levels provides a useful perspective on achieving an optimal solution. Pollution should be reduced to the point where the marginal benefits associated with the last incremental change in pollution are just equal to the marginal costs associated with that level of cleanup. Any additional cleanup would decrease overall welfare, since the extra costs of cleanup would exceed the extra benefits, and any less cleanup wouldn't be optimal, since each incremental change in cleanup is generating more extra benefits than extra costs. It should be kept in mind that an economically optimal level of cleanup may not be an optimum from an ecological perspective.

Learning Objectives

After completing this chapter, you should be sure that you are able to:

- understand and define positive and negative externalities for both production and consumption activities.

- show how positive and negative externalities can be incorporated into demand and supply analysis and graphs.

- understand the free rider concept and the difficulties free riders create in resolving problems associated with externalities.

- understand why inadequately defined property rights and the existence of excessive transactions costs result in obstacles that delay or prevent the development of solutions to externalities problems.

- understand how taxes and subsidies can be used to offset the inefficiencies and losses associated with negative and positive externalities.

- explain the concept of an "optimum" level of pollution and how the marginal costs and benefits associated with various levels of cleanup influence the optimum level of pollution.

- understand how a market in pollution credits or rights would function and how the trading of such credits would allow society to decrease pollution in an efficient fashion.

- understand how social costs/benefits could be measured and thus facilitate cost/benefit analysis.

Self Evaluation

List of Terms

Emissions Trading
Externalities
Free Rider
Marginal Cost of Pollution Damage
Marginal Cost of Pollution Prevention
Market Failure
Negative Externality

Positive Externality
Private Marginal Benefits
Private Marginal Costs
Property Rights
Social Benefits
Social Costs
Transactions Costs

For the statements below, fill in the term from the list above which provides the best fit.

1.) One reason that it is often difficult for society to solve problems associated with social costs is the existence of relatively large _____.

2.) Vaccinations are examples of activities which have _____ associated with them.

3.) _____ occur wherever third parties are affected by private transactions.

4.) Whenever social costs exceed private costs for a given activity, a _____ exists.

5.) As the level of pollution decreases, the _____ decreases.

6.) An _____ program allows firms to buy/sell pollution rights.

7.) The _____ problem occurs whenever individuals have no incentive to change their actions, because it will not correct or significantly affect a particular problem.

8.) In the absence of externalities, the market demand curve can be viewed as the summation of the _____ of all the buyers in the market.

9.) _____ are defined as costs imposed on third parties without their knowledge and/or permission.

10.) If a _____ exists, then proper corrective action consists of subsidizing the activity in question.

11.) Many externalities occur because _____ are not adequately defined.

12.) In the absence of externalties, the market supply curve can be viewed as the summation of individual firms' _____.

13.) As the level of pollution increases, the _____ increases.

14.) The existence of externalites means that market outcomes can no longer be considered optimal and thus represents an example of _____.

Problems

An Application of Marginal Analysis -- Cleaning Up the Environment

This problem shows how marginal analysis (the comparison of the extra costs and extra benefits of a particular action) can be used to determine the optimal amount of pollution cleanup for a hypothetical community. Economic analysis dictates that a community should clean up to the point where the extra costs of the last unit of pollution cleaned up are just equal to the perceived extra benefits that society derives from the incremental unit of the resource in question (in this case water-based recreation.) As this problem will show, by cleaning up to that point, society will maximize its net welfare.

Specific economic activities should not necessarily be carried out to their ultimate degree. In this case, even though cleaning up pollution is clearly a desirable goal for society as a whole, society should not necessarily cleanup to the 100 % level. It may simply be too costly to achieve that goal, given the benefits that result from it. In every instance, costs, as well as benefits, must be taken into account in order to make an optimal decision.

Assume that the city of Moorhead is considering a new sewage treatment plant. They are undecided as to how much they should treat the water, i.e. -- they don't know what the "**optimal**[1]" amount of cleanup should be? Economists would define the optimal amount in the following way:

The amount of river cleanup will be optimal when the extra or marginal cost of cleaning up to a particular degree is just equated with extra or marginal benefits associated with the extra cleaning-up.

Marginal Cost (MC) = the extra cost associated with an additional amount of cleanup

example => the additional expenditure necessary to cleanup an additional 5 % percent of sewage wastes

Marginal Benefits (MB) = the extra benefits associated with an additional amount of cleanup

example => the additional benefits (valued in dollars) a community expects to receive from cleaning up an additional 5 % percent of sewage wastes

Using the terminology from your text, the marginal cost of cleaning up pollution is called the marginal cost of pollution prevention (MCP), and your text doesn't discuss benefits directly but rather in terms of the marginal cost of damage from pollution (MCD). The point of optimality is conceptually the same but the rule would be stated: to achieve an optimal level of cleanup, a community should cleanup to the point where the marginal cost of pollution prevention (MCP) just equals the marginal cost of damage associated with the pollution (MCD). No matter what terminology you use, the logic and analysis are exactly the same.

---

[1] Note that optimality in this instance is defined in terms of the economic welfare of society and not in terms of what is optimum from an ecological perspective. Ecological considerations may well dictate that the amount of cleanup should be carried out well past the point of economic optimality. Economic factors and influences typically take precedence in our society, reflecting our interest in material goods and services.

Two important assumptions are critical to this analysis:

1.) **Increasing marginal costs**:

   On a scale of 0-100% cleanup, initial percentages of cleanup are less costly than subsequent units of cleanup. Simply stated: it is more expensive to cleanup from 90% to 95% than from 0% to 10%. This is an application of the **law of increasing marginal costs**, which states that the production of additional units of any commodity requires larger sacrifices in terms of other commodities, since resources must be bid away from other competing uses.

2.) **Decreasing marginal utility or benefits**:

   As the river is cleaned up, successive units of cleanup are valued less and less. It is assumed that people in the community are more willing to pay to cleanup the river from 0% to 30% than from an 80% to 95% cleanup. Perhaps they obtain many more direct benefits from achieving this lower level of cleanup than they d application of the **law of diminishing marginal utility**.

Suppose you are given the following information about costs and benefits involving the Red River of the North, the river that passes through Moorhead.

Table 10-1

Percent of Clean-up	Total Cost Required to to Achieve a Given Level of Clean Up TC	Marginal Costs MC	Total benefits Perceived by Residents for a Given Level of Clean Up TB	Marginal Benefits MB	Total Net Benefits TB - TC
0%	$ 0	$ _____	$ 500,000	$ _____	$ _____
10%	$ 300,000	$ _____	$ 2,000,000	$ _____	$ _____
20%	$ 800,000	$ _____	$ 4,000,000	$ _____	$ _____
30%	$ 1,500,000	$ _____	$ 6,500,000	$ _____	$ _____
40%	$ 2,500,000	$ _____	$ 8,500,000	$ _____	$ _____
50%	$ 3,700,000	$ _____	$10,000,000	$ _____	$ _____
60%	$ 5,000,000	$ _____	$11,000,000	$ _____	$ _____
70%	$ 6,500,000	$ _____	$11,600,000	$ _____	$ _____
80%	$ 8,500,000	$ _____	$12,000,000	$ _____	$ _____
90%	$11,000,000	$ _____	$12,300,000	$ _____	$ _____
100%	$14,000,000	$ _____	$12,500,000	$ _____	$ _____

1.) Calculate the marginal cost and marginal benefits from the information provided in the table above:
   for example: If in cleaning-up from 0% to 10%, total costs increased from $50,000 to $150,000, then the extra or marginal cost of that extra 10% of cleanup would be $100,000. Similarly, if the total benefits associated with cleaning up from 0% to 10% increased from $500,000 to $1,000,000, then the marginal benefits of that incremental 10% cleanup are $500,000.

2.) At what point in the cleanup process are marginal costs equal to marginal benefits? _____ % cleanup

3.) How would you explain to someone who has never had an economics course before why that amount of cleanup represents an optimum for this particular city?

_____

_____

_____

4.) Graph marginal costs and marginal benefits, on the following figure, clearly labeling each curve. Indicate the point of optimum cleanup.

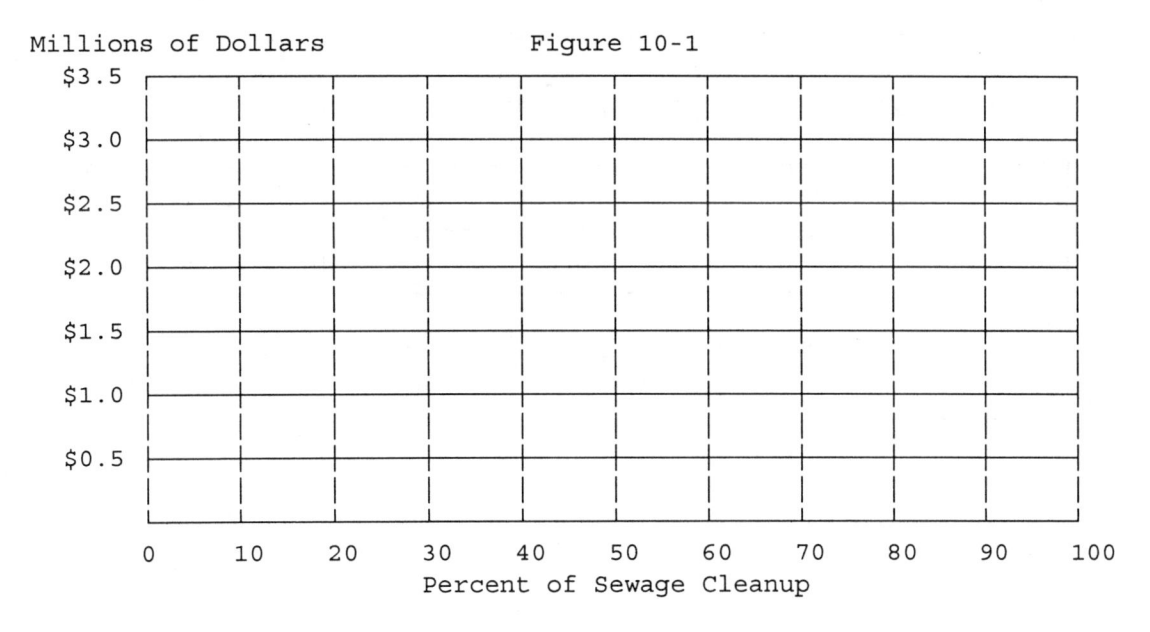

Millions of Dollars   Figure 10-1

[Graph with y-axis from $0.5 to $3.5 in $0.5 increments, x-axis labeled "Percent of Sewage Cleanup" from 0 to 100 in increments of 10]

5). Using the other data from Table 10-1, calculate total net benefits.

   Total Net Benefits = Total Benefits (TB) - Total Costs (TC)

   Note that calculation of total net benefits will provide a check on your marginal analysis. Total net benefits (a measure of society's well-being) from the treatment plant should be a maximum at the point where marginal costs of cleanup are just equal to the marginal benefits of cleanup: MC = MB.

Graph total benefits, total costs, and total net benefits on the graph below. The point where the vertical distance is the greatest positive distance between TB and TC is the point of maximum total net benefits. Label that point on your graph.

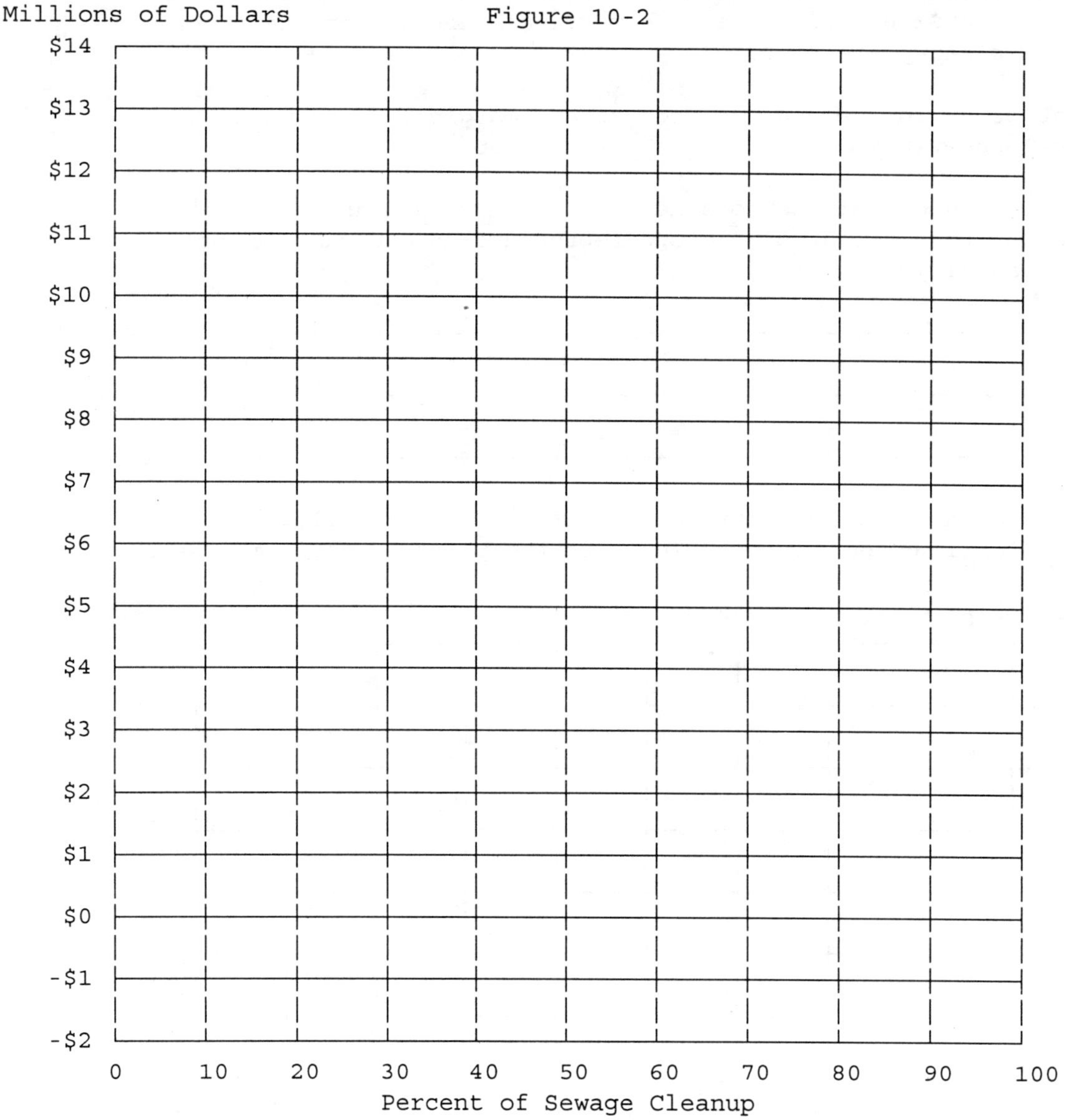
Millions of Dollars
$14
$13
$12
$11
$10
$9
$8
$7
$6
$5
$4
$3
$2
$1
$0
-$1
-$2
0
10
20
30
40
50
60
70
80
90
100
Percent of Sewage Cleanup

Figure 10-2

6.) The figure below illustrates what typically shaped marginal cost and marginal benefits curves might look like. Their intersection determines the point of optimality.

Figure 10-3

Dollars of Costs/Benefits

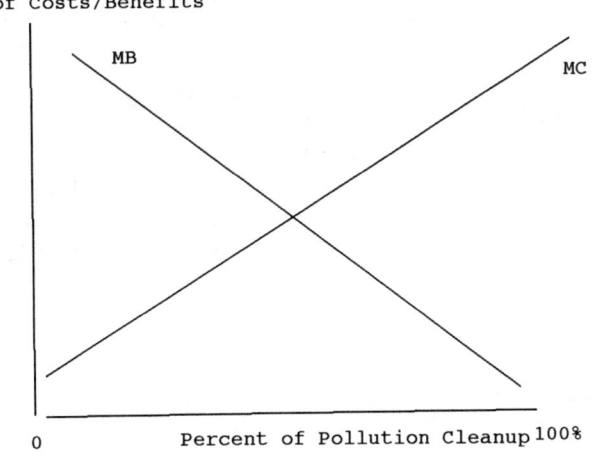

```
         MB                              MC




                    X


     0         Percent of Pollution Cleanup  100%
```

a. Label the point of optimum cleanup, Q_o This will be your point of reference for all subsequent changes. Do not cumulate your changes, always reference all changes back to the original equilibrium position.

b. Show graphically what would happen if there were now larger marginal costs associated with each level of pollution (i.e., -- it becomes more expensive to cleanup pollution). Label the new optimum level of pollution cleanup (B).

c. Show graphically what would happen if there were now lower marginal costs associated with each level of pollution (i.e., -- it becomes less expensive to cleanup pollution). Label the new optimum level of pollution cleanup (C).

d. Show graphically what would happen if there were now larger marginal benefits associated with each level of pollution (i.e., -- people place more value on each level of cleanup than before). Label the new optimum level of pollution cleanup (D).

e. Show graphically what would happen if there were now smaller marginal benefits associated with each level of pollution (i.e., -- people place less value on each level of cleanup than before). Label the new optimum level of pollution cleanup (E).

Comparing the Economic Efficiency of a Tax on Pollution Versus Governmental Standards

The economic way of addressing pollution problems involves the imposition of a tax per unit of pollution emitted. This approach effectively internalizes the pollution externality, allowing each firm to deal with the pollution cleanup problem according to its own individual costs and circumstances. In contrast, the regulatory approach would require every firm to cleanup to the same standard, or perhaps the requirement would require the utilization of some specified technology. The purpose of this exercise is to show how the economic approach is more economically efficient (i.e., achieves a given level of cleanup at a lower total cost). The difference in overall efficiency becomes more apparent when the firms in an industry differ in their age, technology, and the marginal costs they face in cleaning up.

Let's examine how a tax on pollution would affect a single representative firm. For purposes of this exercise, assume that the industry in question is purely competitive, made up of many small firms. Each firm has the potential to generate 10 units of pollution. Assume a typical firm's marginal cost schedule for cleaning up pollution is given below:

Table 10-2

Typical Firm's Marginal Cost of Cleanup Schedule

Tons of Pollution Cleaned Up	Marginal Cost ($/ton)		Pollution Tax ($/ton)
0	$ 0	<	$5,000
1	$ 400	<	$5,000
2	$ 900	<	$5,000
3	$ 1,600	<	$5,000
4	$ 2,500	<	$5,000
5	$ 3,500	<	$5,000
6 (OPTIMUM CLEANUP LEVEL)	$ 4,800	<	$5,000
7	$ 6,500	>	$5,000
8	$ 8,500	>	$5,000
9	$11,500	>	$5,000
10	$16,000	>	$5,000

After a careful study, the government determines that the social cost per ton of pollution is approximately $5,000. That estimate of the social cost could then be used to justify a tax of $5,000 per ton of pollution. How would a representative firm respond to such a tax? Since the firms are profit maximizers, they want to cleanup in the most cost-efficient, least cost way. As long as it is less expensive to clean up the pollution than to pay the tax, they will do so. When the cleanup cost becomes greater than the tax, it will be cheaper to pay the tax. The firm's decision rules are:

If the marginal cost of cleanup < pollution tax, then the firm cleans up the pollution.

If the marginal cost of cleanup > pollution tax, then the firm pays the tax and does not cleanup.

If the marginal cost of cleanup = pollution tax, then the firm would be indifferent as to whether it cleaned up itself or paid the tax.

In this specific instance, given a pollution tax of $5,000, the firm would respond by cleaning up 6 tons of pollution and paying the tax for the other 4 tons of pollution emitted. The cost of cleaning up the seventh ton is $1,500 greater than paying the tax, so it would be less expensive to pay the tax for the seventh ton and all successive pollution after that. Note that the total cost involved with the firm's cleanup can be calculated by summing the appropriate marginal costs. For example, the total cost involved in cleaning up six tons of pollution would be:

$400 + $900 + $1,600 + $2,500 + $3,500 + $4,800 = $13,700

A graph is also useful in illustrating the relationship between marginal cleanup costs and a pollution tax. Graph the marginal cost schedule given above and the $5,000 pollution tax. The intersection of the two schedules marks the point of optimal cleanup.

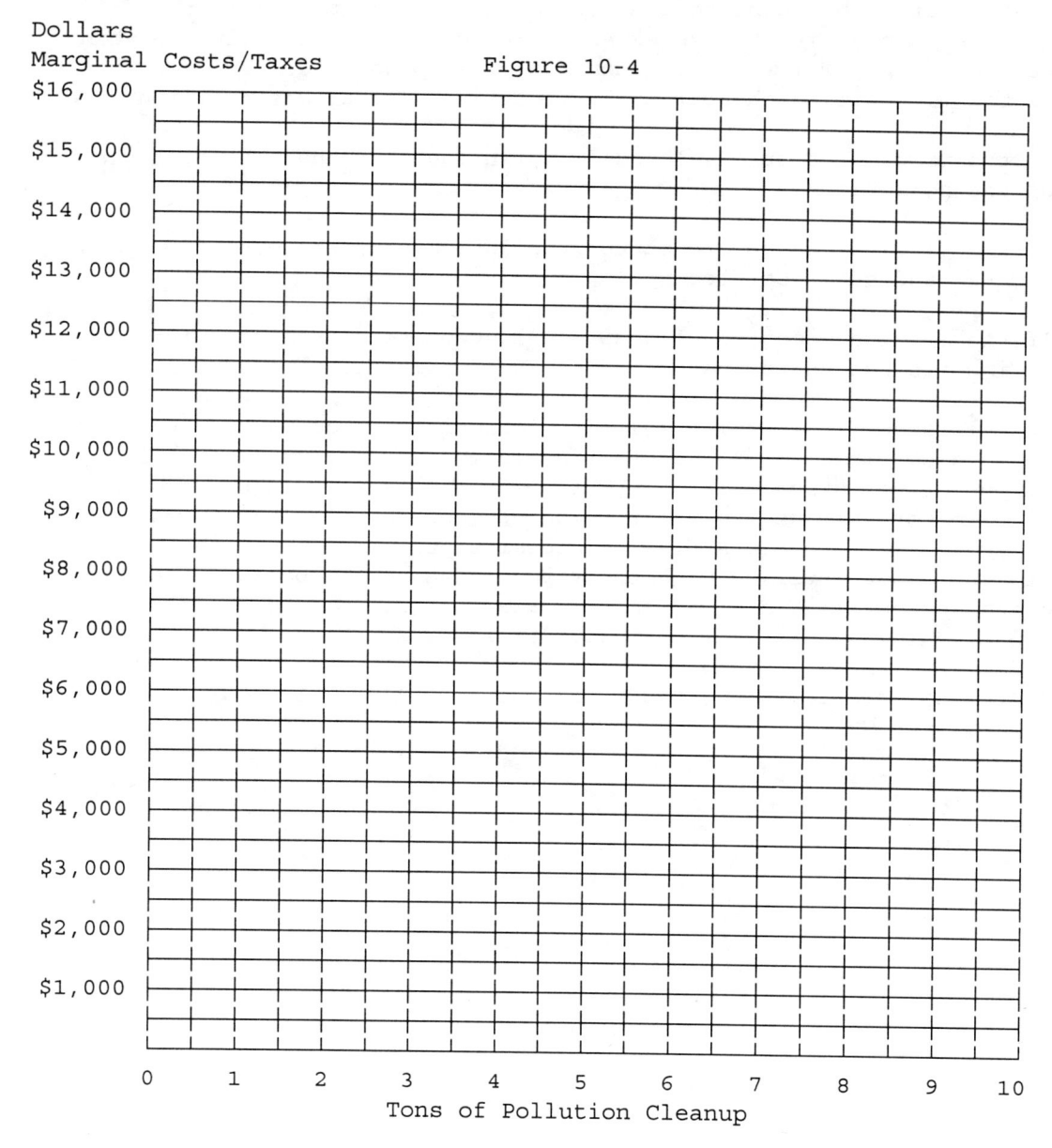

Dollars
Marginal Costs/Taxes   Figure 10-4

[Blank graph: y-axis labeled from $1,000 to $16,000 in $1,000 increments; x-axis labeled "Tons of Pollution Cleanup" from 0 to 10.]

Check your understanding of the economic principle involved by determining how many tons of pollution the firm would cleanup given pollution taxes of $1,000 per ton and $7,000 per ton. Indicate the two new tax levels on the figure above. (The graphical solution may be a bit different from your own, since it is based on continuous pollution cleanup rather than cleaning up in discrete units of pollution (1,2,3,.... tons of pollution).

Tons of cleanup with pollution tax of $1,000/ton: _____

Total cleanup costs associated with that level of cleanup: $ _____

Tons of cleanup with pollution tax of $7,000/ton: _____

Total cleanup costs associated with that level of cleanup: $ _____

True/False Statements

Indicate whether you think the statements below are true or false. These questions are designed to make you think about the concepts presented in the text. There may not be any easy clear-cut answers. Some thoughts about the answers are presented at the end of the chapter.

1.) _____ If negative externalities are associated with the production of a particular good, the full cost of producing the commodity exceeds its private cost.

2.) _____ Education generates significant positive externalities for society as a whole. A free market, private enterprise capitalistic economy takes that into account and provides an optimum amount of education.

3.) _____ A capitalistic, free market economy will generate allocatively efficient results only if there are no externalities (positive or negative).

4.) _____ If negative production externalities are associated with the production of a specific commodity, the overall costs of production will outweigh the overall benefits derived by society from the production of the good in question.

5.) _____ If a negative externality is associated with the consumption of widgets, it means that the social marginal benefits are less than the private marginal benefits.

6.) _____ If the consumption of a good yields positive externalities, then a market-based economy will produce too little of the good in question.

7.) _____ If property rights are clearly and perfectly defined, the market system would allocate resources in an optimum fashion.

8.) _____ If the transactions costs associated with an externality are very large, society will be better off with the status quo rather than solving the externality problem.

9.) _____ The free rider problem complicates efforts to reduce negative consumption externalities since no one individual will have any incentive to change his/her behavior.

10.) _____ Taxing producers for each unit of pollution they generate will not completely eliminate the allocative inefficiency associated with the pollution.

11.) _____ Generally speaking, the imposition of taxes to eliminate the effects of negative externalities is a more economically efficient method of dealing with the problem than the imposition of governmental regulations and/or standards.

12.) _____ If it can be shown that a negative externality harms the environment, it is in society's best interest to eliminate the externality altogether.

13.) _____ Society should cleanup pollution up to the point where the marginal cost of pollution prevention (MCP) just equals the marginal cost of damage from pollution (MCD).

14.) _____ If the marginal damage costs associated with pollution increase, then society should cleanup more to compensate for the increased damage costs.

15.) _____ If an accurate estimate of the social costs associated with either the production or consumption of a particular good can be obtained, imposing a tax/unit of pollution equal to the estimated social costs will achieve an optimum level of pollution cleanup.

16.) _____ Emission trading is a more economically efficient method of cleaning up pollution since firms with the greatest financial resources will cleanup the most.

Multiple-Choice Questions

Select the "best" answer from the alternatives provided.

1.) When negative externalities are present in production are present,
   a. the market system will set too low a price, and allocative efficiency is impaired.
   b. the market system will set too high a price, and allocative efficiency is impaired.
   c. the market system will set too low a price, and allocative efficiency is not impaired.
   d. the market system will set too high a price, and allocative efficiency is not impaired.
   e. the market system will set a correct price, and allocative efficiency is not impaired.

2.) When a positive production externality exists, the market system will
   a. set a market price that is too high and will overallocate resources to the production of that commodity.
   b. set a market price that is too low and underallocate resources to the production of that commodity.
   c. set a market price that is too high and underallocate resources to the production of that commodity.
   d. set a market price that is too low and overallocate resources to the production of that commodity.
   e. set a correct market price and properly allocate resources to the production of that commodity.

3.) Which of the following best describes the free rider problem?
   a. An outdoor rock concert where some portion of the audience has not paid, successfully evading the concert's security guards.
   b. Shoplifting and employee theft.
   c. Government programs which give away free food and clothing to low income families.
   d. Commercial free public television where it is impossible to determine which households are actually watching the station's programs.

4.) The free rider problem greatly complicates efforts to deal with negative consumption externalities, because
   a. there is no generally accepted payment system that would allow consumers to pay for the pollution damage they are causing.
   b. it is impossible to specifically identify who is consuming the commodity.
   c. people have no economic incentive to change their behavior since their actions will not affect the problem one way or the other.
   d. consumers who are free riders feel that the government should properly be the agency that pays for their pollution.
   e. none of the above.

5.) When comparing the regulatory approach of government to market-oriented methods of controlling pollution
   a. governmental regulations and standards are more economically efficient because they apply equally to all affected parties (i.e., firms and/or consumers).
   b. governmental regulations and standards are preferred, since they generally do not result in higher prices for the commodity.
   c. governmental regulations and standards are less efficient than market-oriented methods, since they do not take into account differences in firms or consumers and their ability to cleanup.
   d. governmental regulations and standards increase firms' incentives to develop new and improved technologies for dealing with pollution.
   e. none of the above.

6.) When externalities are present (either positive or negative), appropriate governmental policy would be to
   a. tax both positive and negative externalities.
   b. tax positive externalities and subsidize negative externalities.
   c. subsidize positive externalities and tax negative externalities.
   d. subsidize both positive and negative externalities.
   e. pass a law effectively prohibiting both kinds of externalities.

7.) Concerning the economically optimal level of pollution cleanup
   a. society should try as hard as it can to eliminate the pollution entirely (for obvious reasons).
   b. society should cleanup to the point as determined by the best available technology.
   c. society should cleanup to the point where the most pollution can be cleaned up for the lowest cost.
   d. society should cleanup as much as it can based upon its ability and willingness to pay for the cleanup.
   e. society should cleanup to the point where the marginal cost of cleaning up pollution just equals the marginal benefits associated with that extra level of cleanup.

8.) Concerning the economically optimal level of pollution cleanup
   a. society should cleanup more if the marginal cost of preventing pollution (MCP) increases.
   b. society should cleanup more if the marginal cost of pollution damage (MCD) increases.
   c. society should cleanup less if the marginal cost of preventing pollution (MCP) increases.
   d. society should cleanup more whenever the pollution technology becomes more effective.
   e. both (b) and (c).

9.) When a tax per unit of pollution emitted is levied on firms
   a. polluting firms will pay the tax as long as the tax exceeds the marginal cost of pollution prevention.
   b. polluting firms will cleanup as long as the tax exceeds the marginal cost of pollution prevention, then after that point they will pay the tax.
   c. those firms whose marginal cost of pollution prevention is lower than the tax will cleanup their pollution, and those firms whose marginal cost of pollution prevention is greater than the tax will pay the tax.
   d. most firms will end up paying the tax, since it is less expensive than cleaning up the pollution.
   e. both (b) and (c).

10.) Suppose the government allows polluting firms in a particular industry to participate in a market for emissions-reduction credits. As a result, we would likely see
   a. the biggest firms (with the most financial assets) buy up the most emissions-reduction credits.
   b. older, more established firms selling most of the emission-reduction credits based on the initial allocation of credits.
   c. the firms with the lowest marginal cost of pollution prevention schedules would cleanup the most and sell the most emission-reduction credits.
   d. most firms cleaning up to the same degree as they would under governmental legislation which mandates specific pollution limits.
   e. the emissions-reduction credit market being most widely used when the marginal cost of pollution prevention schedules for the firms in the affected industry are all about the same.

11.) Efforts to deal with global negative externalities like global warming
   a. were agreed upon at the Earth Summit in 1992, with all nations agreeing to reduce carbon dioxide emissions by twenty percent.
   b. are not subject to the free rider effect, since the earth as a whole is a closed ecological system and no country has any incentive not to go along with an emissions reduction program.
   c. must in the future deal primarily with the developed countries which have the greatest per capita carbon dioxide emissions.
   d. are likely to be opposed by many of the lesser developed countries that are still in the process of industrializing their economies.

(assume that the initial position is represented by MCP_0 and MCD_0)

Dollars of Costs/Benefits

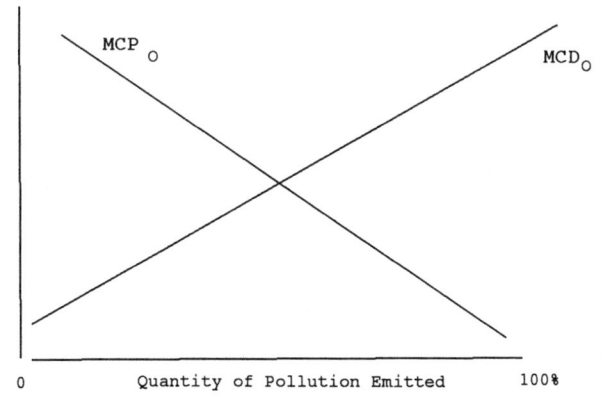

[Graph showing MCP_0 curve rising from origin and MCD_0 curve falling, intersecting in the middle. X-axis: Quantity of Pollution Emitted, from 0 to 100%]

Please refer to the graph above for the next 3 questions.

The graph above represents the marginal cost of pollution prevention curves and the marginal cost of damage from pollution curves for water pollution coming from a paper mill on the Clark's Fork River, with an initial equilibrium position at the intersection of MCP_0 and MCD_0.

12.) What will be the new optimum level of pollution if fishing on the Clark's Fork River suddenly becomes much better because of sustained efforts by the Department of Natural Resources (DNR)?
   a. The marginal cost of pollution prevention increases, shifting the MCP curve to the right, increasing the optimum level of pollution.
   b. The marginal cost of pollution prevention decreases, shifting the MCP curve to the left, decreasing the optimum level of pollution.
   c. The marginal cost of damage from pollution increases, shifting the MCD curve to the left, decreasing the optimum level of pollution.
   d. The marginal cost of damage from pollution decreases, shifting the MCD curve to the right, increasing the optimum level of pollution.
   e. None of the above, since changes in the the quality of fishing should not affect how much pollution is cleaned up.

13.) Again, referring to the preceding diagram, what will be the new optimum level of pollution if additional filtering of the effluent at the paper mill must be done to eliminate a potentially dangerous pollutant?
   a. The marginal cost of pollution prevention increases, shifting the MCP curve to the right, increasing the optimum level of pollution.
   b. The marginal cost of pollution prevention decreases, shifting the MCP curve to the left, decreasing the optimum level of pollution.
   c. The marginal cost of damage from pollution increases, shifting the MCD curve to the left, decreasing the optimum level of pollution.
   d. The marginal cost of damage from pollution decreases, shifting the MCD curve to the right, increasing the optimum level of pollution.
   e. None of the above, since the additional filtering that is required should not affect how much pollution is cleaned up.

14.) Again, referring to the preceding diagram, what will be the new optimum level of pollution if a new technology is developed which dramatically lowers the cost of cleaning up the paper mill's effluent and, at the same time, the population downstream of the paper mill increases and along with the increased population is an increased interest in water-based recreation?
   a. The optimum level of pollution would increase.
   b. The optimum level of pollution would decrease.
   c. The optimum level of pollution would remain unchanged.
   d. Unable to determine the effect on the optimal level of pollution since the magnitude of the changes is unknown.

$ |
  |
  |
  |
  |
  |
  |
  |
  |
  |_____
              Quantity

15.) Referring to the diagram above, what is the **net economic cost** of the negative production externality?
   a. the area defined by ABD.
   b. the area defined by ACD.
   c. the area defined by BDE.
   d. the area defined by BCD.
   e. can't be determined, since the concept of net economic cost is subjective.

Discussion Questions

1.) How would a carbon tax (a tax which is levied on the amount of carbon emissions associated with a particular fuel) address the problem of global warming? Would such a tax be more efficient than government regulations which have specific carbon emission standards?

2.) Many environmentalists take the position that pollution should be cleaned up to the maximum extent possible as determined by the latest technology. As an economist, how would you respond to their position?

3.) It is said that a tax on pollution internalizes the cleanup cost for the affected firms. What is meant by that statement, and is it a good idea to internalize such costs?

233

4.) Is higher education an example of a positive externality? Explain and indicate what appropriate public policy would be if it is.

5.) Only a small percentage of taxpayers are able to actually attend professional football games. Of course, a larger percentage of taxpayers are football fans, yet it may be the case that a majority of taxpayers and the population at large are not interested in what happens on the football field. If that is the case, on what grounds could a publicly-financed football stadium be justified? Much the same question could be asked about art museums and airports.
Hint: consider the role of positive externalities.

Answers and Solutions to Problems and Exercises

Completing Statements from the List of Terms

1.) Transactions Costs
2.) Social Benefits
3.) Externalities
4.) Negative Externality
5.) Marginal Cost of Pollution Damage
6.) Emissions Trading
7.) Free Rider
8.) Private Marginal Benefits
9.) Social Costs
10.) Positive Externality
11.) Property Rights
12.) Private Marginal Costs
13.) Marginal Cost of Pollution Prevention
14.) Market Failure

Problems

An Application of Marginal Analysis -- Cleaning Up the Environment

Table 10-1

Sewage Treatment in Moorhead

Percent of Clean-up	Total Cost Required to to Achieve a Given Level of Cleanup TC	Marginal Costs MC	Total benefits Perceived by Residents for a Given Level of Cleanup TB	Marginal Benefits MB	Total Net Benefits TB - TC
0%	$ 0	$ -	$ 500,000	$ -	$ 500,000
10%	$ 300,000	$ 300,000	$ 2,000,000	$ 1,500,000	$ 1,700,000
20%	$ 800,000	$ 500,000	$ 4,000,000	$ 2,000,000	$ 3,200,000
30%	$ 1,500,000	$ 700,000	$ 6,500,000	$ 2,500,000	$ 5,000,000
40%	$ 2,500,000	$ 1,000,000	$ 8,500,000	$ 2,000,000	$ 6,000,000
50%	$ 3,700,000	$ 1,200,000	$10,000,000	$ 1,500,000	$ 6,300,000
60%	$ 5,000,000	$ 1,300,000	$11,000,000	$ 1,000,000	$ 6,000,000
70%	$ 6,500,000	$ 1,500,000	$11,600,000	$ 600,000	$ 5,100,000
80%	$ 8,500,000	$ 2,000,000	$12,000,000	$ 400,000	$ 3,500,000
90%	$ 11,000,000	$ 2,500,000	$12,300,000	$ 300,000	$ 1,300,000
100%	$ 14,000,000	$ 3,000,000	$12,500,000	$ 200,000	-$ 1,500,000

1.) **Calculate the marginal cost and marginal benefits:**

2.) At what point in the cleanup process are marginal costs equal to marginal benefits? **somewhere between 50% - 60%**

at the 50% cleanup level, the marginal benefits of $1.5 million are slightly larger than the marginal costs of $1.2 million so that level of cleanup adds to society's net welfare.

at the 60% cleanup level, the marginal benefits of $1.0 million are slightly lower than the marginal costs of $1.3 million so that level of cleanup decreases society's net welfare.

3.) How would you explain to someone who has never had an economics course before why that amount of cleanup represents an optimum for this particular city. Although it would be difficult to meet anyone who has not taken an economics course, one way to explain the procedure is to relate it in terms of a scale which measures "benefits" and costs against each other. Whenever the extra benefits associated with a specific action exceed the extra costs, then net positive benefits are created, and society is better off for having taken the action. On the other hand, if the extra benefits of an action are less than the extra costs, then there would be a net loss of benefits, and welfare and society are worse off for having undertaken that action. Logically, society will continue this process until marginal benefits just equal marginal costs.

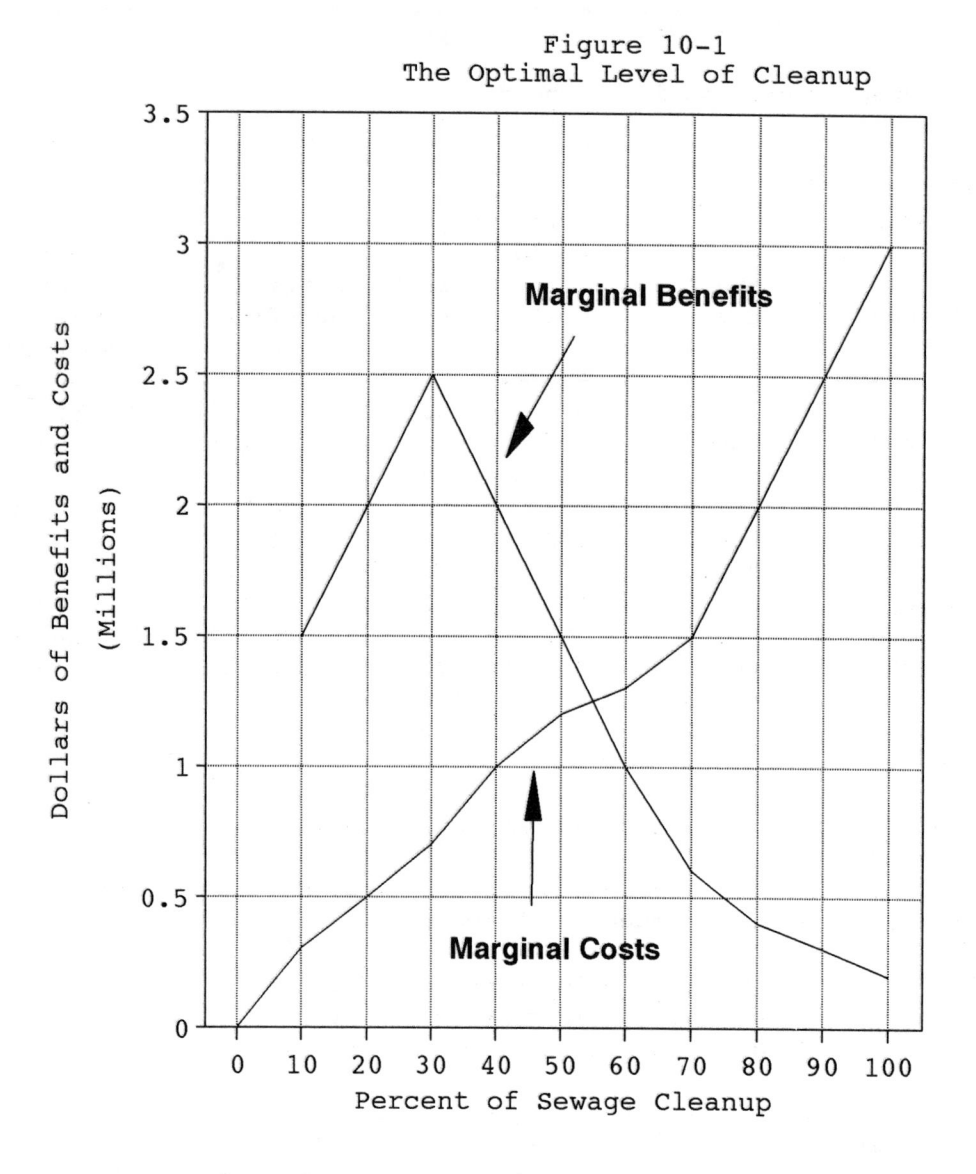

Figure 10-1
The Optimal Level of Cleanup

Figure 10-2
The Optimal Level of Cleanup

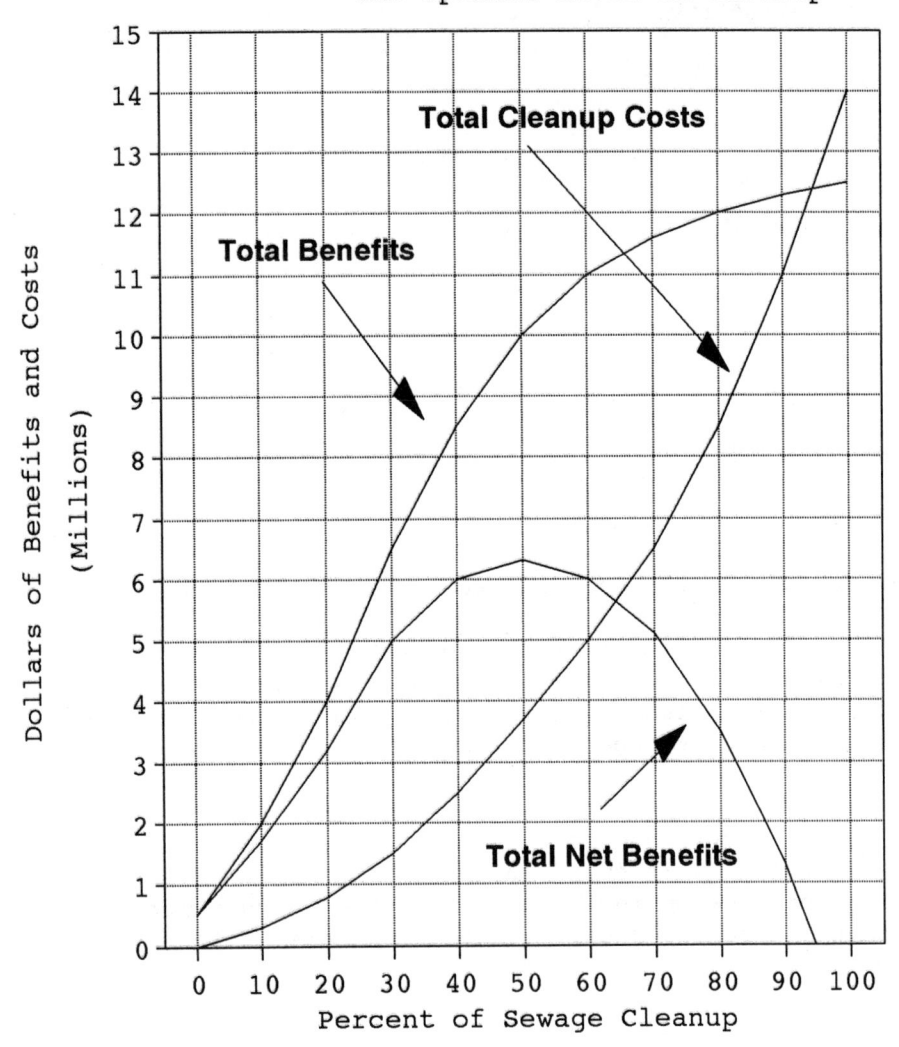

6.) The figure below illustrates what typically-shaped marginal cost and marginal benefits curves might look like. Their intersection determines the point of optimality.

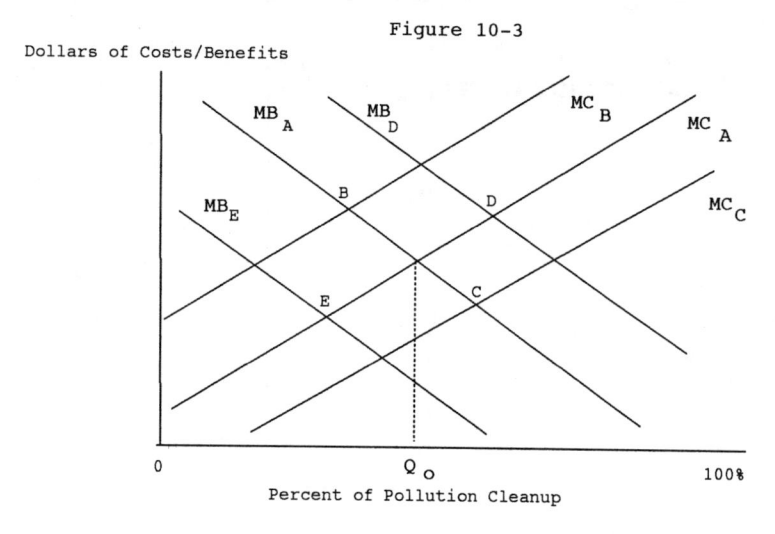

Figure 10-3

Dollars of Costs/Benefits (y-axis)
Percent of Pollution Cleanup (x-axis, from 0 to 100%)

Curves labeled: MB_A, MB_D, MB_E, MC_A, MC_B, MC_C, with intersection points B, C, D, E and original equilibrium at Q_O.

a. Optimum cleanup, Q_O -- the original equilibrium position.

b. Increased marginal costs associated with each level of pollution Denoted (B). **Marginal cost curve shifts to the left -- the optimum level of pollution cleanup decreases. It is now more expensive to cleanup than before, so society engages in less cleanup activity.**

c. Decreased marginal costs associated with each level of pollution. Denoted (C). **Marginal cost curve shifts to the right -- optimum level of pollution cleanup increases. It is now less expensive to cleanup than before, so society engages in more of that type of activity.**

d. Larger marginal benefits associated with each level of pollution. Denoted (D). **Marginal benefits curve shifts to the right -- optimum level of pollution cleanup increases. Society now obtains more marginal benefits from each level of cleanup than before, so society now wants to engage in more cleanup activity.**

e. Smaller marginal benefits associated with each level of pollution. Denoted (E). **Marginal benefits curve shifts to the left -- optimum level of pollution cleanup decreases. Society now obtains less marginal benefits from each level of cleanup than before, so society now wants to engage in less cleanup activity.**

Comparing the Economic Efficiency of a Tax on Pollution Versus Governmental Standards

Figure 10-4

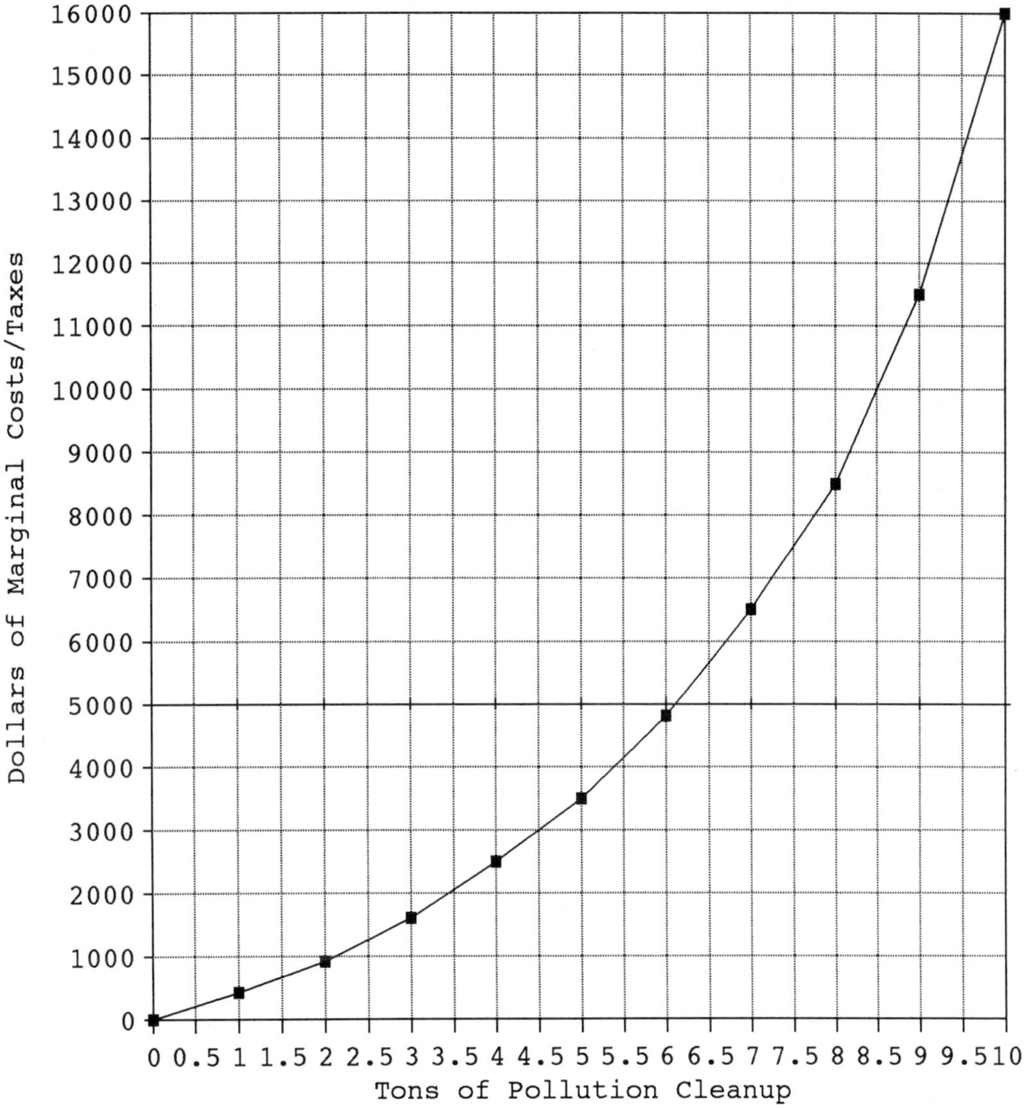

Tons of cleanup with pollution tax of $1,000/ton: **2 tons**
Total cleanup costs associated with that level of cleanup: **$ 1,300**
Tons of cleanup with pollution tax of $7,000/ton: **7 tons**
Total cleanup costs associated with that level of cleanup: **$ 20,200**

Required pollution tax: **$ 5,400 per ton**

True/False Statements

1.) **True.** The negative externality means that some costs associated with the production of the commodity are incurred by third parties (the public at large). The full costs of production should reflect all costs, not just private costs.

2.) **False.** Those individuals attending institutions of higher education are generating benefits for society as a whole. However, since those social benefits are not incorporated into individual student preferences, the actual amount of demand is less than optimal. This could be corrected by a subsidy to students which would shift the demand for higher education to the right.

3.) **True.** When externalities are present, there is a divergence between marginal private benefits and marginal social benefits on the demand side, or a divergence between marginal private costs and marginal social costs on the supply side of the market. Since markets are unable to take these differences into account (by definition of externality), the outcomes of private buyers and sellers can no longer be considered optimal from society's point of view.

4.) **False.** Negative externalities merely raise the full cost of production, reflecting the impact on society. It would be difficult, if not impossible, to state that such an increase in costs would tip the welfare scales in such a way that the commodity would no longer yield any net benefits. As long as people were willing to pay the new price which reflects the full cost of production, then they must feel the purchase of the commodity is worthwhile and enhances their well-being.

5.) **True.** The private consumption of such a commodity has a negative impact on society as a whole and, on a net basis, the individual values an additional unit of the commodity more than society as a whole.

6.) **True.** Since consumers are not compensated for the benefits they are conferring onto society at large, the demand for the commodity will not be optimal from society's viewpoint. The marginal social benefit of the last unit consumed exceeds the corresponding private marginal benefit. Too few resources are being allocated to this commodity, and society should implement a policy to increase the demand for the commodity.

7.) **False.** Many, if not most, of the problems associated with externalities would either disappear or be resolved by affected parties if property rights were better defined. But there would still be problems associated with high transactions costs and imperfect information about property right violations.

8.) **True.** High transactions costs (lawyers fees, court fees, expert witness fees) may well exceed any expected benefits associated with getting rid of the negative externality and make one reconsider initiating a legal action. Thus, small, everyday nuisances typically persist in spite of people complaining about them.

9.) **True.** Why should a commuter stop driving to work when the smog problem will be the same whether he/she drives or not? Besides, no one in authority knows whether you commute to work or not, so there is no way to identify you as someone who contributes to this problem.

10.) **False.** If the tax applied was exactly equal to the social costs imposed on society, then the social cost has been effectively internalized, and there would be a return back to an allocatively efficient solution. Practically, it would be extremely difficult to know what the full social costs would be, so, in practice, the answer to the question may well be true.

11.) **True.** Government regulations generally require that all affected parties (all firms or perhaps all units of output) meet or exceed a set standard, regardless of individual circumstances. On the other hand, the imposition of a tax per unit of pollution allows each individual decision-maker some latitude in deciding whether to clean-up or pay the tax. Firms that can cleanup cheaply and efficiently will do so, and firms that face higher cleanup costs will pay the tax. As mentioned in your text, the regulatory approach may be necessary if the risks or dangers associated with too much pollution are such that society must carefully control the amount of pollution.

12.) **False.** I don't think so! The optimum level of clean up depends upon the marginal costs of cleanup and how much society values the different cleanup levels. The optimum level of cleanup (the one which maximizes society's overall level of satisfaction) would tend to low if it were very expensive to cleanup the pollution, and/or society didn't really care whether or not the pollution was cleaned up.

13.) **True.** At that point, the extra cost associated with cleaning up an extra unit of pollution is just equal to the marginal cost of damage associated with the pollution. Any more cleanup would generate more extra costs than benefits, and any less cleanup would mean that the extra benefits from cleaning up would be larger than the extra costs associated with that last marginal unit.

14.) **False.** If there were now more economic damage associated with various levels of pollution, then there would be more cleanup than before, because there would be more benefits associated with getting rid of the pollution. Put differently, firms would equate their marginal costs of cleanup (pollution prevention) with a higher MCD. Since their MCD is higher, they could go up further on their MCP curve to find the optimum amount of pollution control.

15.) **True.** If the estimate of social costs is indeed accurate, then the tax would be equivalent to the social costs and the commodity's supply curve would shift to the left by the appropriate amount to fully reflect the full cost (private plus social costs) of production.

16.) **False** The emission trading plan is economically efficient because the firms with the lowest cleanup costs will tend to cleanup the most, not necessarily the firms with the greatest financial resources or the deepest pockets.

Multiple-Choice

1.) a   2.) b   3.) d   4.) b   5.) c   6.) c

7.) e   8.) e   9.) e   10.) c   11.) d   12.) c

13.) a   14.) d   15.) d

Discussion Questions

1.) Using the theory and analysis developed in this chapter, a carbon tax would be the most economically efficient way to address the problem of carbon emissions into the atmosphere. Those activities and fuels which contributed the most carbon would be the most heavily taxed, thus giving incentives for both producers and consumers to use other alternatives which are less carbon-intensive. A tax would tend to maximize the flexibility and choices available, whereas government regulations (prescribing specific technologies or setting specific standards) would disregard individual differences in abilities to change and adapt to the new circumstances. Even in the case of global warming (or perhaps especially in the case of global warming), society's goal is still to carry out the decrease in emissions in the least costly fashion.

2.) The law of increasing marginal costs comes into play here. It becomes more and more costly to cleanup pollution as you approach the point of no pollution whatsoever. Water pollution provides an excellent example of this. The first 20 or 40 % of cleanup can be accomplished using inexpensive primary screening techniques. Clean-up past that point involves the use of increasingly sophisticated methods, aeration, chemical treatment, etc. To improve water quality from a 92 % level to a 97 % level may be very expensive indeed. On the other hand, the law of diminishing marginal utility suggests that the perceived marginal benefits that society obtains from using cleaner water resources decreases as cleanup continues. Thus, as cleanup continues, it becomes more expensive, and society values the additional benefits less and less. Marginal analysis suggests that the optimum level of pollution would be the point where the extra cost of cleaning up the last percent of pollution would just be equal to the marginal benefits derived from that last percent of cleanup. It would be a very rare case that society would want to cleanup to the maximum extent possible.

3.) In one sense, the imposition of the tax puts a market price on pollution, since the firm must pay the tax for each unit that it pollutes. The cost of the pollution is thus internalized in that it becomes similar to all the other costs the firms must pay and, best of all, the firm will address its pollution costs in a least cost, economically efficient manner.

4.) One would expect college students and graduates to provide leadership for society in their role as citizens. To that extent, their education can be looked on as a positive externality and, as your text suggests, appropriate public policy is to subsidize positive externalities, since we have less than the optimum amount of those commodities or activities.

5.) Having a professional sports franchise is thought to be a necessary part of a progressive city's infrastructure. It helps attract both firms and potential residents to a city. The games themselves generate significant amounts of spending, some directly related to football and some only indirectly related. These football-related spending injections create jobs and employment, benefiting the community at large.

Summary

Since externalities pose one of the greatest challenges to the effective functioning of the market system, this chapter is extremely important in helping you understand how externalities affect the demand and supply of commodities and how their impacts can be offset. In addition, some valuable perspectives on the economically optimum amount of pollution are presented. Even a strong environmental advocate should be aware of the conceptual framework that is introduced in this chapter.

Cleaning up pollution is an expensive proposition and becomes progressively more expensive as more of it is undertaken. At some point, the question has to be asked whether or not additional units of cleanup are worth the benefits that society will receive from that cleanup. Perhaps, more to the point, society may not value the ecological benefits associated with cleaning up as much as environmentalists would like. If it is felt that society is not addressing various pollution problems as much as it "should," then more needs to be done in the way of informing everyone about those benefits. Obviously, there is considerable controversy about exactly this issue.

Related to this issue is the use of markets and market-oriented policies to reduce the total cost of cleaning up pollution. Economists are generally in favor of establishing emissions-reduction credits and markets and the implementation of taxes and subsidies to deal with externalities. Many environonmentalists are not in favor of taxing pollution, since it allows firms to pay the tax and continue polluting (a so called license to pollute), but to an economist, a tax on pollution internalizes the externality and provides firms with flexibility in finding the least cost approach to the pollution question. The whole issue of whether we as a society should utilize governmental regulations/standards as the main policy approach to pollution as opposed to more market-oriented approaches is a significant one, one in which each of us has a financial stake.

Finally, one of the "ultimate" externalities, global warming, continues to generate discussion. The economic costs associated with reducing carbon emissions are at the core of the discussion. How much should society spend or sacrifice to meet a potential threat of unknown magnitude? Indeed, some have argued that there is no threat at all. Is a world-wide carbon tax the most effective means of reducing carbon dioxide emissions? Will governmental standards be adopted? This chapter provides you with a brief background to help guide you through complex issues like this one.

Chapter 11
Factors of Production: Productivity and Income

Overview of the Chapter

The market model provides some valuable insights into the relationship between the economic productivity of factors of production and the incomes that they receive. Differing market structures play a role here too, and their impact is explored in this chapter. After reading this chapter, you will have a better understanding of the underlying factors which determine the employment of the various factors of production and the factor proportions that firms use.

Using labor as an example, a profit maximizing firm will hire units of labor as long as the value of each additional worker's productivity is greater than the wage that has to be paid. For a given wage level, increases in the marginal revenue product (MRP), whether the result of an increase in worker productivity or an increase in the price of output, will motivate a firm to hire more labor. Similarly, decreases in the wage level will result in more employment, just as wage increases will lead to less employment for a given MRP.

The factor market, through the interaction of demand and supply, determines the price of a specific factor and the amount of a factor that will be employed. The market responds to changes in the productivity of a factor and the price of the output as well as the willingness of the owners of a factor to offer their services to the market. The equilibrium price and quantity employed of a factor will determine the total income paid to owners of that factor and that, in turn, answers the distribution question.

In a multiple factor setting, firms can attain the least cost method of production by comparing the factors' marginal physical production (MPP) to their price per unit. If one factor generates more additional output per dollar than another factor, then more of that factor will be employed and less of the other factors. A firm has achieved an "optimal," least cost combination of factor inputs when each factor's MPP per dollar is the same for all factors.

The initial model for analyzing the factors which affect the equilibrium price and quantity of the factor assumes perfect competition on both the demand and supply sides of the market. Factors will be hired up to the point where the marginal revenue product associated with the last factor employed equals the marginal cost of employing that factor.

There are several different cases involving different market structures on both sides of the factor market which can be analyzed. The cases involve monopoly in the product market, monopsony in the factor market, monopoly in the factor market, and the case of bilateral monopoly (monopoly in the product market and monopsony in the factor market). In each of these cases, the imperfections in either the product or factor market have significant impacts on the final equilibrium solutions that are obtained.

Learning Objectives

After completing this chapter, you should be sure that you are able to:

- discuss the relationship that exists between marginal physical product (MPP) and total physical product (TPP).

- explain the process by which a firm can achieve the least-cost combination of factors of production.

- understand the concept of marginal revenue product (MRP) and how the MRP and the wage rate interact to determine how many workers to hire.

- understand how wages are determined in the labor market and, in a more general sense, how the price of any factor is determined.

- discuss the advantages and disadvantages of an efficient and perfectly competitive factor market, how it determines factor incomes, and issues of fairness.

- modify the perfectly competitive factor market model to account for monopoly in the product market, monopsony in the factor market, and monopoly in the factor market.

- understand the case of bilateral monopoly and why both the wage and quantity of labor hired are indeterminate.

Self Evaluation

List of Terms

Bilateral Monopoly
Compensating Wage Differential
Derived Demand
Marginal Physical Product
Marginal Product
Marginal Revenue Product
Monopsony

For the statements below, fill in the term from the list above which provides the best fit.

1.) The extra output associated with the employment of an additional worker is called _____. It is also referred to as _____.

2.) Generally, the demand for workers of all types is dependent upon the market demand for the product, and that is best described as a _____.

3.) The term _____ is applicable in markets where there is only a single buyer.

4.) A market situation where a single seller faces a single buyer is called a _____.

5.) Workers who are employed in the toxic waste disposal sector are likely to need a _____.

6.) The _____ is the value of an additional worker's productivity.

Problems

The Firm's Production Function and Equilibrium in the Factor Market

QUESTION: "How does the firm determine the optimal (most profitable) number of workers to hire?"

ANSWER: By utilizing marginal analysis to compare the extra cost of each worker with his/her corresponding value of output that he/she contribute to the firm (value of marginal product).

In the short run, one of the most important decisions that must be made by a firm involves the determination of the optimal amount of the variable factor, in most cases, labor. Firms will not attain maximum profits if they can't determine the "correct" number of workers to hire. We are assuming that all factor inputs, with the exception of the labor input, are fixed in the short run. The relationship that exists between various amounts of labor and total output is illustrated by the firm's production function.

In this problem, the firm is assumed to be selling in a perfectly competitive market in which the firm has no market power, taking the market price as given. Similarly, the factor market for labor is also assumed to be perfectly competitive, with the firm being able to hire as many units of labor as it wishes at the going wage rate.

You are given the following production function:

Table 11-1

Units of the Variable Input (Labor = L)	Total Physical Product (TPP)	Marginal Physical Product (MPP) $MP_p = \frac{\Delta TPP}{\Delta L}$	Marginal Revenue Product (MRP) $(P_{output} \times MPP)$	Wage	Total Revenue TR $P_{output} \times TPP$	Total Fixed Cost Plus Total Variable Cost (Wage × Units of L) TC	TR − TC Total Profit Tπ
0	0						
1	16						
2	34						
3	49						
4	62						
5	73						
6	83						
7	90						
8	95						
9	98						
10	100						

Assumptions:
Fixed Capital Expense (K) = $200   (the firm's overhead expense)
Wages = $ 20   (determined in the labor market)
P_{output} = $ 5   (determined in the final output market)

Plot the total physical product (TPP) and the marginal physical product (MPP) on the following graph. Indicate on the graph, the slope of the production function and its relationsh, on the graph, the slope of the production function and its relationship to the marginal productivity of the variable factor.

Figure 11-1

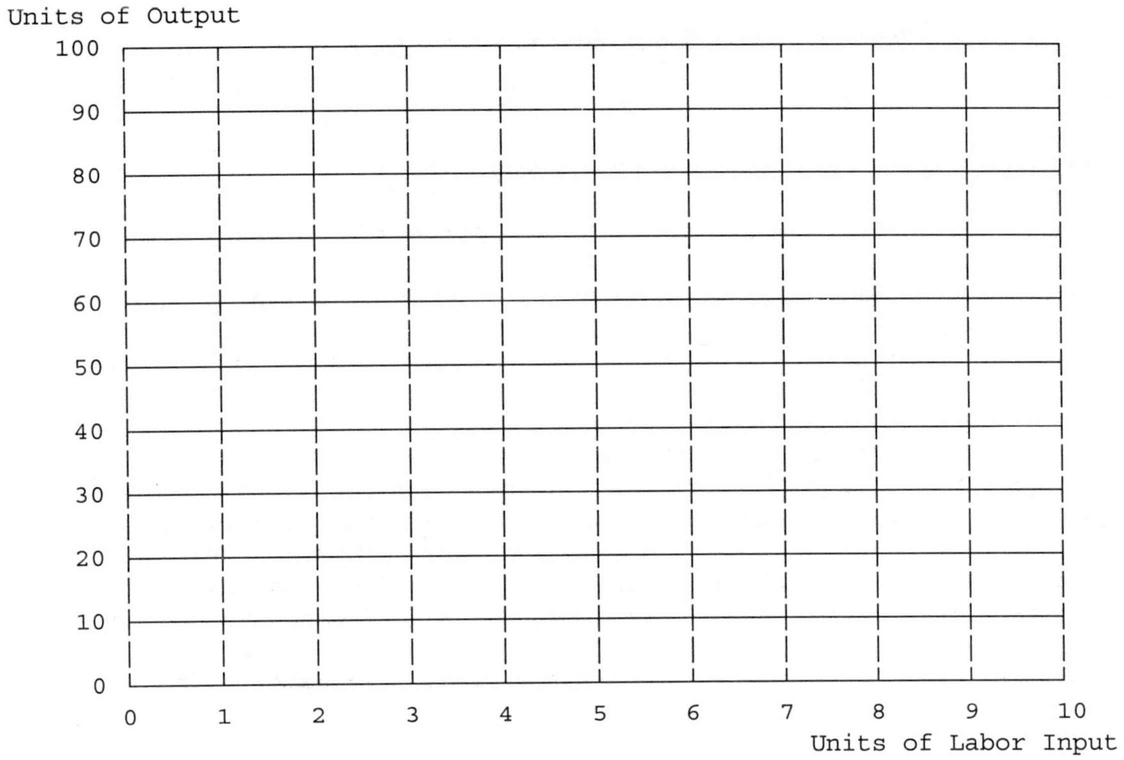
Units of Output
100
90
80
70
60
50
40
30
20
10
0
0
1
2
3
4
5
6
7
8
9
10
Units of Labor Input

On the graph below, plot the firm's marginal revenue product (MRP) and the wage paid. Indicate the optimum number of workers on the graph.

Figure 11-2

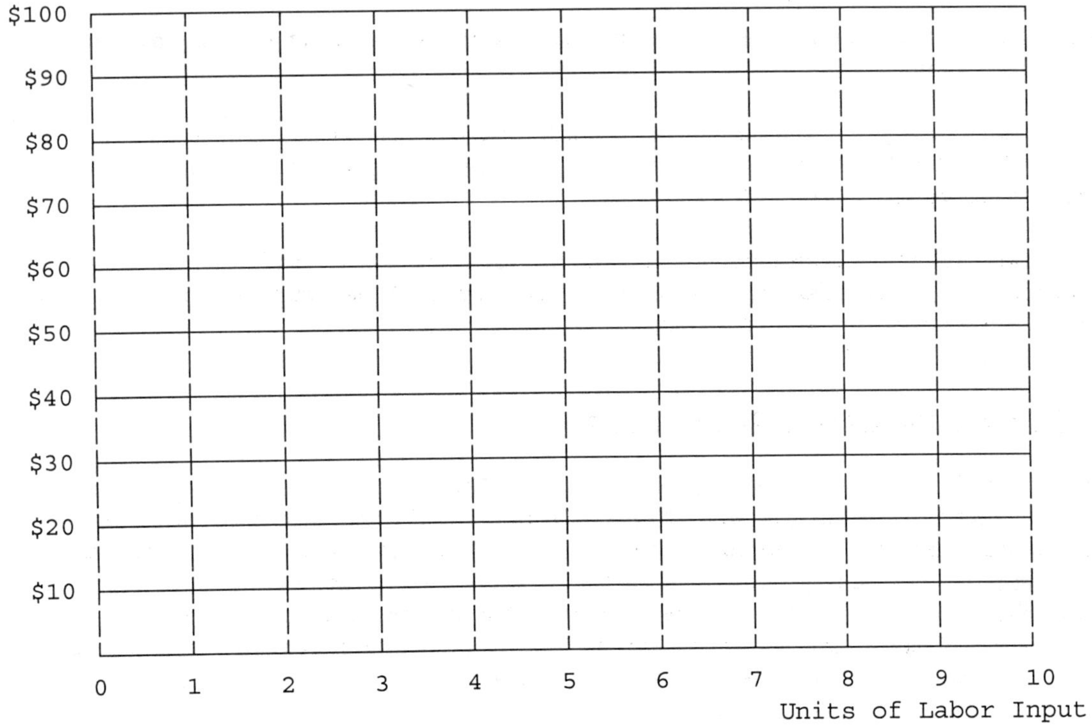
$100
$90
$80
$70
$60
$50
$40
$30
$20
$10
0
1
2
3
4
5
6
7
8
9
10
Units of Labor Input

What is the optimum number of workers for this firm? ____

Determine the effect on the optimum number of workers of:

- changing the wage to $ 30   ===> Optimum # Workers ____
- changing the wage to $ 12   ===> Optimum # Workers ____
- changing the price of output to $ 7   ===> Optimum # Workers ____
- changing the price of output to $ 3   ===> Optimum # Workers ____

(For each case, refer to the initial assumptions, do not cumulate the changes)

In each case, if the optimum number of workers has been hired, the firm will be maximizing its profits at that point. In other words, if the firm achieves equilibrium with respect to hiring the various factors of production, it will attain its goal of maximizing total profits. Check your understanding of the production function and its underlying economic relationships by circling the correct response in the following statements.

If wages increase, firms will tend to hire (**more, less, the same**) units of labor.

If wages decrease, firms will tend to hire (**more, less, the same**) units of labor.

If the price of output increases, firms will tend to hire (**more, less, the same**) units of labor.

If the price of output decreases, firms will tend to hire (**more, less, the same**) units of labor.

If worker productivity increases (i.e., each worker has a larger marginal product associated with his/her labor than before), firms will tend to hire (**more, less, the same**) units of labor.

If worker productivity decreases (i.e., each worker has a smaller marginal product associated with his/her labor than before), firms will tend to hire (**more, less, the same**) units of labor.

The MRP Under Imperfect Competition

The situation illustrated by the data in Table 11-1 reflected perfect competition in both the output and input markets. The firm could sell as much as it wanted at the existing market price, and it could employ as much labor as it wanted at the going wage rate. Let's see what effect imperfect competition has on the employment decision. Assume that a firm has a downward sloping demand curve as shown on the following page, and that the labor market is perfectly competitive as before.

Table 11-2

Units of the Variable Input (Labor = L)	Total Physical Product (TPP)	Product Price (P)	Marginal Physical Productivity (MPP)	Total Revenue Product (TRP)	Marginal Revenue Product (MRP)	Wage
0	0	$10.00	—	0	—	$20
1	16	9.20	16	147.20	147.20	20
2	34	8.30	18	282.20	135.00	20
3	49	7.55	15	369.95	87.75	20
4	62	6.90	13	427.80	57.85	20
5	73	6.35	11	463.55	35.75	20
6	83	5.85	10	485.55	22.00	20
7	90	5.50	7	495.00	9.45	20
8	95	5.25	5	498.75	3.75	20
9	98	5.10	3	499.80	1.05	20
10	100	5.00	2	500.00	0.20	20

Note: The MRP is calculated in this case by taking the change in total revenue rather than multiplying the price of the product by the corresponding marginal physical product. The MRP has to take into account the decrease in price that occurs on all previous units.

Fill in the remaining columns in the table above. On the following graph, plot the firm's MRP (under imperfect competition) and the wage rate. Indicate on your graph how many units of labor would be employed.

Based on your diagram, what is the effect of imperfect competition on the MRP curve of the firm?

Figure 11-3

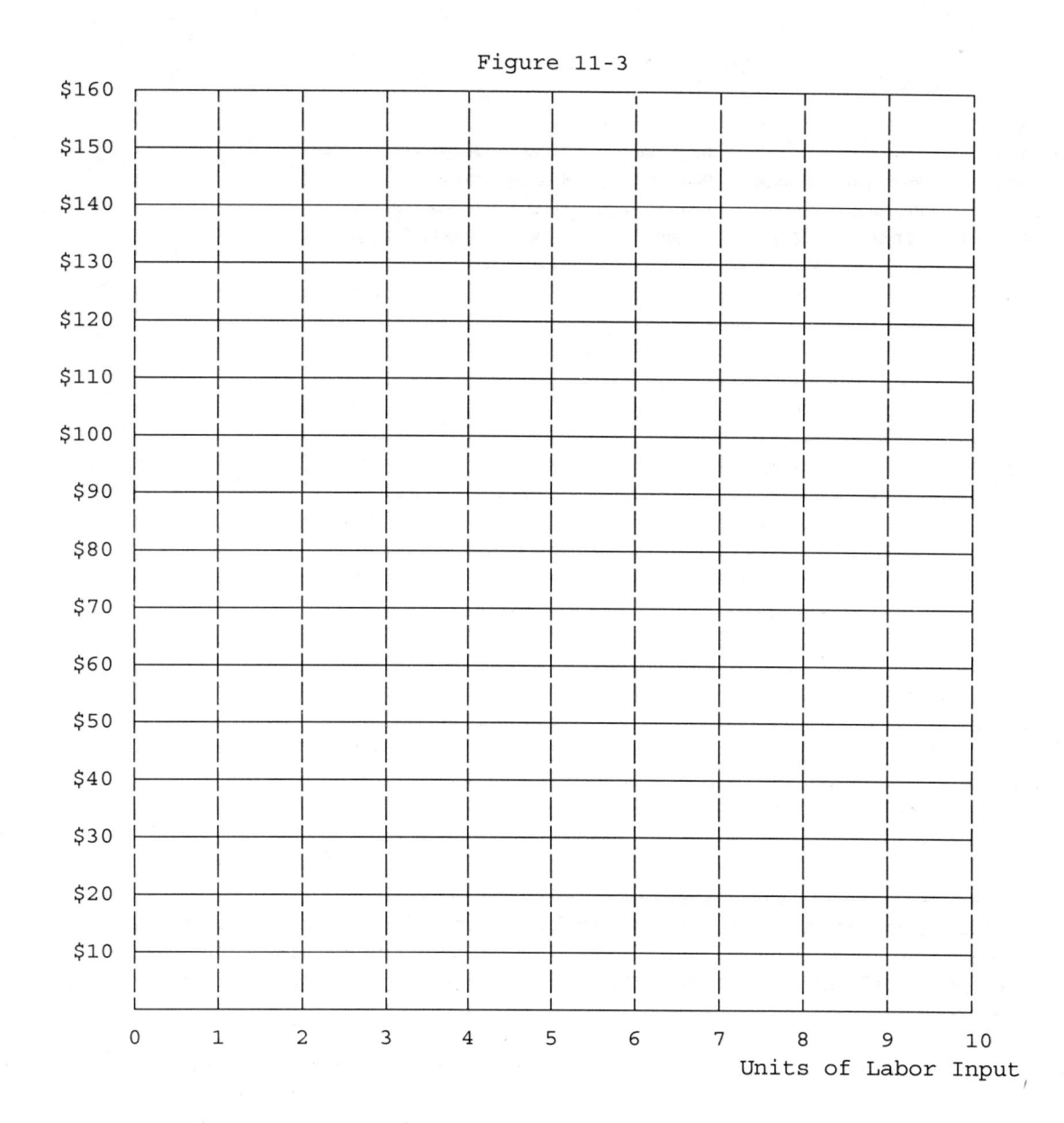

It is also possible to examine the effect of an imperfect labor market on the hiring decision. If the labor market is imperfectly competitive, then the supply curve of labor will be upward sloping -- meaning that more units of labor can hired only if the wage increases. Suppose we return to the original case with perfect competition on the output side and an imperfectly competitive labor market. Fill in the remaining columns in the table below and graph the MRP and the supply curve and marginal cost of labor. What is the optimum number of workers that should be employed?

Table 11-3

Units of the Variable Input (Labor = L)	Total Physical Product (TPP)	Product Price (P)	Marginal Physical Productivity (MPP)	Marginal Revenue Product (MRP)	Wage	Total Wage Cost (Wage X L)	Marginal Cost of Labor
0	0	$5			$12		
1	16	5			15		
2	34	5			18		
3	49	5			21		
4	62	5			24		
5	73	5			27		
6	83	5			30		
7	90	5			33		
8	95	5			36		
9	98	5			39		
10	100	5			42		

Note that the marginal cost of labor is calculated by taking the change in the total wage costs from one unit of labor to another.

Figure 11-4

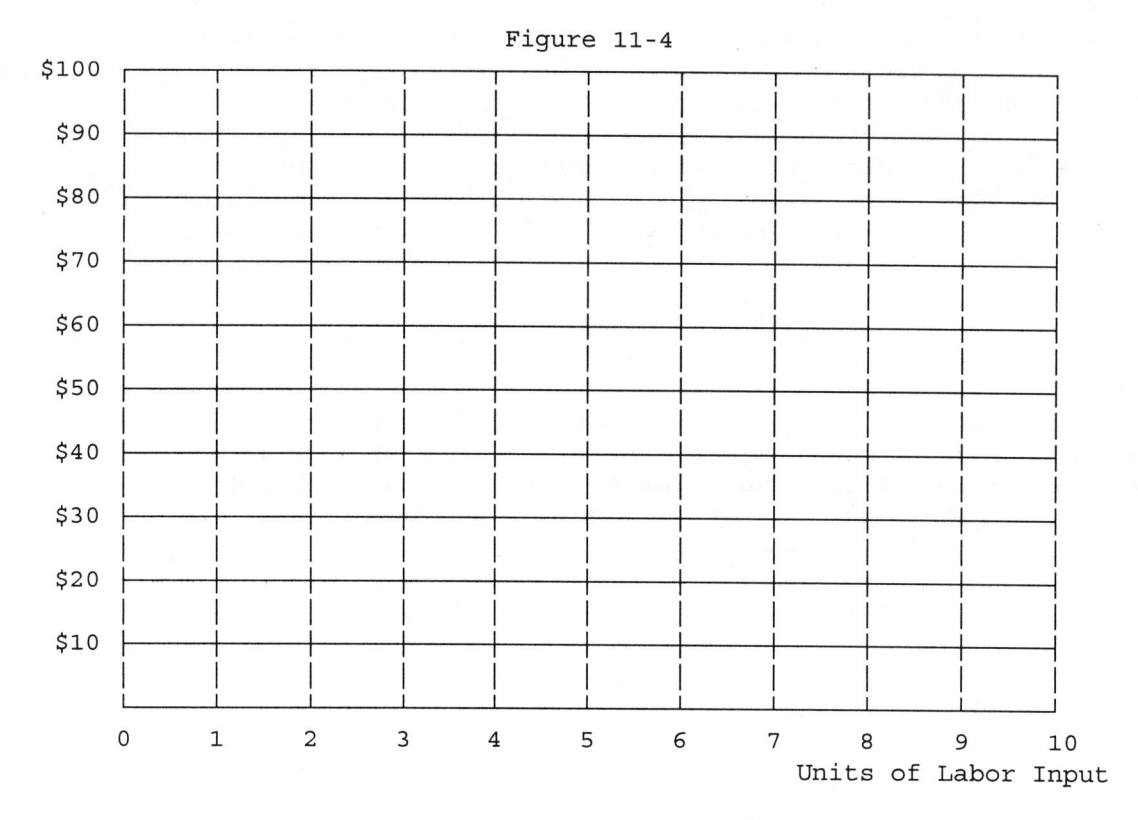

[Blank graph with y-axis labeled from $10 to $100 in increments of $10, and x-axis labeled "Units of Labor Input" from 0 to 10.]

Based on your diagram, what is the effect of imperfect competition in the factor market on the number of workers hired?

_____

True/False Statements

Indicate whether you think the statements below are true or false. These questions are designed to make you think about the concepts presented in the text. There may not be any easy clear-cut answers. Some thoughts about the answers are presented at the end of the chapter.

1.) _____ An increase in the price of the output will increase labor's marginal revenue product.

2.) _____ An increase in the wage rate will result in a firm hiring fewer units of labor.

3.) _____ Workers in dangerous or unpleasant jobs are paid more than their marginal revenue product would warrant, since they receive a compensating wage differential.

4.) _____ A monopolist in the output market will typically hire more workers than its perfectly competitive counterpart, since it faces less competitive pressures.

5.) _____ A monopsonist will pay its workers a wage that is less than the marginal revenue product of the workers.

6.) _____ Compared to a perfectly competitive labor market, a monopoly labor union will lead to less employment for its members.

7.) _____ The equilibrium wage that occurs in the case of a "bilateral monopoly" is higher than would exist in a perfectly competitive labor market.

8.) _____ Although a monopoly labor union has the market power to increase the total wages paid to its members, it is not possible that the deadweight efficiency loss associated with its monopoly power will exceed its members' gain in wages.

9.) _____ If the supply of labor is upward sloping, then the marginal cost of employing an additional worker is higher than the average wage paid.

Multiple-Choice Questions

Select the "best" answer from the alternatives provided.

1.) The marginal physical product (MPP) of labor
   a. is calculated by dividing the total output by the number of workers.
   b. can never be negative.
   c. always increases, then decreases.
   d. always declines when the firm experiences diminishing returns.

2.) A perfectly competitive firm which faces a perfectly competitive labor market would maximize its total profits by
   a. continuing to hire workers as long as MPP is greater than zero.
   b. hiring workers up to the point where MPP is at a maximum.
   c. hiring workers up to the point where MRP of the last worker just equals the wage.
   d. hiring workers up to the point where the difference between the MRP and the wage is the greatest.

3.) The marginal revenue product (MRP) of labor
   a. indicates to the firm how much profit it will make by hiring an additional worker.
   b. increases (shifts to the right) when worker productivity increases.
   c. decreases (shifts to the left) when wages increase.
   d. decreases at a slower rate for a monopoly compared to a perfectly competitive firm.

4.) A perfectly competitive firm can purchase an additional unit of capital for $200, while an additional unit of labor can be purchased for $40. If the marginal physical product of the unit of capital is 1000 units, and the marginal physical product of the unit of labor is 160 units, in order to maximize profits and obtain the least cost combination of factors, the firm should:
a. purchase the additional unit of capital.
b. purchase the additional unit of labor.
c. purchase both the additional capital and labor.
d. purchase neither the labor nor capital.

5.) According to the rule governing the least-cost combination of factors for the firm, the firm will attain the least cost combination when
a. the marginal physical products for all factors are at a maximum.
b. the prices of the factors are the same.
c. the marginal physical products for all the factors are the same.
d. the marginal physical product per dollar of factor cost is the same for all factors.

6.) A perfectly competitive firm which faces a perfectly competitive labor market would
a. hire more workers when wages fall or marginal productivity increases, or the price of output falls.
b. hire less workers when wages increase or marginal productivity decreases, or the price of output falls.
c. hire more workers when wages fall or marginal productivity decreases, or the price of output falls.
d. hire less workers when wages increase or marginal productivity decreases, or the price of output increases.

7.) For the case of monopsony in the factor market,
a. the monopsonistic buyer will pay as low a wage as possible to all workers.
b. workers will receive a lower wage than they would in a perfectly competitive labor market.
c. more workers will be employed than in a perfectly competitive labor market.
d. the workers' MRP is lower than the wage.

8.) When a union has a monopoly in a labor market and is the only supplier of labor,
a. workers receive a higher wage but fewer workers are employed.
b. workers receive the same wage as in a perfectly competitive market but more workers are employed.
c. workers receive a higher wage and more workers are employed.
d. workers receive the same wage as in a perfectly competitive market but fewer workers are employed.

9.) When a bilateral monopoly exists,
   a. the two, the monopoly and the monopsony, offset the market power of the other, yielding a perfectly competitive solution.
   b. the final negotiated outcome would never result in a wage level lower than one associated with a perfectly competitive outcome.
   c. the final negotiated outcome would always result in a wage level higher than one associated with a perfectly competitive outcome.
   d. both the final wage outcome and the level of employment are indeterminate.

Discussion Questions

1.) Suppose that the wage rate for unskilled workers, determined through the interaction of demand for these workers by businesses and the supply of workers, falls substantially below a level necessary to maintain a minimum standard of living. Utilizing the theoretical framework developed in this chapter as a basis for your answer, what relationship exists between the equilibrium wage level and the wage level needed to attain a minimum standard of living? Would a subsistence wage rate be grounds for governmental intervention in the market with, for example, a minimum wage policy?

2.) Your text discusses how a firm uses the prices of factors of production and their marginal physical products (MPPs) to obtain the least cost method of production. Utilizing the equation found on page 274 of Hogendorn's text, briefly discuss why rice production can be capital-intensive in the United States and labor-intensive in the Far East. Different methods of production for the same product! Which one is the most cost efficient?

3.) Using demand and supply diagrams for two labor markets, both of which require about the same set of basic skills, show how a compensating wage differential would develop between the two markets if one of the jobs was particularly onerous, such as working in a slaughter house.

4.) Drawing production functions and equating marginal revenue products with their marginal factor costs works well in the classroom, but in the real world such theory is of little use because it is difficult to know or estimate the specific contribution of each worker. Is this a valid objection to the theories and models presented in this chapter?

5.) Based on your understanding of factor markets, specifically labor markets, how would you explain the fact that some movie stars and musicians earn such large incomes, even though many critics believe that they have little, if any, acting/musical skills?

6.) The market system is widely described as an economic system in which workers' incomes are based on the value of their economic productivity. Similarly, many believe that economic fairness requires that workers receive the value of their marginal product. Based on your knowledge of Chapter 11, to what extent are these principles satisfied in factor markets?

Answers and Solutions to Problems and Exercises

Completing Statements from the List of Terms

1.) Marginal Physical Product; Marginal Product
2.) Derived Demand
3.) Monopsony
4.) Bilateral Monopoly
5.) Compensating Wage Differential
6.) Marginal Revenue Product

Problems

The Firm's Production Function and Equilibrium in the Factor Market

Table 11-1

Price of Output = $5   Wage = $20   Fixed Capital Expense of $200

$$MP_P = \frac{\Delta TPP}{\Delta L}$$

Units of the Variable Input (Labor = L)	Total Physical Product (TPP)	Marginal Physical Product (MPP)	(P_{output} X MPP) Marginal Revenue Product (MRP)	Wage	P_{output} X TPP Total Revenue TR	Total Fixed Cost Plus Total Variable Cost (Wage X Units of L) TC	TR - TC Total Profit Tπ
0	0	0	$0	$20	$0	$200	($200)
1	16	16	$80	$20	$80	$220	($140)
2	34	18	$90	$20	$170	$240	($70)
3	49	15	$75	$20	$245	$260	($15)
4	62	13	$65	$20	$310	$280	$30
5	73	11	$55	$20	$365	$300	$65
6	83	10	$50	$20	$415	$320	$95
7	90	7	$35	$20	$450	$340	$110
8	95	5	$25	$20	$475	$360	$115
9	98	3	$15	$20	$490	$380	$110
10	100	2	$10	$20	$500	$400	$100

Figure 11-1

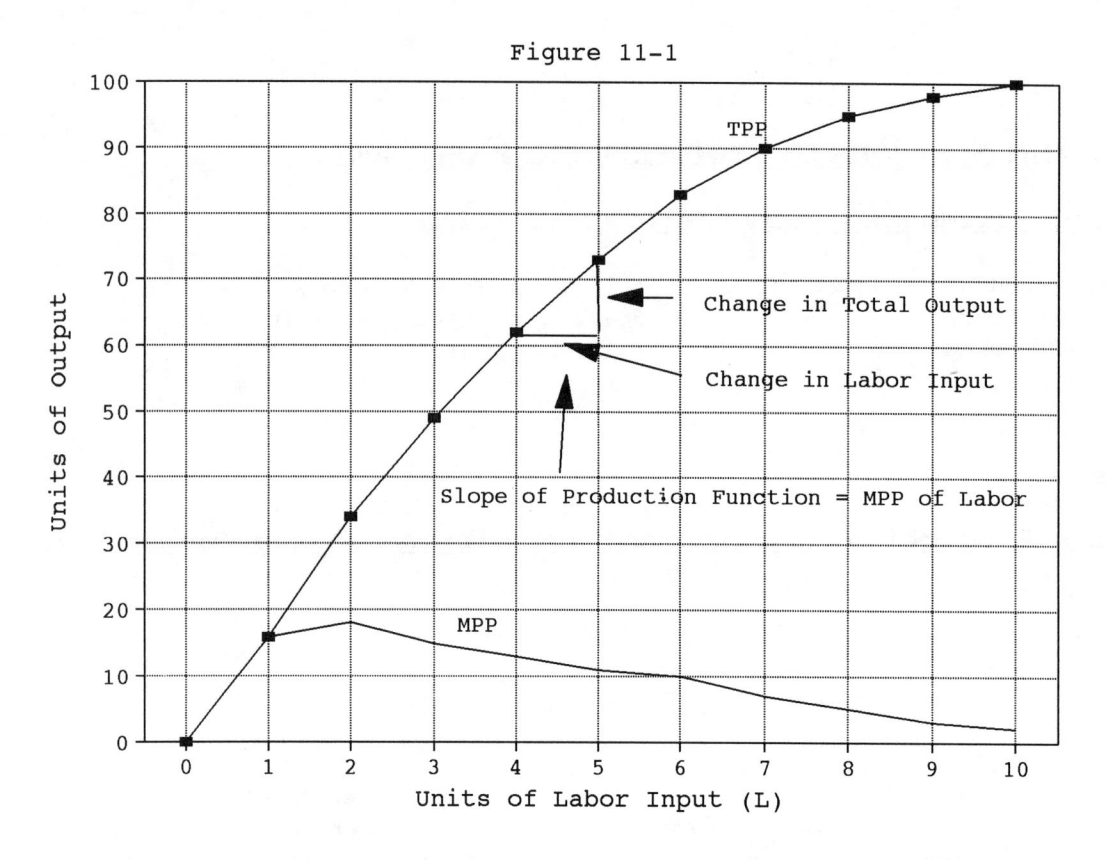

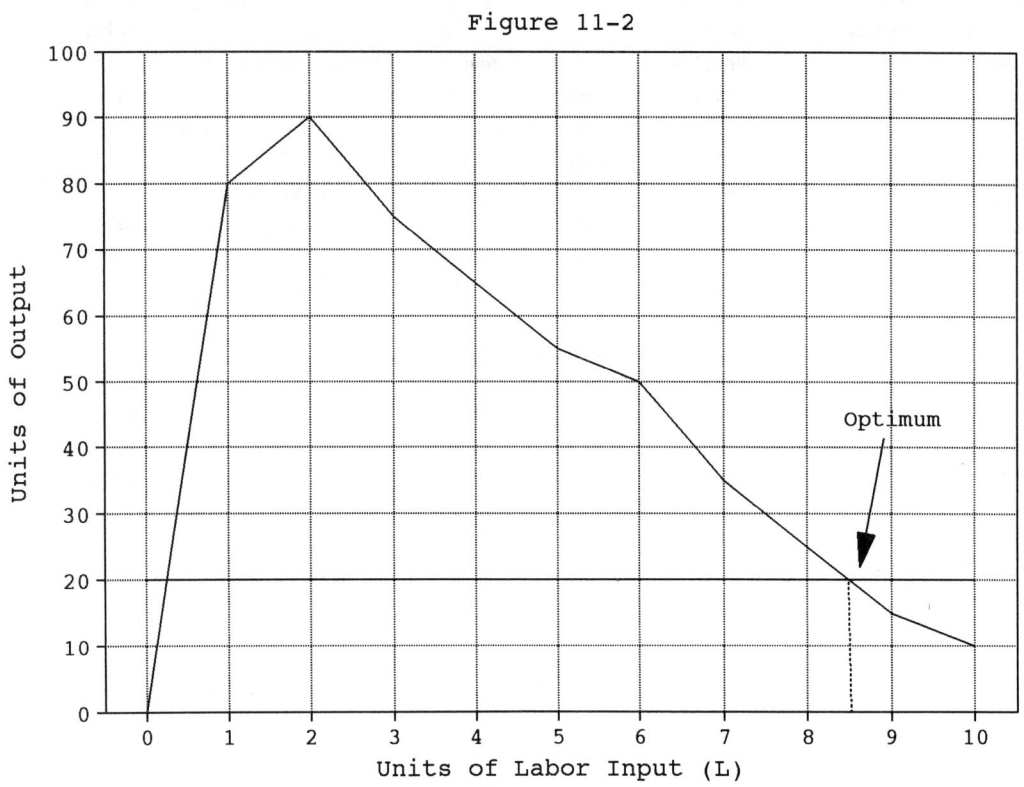

Figure 11-2

What is the optimum number of workers for this firm? **8 workers**

- changing the wage to $ 30   ==> Optimum # Workers **7 workers**
- changing the wage to $ 12   ==> Optimum # Workers **9 workers**
- changing the price of output to $ 7   ==> Optimum # Workers **9 workers**
- changing the price of output to $ 3   ==> Optimum # Workers **7 workers**

If wages increase, firms will tend to hire **(less)** units of labor.

If wages decrease, firms will tend to hire **(more)** units of labor.

If the price of output increases, firms will tend to hire **(more)** units of labor.

If the price of output decreases, firms will tend to hire **(less)** units of labor.

If worker productivity increases (i.e., each worker has a larger marginal product associated with his/her labor than before), firms will tend to hire **(more)** units of labor.

If worker productivity decreases (i.e., each worker has a smaller marginal product associated with his/her labor than before), firms will hire **(less)** units of labor.

The MRP Under Imperfect Competition

Table 11-2

Units of the Variable Input (Labor = L)	Total Physical Product (TPP)	Product Price (P)	Marginal Physical Productivity (MPP)	Total Revenue Product (TRP)	Marginal Revenue Product (MRP)	Wage
0	0	$10.00	0	$0.0	$0.0	$20
1	16	9.20	16	147.20	147.20	20
2	34	8.30	18	282.20	135.00	20
3	49	7.55	15	369.95	87.75	20
4	62	6.90	13	427.80	57.85	20
5	73	6.35	11	463.55	35.75	20
6	83	5.85	10	485.55	22.00	20
7	90	5.50	7	495.00	9.45	20
8	95	5.25	5	498.75	3.75	20
9	98	5.10	3	499.80	1.05	20
10	100	5.00	2	500.00	0.20	20

The optimum number of workers = 6

Based on your diagram, what is the effect of imperfect competition on the MRP curve of the firm? **MRP falls at a faster rate under imperfect competition, because additional output causes the price of all units previously produced to fall.**

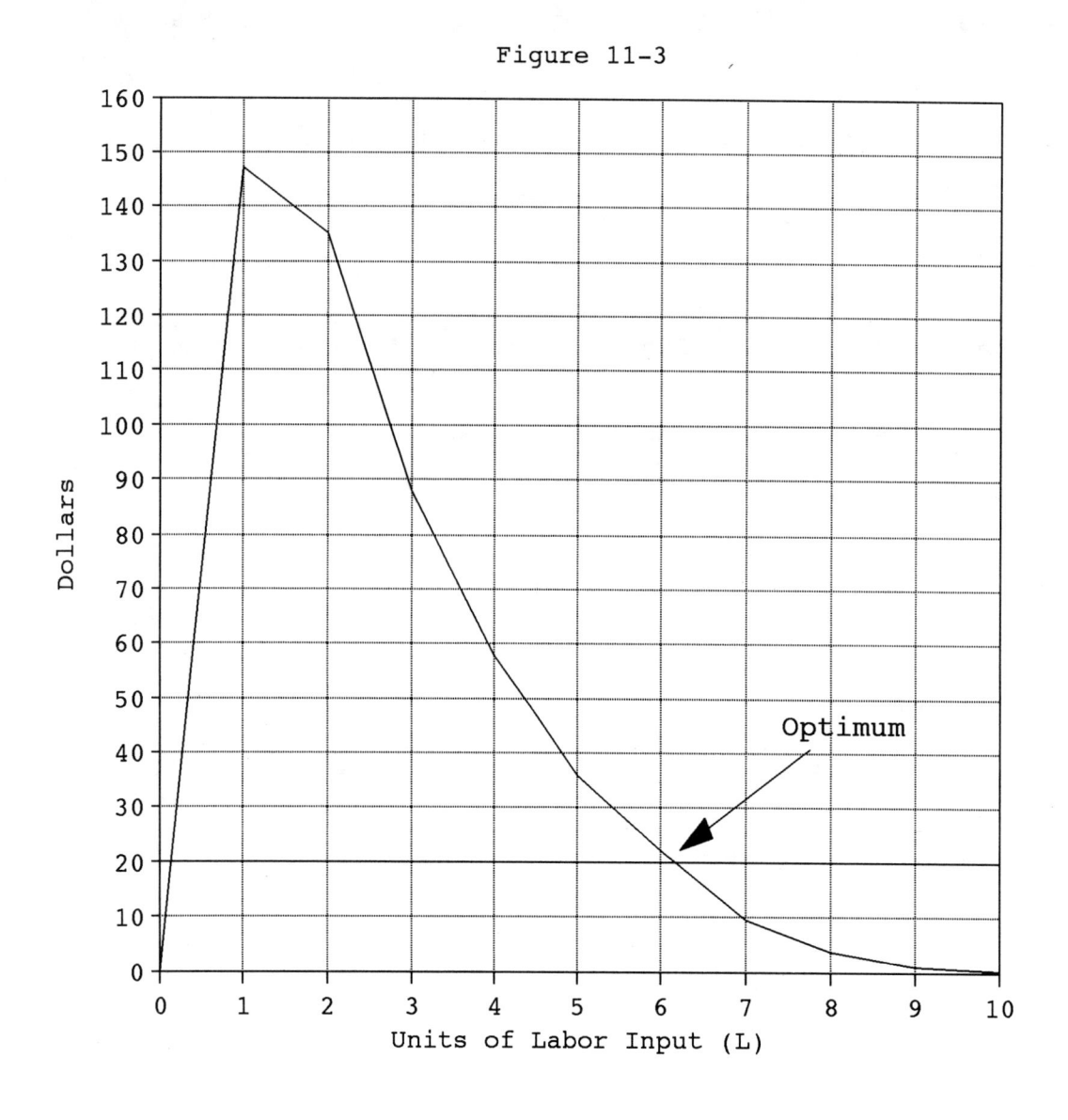

Figure 11-3

Table 11-3

Units of the Variable Input (Labor = L)	Total Physical Product (TPP)	Product Price (P)	Marginal Physical Productivity (MPP)	Marginal Revenue Product (MRP)	Wage	Total Wage Cost (Wage X L)	Marginal Cost of Labor
0	0	$5	0	$0	$12	$0	$0
1	16	5	16	80	15	15	15
2	34	5	18	90	18	36	21
3	49	5	15	75	21	63	27
4	62	5	13	65	24	96	33
5	73	5	11	55	27	135	39
6	83	5	10	50	30	180	45
7	90	5	7	35	33	231	51
8	95	5	5	25	36	288	57
9	98	5	3	15	39	351	63
10	100	5	2	10	42	420	69

The optimum number of workers = **6**

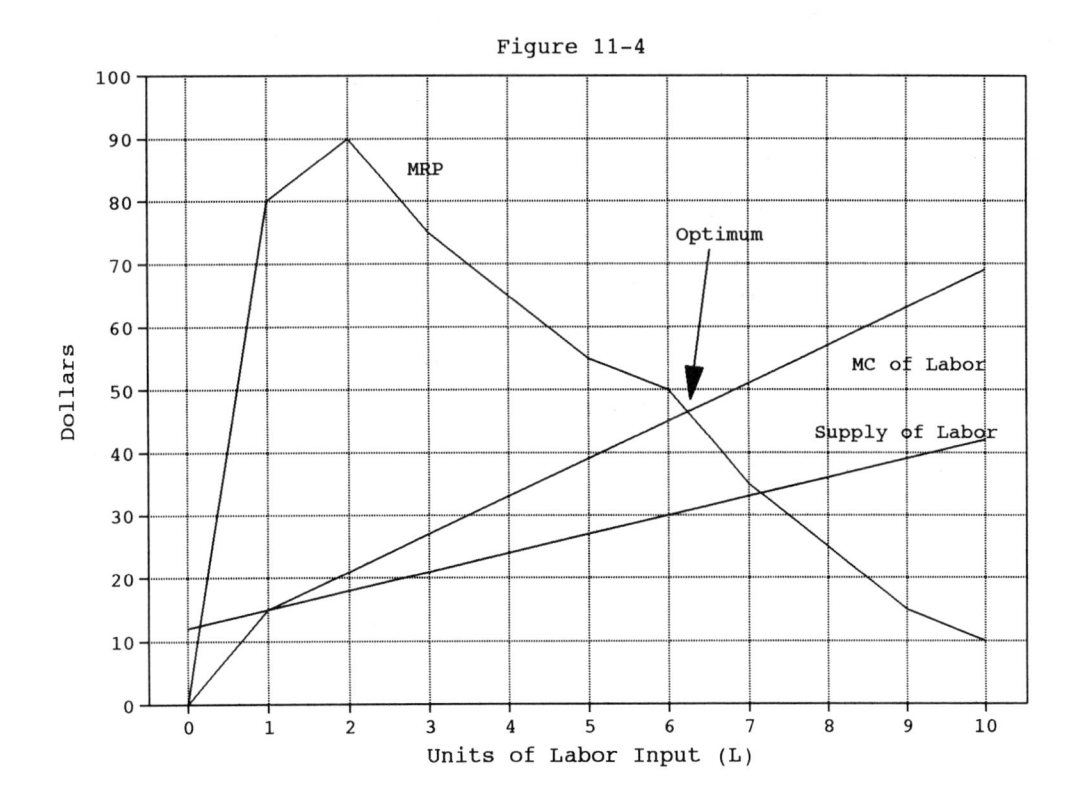

Figure 11-4

Based on your diagram, what is the effect of imperfect competition in the factor market on the number of workers hired? **Since the marginal cost of labor reflects the increase in wages that must be paid to all previously hired workers as well as the cost of a new worker, the marginal cost of** the labor curve lies above the supply curve of labor and would therefore decrease the amount of labor hired.

True/False Statements

1.) **True.** Marginal revenue product is calculated by multiplying the marginal physical product of a factor by the price of the output in order to obtain the dollar value of an additional factor unit. An increase in the price of the output will increase the MRP.

2.) **True.** For a given MRP schedule, a higher wage will mean that fewer units of the factor will be hired, since they must be more productive to justify the higher wage rate.

3.) **False.** Since the supply of workers for such jobs is generally less than for other jobs requiring the same set of skills, the wage rate is higher. The difference in the wage rates between the two is the compensating wage differential. The theory of factor markets presented in the text is still valid for these kinds of factor markets.

4.) **False.** Since a monopolist must reduce price as more output is produced, the MRP falls faster than in a perfectly competitive industry, leading to less employment. Monopoly outcomes involve less output than perfectly competitive outcomes, and typically less labor would be required.

5.) **True.** A monopsonist faces an upward sloping supply curve for labor and a marginal cost of labor curve which lies above the supply curve. Equating the MRP of labor with the MC of labor determines the equilibrium quantity of employment, but the wage paid is less than the MRP.

6.) **True.** The monopoly labor union has the market power to generate higher wages for its members, at the cost of a lower level of employment. Since the monopolist takes into account lower wage levels as employment increases, the equilibrium level of employment is less than that of a perfectly competitive factor market.

7.) **False.** The wage level is indeterminate in the bilateral monopoly case. It could be higher or lower than the perfectly competitive wage level.

8.) **False.** Check the diagram on page 286 of your Hogendorn text. Depending on the position and slope of the MRP curve, it would be possible for labor's gain in wages to be offset by the efficiency loss to society as a whole.

9.) **True.** In order to hire more workers, a higher wage must be paid to all workers, so the marginal cost of an additional worker not only includes the wage of the additional worker but also the change in the wages that must be paid to all other workers.

Multiple-Choice

1.) d   2.) c   3.) b   4.) b   5.) d   6.) b

7.) b   8.) a   9.) d

Discussion Questions

1.) According to the theoretical framework developed in this chapter, the wage level is determined by the interaction of demand and supply, and there is no relationship between what that wage is and the cost of living. One possible solution would be a minimum wage, but that would result in some amount of unemployment. It should also be kept in mind that a full time worker who is earning the current minimum wage would fall below the defined poverty level so apparently that isn't the panacea that society is looking for.

2.) The price of labor in the United States is quite high, relative to the marginal physical product of labor, making labor an expensive proposition with regards to rice production. Capital, on the other hand, is much more expensive but has a much higher MPP. The situation is reversed in the Far East where labor is relatively cheap and capital is relatively expensive (compared to their respective MPPs). Both are cost efficient given their respective factor prices.

3.)

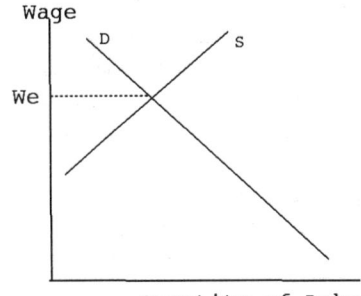

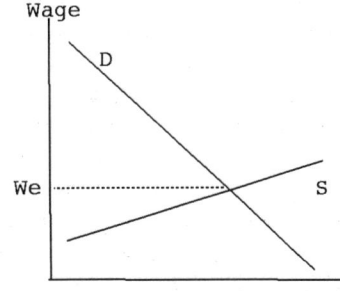

One explanation of the wage differential would be a reduced supply of labor in the high risk or unpleasant sector. That could be interpreted as workers needing a higher wage in that sector to offer each quantity of labor.

4.) While it's true that in the real world it may be difficult to obtain information of this type, especially in operations characterized as team production efforts, the theory presents a number of useful perspectives on how factor markets function. It may be the case that firms can find new ways to measure individual productivity.

5.) Incomes depend on not only productivity but also society's valuation of the product. Apparently, society likes what these people are offering, and the critics must be wrong! More on this issue in Chapter 12 -- a discussion of the concept of economic rent.

6.) When both the factor markets and the output markets are perfectly competitive, firms hire up to the point where the wage equals the MRP of labor. But even in that situation, that equality is based on the last worker hired, and other workers who have higher MRPs do not receive higher wages. In the case of imperfect competition, wages are typically lower than the MRP of labor.

Summary

The labor market models in this chapter provide an in-depth look at how factor markets operate. Equilibrium in factor markets is an extension of the same kind of marginal analysis that was used to analyze the theory of the firm, equating the marginal cost of the factor with its marginal revenue product. Increases in employment will occur when factor productivity increases, the demand for the output increases, or when wages decrease. Understanding how factor markets function is useful when evaluating the effects of a minimum wage policy.

Whether the results of the market are fair, according to some standard of economic justice, is a question filled with controversy. Strictly speaking, in a market economy, earnings and their distribution depend upon the productivity of workers and society's evaluation of the worth of their skills. It is not sufficient to be highly productive in what you do if society does not attach a particularly high value to that skill.

The term exploitation of labor is briefly discussed in terms of workers not receiving the full value of their marginal revenue product, a situation which exists when there is only a single buyer of labor in the factor market. Nurses throughout the country have raised concerns that their pay levels are too low for the level of skills and responsibility that are required in that profession. The monopsony perspective presented in this chapter is especially useful when analyzing that situation. If there is only one hospital in a community and nurses are not organized in a union, then there is the potential for exploitation and, subsequently, lower wages than would otherwise be the case.

Chapter 12
Wages, Rent, Interest, and Profit

Overview of The Chapter

This chapter begins by briefly discussing some historical background relating to unions and the different types of unions that have developed. In terms of judicial history, the Clayton Act, the Norris-La Guardia Act, the Wagner Act, and the Taft-Hartley Act of 1947 are the most important pieces of legislation regulating relations between firms and workers.

The overall effect of unions is mixed. Many people believe that their activities tend to reduce employment, and yet there are circumstances in which union actions increase employment. Their support of restrictive tariffs and advertisements calling for people to buy union products have probably increased employment to some degree. Their impact on non-unionized sectors of the economy is unclear. Profit sharing programs introduce greater wage flexibility by reducing payments to labor during recessions and increasing them during more profitable economic expansions.

Unions can pursue different goals. They can attempt to maximize employment, or that goal can be traded off in favor of maximizing wage levels for union members. There are several ways in which unions can raise wages: (1) by implementing measures which increase the demand or need for labor; (2) by implementing measures which decrease the supply of labor; and (3) by bargaining for higher than equilibrium wages. Measures 2 and 3 are dependent upon the elasticity of demand and will be more successful the more inelastic the demand for labor.

Other countries have had somewhat different experiences and results with labor unions. In the United Kingdom, unions have played more of a political role than in the United States, and the Labour Party has been in power several times in the postwar era. Because of differences in the legal environment and other structural factors, strikes were more frequent and more disruptive than in most other countries. Since the election of Mrs. Thatcher, a conservative, changes were made that have decreased the incidence of strikes and the power of the labor unions. Japan, on the other hand, has been characterized by substantially greater cooperation between labor and management. The concept of lifetime employment, the willingness of workers to change jobs within the firm, and re-training programs provided by the firm have all contributed to relatively good labor/management relations and relatively few strikes in that country.

Whether or not employees in the public sector and in critically important private sectors should be allowed to strike is an important public policy issue. How should society balance the right to strike against its own interests of minimizing the economic disruption and spill-over costs associated with a strike in a key economic sector? Sections of the Taft-Hartley Act provide a mechanism for dealing with this, although it does not call for compulsory arbitration which could also be used.

Discrimination in the workplace has been a serious problem for minority groups in society. Discrimination and barriers to employment interfere with the efficient allocation of resources and inflicts a deadweight loss on society. If markets were purely competitive and completely efficient, efforts to discriminate would eventually be self-defeating since firms which engaged in discrimination would be forgoing valuable human resources and paying higher than necessary wages to favored individuals. But such adjustments are probably more of a long-run adjustment, and many labor markets are imperfectly competitive, thus allowing firms some leeway in their hiring practices.

Comparable-worth policies have been developed in an attempt to address inequities in pay scales among different groups. These policies attempt to compare the skills and responsibilities involved in different occupations and thus provide a basis for comparison of pay scales. The eventual goal would be to have a workplace environment in which jobs with comparable skills, risks, and responsibilities would have similar pay.

Economic rent arises from the fixed supply of a resource and the fact that additional units of the resource cannot be provided to the market. The term quasi-rent is appropriate wherever factors or firms are earning super-normal profits for a period of time after which the profits will be competed away, leaving only normal profits. A temporarily fixed resource would fall into this category. In general, economic rent is generated whenever a factor receives a return that exceeds its opportunity cost. Within that context, a monopolist's super-normal would be classified as economic rent.

The concept of net present value is also discussed in this chapter. Net present value is useful when anlyzing a future stream of earnings. Earnings or income received in the future are worth less than they would be if they were received today, and it is necessary to discount future earnings in order to determine their present value. Discounting is necessary because of the interest forgone -- a classic example of opportunity cost. It must be emphasized that discounting as such is not related to inflation or the fact that the purchasing power of future earnings is likely to be less -- that is a separate factor that must be dealt with on its own terms.

The special characteristics of interest and profits are briefly discussed. One way of thinking about the interest rate is that it is determined by the demand for and supply of loanable funds. The interest rate affects capital investment plans because it represents a relatively risk-free, alternative rate of return for investment funds. The expected rate of return should exceed the relevant interest rate in order for an investment project to be deemed economically feasible. Investors may also want to make an appropriate adjustment for the degree of expected risk associated with a project.

Profit can be thought of as a return for incurring risk and a return for entrepreneurial activities. Super-normal profit -- the profit above the minimum acceptable level of profit -- can be thought of as economic rent. Depending on market structure and the barriers to entry, it may persist or be competed away.

Learning Objectives

After completing this chapter, you should be sure that you are able to:

- describe and graph the different ways that labor unions can raise wages. You should also be sure that you can identify the factors which influence the effectiveness of labor union strategies.

- distinguish among the different kinds of labor shops and have some familiarity with the major provisions of the Wagner Act and the Taft-Hartley Act.

- briefly describe how British and Japanese labor union experiences and policies differ from that of the United States.

- explain the rationale for comparable-worth programs and their strengths and weaknesses.

- understand the concept of economic rent and the role it plays in the factor resource market.

- explain the economic phenomenon of differential rent.

- describe the relationship that exists between economic rent and transfer earnings.

- differentiate between rents and quasi-rents.

- define the concept of the net present value of a stream of future earnings and calculate the net present value given appropriate information. You should also understand the role that the discount rate plays in calculating net present value.

- understand the conceptual basis for both interest and profit.

Self Evaluation

List of Terms

Closed Shop
Comparable Worth
Compulsory Arbitration
Discounting
Economic Rent
Featherbedding
Future Value
Interest Rate
Lifetime Employment
Net Present Value
Open Shop
Profit
Quasi-Rent
Ricardian or Differential Rents
Right-to-Work Laws
Transfer Earnings

For the statements below, fill in the term from the list above which provides the best fit.

1.) Firms are willing to spend larger amounts on training and re-training, and workers are more willing to shift to different kinds of jobs and tasks if there is a commitment to _____ between the firm and the worker.

2.) An _____ is one where workers are not required to join a union as a condition of employment.

3.) _____ is often proposed in those situations in which there are large economic losses associated with labor strikes.

4.) Some states have passed _____ in an attempt to provide greater latitude for workers and counter the power of unions.

5.) _____ is the term applied to restrictive work rules which result in an artificial need for additional workers.

6.) When a _____ exists, workers must belong to a union before they can be hired.

7.) Frustrated by the earnings inequalities that exist between male and female workers, some people have advocated _____ policies which would attempt to equalize earnings for jobs which involve the same set of skills and similar amounts of risk and responsibilities.

8.) The term _____ describes the sum of a discounted stream of future incomes or costs.

9.) _____ is a return attributable to a temporarily fixed resource.

10.) The process of changing the future value of an income or cost to its present value equivalent is known as _____.

11.) The supply and demand for loanable funds determine the _____.

12.) _____ can be thought of as the minimum earnings or payment necessary to induce a resource, with alternative uses, into its most productive use.

13.) Any economic return or payment above that absolutely necessary to supply it to the market is defined as _____.

14.) The economic return for undertaking entrepreneurial activities such as risk-taking is called _____.

15.) Differences in the quality, location, or productivity result in _____ that affect the economic return of the different quality resource units.

16.) The _____ of a payment or stream of incomes is greater than its net present value.

Problem

Net Present Value and The Time Value of Money Formula -- Useful Tools for Your Economics Toolkit

The mathematical relationship between present and future values is derived in Chapter 12 and is shown below with some modification of terminology:

$$P_n = P_o * (1 + r)^n$$

where: P_n = principal or amount at the end of the nth period of the time interval
P_o = principal or amount at the beginning of the time interval
r = average percentage rate of growth (or interest rate)
n = number of time periods (years, quarters, etc.)

The rationale for the formula can be easily shown by referring to a simple financial example. Say you had $1,000 to put into a savings account which had an interest rate of 6 percent (compounded annually). At the end of one year, you would still have the initial principal of $1,000, plus you would have gained 6 percent interest (0.06 X $1,000) = $60 for a total year-end amount of $1,060.

Total at the end of year one:
    initial principal + (interest rate X initial principal)
         $1,060 = $1,000 + (0.06 X $1,000)
                = $1,000 + $60

Using the notation described above: $P_1 = P_o + (P_o \times r) = P_o(1 + r)$

271

If the savings account were left untouched for two years, the amount in the account would equal:

Total at the end of year two:
principal after year one + (interest rate X principal after one year)
$$\$1,123.60 = \$1,060 + (0.06 \times \$1,060)$$
$$= \$1,060 + \$63.60$$

In terms of our previous notation: $P_2 = P_1 + (P_1 \times r) = (P_0(1 + r))(1 + r)$

$$= P_0(1 + r)^2$$

and the formula will continue to change in the same fashion as additional time periods are included.

Formula (1) can be used to determine the following:

a. the future value of an initial amount which increases at a given percentage rate of change or rate of interest

b. the present value of an amount (or a stream of amounts) received in some given future time period

c. the percentage growth rate associated with an initial and final amount over a period of time (which is a bit more complicated and won't be covered here)

Determining the Future Value With a Given Rate of Interest

(1.) You receive a modest inheritance of $15,000 when you are 24 years old. Your financial counselor tells you that over the last twenty years or so the annual average return for the stock market has been about 11 %.

If you invest the $15,000 in a mutual fund that earns the same return as the stock market as a whole and the stock market continues to provide investors with an 11 % return on investment, **what would the $15,000 principal be after 40 years of annually compounded earnings at 11 %?**[1]

$$P_{40} = \$15,000(1 + 0.11)^{40} = \$15,000(65.000867) = \$975,013.01$$

The 11 % annual return would be exceptional over such a long period of time, but the stock market's overall return for the last twenty years has been very close to that figure. The long investment horizon is very helpful for achieving specific financial goals.

---

[1] Computation for these problems is fairly simple with a calculator. For those calculators with an x^y key, simply enter (1 + r), hit the x^y or y^x key -- whichever it is on your calculator and then the appropriate power. Thus, for the problem above, the sequence would be 1.11, then x^y, and then 40 and the answer should be 65.000867. That answer is then multiplied by the 15,000 to obtain the final total of $975,013.01. Check it out!

Next let's change the parameter of the problem to see what happens: suppose that the annual rate of return our investor could get was only 7 %.

Problem 1.) What would the $15,000 principal be after 40 years of annually compounded earnings at 7 %?

A shorter number of time periods also makes a significant difference on the final total as you can see below. Returning to our original example,

Problem 2.) What would the $15,000 principal be after 25 years of annually compounded earnings at 11 %?

Determining the Present Value of an Amount Received at Some Future Point in Time

Manipulating the formula $P_n = P_o * (1 + r)^n$, we obtain:

$P_n/(1 + r)^n = P_o$ (Future value/discount factor = present value)

where $(1 + r)^n$ = the discount factor and r = the discount rate

You receive a modest inheritance of $15,000. However, because of some behavioral problems that characterized your high school days, your deceased aunt has indicated that you will not be able to receive the inheritance until you have settled down at age 40 -- 16 years from now. **What is the net present value of your $15,000 inheritance which will be received 16 years from now? Your personal financial counselor advises you that a 7 % discount rate (interest rate) would be appropriate to use for this exercise.**

P_o (present value) = $15,000/((1 + 0.07)^{16})$ = $15,000/2.952164
         = $5,081.02

In this problem, (1/2.952164) = 0.33873 is known as the discount factor, which indicates how much the future value should be discounted. In this example, using a discount rate of 7 %, each dollar received 16 years from now is worth only $0.33873 at the present time. Another way to look at the relationship between present and future value is that $5,081.02 invested for 16 years at an interest rate of 7 % will yield a total amount of $15,000 at the end of that period of time. The concept of net present value can also be applied to a stream of future earnings or costs.

Problem 3.) What is net present value of the $15,000 inheritance if it is received 25 years from now, assuming a discount rate of 7 %?

Problem 4.) What is net present value of the $15,000 inheritance if it is received 25 years from now, assuming a discount rate of 4 %?

True/False Statements

Indicate whether you think the statements below are true or false. These questions are designed to make you think about the concepts presented in the text. There may not be any easy clear cut-answers. Some thoughts about the answers are presented at the end of the chapter.

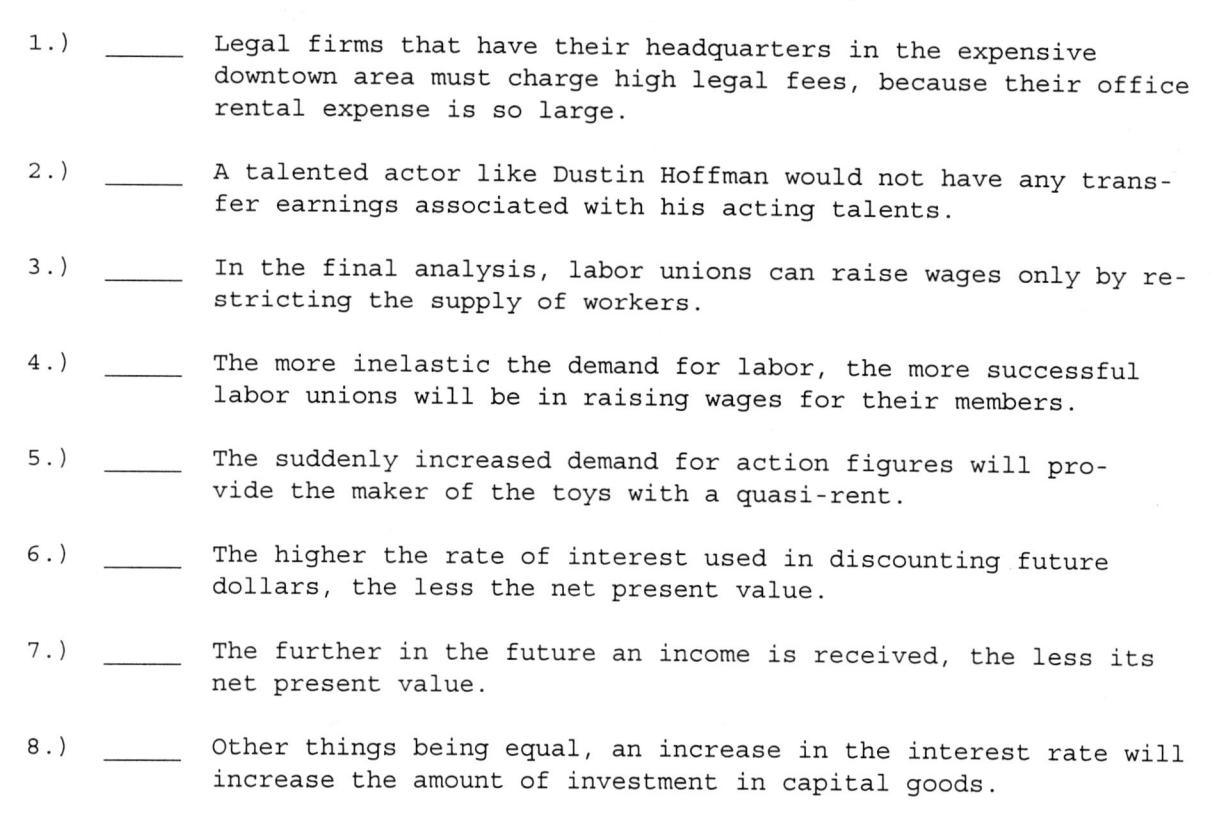

1.) _____ Legal firms that have their headquarters in the expensive downtown area must charge high legal fees, because their office rental expense is so large.

2.) _____ A talented actor like Dustin Hoffman would not have any transfer earnings associated with his acting talents.

3.) _____ In the final analysis, labor unions can raise wages only by restricting the supply of workers.

4.) _____ The more inelastic the demand for labor, the more successful labor unions will be in raising wages for their members.

5.) _____ The suddenly increased demand for action figures will provide the maker of the toys with a quasi-rent.

6.) _____ The higher the rate of interest used in discounting future dollars, the less the net present value.

7.) _____ The further in the future an income is received, the less its net present value.

8.) _____ Other things being equal, an increase in the interest rate will increase the amount of investment in capital goods.

9.) _____ Differential rents can arise only from differences in productivity.

10.) _____ Inflation has no effect on the net present value of an asset.

11.) _____ For a completely unique resource, the amount of economic rent is determined by demand.

Multiple Choice-Questions

Select the "best" answer from the alternatives provided.

1.) There is a plot of land on an island that is unique in the sense that it is the only place in the world where the exotic fruit wamawa can be grown. A permanent increase in the demand for wamawas would
   a. increase the economic rent on the plot of land.
   b. decrease the economic rent on the plot of land.
   c. leave the economic rent on the plot of land unchanged.
   d. affect the economic rent, but it is impossible to know the direction of change.

2.) The difference between economic rent and quasi-economic rent is that
   a. economic rent is based on actual productivity, while quasi-rent can be due to many other factors.
   b. economic rent pertains to land which is the only permanently fixed factor, while quasi-rent applies to individuals and capital goods.
   c. economic rent is a true rent based on a natural inelasticity of a factor, while quasi-rent is due to contrived or artificial factors.
   d. economic rent is based on a long-run inelasticity of supply, while quasi-rent refers to a temporary inelasticity or scarcity of a factor.

3.) In a regional farming area, farmland varies considerably in quality and its productivity. As a result of those natural differences,
   a. land prices would remain the same, but farmers' profits would vary according to land productivity.
   b. land rentals would vary according to land productivity, bidding up rents for productive land until profit margins would be about the same for all land.
   c. land rentals would vary due to many other factors, land productivity being only one of those factors and not necessarily the most important one.
   d. land with low farm productivity would change to another use, only highly productive land would remain in farm production.

4.) Other things being equal, the net present value of a stream of future revenues will
   a. increase with an increase in the interest rate.
   b. increase as the time of payments moves into the future.
   c. decrease with an increase in the interest rate.
   d. remain unchanged when the interest rate changes.

5.) The concept of net present value
   a. is not valid when different interest rates are used.
   b. is based on the fact that inflation reduces the value of any revenues received in the future.
   c. is valid only for relatively short periods of time.
   d. allows one to compare the current dollar value of investments which differ significantly in their future revenue streams.
   e. none of the above.

6.) The theory of loanable funds suggests that when the demand for loanable funds increases (due to favorable economic conditions),
   a. a shortage of loanable funds will develop which the central bank will somehow have to alleviate.
   b. the equilibrium interest rate will rise, encouraging financial institutions to offer more funds to the market.
   c. a surplus of funds develops at first until financial institutions have the time to process the increased number of loans.
   d. some investment projects and loans will be postponed until the supply of loanable funds increases sufficiently.

7.) Efforts by labor unions to increase wages by negotiating a wage level that is above the equilibrium wage level
   a. will create a labor shortage.
   b. will be more successful if the elasticity of demand for labor is elastic.
   c. will be more successful if the elasticity of demand for labor is inelastic.
   d. will never be successful, because wages will eventually return to their original equilibrium levels.

8.) Efforts by labor unions to raise wages will be most successful
   a. in those industries where the MRP of labor exceeds current wage levels.
   b. in those industries that are the most competitive, with many small firms lacking market power.
   c. in those situations where there is a large pool of labor with skills similar to labor union members.
   d. in those sectors of the economy where wages are lowest.

Discussion Questions

1.) Using a framework of Ricardian economic rent, explain what would happen to the price of North Dakota farmland as imports of Canadian wheat increase.

2.) Many court cases involve the time value of money and the net present value of future costs and streams of income. As you know, the discount rate or interest rate that is selected plays an important role in determining the net present value of any stream of costs or incomes. If you were an attorney for a plaintiff who was bringing suit against a company who fired him on the basis of his age, therefore depriving him of a seven year stream of future salaries, would you want your economic consultant to use a high or low discount rate? What would the company's attorney want the discount rate to be? How could a judge decide which discount rate best served the concept of justice?

3.) Is it possible for labor unions to maximize their contractual wage rate and the amount of employment simultaneously?

4.) The compensation of U.S. CEOs is currently a "hot" political question, particularly when their compensation appears to be so much higher than their Japanese counterparts. Utilize the theoretical framework provided in this chapter to analyze this issue and provide some much needed perspective on this issue.

5.) Describe how comparable-worth programs deal with the problem of discrimination in pay scales. What problems are associated with corrective programs like this?

6.) What effects do unions have upon non-unionized sectors of the economy?

7.) Why do you think unions support minimum wage legislation when it applies mostly to unskilled, non-unionized kinds of workers?

8.) Barbers and beauticians must pass a fairly lengthy and rigorous training process and, in many instances, serve as an apprentice for another extended period of time before they are allowed to practice on their own. Do you think this is a question of public safety or a question of economic rent? Would your answer be any different for physicians or airline pilots?

Answers and Solutions to Problems and Exercises

Completing Statements from the List of Terms

1.) Lifetime Employment
2.) Open Shop
3.) Compulsory Arbitration
4.) Right-to-Work Laws
5.) Featherbedding
6.) Closed Shop
7.) Comparable Worth
8.) Net Present Value
9.) Quasi-Rent
10.) Discounting
11.) Interest Rate
12.) Transfer Earnings
13.) Economic Rent
14.) Profit
15.) Ricardian or Differential Rents
16.) Future Value

Problems

Determining the Future Value With a Given Rate of Interest

Problem 1.) What would the $15,000 principal be after 40 years of annually compounded earnings at 7 %?

$$P_{40} = \$15,000 (1 + 0.07)^{40} = \$15,000 (14.9745) = \$224,616.87$$

Problem 2.) What would the $15,000 principal be after 25 years of annually compounded earnings at 11 %?

$$P_{25} = \$15,000 (1 + 0.11)^{25} = \$15,000 (13.5855) = \$203,781.96$$

Determining the Present Value of an Amount Received at Some Future Point in Time

Problem 3.) What is net present value of the $15,000 inheritance if it is received 25 years from now, assuming a discount rate of 7 %?

$$P_{25} = \$15,000/(1 + 0.07)^{25} = \$15,000/(5.42743) = \$2,763.74$$

Problem 4.) What is net present value of the $15,000 inheritance if it is received 25 years from now, assuming a discount rate of 4 %?

$$P_{25} = \$15,000/(1 + 0.4)^{25} = \$15,000/(2.6650) = \$5,626.75$$

True/False Statements

1.) **False.** As Ricardo was able to show over a hundred years ago, rental expenses are high because the attorneys are able to charge high fees. Not the other way around.

2.) **False.** This, of course, is conjecture, but one would think there would be some salary level below which he might do something else besides act.

3.) **False.** Restrictions on supply are perhaps the best known strategy employed by labor unions, but it is not the only strategy. Efforts to increase the demand for union labor and the attainment of a higher than equilibrium wage rate are other strategies.

4.) **True.** With an inelastic demand for labor, the wage rate can be raised with minimal effects on overall employment.

5.) **True.** Quasi-rent is defined as an economic return above the minimum necessary to obtain the product or resource which is due to a temporary situation such as an increase in demand.

6.) **True.** The concept of discounting future dollars is based on the interest forgone when receiving dollars in the future as compared to current dollars which could earn interest up till that time in the future. The higher the interest rate, the greater the interest forgone, and the more that the value of future dollars must be discounted.

7.) **True.** For much the same reasons as question 6 above. The further out in time a dollar is received, the less it is worth in current dollars, because the longer the time span, the greater the interest that could have been earned.

8.) **False.** Increases in the interest rate will make some investment projects unprofitable when compared against the higher interest rate. As the interest rate increases, there are fewer investment projects that have an internal rate of return that will exceed the rate of interest.

9.) **False.** When David Ricardo first discussed differential rents, he stated that they could be attributed to any factor which affected the productivity and revenue-generating ability of the resource. Differential rents could also be caused by differences in the willingness of the suppliers to offer the resource to the market and also to whatever market imperfections that might exist.

10.) **False.** It is important to realize that the rationale for discounting future streams of incomes and costs does not depend upon inflation -- rather, it is based on forgone interest. Even if inflation were zero, future steams of incomes would still need to be discounted. But, to the extent that inflation affects future incomes/costs, it is a factor which should be taken into account.

11.) **True.** A unique resource would have no substitutes and, therefore, would have a completely inelastic supply curve. If supply is completely inelastic, then the market price would be demand determined -- the classic case for rents.

Multiple-Choice

1.) a   2.) d   3.) b   4.) c   5.) d   6.) b

7.) c   8.) a

Discussion Questions

1.) Increased imports of Canadian wheat would tend to lower the market price of wheat in the U.S. market. A lower price of wheat would reduce any super-normal profits that were being earned in the wheat industry, thus lowering any economic rent that North Dakota farmers were earning. The price of land used for growing wheat would decline, reflecting the lower price of wheat.

2.) In this case, the plaintiff who is seeking as large a settlement as possible from the company would prefer to use a lower interest rate in calculating the net present value of the plaintiff's future forgone income. The defendant who wants to minimize the net present value of the future salaries would want to use a higher interest rate. Ultimately, a judge or jury would have to decide which side has made the most effective argument. If the plaintiff wins, then some basic economic and financial understanding is useful, if not necessary, to decide whether the estimates of financial loss are realistic and accurate. The decision to use a particular interest rate in calculating net present value is subjective in the sense that the person doing the analysis must decide what is an appropriate interest rate. There is nothing in the textbooks which tells anyone what interest rate should be used.

3.) No, but unions frequently act as if that should be the case. After negotiating a wage increase, public statements by union officials lead one to believe that they think it is unfair if some jobs are lost as a result of a newly-agreed-upon wage settlement. That would be true only if the demand for labor were perfectly inelastic.

4.) One rationale would be that there is a limited supply of managers who are capable of running large corporations effectively, and, as a result, their salaries are quite high as is the economic rent that they earn. But, an interesting question would be: why would such managers be more scarce in the United States than they are in other countries? Other dimensions of the CEO market must be examined. The inter-relationships that exist among corporate directors and board members may remove the cost efficiency of the market. Larger firms are removed from many of the competitive pressures that characterize perfect competition, so they may have less incentive to keep salaries down.

5. Such programs try to identify and quantify the skills and education, risks, and responsibilities that characterize different jobs and then assign wages on the basis of job characteristics without regard to gender or other factors. One drawback is obviously the difficulty in trying to compare employment in different sectors -- can all the relevant factors be identified? Comparable-worth programs also ignore the other blade of the market scissors, the demand side. Being a well-educated and skilled employee may not be worth very much in the market if society doesn't value the product very much. The other wild card in all of this is market power of unions and market imperfections. The goal of comparable worth is admirable but its implementation is fraught with difficulties.

6.) Wage settlements in unionized sectors of the economy undoubtedly affect workers' expectations about possible wage increases in all sectors of the economy, both unionized and non-unionized.

7.) Minimum wage legislation increases wages at the lower levels, and that may provide some leverage for increasing wages for workers earning more than the minimum wage.

8.) Requirements that are imposed on both barbers and beauticians decreases the number of new entrants into those professions, thus decreasing the supply and increasing the equilibrium wage, *ceteris paribus*. The same applies to physicians and airline pilots. The case for long training programs and rigorous entrance standards is much stronger for the latter professions.

Summary

An awareness of the theory of economic rent is helpful in understanding why the prices of some factor resources are what they are. It helps explain why an obscure second baseman of rather mediocre skills that plays for one of the major league baseball teams can earn over $600,000 a year, while your favorite college teacher, who may have spent as many as 5 to 7 years in graduate school, may earn between $40,000 and $60,000. It helps explain why rents differ so much among various locations and how the market takes into account the different qualities attributable to each location.

Interest rates and the monetary system as a whole will be focused on in much more detail in later macro-economic chapters. But this brief overview in Chapter 12 helps to set the stage for your work later on. Monetary policy

-- controlling the money supply and interest rates to achieve certain macro-economic goals -- is an important component of macro-economic policy, so knowing about the role of interest rates on purchases of capital goods is vital.

The concept of the time value of money and net present value are extremely useful, since there are so many instances in which either costs or revenues or both are received over periods of time. If, for example, a project has very large costs that are incurred at the beginning of a project and revenues that are delayed for some time until the project is completed and then spread out for a number of years in the future, it is essential that both costs and revenues be converted back to their net present dollar values, so an accurate comparison can be made.

Similarly, a couple is getting a divorce, and one of the assets to be divided between the two spouses is a pension plan of the wife that starts at age 65 and pays $1,200 per month until her death. What is the present dollar value of that pension today when she is 53 years old?

While not mentioned specifically in your textbook, the formula for the net present value can also be used to solve for annual rates of %age change when the beginning and ending values are given and the number of time periods involved. If real disposable per capita income in the United States had grown from $9,875 in 1970 to $14,154 in 1990, we could use the net present value formula to solve for (r) - the rate of interest or, in this case, the annual %age rate of change. Without going into the calculation details, (r) turns out to be about 1.82 % per year. The value of knowing the annual %age rate of change is that it then can be compared against other annual rates of change for comparison purposes.

Chapter 13
Income Distribution and Poverty

Overview of the Chapter

Every society, even the most egalitarian, has some degree of income inequality. The degree of income inequality can be depicted graphically by a Lorenz curve. The Gini coefficient is a more quantitative measure of the degree of income inequality, and it can be calculated from the income distribution information contained in the Lorenz curve. Using the Gini coefficient, it is possible to make comparisons of the degree of income inequality among different countries.

The role of the market in determining a society's distribution of income through demand and supply forces in the labor market is shown. Occupations which require relatively little skill are characterized by low demand and abundant supply, and the equilibrium wage is correspondingly low. In contrast, for those occupations which require highly trained workers, the supply of qualified workers is much smaller and the wages higher. Immigration and freer trade have negatively impacted the market of unskilled workers, just as technological change and computers have enhanced the market for workers who are familiar with the new technologies. The effects of discrimination on wages and employment at the individual firm level and at the industry level are explored briefly.

Can the market system eliminate poverty? While no other economic system has as good a track record as the market system in raising a society's overall economic standard of living, poverty and homelessness continue to plague market-oriented economies. Developed countries which have more governmental involvement in the economy have a significantly smaller percentage of their population living below the poverty level, with significantly fewer homeless. Of particular concern here in the United States is the development of what some have called a "culture of poverty" -- a dependency on outside aid and governmental safety net programs that is passed on from generation to generation. It has proven to be very difficult to break down this culture of poverty with traditionally-oriented programs. For that reason, many are now calling for new and innovative welfare reforms to break the cycle of poverty. Workfare, changes in AFDC benefit packages, requiring welfare recipients to enroll in educational and training programs, and specific time limits on welfare payments are some of the reforms being implemented.

Poverty presents a continuing challenge to every society. There is still considerable controversy about the proper role of government in addressing a problem like poverty in a society like the United States which has both capitalistic and socialistic characteristics. It was not so long ago that the government played a very limited role in helping those less fortunate, and a significant number of people refused to go on welfare during the Great Depression because it was so demeaning.

Economic policies designed to alleviate poverty include: high growth macroeconomic policies which minimize the extent of unemployment, thus creating broader employment opportunities for disadvantaged groups; training and education programs designed to increase skill levels, employability, and relocation incentives; and welfare programs which minimize the negative effects on individual initiative. The earned income tax credit which provides direct income assistance to households near the poverty level is currently being used as an alternative to the wide variety of poverty-related programs currently in place.

Learning Objectives

After completing this chapter, you should be sure that you are able to:

- understand how society's distribution of income/wealth can be represented graphically using a Lorenz curve and how a specific individual distribution can be represented mathematically by the Gini coefficient.

- show how the market assigns factor incomes and the role the market plays in determining society's distribution of income.

- identify some of the major reasons for income inequity.

- specify how poverty is officially defined.

- discuss the impact of discrimination on a labor market and whether or not discrimination increases the degree of inequality in society.

- identify the major reasons that have been put forth to explain the persistence of poverty.

- understand how the problem of poverty is addressed within the context of the market system, why continual poverty poses a significant problem for society.

- understand the economic implications of a "culture of poverty."

- identify potential solutions to the poverty problem and their strengths and weaknesses.

- understand how the earned income tax credit works and how it represents an alternative approach to helping those below the defined poverty level.

Applications

One reason that people become frustrated with government policies is that it often appears that although we spend extremely large sums of money on our problems, they either don't get resolved in any meaningful fashion or, on occasion, they get worse. Much of this frustration is caused by policies that do not contain the correct economic incentives which encourage people to act in the way society intended. Instead, we rebuke the individuals involved for not acting the way they were supposed to act.

Welfare and, in particular, the AFDC program typically requires that aid recipients lose their benefits on a one-to-one basis when they have outside earnings. That means that a recipient's income is effectively taxed at a 100 percent rate up to his/her current level of benefits. How many of us would want to seek employment under such an adverse tax plan? But, it gets worse, since almost always there are additional expenses associated with employment -- transportation to and from work, added childcare expenses, additional clothing purchases, and oftentimes larger expenditures for food, both at work and at home. Take the case of a single parent with $800 of AFDC benefits:

Not Working: $800   AFDC Benefits per month

                 $800   Net Income per month

Working: $800   AFDC Benefits per month
               $1,000   Outside Earnings per month
             - $400   Additional Expenses Associated with Working per month
             - $800   Loss in AFDC Benefits

                $600   Net Income per month

With the dollar-for-dollar loss of benefits, it is much easier to see why welfare recipients want to stay on the program and not seek outside employment unless they can find a good high-paying job. That problem can be addressed by changing the loss of benefits to outside earnings ratio. Take, for example, a new ratio of a loss of one dollar in benefits for each three dollars in outside earnings (still representing an effective tax rate of 33 percent on the first $800 of earnings).

Not Working: $800   AFDC Benefits per month

                 $800   Net Income per month

Working: $800   AFDC Benefits per month
               $1,000   Outside Earnings per month
             - $400   Additional Expenses Associated with Working per month
             - $334   Loss in AFDC Benefits

              $1,066   Net Income per month

Changing the loss in benefits/outside earnings ratio to 1:3 results in an increase in monthly income of $466 over the previous example, but net monthly income is still only $266 above what it would be without working at all. Even with the new 1:3 ratio, how many people, if given the choice, would work full time for an increase in monthly income of $266? If healthcare benefits are provided by the government while, under a welfare program but are not provided when one is working full time, the decision to work is made even more tenuous. Healthcare reform with universal coverage might reduce the number of people who remain on welfare for that reason.

Since there are no free lunches in economics, the proposed solution of changing the loss in benefits/outside earnings ratio results in a problem of another sort. It means that some welfare benefits would continue to be paid out to people with higher incomes -- high enough that some people might protest about such a policy. With the modification described above, some welfare benefits would continue to be paid out until outside earnings reached $2,400 per month (i.e., at $2,400, the recipient would lose $800 worth of benefits -- the initial level of benefit payments). Society will have to ask of itself which is the worse problem: people staying on welfare and not having any incentive to leave welfare, or people receiving partial welfare payments even though their monthly income gets well above the poverty level?

Self Evaluation

List of Terms

Broad-Based Discrimination
Earned Income Tax Credit
Economic Development Subsidies
Gini Coefficient

Income Distribution
Limited Discrimination
Lorenz Curve
Poverty
Workfare

For the statements below, fill in the term from the list above which provides the best fit.

1.) One government initiative for reducing poverty and unemployment is to award _____ to inner city areas and selected rural areas.

2.) A country's _____ provides data to compare the degree of inequality that exists between various income classes in a society.

3.) One way to provide a benchmark for the _____ level is by calculating the cost of buying a nutritionally sound diet and multiplying by a factor of three.

4.) One method of providing direct financial assistance to impoverished households through the federal tax system involves the use of the _____.

5.) One way to graphically illustrate a country's distribution of income is through the use of a _____ which shows the degree of inequity in comparison to an equal distribution of income.

6.) Persistent and widespread criticisms of welfare programs have increased interest in _____ requirements which require able-bodied welfare recipients to accept work.

7.) The _____ provides researchers a quantitative measure of a country's income or wealth distribution.

8.) _____ by an entire industry or sector of the economy can result in lower wages for those discriminated against and an increase in inequality for society as a whole.

9.) _____ by a firm may result in higher wages and/or lower productivity, thus ultimately harming the firm.

Problems

Plotting the Distribution of Income

The Lorenz curve can be used to illustrate graphically a country's income distribution, allowing us to compare it with another country's, and it also permits, in a very approximate way, us to calculate the Gini coefficient. Income data for the United States (before and after taxes and transfers) from Chapter 13 of the Hogendorn text are reproduced below.

Table 13-1
Percentage Share of U.S. Household Income, 1991
By Percentile Groups of Households

	Lowest 20% (To $17,000)	Second 20% (To $29,111)	Third 20% (To $43,000)	Fourth 20% (To $62,991)	Highest 20% (Above $ 62,991)
A.	1.1	8.0	15.9	25.3	49.6
B.	5.1	11.1	16.7	24.0	43.0

A -- Before taxes and transfers.
B -- After taxes and transfers (in cash or in kind)
Source: U.S. Bureau of the Census. <u>Statistical Abstract of the United States, 1993</u>, Table 750.

Highlight the diagonal in the following graph. Then, plot the two Lorenz curves for the United States, using the data in the table above. You may find it helpful to cumulate the income data before graphing it.

Table 13-2
Cumulative Income Distribution

	Distribution A	Distribution B
0 Percent of Income Units	0 %	0 %
Bottom 20 Percent of Income Units		
Bottom 40 Percent of Income Units		
Bottom 60 Percent of Income Units		
Bottom 80 Percent of Income Units		
100 Percent of Income Units	100 %	100 %

Figure 13-1

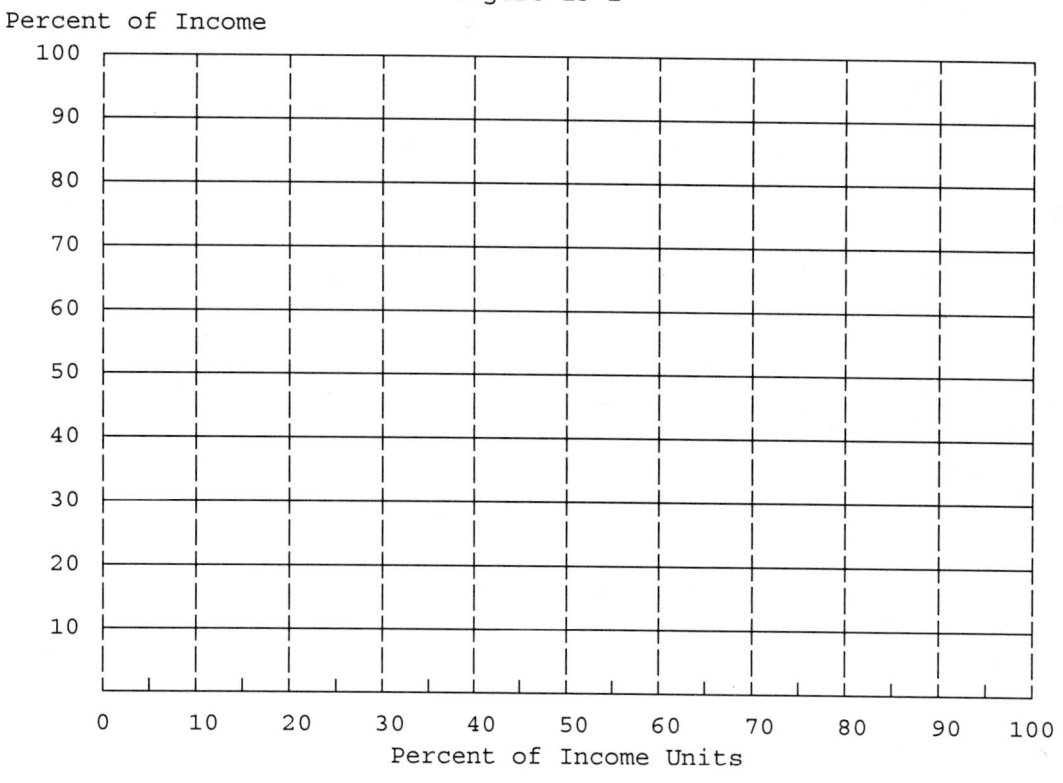

Percent of Income

[Blank graph with y-axis labeled 0 to 100 in increments of 10, and x-axis labeled "Percent of Income Units" from 0 to 100 in increments of 10]

A rough approximation of the Gini coefficient can be made by using the formula a/(a + b) where (a) is the area bounded by the Lorenz curve and the diagonal, and (b) is the area bounded by the Lorenz curve and the right angle of the graph itself. The areas could be approximated by counting squares and parts of squares but would be a bit tedious so we'll skip that this time around.

True/False Statements

Indicate whether you think the statements below are true or false. These questions are designed to make you think about the concepts presented in the text. There may not be any easy clear-cut answers. Some thoughts about the answers are presented at the end of the chapter.

1.) _____ The further a Lorenz curve bows out away from the 45 degree line diagonal, the more inequitable the income distribution.

2.) _____ If an individual firm discriminates against a particular class of people, it will end up harming the firm, since it will face increased labor costs.

3.) _____ Increased labor mobility will tend to reduce geographical differences in per capita incomes.

4.) _____ As income taxes become more progressive, after-tax incomes become more equal.

5.) _____ The market system perpetuates poverty by continually rewarding the rich and successful members of society and penalizing the poorer, less successful members.

6.) _____ Discrimination in the labor market always lowers the wages of those being discriminated against.

7.) _____ Greater geographical mobility tends to reduce income differentials between different regions of the country.

8.) _____ Decreasing welfare benefits when recipients earn outside income creates an incentive to get off welfare.

Multiple-Choice Questions

Select the "best" answer from the alternatives provided.

1.) If a society's income distribution were to become more equally distributed, its Lorenz curve
   a. would be more "bowed out" from the 45 degree line diagonal.
   b. would be less "bowed out" from the 45 degree line diagonal.
   c. would be the same as the 45 degree line diagonal.
   d. would not change, since such a change can not be illustrated on a Lorenz curve.

2.) The Gini coefficient
   a. will be higher the greater society's inequality.
   b. will be lower the greater society's inequality.
   c. can only be calculated for market societies.
   d. can vary between 0 and 1, with 0.5 representing a balance between high and low income classes.

3.) In terms of how labor markets function, inequalities in income can be caused by
   a. high demand and low supply for skilled workers and a high demand and low supply for unskilled workers.
   b. high demand and low supply for skilled workers and a low demand and low supply for unskilled workers.
   c. high demand and low supply for skilled workers and a low demand and high supply for unskilled workers.
   d. low demand and high supply for skilled workers and a high demand and low supply for unskilled workers.

4.) If a firm discriminates against a minority group,
   a. its costs will be the same, and other firms' costs will decrease.
   b. its costs will decrease, and other firms' costs will decrease.
   c. its costs will increase, and other firms' costs will decrease.
   d. its costs will increase, and other firms' costs will remain the same.

5.) If broad-based discrimination exists in a society,
   a. wages will increase in the sector where the discrimination occurs and will decrease in other industries.
   b. firms in the sector where the discrimination occurs will experience higher labor costs.
   c. then the degree of income inequality will increase.
   d. all of the above apply.

6.) With respect to the level of poverty in the United States,
   a. an increase in the cost of a nutritionally sound diet will result in an increase in the defined poverty level.
   b. in-kind assistance from government agencies is included in the government's definition of income.
   c. it is dependent upon the average income of society as a whole.
   d. it has improved dramatically since the inception of a formal definition of poverty in the 1960s.

7.) The earned-income tax credit is an alternative to traditional welfare programs such as AFDC. Comparing the two programs
   a. both programs penalize, to some degree, recipients who have outside earnings.
   b. the earned-income tax credit allows recipients to choose how they want to consume their income subsidy.
   c. the earned-income tax credit is paid only to households with incomes below a prescribed level.
   d. both programs have found that recipients are sensitive to changes in the program' financial incentives.

Discussion Questions

1.) One of the grounds for supporting the North American Free Trade Agreement (NAFTA) was that it made good economic sense -- it combined a high wage, highly capital-intensive economy with a low wage, labor-intensive economy. What impact do you think NAFTA will have upon the wages and employment of relatively unskilled workers in the two countries? the number of people under the poverty level in the two countries?

2.) One proposal supply side economists have made is that welfare and unemployment benefits be taxed so that there are less incentives for not working. During the eighties, supply siders argued that there were too many incentives not to work being provided by the government and a lack of incentives towards work itself. Is this a useful perspective on the problem of poverty and unemployment in the United States?

3.) How does large-scale illegal immigration affect poverty and unemployment problems? Many illegal immigrants argue that the jobs that they obtain are ones that Americans are not interested in having, so their presence does not reduce job opportunities for Americans. Comment.

4.) From a public policy viewpoint, do you think it is better to provide welfare recipients with goods and services in kind or with cash grants?

5.) Should our federal income tax be made progressive (i.e., marginal tax rates increase at a faster rate as income increases) to help alleviate the income inequities that exist in our society today?

Answers and Solutions to Problems and Exercises

Completing Statements from the List of Terms

1.) Economic Development Subsidies
2.) Income Distribution
3.) Poverty
4.) Earned Income Tax Credit
5.) Lorenz Curve
6.) Workfare
7.) Gini Coefficient
8.) Broad-Based Discrimination
9.) Limited Discrimination

Problems

Plotting the Distribution of Income

Table 13-2
Cumulative Income Distribution

	Distribution A	Distribution B
0 Percent of Income Units	0 %	0 %
Bottom 20 Percent of Income Units	1.1 %	5.1 %
Bottom 40 Percent of Income Units	9.1 %	16.2 %
Bottom 60 Percent of Income Units	25.0 %	32.9 %
Bottom 80 Percent of Income Units	50.3 %	56.9 %
100 Percent of Income Units	100.0 %	100.0 %

Figure 13-1

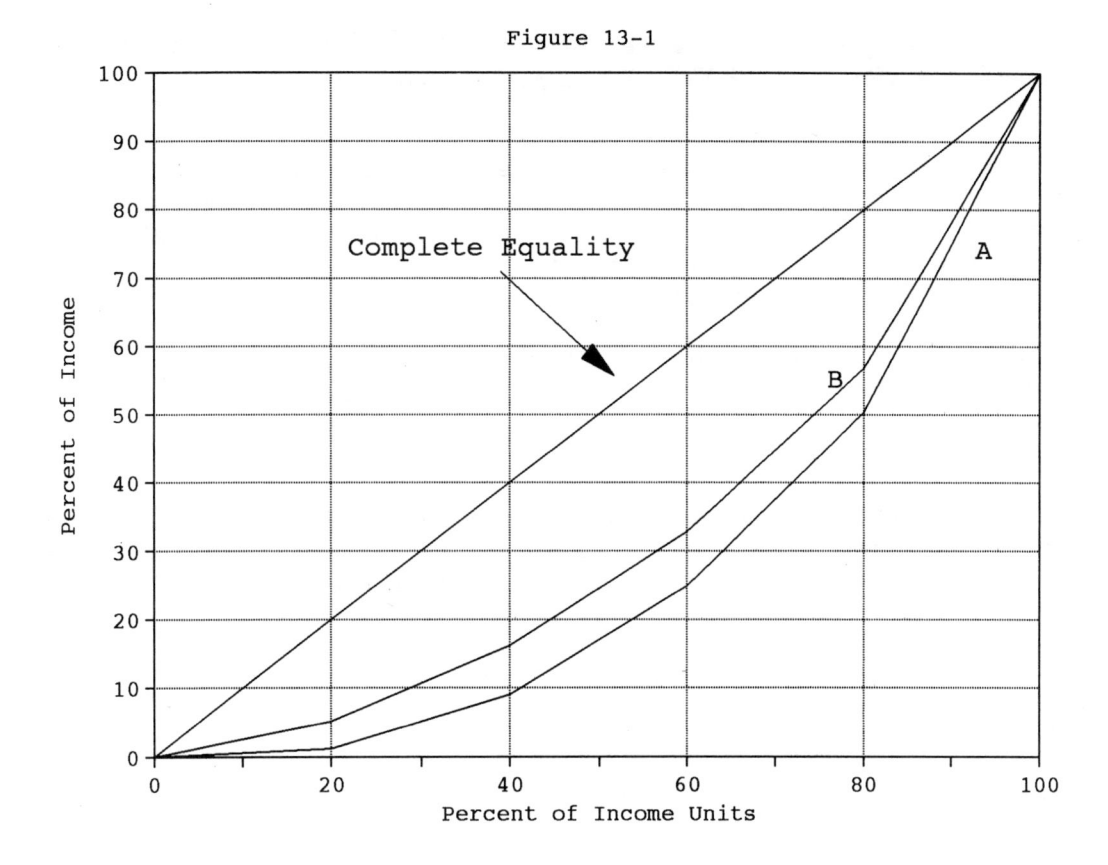

True/False Statements

1.) **True.** If the bottom 20 % of income units received only 5 % of total income, rather than a more equal figure of 12 %, the first point on the Lorenz curve would be well below the diagonal line of complete equality.

2.) **True.** The discriminating firm's supply of labor will shift to the left, raising its wages and labor costs, while other firms will face an increased supply of labor and lower wages.

3.) **True.** This is the classic method for reducing wage and income inequities, with people from low wage areas migrating to areas of higher wages. This labor movement tends to equalize geographical wage differences over time.

4.) **True.** Higher marginal tax rates on upper income units and lower marginal tax rates on lower income units will tend to equalize after-tax incomes. Tax avoidance becomes an issue when marginal tax rates reach some point.

5.) **False.** The market system allows individuals an opportunity to succeed at what they do best, creates economic incentives to better one's economic position, and provides an environment that is generally conducive to change and improvement. Unfortunately, there is also a tendency to concentrate and perpetuate existing wealth and sources of economic and political power.

6.) **True.** As discriminated workers move from sectors where they are discriminated against to other economic sectors, the supply of labor is increased in those sectors where they are moving, and, other things being equal, wages will be lower. On an individual level, discrimination prevents workers from reaching their full potential, thus lowering their income possibilities.

7.) **True.** Workers will tend to migrate from low wage areas to higher wage regions. Greater mobility would facilitate this process. Income differentials within the United States have grown smaller with the greater mobility of today's workers.

8.) **False.** If welfare benefits are reduced on a one-to-one basis when a recipient has outside earnings, the effect is the same as a 100 % percent tax on those earnings, up to the level of their welfare benefits. Not very many people are willing to work under those conditions.

Multiple-Choice

1.) b   2.) a   3.) c   4.) c   5.) d   6.) a

7.) b

Discussion Questions

1. NAFTA will move the two labor markets closer together. Wages for unskilled workers in the United States will either fall or not increase as fast as they would have without the agreement, and, in Mexico, the demand for unskilled workers will increase with resulting increases in wages and employment. If there ever was a reason to finish high school and go on to college to obtain more skills, NAFTA is it!

   Thus, NAFTA is likely to intensify unemployment problems in the United States for a segment of our population that already faces significant economic problems. An increase in poverty rates for the unskilled and uneducated may be a likely prospect. Mexico, on the other hand, may very well see an improvement in the economic prospects for the unskilled component of its population.

   Any trade agreement creates groups of winners and losers. Owners of capital and workers in capital-intensive sectors are expected to come out winners in the United States as are the best trained and most skilled workers. But, as mentioned above, there will be losses that will need to be dealt with.

2.) Economics is concerned with how incentives affect behavior and actions. To the extent that we as a society make our "safety net" programs too lucrative, we already know from experience that some people will choose to stay with such programs, not actively looking for ways to get off the programs. Taxing welfare and unemployment benefits may seem like somewhat odd behavior -- giving people benefits and then taxing those benefits. But, in principle, peoples' incentives to work or not to work would be affected, and, as economists, we would predict that people would change their behavior over time.

3.) This question is getting more and more attention as people analyze the impact of immigration on the U.S. economy. If, at any given period of time, there are only so many jobs available for the unskilled, then an increase in the supply of labor (through illegal immigration) would put downward pressure on wages and possibly result in an increase in unemployment for both groups. There is some truth to the assertion that Americans don't seem to want the most menial, lowest paying jobs in our society. In that case, the illegal aliens provide a real service in being willing to work in these positions. There are, of course, many other economic consequences associated with illegal aliens.

4.) There are arguments to be made on both sides of this position. From a strictly economic perspective, welfare recipients can be made better off with cash grants, since they could use the income received to consume the bundle of goods and services which they preferred the most. Consumer choice is maximized when cash grants are provided; consequently, overall satisfaction is maximized with that approach. If, however, there is concern about some of the items that might be consumed by the recipients (society may prefer that such income not be spent on liquor, cigarettes, or great looking clothes when dependent children are in need of milk, fruit, and cereal), cash grants are apt to result in considerable controversy.

5.) A highly progressive income tax structure can be used to diminish after-tax income inequities, particularly if some of the taxes collected from upper income units is used to finance programs which enhance the standard and quality of living for those under and near the poverty line. However, high marginal rates of taxation may be counter-productive as taxpayers try to evade paying the higher tax rates or start substituting leisure for work. If the high tax rates put a damper on economic growth in the economy, then the resulting increases in unemployment will also affect the economic welfare of those having lower incomes.

Summary

Income distribution and poverty issues always generate a lot of controversial discussion, partly because the notion of fairness is so subjective.

There has been some realization that providing cash assistance through the tax system or by some other means may be a more effective and efficient way of helping people with low incomes. Basing total benefits on family size, while a reasonable approach, has resulted in highly publicized stories about welfare recipients having children simply to obtain more benefits. Yet to deny additional benefits when a new child enters the family may harm the child. When outside earnings are subtracted from welfare benefits on a one-to-one basis, those benefits are effectively taxed at a rate of 100 %. One need not ask why welfare recipients stay on welfare instead of trying to find a job when policies like that are in force.

Education, re-training, and perhaps relocation (with significant economic incentives) are important factors in breaking the culture of poverty that exists in many urban centers today. Workfare, mandatory training programs, changing incentives to work, and time limits on receiving benefits are all being discussed and tried out in various states. Perhaps most importantly, minority and impoverished young people must have a interest in the economic system, so that they feel there are sufficient incentives to participate in the system. Currently, with unemployment rates so high for young adults and minority Americans, many feel as if the economic system has failed them.

Chapter 14
An Introduction to Macroeconomics

Overview of the Chapter

Chapter 14 provides a brief transition to our study of macroeconomics. You will now start to grapple with the sometimes difficult and perplexing but always interesting, problems of business cycles, economic growth, unemployment, and inflation. As your author notes, the economic history of the United States has been characterized by fluctuations, occasionally quite large, in the overall level of economic activity. The problems of unemployment and inflation have become more problematic with the decline in the importance of the agricultural sector of the economy and the increasing interdepedence of households and businesses. These two problems have received the largest amount of attention, since they affect not only those who are economically active but also those who are not.

The length and severity of the Great Depression changed people's views on the economy. John Maynard Keynes, an English economist, presented an entirely different macroeconomic perspective of the economy -- one in which total spending on goods and services played a pivotal role in determining the level of output, income, and employment. The Keynesian view was that excessive unemployment was due to insufficient spending and inflation was due to too much spending.

During recessions and depressions, the economy contracts, output and spending fall, and unemployment rises. The real economic cost of economic downturns is the forgone output that could have been produced had the unemployment not occurred. The stated unemployment rate does not distinguish between full-time and part-time employment nor does it take into account under-employed workers who would like to be working more. Workers who have gotten discouraged from lengthy and unsuccessful job searches are not counted in the official unemployment statistics, since they are no longer in the labor force.

Inflation, on the other hand, is generally associated with economies that have too much spending taking place relative to the economy's productive output. While there are some real costs associated with inflation, its economic effects are much more subtle than those related to excessive unemployment. Unanticipated inflation redistributes income in an arbitrary and capricious manner, creating different sets of winners and losers. If it is anticipated, it is sometimes possible to adjust to higher inflation rates and offset some of its effects.

Inflation usually raises nominal incomes (incomes in terms of current, inflated dollars), however, it does not necessarily follow that increases in people's nominal incomes makes them better off economically. Inflation has the potential to distort our economic decisions, making us think that we are better off when, in fact, we may not be in terms of real purchasing power. As is the case for all economic variables, it is important to distinguish between nominal variables, such as the nominal interest rate, and real economic variables (the real interest rate) which have been adjusted to account for the degree of inflation that has occurred.

Occasionally, moderate inflation accelerates into what has come to be called hyperinflation -- a situation in which inflation grows uncontrollably, wiping out any assets that can't keep up with its increasing spiral. Hyperinflation stops only when a country's monetary authorities quit issuing the new money needed to fuel the inflation.

Learning Objectives

After completing this chapter, you should be sure that you are able to:

- understand the business cycle and its cyclical pattern of expansion and contraction in business activity that has characterized the United States economy since its conception.

- describe the economic and social costs and impacts of recessions and depressions.

- define the real cost of unemployment for society.

- understand the dimensions of unemployment, the concept of under-employment, and the discouraged worker syndrome.

- describe the economic and social costs and impacts of inflation.

- distinguish between the nominal rate of interest and the real rate of interest.

- understand the special case of hyperinflation and its costs and causes.

Self Evaluation

List of Terms

Business Cycle
Depression
Discouraged Workers
Gross Domestic Product
Hyperinflation
Inflation
Macroeconomics
Menu Costs

Nominal Interest Rate
Real Interest Rate
Recession
Shoe Leather Costs
Variable Interest Rates
Under-employed
Unemployment

For the statements below, fill in the term from the list above which provides the best fit.

1.) _____ is an overall increase in the price level.

2.) Inflation often makes it difficult for firms to keep current with price changes, and the inconvenience and expense associated with constantly changing prices are known as _____.

3.) If, while eating at a restaurant, the cost of your meal doubles, you can be sure that _____ has set in.

4.) _____ is the study of the whole economic system, how it performs, and what major problems it faces.

5.) _____ provides an estimate of the total value of economic activity that takes place in a year.

6.) Consumers shopping the specials at each store, firms and consumers paying more attention to cash flow and financial management issues are examples of the _____ associated with inflation.

7.) Workers are considered to be _____ if they are working on a part-time basis but have the capabilities and desire to work full time.

8.) By subtracting the rate of inflation from the nominal interest rate, an estimate of the _____ can be obtained.

9.) Whenever there is a situation in which people are willing to work and are actively looking for work but can't find work, _____ exists.

10.) The output fluctuations that have occurred in the U.S. economy over time are commonly referred to as the _____.

11.) _____ have been employed at some earlier time but have been unable to find employment for an extended period of time and have now dropped out of the labor force.

12.) During periods of inflation, lenders can minimize the risks of incorrectly estimating the rate of inflation by offering loans with _____ to borrowers.

13.) The actual stated rate of interest on a loan agreement is known as the _____.

14.) While there is no universally accepted definition of a _____, it is characterized by very high levels of unemployment and declines in industrial production and total output.

15.) A _____ occurs when real output declines for six months or more.

Problems

Calculating the Real Rate of Interest

You are given the following time series data for interest rates and the rate of inflation for the period 1980 - 1991:

Table 14-1

Nominal Rates of Interest on Selected Securities
and the Rate of Inflation

Year	Interest Rate on 3 Year Government Securities (Percent/year)	Interest Rate on Baa Rating Corporate Bonds (Percent/year)	Rate of Inflation Dec. to Dec. (Percent/year)	Real Rate of Interest 3 Year Government Securities (Percent/year)	Real Rate of Interest Baa Corporate Bonds (Percent/year)
1984	11.89	14.19	3.9		
1985	9.64	12.72	3.8		
1986	7.06	10.39	1.1		
1987	7.68	10.58	4.4		
1988	8.26	10.83	4.4		
1989	8.55	10.18	4.6		
1990	8.26	10.36	6.1		
1991	6.82	9.80	3.1		
1992	5.30	8.98	3.2		
1993	4.44	7.93	2.7		

Source: *Economic Report of the President, Transmitted to the Congress, February, 1992.* Washington, D.C.: United States Government Printing Office, 1992.

Calculate the real rate of interest for three year government securities and the Baa corporate bonds. For purposes of this exercise, you may use the short-cut method of calculation which approximates the actual real rate of interest: **nominal interest rate - inflation rate = real interest rate**

Plot the nominal and real rates of interest for the two different types of securities on the following graphs.

Figure 14-1

Percent per year — Three Year Government Securities

Nominal and Real Interest Rates (18 to -2)

Year: 1984 85 86 87 88 89 90 91 92 93

Figure 14-2

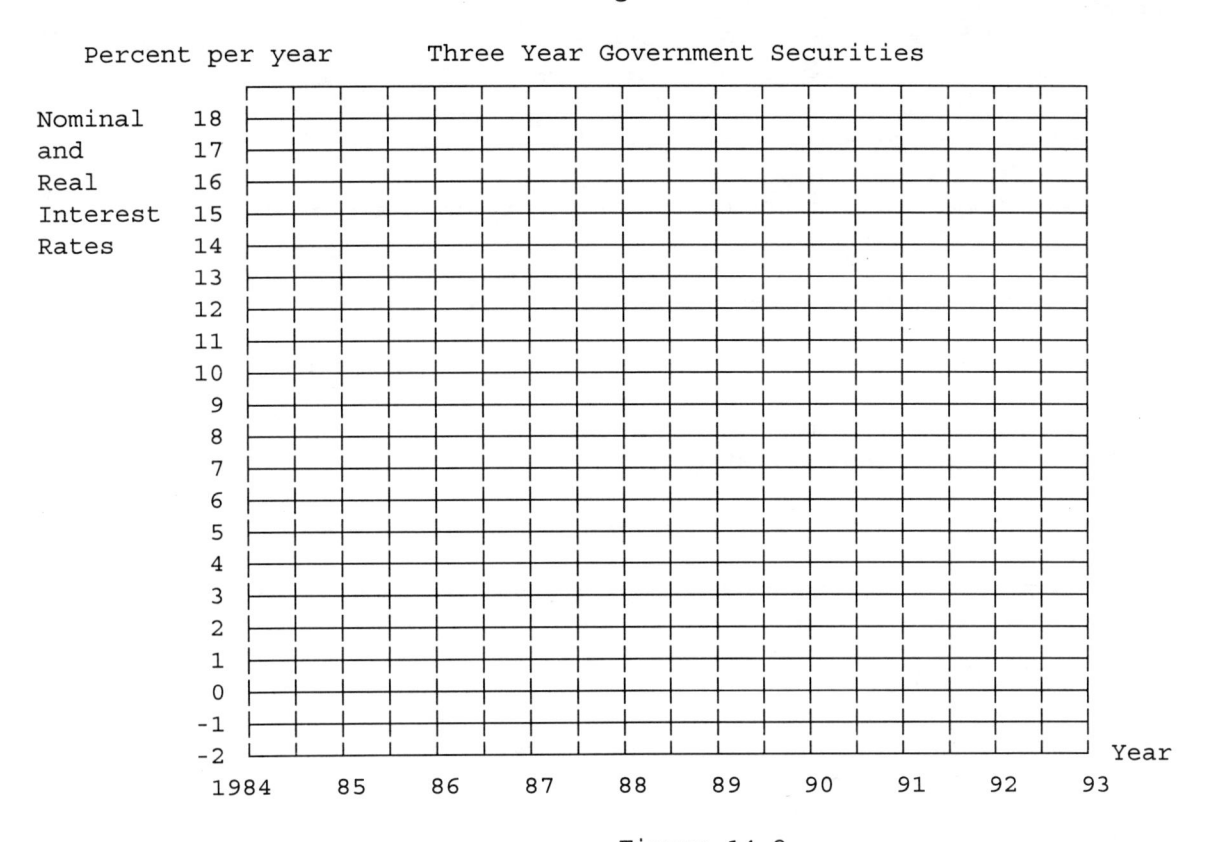

Percent per year — Baa Corporate Bonds

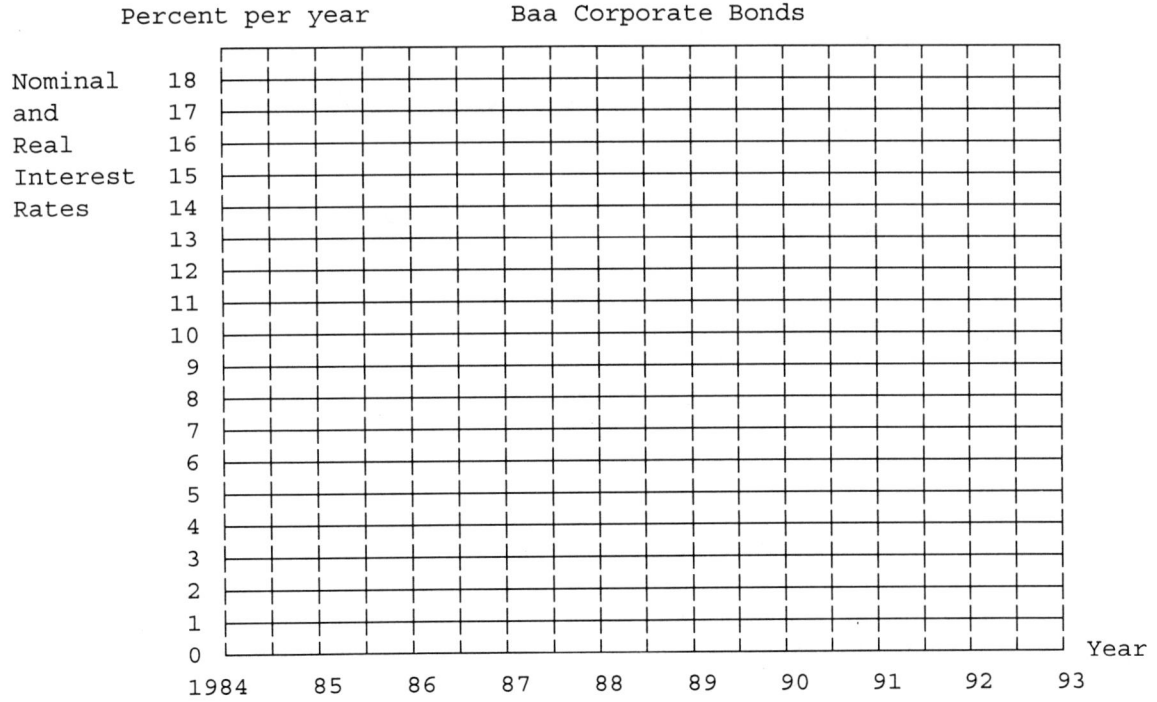

Nominal and Real Interest Rates (18 to 0)

Year: 1984 85 86 87 88 89 90 91 92 93

Why do you think the two real rates of interest are different from one another?

_____

_____

Would you expect the real rate of interest to increase or decrease during periods of significant inflation?

_____

_____

Would you expect the nominal rate of interest to increase or decrease during periods of significant inflation?

_____

_____

True/False Statements

Indicate whether you think the statements below are true or false. These questions are designed to make you think about the concepts presented in the text. There may not be any easy clear-cut answers. Some thoughts about the answers are presented at the end of the chapter.

1.) _____ The real interest rate is always greater than zero.

2.) _____ Hyperinflations are always accompanied by large increases in the supply of money.

3.) _____ Borrowers lose out during periods of unanticipated inflation, while lenders usually do quite well.

4.) _____ Lower nominal interest rates are always preferred by borrowers over higher nominal interest rates.

5.) _____ Real assets, such as land or commodities, should be held during a period of inflation rather than paper assets such as bonds and leases.

6.) _____ Falling imports in the United States may result in a recession being transmitted to other countries.

7.) _____ Recessions and contractions in the level of economic activity have become less frequent and less severe in the post-World War II era.

8.) _____ Governmental units with large amounts of debt outstanding gain during periods of rapid inflation.

Multiple-Choice Questions

Select the "best" answer from the alternatives provided.

1.) The current nominal interest rate on a particular kind of student loan is 12 %. If the rate of inflation over the period of the loan is expected to be 4 %,
   a. the real rate of interest would be 16 %.
   b. the real rate of interest would be 8 %.
   c. the real rate of interest would be also be 12 %.
   d. the real rate of interest can't be determined without additional information.

2.) When your text discusses "menu costs" as part of the cost to society due to inflation,
   a. that means that inflation makes it too expensive for most people to go out to eat because of declining real incomes.
   b. inflation impoverishes people so they steal restaurant menus to slip inside their clothes to keep warm.
   c. the higher prices associated with inflation mean that everyone has to lug around large amounts of coins, with resulting inconveniences for both consumers and firms who have to count all the coins.
   d. constantly changing prices mean that restaurants and other firms have to spend real resources in keeping up with the price changes.
   e. both (c) and (d) apply.

3.) During a period of unanticipated inflation,
   a. wage earners with long-term contracts gain at the expense of their employers.
   b. owners of fixed interest rate bonds come out ahead, since their rate of return is guaranteed.
   c. owners of real assets gain.
   d. creditors gain at the expense of debtors.

4.) If an economy is experiencing hyperinflation,
   a. it is especially important because of the turbulent times to put money away for retirement.
   b. lenders typically gain, since they can raise their interest rates on loans.
   c. it is almost always caused by workers demanding excessive wage increases.
   d. it is prudent for wage earners to get paid as often as possible.

5.) Which of the following groups gain during a period of unanticipated inflation?
   a. bond holders, creditors, pensioners on fixed incomes, and people with little or no debt
   b. owners of real assets, borrowers, pensioners whose incomes are indexed, and people who are heavily in debt.
   c. owners of paper assets, creditors, homeowners with variable rate mortgages, and people who are heavily in debt.
   d. owners of real assets, homeowners with fixed rate mortgages, and people with little or no debt.

6.) During a recession,
   a. unemployment usually remains fairly constant, but people quit entering the labor force.
   b. GDP and total production continue to increase, but unemployment rises.
   c. unemployment increases proportionally for all demographic groups.
   d. GDP will decrease, unemployment will rise, and the percent of capacity utilization will fall.

Discussion Questions

1.) Hyperinflations provide some insights into the relationship that exists between economic stability and political stability for societies. Some people have suggested that there was a relationship between the post-World War I hyperinflation that occurred in Germany and Hitler's rise. What do you think would be the basis for that conclusion?

2.) What can individuals and firms do to avoid the adverse effects of unanticipated inflation?

3.) Does inflation that is widely and accurately anticipated cause the same kind of problems as unanticipated inflation?

4.) Unemployment, with its very high real economic costs, represents a much more serious problem for an economy than inflation which merely redistributes incomes between winners and losers. Comment.

5.) If, as your text indicates, inflation results in some difficult problems for the economy, would deflation (a reduction in the overall price level) create favorable economic conditions?

6.) During a period of inflation, would you expect interest rates to rise or fall?

Answers and Solutions to Problems and Exercises

Completing Statements from the List of Terms

1.) Inflation
2.) Menu Costs
3.) Hyperinflation
4.) Macroeconomics
5.) Gross Domestic Product
6.) Shoe Leather Costs
7.) Under-employed
8.) Real Interest Rate
9.) Unemployment
10.) Business Cycle
11.) Discouraged Workers
12.) Variable Interest Rates
13.) Nominal Interest Rate
14.) Depression
15.) Recession

Calculating the Real Rate of Interest

Table 14-1

Year	Interest Rate on Three Year Government Securities (Percent/year)	Interest Rate on Baa Rating Corporate Bonds (Percent/year)	Rate of Inflation Dec. to Dec. (Percent/year)	Real Rate of Interest 3 Year Government Securities (Percent/year)	Real Rate of Interest Baa Corporate Bonds (Percent/year)
1984	11.89	14.19	3.9	7.99	10.29
1985	9.64	12.72	3.8	5.84	8.92
1986	7.06	10.39	1.1	5.96	9.29
1987	7.68	10.58	4.4	3.28	6.18
1988	8.26	10.83	4.4	3.86	6.43
1989	8.55	10.18	4.6	3.95	5.58
1990	8.26	10.36	6.1	2.16	4.26
1991	6.82	9.80	3.1	3.72	6.70
1992	5.30	8.98	2.9	2.40	6.08
1993	4.44	7.93	2.7	1.74	5.23

Figure 14-1
Three Year Government Securities

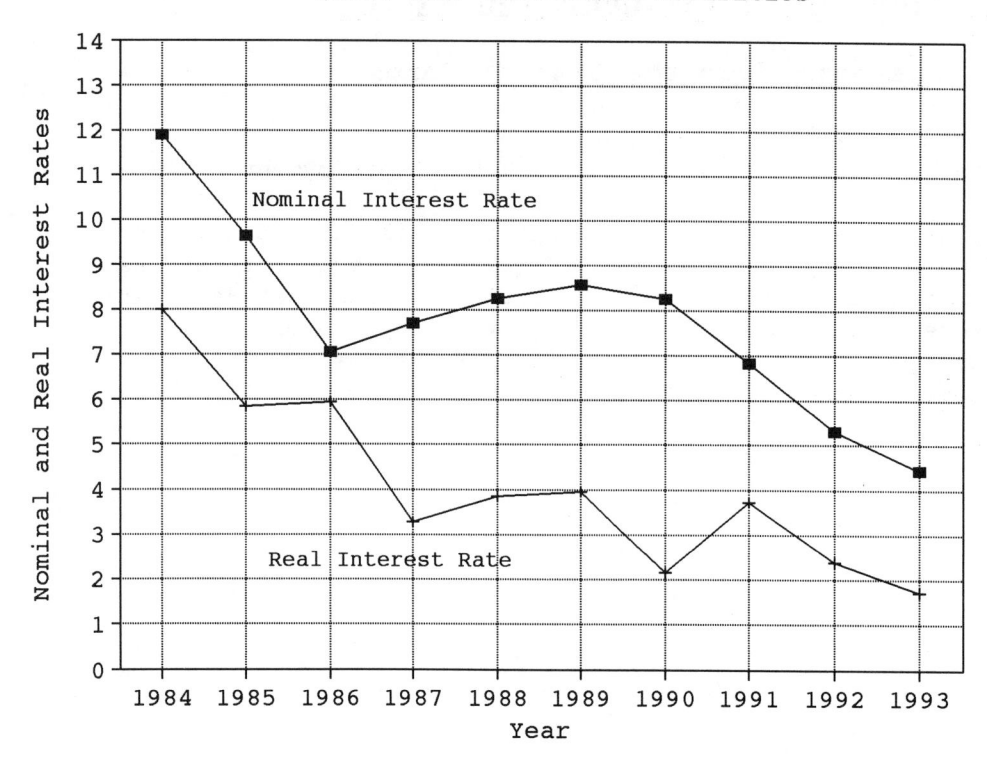

Figure 14-2
Baa Corporate Bonds

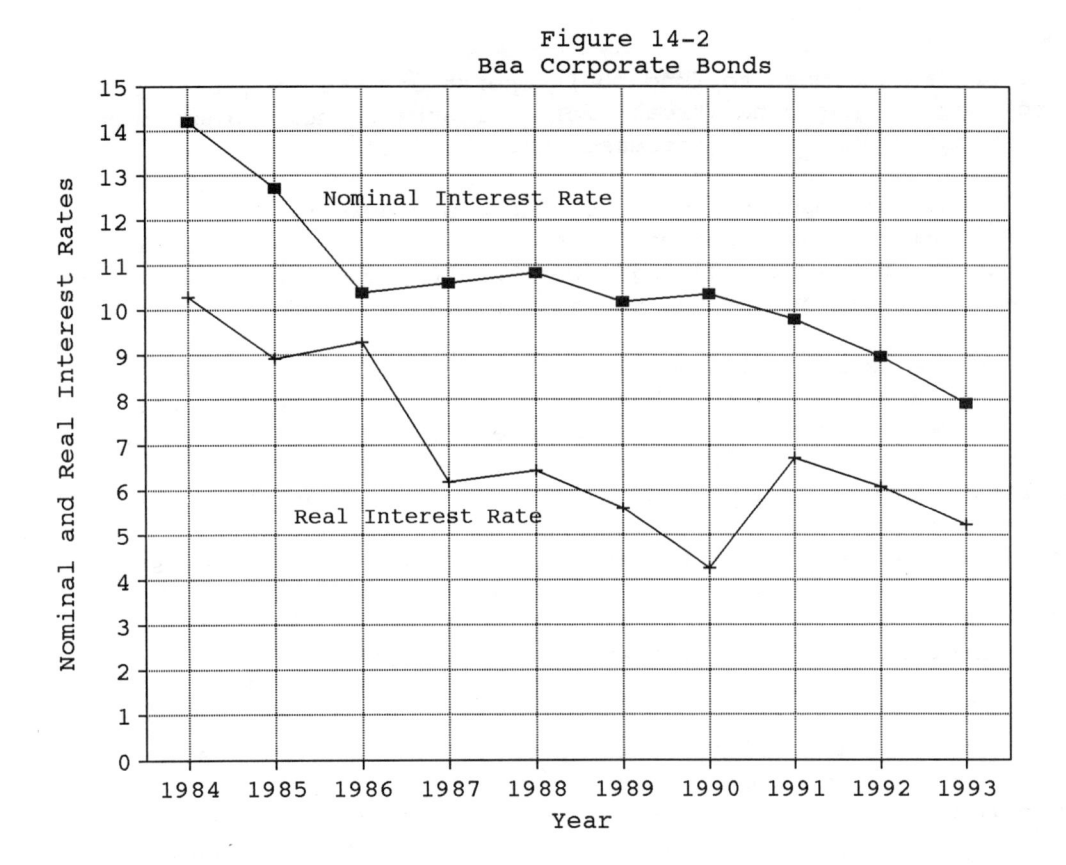

Why do you think the two real rates of interest are different from one another? **The risk factors differ significantly between the two different types of securities. One would expect lenders would want to be compensated more, in real terms, when lending under riskier circumstances.**

Would you expect the real rate of interest to increase or decrease during periods of significant inflation? **That depends upon the ability of lenders to respond to inflationary pressures. Interest rates on short-term securities can be adjusted quickly, those on long-term securities only over a much longer time horizon.**

Would you expect the nominal rate of interest to increase or decrease during periods of significant inflation? **They would increase as lenders attempt to adjust nominal interest rates to keep their real rates of interest the same.**

True/False Statements

1.) **False.** If the inflation rate exceeds the stated nominal interest rate, then the real interest rate will be negative. The real interest rate equals the nominal interest rate minus the rate of inflation.

2.) **True.** Excessive growth in the money supply is necessary to sustain the inflationary spiral associated with hyperinflations. Typically, governments issues the new money when they are unable to generate sufficient tax revenues to fund their operations. It would be difficult to imagine what other "real" forces in the economy might cause such a sustained and rapid increase in the price level.

3.) **False.** Just the opposite, since during a period of inflation, borrowers are able to pay back creditors in dollars that are less valuable in terms of real purchasing power than the ones they were originally lent. Inflation reduces the real burden of debt.

4.) **False.** Not always -- it depends! Other things being equal, a person would always prefer to have a lower nominal interest rate. But during periods of high inflation rates, a loan with a high nominal interest rate might well be preferable to a loan with a lower nominal rate taken out during a period of very low inflation. An illustration:
nominal interest rate = 14% Inflation rate = 9% => Real interest rate = 5%

nominal interest rate = 8% Inflation rate = 2% => Real interest rate = 6%

5.) **True.** During periods of significant inflation, the best assets to have are those whose value will rise with inflation, maintaining their real purchasing power. Paper assets with fixed nominal payments will result in lower and lower real income from the asset.

6.) **True.** As we import less from abroad, foreign exports would fall. Unless replaced by some other source of spending, foreign output, employment, and income would fall, putting contractionary pressures on their economies. While a fall in spending for a country's exports may not be sufficient to put an economy into a full-fledged recession, it certainly could be a major contributing factor.

7.) **True.** While recessions have not yet been eliminated, the historical record indicates that they have been less frequent and less severe since the end of World War II.

8.) **True.** Inflation makes it easier for governmental units to pay back their loans with dollars that have less purchasing power and, thus, are less valuable. Inflation reduces the real burden of debt, no matter whether it is private or public.

Multiple-Choice

1.) b   2.) e   3.) c   4.) d   5.) b   6.) d

Discussion Questions

1.) It has been suggested that hyperinflations destroy the middle class by taking away all of their assets, their pension funds, their savings, etc. This then makes them more susceptible to extreme political solutions, either from the far left or in the case of Hitler, the far right. The viability of the middle class is an important factor in maintaining society's stability. Inflation, since it sets group against group, winner against loser, rips the social fabric that holds us together. From this perspective, proper economic policy becomes vitally important for the long term well-being of society.

2.) They can try, if possible, to get into assets which will maintain their real value. Land, gold, homes, specific commodities -- items whose price will rise with the price level. Paper assets with fixed nominal returns should be avoided. Currency is a paper asset, and inflation can be looked upon as a tax on holding currency. Political power can also be used to offset the effects of inflation. Social Security recipients have their benefits tied to the rate of inflation, so they are no longer hurt by inflation. Market power is also useful in being able to pass on cost increases to other parties in the form of higher prices or wages. The return on savings almost always falls below the rate of inflation, meaning that the real purchasing power of those savings is falling. So, during inflationary periods, spending for consumption makes sense; saving doesn't make as much sense.

3.) No, since if it is anticipated, both firms and individuals can take appropriate steps to lessen the impact of inflation on their activities. Lenders, for example, can raise the interest rate to compensate them for the loss of purchasing power that occurs over the term of a loan, or they can issue variable rate loans instead of fixed rate loans, thus transferring the risk of inflation onto the borrowers. Consumers can change their spending and saving habits.

4.) A difficult question that policy makers have had to grapple with for many years. Unemployment extracts a terrible toll on the economy, on individuals, and on families. Loss of a job in today's society frequently is associated with a loss of respect, a loss of importance. If one doesn't have a job, then worries about inflation seem pretty trivial. However, given our recent experience with inflation and its effect on our rate of economic growth and productivity, it's pretty clear that inflation imposes some significant long-run costs on society.

5.) One might be tempted to think that since inflation causes severe problems for the economy that its opposite, deflation, would be better for the economy. Unfortunately, in this case, neither is very good for the economy. Deflation creates its own set of problems for the economy -- rewarding lenders at the expense of borrowers, changing the distribution of income in favor of holders of fixed return paper assets, etc.

6.) Nominal interest rates will rise as lenders attach larger inflationary premiums to their interest rates. Regarding real interest rates, if nominal rates increase faster than the rate of inflation, they will rise; otherwise, they will fall.

Summary

Economists have studied the business cycle and its consequences for a long time, trying to understand its causes so that it would be possible to control the cycles. A steady growth path for the economy is much more desirable than the unpredictable and variable pattern of expansion and contraction associated with the business cycle. The record of economic growth contained in Figure 14-1 certainly suggests that we have been more successful in the past 50 years in achieving longer expansions and less severe recessions than we experienced in the pre-World War II period.

Full employment and stable prices are the two most important economic goals for developed economies. Employment is closely tied to the growth path of the economy, increasing in expansion part of the cycle and decreasing in contractions. Inflation is also related to the business cycle, although the relationship is much looser, with inflationary pressures tending to develop during expansions and the price level not increasing as rapidly or perhaps even falling during contractions.

Up until the early 1970s, society had a fairly well-defined trade-off that existed between inflation and unemployment (i.e., it could have lower unemployment only at the cost of higher inflation and lower inflation only with higher unemployment). The trade-off meant that society had to choose between achieving one goal or the other, and it is for that reason so much emphasis is put on examining the costs of unemployment and inflation to society. If society has to choose which goal to attain, then it must compare the economic costs to make a knowledgeable decision.

The economic costs of unemployment are readily identifiable in terms of forgone output and income. What is perhaps not so apparent are the other costs -- increased crime rates, a rise in suicides, more mental illness, and the stress on families. The loss of a job means much more than just the loss in income. Inflation, in contrast, redistributes income in an arbitrary fashion among a diverse set of winners and losers. But for society as a whole, redistributing income is a zero sum game with no net loss. There are some very real economic costs associated with inflation but they are much more subtle than those associated with unemployment. Since inflation penalizes saving and complicates long-term investment plans, the growth rate of the economy, as well as productivity increases, is negatively affected as inflation continues. It is no coincidence that our country's growth and productivity problems started soon after we began having problems with inflation (in the 1970s).

Hyperinflation, although a rare phenomenon, is still with us today. As has always been the case, wars put almost insurmountable economic pressures on already weakened economies, and prices have soared in those countries involved with the Bosnian crisis.

Inflation in the United States has averaged under 3 % since 1990, achieving levels which we have not seen since the mid 1960s. There is considerable discussion about whether the Federal Reserve should attempt to implement a zero inflation goal. The fact that such discussions are taking place is a tribute to how well inflation has been controlled.

Chapter 15
Measuring Economic Performance

Overview of the Chapter

Chapter 15 provides an introduction to the most important macro-economic variables, describing their conceptual basis, how they are measured, and some of their limitations. One needn't be an expert in economics to realize the importance and necessity of having an accurate set of statistics for measuring various aspects of the economy's performance.

The chapter discusses and defines several macro-economic variables and national income accounts, providing some valuable insights into some of the problems associated with them. Two different measures of total output (national product) are discussed -- gross national product (GNP) and gross domestic product (GDP). Both GNP and GDP can be thought of in terms of the final market value of all goods and services produced and as the sum of total expenditures in the four basic sectors of the economy. Two sectors of the economy, investment and government, require special attention because of the unique characteristics of those two sectors.

In general, the value of all productive activity in a given period of time should be included in any measure of overall output. There are, however, some transactions which should not or cannot be included in the official GDP figures. Intermediate transactions, financial and government transfers, non-market activities, and illegal activities make up the majority of these non-included transactions.

Both GNP and GDP attempt to measure the value of final economic output produced during a year, but they are not indices of overall welfare and should not be construed as such. They do not take into account changes in the work week (or leisure time for that matter), quality changes, changes in population, pollution, or the distribution of income. No judgement is made about the composition of goods and services comprising GDP -- expenditures on cosmetics, liquor, and cigarettes are included on the same basis as spending for diapers, computers, good books, milk, and baby food.

Another economic variable which is indicative of how well the economy is performing is the level and rate of unemployment. In the United States, a fairly large number of households are sampled each month, and the survey results are used to estimate the total number of unemployed and, from that, the rate of unemployment. The official unemployment rate is not a measure of those members of society who could be working but are not; rather, it is a measure of those who are looking for work and can't find employment.

Because some unemployment is unavoidable and always present, full employment is currently defined to be around six percent. In an economic policy context, it is only when unemployment exceeds six percent that a problem exists. Capacity utilization data represent another way of determining how well the economy is performing.

The rate of inflation in an economy is measured by a price index which is based on the price changes occurring in a market basket of commodities. The consumer price index (CPI) is most appropriately used when dealing with issues involving real wages, real income, or other questions relating to households. The GDP or GNP deflator provides an estimate of price changes taking place for all sectors of the economy and can be used to measure the real GDP or GNP of the economy. The producer price index (PPI) measures price changes for goods in the production process before they get to the final sales level.

By dividing nominal GDP by the GDP deflator, an estimate of real GDP can be obtained. In nominal terms, GDP is measured by multiplying final market prices by appropriate final market quantities. It is possible for nominal GDP to increase simply because final market prices have increased without an actual increase in real output. This problem is known as money illusion.

The chapter concludes with a brief discussion of leading indicators, specific economic variables which lead or precede the overall business cycle of the economy, and the misery index. The Commerce Department currently uses an index of leading indicators which is made up of ten different variables, each of which is thought to lead the business cycle. Alas, it has not had a perfect forecasting record. The misery index is defined as the sum of the rates of inflation and unemployment, the two main economic goals of our economy. By summing the two performance variables, the implication is that the lower the misery index, the more successful an economy has been in achieving its main goals.

Learning Objectives

After completing this chapter, you should be sure that you are able to:

- define, use, and interpret the terms and tools used in measuring various aspects of macro-economic performance.

- define and interpret the different national income and product accounts.

- describe the components of gross investment and their relationship to the economy's capital stock.

- explain the role that inventories play in the economy.

- identify the types of transactions that are not included in gross domestic product and explain the rationale for their exclusion.

- discuss the measurement problems associated with the national income and product accounts.

- distinguish between gross national product and gross domestic product.

- explain the problems associated with using the various national income accounts as a measure of overall welfare.

- explain the different approaches used to measure society's total output.
- discuss the problems associated with measuring the rate of unemployment.
- describe the three different price indices, how they are used, and how they differ from one another.
- explain the role of the leading indicators index and index's relationship to the business cycle.
- define the misery index and how it can be used to measure an economy's macro-economic performance.

Self Evaluation

List of Terms

Business Inventories
Consumer Price Index
Depreciation
Discouraged Workers
Disposable Personal Income
Double Counting
Export Spending
Frictional Unemployment
GDP Deflator
Government Sector
Gross Domestic Product
Gross Investment
Gross National Product

Import Spending
Index of Leading Indicators
Indirect Business Taxes
Misery Index
National Income
Net Economic Welfare
Net Domestic Product
Per Capita GDP
Producer Price Index
Psychic Income
Real GDP
Statistical Discrepancy
Underground Economy
Value Added

For the statements below, fill in the term from the list above which provides the best fit.

1.) The **Index of Leading Indicators** provides economists with information about possible upturns or downturns in the economy before they actually occur.

2.) The difference between the price or selling price of a commodity and the cost of purchased inputs and components is defined as **Value added**.

3.) Full employment is normally considered to be around 5 to 6 % unemployment, because of the existence of **Frictional Unemp** which is temporary and transitional in nature.

4.) When calculating real wages/incomes, the **Consumer Price Index** should be used to deflate nominal wages/incomes.

5.) Payments to all factors of production is known as **National Income**

6.) _____ was developed in an attempt to account for some of the harmful economic activities which tended to reduce over-all welfare as well as some of the non-market activities normally excluded from the official GNP accounts.

7.) Expenditures for both new and replacement capital goods are listed under _____ in the national product accounts.

8.) _____ attempts to measure how much capital was used up in the process of producing the economy's annual output.

9.) If you were searching for the "best" economic measure of how much total income consumers have available for spending for any given year, that measure would be _____.

10.) Because different sources are used to estimate total income generated in the economy and estimated total product and output, it is necessary to include a _____ in the national income accounts.

11.) _____ must be subtracted from GDP and GNP in order to obtain a more accurate indication of total economic activity.

12.) _____ is a better measure than GNP of the amount of economic activity taking place within the geographic borders of a country.

13.) If intermediate economic transactions are inadvertently counted along with final transactions, we must deal with the problem of _____.

14.) Economists call the intangible enjoyment that you obtain from your job or from engaging in certain kinds of activities, _____.

15.) National income plus _____ equals net national product.

16.) The _____ provides an estimate of the prices of the entire spectrum of goods and services produced in the economy.

17.) If total production in a given year exceeds total sales, then _____ will rise.

18.) In order to determine _____, depreciation must be subtracted from GNP.

19.) The final market value of all goods and services produced in an economy over a given period of time is defined as _____.

20.) Purchases of goods and services by non-residents are called _____.

21.) If nominal GDP is adjusted for the amount of inflation that has taken place, we obtain _____.

22.) Workers who are unemployed but who have given up any hope of finding employment are classified as _____.

23.) Legal and illegal activities which generate incomes but which are not reported are included in the _____.

24.) The _____ surveys prices at the wholesale level and thus provides an estimate of future inflationary trends at the consumer level.

25.) Since there is no market for public goods, _____ is valued by summing the value of the factor inputs used in providing or producing goods and services from this sector.

26.) Two economies might have similar total GDPs but quite different population totals. A more realistic comparison of the two economies would be to compare the _____ of the two countries.

27.) The _____ was formulated in an attempt to measure how well society has attained the economic goals of price stability and full employment.

Problems

Identifying National Income Accounts and Concepts

Match the descriptions and/or illustrations in the following table with the national income account or concept that are the best fit.

	Description or Illustration		National Income Account or Concept
a.)	Payment to all factors of production	D	Depreciation
b.)	Total amount available for consumption and saving	H	Transfers
c.)	Total value of new goods and services not in existence the year before	C	Net Domesticd Product
d.)	Amount spent for replacement investment	J	Real GNP
e.)	Sum of all final expenditures in the economy	I	Statistical Discrepancy
f.)	GNP minus net factor income from abroad	K	Consumption Spending
g.)	Taxes paid by firms directly to the government which are not associated with any factors of production	E	GDP
h.)	Not included in GNP since they are not associated with any productive activity	A	National Income NI
i.)	Fudge factor to reconcile different estimates of income and total output	G	Indirect Business Taxes
j.)	Total output adjusted for changes in the price level	B	Disposable Personal Income
k.)	Largest and most stable spending component of GNP	F	GNP

317

The Problem with Double Counting

The problem that double counting presents is illustrated by the example below. There are numerous stages of production involved with most commodities with transactions taking place at each of these stages up to the final stage.

Assume that the production of leather coats involves the following various stages of production and transactions:

Stage of Production	Transactions Price	Value Added*
Rancher	$15.00	15.00
Hide Collector	$22.00	7.00
Tanner	$40.00	18.00
Coat Producer	$155.00	115.00
Clothing Wholesaler	$185.00	30.00
Clothing Retailer	$325.00	140
Totals:	742.00	325.00

* Value added = transactions price - cost of purchased inputs

What is sum of all stages' transactions? 742.00

What is the contribution to GDP for this commodity (the leather coat)? 325.00

What is the sum of the value added for all stages of production? 325.00

The final selling price can be thought of as reflecting the value added of all the various stages of production:
the sum of the value added of all stages of production = final transaction price

A Problem in Calculating Nominal and Real GDP and the Implicit GDP Deflator

One of the methods of calculating nominal GDP is to sum up the final market values of all goods and services produced during a given time period (almost always one year) within the borders of a particular country. If there are (n) goods and services produced in a particular economy, then nominal GDP can be obtained by summing the current price times the final market output for each good produced (P X Q).

(1) Nominal GDP = $P_1Q_1 + P_2Q_2 + P_3Q_3 + \ldots + P_nQ_n$

where the subscripts refer to goods 1 to n, where n is the total number of goods and services produced in the economy

The prices referred to in the equation above are in current dollars of the specific year being examined.

In order to take inflation into account, nominal GDP must be adjusted for the change that has occurred in the prices of the goods and services being produced. To do that, the nominal variable (GDP in this case) must be divided by an appropriate price index. The three most important price indices are the GDP deflator, the Consumer Price Index (CPI), and the Producer Price Index (PPI). When dealing with questions involving GNP or GDP, the appropriate price index would be either the GNP or GDP deflator. Real GDP is obtained by dividing nominal GDP by the GDP deflator. Real GDP for any given year can be thought of as that year's output of goods and services priced in terms of base year prices.

(2) Real GDP = Nominal GDP/GDP Deflator

(3) Real GDP_{1996} = $P_{Base\ Year}Q_{1996}$

Based on the following hypothetical data, calculate nominal and real GDP for the years 1993 through 1996, **using 1993 as the base year.**

Table 15-1

	CDs		Movies		Roller Blades		Cheeseburger Medium Drink Large Fries	
Year	P	Q	P	Q	P	Q	P	Q
1993	$15	200 3000	$4	500 2000	$100	10 1000	$2.50	300 750
1994	$12	300 3600	$4	450 1800	$90	20 1800	$2.80	400 1120
1995	$10	500 5000	$5	400 2000	$80	40 3200	$3.00	600 1800
1996	$8	800 6400	$6	500 3000	$60	60 3600	$2.50	1000 25,000

Nominal GDP	Real GDP	Implicit GDP Deflator
1993 = 6750	1993 = 6750	1993 = 100
1994 = 8320	1994 = 9300	1994 = 89.46
1995 = 12,000	1995 = 14600	1995 = 82.19
1996 = 15,500	1996 = 22,500	1996 = 68.88

6750/6750 × 100
8320/9300 × 100
12000/14600 × 100
15500/22500 × 100

Hint: to calculate the implicit GDP deflator, refer to equation (3) above. Remember, if you know two of the three variables in an equation, you can always solve for the third variable.

Use the following nominal GDP and price data to calculate real GDP and the rate of inflation:

The formula for percentage change: $\left[\dfrac{\text{Final Value} - \text{Initial Value}}{\text{Initial Value}} \right] \times 100$

Table 15-2

Year	Nominal GDP (in Billions of Current $)	Implicit GDP Deflator (1987 = 100)	Real GDP (in Billions of 1987 $)	Rate of Inflation* (Percent/year)
1985	$4,038.7	94.4	4,278.2.8	—
1986	$4,268.6	96.9	4,405.1.6	2.6
1987	$4,539.9	100.0	4,539.9	3.1
1988	$4,900.4	103.9	47,164	3.75
1989	$5,250.8	108.5	4,839.4	4.24
1990	$5,546.1	113.3	5,052.78	4.24
1991	$5,724.8	117.7		3.9
1992	$6,020.2	121.1		2.9
1993	$6,343.3	124.2		2.6

Source: Economic Report of the President, February, 1994.
* Based on the rate of change in the Implicit GDP Deflator.

Plot both nominal and real GDP on the graph which follows.

Figure 15-1

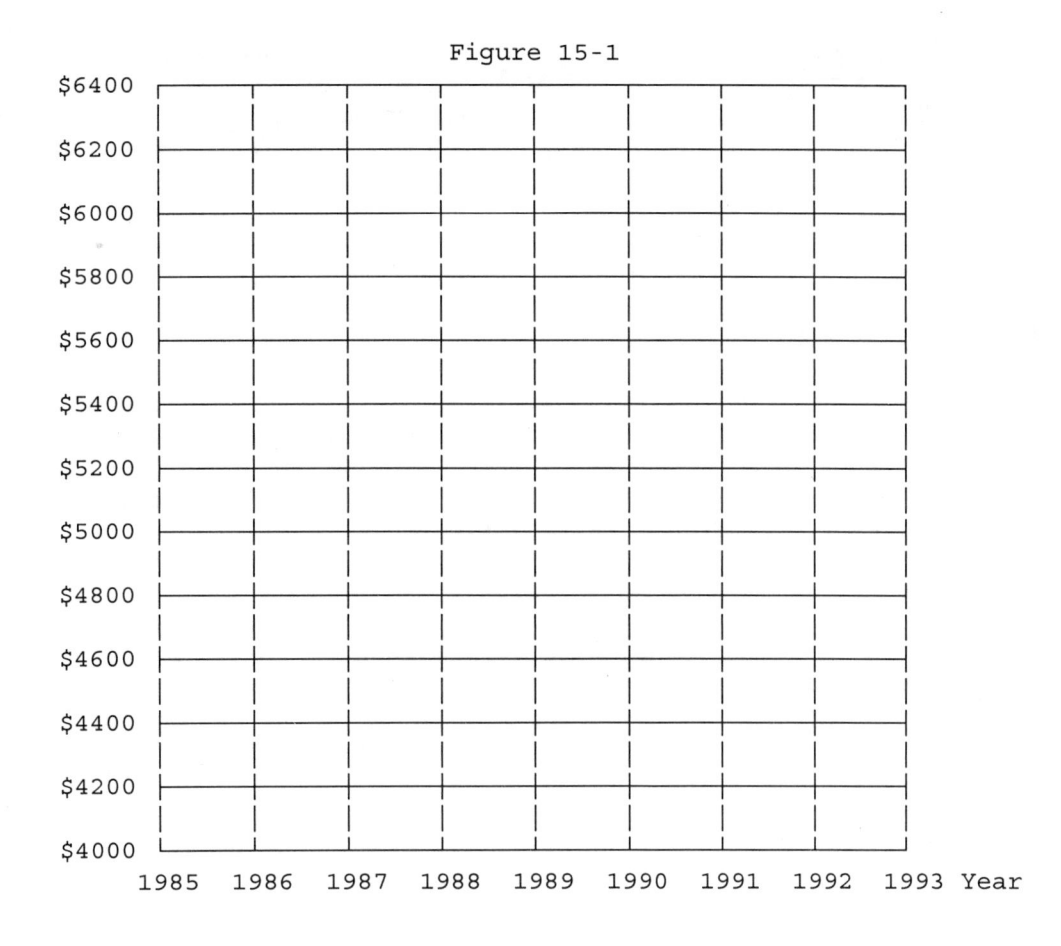

National Income Problem

You are given the following expenditures (in billions of dollars) for a hypothetical economy. Based on that information, calculate the national income accounts listed below.

Indirect Business Taxes	$315
Corporate Taxes	$140
Personal Taxes	$425
Social Security Taxes	$285
Depreciation	$745
Consumption Expenditures	$3476
Receipts of Factor Income from ROW*	$125
Undistributed Corporate Profits	$80
Wages and Salaries	$3890
New Net Investment Spending	$145
Government Transfer Spending	$800
Imports	$560
Payments of Factor Income to ROW*	$113
Government Spending	$971
Exports	$480

* Rest of the World

Gross Domestic Product = $ _____
I + C + G + X − M = GDP

Gross National Product = $ _____
GNP = NI + Depr + indirect taxes

Net Domestic Product = $ _____
GDP − Deprec = NDP

National Income = $ _____
wages + Sal + Rent + Int + profit

Disposable Personal Income = $ _____
PI − income taxes

Balance of Trade (X − M) = $ 480 − 560 = −80

What's Included in GDP?

Determine whether or not the following transactions or events would be included in GDP. If included in GDP, indicate with an **I** and why and where it would show up (which account). If not included in GDP, indicate with an **N** and briefly explain why. If undecided or can't tell on the basis of the information provided, indicate with a **U**.

____ 1.) A homemaker buys ten pounds of flour.

____ 2.) The same homemaker uses the flour to make a loaf of bread and bakes it at home.

____ 3.) A baker buys 1000 pounds of flour from a flour mill for use in her business.

____ 4.) The bakery sells twenty-five loaves of bread to a well-known local restaurant.

____ 5.) The restaurant pays $17.50 per month to the city to take away its garbage.

____ 6.) Your fourteen-year-old brother babysits four hours for a next door neighbor and is paid $12.

____ 7.) A mother buys her daughter a dress for the "Big Dance" at the local thrift store which sells "nice" used clothing. Uh oh!

____ 8.) Your grandfather buys you 100 shares of a fast growing company as a graduation present.

____ 9.) A recently unemployed worker obtains his first $225 unemployment benefits check.

____ 10.) A chemical company dumps two and a half tons of chemical waste products into the river running through your city.

____ 11.) Because of the previous event, the city downstream must spend an additional $75,000 to clean up its drinking water.

_____ 12.) For your first new car, you buy a 1992 model compact car (actually produced in 1992) in the summer of 1993. You get a pretty good deal.

_____ 13.) Your favorite Aunt Betsy sends you $100 in "mad" money.

_____ 14.) A drug deal goes down for $800 in the alley behind the high school.

_____ 15.) Congress passes legislation decreasing income taxes by an average of $675 per family.

_____ 16.) A major corporation buys fourteen new trucks to replace the trucks which wore out during the previous production year.

_____ 17.) You and your spouse finish off the basement in your new house. Should their productive activity be included in GDP?

_____ 18.) You and your spouse consult with a marriage counselor to repair your relationship (consulting fee = $195).

_____ 19.) A farm family grows much of its own food on its four-acre garden.

_____ 20.) Your city's art museum buys the Vincent Van Gogh painting L'Eglise D'Auvers (1890) for $55 million.

True/False Statements

Indicate whether you think the statements below are true or false. These questions are designed to make you think about the concepts presented in the text. There may not be any easy clear-cut answers. Some thoughts about the answers are presented at the end of the chapter.

1.) _____ Payments to all factors of production typically are larger than total national income.

2.) _____ The estimate of inflation provided by the GDP deflator is almost always greater than the inflation rate as measured by the CPI.

3.) _____ Increases in GDP enhance the overall national welfare.

4.) _____ Intermediate transactions can be counted in measuring GDP if they take place between firms in different industries.

5.) _____ In a period of deflation (declining prices), real GDP will be larger than nominal GNP.

6.) _____ Environmental pollution has no effect on overall GDP.

7.) _____ Other things being equal (*ceteris paribus*), an increase in the quality of a commodity will increase GDP.

8.) _____ A natural disaster such as hurricane will increase GDP.

9.) _____ The unemployment rate is a measurement of those who could be working but are not (for whatever reason).

10.) _____ The total value of all economic transactions taking place within a given time period greatly exceeds the value of GDP.

11.) _____ The total value of all productive economic activity equals GDP.

12.) _____ Because of the existence of the underground economy, GDP actually understates the amount of economic production and activity taking place in the economy.

Multiple-Choice Questions

Select the "best" answer from the alternatives provided.

1.) Other things being equal, gross domestic product (GDP) will exceed gross national product if
   a. domestic firms own more foreign subsidiaries.
   b. foreign firms own fewer U.S. subsidiaries.
   c. foreign firms own and operate more factories here in the United States.
   d. the United States imposes higher tariffs to keep out cheap foreign goods.
   e. none of the above.

2.) Nominal GNP and/or GDP
   a. tends to correlate with alternative indices of economic development such as the Human Development Index (HDI).
   b. increases with an increase in the quality of the items produced.
   c. rises with inflation.
   d. is independent of the kinds of goods produced.
   e. (c) and (d).

3.) Economic transactions labeled as transfers
   a. increase personal income but do not affect GDP.
   b. do not affect GDP.
   c. are part of the underground economy.
   d. do affect GDP and are, for the most part, included.
   e. are none of the above.

4.) The index of leading indicators
   a. tells when a recession will occur.
   b. precedes a recession by a specified period of time.
   c. provides advance notice on what the stock market will be doing.
   d. usually turns upwards or downwards in anticipation of changes in the economy's level of production.
   e. does none of the above.

5.) In 1991, nominal gross domestic product (GDP) was $5,671.8 billion, while in 1990 nominal GDP equaled $5,513.8 billion. In 1990, the GDP deflator was 112.9, and in 1991 the deflator was 117.0 (base period 1987 = 100.0). On the basis of that information, we can conclude that
   a. both nominal and real GDP increased.
   b. nominal GDP increased by 1.87 percent.
   c. real GDP decreased by -0.74 percent.
   d. real GDP in 1990 equaled $48.83 billion.
   e. none of the above apply.

Answer the following questions on the basis of the table below:

Year	Commodity A Price	Commodity A Quantity	Commodity B Price	Commodity B Quantity	Commodity C Price	Commodity C Quantity
1990	$5	200	$10	100	$1	500
1991	$6	250	$12	140	$2	400
1992	$6	225	$11	125	$1.50	300

6.) Based on the information contained in the table above, nominal GDP in 1991 was equal to
   a. $2500   b. $4000   c. $1500   d. $3980
   e. can't be determined on the basis of the information above.

7.) Based on the information contained in the table above, nominal GDP increased
   a. by 59 % from 1990 to 1991 and decreased by 20 % from 1991 to 1992.
   b. by 59 % from 1990 to 1991 and increased by 20 % from 1991 to 1992.
   c. by 37 % from 1990 to 1991 and decreased by 25 % from 1991 to 1992.
   d. can't be determined on the basis of the information above.

8.) Based on the information contained in the table above, real GDP for the three years was (base period = 1991)
   a. 2500, 3980, 3175 respectively.
   b. 3400, 3980, 3450 respectively.
   c. 2500, 3050, 2675 respectively.
   d. 3050, 3980, 3640 respectively.
   e. can't be determined on the basis of the information above.

9.) Based on the information contained in the preceding table, the implicit GDP inflator for this hypothetical economy for the three years (base period = 1991) was
   a. 136, 100, 108.7
   b. 92.1, 100, 112.0
   c. 73.5, 100, 92.0
   d. 100, 92, 112
   e. can't be determined on the basis of the information.

10.) Regarding the official unemployment statistics,
   a. they largely ignore frictional unemployment, giving a biased perspective on the unemployment situation.
   b. they represent a weighted average between full-time and part-time employment.
   c. they include a component for so-called "discouraged workers."
   d. they are based on whether or not the people interviewed accurately stated whether or not they were looking for work for the period in question.
   e. both (a), (b), and (c).

11.) Gross domestic product (GDP)
   a. makes no distinction or value judgements about the bundle of goods and services being measured.
   b. generally increases with an increase in the quality of a good.
   c. is adjusted for the change in leisure time that has occurred during the period of measurement.
   d. is a pretty accurate indicator of our national welfare.
   e. necessarily ignores the effects of pollution, since they can't be measured.

12.) Which of the following transactions would not be included in the official measurement of GDP?
   a. sale of high technology F-16 jet fighters to Taiwan.
   b. government construction of a new school.
   c. a local business purchases accounting software from Great Plains software.
   d. purchase of lumber and materials for building your own summer cabin.
   e. selling your 100 shares of Advanced Economic Software stock

Discussion Questions

1.) How is pollution and its economic impacts accounted for in the national income and product accounts?

2.) How would you respond to a person who states that the purchase of his used car should be included in GDP, because the purchase will result in an increase in his economic well-being (otherwise, he wouldn't have bought it).

3.) Would it ever be possible for new net investment to be negative?

4.) What are some of the problems associated with the Consumer Price Index (CPI)? If, as your text suggests, there are reasons to believe that the CPI may overestimate the "true" rate of inflation, what are the macro-economic implications associated with that?

5.) Why is full employment considered to be around 6 % unemployment instead of zero %?

6.) Why aren't transfer transactions of any kind included in GDP?

7.) Why is real GDP (in constant dollars of a base year) a better measure of overall output than nominal GDP (in current dollars)? How does inflation distort economic data and decisions?

Answers and Solutions to Problems and Exercises

Completing Statements from the List of Terms

1.) Index of Leading Indicators
2.) Value Added
3.) Frictional Unemployment
4.) Consumer Price Index
5.) National Income
6.) Net Economic Welfare
7.) Gross Investment
8.) Depreciation
9.) Disposable Personal Income
10.) Statistical Discrepancy
11.) Import Spending
12.) Gross Domestic Product
13.) Double Counting
14.) Psychic Income
15.) Indirect Business Taxes
16.) GDP Deflator
17.) Business Inventories
18.) Net Domestic Product
19.) Gross National Product
20.) Export Spending
21.) Real GDP
22.) Discouraged Workers
23.) Underground Economy
24.) Producer Price Index
25.) Government Sector
26.) Per Capita GDP
27.) Misery Index

Problems

Identifying National Income Accounts and Concepts

d	Depreciation	k	Consumption Spending
h	Transfers	f	GDP
c	Net Domestic Product	a	National Income NI
j	Real GNP	g	Indirect Business Taxes
i	Statistical Discrepancy	b	Disposable Personal Income
		e	GNP

The Problem with Double Counting

Stage of Production	Transactions Price	Value Added
Rancher	$15.00	$15.00
Hide Collector	$22.00	$7.00
Tanner	$40.00	$18.00
Coat Producer	$155.00	$115.00
Clothing Wholesaler	$185.00	$30.00
Clothing Retailer	$325.00	$140.00
Totals:	$742.00	$325.00

What is sum of all stages' transactions? **$742.00**

What is the contribution to GDP for this commodity (the leather coat)?
$325.00 -- the final market price of the leather coat.

What is the sum of the value added for all stages of production?
$325.00 -- the same as the final market price of the leather coat.

Calculating Nominal GDP

Table 15-1

1993 $6,750   1994 $8,320   1995 $12,000   1996 $15,500

Calculating Real GDP

1993 $6,750   1994 $9,300   1995 $14,600   1996 $22,500

Calculating the Implicit GDP Deflator

1993   100.0   1994   89.5   1995   82.2   1996   68.9

Calculating Real GDP and the Rate of Inflation

Table 15-2

	Real GDP	Rate of Inflation
1985	$4,278.3	-
1986	$4,405.2	2.6%
1987	$4,539.9	3.2%
1988	$4,716.5	3.9%
1989	$4,839.4	4.4%
1990	$4,895.1	4.4%
1991	$4,863.9	3.9%
1992	$4,971.3	2.9%
1993	$5,107.3	2.6%

Figure 15-1

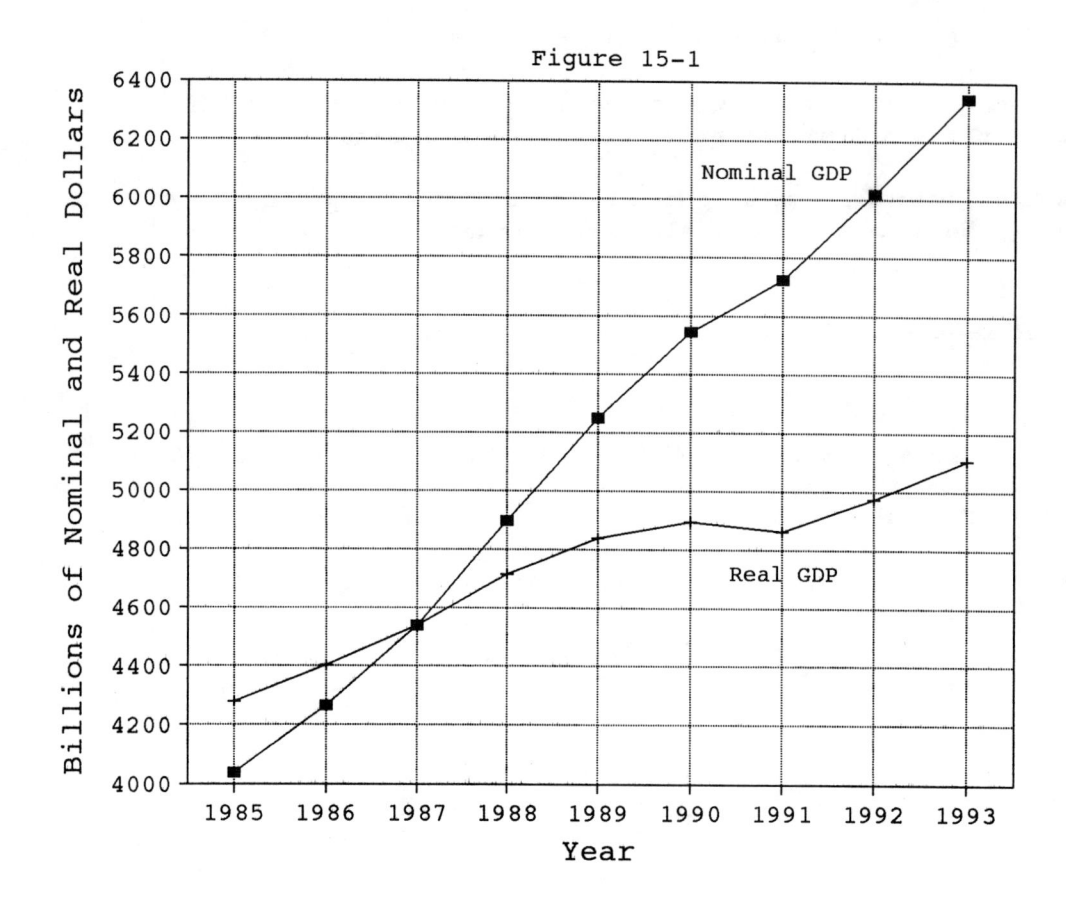

[Figure 15-1: Line chart showing Nominal GDP and Real GDP in Billions of Nominal and Real Dollars from 1985 to 1993. Nominal GDP rises from about 4040 in 1985 to about 6320 in 1993. Real GDP rises from about 4280 in 1985 to about 5080 in 1993.]

National Income Problem

Gross Domestic Product = $ 5,257   Gross National Product = $ 5,269
Net Domestic Product = $ 4,512   National Income = $ 4,209
Disposable Personal Income = $4,079
Balance of Trade (X - M) = - $ 80

What's Included in GDP

1.) Included, C
2.) Not included, non-market activity, no recorded transaction
3.) Not included, intermediate transaction, will be counted as part of her final sales
4.) Not included, intermediate transaction, will be counted as part of the price of the dinners which the restaurant sells
5.) Included, I.
6.) Not included, part of the underground economy (just joking) in which activities are not reported, and therefore, not taxed. It should be included, because it is productive activity, but it is not.
7.) Not included, purchase of used good which has already been counted in GDP
8.) Not included, financial transfer which has no effect on GDP. Any income earned by broker would be included.

9.) Not included, government transfer payment. No productive activity involved.
10.) Not included, but effects of this will, in all probability, show up in GDP.
11.) Included, G. Here is where event 10 shows up.
12.) Not included, previously included in inventories (I)
13.) Not included, personal financial transfer. No productive activity involved. Does serve to maximize student welfare.
14.) Not included, illegal transaction part of underground economy.
15.) Not included, may reduce spending and ultimately reduce GDP
16.) Included, I. Part of replacement investment and as such indistinguishable from new investment.
17.) Not included, non-market activity.
18.) Included, C. No comment.
19.) Interestingly enough, included. Even though it is a non-market transaction, it is included.
20.) Not included, used transaction.

True/False Statements

1.) **False.** National income equals the sum of all payments to factors of production.

2.) **False.** This would be true only if the rate of inflation of consumer goods and services was always less than the rate of change in prices in all other sectors. There is nothing that would lead one to believe that would always be the case -- it might or might not be the case.

3.) **False.** GNP and GDP are national income accounts which attempt to measure the amount of economic output that was produced. Neither of them nor any of the other national income accounts can be construed to be measures of welfare. Welfare is dependent on a number of other factors which are not taken into consideration by these accounts.

4.) **False.** Intermediate transactions can never be counted because they result in double counting, no matter what economic sectors the transactions are occurring in.

5.) **True.** During deflation, price indices will be falling and as a result, nominal economic variables in the process of being deflated are being divided by a decreasing magnitude, making the real variable larger. If today's dollars are more valuable than yesterday's, then for a given level of GDP, real GDP will have increased.

6.) **False.** Any cleanup or any other kind of expenditures associated with or due to environmental pollution will be reflected in GDP. In that sense, the more society pollutes, the more it must spend to clean up that pollution, and the larger GDP will be. That would certainly give society a false feeling of well-being.

7.) **False.** The only way quality changes show up is through any corresponding changes in prices or production that take place because of the quality change. Items like computers that have become smaller and more powerful have decreased significantly in price. For a given number of computers, the overall contribution to GDP would be less than before. However, more people are buying computers than before, so that would tend to offset the price decreases.

8.) **True.** To the extent that natural disasters force society to spend more on repair and reconstruction than they otherwise would have, the statement is true. GDP is a record of all final expenditures, and no questions are asked about why those expenditures were made or why they were necessary.

9.) **False.** The unemployment rate is a measure of those who are looking for work but can't find work. If you are not looking for work, you are not considered to be in the labor force and, therefore, are not considered to be unemployed.

10.) **True.** Think of all the intermediate transactions, the financial transfers, and the volume of used transactions that are taking place in the economy. They would surely be many times larger than the sum total of final market transactions occurring in the economy at any point in time.

11.) **It Depends!** GDP is supposed to be a measure of all productive activity taking place in the economy over a given period of time. Yet, after reading this chapter, you are surely aware of all the productive activity that should be counted as productive but is not included. Do-it-yourself activites as well as the multitude of homemaker activities are all excluded, because it is felt that they can't be measured accurately.

12.) **True.** Since the underground economy lies outside of the scrutiny of the Department of Commerce, all of the productive activities (no matter what their moral and legal ramifications might be) are necessarily excluded from our official statistics.

Multiple-Choice

1.) c 2.) e 3.) a 4.) d 5.) c 6.) d

7.) a 8.) b 9.) c 10.) d 11.) a 12.) e

Discussion Questions

1.) The actual act of polluting is not taken into account by the national income and product accounts. Thus, an oil spill, *per se*, does not show up. However, any final measurable economic transactions that are undertaken as a result of the pollution will be counted and will increase GDP. This leads to a rather curious result: the more we pollute and contaminate our environment, the more that we as a society have to spend to cleanup the environment, and GDP will be larger since there will be increased output, income, and employment associated with the clean-up expenditures. The greater the pollution, the higher the GDP.

One should keep in mind that these expenditures merely attempt to restore what society formerly had available, e.g., clean air and water. Even if there is no cleanup undertaken, total expenditures will undoubtedly rise in response to the effects of pollution, e.g., going to the doctor because of respiratory illness, replacing sulfur dioxide eroded windshield wipers, etc.

2.) Such a statement sounds plausible, but one has to remember that GDP is not a measure of society's overall welfare, but of the value of production. The item was counted once when new and shouldn't be counted again.

3.) Yes, if the depreciation allowance (the amount set aside to replace capital goods used up in the production process) exceeds gross private domestic investment (total expenditures for investment purposes). Exactly this situation occurred during 1933. According to the Economic Report of the President, 1991, in 1933, gross private domestic investment expenditures amounted to only $1.6 billion, while the capital consumption allowance (depreciation) was $7.6 billion. If these figures are correct, then the capital stock of the economy shrank by $6 billion during that year. Times were tough indeed.

4.) Since the CPI bundle is fixed, charting changes in the cost of purchasing the bundle ignores any substitution that consumers would normally carry out as the prices of some items in the bundle rise faster than others. As your text mentions, there is no good way to handle quality changes that occur, and increases in prices due to quality change are not considered to be due to inflation, since consumers would normally pay more for a higher quality item. The CPI methodology also means that only regular, stated prices are recorded, ignoring sales and coupons that might be available.

In terms of the macro-economic implications of overestimating the actual degree of inflation, many wages, salaries, pensions, and government benefits are indexed (linked) to the CPI. Thus, whenever the CPI increases by a certain amount, wages, salaries, etc. will increase. An overestimate would mean that more is paid out for these incomes and benefits than really should have been. That will affect business' costs and government expenditures and the government deficit. There is discussion in Congress about using the CPI minus one % to index social security, recognizing the reality that there is an upward bias in the CPI. Whether that bias is one % or not is not known.

From a policy standpoint, it's difficult to conduct meaningful policy when your economic statistics are not accurate. If inflation is not really as bad as policymakers believe, inappropriate contractive policies might well be implemented when they shouldn't be.

5.) The level of full employment is determined by the amount of frictional unemployment that is considered normal or typical. Most economists have agreed that somewhere around 6 % is a reasonable estimate for that kind of unemployment. Frictional unemployment is not considered to be a problem -- it reflects normal and expected changes in employment, seasonal variations in employment, and the period of unemployment that normally occurs for first-time job entrants. Only when the rate of unemployment exceeds the level of frictional unemployment does society have an "unemployment problem."

6.) Transfers, by definition, are not linked to any productive economic activity and, therefore, should not be included in GDP. Only productive activity should be included. It should be noted that transfers do result in changes in personal income and do show up in the personal income and disposable personal income accounts.

7.) Inflation has the capacity to distort our economic decisions, fooling us into thinking we are better off or worse off than we really are. We even have a name for that: money illusion. People commit the fallacy of money illusion when they base their decisions on nominal variables rather than real variables. Your nominal income rises by 6 % and on that basis you go out and purchase that new car you have been wanting, because you feel you are better off than before. Unfortunately, you may not be better off if the rate of inflation (which measures the increase in the prices of the items you are buying) is more than 6 %.

Inflation must be accounted for, so that incomes can be stated in real terms, and that is accomplished by dividing nominal incomes by an appropriate index of prices. Real variables represent a "truer" measure of actual purchasing power (control over real goods and services).

Summary

One of the most important realizations that you as a student can gain from this chapter is that all of the most important macroeconomic statistics (GDP or GNP, the rate of unemployment, the rate of inflation, and the rate of capacity utilization) need to be carefully interpreted, with full knowledge of their limitations, flaws, and potential inaccuracies. It is absolutely essential that the general public be aware of the fact that full employment is actually about 6 % unemployment, and it is only when the rate of unemployment exceeds 6 % that an unemployment problem exists. To a lesser extent, it is also important for society to be aware of the fact that the official rate of unemployment makes no distinction between part-time and full-time employment and does not reflect discouraged workers.

In a similar vein, there are several reasons why the consumer price index (CPI) overestimates the actual rate of inflation -- any fixed weight index necessarily ignores the effect of consumers substituting out of those commodities increasing in price and the upward bias introduced by quality changes. With so many labor contracts and pensions indexed to the CPI by means of a COLA, the cost implications of an upward bias in the CPI are significant. The monetary aspects are so great that when the Bureau of Labor Statistics announced a few years ago that it was revising its procedures to correct a faulty methodology, one affected party opposed the revision on the grounds that it would harm the members of his organization, even though it was recognized that the revision would correct an error!

National income accounting may not be everyone's cup of tea, but it is useful to know about the distinction between GNP and GDP and its significance. There have been occasions when specific projects have been justified on the grounds that an increase in GDP is equivalent to an increase in society's overall welfare or standard of living. In this era of increased environmental and resource awareness, an alternative welfare index which takes into account resource depletion, environmental pollution, and some of the non-market activities not included in the standard national income accounts becomes more of a priority. The problem with such indices is, of course, their elements of subjectivity.

The variables discussed in Chapter 15 are among the most publicized and most discussed of the ones that are available to the public. Greater knowledge of exactly what they are measuring, what they represent, and what their shortcomings are can only enhance public debate on public policy and macroeconomic performance.

Chapter 16
How the Level of Output is Determined: The Concept of Macroeconomic Equilibrium

Overview of the Chapter

Chapter 16 addresses the important concept of macroeconomic equilibrium. Although the economy may not always be at its equilibrium level of income, it will necessarily be moving towards that level. From an economic policy perspective, it is vitally important to have an understanding of the economic forces which determine the equilibrium level of income. This chapter focuses on the role that total spending plays in the economy and how it affects equilibirium income.

The labor market provides the basic conceptual framework for analyzing unemployment and the determination of the equilibrium real wage. Equilibrium in the labor market is always a position of full employment, since at that point the quantity of labor demanded by employers just equals the quantity of labor supplied by the labor force. If wages exhibit some rigidity, some resistance to decreasing, then it is possible for extended unemployment to occur. Thus, the assumptions about labor market flexibility or rigidity are critical in explaining how unemployment occurs within the macroeconomic system.

Classical and neo-classical economic theory emphasized the self-regulating characteristics of the economy and the expectation that problems of unemployment and inflation were likely to be temporary in nature. Since the neo-classicists believed in wage flexibility, unemployment was thought to be transitory with market forces within the labor market correcting any unemployment through decreases in the real wage -- unemployed workers would compete the real wage down to the point where equilibrium was achieved once again.

Keynesian economic theory, on the other hand, emphasizes that firms and workers resist decreases in their prices and wages, making it difficult to achieve swift adjustment in a downward direction. Thus, according to the Keynesian theory, it is possible to have an extended period of unemployment, with the labor market being unable to adjust properly. Macroeconomic equilibrium occurs where aggregate demand equals aggregate supply. At that point, the equilibrium level of real output and the price level will be determined. If total spending and total output are not equal, inventories will change and signal the economic system that there was either too much or too little production, and the size of the income flow will change accordingly. Changes in inventories play a crucial role in the Keynesian model. The key point to remember is that changes in aggregate demand and supply will affect the equilibrium levels of real output.

The interaction that exists between income, output, and employment and total spending is perhaps most easily understood through the circular flow diagram. The production costs of the business sector (factor costs, for example) represent income to the household sector which uses that income for consumption expenditures. These expenditures have now come full circle, since they are receipts (income) for the business sector, and the cycle begins anew. This model stresses the interdependence of the various sectors of the economy.

Leakages from the income flow, such as savings, may cause problems, since they mean that not all of the factor incomes will be returned to the business sector, and it is important that that particular sector get back all of its costs or the level of production may be cut back. However, the saving leakage can be offset by an injection which will return the amount saved to the spending flow.

The level of spending occupies the central role in the Keynesian fixed price model. In the simple two-sector model (consisting of only consumption and investment sectors), equilibrium occurs when total output (C + S) equals total spending (C + I). Consumption spending (C) is assumed to be positively related to income, and the relationship between consumption (C) and income (Y) is depicted by the the consumption function.

Total investment spending is related to the interest rate, the overall level of spending, and changes in spending. Firms are assumed to compare an investment project's projected rate of return with the interest rate, investing in the project when the expected rate of return exceeds the interest rate that could be earned on the investment funds. Investment, then, is assumed to be inversely related to the interest rate, other things being equal.

Investment spending fluctuates the most of any of the spending sectors in the economy. One model, the accelerator, attempts to explain that instability by linking investment spending to changes in the level of income. Relatively small changes in income and output levels can cause investment spending to fluctuate widely in response as firms attempt to maintain specific ratios between their total output and their capital.

Learning Objectives

After completing this chapter, you should be sure that you are able to:

- understand how the labor market functions, the role of the real wage in determining the equilibrium level of employment and the level of unemployment.

- explain how wage rigidities can result in extended involuntary unemployment.

- understand the rationale of the circular flow model, the importance of income leakages and injections and how they affect the level of economic activity in the economy.

- understand the role that total spending (aggregate demand) plays in determining the overall level of economic activity and the equilibrium level of income, output, and employment.

- understand the concept of macroeconomic equilibrium and the conditions necessary to obtain it.

- understand how the economy can be in a disequilibrium condition and the process that occurs in returning to a postion of equilibrium.

- understand the rationale behind the consumption and saving functions and their average and marginal propensities.

- identify the economic factors which affect and shift the consumption function.

- understand the relationship that exists between the consumption function and the saving function.

- identify the economic factors which affect the level of investment spending in the economy.

- explain the concept of the accelerator and its implications for the economy.

Self Evaluation

List of Terms

Accelerator
Actual Investment
Actual Saving
Aggregate Demand
Aggregate Supply
Average Propensity to Consume
Average Propensity to Save
Business Sector
Circular Flow
Consumption Function
Desired Investment
Desired Saving
Expected Net Return

Household Sector
Induced Investment
Injection
Investment
Leakage
Macroeconomic Equilibrium
Marginal Propensity to Consume
Marginal Propensity to Save
Permanent-Income Hypothesis
Real Balances Effect
Saving
Wage Flexibility
Wage Rigidity
Wealth

For the statements below, fill in the term from the list above which provides the best fit.

1.) The _____ allows one to determine the amount of consumption spending given a certain level of income.

2.) The level of _____ is functionally related to the level of profits and income.

3.) _____ is one of the factors which shift the consumption function up or down.

4.) That portion of investment spending which is directly related to the level of income and spending in the economy is known as _____.

5.) The ratio of the change in consumption spending that occurs for a given change in the level of income is defined as _____.

6.) When the change in inventories is added to planned investment, one obtains _____.

7.) Equilibrium in the macroeconomy occurs when _____ equals _____.

8.) The interdependency of the _____ and the _____ is illustrated by _____ models.

9.) When the level of income and output in the economy shows no tendency to change, the economy is in a position of _____.

10.) The _____ is an important determinant of investment spending.

11.) The _____ model hypothesizes that investment spending is functionally related to changes in the level of income.

12.) By definition, _____ is always equal to actual investment.

13.) The difference between income and consumption equals _____.

14.) In the context of the circular flow model, investment spending, government spending, and export spending are all examples of an income _____.

15.) The percent of total income spent on consumption is known as _____.

16.) In the context of the circular flow model, savings, income taxes, and imports are all examples of an income _____.

17.) The _____ suggests that unexpected or temporary changes in income may not affect total spending all that much.

18.) The percent of total income saved is known as _____.

19.) The ratio of the change in saving that occurs for a given change in the level of income is defined as _____.

340

20.) The _____ suggests that given a certain amount of assets, a decline in the price level would increase the purchasing power of those assets and would result in increased total spending.

21.) The total value of spending in the economy is known as _____.

22.) If sufficient _____ exists, then any involuntary unemployment is likely to be only temporary.

23.) The total value of what was produced in the economy is known as _____.

24.) If a labor market is characterized by significant _____ then it is possible to experience involuntary unemployment over an extended period of time.

Problems

Working with the Consumption Function

You are given the following consumption function: **C = 200 + 0.6Y**[1] Use this equation to determine the amount of consumption spending and saving for each of the levels of income specified in the following table. This is accomplished by plugging the different levels of income (Y) into the equation above. Once you have done that, you will then be able to calculate the MPC, MPS, APC, and APS.

---

[1] Since Y = C + S, once the consumption function is known, the saving function is easily determined, since S = Y - C. Using the consumption function specified above, we can substitute:
S = Y - C = Y - (200 + 0.6Y) = **-200 + 0.4Y**

Table 16-1

A	B	C	D	E	F	G
Possible Levels of Income (Y)	Planned Consumption Spending (C)	Planned Saving (S)	Marginal Propensity to Consume (MPC)	Marginal Propensity to Save (MPS)	Average Propensity to Consume (APC)	Average Propensity to Save (APS)
Given Below	C = 200+0.6Y	S = -200+0.4Y	($\Delta C/\Delta Y$)	($\Delta S/\Delta Y$)	(C/Y)	(S/Y)
0						
100						
200						
300						
400						
500						
600						
700						
800						
900						
1000						

All spending data in billions of dollars

Using the data in the Table 16-1 above:

- Plot the consumption function on Graph 16-1. Be sure to include your 45 degree reference line.

- Indicate the following on Figure 16-1:

    - the slope between two of the points in the table above
    - the average propensity to consume at Y = 800

- Suppose that the Federal Reserve decreases interest rates to offset a recession and, as a result, the consumption function changes to: **C = 300 + 0.6Y**

- Plot the new consumption function on Figure 16-1.

- Comparing the original consumption function with the new consumption function, compare the following:

	Original Function	New Function
MPC	_____	_____
MPS	_____	_____
APC at Y = 600	_____	_____
APS at Y = 600	_____	_____

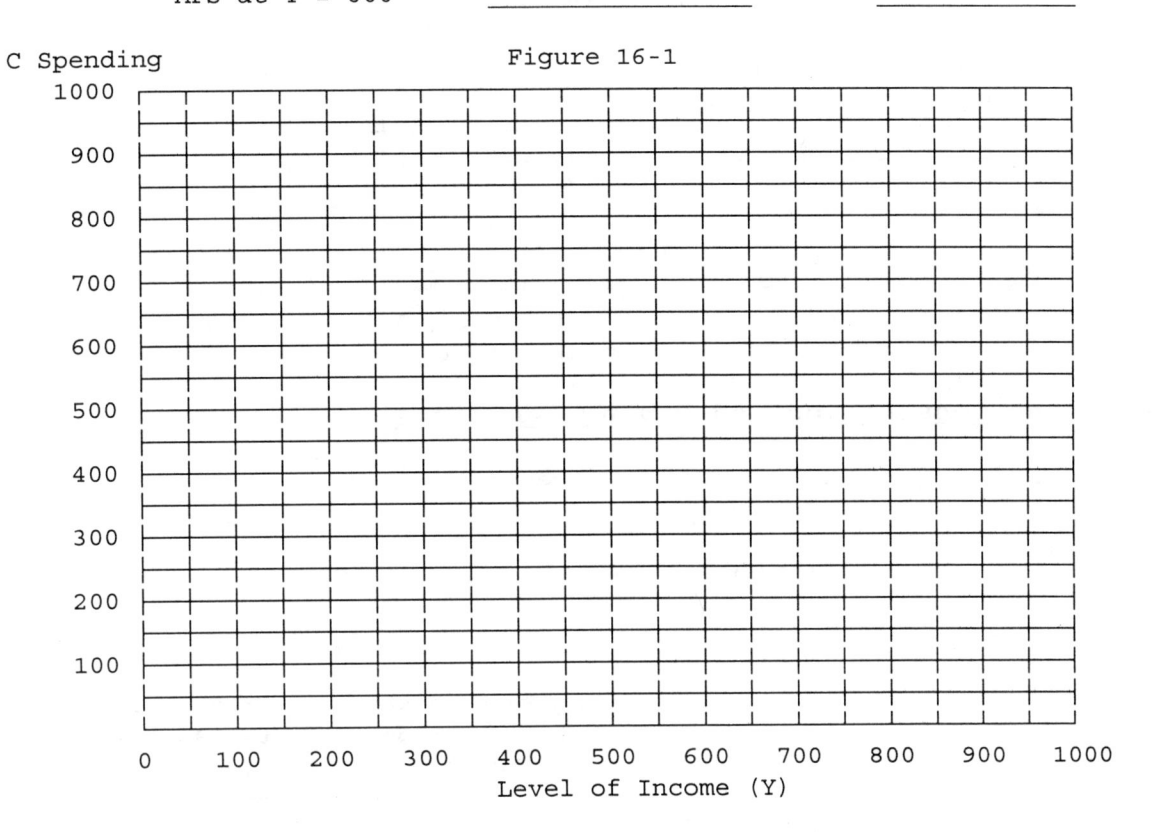

C Spending   Figure 16-1

- On the graph above, indicate the level of income, consumption spending, and the level of saving for the following three income levels: Y = 200   Y = 400   Y = 1000

- Plot the original saving function on Figure 16-2. Note that this graph will necessarily include both positive and negative values.

- Indicate the following on Figure 16-2:
  - the slope between two of the points on the graph above
  - the average propensity to save at Y = 800

- As mentioned on the preceding page, suppose that the Federal Reserve decreases interest rates to offset a recession and as a result, the consumption function changes in the following way:
  C = 300 + 0.6Y   What is the new saving function?

- Plot the new saving function on Figure 16-2.

Saving (S)   Figure 16-2

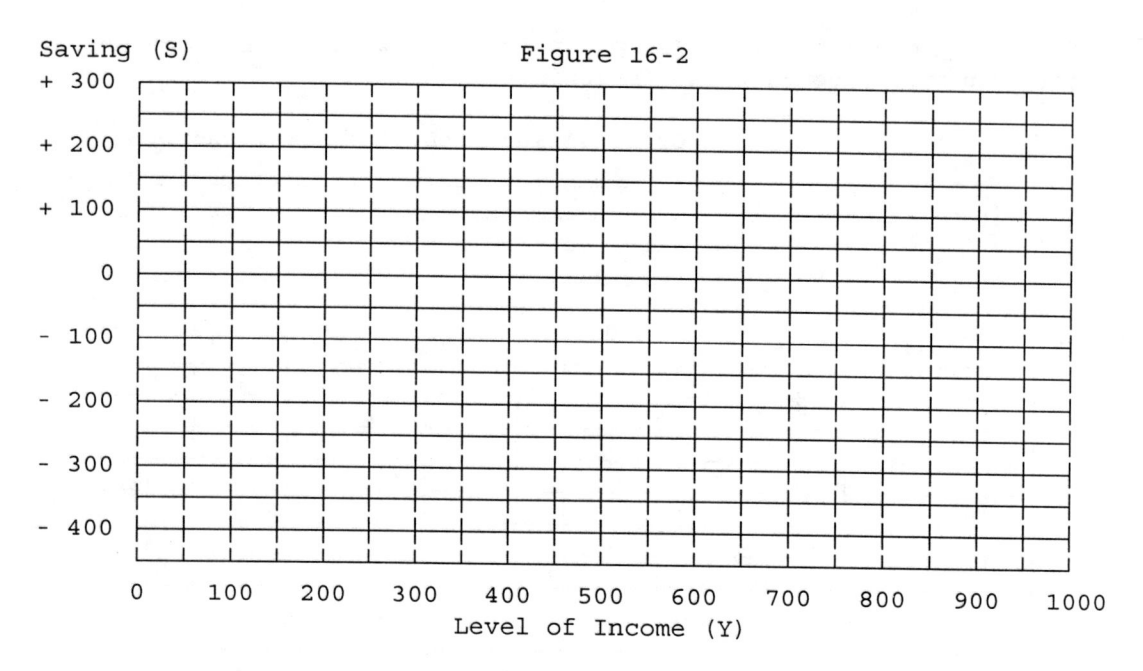

[Graph with vertical axis Saving (S) ranging from -400 to +300, and horizontal axis Level of Income (Y) ranging from 0 to 1000]

Shifts in the Consumption and Saving Functions

Indicate the effect of the following events on the consumption and saving functions:

U = Shift Up   **D** = Shift Down   **A** = Movement Along the Curve

Table 16-2

Event	Effect on the Consumption Function	Effect on the Saving Function
An increase in interest rates		
Expectation of lower prices in the future		
Home equities (a major component of wealth) decrease		
Increased use of credit cards		
Consumers feel their stock of durable goods is too large		
Introduction of new, technologically sophisticated products		
Household attitudes towards thrift improve		
Total household income increases		

Macroeconomic Equilibrium (Using the Fixed Price Model)

You are given the following Keynesian model of the economy:

- Fill in the empty columns in the table below to determine the equilibrium level of income for the first model.

Table 16-3

A	B	C	D	E	F	G
Possible Levels of Income and Output (Y)	Consumption Spending (C)	Saving (S)	Investment Spending (I)	Total Spending on Output of Business = Business Receipts = (C) + (I)	Payments Made by Business Sector (= Income)	Change in Inventories: Total Output Minus Total Spending
Given Below	Given Below	Column A − Column B	Given Below	Column B + Column D	Identical to Column A	Column A − Column E
0	400		100			
100	450		100			
200	500		100			
300	550		100			
400	600		100			
500	650		100			
600	700		100			
700	750		100			
800	800		100			
900	850		100			
1000	900		100			
1100	950		100			
1200	1000		100			
1300	1050		100			
1400	1100		100			

What is the MPC for this economic model? _____

What is the MPS for this economic model? _____

Given the spending plans for consumers and businesses that were specified in the preceding table, what is the equilibrium level of income\output? _____

What are the equilibrium values of Y, C, S, I?

Y = _____   C = _____   S = _____   I = _____

Briefly explain why that level of income/output is an equilibrium level of income/output.

_____

_____

True/False Statements

Indicate whether you think the statements below are true or false. These questions are designed to make you think about the concepts presented in the text. There may not be any easy clear-cut answers. Some thoughts about the answers are presented at the end of the chapter.

1.) _____ Macroeconomic equilibrium occurs when planned spending equals total business outlays.

2.) _____ Consumers respond more to changes in temporary income than they do to changes in permanent income.

3.) _____ When graphed one below the other, the consumption function and the savings function have the same slope.

4.) _____ The percentage of income devoted to consumption falls as income rises.

5.) _____ The circular flow model suggests that all income received by the household sector will in turn be spent.

6.) _____ The circular flow of income will be stable when leakages equal injections.

7.) _____ When planned savings are greater than planned investment, then total output will be greater than total spending.

8.) _____ When total spending is less than total output, inventories will rise, signaling the business sector to produce less.

9.) _____ An increase in the stock market would be expected to shift the consumption function upward.

10.) _____ As long as the expected rate of return on an investment project equals the current rate of interest, there will be economic incentives to proceed with the project.

11.) _____ The accelerator suggests that the retained earnings of firms play a key role in investment decisions and helps explain why investment spending is so unstable.

12.) _____ With respect to after-tax income (disposable personal income), the sum of the marginal propensity to consume (MPC) and the marginal propensity to save (MPS) must equal one.

13.) _____ If the consumption function shifts upwards because of the introduction of new, technologically advanced goods, the saving function will shift downward.

Multiple-Choice Questions

Select the "best" answer from the alternatives provided.

Use the table below to answer the following questions:

Disposable Income Y	Consumption C
0	300
100	350
200	400
300	450
400	500
.	.
.	.

1.) Based on the information contained in the table above, the formula for the consumption function is:
   a. C = 0.5Y
   b. C = 100 + 0.5Y
   c. C = 300 + 0.5Y
   d. C = 300 + 0;75Y
   e. unable to determine from the information available.

2.) Based on the information contained in the preceding table, the break-even level of income is:
   a. 400   b. 500   c. 600   d. 700
   e. unable to determine from the information available.

3.) Based on the information contained in the preceding table, the marginal propensity to consume (MPC) and the marginal propensity to save (MPS) for this consumption function are:
   a. 0.6, 0.4
   b. +1, -1
   c. 0.7, 0.3
   d. 0.5, 0.5
   e. 0.5, 0.4

4.) Based on the information contained in the preceding table, the average propensity to consume at an income level of 300 is:
   a. 0.6667
   b. 1.5
   c. 1
   d. 150
   e. 300

5.) Based on the information contained in the preceding table, the average propensity to save (MPS) at an income level of 500 is:
   a. -0.1
   b. 0.1
   c. -50
   d. 550
   e. -300

6.) Based on the information contained in the preceding table, the amount of consumption spending at an income level of 1000 would be:
   a. 400
   b. 500
   c. 600
   d. 700
   e. 800

7.) If society wants to spend more than the value of total output,
   a. inventories will accumulate.
   b. C + S > C + I.
   c. C + I > C + S.
   d. inventories will be depleted.
   e. both (c) and (d).

8.) The circular flow model reveals that
   a. the level of consumption spending largely dictates whether an economy will be in a state of equilibrium or not.
   b. the spending of one sector of the economy represents the income of another sector.
   c. if investment (I) spending is larger than saving (S), then the economy will be in good condition.
   d. saving is specified to be a positive function of the interest rate.
   e. none of the above.

9.) If inventories are being depleted in the Keynesian fixed price model, then
   a. total leakages from the flow of income are larger than total injections.
   b. total output exceeds total spending.
   c. consumption spending is too large for the economic system and the flow of income.
   d. total planned spending is greater than total output.
   e. actual spending is greater than total output.

10.) If the consumption function is assumed to be a linear function of the level of disposable income, then
   a. the MPC will be larger than the MPS.
   b. the MPC + MPS = 1 for a two-sector model.
   c. the savings function could be linear or non-linear depending upon different circumstances.
   d. the MPC will decline as income increases.
   e. the MPC will remain constant as income increases or decreases.

11.) The marginal propensity to consume (MPC)
   a. is the fraction of a change in income that is consumed.
   b. is the fraction of total income that is consumed.
   c. increases as the level of income increases.
   d. declines when the MPS declines simultaneously.
   e. both (b) and (c)

12.) When the stock of usable consumer durables decreases (perhaps because of a recent recession when some durables were allowed to wear out),
   a. the consumption function will not shift; however, the saving function will shift downwards as consumers use their savings to buy durables.
   b. the consumption function will shift upwards, the saving function downwards.
   c. no change in either the consumption or saving function.
   d. consumers will move along their existing consumption and saving functions.
   e. none of the above.

13.) As the level of disposable income increases,
   a. the consumption function will shift upward.
   b. the MPC will increase, the MPS decrease.
   c. the MPC will decrease, the MPS increase.
   d. consumers will move along the existing consumption and saving functions.
   e. none of the above.

Use the table below to answer the following questions:

Total Output Y	Consumption C	Saving S	Planned Investment I
3000	2650		500
3200	2800		500
3400	2950		500
3600	3100		500
3800	3250		500
4000	3400		500

14.) Given planned spending schedules for consumption and investment shown above, then the level of equilibrium income will be:
   a. 3200
   b. 3400
   c. 3600
   d. 3800
   e. 4000

15.) The MPC for this hypothetical economy is:
   a. 0.861
   b. 0.75
   c. 0.50
   d. 0.8
   e. not able to be determined from the information above.

16.) Total planned spending when Y = 3200 would be:
   a. 2650
   b. 3200
   c. 3300
   d. 3400
   e. 3600

17.) At an income level of 3800, the change in inventories will be:
   a. -100
   b. 0
   c. +50
   d. +100
   e. can't be determined since inventory changes are an unplanned component of spending.

18.) If the level of investment spending changed to 600, what would the new equilibrium level of income be?
   a. 3200
   b. 3400
   c. 3600
   d. 3800
   e. 4000

Discussion Questions

1.) Most of us have been told since childhood that saving for that proverbial rainy day is something that we all ought to do more of. Briefly explain, why, in terms of the circular flow model, the act of saving can be potentially troublesome for the economy. Why only potentially troublesome?

2.) Why do you think that household saving as a percent of disposable personal income is lower in the United States than in most other developed countries? What are the macroeconomic implications of lower saving rates?

3.) Neo-classicists believed that unemployment was possible only if the real wage was too high. Using a demand and supply diagram of the labor market, briefly explain their viewpoint.

How does that view differ from that of Keynesian economists about the cause of involuntary unemployment?

4.) From the viewpoint of macroeconomic policy when trying to control consumption spending, would it make any difference whether permanent or current income was the biggest factor in determining consumption expenditures?

5.) Using the circular flow model, work through the effects on the economy as a whole of a sudden fall in investment spending.

6.) In comparing a low income household with a high income household, how do you think the MPC, MPS, APC, and APS would differ?

7.) What implications does the accelerator have for achieving a stable growth path for the economy?

Answers and Solutions to Problems and Exercises

Completing Statements from the List of Terms

1.) Consumption Function
2.) Investment
3.) Wealth
4.) Induced Investment
5.) Marginal Propensity to Consume
6.) Actual Investment
7.) Desired Investment
   Desired Saving
8.) Household Sector
   Business Sector
   Circular Flow
9.) Macroeconomic Equilibrium
10.) Expected Net Return
11.) Accelerator
12.) Actual Saving
13.) Saving
14.) Injection
15.) Average Propensity to Consume
16.) Leakage
17.) Permanent-Income Hypothesis
18.) Average Propensity to Save
19.) Marginal Propensity to Save
20.) Real Balances Effect
21.) Aggregate Demand
22.) Wage Flexibility
23.) Aggregate Supply
24.) Wage Rigidity

Problems

Working With the Consumption Function

Table 16-1

A	B	C	D	E	F	G
Possible Levels of Income (Y)	Planned Consumption Spending (C)	Planned Saving (S)	Marginal Propensity to Consume (MPC)	Marginal Propensity to Save (MPS)	Average Propensity to Consume (APC)	Average Propensity to Save (APS)
Given Below	C = 200+0.6Y	S = -200+0.4Y	(ΔC/ΔY)	(ΔS/ΔY)	(C/Y)	(S/Y)
0	200	-200	Undef.	Undef.	Undef.	Undef.
100	260	-160	60/100 = 0.6	40/100 = 0.4	2.60	-1.60
200	320	-120	60/100 = 0.6	40/100 = 0.4	1.60	-.60
300	380	-80	60/100 = 0.6	40/100 = 0.4	1.27	-.27
400	440	-40	60/100 = 0.6	40/100 = 0.4	1.10	-.10
500	500	0	60/100 = 0.6	40/100 = 0.4	1.00	.00
600	560	40	60/100 = 0.6	40/100 = 0.4	.93	.07
700	620	80	60/100 = 0.6	40/100 = 0.4	.89	.11
800	680	120	60/100 = 0.6	40/100 = 0.4	.85	.15
900	740	160	60/100 = 0.6	40/100 = 0.4	.82	.18
1000	800	200	60/100 = 0.6	40/100 = 0.4	.80	.20

C = 300 + 0.6Y

	Original Function	New Function
- MPC	0.6	0.6
- MPS	0.4	0.4
- APC at Y = 600	0.933	1.10
- APS at Y = 600	0.067	-0.10

Figure 16-1

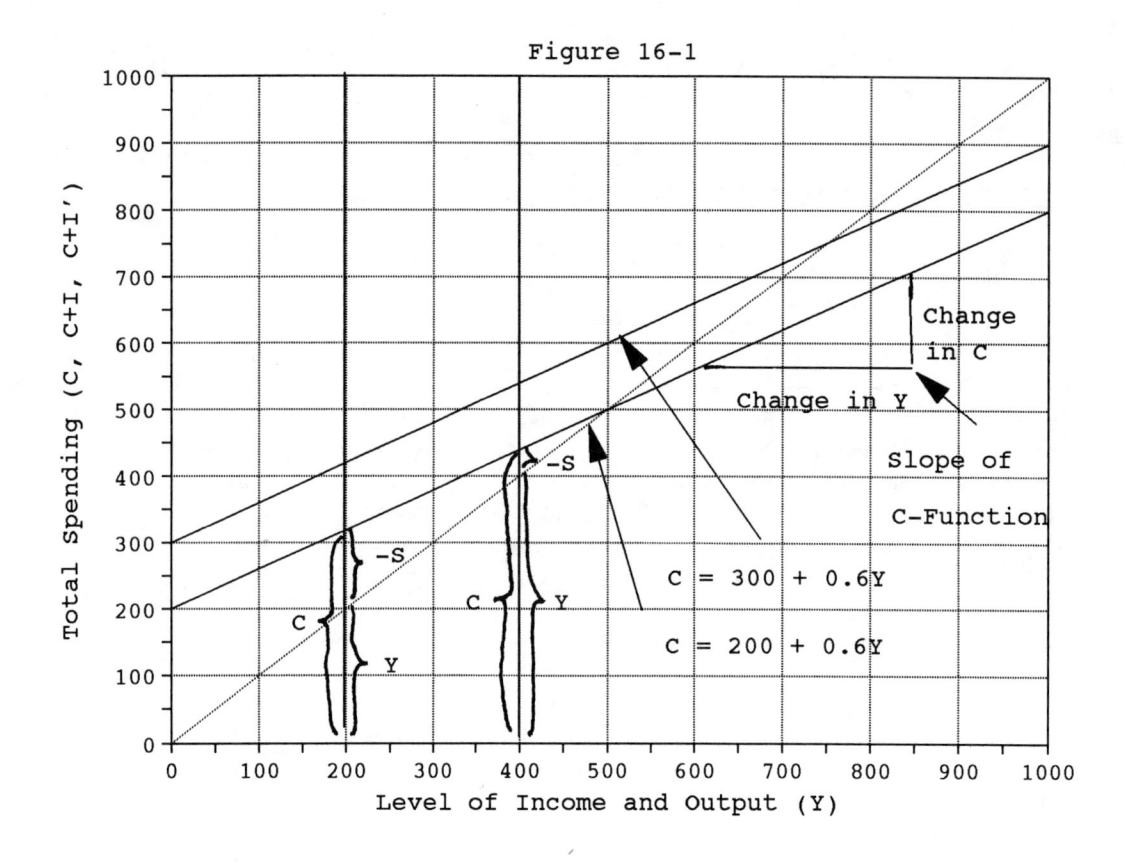

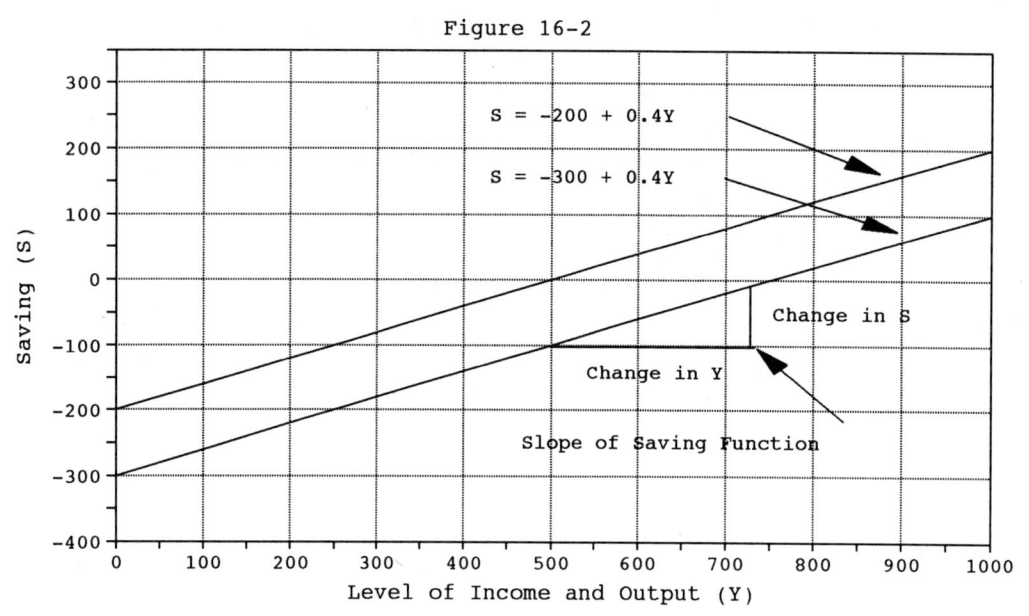

Figure 16-2

Shifts in the Consumption and Saving Functions

Event	Effect on the Consumption Function	Effect on the Saving Function
An increase in interest rates	D	U
Expectation of lower prices in the future	D	U
Home equities (a major component of wealth) decrease	D	U
Increased use of credit cards	U	D
Consumers feel their stock of durable goods is too large	D	U
Introduction of new, technologically sophisticated products	U	D
Household attitudes towards thrift improve	D	U
Total household income increases	A	A

Macroeconomic Equilibrium (Using the Fixed Price Model)

Table 16-3

A	B	C	D	E	F	G
Possible Levels of Income and Output (Y)	Consumption Spending (C)	Saving (S)	Investment Spending (I)	Total Spending on Output of Business = Business Receipts = (C) + (I)	Payments Made by Business Sector (= Income)	Change in Inventories: Total Output Minus Total Spending
Given Below	Given Below	Column A - Column B	Given Below	Column B + Column D	Identical to Column A	Column A - Column E
0	400	- 400	100	500	0	- 500
100	450	- 350	100	550	100	- 450
200	500	- 300	100	600	200	- 400
300	550	- 250	100	650	300	- 350
400	600	- 200	100	700	400	- 300
500	650	- 150	100	750	500	- 250
600	700	- 100	100	800	600	- 200
700	750	- 50	100	850	700	- 150
800	800	0	100	900	800	- 100
900	850	+ 50	100	950	900	- 50
1000	900	+ 100	100	1000	1000	0
1100	950	+ 150	100	1050	1100	+ 50
1200	1000	+ 200	100	1100	1200	+ 100
1300	1050	+ 250	100	1150	1300	+ 150
1400	1100	+ 300	100	1200	1400	+ 200

What is the MPC for this economic model? **0.5**

What is the MPS for this economic model? **0.5**

Given the spending plans for consumers and businesses that were specified in the table above, what is the equilibrium level of income\output? **1000**

What are the equilibrium levels of Y, C, S, I?

Y = **1000**   C = **900**   S = **100**   I = **100**

Briefly explain why that level of income/output is an equilibrium level of income/output. Only at an income and output level of 1000 do aggregate demand and aggregate supply equal one another, and that means that the economy is spending at the same rate as it is producing -- a condition of macroeconomic equilibrium. Also at an income level of 1000, the change in inventories equals zero, so there is no signal to producers to change their level of production. Finally, only at 1000 do we find that planned saving equals planned investment. These are all conditions of equilibrium, and if one holds they all hold.

True/False Statements

1.) **True.** The circular flow of income is stable when total spending (aggregate demand) equals all of the costs that were incurred by the business sector.

2.) **False.** The existing body of evidence indicates that is not true. Expectations of permanent income largely dictate how consumers behave.

3.) **False.** This statement would be true only if the MPS equals the MPC, and that is possible only when the MPC and MPS equal 0.5. The MPC is the slope of the consumption function, and the MPS is the slope of the savings function.

4.) **True.** The fraction of total income consumed is defined as the average propensity to consume (APC), and the APC falls as income increases. One of the reasons for this phenomenon is that many consumption expenditures tend to be regressive in nature -- less is spent on them as one's income rises. Take food, for example -- while higher income units can spend more on more expensive, higher quality food, for the most part, the amount spent on food consumption will not change in direct proportion to income.

5.) **False.** It might all be spent, but some of the income received will, in all probability, leak out of the income flow (e.g., savings, taxes, imports).

6.) **True.** Intuitively obvious -- the circular flow of income will not change (i.e., it will be at equilibrium) when all the leakages are re-injected into the system.

7.) **True.** When planned savings are greater than planned investment expenditures, a net leakage from the circular flow results. That, in turn, means that there will be an unexpected accumulation of inventories, and that will signal producers to decrease production in the next time period. Inventory accumulation is direct evidence that total output exceeds total spending.

8.) **True.** Refer to the answer above.

9.) **True.** To the extent that stock market investments are perceived as part of the wealth of consumers, increases in that component of consumer wealth should shift the consumption function upwards.

10.) **False.** The expected rate of return on an investment project needs to exceed the relevant rate of interest. The risk on investment projects is probably larger than putting investment funds into a financial institution, and an investor needs to have a higher rate of return to compensate for the higher degree of risk.

11.) **False.** The accelerator is based on changes in income and output and their impact on investment spending.

12.) **True.** After taxes have been taken out of personal income, consumers can either consume or save their income. Given a change in disposable personal income, the sum of the change in consumption plus the change in saving must necessarily equal the change in income. Similarly, the percentage of the change in disposable personal income spent on consumption plus the percentage of the change in income devoted to saving must add up to 100 percent.

13.) **True.** For any given level of income, if consumption spending increases, the amount set aside for saving must decrease. If the consumption function shifts upward, then the saving function must necessarily shift downward.

Multiple-Choice

1.) c   2.) c   3.) d   4.) b   5.) a   6.) e

7.) e   8.) b   9.) d   10.) e   11.) a   12.) b

13.) d   14.) c   15.) b   16.) c   17.) c   18.) e

Discussion Questions

1.) The act of saving creates a net leakage in the flow of income, and that means that there will be insufficient purchasing power available to buy back what was produced. As a result, inventories (unsold goods) will start to accumulate -- an economic signal to the business sector that it produced more than society was willing to spend. In response, the business sector will cut back on production which will, in turn, reduce factor incomes and consumption spending. The flow of income will become smaller as a result of the saving leakage. If however, as is usually the case, savings are reinjected into the economy, the flow of income will remain stable and saving will not be a problem for the economy.

2.) The United States is a very consumption-oriented economy for a variety of reasons. The ever increasing introduction of appealing, technologically innovative new goods undoubtedly plays a role in encouraging us to spend more of our incomes. The pervasiveness and effectiveness of advertising constantly tempting us is another factor. Credit cards have made it all too easy for people to spend more than perhaps they should with corresponding negative effects on saving.

Even demographics plays a role in our low saving -- the majority of the baby boom population bulge is in that part of their life cycle where spending often exceeds income (buying and furnishing their homes, large expenditures for their children.)

Low savings ultimately means less resources available for investment activities which are closely associated with our rate of economic growth and the level of productivity. Our future standard of living is largely determined by the saving/investment decisions that we are making today. By saving less today, we are making a decision about our future productive capacity and ability to produce and consume. So it is an important decision for our society.

3.) If the labor market was in equilibrium, the quantity of labor demanded by employers would just equal the quantity of labor supplied by the labor force -- a situation of full employment. If the real wage was above its equilibrium level, then a surplus of labor would occur, and the surplus would represent the amount of unemployment. Competition among workers was assumed to drive the real wage back down towards its equilibrium level. So, the only way that persistent unemployment could exist was to have a real wage that was too high and, for some reason, could not return to its equilibrium level.

Keynesians emphasize believe that the level of total spending in the economy determines the level of output, income, and employment. To a Keynesian economist, if persistent unemployment exists, it is a sign that there is inadequate aggregate demand in the system. Lowering wages, according to their viewpoint, would not be helpful in reducing unemployment, since it does nothing to enhance total spending.

4.) Yes, it could make a big difference. According to the permanent-income hypothesis, any tax designed to reduce consumption expenditures would not be effective if it was known to be temporary. Temporary income tax surcharges would tend to be financed out of savings rather than reducing consumption expenditures as intended.

5.) Since investment spending is an injection in the circular flow model, a decrease in investment spending would result in a fall in the flow of the model (i.e., a decrease in income). The economy would have a net leakage (since saving would be greater than investment), and this would continue until saving and investment were equal once again (or in terms of the circular flow model, until leakages equalled injections).

6.) As household income increases, we would expect to see the following changes: the MPC would decrease, the MPS would increase, the APC would decrease, and the APS would increase. Lower income units would tend to spend a high proportion of any increase in income, saving a small proportion of the increase. The same would hold true for the average propensities out of total income. Higher income households would be expected to save a larger proportion of their total income as well as any increase in income.

7.) The accelerator introduces an element of instability into the macroeconomy, since it suggests that investment spending is capable of wide fluctuations in response to relatively small changes in sales. The accelerator assumes that firms attempt to maintain a fixed ratio between their sales and capital stock. Since the capital output ratio is greater than one, a sales increase implies that investment spending will increase more than proportionately.

Summary

This chapter provides you with a brief introduction to some of the simplest and most useful macroeconomic models that are incorporated in a beginning economics course. The circular flow model, with its emphasis on leakages and injections from the income stream, provides many new and worthwhile insights about the economy: (1) the linkages that exist among the different sectors of the economy; (2) the importance of returning any leakages from the income stream to the income flow; and (3) the mechanisms (such as the financial markets) which facilitate the return of savings to the income flow in the form of investment expenditures.

There are more complicated versions of the circular flow model which contain more sectors (such as the government sector and the foreign trade sector) which provide more detailed insights into the functioning of the economy. Very few economic models are as easy to learn, yet generate so many useful insights into how the economy works.

To be economically literate, one must have had at least a passing exposure to Keynesian economics and its policy prescriptions for the economy. Even though there are many who believe that Keynesian economics no longer offers valid insights into how the economy operates, in one sense **"we are all Keynesians now."** Keynes put total spending and aggregate demand into the economic spotlight as the single most important macroeconomic variable to the exclusion of most other factors. It is important to be familiar with the Keynesian solutions for unemployment (to increase total spending) and inflation (to decrease total spending).

One other extremely important point that is brought out in this chapter involves the role that inventories play in the macroeconomy. Inventories provide the economic signals to producers that help bring production plans in line with current sales -- it is the mechanism by which the system adjusts itself and moves towards equilibrium. If the amount being spent by all sectors of the economy is lower than the current output and production, then inventories will rise, and firms will adjust their production downwards. As a result, output, income, and employment will move towards a position where total spending equals the value of what is being produced. An understanding of inventories is essential to understanding the macroeconomy.

Chapter 17
Pursuing the Fixed-Price (Keynesian) Analysis

Overview of the Chapter

Once you have mastered the concepts in Chapter 17, you will have a good grasp of how the Keynesian model can be used in an economic policy context. Much of the analysis in the chapter utilizes the Keynesian cross diagram as a vehicle for explaining and diagramming the different equilibrium positions of the economy.

With the investment sector added, the total spending curve now represents the sum of both consumption spending and investment spending. The model can also be made to be more realistic by making investment a function of income (I = f(Y)). The concept of equilibrium remains the same -- the intersection of the total spending curve (C + I) and the 45 degree line. It's important to remember that as more economic sectors are added to the model and it becomes more sophisticated, the concept of equilibrium remains exactly the same as it was for the simplest model.

Equilibrium is also defined as the equality between planned saving and investment. If S exceeds I, then by definition total output must exceed total spending which will lead to inventory accumulation, and that is a signal for firms to decrease the level of output, income, and employment. If, on the other hand, I is greater than S, then total spending is larger than total output and declining inventories will lead firm to increase their orders to final producers, thus increasing output and income.

Using the graphics associated with the Keynesian model, it is easy to show changes in macroeconomic equilibrium and how they are related to changes in total spending. If total spending decreases because of either a decrease in consumption spending or a decrease in investment spending, then the total spending curve shifts downward at each level of total output, and the equilibrium level of income and output in the economy decreases. An increase in spending will cause the total spending curve to shift upwards, thus increasing equilibrium output and income.

One of the most important contributions of Keynesian economics was the economic multiplier -- the concept that a change in spending results in a change in income that is larger than the original change in spending. When spending increases, for example, there will be a corresponding change in the incomes of those firms and individuals providing the goods and services related to that spending, and those income recipients will then spend part of their increased incomes and save part. Their new spending will result in new incomes to others who will, in turn, spend part of their new income, and so on. The importance of the multiplier concept is that induced, secondary indirect impacts are important and must be taken into consideration when analyzing the macroeconomy.

Since so much time is spent discussing equilibrium, it is only natural that students associate equilibrium with a desirable outcome. However, in the Keynesian model, the equilibrium level of income -- the stable level of income where there are no changes in income -- is not necessarily the full employment level of income -- our target income level.

The level of full employment can be indicated on the Keynesian cross diagram and compared with the point at which equilibrium is achieved. If the equilibrium level of income lies below the income and output level necessary to achieve full employment, then a recessionary gap exists which represents the amount of additional spending necessary to reach full employment. A situation can also exist where there is an excessive amount of total spending, in which case, the equilibrium level of income will be larger than the full employment level of income. In that case, an inflationary gap exists.

The addition of government spending and taxation to the model allows us to explore the effects of fiscal and monetary policy on the economy. It is a much richer and robust model than the simpler model. When facing a recession and the prospect of excessive unemployment, the Keynesian model provides a framework for analyzing appropriate fiscal and monetary policy. An upward shift in the total spending curve will increase the level of equilibrium income and output, so appropriate fiscal policy should stimulate overall spending through either an increase in government spending (G), a decrease in taxes (T), or some combination of both. Monetary policy should attempt to lower interest rates which would stimulate interest-sensitive spending, primarily investment spending.

When inflation occurs because of excessive total spending, appropriate macro policy lies in shifting the total spending curve downwards through a combination of decreases in government spending, increases in taxes, and increasing interest rates. Because changes in taxes result in corresponding changes in disposable income and then spending according to the MPC, tax changes are less powerful than equivalent changes in government spending. There is an interesting conclusion that can be drawn from this. If a government budget is balanced to begin with and then government spending and taxation are changed by an equal amount, the government budget would remain balanced, but since government expenditure dollars are more powerful than taxation dollars, the level of equilibrium income increases.

With the inclusion of the foreign sector, the total spending curve now becomes C + I + G + X, and when total spending equals total output (C + S + T + M), equilibrium will occur. This model includes an induced investment function, a marginal propensity to tax (MPT), and/or a marginal propensity to import (MPM). With addition of these marginal propensities, the value of the economic multiplier also changes. The MPT and MPM are associated with leakages from the flow of income in the model and cause the equilibrium level of income to fall. With inclusion of these two marginal propensities, the multiplier becomes 1/(MPS + MPT) and 1/(MPS + MPM).

Learning Objectives

After completing this chapter, you should be sure that you are able to:

- graph the two-sector Keynesian fixed price model to illustrate and identify the concept of equilibrium income.

- understand the significance of the 45 degree line and its role in the diagrammatic model.

- understand how changes in society's spending plans affect the level of equilibrium income and how those changes can be illustrated in the graphic model.

- understand the Keynesian economic multiplier and the relationship of the multiplier to the marginal propensity to consume and other spending propensities.

- understand the paradox of thrift and how it can be explained in the context of the Keynesian model.

- understand the relationship that exists between the level of equilibrium income and the full employment level of income.

- define recessionary and inflationary gaps and explain their significance with respect to appropriate economic policy.

- understand how the government sector and the foreign trade sector can be added to the Keynesian two-sector model and that you understand the broader policy context of the more complex model.

- define fiscal and monetary economic policy and understand the economic mechanisms through which they work.

- understand why changes in government spending have more of a multiplier effect than an equivalent change in tax receipts.

- explain the economic rationale behind the balanced budget multiplier.

- understand how the value of the economic multiplier changes when induced investment spending, government taxes, and import spending are added to the model.

Self Evaluation

List of Terms

Balanced-Budget Multiplier
Fiscal Policy
GDP Gap
Inflationary Gap
Keynesian Multiplier

Monetary Policy
Multiplier Effect
Okun's Law
Open Economy
Paradox of Thrift
Recessionary Gap

For the statements below, fill in the term from the list above which provides the best fit.

1.) The _____ suggests that contrary to your intuition, equal changes in government spending (G) and taxes (T) -- leaving the net budget status of the government unchanged -- will affect the level of equilibrium income.

2.) When the equilibrium level of income falls below the level necessary to maintain full employment, the _____ provides an estimate of how much total spending will have to increase to achieve full employment.

3.) The _____ refers to the economic process in which changes in spending result in larger changes on income/output.

4.) An _____ is one which interacts and has trade with other economies.

5.) Macroeconomic policy which consists of changes in the level of government spending and the level and rate of taxes in an attempt to change the equilibrium level of income is called _____.

6.) Efforts to save more (i.e., an upward shift in the saving function) may ultimately result in less total saving for the economy as a whole. This is known as the _____.

7.) When the equilibrium level of income is lower than the full employment level of income, the _____ provides an estimate of how much total spending will have to increase to achieve a position of non-inflationary full employment.

8.) When the equilibrium level of income is higher than the full employment level of income, the _____ provides an estimate of how much total spending will have to decrease to achieve a position of non-inflationary full employment.

9.) The difference between the current output level and the output level associated with full employment is known as the _____.

10.) _____ involves changes in the money supply, the level of credit, and interest rates.

11.) _____ stipulates that real income must increase by about two percentage points in order to reduce the level of unemployment by one percentage point.

Problems

Graphing the Keynesian Model

The graphs associated with the Keynesian model will strengthen your understanding of the model and how it functions. The main diagram shows equilibrium as the intersection between total spending which increases with the level of income/output and total output, the latter depicted by a 45 degree line. This graph is commonly refered to as the Keynesian cross diagram. If not otherwise noted, all data and graphs are in real terms.

The first Keynesian model to be graphed will be the first one presented in the last chapter of the Hogendorn text. That model, if you recall, had an equilibrium level of income of $1000. Its table of values is reproduced on the following page.

Table 17-1

A	B	C	D	E	F	G
Possible Levels of Income and Output (Y)	Consumption Spending (C)	Saving (S)	Investment Spending (I)	Total Spending on Output of Business = Business Receipts = (C) + (I)	Payments Made by Business Sector (= Income)	Change in Inventories: Total Output Minus Total Spending
Given Below	Given Below	Column A − Column B	Given Below	Column B + Column D	Identical to Column A	Column A − Column E
0	400	− 400	100	500	0	− 500
100	450	− 350	100	550	100	− 450
200	500	− 300	100	600	200	− 400
300	550	− 250	100	650	300	− 350
400	600	− 200	100	700	400	− 300
500	650	− 150	100	750	500	− 250
600	700	− 100	100	800	600	− 200
700	750	− 50	100	850	700	− 150
800	800	0	100	900	800	− 100
900	850	+ 50	100	950	900	− 50
1000	900	+ 100	100	1000	1000	0
1100	950	+ 150	100	1050	1100	+ 50
1200	1000	+ 200	100	1100	1200	+ 100
1300	1050	+ 250	100	1150	1300	+ 150
1400	1100	+ 300	100	1200	1400	+ 200

Plot the consumption function (C) and total spending (C + I) on Figure 17-1, based on the values contained in Table 16-3. Label both curves clearly.

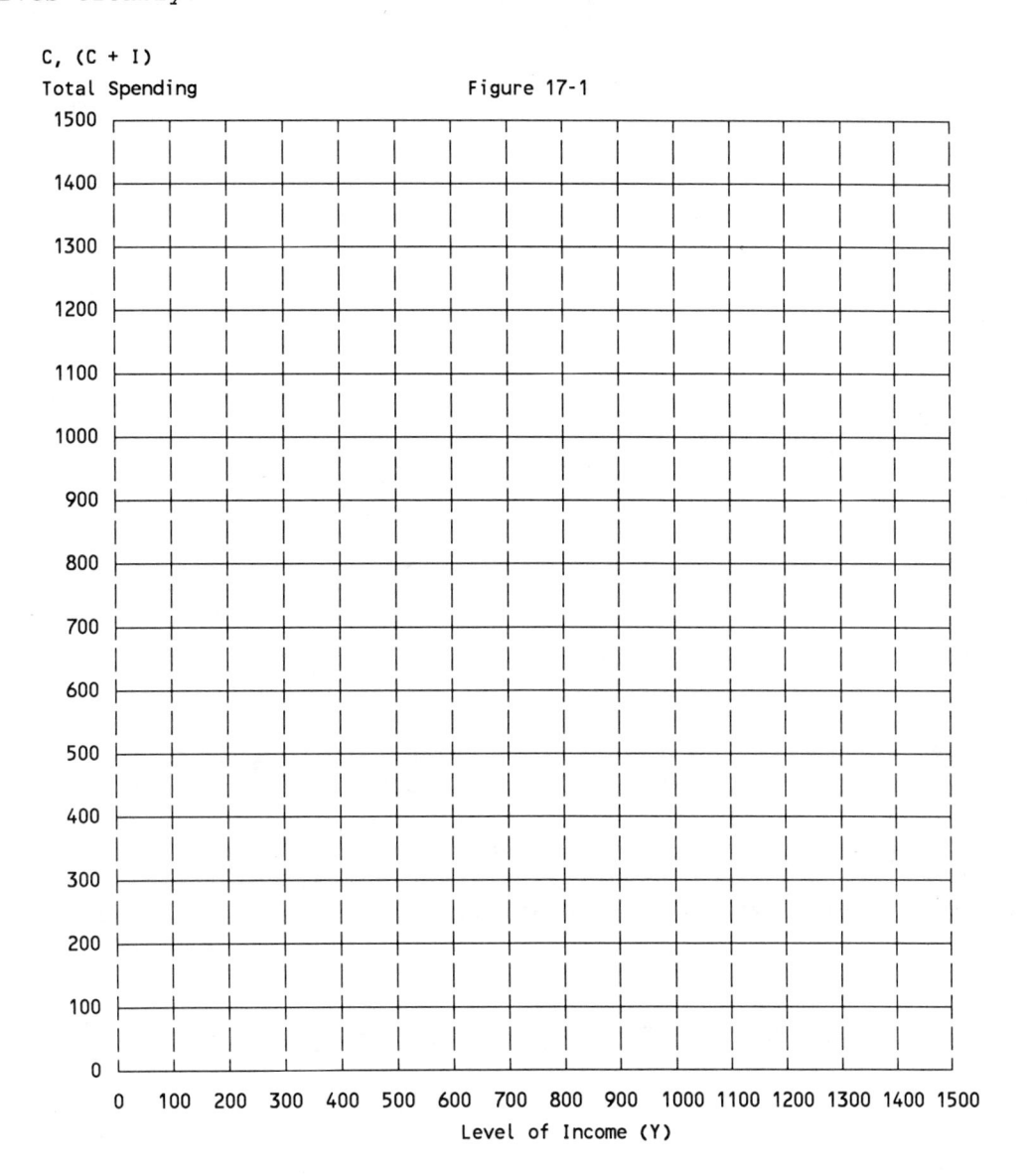

C, (C + I)
Total Spending   Figure 17-1

[Blank graph with y-axis labeled from 0 to 1500 in increments of 100, and x-axis labeled "Level of Income (Y)" from 0 to 1500 in increments of 100.]

Clearly indicate the equilibrium level of income, labeling it Y_e.

Changes in inventories indicate where the level of income is headed in the Keynesian system with inventory accumulation signifying overproduction and leading to less production and income, inventory depletion signifying underproduction (or overspending?) and leading to more production and income, and constant inventory levels indicating that total production and output are equal to total spending.

Plot saving (S) and investment (I) on Figure 17-2, based on the values contained in Table 17-1.

S, I
Saving, Investment   Figure 17-2

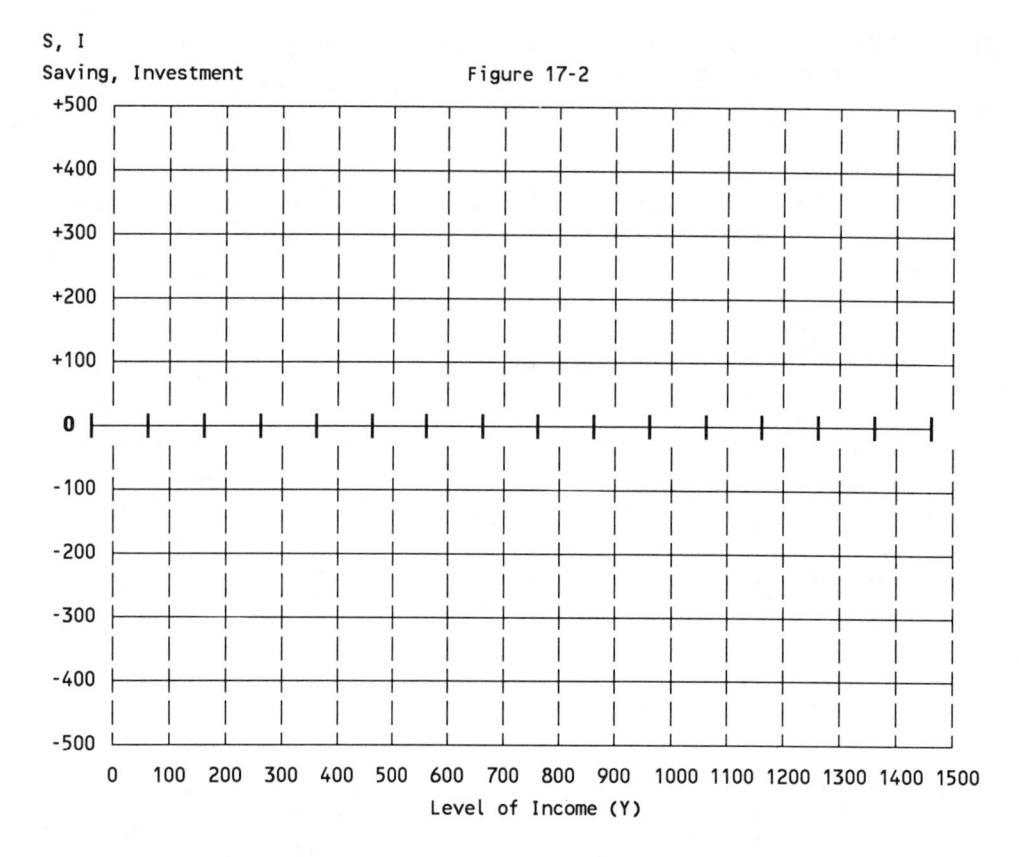

[Graph: vertical axis labeled S, I with values from -500 to +500 in increments of 100; horizontal axis labeled "Level of Income (Y)" with values from 0 to 1500 in increments of 100. Grid is empty.]

Put the label "leakage" on the saving curve and "injection" on the investment curve. Note that the saving and investment curves should intersect at the same level of income as did the total output and total spending curves in the previous graph. At income levels below equilibrium (less than 1000), the investment injection is larger than the saving leakage, thus increasing the level of income. Draw an arrow in the gap between the two curves that points towards equilibrium.

The Keynesian Economic Multiplier and Other Multipliers

The economic multiplier concept is an extremely useful concept, and it has to be ranked as one of the greatest contributions of Keynes. Because of the interconnected nature of the modern economy, changes in spending have a total final impact that is greater than the initial change. It constantly reminds us of the importance of the induced, secondary impacts that are associated with spending changes in either the entire economy or some specified region or local economy.

From a policy perspective, the existence of multiplier means that desired changes in government spending (▲ G) or taxes (▲ T) or, for that matter, (▲ C) or (▲ I), need be only some fraction of the total intended change. The economic multiplier will do the rest.

It is particularly important for students to realize that the multiplier and its formula depend upon the way in which the economic model is specified. If, for example, the only marginal propensity in the model is the marginal propensity to consume, the simple multiplier is applicable, k = 1/1-MPC or 1/MPS. If there is also a marginal propensity to tax specified in the model (i.e., taxes are specified as a function of income), then the applicable multiplier k = 1/(MPS + MPT). Leakages such as taxes always decrease the value of the multiplier, while injections like the marginal propensity to invest (specifying that investment increases with the level of income) increase the value of multiplier.

Thus, when the marginal propensity to import (MPM) is added to an economic model, the economic multiplier will incorporate that leakage into its formula, k = 1/(MPS + MPM).

To summarize:

- injections to the income stream increase the value of the economic multiplier.

    - increases in the marginal propensity to consume increase the multiplier.

- leakages to the income stream decrease the value of the economic multiplier.

    - increases in the marginal propensity to save decrease the multiplier.

    - increases in the marginal propensity to tax decrease the multiplier.

    - increases in the marginal propensity to import decrease the multiplier.

There are other economic multipliers that you should be familiar with as well. The government transfers multiplier is based on the same economic groundwork as the simple economic multiplier. The only difference is that when a government transfer is paid out, income is increased by that amount, but part of it is saved. Thus, the change in consumption spending will be less than the original amount of the transfer payment. That change in consumption will, however, be multiplied by the simple multiplier. In essence, the government expenditures multiplier is larger than the government transfers multiplier, because all of the increase in government expenditures gets injected into the economy, while some of the transfer payment is saved, and the increase in consumption spending is necessarily less than the original increase in the transfer payment.

Problem 1.) Assume an economy has a current equilibrium income level of $5,000. The economy's MPC = 0.75. How much of a change in government expenditures would it take to increase equilibrium income by $500?

Problem 2.) How much of an increase in government transfer payments would it take to increase equilibrium income by $500?

The other multiplier, the balanced-budget multiplier, is based on the assumption that all of an increase in government expenditures gets injected into the economy, while part of any change in taxes is saved. Because of that, the impact of a change in government expenditures is larger than the impact of a similarly sized change in taxes. Government expenditure dollars have more economic bang per buck than tax dollars. Thus, if government spending and taxes are both increased by the same amount, there will be a change in equilibrium income because the multiplied impacts of the two changes are not the same. The balanced-budget multiplier equals one, because if government spending and taxes are changed by the same amount, equilibrium income will change by the amount of the change in G and T.

Problem 3.) Assume, as in the problem above, that the level of equilibrium income equals $5,000 that the MPC = 0.75, and that the government budget is balanced with G = 800 and T = 800. What will the level of equilibrium income be if both G and T change by +200?

Again, using the first Keynesian model from the previous chapter, we can analyze the impact of changes in either consumption or investment spending on the level of equilibrium income. Keep in mind that the level of equilibrium income from that model was 1000. The revised model which follows has an increased level of investment spending, I' = 200.

- Fill in the empty columns in the table below to determine the equilibrium level of income for this two-sector economic model with revised investment spending.

Table 17-2

A	B	C	D	E	F	G
Possible Levels of Income and Output (Y)	Consumption Spending (C)	Saving (S)	New Level of Investment Spending (I')	Total Spending on Output of Business = Business Receipts = (C) + (I')	Payments Made by Business Sector (= Income)	Change in Inventories: Total Output Minus Total Spending
Given Below	Given Below	Column A − Column B	Given Below	Column B + Column D	Identical to Column A	Column A − Column E
0	400		200			
100	450		200			
200	500		200			
300	550		200			
400	600		200			
500	650		200			
600	700		200			
700	750		200			
800	800		200			
900	850		200			
1000	900		200			
1100	950		200			
1200	1000		200			
1300	1050		200			
1400	1100		200			
1500	1150		200			

All spending data in billions of dollars

What is the new level of equilibrium income for this economic model? _____

What are the new equilibrium values of C, S, I?

C = _____   S = _____   I = _____

Investment spending increased by _____, yet equilibrium income increased by _____. Briefly explain why the increase in the equilibrium level of income increased by more than the original spending change.

_____

_____

_____

Three different ways of looking at the multiplier:

(1.) economic multiplier = $\dfrac{\text{total change in income}}{\text{initial change in spending}} = \dfrac{\Delta Y\ =}{\Delta I\ =} =$

(2.) economic multiplier = $\dfrac{1}{1 - \text{MPC}} = \dfrac{1}{1 - } =$

(3.) economic multiplier = $\dfrac{1}{\text{MPS}} = \dfrac{1}{} =$

Draw the new total spending curve based on the increased investment expenditures on Figure 17-1 on page 368 of your study guide. Label the new point of equilibrium Y'_e. Do the same for the new investment curve, drawing it on Figure 17-2 (again on page 368). Label the new point of equilibrium Y'_e.

Be sure to check that all the equilibrium conditions are satisfied at the new level of equilibrium:

    (1.) Total output = total spending C + I'

    (2.) no change in inventories: Δ inventories = 0

    (3.) leakages = injections
           S = I

Macroeconomic Equilibrium and the Full Employment Level of Income

The level of equilibrium income associated with current spending patterns may not be the full employment level of income. The economy would then face a problem, because it would always be moving towards an income level which would not provide for full employment. If Y_e is less than the full employment level of income Y_f, then the economy will be characterized by excessive unemployment.

It is also possible for the level of equilibrium to be higher than that necessary to achieve full employment -- $Y_e > Y_f$. In that case, the economy will try to achieve an income level that is greater than what can be achieved when all resources are fully employed. The only way that can happen is through an increase in the price level (P). Once resources are fully employed, more income can be generated only through inflation.

The macroeconomic policy challenge now becomes one of adjusting total spending in the economy so that the level of equilibrium income equals the full employment level of income (Y_f) or some other target level of income that society has agreed upon. If the level of equilibrium income is below that required to generate full employment, then total spending should be increased, shifting the C + I curve upwards to a new, higher level of equilibrium income. If, on the other hand, the level of equilibrium income lies above the full employment level of income, then total spending should be decreased, shifting the C + I curve downwards to a new, lower level of equilibrium income.

Because of the economic multiplier, the required change in total spending will be only a fraction of the difference between the full employment level of income and the equilibrium level of income. For example, if the marginal propensity to consume (MPC) for an economy was equal to 0.8 and the current equilibrium level of income is Y = 3700 and the full employment, target income was determined to be Y = 4200, then the desired macroeconomic policy would be to design a fiscal policy package which would raise income by a total of 500. The critical fiscal policy question would be: **How much would consumption or investment spending have to increase in order to raise equilibrium income by 500?**

To answer this question, we first must calculate the value of the economic multiplier:

$$\text{Multiplier} = \frac{1}{1 - \text{MPC}} = \frac{1}{0.2} = 5$$

Next, the difference between equilibrium income and full employment income, determined. The required change in spending is found by dividing the income difference by the appropriate multiplier.

$$\text{Required } (\blacktriangle C \text{ or } \blacktriangle I) = \frac{Y_f - Y_e}{\text{Multiplier}} = \frac{\$4200 - \$3700}{5} = \frac{\$500}{5} = \$100$$

Our general rule for determining how much total spending will have to change to reach the full employment level of income is shown below:

$$\text{Required spending change } (\Delta \text{ spending}) = \frac{\text{Difference between } Y_f \text{ and } Y_e}{\text{appropriate economic multiplier}}$$

The appropriate economic multiplier depends upon what economic model is being specified (i.e., whether or not the model includes marginal propensities to invest, tax, and import).

Problem 1.) An economy is currently attaining an income level of $1800. The full employment level of income is estimated to be $1250. Research indicates that this society saves one third of an increase in income. Using fiscal policy, what should be done to achieve full employment without inflation? Be specific in terms of the size of any spending change and its direction.

Problem 2.) At the present time, consumption spending (C) is $2000 and investment spending (I) equals $350 for a total equilibrium income of $2,350. If income (Y) were to increase an additional $200, consumption spending would increase by $125 ($\Delta$C). This economy would like to attain an income level of $3000 where there would be acceptable performance for both unemployment and inflation. If fiscal policy were used to attain this income goal, how much should total spending change?

True/False Statements

Indicate whether you think the statements below are true or false. These questions are designed to make you think about the concepts presented in the text. There may not be any easy clear-cut answers. Some thoughts about the answers are presented at the end of the chapter.

1.) _____ Equilibrium income is the best overall level of income for the economy, since it is the point of stability.

2.) _____ If the level of equilibrium income is greater than the full employment level of income, then total spending should be decreased.

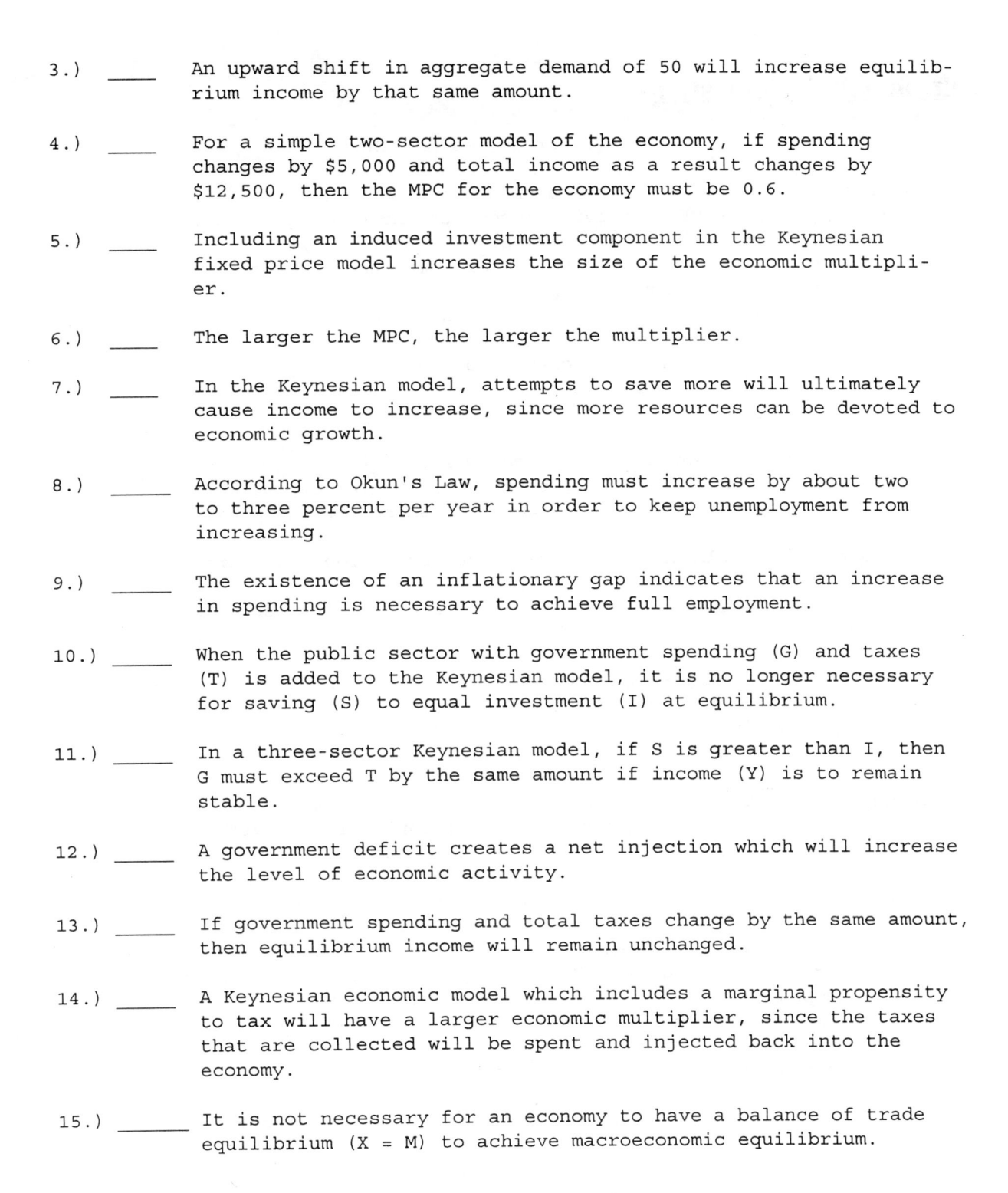

3.) _____ An upward shift in aggregate demand of 50 will increase equilibrium income by that same amount.

4.) _____ For a simple two-sector model of the economy, if spending changes by $5,000 and total income as a result changes by $12,500, then the MPC for the economy must be 0.6.

5.) _____ Including an induced investment component in the Keynesian fixed price model increases the size of the economic multiplier.

6.) _____ The larger the MPC, the larger the multiplier.

7.) _____ In the Keynesian model, attempts to save more will ultimately cause income to increase, since more resources can be devoted to economic growth.

8.) _____ According to Okun's Law, spending must increase by about two to three percent per year in order to keep unemployment from increasing.

9.) _____ The existence of an inflationary gap indicates that an increase in spending is necessary to achieve full employment.

10.) _____ When the public sector with government spending (G) and taxes (T) is added to the Keynesian model, it is no longer necessary for saving (S) to equal investment (I) at equilibrium.

11.) _____ In a three-sector Keynesian model, if S is greater than I, then G must exceed T by the same amount if income (Y) is to remain stable.

12.) _____ A government deficit creates a net injection which will increase the level of economic activity.

13.) _____ If government spending and total taxes change by the same amount, then equilibrium income will remain unchanged.

14.) _____ A Keynesian economic model which includes a marginal propensity to tax will have a larger economic multiplier, since the taxes that are collected will be spent and injected back into the economy.

15.) _____ It is not necessary for an economy to have a balance of trade equilibrium (X = M) to achieve macroeconomic equilibrium.

Multiple-Choice Questions

Select the "best" answer from the alternatives provided.

1.) The economic multiplier is based on the concept that
   a. a change in the MPC can cause income to increase by an amount several times as large as the initial change in the MPC.
   b. changes in spending will result in income changes that are larger than the initial change in spending.
   c. changes in income induce changes in investment spending.
   d. changes in consumption spending lead to larger changes in income than similar changes in investment or government spending, since the consumption sector is so much larger.
   e. none of the above.

2.) Other things being equal (*ceteris paribus*),
   a. the economic multiplier will be smaller the larger the MPS.
   b. the economic multiplier is larger over short periods of time than over longer periods.
   c. the economic multiplier will be larger the larger the marginal propensity to tax.
   d. the economic multiplier will be smaller the smaller the MPC.
   e. none of the above.

3.) In a three-sector Keynesian model, if government spending increases by $30 billion with no other spending changes,
   a. equilibrium income will increase by $30 billion.
   b. taxes will change by MPT X $30 billion.
   c. equilibrium income will increase by $30 billion X MPS.
   d. equilibrium income will increase by $30 billion X (1/MPS).
   e. it is impossible to determinie if equilibrium income will increase on the basis of the information given.

4.) If the current equilibrium level of income equals $3700 billion and the MPC is 0.8 and it has been determined that the income level necessary to achieve full employment is $4200 billion, then
   a. a change in spending of $500 billion will be necessary to achieve full employment.
   b. a change in spending of $400 billion will be necessary to achieve full employment.
   c. full employment can be achieved if total saving falls by $80 billion.
   d. full employment can be obtained with a change in consumption spending of $100 billion.
   e. an increase in government spending of $200 billion along with a tax cut of $300 billion could achieve the full employment income level of $4200.

5.) Assume an economy that has an MPC of 0.75 is currently at an equilibrium level of income of $5000 billion. The government budget is balanced, with government spending (G) equaling $700 billion and total taxes (T) at $700 billion. If both G and T increase by $200 billion, maintaining a balanced-budget,
   a. the equilibrium level of income will decrease by $200 billion.
   b. the equilibrium level of income will increase by $800 billion (4 X $200 billion).
   c. the equilibrium level of income will not change, since the budget remains balanced and there is no net public sector leakage or injection.
   d. the equilibrium level of income will increase by $200 billion.
   e. the equilibrium level of income will increase by $100 billion.

6.) If an economy has a recessionary gap, appropriate fiscal policy for this economy would be
   a. to have a balanced-budget to maintain fiscal stability.
   b. to increase government spending (G) by the amount of the recessionary gap.
   c. to increase taxes by the amount of the recessionary gap.
   d. to increase both (G) and (T) by the amount of the recessionary gap.
   e. both (b) and (d)

7.) A four-sector Keynesian model has a balance of trade deficit (M>X) and a private sector leakage (S>I). Appropriate fiscal policy to maintain a position of equilibrium will be
   a. to run a deficit equal to the sum of the foreign sector leakage and the private sector leakage.
   b. to run a surplus equal to the sum of the foreign sector leakage and the private sector leakage.
   c. to have a balanced-budget (G = T).
   d. to run a deficit equal to the private sector leakage.
   e. none of the above.

8.) An inflationary gap can be thought of as
   a. the difference between an equilibrium level of income that is higher than full employment and the level of full employment income.
   b. the increase in spending necessary to bring the equilibrium level of income up to the full employment level of income.
   c. the decrease in spending necessary to bring the equilibrium level of income down to the full employment level of income.
   d. the difference between government spending and taxes.
   e. being equal to the accumulation in inventories that is taking place.

9.) If society decides to save more at each and every level of income because of widespread anticipation of an upcoming recession
   a. the increased savings will provide additional funds for investment purposes which will help alleviate the recession.
   b. the increased savings can be offset by increasing taxes which will reduce total savings.
   c. the increased savings will intensify the recessionary pressures in the economy.
   d. the increased savings will decrease equilibrium income, and total savings at the new level of equilibrium income will be lower than what they were initially.
   e. both (c) and (d)

Answer the following questions on the basis of the information contained in the graph below.

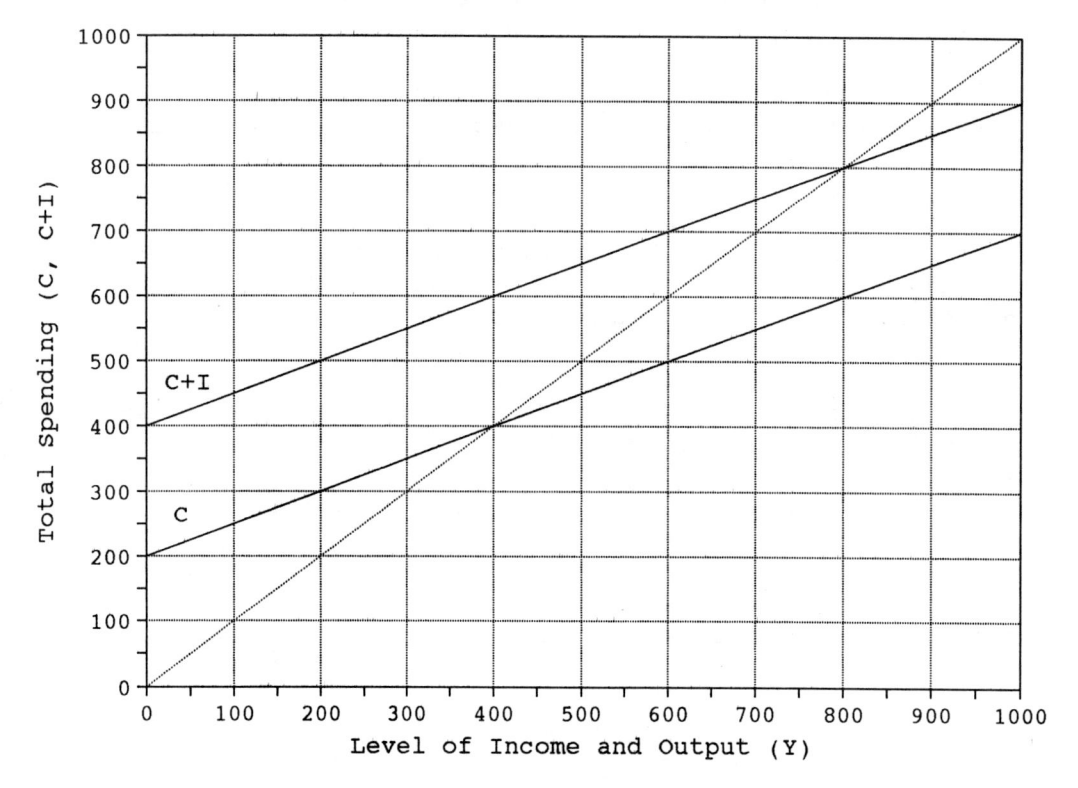

10.) The break-even level of income for the consumption function equals:
   a. 0   b. 100   c. 200   d. 500   e. 600

11.) The amounted saved at an income level of Y = 500 equals
   a. 0   b. 50   c. 100   d. 150   e. 200

12.) The MPC for this economy is
   a. 0.4   b. 0.5   c. 0.6   d. 0.75
   e. cannot be determined graphically.

13.) The equilibrium level of income for the two-sector model represented on the preceding page is:
a. 200   b. 500   c. 600   d. 800
e. cannot be determined graphically.

14.) At an income level of 800, the change in inventories equals:
a. 0   b. 50   c. 100   d. 150
e. cannot be determined graphically.

15.) If government spending of 100 were added to this model with no added taxes, the new equilibrium level of income would be:
a. 600   b. 700   c. 800   d. 900   e. 1000

16.) If the full employment level of income is $3000 billion and at the present time C = $2100 billion, I = $400 billion, total taxes T = $600 billion, and G = $700 billion,
a. the economy is at a position of equilibrium.
b. total spending in the economy should be decreased to reduce inflationary pressures.
c. total spending in the economy should be increased to reduce the amount of excessive unemployment.
d. the government budget should be balanced in order to attain equilibrium.

17.) If an economy has an MPC and a marginal propensity to tax and import as well,
a. the economic multiplier will be larger than the multiplier based only on the MPC.
b. the economic multiplier will be smaller than the multiplier based only on the MPC.
c. the economic multiplier will be about the same as the multiplier based only on the MPC.
d. the equilibrium level of income will depend upon the fixed levels of spending rather than the multiplier associated with the model.

Discussion Questions

1.) Various studies have estimated that the marginal propensity to consume (MPC) in the United States is quite high, possibly in the 0.9 - 0.95 range. Those results would suggest a fairly large multiplier, yet the multiplier studies that have been done indicate that the actual, real world multiplier is somewhere between 2.5 - 3, much lower than would be the case with the high MPC. Why do you think the actual multiplier is so much lower than what the estimated MPC would indicate? [Hint: think about the various factors which affect the size of the multiplier]

2.) Using the Keynesian concepts developed in this chapter, explain why so many countries are interested in increasing their exports to the rest of the world and minimizing their imports.

3.) A well-known business forecaster predicts that a recession is on the horizon. Would it make any difference whether her forecast is correct or completely off the mark?

4.) Upon hearing the above foreaster's gloomy economic prediction, many households start to save more of their income in anticipation of possibly losing their jobs. What advice would you give them?

5.) Why would you expect the balance of trade to deteriorate when the United States economy comes out of a recession?

6.) Using Keynesian analysis, describe the mechanism by which a recession in the United States can be transmitted to its main trading partners.

7.) If exports increase by $50 billion, why would you expect the balance of trade to increase by less than that amount?

8.) Assume that taxes are functionally related to the level of income, $T = f(Y)$. If the government's budget is balanced and the economy goes into a recession, what would you expect to happen to the government budget position? Would that help or hinder the recession?

Answers and Solutions to Problems and Exercises

Completing Statements from the List of Terms

1.) Balanced-Budget Multiplier
2.) Keynesian Multiplier
3.) Multiplier Effect
4.) Open Economy
5.) Fiscal Policy
6.) Paradox of Thrift
7.) Recessionary Gap
8.) Inflationary Gap
9.) GDP Gap
10.) Monetary Policy
11.) Okun's Law

Problems

Graphing the Keynesian Model

Figure 17-1

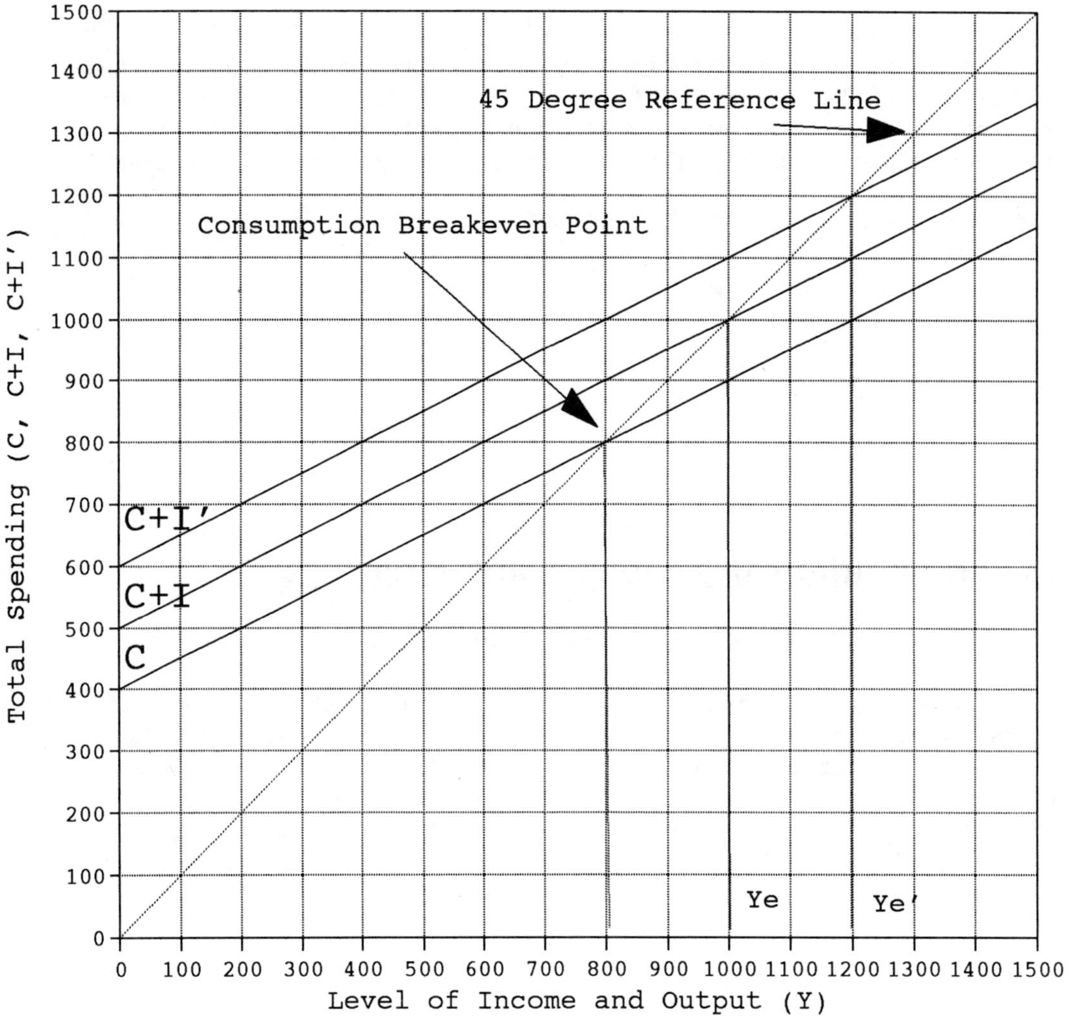

Figure 17-2

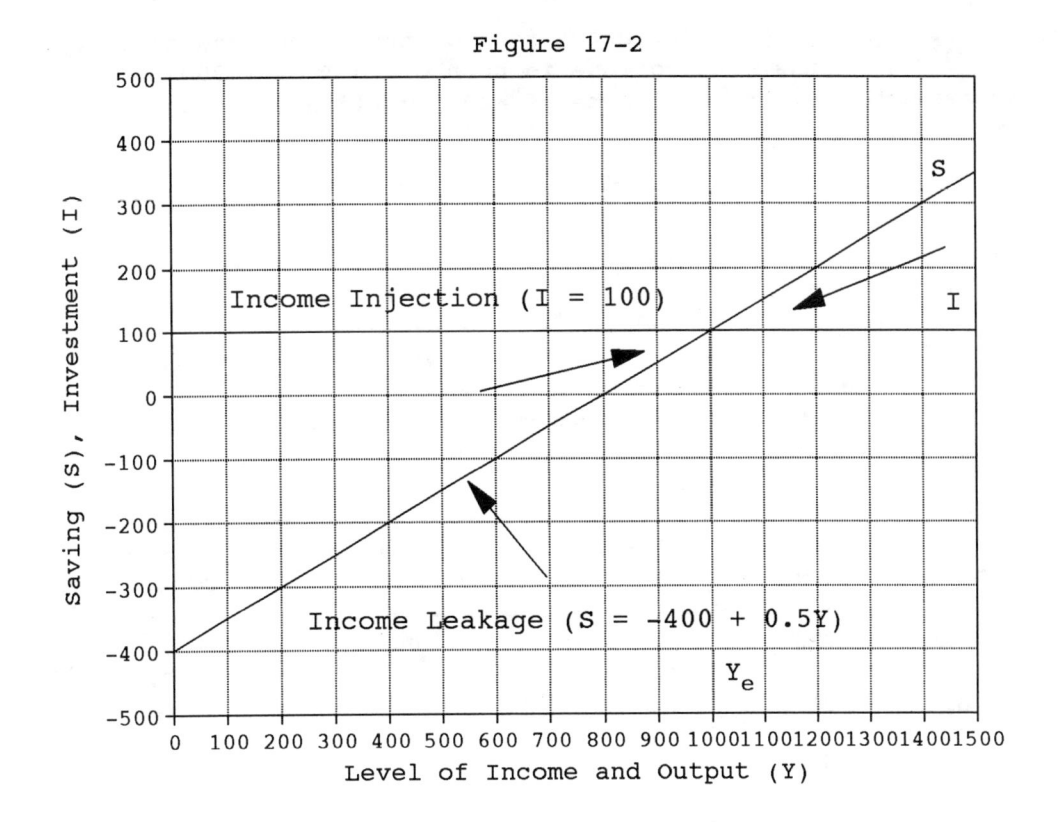

[Graph showing Saving (S), Investment (I) on y-axis from -500 to 500, and Level of Income and Output (Y) on x-axis from 0 to 1500. Horizontal line labeled "Income Injection (I = 100)" at I=100. Upward sloping line labeled "Income Leakage (S = -400 + 0.5Y)" crossing the investment line at Y_e near 1000.]

The Keynesian Economic Multiplier and Other Economic Multipliers

Problem 1.) The economic multiplier equals 4. The required spending change in government spending can be calculated by dividing the required change in income by the appropriate multiplier ($500/4 = $125).

Problem 2.) If government transfers were to increase by the same amount as above ($125), seventy five percent of the transfer payment would be consumed (equal to $93.75) and twenty five percent would be saved (equal to $31.25). The change in consumption would be subject to the multiplier of 4 for a total change in income of $375 -- less than the required increase in income. Therefore, the increase in transfer payments necessary to increase equilibrium income by $500 would be $166.67. With an increase in government transfers of $166.67, consumption spending would increase by $125, and the total multiplied impact would be equal to the required $500. The required amount of spending is found by setting up an equation:
(x) (0.75) = 125 in words: we are looking for the value of transfer payments such that when seventy five percent of the increase is consumed, it will result in an increase in consumption spending of $125.

Problem 3.) It is useful to separate the change in government spending and the change in taxes. If only government spending changed by 200, equilibrium income would increase by +800 (+200 X 4 = +800) If, on the other hand, only taxes increased by +200, equilibrium income would decrease by 600 (↑taxes of 200 → ↓disposable income of 200 → ↓C of 150 and ↓S of 50). The change in consumption of 150 would result in a decrease in equilibrium income of -600   (-150 X 4 = -600). The net effect of these two changes is + 200 (+800 - 600 = +200). Thus, an increase in both G and T of + 200 resulted in an incrase in equilibrium income of +200, yielding a balanced-budget multiplier of 1.

Table 17-2

A	B	C	D	E	F	G
Possible Levels of Income and Output (Y)	Consumption Spending (C)	Saving (S)	New Level of Investment Spending (I')	Total Spending on Output of Business = Business Receipts = (C) + (I')	Payments Made by Business Sector (= Income)	Change in Inventories: Total Output Minus Total Spending
Given Below	Given Below	Column A - Column B	Given Below	Column B + Column D	Identical to Column A	Column A - Column E
0	400	-400	200	600	0	-600
100	450	-350	200	650	100	-550
200	500	-300	200	700	200	-500
300	550	-250	200	750	300	-450
400	600	-200	200	800	400	-400
500	650	-150	200	850	500	-350
600	700	-100	200	900	600	-300
700	750	- 50	200	950	700	-250
800	800	0	200	1000	800	-200
900	850	+ 50	200	1050	900	-150
1000	900	+100	200	1100	1000	-100
1100	950	+150	200	1150	1100	- 50
1200	1000	+200	200	1200	1200	0
1300	1050	+250	200	1250	1300	+ 50
1400	1100	+300	200	1300	1400	+100
1500	1150	+350	200	1350	1500	+200

What is the new level of equilibrium income for this economic model? **1200**

What are the new equilibrium values of C, S, I? **C = 1000   S = 200   I = 200**

Investment spending increased by **100**, yet equilibrium income increased by **200**. Briefly explain why the increase in the equilibrium level of income increased by more than the original spending change? **Because of the economic multiplier. In this case, investment spending increased by +100, and the economic multiplier equaled 2 (1/1-0.5), for a final change in income of 200. The initial change in spending resulted in another 100 of induced, secondary spending as the original amount was spent and respent.**

Macroeconomic Equilibrium and The Full Employment Level of Income

Problem 1.) In this case, there is an inflationary gap of $550, since the equilibrium level of income exceeds the full employment level of income by that amount. With a marginal propensity to save of 0.333, the simple economic multiplier would be 3. The required change in spending would equal -$550/3 or -$183.33. If total spending in this economy were reduced by that amount (-$183.33), total income would fall by $550, and the new level of equilibrium income would be $1,250.

Problem 2.) This economy has a deflationary gap of $650. Based on the information in the problem, the MPC for this economy equals 0.625, and the simple economic multiplier would be 2.6667. Dividing the recessionary gap of $650 by the multiplier of 2.6667 yields the required increase in spending of $243.75 needed to obtain an equilibrium level of income of $3,000. If either C or I spending or both increase by a total of $243.75, this economy will achieve a new equilibrium level of income of $3,000.

True/False Statements

1.) **False.** In this case, the optimal level of income depends upon what society's target level of income is -- typically the level of income necessary to achieve full employment. If equilibrium income is greater than the full employment level of income, then inflation will result. If equilibrium income is lower than the full employment level of income, then unemployment will result.

2.) **True.** Total spending should be decreased in this case.

3.) **False.** The Keynesian economic multiplier tells us that any spending change that takes place will have a "multiplied" impact on income, so income will change by more than 50, specifically 50 times the multiplier.

4.) **True.** An MPC of 0.6 yields an economic multiplier of 2.5. $5,000 X 2.5 = $12,500.

5.) **True.** When induced investment is part of the Keynesian model, the multiplier becomes larger, because income changes result in not only more consumption spending but also additional investment expenditures as well which, in turn, are subject to the entire multiplier process. When induced investment is included in the simple two-sector model, the multiplier associated with the model is sometimes called the "Super Multiplier."

6.) **True.** The larger the MPC, a larger proportion of income change in the multiplier process is spent, causing successive income changes to also be that much larger. All of the income/spending stages of the multiplier are increased with a larger MPC.

7.) **False.** Saving is a leakage from the flow of income and results in lower income levels. Attempts to save more will decrease income and less will be saved at the lower level of income than before. This is known as the "paradox of thrift."

8.) **True.** The economy has certain built-in growth requirements which means that total spending must increase at roughly the same rate as those growth requirements or else unemployment will increase.

9.) **False.** Just the opposite is true. An inflationary gap measures the amount that spending must be decreased in order to get back to full employment.

10.) **True.** To achieve equilibrium, it is necessary only that total leakages equal total injections. It is not necessary for each corresponding set of leakages (S and I, G and T, and X and M) to be equal to one another, only that the totals be equal.

11.) **True.** When S exceeds I, a net leakage is created that can be offset by a net injection in the public sector of an equivalent amount: (G - T) must equal (S - T) for equilibrium to occur.

12.) **True.** When government spending (G) exceeds taxes (T), a net injection is created, and injections increase the flow of income.

13.) **False.** Government spending dollars are more powerful (i.e., have more economic impact -- a greater multiplier effect) than tax dollars which have to go through the consumption function. Thus, if G and T change by the same amount, there will be an effect on equilibrium income. As a matter of fact, equilibrium income will change by the same amount as the changes in G and T and in the same direction.

14.) **False.** Taxes are a leakage and their inclusion in the model will tend to reduce the size of the multiplier effect. For each change in income, less will be consumed and saved at each period since taxes must be paid.

15.) **True.** It is necessary only that total leakages equal total injections, and that can occur when exports are not equal to imports.

Multiple-Choice

1.) b   2.) d   3.) d   4.) d   5.) d   6.) e

7.) a   8.) c   9.) e   10.) c   11.) d   12.) b

13.) c   14.) c   15.) c   16.) b   17.) b

Discussion Questions

1.) In the real world, there are a number of other leakages and injections that affect the actual size of the multiplier. The factors that would tend to reduce the size of the multiplier include the marginal propensity to tax (MPT), the marginal propensity to import (MPM), and business savings which represent another leakage. Taxes probably have the greatest impact, since they are quite pervasive.

2.) Exports are an injection into the income stream, creating income and employment, while imports are a leakage from the income stream, causing the income flow to decline. Income growth and full employment are important domestic economic goals, and a surplus in the balance of trade helps achieve those goals.

3.) As long as people act on their beliefs, it really doesn't make any difference whether or not their actions are based on correct perceptions of what is going to happen. Any forecast has the potential to become a self-fulfilling prophecy -- if you think a recession is on the way and cut back on spending to prepare for it, a recession will occur.

4.) This relates to the paradox of thrift -- efforts to save more will result in actions which will cause saving to decline. Saving, in the Keynesian scheme of things, is a leakage and has the potential to disrupt the circular flow of income. Saving in anticipation of a recession is exactly the wrong thing to do, since it will cause income to decline. People should increase their spending.

5.) Imports, are function of income, and, as income increases, the level of import spending will also increase. If exports remain constant, then the balance of trade will move towards a deficit position as the domestic economy recovers from a recession.

6.) A recession in the United States will lower income levels, causing imports to decrease. Our imports are other countries' exports, thus the exports of our trading partners will decline. A decrease in exports is subject to a multiplier effect and will result in overall income falling by some multiple of the initial decrease in exports. Thus, recessionary pressures are transmitted to other countries, the magnitude of which depends on how much they trade with the United States.

7.) An increase in exports will cause a multiplied increase in income, which in turn will result in increased spending for imports. The increase in imports will partially offset the initial increase in exports.

8.) A recession will decrease national income and reduce government tax receipts, moving the government budget towards a deficit. Since a deficit is an injection into the income stream and stimulates the economy, it will tend to offset the severity of the recession.

Summary

This chapter completes the Keynesian model, adding the government and foreign sectors to the basic model described in Chapter 16. This more realistic and complex macro model provides an excellent conceptual framework for examining how the economy functions. It provides a basis for understanding the various policy options that can be used to address macroeconomic problems such as excessive unemployment and inflation. The Keynesian perspective is one of short-run active demand management, or what was commonly referred to as "fine tuning the economy." Although that approach has been criticized because of the inherent difficulties involved in timing spending changes and the varying amount of time it takes for policy changes to have an impact on economic behavior, it is still useful to have an understanding of the Keynesian policy orientation.

The inclusion of the public sector provides a rationale for using fiscal policy -- changing government expenditures, taxes, and the budget deficit -- to change the equilibrium level of income. Keynes felt that the budget should be balanced over the business cycle, with the government running a deficit during recessions and a surplus during business expansions. During a recession or depression, the government should be a spender of last resort, increasing its spending if private spending proves to be less than adequate to insure full employment.

The inclusion of the foreign sector allows us to explore the linkages that exist among the various economies of the world as well as the impact of the balance of trade on equilibrium income. At no time was that more important than during the two oil crises of the mid and late 1970s. The increase in the price of imported petroleum resulted in a tremendous import leakage to members of OPEC, with consequent impacts on unemployment (as well as inflation). More recently, the coordination of the economic policies of the OECD countries (consisting primarily of the United States, Canada, Japan, Australia, New Zealand, and Western European countries) has been a prime concern. The United States came out of its recession earlier than many of its trading partners, and, as a result, imports increased at a faster rate than exports.

Chapter 18
A Contemporary Model of Aggregate Supply and Aggregate Demand

Overview of the Chapter

This chapter develops a broader model of the economy -- the aggregate demand (AD)/aggregate supply (AS) model. The AD/AS model incorporates the overall price level (P) and the level of real output (Q) and through the AS curve allows us to investigate the effects of different supply conditions on macroeconomic performance. Within the framework of the AD/AS model, we can analyze the effects that different events and macro-policies have on the price level (P) and the level of real output (Q). With this model, economies with significant unemployment and slack resources can be analyzed as well as economies at full employment and no unemployed resources.

Similar to the Keynesian fixed price model, macroeconomic equilibrium occurs when the total value of production (AS) equals the level of total spending (AD). Graphically, equilibrium is depicted by the intersection of the AD and AS curves. If the price level (P) is too high for equilibrium, AD will be less than AS, causing inventories to accumulate, and the price level will fall as firms attempt to decrease the level of inventories.

While both aggregate curves have the same shape as the demand and supply curves for individual commodities, the rationales for their shapes are quite different. For the AD curve, a lower price level brings about lower interest rates which, in turn, stimulates spending in the interest-sensitive sectors of the economy, thus lower prices are associated with a higher total spending. Exports also increase as prices decrease, providing another reason for the AD sloping downward.

The slope of the AS curve depends upon how many unemployed resources exist in the economy. If the economy contains a significant amount of unutilized resources, total output can be increased with little or no increase in the overall price level. As the economy approaches full employment, increases in output are associated with increases in the price level, the amount of inflation depending upon how close the economy is to full employment. When the economy attains full employment, no further increases in output are possible, and increases in total spending call forth only increases in the price level. Price rigidity and wage stickiness also play an important role in providing an explanation for the horizontal and upward sloping components of the AS curve.

With the inclusion of the long aggregate supply curve (LRAS), different time horizons can be included in our analysis -- a valuable dimension. Including the LRAS in our analysis allows us to analyze what will happen over time if AD and SRAS equilibrate at a level of real output that is different from the potential level of output. This analytical framework illustrates a process by which the economy will always be moving towards the potential level of output and natural rate of unemployment.

A vertical LRAS emphasizes the importance of "real" factors such as technological change, capital formation, and increases in productivity in achieving long-term growth and points out the difficulty of permanently attaining levels of unemployment that are below the natural rate of unemployment. While it is possible to reduce unemployment below that level in the short run, over the long-run induced changes in the costs of production, wages, and prices will return the economy to its natural rate.

The chapter concludes with a brief discussion of the business cycle phenomenon and the role that such real factors as changes in investment spending and declines in consumer spending. Changes in interest rates and the lending policies of financial institutions as well as credit rationing also contribute to economic instability. Confidence factors for both consumers and businesses have an impact on spending and production plans, although it is obviously more difficult to quantify such a factor.

Learning Objectives

After completing this chapter, you should be sure that you are able to:

- understand the aggregate demand/aggregate supply model, the concept of macroeconomic equilibrium within the model, and the rationale for the shapes of the AD and AS curves.

- identify the factors which cause the AD and AS curves to shift.

- understand the interrelationship that exists between the short-run aggregate supply curve (SRAS) and the long-run aggregate supply curve (LRAS).

- define the potential level of output and the natural rate of unemployment and their significance within the AD/AS model.

- understand the long-run equilibrating process in the AD/AS model.

- the role of "real" factors in the business cycle.

Self Evaluation

List of Terms

Aggregate Demand Curve
Aggregate Supply Curve
Efficiency Wage
Long-Run Aggregate Supply Curve (LRAS)
Money Illusion
Natural Rate of Unemployment
NAIRU

Political Business Cycle
Potential Level of Output
Ratchet Effect
Real Balances
Short-Run Aggregate Supply
Stagflation

For the statements below, fill in the term from the list above which provides the best fit.

1.) The _____ slopes upward and to the right because the production of additional output involves the use of more costly resources.

2.) Whether it is referred to as the _____ or _____, both terms relate to the rate of unemployment which is compatible with stability in the overall price level.

3.) Even if total aggregate demand falls, the price level may not decrease because of the _____.

4.) If the short-run aggregate supply curve (SRAS) shifts to the left, and aggregate demand remains constant, the economy will experience _____.

5.) There is increasing evidence of a _____ in which the level of economic activity is correlated with elections.

6.) There are several reasons why the _____ slopes downward and to the right, but the role of interest rates is probably the most important.

7.) Firms sometimes pay an _____ in the expectation that worker morale, commitment, and productivity will more than offset the increased costs.

8.) The shape of the _____ determines whether or not an increase in aggregate demand will result in higher output or higher prices or a combination of both.

9.) If workers suffer from _____, then they may not realize that their real wage is decreasing during a period of inflation.

10.) The level of output beyond which labor costs and other input costs will begin to rise is known as the _____.

11.) The _____ is vertical, because the costs of production (including wages) rise as output prices rise.

12.) If the price level decreases, a household with a given amount of cash on hand would experience an increase in its _____.

Problems

Factors Affecting Aggregate Demand and Aggregate Supply

Show the effect of each of the following events on aggregate demand or aggregate supply or both. Also indicate whether the event would increase, decrease, or have no effect on the overall price level (P) and the level of real output (Q) in the economy. Use the following notation: **I** -- Increase **D** -- Decrease **U** -- Unchanged **A** -- Ambiguous, unable to determine without more information

Change in Aggregate Demand (ΔAD)	Change in Aggregate Supply (ΔAS)	Change in Equilibrium Price Level (ΔP)	Change in Equilibrium Real Output (ΔQ)	
				1.) Investment spending increases.
				2.) Technological change occurs, making production more efficient.
				3.) The stock market posts a substantial, long-term gain.
				4.) Workers receive substantial wage increases.
				5.) Income taxes increase.
				6.) Government deficit increases.
				7.) Major drought hits midwest farm states.
				8.) Federal Reserve increases interest rates.
				9.) OPEC initiates a major increase in the price of petroleum.
				10.) Export spending climbs as major trading partners come out of the recession.
				11.) Consumption spending declines as consumers become more cautious.
				12.) Government spending increases.

Applying The AD/AS Model to Real World Situations

For each of the economic situations described below, show how the situation could be presented in terms of the AS/AD model described in this chapter. Assume the natural rate of unemployment is 6 %.

1.) The government increases its deficit in the Great Depression.

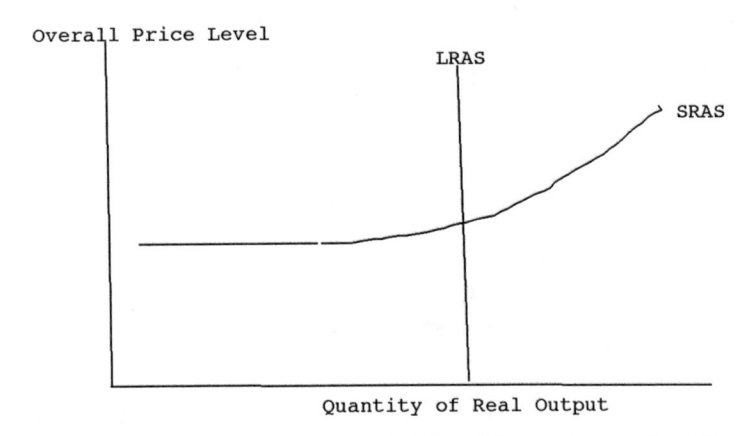

Overall Price Level vs. Quantity of Real Output graph with LRAS and SRAS curves.

2.) OPEC increases the world wide price of oil causing United States imports to increase and domestic prices to rise. Unemployment is slightly below full employment.

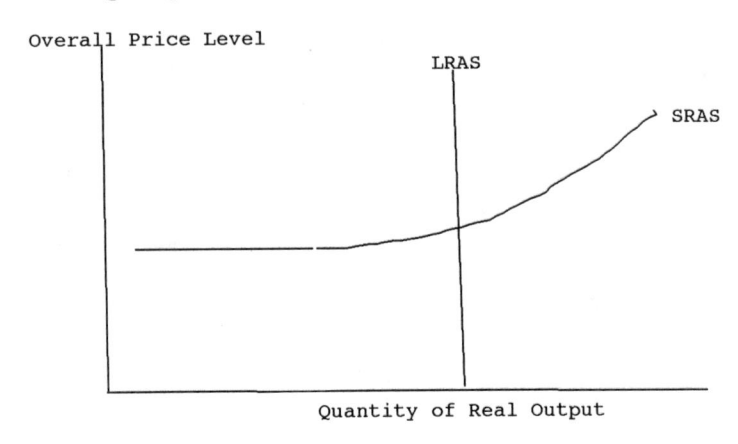

Overall Price Level vs. Quantity of Real Output graph with LRAS and SRAS curves.

3.) Heavy investment in computers and information-related technology increases productivity. Assume that the economy is fully employed.

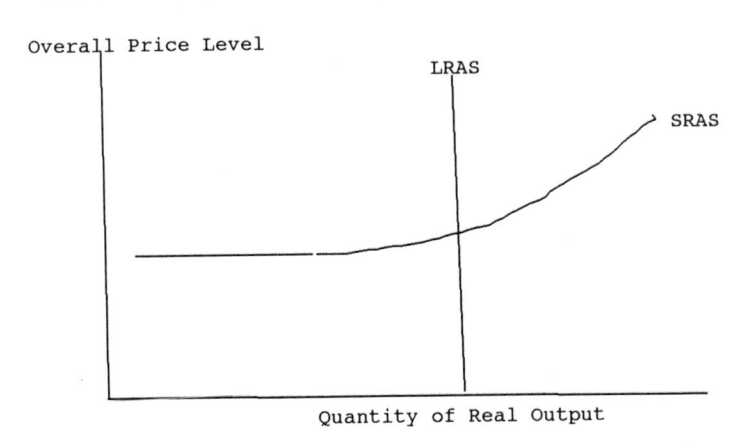

Overall Price Level vs. Quantity of Real Output graph with LRAS and SRAS curves.

4.) The economy recovers from a recession, with the unemployment rate reaching 5.5 %.

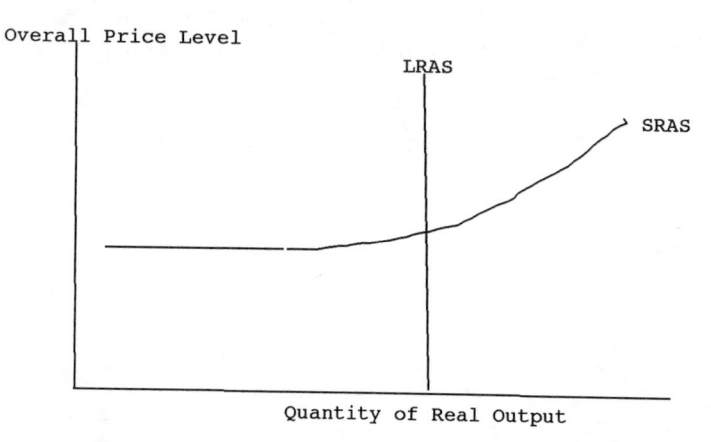

Overall Price Level

LRAS

SRAS

Quantity of Real Output

5.) Congress passes a balanced-budget amendment and immediately cuts spending to move towards that goal. Unemployment is 6.5 %.

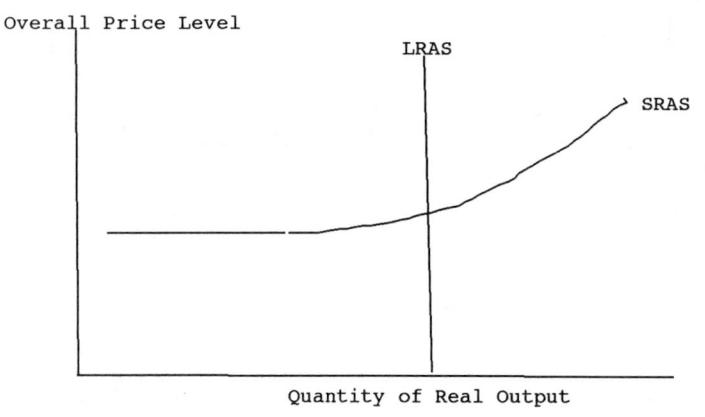

Overall Price Level

LRAS

SRAS

Quantity of Real Output

6.) Congress passes legislation which decreases the marginal rates of taxation for individuals and the tax rate on corporate profits. Unemployment has been hovering around 7 %.

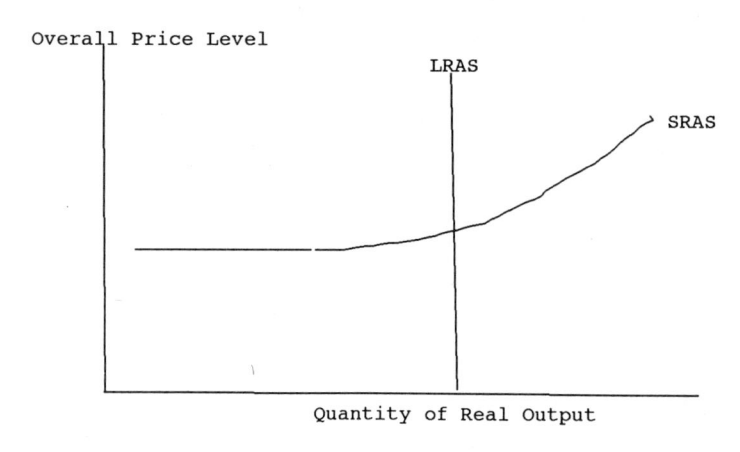

Overall Price Level

LRAS

SRAS

Quantity of Real Output

True/False Statements

Indicate whether you think the statements below are true or false. These questions are designed to make you think about the concepts presented in the text. There may not be any easy clear-cut answers. Some thoughts about the answers are presented at the end of the chapter.

1.) _____ If OPEC increases the price of oil, the SRAS will shift to the left.

2.) _____ Spending changes will shift the aggregate demand (AD) curve, but tax changes leave the curve unchanged.

3.) _____ An increase in interest rates will shift the AD curve to the left.

4.) _____ The more responsive investment spending and other interest sensitive spending is to changes in the interest rate, the flatter the AD curve will be.

5.) _____ The Keynesian fixed-price model is consistent with an short-run aggregate supply curve (SRAS) which is perfectly horizontal.

6.) _____ The accelerator provides an explanation of why investment spending is capable of such wide swings, and the economic multiplier indicates how much those spending changes will be amplified.

7.) _____ The political business cycle refers to the actions and policies the Congress takes to control the cycle and bring about full employment.

8.) _____ If equilibrium in the short-run occurs at a point which is less than the economy's potential level of output, the AD and SRAS curve will both shift to the right.

9.) _____ A shift to the right in the SRAS will help reduce inflationary problems.

10.) _____ By constantly increasing AD, shifting the curve to the right, it is possible to keep the rate of unemployment below the natural rate of unemployment.

11.) _____ In the long-run, there is an adjustment process which tends to bring the economy towards the potential level of output.

12.) _____ One of the reasons that the AD curve slopes downward and to the right is that exports will increase as real output increases.

13.) _____ If wages are sticky, taking some time to adjust to changes, firms' profits will increase as production increases.

Multiple-Choice Questions

Select the "best" answer from the alternatives provided.

1.) The aggregate demand/aggregate supply macroeconomic model provides a framework for identifying the equilibrium levels of
   a. the rate of interest and the level of unemployment.
   b. the price level and the level of employment.
   c. nominal and real spending on GDP.
   d. the price level and the level of real output in the economy.

2.) If aggregate supply is greater than aggregate demand at a given price level,
   a. then inventories will increase.
   b. then inventories will decrease.
   c. then aggregate demand will shift to the left.
   d. then aggregate demand will shift to the right.

3.) The aggregate demand curve will shift to the right when
   a. taxes increase.
   b. the government budget moves towards a surplus.
   c. interest rates decrease.
   d. taxes decrease.

4. The aggregate demand (AD) curve
   a. slopes downward, because interest rates increase as society produces more real output.
   b. slopes downward, because a lower price level results in greater imports and decreased exports.
   c. slopes downward, because lower prices result in larger real balances and more real spending.
   d. slopes downward, because lower prices result in firms producing more output.

5.) The short-run aggregate supply curve will shift to the right when
   a. taxes increase.
   b. the government decreases costly regulations.
   c. the cost of labor and energy increase.
   d. firms produce more output.
   e. the government deficit is reduced.

6.) If the short-run aggregate supply curve is perfectly inelastic (vertical)
   a. an increase in AD will increase real output.
   b. an increase in AD will decrease real output.
   c. an increase in AD will increase the price level.
   d. an increase in AD will decrease the price level.

7.) Stagflation -- a situation of increasing inflation and rising unemployment -- could be explained in the AD/AS model in terms of
   a. a movement along an existing AS curve.
   b. a shift to the right in the AD curve.
   c. a simultaneous shift with AD shifting left and AS shifting right.
   d. a shift to the left in the existing AS curve.

8.) If the Federal Reserve Board increased interest rates
   a. AD would shift to the left.
   b. AD would shift to the right.
   c. AD would remain unchanged, and AS would shift to the right.
   d. neither AD or AS would shift, since the monetary factors don't affect the model.

9.) The long-run aggregate supply curve (LRAS) is vertical because
   a. in the long-run AD is relatively constant.
   b. wages increase at a faster rate than prices, thus firms have no incentive to change their output.
   c. prices increase at a faster rate than wages, thus firms can increase their profitability while maintaining their output.
   d. in the long-run higher costs of production increase as prices increase, thus firms have no incentive to change their output.

10.) If the AD and SRAS curves intersect at a level of real output which is to the right of the LRAS curve, then
   a. AD will decrease until full employment is attained.
   b. LRAS will gradually shift to the left until AD and SRAS intersect with the LRAS.
   c. AS will shift upwards as inflationary pressures raise the costs of production.
   d. AS will shift downwards until an intersection with the LRAS is achieved.

11.) The long-run aggregate supply curve would shift to the right when
   a. wages increase.
   b. AD increases significantly over time.
   c. the overall level of prices increases.
   d. technology increases the productivity of the work force.

12.) If the AD and SRAS curves intersect at a level of real output which is to the left of the LRAS curve, then
   a. AD will gradually increase over time, moving the level of equilibrium real output towards full employment.
   b. AD will gradually decrease over time, moving the level of equilibrium real output towards full employment.
   c. AS will gradually decrease over time, moving the level of equilibrium real output towards full employment.
   d. AS will gradually increase over time, moving the level of equilibrium real output towards full employment.
   e. AD and AS will remain unchanged, and the economy will experience persistent unemployment.

13.) A political business cycle can be best described as
   a. a constant cycle of upturns and downturns in the economy caused by the politicians' inappropriate economic policies.
   b. a constant cycle of upturns and downturns in the economy caused by the political gridlock and lack of action in the Congress.
   c. a recession or downturn in the economy in the months after an election and an upturn and period of prosperity in the months preceding the next election.
   d. an upturn or period of prosperity in the economy in the months following an election and a downturn or recession in the months preceding the next election.

Discussion Questions

1.) What new perceptions and insights does the AS/AD model offer about the behavior of the economy that are different from those provided by the Keynesian macroeconomic model?

2.) How can stagflation be accounted for in the AS/AD model? Why does stagflation present problems for the traditional Keynesian model?

3.) What kinds of macroeconomic policies could be used to facilitate increases in aggregate supply?

4.) If the long-run aggregate supply curve (LRAS) is completely vertical, what kinds of macroeconomic policies could be used to shift the LRAS to the right? Why would that be desirable?

5.) If the LRAS is vertical, what does that imply about the effectiveness of traditional demand management policies?

6.) In late 1994 and early 1995, unemployment was less than 6 % -- the level usually associated with full employment. Using the AD/AS model, explain why many people thought that was cause for concern about future inflation increases.

Answers and Solutions to Problems and Exercises

Completing Statements from the List of Terms

1.) Aggregate Supply Curve
2.) Natural Rate of Unemployment; NAIRU
3.) Ratchet Effect
4.) Stagflation
5.) Political Business Cycle
6.) Aggregate Demand Curve
7.) Efficiency Wage
8.) Short-Run Aggregate Supply Curve (SRAS)
9.) Money Illusion
10.) Potential Level of Output
11.) Long-Run Aggregate Supply Curve (LRAS)
12.) Real Balances

Problems

Factors Affecting Aggregate Demand and Aggregate Supply

Change in Aggregate Demand (ΔAD)	Change in Aggregate Supply (ΔAS)	Change in Equilibrium Price Level (ΔP)	Change in Equilibrium Real Output (ΔQ)		
I	U	I	I	1.)	Investment spending increases.
U	I	D	I	2.)	Technological change occurs, making production
I	U	I	I	3.)	The stock market posts a substantial, long-term gain.
I	D	I	A	4.)	Workers receive substantial wage increases.
D	U	D	D	5.)	Income taxes increase.
I	U	I	I	6.)	Government deficit increases.
U	D	I	D	7.)	Major drought hits midwest farm states.
D	U	D	D	8.)	Federal Reserve increases interest rates.
D	D	I	D	9.)	OPEC initiates a major increase in the price of petroleum.
I	U	I	I	10.)	Export spending climbs as major trading partners come out of the recession.
D	U	D	D	11.)	Consumption spending declines as consumers become more cautious.
I	U	I	I	12.)	Government spending increases.

Applying The AD/AS Model to Real World Situations

1.) The government increases its deficit in the Great Depression.

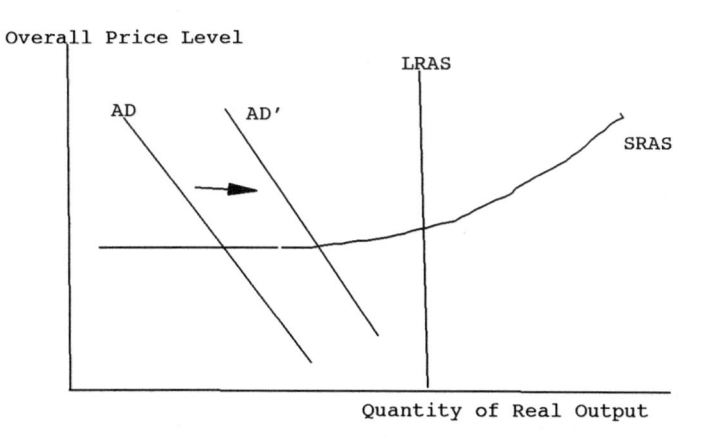

Overall Price Level vs. Quantity of Real Output; AD shifts right to AD', with LRAS vertical and SRAS upward-sloping.

2.) OPEC increases the world wide price of oil causing United States imports to increase and domestic prices to rise. Unemployment is slightly below full employment.

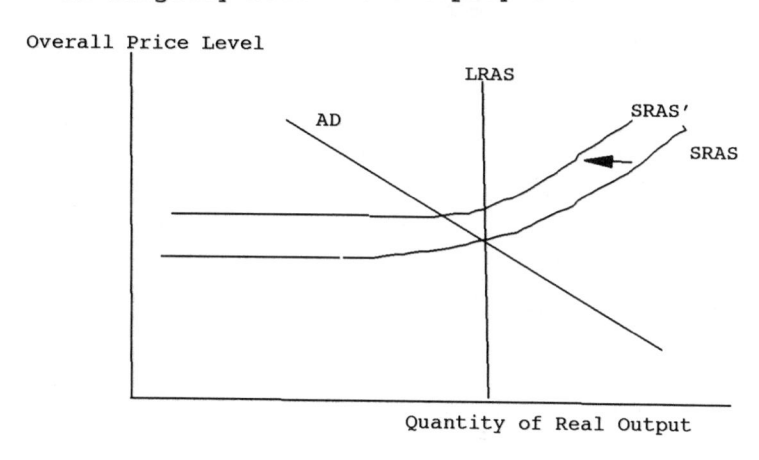

Overall Price Level vs. Quantity of Real Output; SRAS shifts left to SRAS', with AD downward-sloping and LRAS vertical.

3.) Heavy investment in computers and information-related technology increases productivity. Assume that the economy is fully employed.

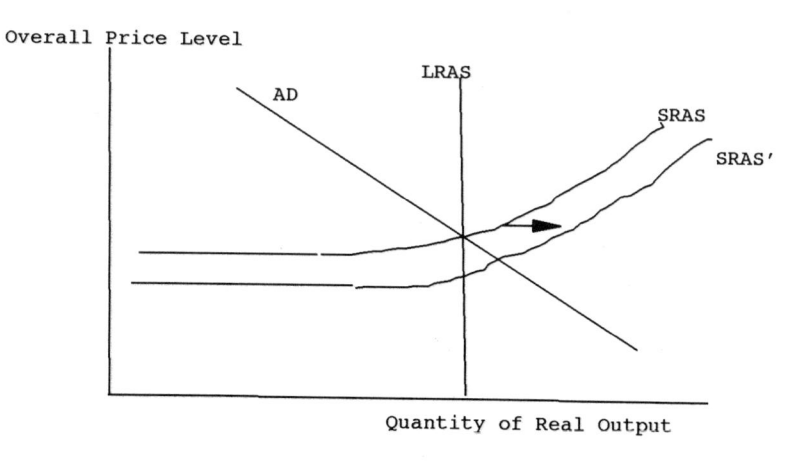

Overall Price Level vs. Quantity of Real Output; SRAS shifts right to SRAS', with AD downward-sloping and LRAS vertical.

4.) The economy recovers from a recession, with the unemployment rate reaching 5.5 %.

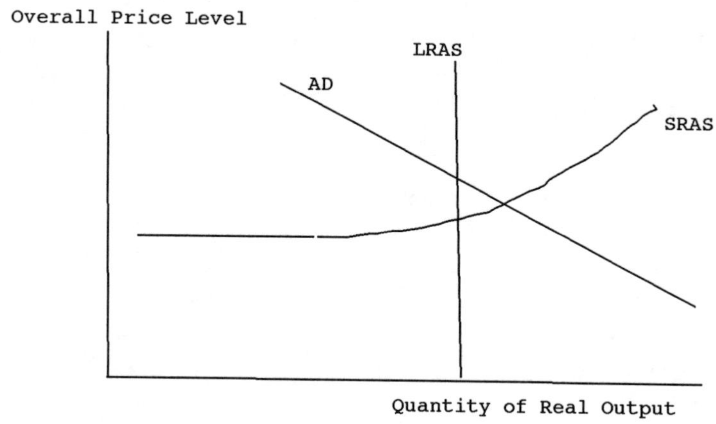

5.) Congress passes a balanced-budget amendment and immediately cuts spending to move towards that goal. Unemployment is 6.5 %.

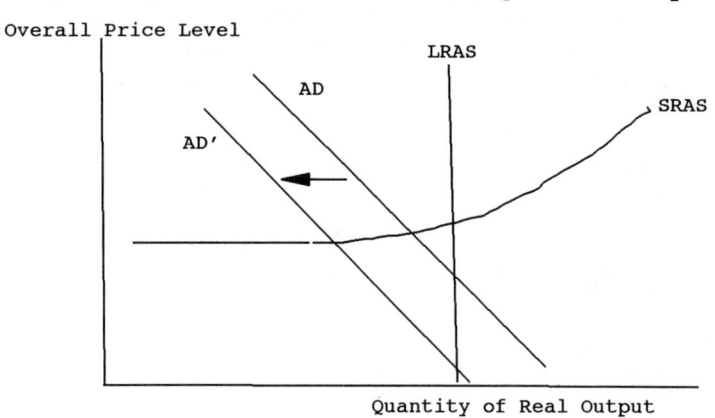

6.) Congress passes legislation which decreases the marginal rates of taxation for individuals and the tax rate on corporate profits. Unemployment has been hovering around 7 %.

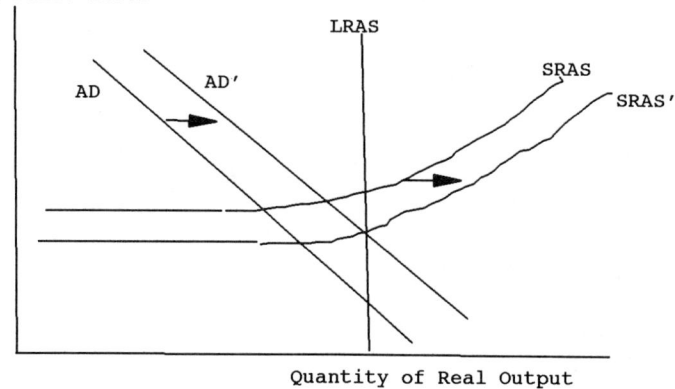

True/False Statements

1.) **True.** Factors such as the price of widely used commodities will affect the cost of production and will shift the SRAS upwards.

2.) **False.** Both spending changes and tax changes will shift the SRAS. Increases in spending and decreases in taxes shift the curve to the right.

3.) **False.** Changes in interest rates *per se* do not shift the AD curve, but the curve will shift in response to spending changes that result from the change in interest rates (changes in consumption and investment spending).

4.) **True.** To the extent that investment spending and other interest-sensitive sectors are more sensitive to interest rate changes, real output will be greater than it otherwise would be, and the AD curve will be flatter.

5.) **True.** In the Keynesian model, increases in spending (AD) do not result in increases in the price level, and that is consistent with changes in AD along the horizontal portion of the AS in the AD/AS model.

6.) **True.** These concepts are not the same thing. The accelerator provides a framework for understanding why investment that is often based on a fixed capital/output ratio varies so much. The multiplier indicates that changes in spending will have a final impact that is greater than the initial spending change. The old saying was that the multiplier tells us how the tail can wag the dog. We can extend that further and state that the accelerator tells us why the tail wags so much.

7.) **False.** The political business cycle is the term used to suggest that the economy's ups and downs are becoming increasingly correlated with election dates.

8.) **False.** If equilibrium is at a point that is less than the potential level of output, the SRAS will shift downward, gradually increasing the equilibrium level of real output until it corresponds to the potential level of output. Shifts in AD are not part of the process -- they are assumed to be discretionary.

9.) **True.** A shift to the right by the SRAS would, if AD remained constant, increase real output and lower the price level, thus reducing inflationary pressures by having more output available.

10.) **False.** Economists are increasingly skeptical of attempts to reduce unemployment below the natural rate of unemployment without bearing the cost of increased inflation and the very real risk of creating an inflationary wage and price spiral -- in spite of what the politicians may tell us.

11.) **True.** If the economy is not equilibrating at its potential level of output, the SRAS will shift in a direction that will move equilibrium real output towards the potential level of output. Changes in production costs and wages are the mechansim by which the SRAS will shift -- with increasing costs/wages if equilibrium is too high and decreasing costs/wages if equilibrium is too low.

12.) **True.** But not for the reason stated. Exports will increase as the price level falls.

13.) **True.** This provides a rationale for the upward sloping portion of the SRAS.

Multiple-Choice

1.) d   2.) a   3.) c   4.) c   5.) b   6.) c

7.) d   8.) b   9.) d   10.) c   11.) d   12.) d

13.) c

Discussion Questions

1.) (1) The incorporation of the price level into the model brings into the analysis an important variable; (2) The differently sloped ranges of the SRAS reflecting different conditions about unemployment and slack resources; and (3) The ability to incorporate different time horizons for the aggregate supply curve.

2.) Stagflation can occur with a leftward shift in the SRAS along an existing AD curve. A extensive drought or increase in oil prices could cause a shift of that kind, with resulting increases in both inflation and unemployment.

For the traditional fixed-price Keynesian model as presented in your text, if equilibrium income is not at full employment, then there is either too much aggregate demand, and the price level increases or there is insufficient aggregate demand to generate full employment, then unemployment will be a problem.

3.) Policies which encourage incentives to work and invest, and policies which reduce the costs of production for firms. Decreasing the marginal rate of taxation on earned income should increase incentives to work over time, and reducing business taxes would provide incentives for firms to produce more. Business costs could be reduced by scaling back government regulations.

4.) Policies which increase the rate of technological change, enhance productivity, or increase the amount or quality of the factors of production would all shift the LRAS curve to the right. Government policies towards research and development and education would affect the LRAS. Lowering marginal rates of taxation would encourage both labor and capital inputs.

It would be desirable for the LRAS to be as far right as possible, because that would mean that there would be more employment and output for society without upward pressures on the price level.

5.) It implies that efforts to sustain unemployment rates below the natural rate of unemployment (associated with the LRAS) are not going to be successful over the long-run. Macro policies designed to decrease unemployment below that level will generate inflationary pressures which cause the SRAS to shift upward and will kindle inflationary expectations on both the part of labor and management which have historically been very difficult to eliminate.

6.) This economic situation would be depicted as a short-run equilibrium position to the right of the LRAS. The AD/AS model would predict that the AS curve would shift upward in response to cost pressures, eventually attaining an equilibrium consistent with the level of unemployment associated with the LRAS.

Summary

Since the AD/AS model is widely used by economists of different schools of thought, some familiarity with the model is very helpful in understanding the macroeconomic impacts of a variety of events and policies. Its conceptual framework is sufficiently broad that both Keynesian and supply-side perspectives can be depicted and explained. Incorporation of the price level into the analysis is especially worthwhile, since many policies have the potential to affect the price level.

The AD/AS model allows us to bring time explicitly into our macroeconomic analysis. Unfortunately, it is impossible to accurately specify how long it will take the economy and the SRAS to adjust and move towards the long-run equilibrium position. Keynesian macroeconomic policies can be best described as being in the demand management category, with an emphasis on fiscal policy and the economic multiplier. Since aggregate demand changes can be instituted fairly quickly, demand management policies can be characterized as short-run. One of John Maynard Keynes' most famous quotes was "In the long-run, we are all dead." By that he meant that short-run crises (such as a severe recession) have to be dealt with, and policies which may be optimal over the long-run may not be appropriate in dealing with a short-run problem.

Changes in AS, on the other hand, tend to take place over a much longer period of time and can be characterized as more long-run in nature. A policy of decreasing marginal tax rates so as to encourage workers to substitute work for leisure will have an impact on the overall productivity of the economy only after workers have had a chance to respond and adjust to the marginal change in tax rates -- changes that will take place over a much longer period of time.

In spite of the more sophisticated economic models that we have available today, policy-makers still have to struggle with the seemingly endless progression of expansions and contractions that are known as the business cycle. A classic article by Nobel prize winner Paul Samuelson showed that the interaction of the economic multiplier and the investment accelerator could create a business cycle from an initial change in spending from within the macroeconomic system. Real spending changes in any of the four sectors of the economy -- consumption, investment, government, and foreign trade -- are constantly occurring as are external shocks to the economy. These spending changes which are multiplied as they circulate through the economic system make it difficult to achieve a nice smooth secular growth path for the economy.

Compounding the effects of the changes mentioned above are psychological factors which result in economic expansions which become too ambitious, sowing the seeds of the economy's eventual decline with overly optimistic forecasts and subsequent overbuilding and excessive spending. In financial markets, interest rates rise, loan defaults increase, and banks may have to resort to credit rationing to retain their best customers.

Chapter 19
Money and the Banking System

Overview of the Chapter

Up to now, the role of money on the overall level of economic activity has largely been ignored. Chapters 19 - 22 begin an in-depth exploration of how changes in the money supply affect the major macroeconomic variables in the economy. Our first task involves defining what is meant by the term "supply of money." There are a number of different definitions of the money supply, differing according to the liquidity of the assets that are included in the money supply.

The demand for money (or, as it is sometimes called, the demand for cash balances) is closely linked to the concept of liquidity which refers to the ease with which an asset can be turned into cash. The opportunity cost of holding money as an asset is the interest that is foregone. Thus, the demand for money is inversely related to the interest rate. Another major reason for holding cash balances is to facilitate transactions. As the level of economic output increases, more money is needed to finance the increased number of transactions taking place. Thus, this component of the demand for money is postively related to the level of income in the economy.

The Fed controls the supply of money and that, in conjunction with the demand for money, determines the equilibrium rate of interest. At the equilibrium interest rate, the amount of money demanded by society just equals the supply of money. Changes in either the demand or supply of money affect the rate of interest in the same way as in any other market. In turn, changes in the interest rate can affect each of the four major components of aggregate demand. Investment spending (I) is probably the most interest-sensitive sector.

The effect of changes in the supply of money can also be shown by manipulating the Fisher equation, the so-called equation of exchange. The equation is based on the identity that the money supply times the number of times each unit of currency "turns over" must necessarily equal the nominal value of final output (overall price level multiplied by total real output). In the short run, V and Q can be assumed to be constant, and thus changes in the money supply (M) will result in direct and proportional changes in the price level (P).

More recently, the Monetarists have based their belief in the importance of the money supply on a stable velocity. If velocity (V) is relatively stable, then changes in the money supply will have a predictable effect on nominal GDP (PQ). There is, however, considerable controversy within the economics profession about whether or not velocity is stable and predictable. If V changes in an offsetting or unpredictable manner, then changes in the money supply and nominal GDP will no longer be closely correlated with one another, seriously undermining the Monetarist position.

Central banks, such as the Fed, have responsibility for regulating the money supply, banking system, and conducting monetary policy. The most important aspects of this chapter involve the process by which the commercial bank system as a whole can expand and contract the supply of money. The U.S. banking system can be characterized as a fractional reserve system, because member banks are required to have only a small fraction of their total demand deposits on hand at any time, either in the form of vault cash or in a reserve deposit with The Fed. The remainder can be loaned out or used to purchase interest-bearing securities.

The process by which the money supply is increased by the banking system is very similar to the economic multiplier process discussed earlier in your text and is referred to as the money multiplier. In each case, an initial stimulus results in significant secondary effects, the size of which depend on either the fraction of each change in income that is saved or the fraction of each new deposit that is kept as a required reserve.

The total increase in demand deposits (and the money supply) that occurs depends on the required reserve ratio set by the Fed -- the higher the required reserve ratio, the smaller the total expansion in the money supply; the lower the required reserve ratio, the larger the monetary expansion. While no single bank "creates" money on its own or violates any rules of accounting, the banking system as a whole, when operating as described above, does have the power to create or destroy money -- a seemingly magical process.

Learning Objectives

After completing this chapter, you should be sure that you are able to:

- define what is meant by money and specify its components.

- list the three components that make up the demand for money.

- understand how the demand and supply of money interact to determine an equilibrium rate of interest.

- understand the relationship that exists between bond prices and the interest rate.

- understand how changes in the money supply affect the overall level of economic activity (how each of the major spending sectors is affected).

- understand the role of monetary policy in dealing with the problems of recession and inflation.

- understand the basis for the equation of exchange and its relationship to the Quantity Theory of Money.

- understand the concept of the velocity of money and why its stability is important to the Monetarist viewpoint.

- understand how the commercial banking system can expand and contract the supply of money.

- understand the concept of the "money multiplier" and how the required reserve ratio, excess reserves, and cash withdrawals affect its size.

Self Evaluation

List of Terms

Bank Run
Cash Drain (Leakage)
Central Bank
Commercial Bank Reserves
Demand Deposits
Demand for Money
Easy Money
Excess Reserves
Federal Deposit Insurance Corporation (FDIC)
Liquidity Preference
M1

Monetarists
Money Multiplier
Precautionary Demand
Quantity Theory of Money
Reserve Requirement
Speculative Demand
Supply of Money
T-Account
Tight Money
Transactions Demand
Vault Cash
Velocity of Circulation

For the statements below, fill in the term from the list above which provides the best fit.

1.) The term _____ perhaps best describes why the public wants to hold cash balances.

2.) The _____ is a well known mathematical identity which states that total expenditures on goods and services must necessarily equal the final market value of those goods and services.

3.) In analyzing monetary policy and the behavior of the banking system and its member banks, a _____ is often used to keep track of assets and liabilities and how they change.

4.) When an economy grows, and more sales and purchases take place, there will likely be an increase in the _____ component of the demand for money.

5.) Checking accounts are technically known as _____ because they are payable upon demand when presented at the issuing financial institution.

6.) _____ believe that changes in the money supply are the primary determinants of changes in nominal GDP and the price level.

7.) The mass withdrawal of deposits by the public is known as a _____.

8.) Member banks may occasionally accumulate _____ when lending conditions are not optimal for them.

9.) During periods of recession and significant unemployment, the Federal Reserve will likely pursue an _____ policy.

10.) Holding cash balances for possible declines in the prices of assets makes up the _____ for money.

11.) _____ can be estimated by dividing the nominal value of final output (gross domestic product - GDP) by the supply of money (M).

12.) During a period of inflation and excessive spending, the Federal Reserve will likely pursue a _____ policy.

13.) The deposit expansion process associated with new demand deposits is effectively reduced by a _____ at each stage of the process.

14.) The ratio of the final total change in demand deposits for the banking system as a whole that result from an initial deposit is known as the _____.

15.) Since forgone interest is a cost of holding cash balances, the interest rate is likely to have a significant effect on the _____.

16.) The simplest and most basic definition of the _____ consists of checking accounts, coins, and currency.

17.) The _____ was developed to increase society's confidence in its financial system and thus help to prevent bank runs.

18.) Because of the risks and opportunity costs involved, financial institutions typically try to minimize the amount of _____ they keep on hand.

19.) The need to hold cash balances in anticipation of possible future emergencies or other unexpected contingencies provides the rationale for the _____ for money.

20.) The responsibility for regulating the banking system and conducting monetary policy rests with the _____ of a country.

21.) The sum of vault cash and commercial bank deposits with the Fed make up _____.

22.) The _____ dictates how much of each demand deposit banks must hold as either vault cash or in a Federal Reserve account.

23.) The simplest measure of the money supply consists of checking accounts, coins, and currency and is known as _____.

Problems

Analyzing the Equation of Exchange

The quantity theory of money provides a number of interesting perspectives about the interaction of the money supply, the price level, and the level of real output in the economy. The quantity theory is based on the equation of exchange which states:

$$M V \equiv P Y$$

where: M = the supply of money
V = the velocity of money circulation (turnover)
P = the price level (as measured by the implicit GDP deflator)
Y = real output (real GDP)

While velocity cannot be directly observed, it can be calculated if data are available for M, P, and Y. Manipulating the formula above, we obtain:

$$V = \frac{PY}{M} \quad \text{and correspondingly:} \quad 1/V = \frac{M}{PY}$$

The reciprocal of velocity (1/V) is perhaps easier to understand than the concept of velocity itself. As shown above, (1/V) equals M/PY. This ratio becomes easier to understand with some substitutions. The money supply (M) also equals the amount of cash balances held by society at large, since in equilibrium the supply of money must equal the demand for cash balances. The term (PY) can be thought of as a total nominal income, since it is the product of the price level (P) times the level of real output (Y). Making those substitutions, (1/V) equals the ratio of cash balances to nominal income:

$$(1/V) = \frac{\text{cash balances}}{\text{nominal income}} = \text{percent of nominal income held as cash balances}$$

If, for example, (1/V) = .15, that indicates that society is holding fifteen percent of its income in the form of cash balances. One over V would tend to be stable in the short run, since it is not likely that individuals or corporations would rapidly change the percentage of income held as cash balances. But viewed in this perspective, it is clear that other factors such as interest rates might play a factor in determining the amount of cash balances held by the public. The opportunity cost of holding cash balances is the interest forgone, and as interest rates rise, those opportunity costs also increase.

Nominal cash balances (M) are defined as the sum of currency held by the non-banking public and the total of demand deposits (DD). Real cash balances (M/P) are, of course, nominal cash balances divided by an index of overall prices (P).

The initial version of the quantity theory of money assumed that velocity (V) and real output (Y) were fixed or stable in the short run. Given those assumptions, the quantity theory provides a direct linkage between changes in the money supply (M) and the overall price level (P).

$$M V = P Y$$

Bringing the constants to the left side of the equation, we obtain

$$\frac{M \bar{V}}{\bar{Y}} = M (\bar{V}/\bar{Y}) = P \quad \text{(Bars over the variables indicate constants)}$$

Thus, the money supply times a ratio of constants equals the price level. This means that changes in the money supply lead to direct and proportional changes in the price level -- a useful approximation when the economy is fully employed:

$$M \text{ (constant)} = P \quad \text{and}$$
$$\blacktriangle M \text{ (constant)} = \blacktriangle P$$

If we allow real output to vary (i.e., acknowledge the existence of output levels below full employment), then with a stable velocity, changes in the money supply have a direct impact on either the price level or the level of real output, both of which make up nominal GDP.

$$\bar{M} V = P \times Y = \text{Nominal GDP}$$
$$\text{and} \quad \blacktriangle \bar{M} V = \blacktriangle \text{Nominal GDP}$$

If velocity is assumed to be stable, we then have a relationship between changes in the money supply and changes in nominal GDP; in other words, changes in the money supply drive changes in nominal GDP -- a statement of the monetarist macroeconomic position. The state of the economy will ultimately determine which variable (P or Y) is impacted the most when the money supply chnages. If there is a slack economy with a considerable amount of excess unemployment, then most of the change in the money supply will affect real output ($\blacktriangle Y$). If, on the other hand, the economy is near or at full employment, then most of the change resulting from a change in the money supply will impact the price level ($\blacktriangle P$). Obviously, a stable velocity is of critical importance if changes in the money supply are to have the predicted effect.

Plotting the velocity of money is a useful exercise which will provide you with some insights into the relationships we've just discussed.

Fill in the following table of values using the data contained in columns two through four.

Table 19-1

Year	Money Supply M (Billion $)	GDP Deflator P (1987 = 100)	Real Output Y (B of 1987 $)	Nominal GDP P X Y (Billion $)	GDP/M Velocity V	Percentage of Income Held As Cash Balances (1/V) (Percent)	Real Cash Balances (M/P) (B of 1987 $)
1982	474.4	83.8	3,760.3				
1983	521.2	87.2	3,906.6				
1984	552.4	91.0	4,148.5				
1985	620.1	94.4	4,279.8				
1986	724.5	96.9	4,404.5				
1987	750.0	100.0	4,539.9				
1988	787.1	103.9	4,718.6				
1989	794.6	108.5	4,838.0				
1990	827.2	113.3	4,897.3				
1991	899.3	117.7	4,861.4				
1992	1,026.6	121.1	4,986.3				
1993	1,131.2	124.2	5,132.7				

Note: Data for 1993 are preliminary.
Source: <u>Economic Report of the President</u>, Transmitted to the Congress, February, 1994.

Plot the velocity of the money supply (M_1) on the graph below.

Figure 19-1

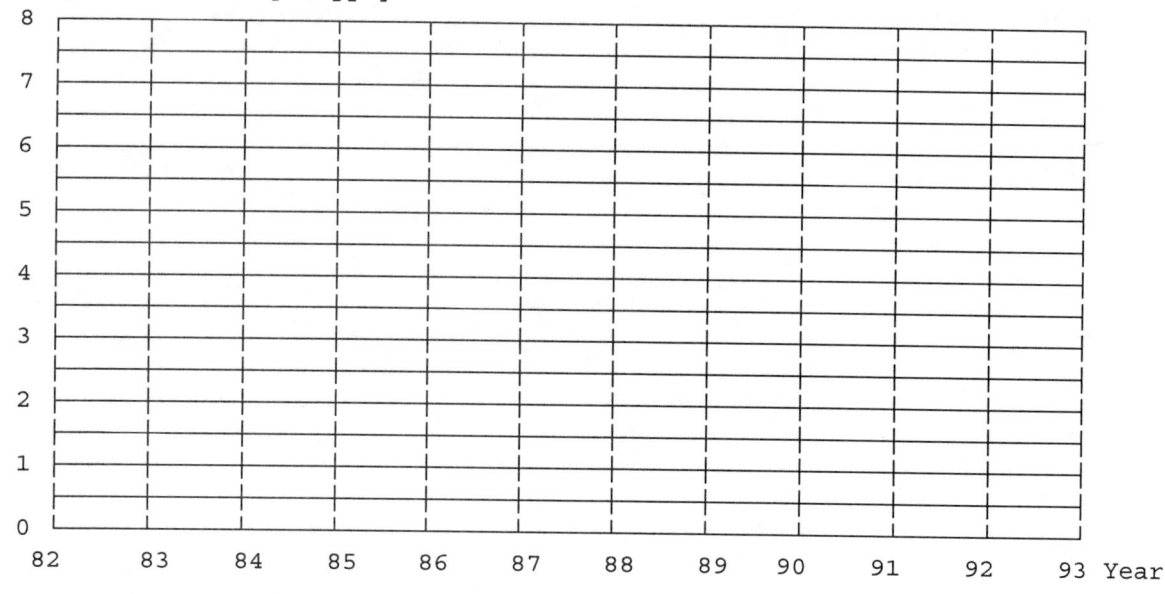

Velocity of the Money Supply

[Graph: y-axis 0 to 8, x-axis years 82 to 93]

Based on the data in Table 19-1 and the figure above, would you say that velocity remained relatively stable from 1980 - 1993?

___

The Process of Deposit Expansion/Contraction

Assume that the Federal Reserve has prescribed a ten % reserve ratio for member banks and that member bank #1 below has just received a new $1,000 demand deposit.

You are given the following T-account for a commercial bank:

Remember that total assets must equal total liabilities in a T-account and that a change on one side of the T-account must be balanced by a change on the other side of the T-account or an offsetting change on the same side of the T-account.

Member Bank #1

Assets		Liabilities	
Vault Cash	$ 200	Previous Demand Deposits	$4000
Reserves	$1200	New Demand Deposit	$1000
Loans	$3000	Total Demand Deposits	$5000
Securities	$600		

Based on the ten % reserve ratio, how much in the way of excess reserves does this member bank have on hand? _____

How can member banks determine the maximum amount that they can safely loan out?

_____

Assuming the member bank wants to be fully loaned up (i.e., not have any excess reserves), what is the largest loan that this bank can safely make? _____

If a loan in the amount specified above is provided as a demand deposit, show below what the member bank's T-account will be like after the loan is made:

Member Bank #1's T-account After Loan

Assets	Liabilities
Vault Cash	Demand Deposits
Reserves	
Loans	
Securities	

Assume that after the loan is granted, the loan recipient writes a check on his/her checking account in member bank #1 for the amount of the loan to a retailer who banks with member bank #2. Show the effect of this transaction on both member banks' T-accounts below:

Show the T-account after the check for the loan has been written and cleared against bank #1.

Member Bank #1's T-account

Assets	Liabilities
Vault Cash	Demand Deposits
Reserves	
Loans	
Securities	

Show just the changes in the T-account that occur as a result of the check from bank #1 being deposited in the retailer's demand deposit.

Member Bank #2's T-account

Assets	Liabilities
Vault Cash	Demand Deposits
Reserves	
Loans	
Securities	

Based on the ten % reserve ratio, how much in the way of excess reserves does member bank #2 have on hand? _____

Assuming the member bank wants to be fully loaned up (i.e., not have any excess reserves), what is the largest loan that member bank #2 can safely make? _____

Every time a new loan and demand deposit are created in response to a new demand deposit, the money supply (defined here as currency plus demand deposits) will increase. The process for each bank will continue as described above. Based on the information above, fill in the following table:

Deposit Expansion Process with 10 Percent Reserve Ratio

    Initial new deposit: _____

    First round: newly created demand deposit, bank #1: _____

    Second round: newly created demand deposit, bank #2: _____

    Third round: newly created demand deposit, bank #3: _____

    Fourth round: newly created demand deposit, bank #4: _____

    Fifth round: newly created demand deposit, bank #5: _____

    Sixth round: newly created demand deposit, bank #6: _____

    All other rounds: _____

    Total change in the money supply: _____
$\Delta M = \Delta DD$ = (new deposit) X (1/reserve ratio) = _____ X _____ = _____
The last two lines above should be equal.

To show the effect of change in the reserve ratio on the size of the money multiplier and the entire deposit expansion process, let's assume that the reserve ratio changes to 15% as the Fed tightens up on its monetary policy. Assume the initial situation for member bank #1 is the same as it was previously.

Revised Deposit Expansion Process with 15 Percent Reserve Ratio

    Initial new deposit: _____

First round: newly created demand deposit, bank #1: _____

Second round: newly created demand deposit, bank #2: _____

Third round: newly created demand deposit, bank #3: _____

Fourth round: newly created demand deposit, bank #4: _____

Fifth round: newly created demand deposit, bank #5: _____

Sixth round: newly created demand deposit, bank #6: _____

All other rounds: ⋮

_____

Total change in the money supply: _____

▲ M = ▲ DD = (new deposit) X (1/reserve ratio) = _____ X ____ = _____
Again, the last two lines above should be equal.

Keep in mind that a cash withdrawal at any stage of the deposit expansion process stops the expansion at that point.

True/False Statements

Indicate whether you think the statements below are true or false. These questions are designed to make you think about the concepts presented in the text. There may not be any easy clear-cut answers. Some thoughts about the answers are presented at the end of the chapter.

1.) _____ The supply of money decreases when people take cash withdrawals from their demand deposits.

2.) _____ There is a larger quantity demanded of money at lower interest rates than at higher interest rates.

3.) _____ The primary reason that cash is useful as an asset is its convenience.

4.) _____ An increase in interest rates will generally decrease the prices of bonds.

5.) _____ Higher interest rates will tend to reduce exports.

6.) _____ Higher interest rates will raise the value of the dollar.

7.) _____ The quantity theory of money illustrates how changes in prices can affect the supply of money.

8.) _____ The velocity of money (V) will increase as the rate of inflation increases.

9.) _____ If the velocity of money (V) is stable, then changes in the supply of money will cause direct and proportional changes in nominal GDP.

10.) _____ The higher the required reserve ratio, the higher the money multiplier.

11.) _____ The velocity of money (V) equals nominal GDP divided by the money supply.

Multiple-Choice Questions

Select the "best" answer from the alternatives provided.

1.) If the money supply (M) = 200, and the velocity of money (V) = 5, and real output (Y) = 100, then
   a. the price level (P) must equal 2.
   b. the price level (P) must equal 5.
   c. the price level (P) must equal 1.
   d. the price level (P) must equal 10.
   e. can't be determined from the above information.

2.) If nominal GDP (PY) is equal to $4,000 billion, and the money supply (M) was $800 billion, then
   a. the velocity of money (V) must equal 10.
   b. the velocity of money (V) must equal 5.
   c. the velocity of money (V) must equal 1.
   d. the velocity of money (V) must equal 6.
   e. can't be determined from the above information.

3.) If the required reserve ratio = 10 %, and there are no excess reserves or cash withdrawals, then a new demand deposit (▲ DD) of $5,000 would
   a. increase the money supply by $10,000.
   b. increase the money supply by $50,000.
   c. increase the money supply by $5,000.
   d. not increase the money supply, since cash in circulation has gone down by $5,000 as a result of the new demand deposit.
   e. unable to determine from the information provided.

4.) If the required reserve ratio equals 15 % and banks keep 5% of each deposit as excess reserves, then
   a. the money multiplier = 6.667.
   b. the money multiplier = 1.0.
   c. the money multiplier = 5.0.
   d. the money multiplier = 10.
   e. unable to determine from the information provided.

5.) If Homer Smith takes $1,000 in cash out of his coin collection and deposits it into his checking account,
   a. the money supply (M1) has increased.
   b. the money supply (M1) has decreased.
   c. the money supply (M1) has remained constant.
   d. the money supply may or may not change depending on what the bank does with the new deposit.
   e. none of the above.

6.) When the Fed increases the money supply, it puts into effect which sequence of events which results in
   a. an increase in the price level which, in turn, results in an increase in nominal GDP.
   b. an increase in the rate of interest, an increase in earnings on saving and other deposits, and an increase in nominal GDP.
   c. an increase in people's cash balances, increased spending on goods and services, and an increase in nominal GDP.
   d. a decrease in the rate of interest, an increase in interest-sensitive spending, and a multiplied effect on GDP.

7.) The relationship that exists between the prices of bonds and the interest rate can be best described as
   a. the higher the market rate of interest, the higher the prices of bonds.
   b. the lower the market rate of interest, the lower the prices of bonds.
   c. no inherent relationship, although sometimes bond prices do rise when market interest rates fall.
   d. the higher the market rate of interest, the lower the prices of bonds.

8.) In hyperinflations,
   a. the velocity of money stays relatively constant, but the money supply increases very rapidly.
   b. the velocity of money increases rapidly as people attempt to spend their cash balances before purchasing power is lost.
   c. the real value of saving accounts increases because of increases in the interest rate due to inflation.
   d. people hoard their money in an attempt to avoid the effects of hyperinflation.

9.) Excess reserves
   a. are necessary to protect a bank in case of a run on the bank.
   b. create an additional leakage from the deposit expansion process, thus lowering the money multiplier
   c. are required by the Federal Reserve as an additional protection for banking customers.
   d. reduce the income-generating potential for a bank holding them.
   e. both (b) and (d).

10.) You are given the following T-account for a member bank. Ignore any account that is not listed below: (M stands for million)

Fourth International Bank of Dilworth

Assets	Liabilities
Reserves $7M	Demand Deposits $50M

If the required reserve ratio is 10 %, the maximum amount that this bank can lend out and still be in compliance with the Fed's regulations is
a. $7M
b. $5M
c. $2M
d. $1M
e. the bank has no basis to make any loans.

11.) If the bank above lends out the maximum amount that it can, given the ratio of demand deposits and reserves that are shown above, the banking system as a whole could increase the money supply by a maximum of (assuming no cash withdrawals at any stage of the process)
a. $2M.
b. $5M.
c. $10M.
d. $20M.
e. $25M.

12.) The money multiplier associated with the deposit expansion process
a. increases with the percentage of excess reserves.
b. is significantly lower if bank reserves are kept as vault cash instead of in the form of deposits with the Fed.
c. increases as the required reserve ratio increases.
d. depends largely upon existing lending conditions and interest rates.
e. increases as the required reserve ratio decreases.

13.) When a bank receives a new demand deposit
a. it can make new loans equal to that demand deposit.
b. it can make new loans equal to its total reserves.
c. it can make new loans equal to its excess reserves.
d. it can make new loans equal to (1/required reserve ratio) X its excess reserves.

Discussion Questions

1.) Would the Federal Deposit Insurance Corporation (FDIC) be effective in the face of a large and massive run on the banking system as a whole?

2.) If you believe, as Monetarists do, that changes in the supply of money are the primary factor in determining the overall level of economic activity and the price level, why is it so important that velocity (V) be stable?

3.) In the first few months of 1995, the dollar fell against the Yen (¥) and the Deutschemark (DM). What could the Fed have done in terms of monetary policy to strengthen the dollar? Would this have helped or hurt the U.S. domestic economy?

4.) Briefly discuss how the effectivness of monetary policy would be affected if it turned out that investment spending was not very sensitive to interest rate changes.

5.) Why would you expect velocity to increase dramatically during hyperinflations?

6.) If you obtained a loan at a local bank to help with college expenses, why would the bank prefer that the loan proceeds be credited to a checking account instead of taking the loan proceeds as cash?

7.) Suppose a tourist buys a piece of local art, valued at $1,200, as she is passing through Jackson, Wyoming. The tourist's check is deposited in the local art dealer's checking account at the First State of Jackson. The Fed has set a reserve requirement of 8 %, and the bank's excess reserves increase by $1,104.

You are a new loan officer with the bank (having been lured to Jackson because of the skiing). Given the increase in excess reserves that occurred, you make a loan of $13,800 to a prominent local business person. Your rationale is that with an 8 % reserve requirement, the $1,104 represents the amount that the bank must hold as reserves against the $13,800 loan. Thus, the bank will be fully loaned up. The loan is brought to the attention of the bank's president. Will you be fired or promoted? Explain.

Answers and Solutions to Problems and Exercises

Completing Statements from the List of Terms

1.) Liquidity Preference
2.) Quantity Theory of Money
3.) T-Account
4.) Transactions Demands
5.) Demand Deposits
6.) Monetarists
7.) Bank Run
8.) Excess Reserves
9.) Easy Money
10.) Speculative Demand
11.) Velocity of Circulation
12.) Tight Money
13.) Cash Drain (Leakage)
14.) Money Multiplier
15.) Demand for Money
16.) Supply of Money
17.) Federal Deposit Insurance Corporation (FDIC)
18.) Vault Cash
19.) Precautionary Demand
20.) Central Bank
21.) Commercial Bank Reserves
22.) Reserve Requirement
23.) M1

Problems

Analyzing the Equation of Exchange

Table 19-1

Year	Money Supply M (Billion $)	GDP Deflator P (1987 = 100)	Real Output Y (B of 1987 $)	Nominal GDP P X Y (Billion $)	Velocity V	Proportion of Income Held As Cash Balances (1/V)	Real Cash Balances (M/P) (B of 1987 $)
1982	474.4	83.8	3760.3	3151.1	6.64	0.151	566.1
1983	521.2	87.2	3906.6	3406.6	6.54	0.153	597.7
1984	552.4	91.0	4148.5	3775.1	6.83	0.146	607.0
1985	620.1	94.4	4279.8	4040.1	6.52	0.153	656.9
1986	724.5	96.9	4404.5	4268.0	5.89	0.170	747.7
1987	750.0	100.0	4539.9	4539.9	6.05	0.165	750.0
1988	787.1	103.9	4718.6	4902.6	6.23	0.161	757.6
1989	794.6	108.5	4838.0	5249.2	6.61	0.151	732.4
1990	827.2	113.3	4897.3	5548.6	6.71	0.149	730.1
1991	899.3	117.7	4861.4	5721.9	6.36	0.157	764.1
1992	1026.6	121.1	4986.3	6038.4	5.88	0.170	847.7
1993	1131.2	124.2	5132.7	6374.8	5.64	0.177	910.8

Note: Data for 1993 are preliminary.
Source: *Economic Report of the President*, Transmitted to the Congress, February, 1994.

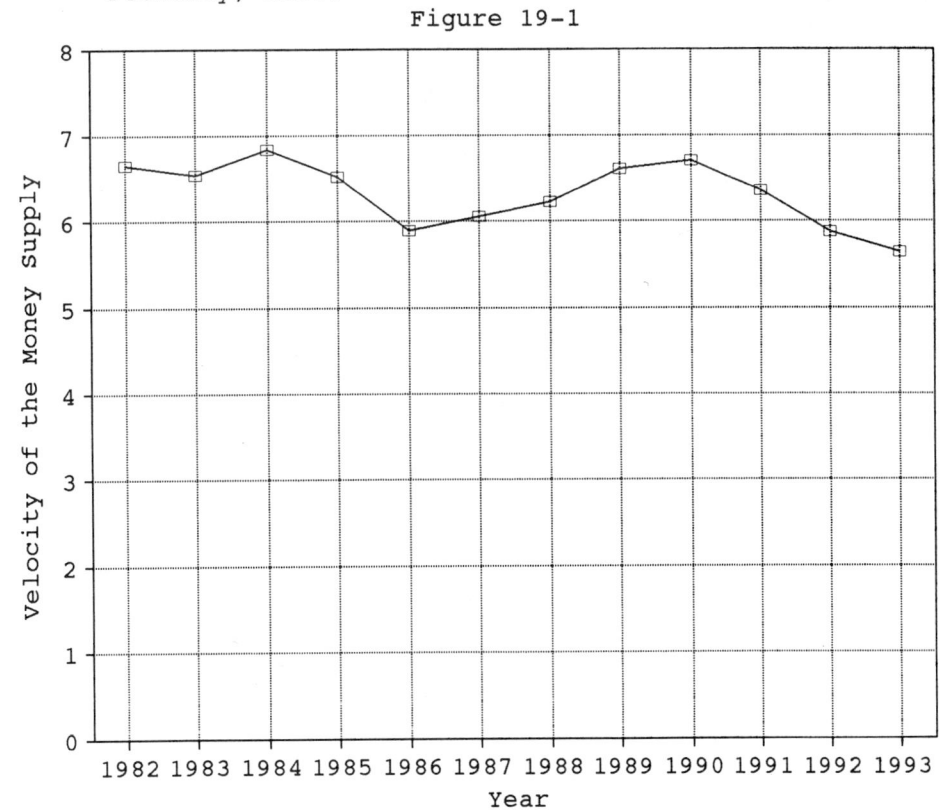

Figure 19-1

Based on the data in Table 17-1 would you say that velocity remained stable from 1982 - 1993? **Over this period of time, velocity ranged from a high of 6.83 to a low of 5.64. While this is not a large absolute variation, it is a sizeable variation in terms of its impact upon GDP. For example, velocity changed from 6.52 in 1985 to 5.89 in 1986. If you were basing your estimates of GDP upon a constant velocity, that would have resulted in an unacceptably large error. If velocity is stable, the money supply does indeed drive GDP, but if velocity varies, as it does in the preceding graph, the relationship between the money supply and GDP is too variable to be of much use.**

The Process of Deposit Expansion/Contraction

Member Bank #1

Assets		Liabilities	
Vault Cash	$200	Previous Demand Deposits	$4000
Reserves	$1200	New Demand Deposit	$1000
Loans	$3000	Total Demand Deposits	$5000
Securities	$600		

Based on the ten % reserve ratio, how much in the way of excess reserves does this member bank have on hand? **$900**

How can member banks determine the maximum amount that they can safely loan out? **Banks can safely loan out the amount of their excess reserves. When they do that, the new loan is fully backed on a one-to-one basis by the excess reserves. Since the loan recipient may take the loan proceeds to a different bank, the loan needs to be backed completely by reserves. Banks must deal with adverse clearing balances when checks are written on accounts with their banks. When the check is cleared against it, a bank has to have sufficient reserves to fully back the check.**

Assuming the member bank wants to be fully loaned up (i.e., not have any excess reserves), what is the largest loan that this bank can safely make? **$900**

If a loan in the amount specified above is provided as a demand deposit, show below what the member bank's T-account will be like after the loan is made:

Member Bank #1's T-account After Loan

Assets		Liabilities	
Vault Cash	$200	Demand Deposits	$5900
Reserves	$1200		
Loans	$3900		
Securities	$600		

The changes to member bank #1's T-account:

Assets	Liabilities
Loans +$900	Demand Deposits +$900

Member Bank #1's T-account

Assets		Liabilities
Vault Cash	$200	Demand Deposits $5000
Reserves	$300	
Loans	$3900	Note that after the loan check has been cleared against bank #1, it is now fully loaned up.
Securities	$600	

Member Bank #2's T-account

Assets		Liabilities
Vault Cash		Demand Deposits +$900 (retailer's account)
Reserves	+$900	
Loans		
Securities		

Based on the ten % reserve ratio, how much in the way of excess reserves does member bank #2 have on hand? **$810**

Assuming the member bank wants to be fully loaned up (i.e., not have any excess reserves), what is the largest loan that member bank #2 can safely make? **$810**

Deposit Expansion Process with 10 Percent Reserve Ratio

Initial new deposit:		**$1000**
First round:	newly created demand deposit, bank #1:	**$900**
Second round:	newly created demand deposit, bank #2:	**$810**
Third round:	newly created demand deposit, bank #3:	**$729**
Fourth round:	newly created demand deposit, bank #4:	**$656.10**
Fifth round:	newly created demand deposit, bank #5:	**$590.49**
Sixth round:	newly created demand deposit, bank #6:	**$531.44**
All other rounds:		※
Total change in the money supply:		**$10000**

$\Delta M = \Delta DD$ = (new deposit) X (1/reserve ratio) = 1000 X (1/10) = 10000
The last two lines above should be equal.

Revised Deposit Expansion Process with 15 Percent Reserve Ratio

Initial new deposit:		$1000
First round:	newly created demand deposit, bank #1:	$850
Second round:	newly created demand deposit, bank #2:	$722.50
Third round:	newly created demand deposit, bank #3:	$614.13
Fourth round:	newly created demand deposit, bank #4:	$522.01
Fifth round:	newly created demand deposit, bank #5:	$443.71
Sixth round:	newly created demand deposit, bank #6:	$377.15
All other rounds:		⋮
Total change in the money supply:		$6666.67

$\Delta M = \Delta DD$ = (new deposit) X (1/reserve ratio) = 1000 X (1/.15) = 6666.67
Again, the last two lines above should be equal.

True/False Statements

1.) **True.** Cash withdrawals absorb reserves on a one-to-one basis. Since banks keep only a fraction of each deposit on hand for daily transactions, cash withdrawals result in a multiplied contraction of the money supply.

2.) **True.** The cost of holding cash balances as an asset is forgone interest. The lower the interest rate, the smaller the forgone interest (a classic opportunity cost), and the larger we would expect cash balances to be.

3.) **False.** The primary reason for holding cash assets is the liquidity it provides.

4.) **True.** Interest rates and bond prices are inversely related. If a bond has been purchased at a stated interest rate of eight %, and interest rates subsequently decrease, the price of the bond will rise, since a bond with a higher price will now yield the new lower interest rate.

5.) **True.** The sequence of events would go something like this: Higher interest rates will increase the value of the dollar on foreign exchange markets, as foreign investors increase their demand for dollar-denominated assets. The increased value of the dollar will mean that it now takes more units of a foreign currency to buy a dollar, effectively raising the price of all U.S. exports. As the price of U.S. exports rise, less American goods and services will be purchased by foreigners.

6.) **True.** See the explanation for question 5.

7.) **False.** Just the opposite is true. The quantity theory of money provides a framework for showing how changes in the money supply will have an effect on the price level.

8.) **True.** Since prices may change quickly during an inflationary period, it will be costly for individuals to wait very long after being paid to purchase any of their commodities. Money turns over more quickly, since there are substantial costs to holding money as an asset.

9.) **True.** This follows directly from the quantity theory of money. If V and Q are assumed constant in the short run, then changes in M will have a direct and proportional impact on P.

10.) **False.** If banks are required to set aside a larger proportion of each demand deposit in the form of required reserves, then the money multiplier will be smaller, because each member bank will loan out smaller amounts at each stage of the deposit expansion process. The cumulative value of the various loans made and subsequent demand deposits will be smaller.

11.) **True.** This can be shown by algebraic manipulation of the equation of exchange. Velocity (V) can be isolated by dividing both sides of the equation by M. V thus equals PQ divided by M -- PQ is nominal GDP and M is the money supply.

Multiple-Choice

1.) d   2.) b   3.) b   4.) c   5.) c   6.) d

7.) d   8.) b   9.) e   10.) c   11.) d   12.) e

13.) c

Discussion Questions

1.) The FDIC was created to revive confidence in the nation's banking system after its virtual collapse in the early 1930s. Runs on banks would be less prevalent if the public knew that their deposits were protected by an agency of the Federal Government. However, the FDIC is funded to deal with the occasional bank failure due to mismanagement or fraud and it would have difficulty dealing with a large scale failure involving numerous banks. While the Fed can print as much money as it needs for such purposes, the value of money would drop dramatically.

2.) According to the equation of exchange, changes in the money supply are transmitted to nominal GDP (PQ) via the velocity of money (V).

▲ M * V = P * Q = nominal GDP

If V changes in an offsetting or unpredictable fashion when the money supply changes, then changes in the money supply will no longer have a close relationship with changes in the overall level of economic activity as measured by nominal GDP. A close linkage between the money supply and nominal GDP is important to the Monetarist view of the world.

3.) If the Fed pursues a tighter monetary policy, domestic interest rates would increase, making dollar-denominated securities and investments more attractive to foreign investors. To get into dollar investment opportunities, they would demand dollars and supply their own currency -- thus increasing the value of the dollar.

4.) Monetary policy affects the level of economic activity in the economy through changes in interest rates and consequent changes in interest-sensitive spending components of GDP. If investment spending was interest inelastic, interest rate changes would not result in significant changes in investment spending, and GDP would not change very much. Monetary policy would be largely ineffective.

5.) Currency turnover would increase as people tried to minimize their cash balances. Income would be spent as soon as it was received in order to minimize the effect of rapid price increases.

6.) Cash withdrawals from a bank decrease reserves on a one-to-one basis. If the loan proceeds are in a demand deposit, chances are that some of the loan will remain within the bank for a longer time.

7.) Better look into that job at the ski resort. The rule of thumb is that banks can loan out their excess reserves, meaning that such loans are fully backed. Once the loan recipient writes a check to someone at another bank, the initial bank will have an adverse credit balance with the second bank and will have to transfer reserves equal to the amount of the check. While it might seem logical to keep only an 8 % reserve ($1,104) behind the loan, it is not good banking practice.

Summary

The Federal Reserve's main responsibility as the nation's central bank is to control the nation's supply of money, but that is becoming more and more difficult with the changes that are occurring in financial markets. The simplest definition of money, M1, no longer is as closely related to nominal GDP as it was in the past. The velocity of M1 is not as stable as it once was and, as a result, the Federal Reserve is looking for other monetary variables to see if one can be found which has a more stable relationship with nominal GDP.

Monetary policy continues to be the macroeconomic policy of choice in dealing with short-run economic fluctuations in a timely fashion. The traditional linkage between the money supply and the level of economic activity operates through interest rates and their effect on interest-sensitive sectors of the economy. The spending changes that occur in those sectors will have a multiplied impact on GDP. As noted in your text, each of the four sectors of GDP have interest-sensitive sectors including the government sector and the foreign trade sector along with the more visible consumption and investment sectors.

Concerning your understanding of monetary policy, one of the most important points to remember is that it is not equally effective in dealing with recession and inflation. A tight money policy by the Fed can effectively reduce inflationary lending and spending even if opposed by the banking system. The Fed has the tools to reduce excess reserves and the lending potential of member banks. An easy money policy designed to get the economy back onto an expansionary growth path may not be effective because the Fed cannot force banks to make loans; it can only create the excess reserves necessary for making new loans. Thus, monetary policy is asymmetrical.

The quantity theory of money provides some interesting new insights into how the money supply affects the price level and real level of output. In the short run when the economy is fully employed, changes in the money supply will have a direct and proportional effect on the price level if the velocity of money is held constant. The stability of velocity is of crucial importance to economists who consider themselves to be Monetarists. If velocity is not stable, then it is difficult to argue that changes in the money supply are the driving force in determining nominal GDP.

It's a little bit magical and mysterious the way the banking system as a whole creates new money from a new demand deposit. If you interviewed each banker, they would, of course, deny that they created any new money, since they loan out only the amount of their excess reserves. But, in a process very similar to the economic multiplier process, a portion of the new deposit is set aside for required reserves, and the remainder (excess reserves) is loaned out. The significance of the money multiplier is that if the Fed wants to increase or decrease the money supply, the necessary change in excess reserves need be only a fraction of the total anticipated change.

Chapter 20
The Tools of Monetary Policy

Overview of the Chapter

Chapter 20 discusses monetary policy and the various tools that the Fed has available to change the money supply as well as the volume of credit, interest rates, and ultimately total spending. Since monetary policy is conducted on a regular basis, it is especially important to understand how it works and what it can and can't do.

The reserve requirement is the most powerful tool that the Fed can use to adjust the money supply. By changing the reserve requirement, it can either increase or decrease excess reserves within the banking system, thus affecting directly commercial banks' ability to make loans.

A significant limitation to decreasing the reserve requirement is that increasing excess reserves may not be sufficient to increase the volume of bank loans, since banks may be reticent to make loans during recessionary conditions. Another problem is that the Fed's intention to use this powerful tool may change businesses' expectations about the future which, in turn, may defeat the effectiveness of the policy change.

The discount rate is the second major tool that the Fed has at its disposal. By changing the discount rate, the Fed can either discourage or encourage member bank borrowing from the Fed which can be used to expand their effective excess reserves. This tool also has limited effectiveness, since the Fed can't force commercial banks to borrow from them -- compounding the problem is that banks have shown more willingness to use the Federal Funds market which provides any needed funds from other banks. Since changes in the discount rate have only a marginal effect on the size of the money supply, its monetary policy value lies largely in its role as an indicator of the Fed's views on the economy. Member banks may change their lending and interest rate guidelines as a result of that information.

Open market operations (the Fed's buying and selling of U.S. government securities) represent the Fed's main monetary policy tool for several reasons: such transactions usually attract little if any national publicity and are capable of changing member bank reserves to any required degree, large or small. The Fed can increase member bank reserves by conducting open market purchases. When the Fed buys government securities from member banks, the Fed takes over ownership of the securities, and it makes payment simply by crediting member bank reserve accounts that they have with the Fed. Member banks have traded the government security they owned for an equal amount of excess reserves on deposit with the Fed -- a change in the composition of member bank assets. The increase in excess reserves can then be loaned out, although as with other monetary policy tools, there is no way to require member banks to make loans.

The sequence of events is much the same when the Fed purchases government securities from individuals instead of member banks. In both cases, the money multiplier associated with an increase in demand deposits means that the total impact of open market operations on the overall money supply will be larger than the amount of the initial purchase of securities.

When the Fed wants to decrease the lending ability of the banking system as a whole, then it will sell government securities. When member banks make payment to the Fed, their reserve deposits are debited and their excess reserves are reduced. If there are no excess reserves, then payment for the securities must be made from member banks' reserves which will result in a multiplied reduction in the money supply as banks decrease their outstanding loans. The Fed can also offer inducements to banks and the public to purchase securities in the form of higher securities prices -- by selling larger quantities of bonds, the Fed can lower the price of securities and at the same time raise interest rates, making government securities a more attractive investment.

The Fed also has several other less publicized monetary policy tools -- moral suasion (the Fed's persuasive powers) as well as several selective controls such as control over the margin requirement on stock purchases. The Fed used to have control over the minimum down payment required and the maximum period of financing on credit purchases, but these powers have not been renewed since 1952-53.

Learning Objectives

After completing this chapter, you should be sure that you are able to:

- explain how changes in the reserve requirement can potentially change the money supply.

- understand why changes in the reserve requirement may not be effective in offsetting recessionary conditions.

- understand how changes in the Fed's discount rate can affect member bank reserves and lending ability.

- understand the role and importance of the Federal Funds Market.

- understand how open market operations can affect member bank reserves, loans, and ultimately the money supply.

- understand the constraints and limitations associated with monetary policy.

- understand the Fed's role in the check-clearing process.

- list advantages and disadvantages of the various non-monetary policy tools that the Fed has at its disposal.

Self Evaluation

List of Terms

Bank Run
Discount Rate
Federal Funds Market
Federal Open Market Committee
Float

Margin Requirement
Moral Suasion
Open Market Operations
Selective Controls
Reserve Requirement

For the statements below, fill in the term from the list above which provides the best fit.

1.) The Fed can either encourage or discourage member bank borrowing from it by changing the _____.

2.) Decisions about the direction and extent of the Fed's purchases and sales in the government securities market are made by the _____.

3.) The larger the _____, the smaller the total potential expansion of the money supply for new deposits.

4.) Speculation on the stock market can be controlled to some extent through adjustments in the _____.

5.) Although infrequently used, the Fed has several _____ which it can use to control credit purchases.

6.) In addition to its main monetary tools, the Fed has on occasion used _____ to try and persuade member banks to support monetary policy.

7.) _____ represent the Fed's main monetary policy tool for fine-tuning member bank reserves and controlling the money supply.

8.) Even with the latest technology, a _____ of some size exists because checks can not be cleared instantaneously.

9.) For many member banks, the _____ represents an effective alternative to borrowing from the Fed.

10.) A _____ creates a short-term liquidity crisis for banks which can eased by the Fed.

Problems

Conducting Monetary Policy

Assume that the economy currently has 7.5 % unemployment and that the rate of capacity utilization in the production sector is well below its maximum. You are given the T-accounts below for the Fed and two member banks. The required reserve requirement is **10 %**. Assume that the member banks can buy government securities up to the amount of their excess reserves. The assets and liabilities of the Fed are greater than the totals represented by the two member banks.

FEDERAL RESERVE		MEMBER BANK #1		MEMBER BANK #2	
Assets	Liabilities	Assets	Liabilities	Assets	Liabilities
$10,000 Govt. Sec.	$10,000 Reserves	$500 Reserves $500 Govt. Sec. $4,000 Loans	$5,000 DD	$1,000 Reserves $1,000 Govt. Sec $8,000 Loans	$10,000 DD

What are the total excess reserves of the two member banks? _____

Why do member banks typically want to minimize their excess reserves?

_____

_____

Given the economic situation described above, list the three main monetary policy tools that the Fed can utilize and indicate what should be done:

(1) _____

(2) _____

(3) _____

434

If the Fed decides to lower the required reserve requirement to eight %, indicate the effect of that action on the three T-accounts:

FEDERAL RESERVE		MEMBER BANK #1		MEMBER BANK #2	
Assets	Liabilities	Assets	Liabilities	Assets	Liabilities
_____	_____	_____	_____ DD	_____	_____ DD
Govt. Sec.	Reserves	Req. Res.		Req. Res.	
		Excess Res.		Excess Res.	
		Govt. Sec.		Govt. Sec.	
		Loans		Loans	

Why might the member banks not want to loan out their excess reserves given the current economic situation?

_____

_____

If the member banks loaned out their newly created excess reserves, indicate the effect of that action on the three T-accounts:

FEDERAL RESERVE		MEMBER BANK #1		MEMBER BANK #2	
Assets	Liabilities	Assets	Liabilities	Assets	Liabilities
_____	_____	_____	_____ DD	_____	_____ DD
Govt. Sec.	Reserves	Req. Res.		Req. Res.	
		Excess Res.		Excess Res.	
		Govt. Sec.		Govt. Sec.	
		Loans		Loans	

What is the maximum potential change in the money supply that could occur if the member banks loaned out their excess reserves (assuming no cash withdrawals)? _____

Returning to the initial situation, the Fed could lower the discount rate instead of lowering the required reserve requirement. Briefly explain how that would help stimulate the economy.

_____

_____

_____

The most frequently used monetary tool involves open market operations by the Fed. Explain what the Fed should do in this particular case.

_____

_____

Assume the Fed carries out its open market activities to the maximum extent possible, given the amount of government securities the member banks currently hold. Indicate the effect of that action on the three T-accounts. (This action takes place after the reduction in the required reserve requirement.)

```
       FEDERAL RESERVE              MEMBER BANK #1              MEMBER BANK #2

    Assets  |  Liabilities        Assets  |  Liabilities      Assets  |  Liabilities
_____|_____       _____|_____     _____|_____
        ____|____                    _____|_____ DD              _____|_____ DD
 Govt. Sec. | Reserves          Req. Res. |                 Req. Res. |
            |                             |                           |
            |                    _____    |                    _____  |
            |                   Excess Res.|                 Excess Res.|
            |                             |                           |
            |                    _____    |                    _____  |
            |                   Govt. Sec.|                  Govt. Sec.|
            |                             |                           |
            |                    _____    |                    _____  |
            |                    Loans    |                    Loans  |
```

What are the member banks' excess reserves after the Fed's open market operation? _____

If the member banks loaned out those newly acquired excess reserves, what would be the maximum potential increase in the money supply? _____

Now assume that the economic situation has changed and that the inflation rate has reached five % and is starting to accelerate.

Given the economic situation described above, list the three main monetary policy tools that the Fed can utilize and indicate what should be done:

(1) _____

(2) _____

(3) _____

True/False Statements

Indicate whether you think the statements below are true or false. These questions are designed to make you think about the concepts presented in the text. There may not be any easy clear-cut answers. Some thoughts about the answers are presented at the end of the chapter.

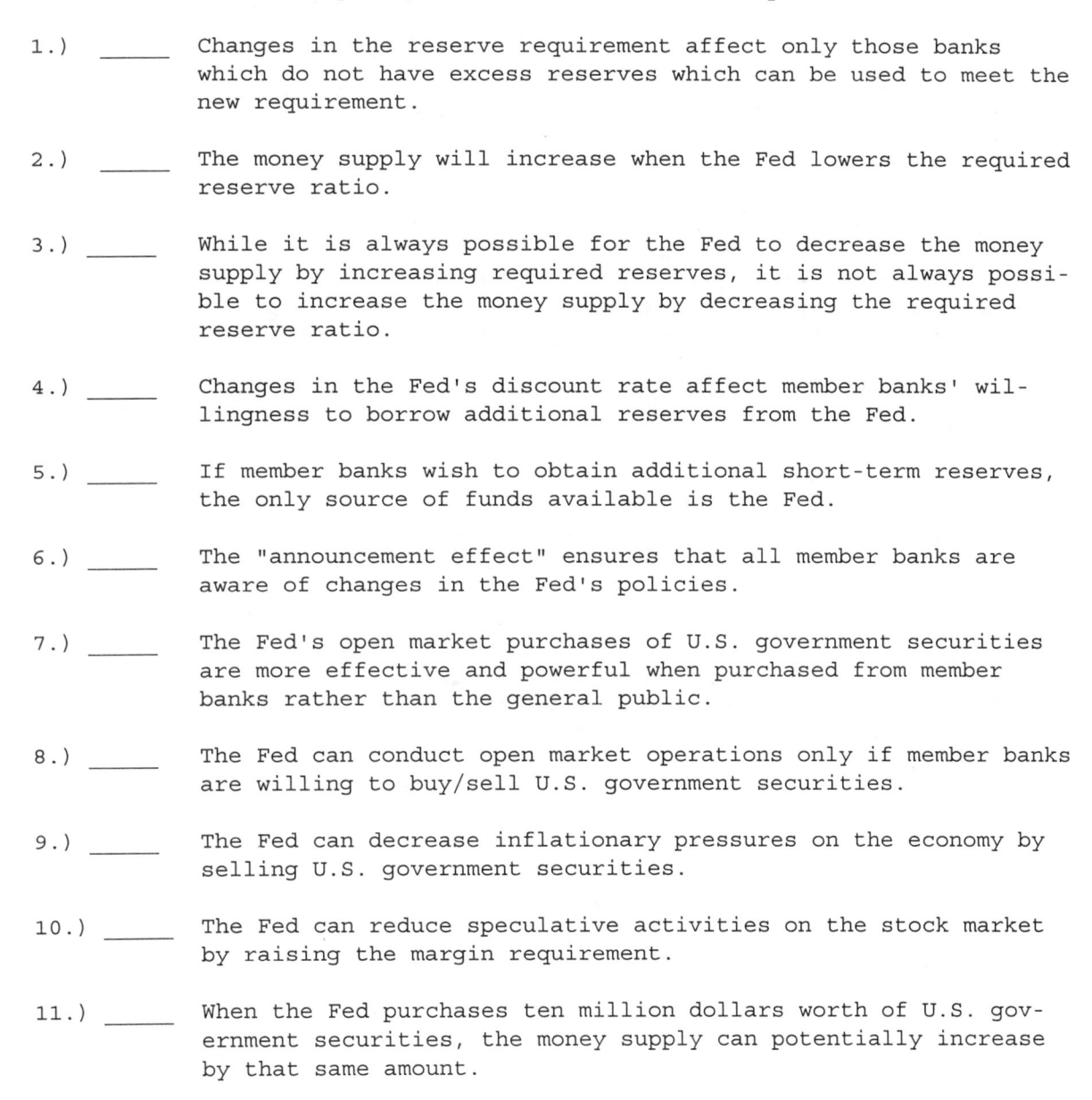

1.) _____ Changes in the reserve requirement affect only those banks which do not have excess reserves which can be used to meet the new requirement.

2.) _____ The money supply will increase when the Fed lowers the required reserve ratio.

3.) _____ While it is always possible for the Fed to decrease the money supply by increasing required reserves, it is not always possible to increase the money supply by decreasing the required reserve ratio.

4.) _____ Changes in the Fed's discount rate affect member banks' willingness to borrow additional reserves from the Fed.

5.) _____ If member banks wish to obtain additional short-term reserves, the only source of funds available is the Fed.

6.) _____ The "announcement effect" ensures that all member banks are aware of changes in the Fed's policies.

7.) _____ The Fed's open market purchases of U.S. government securities are more effective and powerful when purchased from member banks rather than the general public.

8.) _____ The Fed can conduct open market operations only if member banks are willing to buy/sell U.S. government securities.

9.) _____ The Fed can decrease inflationary pressures on the economy by selling U.S. government securities.

10.) _____ The Fed can reduce speculative activities on the stock market by raising the margin requirement.

11.) _____ When the Fed purchases ten million dollars worth of U.S. government securities, the money supply can potentially increase by that same amount.

Multiple Choice-Questions

Select the "best" answer from the alternatives provided.

1.) When the Federal Reserve increases the required reserve requirement
   a. member banks with excess reserves are not affected.
   b. member banks must borrow additional reserves from the Federal Reserve.
   c. it must do so with the expressed consent of the Congress.
   d. banks with no excess reserves must cut back their loans.
   e. only the smaller banks with limited financial resources will be affected.

2.) Under what conditions would the Federal Reserve be most likely to raise the reserve requirement?
   a. In the midst of a recession when the public is questioning the overall safety of keeping their funds in banks.
   b. When bank profits are considered to be excessively large.
   c. When total spending in the economy is at a level where inflation is likely to increase.
   d. When the level of unemployment in the economy is just starting to increase.

3.) When the Federal Reserve conducts an "easy" money policy designed to get the economy out of a recession,
   a. the Fed should increase the required reserve ratio, decrease the discount rate, and buy government securities.
   b. the Fed should decrease the required reserve ratio, decrease the discount rate, and buy government securities.
   c. the Fed should decrease the required reserve ratio, decrease the discount rate, and sell government securities.
   d. the Fed should decrease the required reserve ratio, increase the discount rate, and buy government securities.

4.) When the Federal Reserve lowers the discount rate,
   a. it can't be certain that member banks will borrow more, and there is no guarantee that banks will use the additional reserves to make new loans.
   b. it has little or no effect on member bank borrowing, since most banks use the Federal Funds Market to obtain needed funds.
   c. it has little or no effect on member bank borrowing and is used mainly to alert member banks about the Fed's expectations about the future state of the economy.
   d. all of the above apply.

5.) When the Federal Reserve conducts an open market operation,
   a. it will buy government securities when it wants to contract the money supply.
   b. it will buy government securities when it wants to expand the money supply.
   c. it will sell government securities when it wants to expand the money supply.
   d. it can print new money which can be injected into the economy through the banking system.

6.) If the required reserve ratio is set at 20 % by the Federal Reserve, and the member banks are fully loaned up, then a $1 million purchase of government securities by the Fed from member banks will potentially (assuming no cash withdrawals)
   a. increase the money supply by $1 million.
   b. increase the money supply by $5 million.
   c. decrease the money supply by $1 million.
   d. decrease the money supply by $5 million.
   e. unable to determine

7.) When the Federal Reserve sells government securities on the open market,
   a. member banks are usually interested in buying the securities because of the relatively high interest rates on government securities.
   b. member banks will have less reserves and a reduced ability to make new loans.
   c. member banks will have more reserves and an increased ability to make new loans.
   d. the sale will not affect the money supply, since no new demand deposits are created.

8.) A coordinated policy to fight inflation would include
   a. an increase in taxes, increased government spending, an increase in the required reserve ratio, a decrease in the discount rate, and the purchase of government securities by the Federal Reserve.
   b. a decrease in taxes, increased government spending, a decrease in the required reserve ratio, a decrease in the discount rate, and sale of government securities by the Federal Reserve.
   c. an increase in taxes, reduced government spending, a decrease in the required reserve ratio, a decrease in the discount rate, and the purchase of government securities by the Federal Reserve.
   d. an increase in taxes, reduced government spending, an increase in the required reserve ratio, an increase in the discount rate, and sale of government securities by the Federal Reserve.

9.) A coordinated policy to fight unemployment would include
   a. an increase in taxes, increased government spending, an increase in the required reserve ratio, a decrease in the discount rate, and the purchase of government securities by the Federal Reserve.
   b. a decrease in taxes, increased government spending, a decrease in the required reserve ratio, a decrease in the discount rate, and the purchase of government securities by the Federal Reserve.
   c. an decrease in taxes, reduced government spending, a decrease in the required reserve ratio, a decrease in the discount rate, and the purchase of government securities by the Federal Reserve.
   d. an increase in taxes, reduced government spending, a decrease in the required reserve ratio, a decrease in the discount rate, and sale of government securities by the Federal Reserve.

10.) If the Federal Reserve buys government securities from the general public instead from member banks,
   a. the total overall effect on the money supply is exactly the same as when the purchase is from member banks.
   b. the total overall effect on the money supply is less than it would be when the purchase is from member banks.
   c. the total overall effect on the money supply is greater than it would be when the purchase is from member banks.
   d. it is not possible to predict whether the effect on the money supply will be the same or greater or less than a similar purchase from member banks.

11.) The main determinant of how much the money supply will expand in response to a new demand deposit is
   a. how much of the deposit is spent for goods and services.
   b. the required reserve requirement.
   c. the interest rate.
   d. the discount rate.

Discussion Questions

1.) Should the Federal Reserve be independent from the administration and Treasury as it is now in order to provide a check and balance against the potential abuse of economic policy-making by the administration to stay in office, or should it be made more accountable to the president who is ultimately responsible to the public for the performance of the economy?

2.)   In late 1994, the Federal Reserve Board raised the discount rate even though inflation (as measured by the CPI) was a moderate 2.8 % per year. The Fed's actions run the risk of shutting down a recovery that was widely considered to be erratic and inconsistent. Should the Fed be allowed to pursue whatever monetary policy it wants, no matter what the cost?

3.)   Would you be in favor of granting the Fed the power to set minimum down payment percentages on larger item consumer purchases, such as automobiles and other consumer durables? Wouldn't this be as effective a tool in controlling spending as efforts to control the amount of credit or interest rates?

4.)   The Fed has the monetary tools to increase or decrease bank reserves, with or without the approval of member banks. Yet, in terms of expanding the money supply, some would argue that the Fed has very little power, since it can only provide increased reserves -- it has no power to force banks to make new loans. Would you agree?

5.)   Your text mentions that several countries do not require their member banks to hold reserves. Since changes in the reserve requirement are being used less frequently and banks are complaining about the loss of interest on their reserve deposits with the Fed, would you be in favor of abolishing the legal reserve requirement?

Answers and Solutions to Problems and Exercises

Completing Statements from the List of Terms

1.) Discount Rate
2.) Federal Open Market Committee
3.) Reserve Requirement
4.) Margin Requirement
5.) Selective Controls
6.) Moral Suasion
7.) Open Market Operations
8.) Float
9.) Federal Funds Market
10.) Bank Run

Problems

Conducting Monetary Policy

What are the total excess reserves of the two member banks? **$0**

Why do member banks typically want to minimize their excess reserves? **Because excess reserves can be loaned out, earning interest income. Reserve accounts with the Fed do not earn interest.**

Given the economic situation described above, list the three main monetary policy tools that the Fed can utilize and indicate what should be done: **(1) Decrease the required reserve ratio, (2) Lower the discount rate, and (3) Buy government securities.**

FEDERAL RESERVE		MEMBER BANK #1		MEMBER BANK #2	
Assets	Liabilities	Assets	Liabilities	Assets	Liabilities
$10,000 Govt. Sec.	$10,000 Reserves	$400 Req. Res.	$5,000 DD	$800 Req. Res.	$10,000 DD
		$100 Excess Res.		$200 Excess Res.	
		$500 Govt. Sec.		$1,000 Govt. Sec.	
		$4,000 Loans		$8,000 Loans	

Why might the member banks not want to loan out their excess reserves given the current economic situation? **Typically, lending conditions are very soft during recessions, with higher than normal bankruptcy rates and higher than normal rates of unemployment. Consumer spending is not growing or is even perhaps declining, and firms are laying off employees.**

```
    FEDERAL RESERVE            MEMBER BANK #1              MEMBER BANK #2

   Assets  |  Liabilities      Assets  |  Liabilities      Assets  |  Liabilities
   --------+------------       --------+------------       --------+------------
   $10,000 |  $10,000           $400   |  $5,000 DD         $800   |  $10,000 DD
   Govt. Sec.| Reserves       Req. Res.|                 Req. Res. |
           |                    $100   |                   $200    |
           |                 Excess Res.|               Excess Res.|
           |                    $500   |                  $1,000   |
           |                  Govt. Sec.|                Govt. Sec.|
           |                   $4,100  |  $100 new DD      $8,200  |  $200 new DD
           |                   Loans   |                   Loans   |
```

What is the maximum potential change in the money supply that could occur if the member banks loaned out their excess reserves (assuming no cash withdrawals)? **$300 X (1/0.08) = $300 X 12.5 = $3,750**

Returning to the initial situation, the Fed could lower the discount rate instead of lowering the required reserve requirement. Briefly explain how that would help stimulate the economy. **Lowering the discount rate would make borrowing from the Fed more attractive to member banks. Borrowing reserves would allow banks to increase their loans, and the money supply would subsequently increase.**

The most frequently used monetary tool involves open market operations by the Fed. Explain what the Fed should do in this particular case. **The Fed should buy government securities, and that will increase the excess reserves of member banks.**

```
    FEDERAL RESERVE            MEMBER BANK #1              MEMBER BANK #2

   Assets  |  Liabilities      Assets  |  Liabilities      Assets  |  Liabilities
   --------+------------       --------+------------       --------+------------
   $11,500 |  $11,500           $400   |  $5,100 DD         $800   |  $10,200 DD
   Govt. Sec.| Reserves       Req. Res.|                 Req. Res. |
           |                    $600   |                  $1,200   |
           |                 Excess Res.|               Excess Res.|
           |                    $0     |                   $0      |
           |                  Govt. Sec.|                Govt. Sec.|
           |                   $4,100  |                   $8,200  |
           |                   Loans   |                   Loans   |
```

What are the member banks' excess reserves after the Fed's open market operation? **$1,800 -- $1,500 created with open market operations**

If the member banks loaned out those newly acquired excess reserves, what would be the maximum potential increase in the money supply?
$1,500 X 12.5 = $18,750

Given the economic situation described above, list the three main monetary policy tools that the Fed can utilize and indicate what should be done.
(1) Increase the required reserve ratio, (2) Increase the discount rate, and (3) Sell government securities.

True/False Statements

1.) **False.** Banks that are fully loaned up will necessarily have to reduce their loans outstanding in order to meet the higher reserve requirements. Banks with excess reserves will have to commit part of them to required reserves, thus reducing their ability to make new loans.

2.) **Maybe.** A lower reserve requirement will free up bank reserves, making it possible for banks to make more loans. However, if lending conditions are not very favorable (i.e., an ongoing recession), then member banks may choose not to make the loans. If banks don't use their newly created excess reserves to make loans, then the money supply won't increase.

3. **True.** The Fed can always decrease excess reserves in the banking system, thus reducing lending potential, and, if necessary, required reserves can be increased sufficiently to reduce the total volume of demand deposits. On the other hand, the creation of new excess reserves may not be sufficient, because there is no guarantee that new loans will be made. (See the answer above.)

4.) **True.** By raising the discount rate, the Fed can discourage member bank borrowing.

5.) **False.** The Federal Funds Market provides an excellent alternative to borrowing from the Fed, with none of the regulatory overtones associated with borrowing from the Fed.

6.) **False.** The "announcement effect" refers to the change in expectations that may occur when the public at large learns about the Fed's policy. The announcement that the Fed is going to reduce the discount rate must mean the Fed believes the economy is faced with some threat of recession. That, in itself, may cause certain kinds of spending to decrease.

7.) **False.** The total potential impact on the money supply is exactly the same.

8.) **True, but ...** True in the obvious sense that banks must participate if the transactions are to take place. But even if banks are reluctant to work with the Fed, the Fed can use the threat of changing the required reserve requirement, or they can change the price of the security to make it more attractive.

9.) **True.** Selling securities will reduce member banks' excess reserves and their lending potential.

10.) **True.** Raising the margin requirement would mean that investors would have to put up more money for their purchases, giving them less financial leverage and reducing their ability to make speculative purchases.

11.) **False.** The money supply could potentially change by some multiple of that amount, according to the size of the money multiplier.

Multiple-Choice

1.) d   2.) c   3.) b   4.) d   5.) b   6.) b

7.) b   8.) d   9.) b   10.) a   11.) b

Discussion Questions

1.) Strong arguments can be made for each side of this issue. Personal beliefs towards the power of the presidency probably determine which viewpoint a person supports. If one is suspicious of presidential power and what an incumbent president might do to retain the office, then the quasi-independence of the Federal Reserve is absolutely essential to restrain that branch of government from implementing policies which may be short-sighted and harmful to the effective functioning of the economic system.

On the other hand, having two different policy-makers can obviously lead to coordination problems, especially if the policies oppose each other (e.g., the Fed running a tight money policy and the president and Congress running a large federal deficit). Whether or not you believe the electorate is sufficiently economically literate and informed to make intelligent and rational decisions concerning sophisticated macroeconomic policy is another matter. But it is certainly possible to understand the frustration of a president that may or may not be re-elected on the basis of his/her economic performance, only to have that performance significantly affected by the independent Fed.

2.) This question is related to the one above but also is concerned with the issue of having discretionary policy-making power. There are many that have disagreed with the Fed's policy, stating that key interest-sensitive sectors were already experiencing decreases in spending. The Fed's policy is all the more controversial since the inflation picture was relatively good. The Fed's primary responsibility has always been to fight inflation, and apparently their prognosis is that inflation lies on the horizon. It is important to note that with the lag times that are built into macroeconomic policy, policy changes often have to be undertaken at times when it seems inappropriate. Only time will tell whether the raising of the discount rate was effective or not.

3.) Such a tool would certainly have an impact on total spending; however, it would tend to be focused on a relatively small component of overall consumer spending. Many other types of spending would not be affected at all. There is no doubt that many people would view such power as an infringement on their basic "consumer" rights. The other argument against the Fed's use of this tool is that it unfairly targets lower income units. Presumably upper income units would not be affected to any great degree. On the plus side, there is something to be said for forcing society to save something before purchasing a big ticket consumer item. Pragmatically, this would be a difficult sell in political terms.

4.) Monetary policy is asymmetric. The Fed definitely has the tools and the power to decrease member bank reserves, thereby reducing the volume of credit and loans in its fight against inflationary pressures. To stimulate the economy out of recession, the Fed can only create the needed excess reserves; it can't force member banks to make loans. Loan conditions during a recession may not be very favorable from the bank's perspective. Providing banks with the necessary funds is an important prerequisite for stimulating the economy. It may not be sufficient, however.

5.) It is important to remember that member banks are not required to keep reserves in order to provide a measure of safety for customer deposits -- the required reserve ratio is a tool which allows the central bank to control the money supply. One argument for dispensing with the requirement might be that it is infrequently used and therefore not needed. It is a very powerful tool, particularly against severe inflationary forces. Since fiscal policy is not being utilized because of concern over the size of the budget deficit (or, alternatively, the balanced-budget amendment would effectively eliminate fiscal policy), it may be good judgement to retain the monetary tools we currently have available.

Summary

After studying this chapter, you should have a much better understanding of the Federal Reserve's monetary policy tools, and you'll have some insights about the historical background of each tool and why each tool is used in distinctly different ways. Knowing that the reserve requirement is changed on an infrequent basis provides some insights into the Fed's assessment of the current situation that might otherwise not be evident (i.e., a change in the reserve requirement may mean the Fed believes there is a serious problem with the economy, or it may be an indication of its resolve). Similarly, knowing that changes in the discount rate represent more of a attempt by the Fed to signal what they think is going to happen in the near-term future is helpful. Open market operations are utilized much more frequently, but it is much more difficult to verify what is being done by the Fed.

Selective controls are not very popular with the public, since they directly impact certain consumer transactions, but they would be useful in slowing down unrestrained consumer spending during an inflationary period. Some selective controls on credit card usage was used to control inflation during the early 1980s, with limitations on minimum monthly payments and some restrictions on credit card issuers. One advantage of selective controls is that they impact consumption spending rather than investment spending and, thus, have less impact on the future growth path of the economy.

Chapter 21
The Conduct of Monetary Policy

Overview of the Chapter

While monetary policy can be implemented in a much quicker fashion than fiscal policy, it is not without its own set of problems. Chapter 21 provides some interesting insights into the effectiveness of monetary policy in dealing with the problems of inflation and recession.

One significant disadvantage of monetary policy involves its selective impact on the economy -- not all sectors are equally affected by changes in interest rates. Interest-sensitive sectors such as housing, construction, and consumer durables can be significantly affected by monetary policy, much more than other sectors.

Of even greater importance from a policy perspective is monetary policy's ability to counteract recessionary conditions. While the Fed can lower interest rates and provide member banks with additional reserves for making loans, such measures may not be effective because of hesitancy on the part of lending institutions. Conditions during periods of slack demand, rising business failures, and high unemployment are not likely to be looked upon as being very favorable for lending by financial institutions.

Lately economists have been paying more attention to the impact of the various time lags associated with monetary policy. If, as some people believe, the response lag to changes in interest rates is both "long and variable," then it will be difficult, if not impossible, to conduct monetary policy in an effective fashion. By the time firms and individuals have responded to the interest rate changes and changed their behavior, the economic impact may not be appropriate for that stage of the business cycle. Because of the difficulties presented by variable time lags, some monetarists have advocated that the Fed change the money supply in a steady and predictable fashion.

As has been previously noted, expectations may play a role in counteracting monetary policy, reducing its effectiveness. The Fed's efforts to expand the money supply to fight unemployment may instead be regarded as inflationary, creating an entirely different set of lending conditions and expectations. Since interest rates include an inflationary premium, the expectation of higher future inflation may result in an increase in interest rates rather than a decrease.

Monetary policy has significant impacts on the foreign sector of the economy. A tight money policy raises domestic interest rates and, in turn, attracts funds from investors in other countries seeking the highest possible returns for their investments. The increased demand for dollars raises the value of the dollar, subsequently leading to less exports and more imports. As the net export component of GDP falls, aggregate demand (AD) also declines as the Fed originally intended with its tight money policy.

But the inflow of foreign funds tends to offset the Fed's efforts to contract the money supply, complicating their stabilization task.

Recent developments in financial markets have also complicated the Fed's ability to control the money supply -- the Fed no longer announces what it thinks will happen to the most basic definition of money -- M1. Depositors transfering funds between their demand deposits, their money market accounts, and certificates of deposits (CDs) have made life more complicated for the Fed and made it more difficult for the Fed to achieve its monetary goals.

Achieving prescribed targets for the money supply is made more difficult simply because of the normal fluctuations that occur in the money supply associated with the demand for currency. Cash withdrawals from demand deposits deplete bank reserves on a one-to-one basis -- with the potential to decrease the money supply by some multiple of the initial cash withdrawal. Seasonal changes in the demand for coins and currency must be accounted for by the Fed, or unwanted seasonal variations in the money supply will take place.

Since monetary policy works primarily through changes in interest rates and subsequent changes in spending in interest-sensitive sectors, the Fed initially set "target" rates of interest which it thought would enable it to achieve its announced macroeconomic goals. If a recession was imminent, the Fed would lower interest rates to encourage spending, thus offsetting the recession. However, experience with targeting interest rates has shown that such a policy can be destabilizing, because increasing the money supply can also create inflationary pressures and increase interest rates.

If the Fed attempts to attain interest rate targets, then the money supply will have to be set at whatever level facilitates the achievement of its target. On the other hand, if the Fed were to target growth rates of the money supply as advocated by the monetarist school of thought, interest rates would have to be allowed to fluctuate accordingly. The crux of all this is that the Fed has control over one of the variables (either the interest rate or the money supply), but not both simultaneously.

Further complicating the Fed's task in achieving its economic goals has been the instability of velocity (V). Changes in the money supply have a direct and proportional effect on nominal GDP if velocity is stable. However, if velocity is unstable it creates considerable uncertainty about what will happen to nominal GDP, since the linkage between the money supply and the level of income and output is no longer a stable one.

Learning Objectives

After completing this chapter, you should be sure that you are able to:

- describe why monetary policy affects certain economic sectors more than others.

- explain why monetary policy may not be sufficient to get the economy out of a recession.

- list the different time lags associated with monetary policy.

- understand how variable time lags make it more difficult to use monetary policy effectively.

- understand how "rational expectations" can frustrate monetary policy.

- understand the effects of monetary policy on the foreign trade sector of the economy and on international capital flows.

- understand the effects of changes in financial markets and newly evolving financial instruments on the implementation of monetary policy.

- understand how seasonal and random changes in the demand for currency can affect the money supply and how the Fed deals with these unexpected changes.

- differentiate between the Fed's targeting of interest rates as opposed to levels of a monetary aggregate.

- understand why the Fed can control either interest rates or the money supply and its growth rate but not both variables simultaneously.

- understand the impact of changes in the velocity of money (V) on monetary policy.

- understand why control of the money supply necessarily means greater fluctuations in interest rates.

Self Evaluation

List of Terms

Credit Rationing
Dynamic Monetary Policy
Floating Rate Mortgages
Implementation Lag
L

M2
M3
Rational Expectations
Recognition Lag
Response Lag
Sterilization

For the statements below, fill in the term from the list above which provides the best fit.

1.) _____ refers to the policies that central banks use to offset and manage changes in their domestic supply of money caused by foreign deposit transfers.

2.) The least liquid definition of money contains government savings bonds and short-term government securities and is called _____.

3.) The Federal Reserve's active policies in response to inflationary or recessionary pressures is commonly referred to as its _____.

4.) There are a number of different definitions of the money supply -- the one which contains currency, demand deposits, savings deposits, savings certificates, and money market funds is called _____.

5.) The time it takes for monetary policy to have an impact on the behavior of the different economic units in the economy is known as the _____.

6.) Macroeconomic policy may be ineffective if people's behavior is based upon _____.

7.) In lieu of raising interest rates, financial institutions may resort to _____ to prevent losing their best customers.

8.) Monetary policy has a much shorter _____ than fiscal policy since it doesn't have to be authorized by Congress.

9.) There are a number of different definitions of the money supply -- the one which contains currency, demand deposits, savings deposits, savings certificates, money market funds, and large certificates of deposits is called _____.

10.) Because of the widespread use of _____, the Federal Reserve's efforts to raise interest rates will not only result in fewer housing starts but will also decrease consumption expenditures as monthly housing payments increase.

11.) The time it takes to realize that a macroeconomic problem exists and that some kind of policy needs to be taken is known as the _____.

Problems

The Problem with Unstable Monetary Velocities

Monetarists believe that velocity and the demand for cash balances are relatively stable in the short run. If one accepts that viewpoint, then according to the Fisher equation of exchange, changes in the money supply would result in direct changes in nominal GDP (PY).

$$MV = PY$$

$$\Delta M \, (\bar{V}) \rightarrow \Delta (PY) = \Delta \text{ nominal GDP (the bar above V denoting a constant)}$$

Although this represents a much simplified version of the monetarist theory, it provides a conceptual framework for understanding why monetarists were in favor of targeting the growth rates of monetary aggregates such as M1 or M2. Relatively constant percentage changes in the monetary aggregate (say M2) would result in predictable and relatively constant changes in nominal GDP.

For example, the 1992 values for the variables in the equation were as follows:

M	V	P	Y	Nominal GDP
$3,494.8 (V) =	1.211	($4986.3) =	$6,038.41

Calculate the M2 velocity for 1992: _____ (V = PY/M)

If the Fed's goal for 1993 was to achieve an increase in nominal GDP of 3.5 percent, then, with a stable M2 velocity, how much of an increase in M2 would be needed to achieve that goal? _____ percentage increase
_____ 1993 M2

If velocity remains constant and M2 increases by the amount required to achieve the 1993 goal, what will 1993 nominal GDP equal? _____

In other words, based on the expectation of a constant and stable velocity, the Fed could estimate what value of M2 would allow it to achieve its 1993 nominal GDP target?

However, in 1993, the actual velocity turned out to be 1.795, an increase of 3.88 percent over its 1992 value.

With the actual velocity of 1.795 and the targeted 3.5 percent growth rate in M2, determine what nominal GDP would actually be:

M2	V	=	Nominal GDP
( )	1.795	=	( )

Given the change in velocity from 1992 to 1993, how much would actual GDP differ from targeted GDP? $ _____ billion

True/False Statements

Indicate whether you think the statements below are true or false. These questions are designed to make you think about the concepts presented in the text. There may not be any easy clear-cut answers. Some thoughts about the answers are presented at the end of the chapter.

1.) _____ Monetary policy is more effective in reducing inflation than it is in lowering the rate of unemployment.

2.) _____ The theory of rational expectations implies that monetary policy will be more effective, because everyone is assumed to understand and anticipate what the Fed is attempting to accomplish.

3.) _____ When the Fed sells government securities on the open market, the value of the dollar would normally be expected to appreciate.

4.) _____ When the Fed buys government securities on the open market, exports will rise and imports will fall, thus increasing total aggregate demand.

5.) _____ Foreign capital flows that occur in response to the Fed's open market operations reinforce what the Fed is attempting to accomplish.

6.) _____ With the innovations and changes that have occurred in financial markets, the most basic measure of money, M1, plays a more important role than before.

7.) _____ In order to keep the supply of money constant, the Fed should sell government securities on the open market when there is an increased demand for currency by the public.

8.) _____ The Fed can more easily control the money supply than the interest rate.

9.) _____ By carefully controlling the demand and supply for money, the Fed can usually achieve its targeted interest rate.

10.) _____ A more stable velocity of money (V) makes it easier for the Fed to achieve its monetary policy goals.

Multiple-Choice Questions

Select the "best" answer from the alternatives provided.

1.) The selective impact of monetary policy refers to
   a. the fact that some interest rates change more than others in response to monetary policy.
   b. the fact that some types of monetary policy are more effective than others.
   c. the fact that some banks are affected by Federal Reserve policies, but not all member banks are.
   d. the fact that some sectors of the economy are affected to a much greater extent than other sectors.

2.) With respect to the time lags associated with monetary policy,
   a. the implementation lag is probably shorter than it is for fiscal policy.
   b. the response lag is the longest and most difficult to predict.
   c. the recognition lag is becoming shorter with the prompt publication of economic data.
   d. all of the above apply.

3.) According to the rational expectations approach,
   a. monetary policy becomes even more effective as more people become aware of it and anticipate its results.
   b. monetary policy becomes ineffective as more people become aware of it and anticipate its results.
   c. monetary policy shouldn't be affected, since the theory only changes assumptions about how people incorporate information into their decisions.
   d. fiscal policy becomess less effective as people anticipate its results, but monetary policy is not affected.

4. Increasingly, the Federal Reserve has had to take into account the behavior and reactions of foreigners when it tries to implement a tight money policy. When foreign reaction is taken into account, the effectiveness of the tight money policy:
   a. is increased, because of the cooperation of other central banks.
   b. is decreased, because foreign investors will move their capital out of the country.
   c. is increased, because a tight money policy affects foreigners in the same way as it affects Americans.
   d. is decreased, because foreign investors will move their capital into the country.

5.) If the Federal Reserve implements an easy money policy in an attempt to help get the economy moving again, there will also be an effect on the value of the dollar which will:
   a. reinforce the easy money policy by depreciating the dollar and increasing exports and reducing imports.
   b. reinforce the easy money policy by appreciating the dollar and increasing exports and reducing imports.
   c. offset the easy money policy by depreciating the dollar and increasing exports and reducing imports.
   d. offset the easy money policy by depreciating the dollar and decreasing exports and increasing imports.
   e. none of the above apply.

6.) In examining the various definitions of the money supply that have been developed by the Fed,
   a. they all move in the same direction because of the way that they are defined.
   b. M2, M3, and L have higher income velocities than M1.
   c. M1 is a broader measure of liquidity than M2 or M3.
   d. the money supply measure with the most stable income velocity is the most correlated with GDP.

7.) During the Christmas holiday season,
  a. the demand for cash increases, causing the money supply to increase.
  b. the demand for cash declines as people use credit cards for those special Christmas purchases.
  c. the demand for cash increases, causing the money supply to decline.
  d. there is no effect on the money supply, since cash holdings are increased and demand deposits fall by an equivalent amount.

8.) Concerning the Fed's main "instrumental target variable,"
  a. the Fed can target both interest rates and growth in the money supply in implementing its monetary goals.
  b. it is difficult for the Fed to target or control either interest rates or growth in the money supply.
  c. targeting monetary growth rates is effective only if the velocity of circulation is stable.
  d. targeting monetary growth rates is effective regardless of whether or not the velocity of circulation is stable.

9.) Concerning the velocity of circulation (V in the equation of exchange),
  a. velocity will tend to increase when interest rates are lowered.
  b. velocity appears to be unaffected by changes in the interest rate.
  c. velocity will tend to decrease when interest rates are lowered.
  d. velocity will tend to increase when prices are decreasing.

10.) Federal Reserve attempts to control the money supply have been made more difficult by,
  a. unpredictable changes in velocity.
  b. rapidly increasing utilization of credit cards.
  c. new innovative accounts in banking and financial markets.
  d. all of the above.

Discussion Questions

1.) It has been said that if the Fed utilized a Keynesian theoretical framework, it would target interest rates, while if it utilized a monetarist theoretical framework, it would target growth rates of some selected monetary aggregates (such as M1 or M2). Explain.

2.) Unless the Fed takes specific actions, one would expect the money supply to decline during the Christmas season. Explain why and what actions the Fed should take.

3.) With global financial markets growing more efficient, explain why a country like the United States may have difficulty in controlling its own money supply.

4.) Why do tight monetary policies tend to reduce the future growth of the economy?

5.) Fiscal policy should be utilized during recessions and/or depressions, because changes in spending can be relied upon to have a definite multiplied effect each time. Monetary policy, on the other hand, cannot be relied on to counteract recessions or depressions. Comment.

6.) How do variable time lags complicate economic policy-making?

Answers and Solutions to Problems and Exercises

Completing Statements from the List of Terms

1.) Sterilization
2.) L
3.) Dynamic Monetary Policy
4.) M2
5.) Response Lag
6.) Rational Expectations
7.) Credit Rationing
8.) Implementation Lag
9.) M3
10.) Floating Rate Mortgages
11.) Recognition Lag

Problems

The Problem with Unstable Monetary Velocities

Calculate the M2 velocity for 1992: **1.728**

If the Fed's goal for 1993 was to achieve an increase in nominal GDP of 3.5 percent, then, with a stable M2 velocity, how much of an increase in M2 would be needed to achieve that goal? **3.5 percent increase**

Targeted 1993 M2 = **$3,617.1 billion**

If velocity remains constant and M2 increases by the amount required to achieve the 1993 goal, what will 1993 nominal GDP equal?
3,617.1 billion   X   1.728 = $6,250.4 billion

3,617.1 billion   X   1.795 = $6,492.7 billion

Given the change in velocity from 1992 to 1993, how much would actual GDP differ from targeted GDP?   **$242.4 billion**

True/False Statements

1.) **True.** The Fed has the tools to increase required reserves which will decrease the money supply and amount of loans outstanding, which will, in turn, raise interest rates. Tight money policies can reduce excess spending and inflationary pressures. Efforts to increase spending may or may not succeed, depending upon the willingness of the banking system to make new loans.

2.) **False.** One of the predictions of rational expectations theory is that individuals will have full knowledge of what is happening and will take appropriate actions to anticipate the effects of government policies. By anticipating the effects of economic policies, society may decrease their effectiveness and impact. For example, if an investment tax credit was passed by Congress each time there was a recession, firms might start postponing their investment spending until they can obtain a tax credit, thereby intensifying the business cycle. In such a case, the investment tax credit changes from a counter-cyclical fiscal policy to a pro-cyclical policy, making the economic situation worse rather than better.

3. **True**. When the Fed sells government securities, member banks will use their excess reserves to purchase them -- resulting in less lending potential. To the extent that the money supply is smaller than it otherwise would be, interest rates will be higher, attracting foreign funds, and increasing the value of the dollar as foreign investors increase their demand for dollars.

4.) **True**. When the Fed buys government securities (to stimulate the economy), member banks will have more excess reserves and be able to make more new loans. Interest rates should fall as the supply of money is increased, decreasing the value of the dollar. As the dollar depreciates, exports will increase and import will decrease, thus enhancing total aggregate demand.

5.) **False**. Foreign capital flows tend to offset what the Fed is trying to do, making it more difficult to achieve its policy goal. An example: to wring excess spending out of the economy, the Fed will run a "tight" money policy which will raise interest rates, thus reducing interest-sensitive spending. But the higher interest rates will be attractive to foreign investors, and their efforts to invest in dollar-denominated securities will result in a capital inflow which will offset, to some extent, the efforts of the Fed to reduce the supply of money.

6.) **False**. The innovations and changes have made it more difficult for the Fed to control the means of spending. The linkage between the money supply and the level of economic activity is no longer as close as it once was. The emergence of credit cards as a major source of credit and spending provides an excellent example of a structural change that has greatly complicated the Fed's efforts to control spending.

7.) **False**. When the public's demand for currency increases, the money supply will decline, other things being equal (*ceteris paribus*). To offset the impact of that downward pressure, the Fed should buy, not sell government securities to create additional excess reserves.

8.) **True**. Although the Fed does not have perfect control over the money supply, it should be easier to control, since interest rates also depend on the demand for credit as well as the banking system.

9.) **False**. The Fed has very little control over the demand for money, and it has only partial control over the supply of money.

10.) **True**. If velocity (V) remains stable in the short run, the Fed can have more confidence in what they do. Changes in V can offset what the Fed is attempting to accomplish, making it difficult to achieve its goals for nominal GDP and other macro variables.

Multiple-Choice

1.) d   2.) d   3.) b   4.) d   5.) a   6.) d

7.) c   8.) c   9.) c   10.) d

Discussion Questions

1.) The Keynesian monetary transmission mechanism runs as follows: changes in the supply of money lead to changes in the rate of interest which, in turn, lead to changes in investment spending, which causes GDP to increase by a multiple of the change in investment spending.

In the Keynesian explanation, changes in interest rates are the prime means of changing investment spending. The monetarist theoretical framework, on the other hand, is dependent upon a stable demand for money and a stable velocity of money. Since the money supply (M) times the velocity of money (V) equals nominal GDP, the monetarist emphasis is on growth rates of the money supply.

2.) This could be the Grinch that stole Christmas! Increased demands for currency and cash balances during the Christmas season will put downward pressure on the money supply if the Fed doesn't react. Cash withdrawals eat up reserves on a 100 % basis! The Fed should take whatever measures it feels are necessary to keep the money supply from declining -- purchasing more government securities.

3.) How very true. As we move towards the global village, it will be more difficult for individual countries to go their own way. If the Fed attempts to run a tight money policy, the higher interest rates that would result will attract more funds from abroad -- offsetting what the Fed is attempting to do.

4.) Tight money leads to higher interest rates and less investment spending. Investment spending affects the economy's capital stock, which plays an important role in how fast the economy grows.

5.) Basically a true statement, especially if you are a bona fide Keynesian. Monetary policy with its easy money policy and low interest rates may not be sufficient to get the economy out of a severe recession. However, deficit spending will have a multiplied impact on overall income, no matter what.

6.) The issue of variable and erratic time lags is a tough one for those who believe that the economy can be "fine tuned." If policy-makers are always uncertain about when the full impact of a particular policy will take place, policy-making becomes very difficult indeed.

Summary

This chapter does an excellent job of summarizing the strengths and weaknesses of monetary policy -- what it can and can't do. Reflecting the increasing amount of skepticism towards the overall effectiveness of governmental policy in general, the list is weighted more heavily on the "con" side. To start with, interest-sensitive sectors of the economy bear the brunt of monetary policy. Thus, efforts by the Fed to control inflation tend to decrease investment in new factories and capital goods, both of which affect the economy's rate of economic growth and productivity.

On the flip side of the policy coin, efforts by the Fed to prevent recessions or lessen their impact, are not nearly as effective as its efforts to control inflation. Bankers may not lend, and businesses may not borrow, in spite of the best efforts of the Fed to increase excess reserves and lower interest rates. Bankruptcies of both businesses and consumers and unemployment are both higher during recessionary periods, factors which are not conducive to profitable lending. Real total spending decreases during recessions, making it less likely that firms will need to expand their facilities.

Monetary policy does have a major advantage over fiscal policy in that it can be implemented fairly quickly, not having to be debated and modified by Congress. Even so, it probably takes a full year (perhaps a year and a half) for its full impact to be felt. That means that a monetary policy measure would have to be considered and agreed upon for a year to a year and a half in advance for its timing to be optimal. It's hard to believe that would happen very often.

The ease with which investment capital moves around the world is making it much more difficult to pursue an independent monetary policy. A tight money policy by the Fed attracts funds from abroad, an easy money policy lowers interest rates and drives investment funds to other parts of the world, counteracting the Fed's policy.

Rational expectations on the part of society's economic participants can negate either monetary or fiscal policy, leading some economists to argue that government policies should be as consistent and predictable as possible, so people can incorporate government policies into their plans and behavior.

Changes in monetary institutions and instruments, indeed the whole financial environment, have complicated the Fed's task enormously. In the old days, M1 velocity was a pretty reliable guide for targeting the nominal GDP. With all the innovations and changes that have occurred, the close association that existed between M1 and GDP appears to have changed. Since the Fed changed from targeting interest rates to targeting some measure of the money suppply, the instability of velocity has taken on a new significance. A steady growth rate in some monetary aggregate combined with a constant (or at least predictable) velocity measure would assure a steady growth path for GDP. Efforts to find a new variable which has a more stable relationship with GDP have not been all that successful.

Chapter 22
Fiscal Policy:
Taxation and Spending

Overview of the Chapter

Chapter 22 provides us with greater detail and realism about the dimensions of fiscal policy -- taxation and government spending. The standard Keynesian policy prescription for addressing recessions is to decrease taxes. Lower taxes will, in turn, increase disposable income and, depending upon the marginal propensities to consume and save, consumption and saving will increase by some fraction of the tax decrease. The increase in consumption spending is subject to the economic multiplier effect, so the change in total income will be larger than the initial change in taxes. The full multiplied impact of the tax change will be somewhat less than the full multiplied impact of an equal change in government spending, since only part of the tax change results in a change in consumption. In the aggregate supply/aggregate demand framework, the decrease in taxes increases aggregate demand with corresponding increases in real income and the price level. The increase in the price level reduces the size of the multiplier from what it would otherwise be.

If, on the other hand, inflation and excessive spending are the problems that we are concerned about, appropriate fiscal policy would be to increase taxes to decrease disposable personal income, thereby reducing both consumption and saving. The aggregate demand curve (AD = C + I + G) would shift downward in the Keynesian cross diagram, and the AD curve would shift to the left in the AS/AD framework, reducing both real income and the price level.

In the political arena, all tax increases face intense opposition from a variety of affected parties, while tax cuts have proven to be enormously popular with voters. Tax changes have significant secondary effects associated with them, and any proposal to change taxes should keep them in mind: (1) the question of actual tax incidence; (2) total collection costs; (3) the economic effects of the tax change on factor inputs, particularly labor; and (4) possible shifts to non-taxable activities.

Income taxes tend to be the most visible of the taxes levied. Depending upon how an income tax is structured, it can be either progressive, proportional, or regressive in terms of its impact on the various income classes. Sales taxes on necessities (such as food, clothing, or medicine) can also be characterized as regressive even though they are levied at a constant rate for all expenditures, since lower income units spend a larger proportion of their incomes on necessities.

Income taxes represent a leakage from the flow of income. Thus, as income increases, so do total tax receipts -- creating ever larger leakages -- and declines in income result in lower tax receipts and smaller leakages. Since total income tax receipts vary directly with the level of income, income taxes are called automatic stabilizers -- they offset the prevailing business cycle, stabilizing and moderating the level of income. Perhaps best of all, no Congressional action is required.

As economists became more familiar with Keynesian policies and their impact on the economy, they learned that the effect of a temporary tax cut differs significantly from one considered to be permanent. Households tend to finance out of savings tax increases that are thought to be temporary, whereas tax increases that are viewed to be more permanent in nature have more of an impact on consumption spending. The supply side policies of the Reagan administration emphasized decreases in marginal tax rates (especially at the upper end of the income spectrum) as a way of creating greater incentives to work and changing the relative values of work/leisure.

The Federal budget deficit was also of concern and, somewhat paradoxically, it was argued that it was possible to cut tax rates and still generate more tax revenue. This, of course, could occur only if the tax cuts led to an increase in the tax base (which could result if people worked harder and earned more income as a result of the tax cut). The Laffer curve illustrates the relationship that is said to exist between the tax rate and total tax receipts.

Spending changes represent the other side of fiscal policy, with increases in government spending resulting in a spending injection which will increase nominal GDP, lower the rate of unemployment, and possibly create some inflationary pressures for the economy, depending upon how how much slack capacity exists. With the presence of large federal budget deficits, the challenge has been to find specific programs where spending could be cut. The size of the deficit has severely compromised the effectiveness of deficit spending in addressing recessionary conditions.

Learning Objectives

After completing this chapter, you should be sure that you are able to:

- understand how fiscal policy can be used to stimulate or contract GDP.

- illustrate the effects of changes in government spending and taxes on aggregate demand (AD) in both the Keynesian and AD/AS models.

- identify the different types of taxes and the basic characteristics of each tax, including the VAT which is not currently used in the United States.

- explain the concept of tax indexing and why it is used.

- describe the controversy surrounding the capital gains tax.

- understand how automatic stabilizers function in the economy.

- list the non-spending impacts of tax changes.

- analyze the different economic impacts of permanent and temporary tax changes.

- understand the rationale behind the Laffer curve and its implications for tax policy.

- specify the rationale for public works and public employment programs and related legislation such as CETA.

- discuss the role that the so-called entitlements play in the federal budget and their impact on the budget deficit.

- understand the limitations that large budget deficits have placed on current and future fiscal policy.

Self Evaluation

List of Terms

Automatic Stabilizer
Capital Gains Tax
Compliance Costs
Counter-Cyclical Fiscal Policy
Double Taxation
Entitlements
Fiscal Dividend
Fiscal Drag
Fiscal Policy

Implementation Lag
Inheritance Taxes
Investment Tax Credit
Laffer Curve
Progressive Income Tax
Public Works Spending
Response Lag
Value-Added Tax

For the statements below, fill in the term from the list above which provides the best fit.

1.) _____ refers to the situation in which an income tax is levied on corporate income and then taxed again when recipients receive dividends from the corporation.

2.) With sufficiently high rates of taxation on estates, _____ could prevent large scale transfers of wealth from one generation to another.

3.) One advantage of a comprehensive _____ would be that it would decrease consumption and promote saving.

4.) If income taxes are too progressive, _____ may result, restricting the growth in income as the tax leakages become larger and larger.

5.) If a recession appears imminent, a temporary _____ may boost investment spending by firms, thus stimulating the economy.

6.) The basis for the _____ is that it assumes that the government can collect larger tax revenues with lower tax rates.

7.) If a simplified one-page federal tax form were adopted, with no tax deductions or tax credits, _____ would be lowered.

8.) Given the time period that it takes Congress to pass tax legislation, the _____ of tax changes is probably too long for taxes to be an effective counter-cyclical policy tool.

9.) The federal income tax is an example of an _____, since a recession reduces incomes, lowering tax revenues, thus increasing the Federal deficit -- without Congressional action.

10.) One of the fastest growing components of federal spending has been in _____, government programs in which qualified recipients receive benefits without a means test.

11.) One of the most controversial areas of taxation involves the _____ which is based on the appreciation in the value of assets such as land and stocks and bonds.

12.) _____ consists of running a budget surplus during expansions and potentially inflationary periods and a budget deficit during recessions.

13.) One of the best examples of an automatic stabilizer is the _____.

14.) The increased tax receipts associated with economic growth and a highly progressive tax structure resulted in a _____ which politicians could use to fund new projects.

15.) The time it takes for households and firms to change their spending patterns due to a policy change is known as the _____.

16.) _____, while popular in the depression of the 30s, has not been extensively used as an anti-recession policy tool.

17.) When the government changes tax rates and the level of government spending, it is engaged in _____.

Problems

Attempting to Balance the Budget

Balancing the budget involves making some difficult decisions about spending and taxes. As your text mentions, political constituencies develop around ongoing programs, and any decision to cut program spending risks alienating a group of voters that might be crucial come election time. The political risk surrounding efforts to increase taxes has been well publicized, with President Bush's famous sound bite **"Read my lips -- no new taxes"** coming back to haunt him when he ran for re-election in 1992. The following worksheet is designed to give you an appreciation of the difficulties that are associated with balancing the budget and more importantly, from an economic standpoint, an appreciation of the importance of economic assumptions.

Assumptions:

A Simple Budget Forecasting Model

Initial value of nominal GDP:	$6,700 billion
Growth rate of nominal GDP:	4.7 percent/year
Initial value of government expenditures:	$1,500 billion
Baseline growth rate in govt. expenditures:	3 percent/year
Initial value of government tax revenues:	$1,307 billion
Government tax revenues as a percent of GDP:	19.50 percent

Scenario One -- Business As Usual

	Baseline Year 1	Year 2	Year 3	Year 4	Year 5
Gross Domestic Product	$6,700	$7,015			
Government Expenditures:	$1,500	$1,541			
Govt. Expend. as % of GDP:	22.39%	21.97%			
Government Tax Revenues:	$1,307	$1,388			
Govt. Tax Rev. as % of GDP:	19.51%	19.50%			
Government Budget Status:	- $194	- $173			
Deficit/Surplus as % of GDP:	- 2.89%	- 2.47%			

Year 2 is completed for you, so you can see how this simplified budget model works. Second year GDP is obtained by multiplying year 1 GDP times 1.04 (4 % growth rate.) Government expenditures are calculated in the same fashion -- by multiplying year 1 government expenditures by 1.03, and government revenues are equal to 20 % of year 2 GDP. Year 2 budget status is determined by subtracting government expenditures from government tax revenues, and the deficit as a percent of GDP is simply the deficit (or surplus) divided by total GDP multiplied by 100 to express it in percentage terms.

- Using the procedure described above, calculate the values of the budget table for the remaining years 3 - 5. Graph total government expenditures and revenues (with the deficit or surplus being the difference between the two). This graph will be similar to Figure 22.6 in the Hogendorn text, except that it will be in billions of dollars instead of percent of GDP.

Figure 22-1
Budget Scenario One
Government Expenditures and Revenues

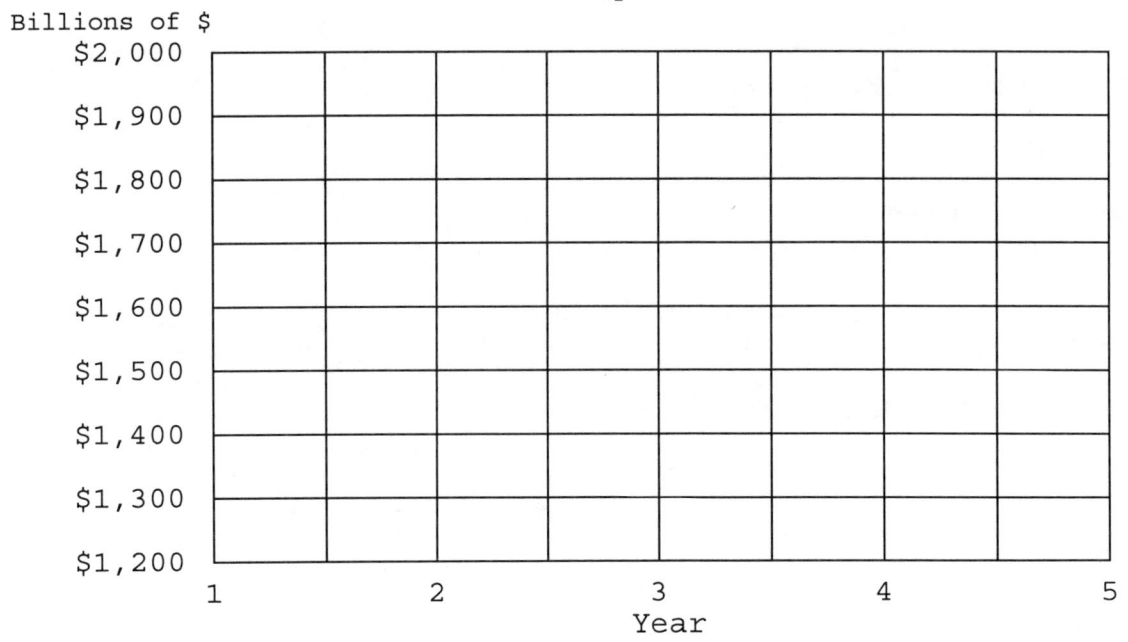

Billions of $

(empty grid from $1,200 to $2,000 on y-axis, Years 1 to 5 on x-axis)

Scenario Two -- Lower GDP Growth Rate

The second scenario examines the impact of a lower growth rate in GDP on the government budget deficit, everything else being held constant. In this scenario, GDP is assumed to grow at a 3.5 % per year instead of 4.7 % per year. Again, the first two years are filled in for you, leaving years 3 - 5 for you to calculate.

	Baseline Year 1	Year 2	Year 3	Year 4Y	Year 5
Gross Domestic Product	$6,700	$6,935			
Government Expenditures:	$1,500	$1,541			
Govt. Expend. as % of GDP:	22.39%	22.23%			
Government Tax Revenues:	$1,307	$1,352			
Govt. Tax Rev. as % of GDP:	19.51%	19.50%			
Government Budget Status:	- $194	- $189			
Deficit/Surplus as % of GDP:	- 2.89%	- 2.73%			

Year 2 is completed for you, so you can see how this simplified budget model works. Second year GDP is obtained by multiplying year 1 GDP times 1.04 (4 % growth rate). Government expenditures are calculated in the same fashion -- by multiplying year 1 government expenditures by 1.03, and government revenues are equal to 20 % of year 2 GDP. Year 2 budget status is determined by subtracting government expenditures from government tax revenues, and the deficit as a percent of GDP is simply the deficit (or surplus) divided by total GDP multiplied by 100 to express it in percentage terms.

- Using the procedure described above, calculate the values of the budget table for the remaining years 3 - 5. Graph total government expenditures and revenues (with the deficit or surplus being the difference between the two). This graph will be similar to Figure 22.6 in your text, except that it will be in billions of dollars instead of percent of GDP.

Figure 22-2
Budget Scenario Two
Government Expenditures and Revenues

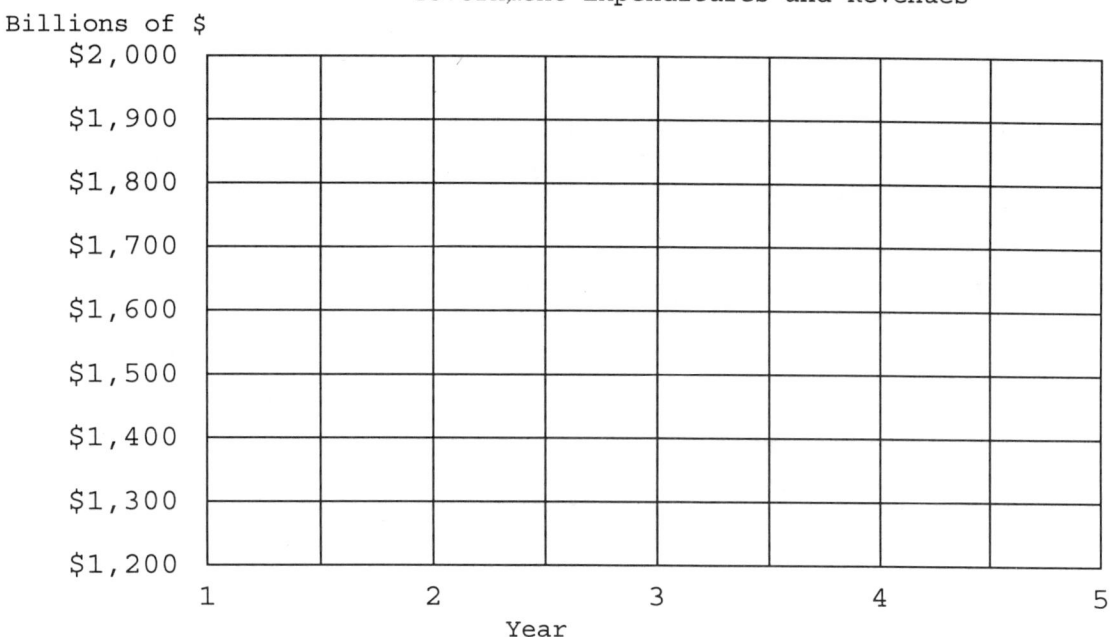

Scenario Three -- Declining Growth Rate in Expenditures and Taxes as Increased Percentage of GDP

The third scenario examines the impact of a decreased growth rate in federal expenditures and taxes as an increasing percentage of GDP on the government deficit, everything else being held constant. In this scenario, GDP is assumed to grow at the original 4.7 % per year. The growth rate in government expenditures is assumed to fall by 0.2 % per year, changing from 2.75 % to 2.55 % to 2.35 % to 2.15 % and, finally, 1.95 %. Note that these are growth rates, so federal spending is still increasing, just at a lower and lower growth rate per year. Government tax revenues, on the other hand, are assumed to increase as a percent of GDP by 0.2 % per year -- 19.5%, 19.7%, 19.9%, 20.1%, and, finally, 20.3% of GDP. Again, the first two years are filled in for you, leaving years 3 - 5 for you to calculate.

	Baseline Year 1	Year 2	Year 3	Year 4	Year 5
Gross Domestic Product	$6,700	$7,015			
Government Expenditures:	$1,500	$1,538			
Govt. Expend. as % of GDP:	22.39%	21.93%			
Government Tax Revenues:	$1,307	$1,382			
Govt. Tax Rev. as % of GDP:	19.51%	19.70%			
Government Budget Status:	- $194	- $156			
Deficit/Surplus as % of GDP:	- 2.89%	- 2.23%			

Year 2 is completed for you, so you can see how this simplified budget model works. Second year GDP is obtained by multiplying year 1 GDP times 1.04 (4 % growth rate). Government expenditures are calculated in the same fashion -- by multiplying year 1 government expenditures by 1.03, and government revenues are equal to 20 % of year 2 GDP. Year 2 budget status is determined by subtracting government expenditures from government tax revenues, and the deficit as a % of GDP is simply the deficit (or surplus) divided by total GDP multiplied by 100 to express it in percentage terms.

- Using the procedure described above, calculate the values of the budget table for the remaining years 3 - 5. Graph total government expenditures and revenues (with the deficit or surplus being the difference between the two). This graph will be similar to Figure 22.6 in your text, except that it will be in billions of dollars instead of percent of GDP.

Figure 22-3
Budget Scenario Three
Government Expenditures and Revenues

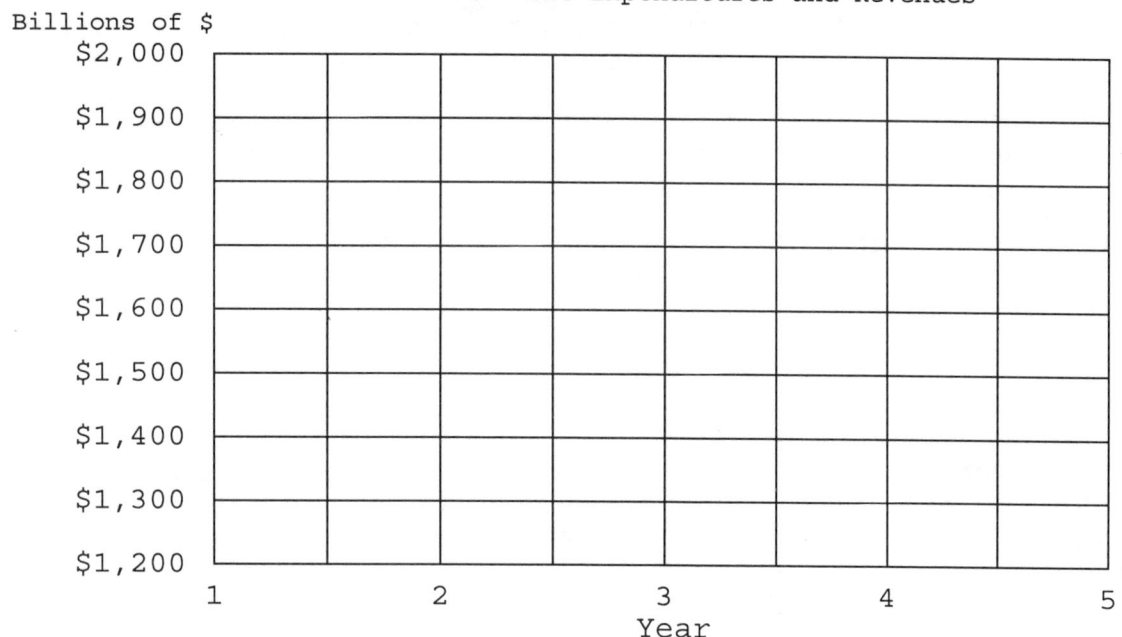

Billions of $

(blank graph with y-axis from $1,200 to $2,000 in $100 increments, x-axis Year 1 to 5)

True/False Statements

Indicate whether you think the statements below are true or false. These questions are designed to make you think about the concepts presented in the text. There may not be any easy clear-cut answers. Some thoughts about the answers are presented at the end of the chapter.

1.) _____ Tax decreases and increases in government expenditures are equally effective in fighting recessions.

2.) _____ Social Security payments represent a large automatic stabilizer for the U.S. economy.

3.) _____ A progressive income tax will generate a fiscal drag in an economic expansion.

4.) _____ Tax indexing effectively eliminates bracket creep during inflationary periods.

5.) _____ The controversy over the capital gains tax revolves around its effect on investment and economic growth.

6.) _____ One reason for the adoption of the VAT would be that it might increase economic growth.

7.) _____ Permanent tax changes affect savings more than temporary tax changes.

8.) _____ The Laffer curve can be used to show that more taxes can be collected by lowering marginal rates of taxation.

9.) _____ To combat inflation, an appropriate fiscal policy would be to decrease government spending and increase taxes.

10.) _____ The large existing government debt makes it easier to engage in expansionary fiscal policy.

Multiple-Choice Questions

Select the "best" answer from the alternatives provided.

1.) The Laffer curve suggests that
   a. increasing tax rates always reduces incentives to work.
   b. decreasing tax rates always increases incentives to work.
   c. decreasing tax rates will always result in enhanced tax revenues.
   d. raising tax rates will increase tax revenues up to a point, then further increases will decrease tax revenues.

2.) If it is thought that inflationary pressures are building up in the economy, appropriate fiscal policy would consist of
   a. increasing government spending programs on basic research and development.
   b. increasing taxes and government spending by roughly the same amount.
   c. increasing the marginal rate of taxation and decreasing tax deductions.
   d. decreasing the money supply and raising interest rates.

3.) If it is thought that the economy is headed into a recession, appropriate fiscal policy would consist of
   a. the president holding a fireside chat to encourage people to keep up their confidence.
   b. cutting defense expenditures and reallocating the extra funds towards essential social programs.
   c. initiating a temporary investment tax credit for any new investment above the previous year's investment.
   d. increasing taxes to balance the budget, which would send the message that the government is in good financial shape.

4.) An increase in taxes will have the effect of
   a. shifting the aggregate demand curve upwards in the Keynesian diagram by the full amount of the tax increase.
   b. shifting the aggregate demand curve downwards in the Keynesian diagram by the tax increase times the MPC.
   c. shifting the aggregate demand curve downwards in the Keynesian diagram by the full amount of the tax increase.
   d. not shifting the aggregate demand curve but moving down the existing aggregate demand curve

5.) If taxes remain the same and government expenditures increase,
   a. the aggregate demand curve will shift upwards in the Keynesian diagram by the change in expenditures, and equilibrium income will shift to the right by more than the change in government expenditures.
   b. the aggregate demand curve will shift upwards in the Keynesian diagram by the change in expenditures, and equilibrium income will shift to the right by the change in government expenditures.
   c. the aggregate demand curve will shift upwards in the Keynesian diagram by more than the change in expenditures, and equilibrium incomewill shift to the right by the same amount.
   d. the aggregate demand curve will remain the same in the Keynesian diagram, but there will be a movement along the existing aggregate demand curve to the new higher level of income.

6.) A decrease in marginal tax rates would be expected to
   a. shift the aggregate demand curve (AD) to the right and shift the aggregate supply curve (AS) to the left in the AD/AS model.
   b. shift the aggregate demand curve (AD) to the right and shift the aggregate supply curve (AS) to the right in the AD/AS model.
   c. shift the aggregate demand curve (AD) to the right and leave the aggregate supply curve (AS) unchanged in the AD/AS model.
   d. leave the aggregate demand curve (AD) unchanged and shift the aggregate supply curve (AS) to the right in the AD/AS model.

7.) Fiscal drag refers to
   a. the fact that high tax rates discourage new investment spending.
   b. a situation in which tax rates are set too high, causing equilibrium income to fall below full employment.
   c. the increase in the budget surplus due to a highly progressive income tax.
   d. the effect that high taxes have on incentives to work.

8.) Automatic stabilizers
   a. refer to certain policies that Congress stands ready to pass when either inflation or recession may occur.
   b. dampen the business cycle, making recessions less severe and expansions less inflationary.
   c. increase expenditures when the economy starts to go into a recession and decrease expenditures when the economy starts to heat up.
   d. are activated by presidential decree without having to have the consent of Congress.
   e. both (b) and (c) apply.

Discussion Questions

1.) If investment tax credits are used on a regular basis as part of expansionary fiscal policy to fend off recessions, how might firms react to the ITC after it has been used several times? (Hint: think about it in terms of rational expectations.)

2.) Discuss the pros and cons of allowing the president the discretion to change tax rates by a plus or minus five % without having to obtain Congressional approval.

3.) Discuss the impact of the balanced-budget amendment on the implementation and effectiveness of fiscal policy.

4.) Describe how a sales tax or a VAT would be regressive in its impact. Many states -- Minnesota is a prime example -- have tried to reduce the regressivity of their taxes by placing more reliance on progressive income taxes which are based on an ability to pay. Why do you think that they have moved in this direction? Is there any way that a sales tax or VAT could be made less regressive? Would there be any advantages associated with a regressive tax?

5.) Some politicians and economists have been proposing that we adopt a flat tax of 17 % for individuals and households, getting rid of the current system which is renowned for its complexity. A single deduction would be allowed for a household and the 17 % tax applied to the remaining income. What advantages and disadvantages would such a tax have over the present system?

Answers and Solutions to Problems and Exercises

Completing Statements from the List of Terms

1.) Double Taxation
2.) Inheritance Taxes
3.) Value-Added Tax
4.) Fiscal Drag
5.) Investment Tax Credit
6.) Laffer Curve
7.) Compliance Costs
8.) Implementation Lag
9.) Automatic Stabilizer
10.) Entitlements
11.) Capital Gains Tax
12.) Counter-Cyclical Fiscal Policy
13.) Progressive Income Tax
14.) Fiscal Dividend
15.) Response Lag
16.) Public Works Spending
17.) Fiscal Policy

Problems

Attempting to Balance the Budget

	Baseline Year 1	Year 2	Year 3	Year 4	Year 5
Gross Domestic Product	$6,700	$7,015	$7,345	$7,690	$8,051
Government Expenditures:	$1,500	$1,541	$1,584	$1,627	$1,672
Govt. Expend. as % of GDP:	22.39%	21.97%	21.56%	21.16%	20.77%
Government Tax Revenues:	$1,307	$1,388	$1,432	$1,500	$1,570
Govt. Tax Rev. as % of GDP:	19.51%	19.50%	19.50%	19.50%	19.50%
Government Budget Status:	- $194	- $173	- $151	- $128	- $ 102
Deficit/Surplus as % of GDP:	- 2.89%	- 2.47%	- 2.06%	- 1.66%	- 1.27%

Figure 22-1
Budget Scenario One

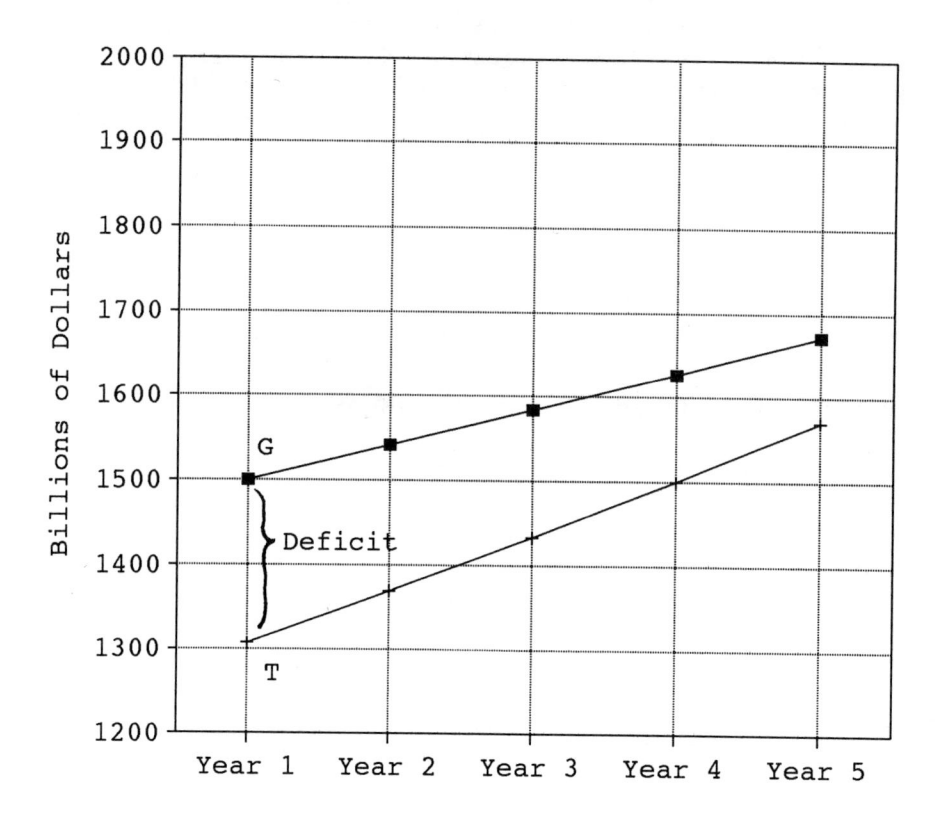

[Chart showing Billions of Dollars (1200-2000) over Year 1 through Year 5. Line G starts at 1500 in Year 1 and rises to ~1660 by Year 5. Line T starts at ~1305 in Year 1 and rises to ~1560 by Year 5. The gap between G and T in Year 1 is labeled "Deficit".]

Scenario Two -- Lower GDP Growth Rate

	Baseline Year 1	Year 2	Year 3	Year 4	Year 5
Gross Domestic Product	$6,700	$6,935	$7,177	$7,428	$7,688
Government Expenditures:	$1,500	$1,541	$1,584	$1,627	$1,672
Govt. Expend. as % of GDP:	22.39%	22.23%	22.06%	21.90%	21.75%
Government Tax Revenues:	$1,307	$1,352	$1,400	$1,449	$1,499
Govt. Tax Rev. as % of GDP:	19.51%	19.50%	19.50%	19.50%	19.50%
Government Budget Status:	- $194	- $189	- $184	- $179	- $173
Deficit/Surplus as % of GDP:	- 2.89%	- 2.73%	- 2.56%	- 2.40%	- 2.25%

Figure 22-2
Budget Scenario Two

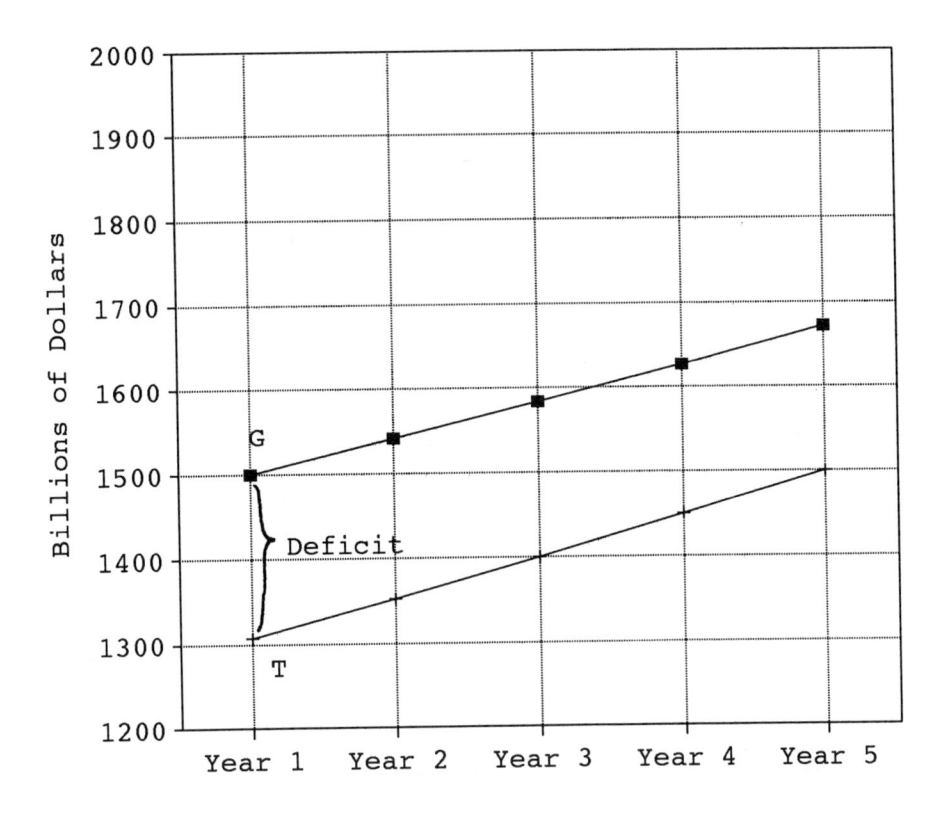

[Graph showing Billions of Dollars (y-axis, 1200-2000) vs. Year 1 through Year 5 (x-axis). Upper line labeled G starts at ~1500 in Year 1 and rises to ~1680 in Year 5. Lower line labeled T starts at ~1307 in Year 1 and rises to ~1510 in Year 5. The gap between them in Year 1 is labeled "Deficit".]

Scenario Three -- Declining Growth Rate in Expenditures and Taxes as Increased Percentage of GDP

	Baseline Year 1	Year 2	Year 3	Year 4	Year 5
Gross Domestic Product	$6,700	$7,015	$7,345	$7,690	$8,051
Government Expenditures:	$1,500	$1,538	$1,574	$1,608	$1,640
Govt. Expend. as % of GDP:	22.39%	21.93%	21.44%	20.91%	20.36%
Government Tax Revenues:	$1,307	$1,382	$1,462	$1,546	$1,634
Govt. Tax Rev. as % of GDP:	19.51%	19.70%	19.90%	20.1.%	20.3%
Government Budget Status:	- $194	- $156	- $113	- $63	- $5
Deficit/Surplus as % of GDP:	- 2.89%	- 2.23%	- 1.54%	- 0.81%	- 0.06%

Figure 22-3
Budget Scenario Three

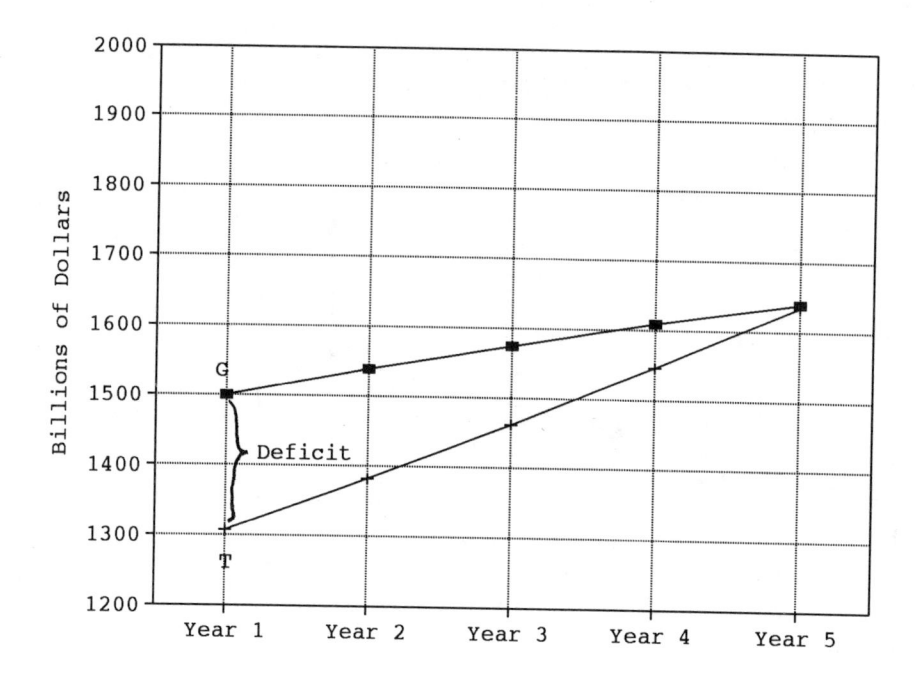

True/False Statements

1.) **False.** Government expenditure dollars have more economic impact than tax dollars. The two have different implementation and response lags.

2.) **True.** Social Security payments will change mainly according to demographic factors rather than economic conditions. When inflation hits, such payments will not rise.

3. **True.** As incomes rise, taxes will increase more than proportionately because of the progressivity of the income tax, moving the government budget towards a surplus.

4.) **It depends!** If only the personal deduction is indexed, the statement is false, since the deduction would only partially offset the increase in incomes due with inflation. If the tax brackets and deductions are indexed, then the statement would be considered true.

5.) **True.** Critics argue that reducing the capital gains tax would only reduce the tax liability associated with the increase in the value of assets, many of which do not affect real investment or productivity. Proponents believe that the capital gains tax discourages investment opportunities and results in a lower rate of economic growth.

6.) **True.** A VAT is esentially a tax on consumption spending, and it should discourage consumption and encourage saving, which would release resources for investment. Greater reliance on the revenues from a VAT would reduce the tax burden on upper income units.

7.) **False.** If a tax increase is temporary, then households will attempt to maintain their current standard of living and finance the extra taxes by drawing down their savings. Thus, savings will vary more with temporary tax changes than with permanent changes.

8.) **True.** If society is on the right hand portion of the curve, as many conservatives believe, then reducing tax rates will result in greater tax revenues as people work more.

9.) **True.** Aggegate demand needs to be reduced, and a combination of these two actions will accomplish that end.

10.) **False.** The large cumulative debt of the United States has made it more difficult to stimulate the economy with budget deficits. Past deficits have been so large that there is widespread concern about running larger deficits, even to mitigate recessions.

Multiple-Choice

1.) d   2.) c   3.) c   4.) b   5.) a   6.) b

7.) c   8.) e

Discussion Questions

1.) According to the rational expectations theory, government policy can be effective only when it catches people by surprise. As time passes, both firms and households incorporate past experience into their actions and in so doing, blunt the effectiveness of the policy. After having seen ITCs used several times to offset recessions, firms may start to postpone needed investment, waiting for the next ITC. What started out as a counter-cyclical policy becomes pro-cyclical, intensifying the business cycle.

2.) The positive side of the proposal would be that the implementation lag associated with tax changes would be dramatically reduced, making it easier to incorporate tax changes as a part of an effective fiscal policy. On the negative side, the pressures of retaining office may be so great that discretionary use of tax rates may invite misuse of this tool.

3.) Passage of this amendment would mean the end of fiscal policy, although GDP could be somewhat affected through equal changes in government spending and taxes via the balanced budget-multiplier. Monetary policy would be the only game in town.

4.) Lower income consumers spend a larger proportion of their income on consumption goods, so a tax on consumption goods would mean that they would pay a larger percent of their income towards the tax -- a regressive tax. Regressive taxes are generally opposed on equity grounds; such taxes violate our sense of economic fairness. In

Minnesota's case, the regressivity of the state sales tax is reduced by exempting food and clothing from the tax. It might be justified by reducing the tax liability of upper income households who do most of the saving and investment. This would be a classic trickle down theory -- tax the rich less so that they can save and invest more, thus creating more jobs and greater economic growth, benefiting society as a whole.

5.) One advantage would certainly be a reduction in compliance costs. A significant amount of resources is now devoted to completing the present tax forms, and the flat tax as described would reduce the resources needed to comply. Another advantage is that because the single flat rate is so low, it reduces the incentive to misrepresent earned income. On the other hand, the wide variety of tax credits and deductions can no longer be used to encourage or discourage certain kinds of actions. The flat tax is a movement away from the ability to pay principle which has characterized the federal income tax.

Summary

When the Republicans took control of both houses of Congress in 1994, almost every aspect of fiscal policy was questioned, and a number of new initiatives were proposed. The emphasis on balancing the budget drew support from both Republicans and Democrats. One area of controversy involved Social Security funding, with a number of senators arguing that efforts to balance the budget should not depend on cutting Social Security benefits. On the tax side, proposals included a $500 per child tax credit, a flat tax of 17 %, and a consumption tax of 17 %. Pertinent to all of these proposals are concepts included in this chapter, such as regressivity of the tax structure, compliance costs, and the effects on economic growth and investment.

The length and variability of the time lags associated with both fiscal and monetary policy continue to be of concern to policy-makers. Without knowing how long the time lags are, the task of conducting effective macroeconomic policy becomes extremely difficult. With Congress being increasingly reluctant to increase the federal budget deficit, monetary policy with its shorter implementation lag is being called upon to bear the brunt of anti-inflation and anti-recession efforts. Although public employment and public works programs have fallen into disfavor, the government may become more involved in providing jobs if welfare programs are significantly changed so that recipients must accept work to retain their benefits.

Interest on the national debt now constitutes the fourth largest expenditure category in the federal budget. Monetary policy directly impacts the amount of interest the Treasury must pay on its outstanding debt. Since a larger proportion of the Treasury's debt in now in shorter, term debt, that portion of the budget will vary much more than it has in the past, as interest rates change in response to changing economic conditions.

Chapter 23
Deficits and Debt in a Modern Economy

Overview of the Chapter

This chapter explores is some detail how debt impacts our economy, different methods of financing the federal debt, the relationship that exists between actual budget deficits and structural deficits, some pros and cons on the balanced-budget amendment, and finally, a discussion on the significance of the national debt and whether or not future generations will be burdened by today's budget deficits.

Do deficits affect the level of income in an economy? Keynesians believe they do, and monetarists believe they do not. Do government deficits crowd out private spending through their effect on interest rates and credit markets? If the economy has considerable excess capacity with lower levels of investment spending, then the crowding-out effect may well be negligible, and expansionary fiscal policy will stimulate the economy along the lines discussed in Chapters 17 and 22. If investment spending is vigorous, then additional government demands for funds may well increase interest rates, discouraging investment spending to some degree.

If interest rates do increase, the value of the dollar will increase as foreign investors shift funds to the United States to maximize their returns on their capital. If that occurs, U.S. exports will decline, and imports will increase, reducing private sector spending and reinforcing the crowding-out effect offset to the government deficit. However, it should be noted that the inflow of foreign capital helps finance the deficit, minimizing any crowding-out effect.

Government deficits can be financed in several ways. Less expansion occurs, and fewer inflationary pressures are generated when the Fed borrows from the private sector as opposed to when the deficit is monetized by the Fed by the creation of new money. The adverse economic impacts of deficits can be difficult to discern but are thought to involve higher real interest rates, the absorption of private savings by the deficit, and subsequent lower net investment and lower real growth rates as well as smaller increases in productivity.

The concept of structural deficits complicates the whole issue of whether deficits are actually stimulating the economy, since it suggests that the appropriate benchmark for gauging fiscal policy is the budget status when the economy achieves a level of high employment. Only if there is a structural or high employment deficit can fiscal policy be considered stimulatory. Although structural budget deficits are not as high currently as they have been in the past, they still average over three percent of GDP.

Arguments will undoubtedly continue for some time to come about how harmful the existing and projected levels of national debt are to our economy. While there are some arguments that can be rejected out of hand, several issues worthy of our attention include: the effect of large national debt on the degree of income inequality in our society, the amount of the debt held by foreigners as opposed to U.S. citizens, whether or not the borrowed funds were utilized for projects which enhanced productivity and future real income, and the effect of higher tax rates needed to finance the national debt.

As a result of the concern over the impact of the national debt, there is renewed interest in passage of a balanced-budget amendment to provide Congress with the necessary willpower to gain control over the deficit. Passage of the amendment would effectively limit fiscal policy as a policy tool, forcing us to rely on monetary policy. It also turns what has been an effective counter-cyclical instrument into a pro-cyclical instrument, perhaps causing wider fluctuations in the business cycle.

Learning Objectives

After completing this chapter, you should be sure that you are able to:

- describe the relationship that exists between the federal budget deficit and the national debt.

- analyze the effect of a government deficit on the demand for money, interest rates, and the private sector credit market.

- explain the rationale for the "crowding-out effect" and how it impacts foreign capital markets and exchange rate markets.

- explain the different, offsetting effects of expansionary fiscal and monetary policy when the international sector responses are considered.

- compare and contrast the four different ways a central bank can finance a budget deficit.

- explain why budget deficits that are monetized are more inflationary than those that are not monetized.

- describe the effects of successive budget deficits on investment spending, the growth in productivity, and the rate of economic growth.

- explain the concept of Ricardian equivalence and how it would affect the effectiveness of fiscal policy.

- understand that whether or not an actual budget deficit has an expansionary impact on the economy depends upon the status of the structural or high employment budget.

- carefully evaluate the different arguments about the actual economic threat of a sizable national debt.

- list the economic pros and cons associated with the balanced-budget amendment.

- assess the effectiveness of the proposals that have been advanced to control the budget deficit.

Self Evaluation

List of Terms

Balanced-Budget Amendment   Ricardian Equivalence
Crowding--Out Effect   Structural Deficit
Monetizing the Deficit   Structural Surplus

For the statements below, fill in the term from the list above which provides the best fit.

1.) A _____ would occur if the government tax revenues exceeded government expenditures at a full employment level of income.

2.) If the economy goes into a recession, the _____ would require that either taxes be increased or government spending be decreased.

3.) According to the theory behind the concept of _____, if the government runs a deficit, taxpayers will save more in expectation of having to pay higher taxes.

4.) A government budget deficit is truly stimulatory only if it generates a _____.

5.) According to the _____, government deficits will raise interest rates and result in lower private spending.

6.) If the federal Reserve creates new money to help finance a budget deficit, then we say it is _____.

Problems

A Closer Look at the Crowding-Out Effect

Monetarists believe that fiscal policy is ineffective in changing the equilibrium level of income, while Keynesians believe that government deficits can effectively stimulate the economy. The crowding-out effect provides the basis for the monetarist position -- the view that public sector deficits increase interest rates which then "crowd out" private sector spending. Any increase in the deficit is either fully or partially offset by a decrease in private spending.

While this issue is never likely to be resolved to the satisifaction of the two parties involved, it is instructive to examine and analyze the data to determine whether or not there is empirical support for the monetarist perspective. There are a number of different interest rates that could be used -- the three year Treasury Bill Rate was selected. To obtain the real rate of interest, the consumer price index (CPI) is subtracted from the nominal three year Treasury Bill rate: (you may want to reread the section in the Hogendorn text on real interest rates, pp. 349 - 352).

Real interest rate = nominal interest rate - inflation rate

The federal deficit is expressed as a percentage of GDP to indicate its magnitude relative to the size of the economy. Using the data contained in Table 23-1, calculate the real three year Treasury bill rate and the ratio of the federal deficit to nominal GDP. Use Figure 23-1 to plot those two variables. Put the year next to each of the data observations.

Table 23-1

Year	Three Year Treasury Bill Rate (in Percent)	Rate of Inflation (in Percent)	Real Treasury Bill Rate (in Percent)	Federal Government Deficit (in Billions)	Gross Domestic Product (in Billions)	Ratio of federal Government Deficit to Gross Domestic Product (in Percent)
1980	11.55	12.5		-73.8	2708.0	
1981	14.44	8.9		-79.0	3030.6	
1982	12.92	3.8		-128.0	3149.6	
1983	10.45	3.8		-207.8	3405.0	
1984	11.89	3.9		-185.4	3777.2	
1985	9.64	3.8		-212.3	4038.7	
1986	7.06	1.1		-221.2	4268.6	
1987	7.68	4.4		-149.8	4539.9	
1988	8.26	4.4		-155.2	4900.4	
1989	8.55	4.6		-152.5	5250.8	
1990	8.26	6.1		-221.4	5546.1	
1991	6.82	3.1		-269.2	5724.8	
1992	5.30	2.9		-290.4	6020.2	
1993	4.44	2.7		-255.1	6343.3	
1994	6.27	2.7		-203.2	6738.4	

Source: <u>The Economic Report of the President</u>, Transmitted to the Congress, February, 1995.

Real Rate of Interest (%) Figure 23-1

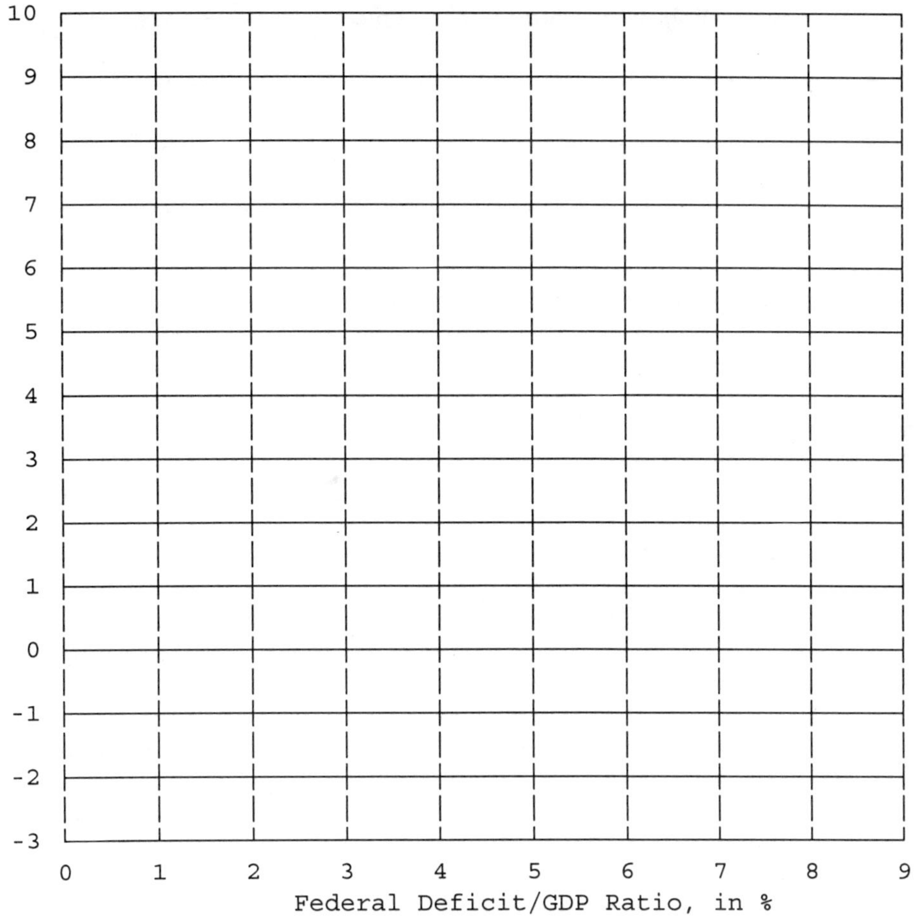
10
9
8
7
6
5
4
3
2
1
0
-1
-2
-3
0 1 2 3 4 5 6 7 8 9
Federal Deficit/GDP Ratio, in %

If the crowding-out hypothesis were correct, what kind of relationship would we expect to see among the data above?

____

____

____

Given the information provided by Figure 23-1, what would you conclude about the crowding-out effect?

____

____

____

If a federal deficit of six percent of GDP were projected, what real interest rate would you anticipate on the basis of the information contained in your graph? How much confidence would you have in that estimate?

_____

_____

_____

The Effect of the Balanced-Budget Amendment

Assume you are given the following economic model of the economy:

GDP -- given
Personal Income = 0.80 X GDP
Personal Tax Receipts = -150 + (Marginal Tax Rate) X (Personal Income)
Government Expenditures = 0.20 X GDP
Government Deficit/Surplus = Personal Tax Receipts - Government Expenditures
Government Deficit/Surplus as a Percent of GDP = (Government Deficit/Surplus/GDP) X 100

Given the formulas above, calculate personal income, personal tax receipts, government expenditures, the government deficit/surplus, and the government deficit/surplus as a percent of total GDP.

Table 23-2

Time Period	1	2	3	4	5	6	7	8	9	10
Gross Domestic Product	5000	5075	5175	5300	5500	5480	5450	5400	5300	5150
Personal Income										
Marginal Tax Rate	0.26	0.26	0.26	0.26	0.26	0.26	0.26	0.26	0.26	0.26
Personal Tax Receipts										
Government Expenditures										
Government Deficit/Surplus										
Government Deficit/Surplus as a Percent of GDP										

Explain how the federal budget acts as an automatic stabilizer on the economy.

Would the automatic stabilizer characteristic of the federal budget be enhanced or dampened if a "flat tax" of 19 percent for taxpayers of all income brackets were adopted?

Explain how the data contained in Table 23-2 illustrate that concept.

Explain in general terms what would have to be done in the above scenario if a balanced-budget amendment were passed.

It has been said that if the balanced-budget amendment were passed, the federal budget would change from being counter-cyclical (moving against the business cycle) to pro-cyclical (intensifying the business cycle, magnifying both recessions and inflationary situations). Explain.

True/False Statements

Indicate whether you think the statements below are true or false. These questions are designed to make you think about the concepts presented in the text. There may not be any easy clear-cut answers. Some thoughts about the answers are presented at the end of the chapter.

1.) _____ If the balanced-budget amendment were passed, business cycles would fluctuate more than they have in the past.

2.) _____ The crowding-out effect occurs when banks limit their credit during periods of expansion and high credit demand.

3.) _____ The response of international investors intensifies the effects of expansionary monetary policy.

4.) _____ Treasury borrowing from the public or from commercial banks is less inflationary than the creation of new bank reserves by the Fed.

5.) _____ Fear of inflation is the main reason that the Fed is reluctant to monetize the deficit.

6.) _____ Because of the crowding-out effect, monetarists believe that budget deficits don't really matter, i.e., they don't stimulate the economy.

7.) _____ If society saves more of its income, in anticipation of higher future taxes associated with a budget deficit, it is as if a budget deficit had been financed with current taxes.

8.) _____ If the government is running a budget deficit, it is conducting an expansionary fiscal policy.

9.) _____ The government is engaging in a neutral fiscal policy if the budget is balanced at full employment.

10.) _____ Economists are generally in agreement that continuing budget deficits will be a burden to future generations.

Multiple Choice-Questions

Select the "best" answer from the alternatives provided.

1.) The crowding-out effect
   a. offsets the effects of expansionary fiscal policy.
   b. is the term applied when fiscal deficits actually reduce the level of income.
   c. occurs when government public sector spending is replaced by private sector spending.
   d. occurs when taxes crowd out private sector spending.

2.) If a government deficit results in higher domestic interest rates,
   a. private sector borrowing will increase to pay for the higher interest rates.
   b. private sector borrowing will be largely unaffected, since government borrowing does not affect private borrowing.
   c. private sector borrowing may decrease, particularly when the economy is in a recession.
   d. private sector borrowing may decrease, particulary when the economy is near full employment.

3.) The federal Reserve is said to "monetize the deficit" when
   a. it purchases government securities on the open market.
   b. it sells government securities on the open market.
   c. it purchases government securities directly from the Treasury.
   d. it creates new member bank reserves.
   e. both (c) and (d) apply.

4. The Ricardian equivalence holds that
   a. people anticipate the future inflationary consequences of a deficit and consume more before the inflation begins.
   b. society believes that future generations will bear the tax burden of a current deficit.
   c. society will consume more in anticipation of future higher taxes when the government runs a deficit.
   d. society will save more in anticipation of future higher taxes when the government runs a deficit.

5.) If a structural or high employment deficit exists,
   a. there is no way to determine if the government's fiscal stance is expansionary.
   b. the government's fiscal stance is always expansionary.
   c. the actual budget status could be in surplus, balanced, or in deficit.
   d. the government's fiscal stance is always contractionary.

6.) Which of the following is a fallacious argument about the national debt?
   a. The national debt redistributes income from middle class taxpayers to upper income bond holders.
   b. Foreign-held debt results in more of an economic burden than domestically-held debt.
   c. Higher taxes needed to pay for interest on the debt could result in incentive problems.
   d. Future generations will be substantially harmed by the high level of public debt we are currently incurring.

7.) If a balanced-budget amendment is adopted,
   a. fiscal policy will continue to play an important role in economic policy-making.
   b. fiscal policy will no longer have any economic impact on the economy.
   c. fiscal policy will change from being pro-cyclical to counter-cyclical.
   d. fiscal policy will change from being counter-cyclical to pro-cyclical.

8. Assuming that the crowding-out effect is valid, which of the following best describes the relationship that exists between government deficits and interest rates?
   a. Interest rates will typically fall, resulting in an outflow of foreign investment funds.
   b. Interest rates will typically rise, increasing domestic savings.
   c. Interest rates will typically not be affected, since such changes are involved with monetary policy.
   d. Interest rates will typically increase, resulting in a decrease in interest-sensitive spending.

Discussion Questions

1.) Using the concept of the structural high employment budget, how would you explain to someone who hasn't had any economics that the current government budget deficit is not expansionary and may, in fact, be contractionary?

2.) Discuss the implications for the future if the proportion of the national debt that is owned by foreigners continues to increase. If foreigners are willing to invest in the United States, purchasing government securities, isn't that a good for our economy?

3.) Do you think it makes any difference if government deficit spending goes towards people-oriented social programs or for infrastructure projects or for high technology research and development projects?

4.) A recent report indicated that the United States had the greatest degree of income inequity of any of the developed countries. Indicate how a rapidly increasing national debt could possibly contribute to that degree of inequity.

5.) In a recent debate over the balanced-budget amendment, someone stated that we shouldn't amend the constitution to add a provision which would indicate how the annual budgetary affairs of the government should be conducted. Furthermore, if Congress wanted to balance the budget, all they would have to do is vote for that result and it would be accomplished. Why do you think so many people were arguing that the amendment was an absolute necessity for balancing the budget?

6.) How do Keynesian and monetarist perspectives on the crowding-out effect tie in with their theories about the way the economy works?

7.) Why do you think the Fed has not been very interested in monetizing the Treasury's debt through direct borrowing?

Answers and Solutions to Problems and Exercises

Completing Statements from the List of Terms

1.) Structural Surplus
2.) Balanced-Budget Amendment
3.) Ricardian Equivalence
4.) Structural Deficit
5.) Crowding-Out Effect
6.) Monetizing the Deficit

Problems

A Closer Look at the Crowding Out Effect

Table 23-1

Year	Three Year Treasury Bill Rate (in Percent)	Rate of Inflation (in Percent)	Real Treasury Bill Rate (in Percent)	Federal Government Deficit (in Billions)	Gross Domestic Product (in Billions)	Ratio of Federal Government Deficit to Gross Domestic Product (in Percent)
1980	11.55	12.5	-0.95	-73.8	2708.0	2.73
1981	14.44	8.9	5.54	-79.0	3030.6	2.61
1982	12.92	3.8	9.12	-128.0	3149.6	4.06
1983	10.45	3.8	6.65	-207.8	3405.0	6.10
1984	11.89	3.9	7.99	-185.4	3777.2	4.91
1985	9.64	3.8	5.84	-212.3	4038.7	5.26
1986	7.06	1.1	5.96	-221.2	4268.6	5.18
1987	7.68	4.4	3.28	-149.8	4539.9	3.30
1988	8.26	4.4	3.86	-155.2	4900.4	3.17
1989	8.55	4.6	3.95	-152.5	5250.8	2.90
1990	8.26	6.1	2.16	-221.4	5546.1	3.99
1991	6.82	3.1	3.72	-269.2	5724.8	4.70
1992	5.30	2.9	2.4	-290.4	6020.2	4.82
1993	4.44	2.7	1.74	-255.1	6343.3	4.02
1994	6.27	2.7	3.57	-203.2	6738.4	3.02

Source: *The Economic Report of the President*, Transmitted to the Congress, February,

Real Interest Rates and the Federal Deficit -- The Crowding-Out Effect

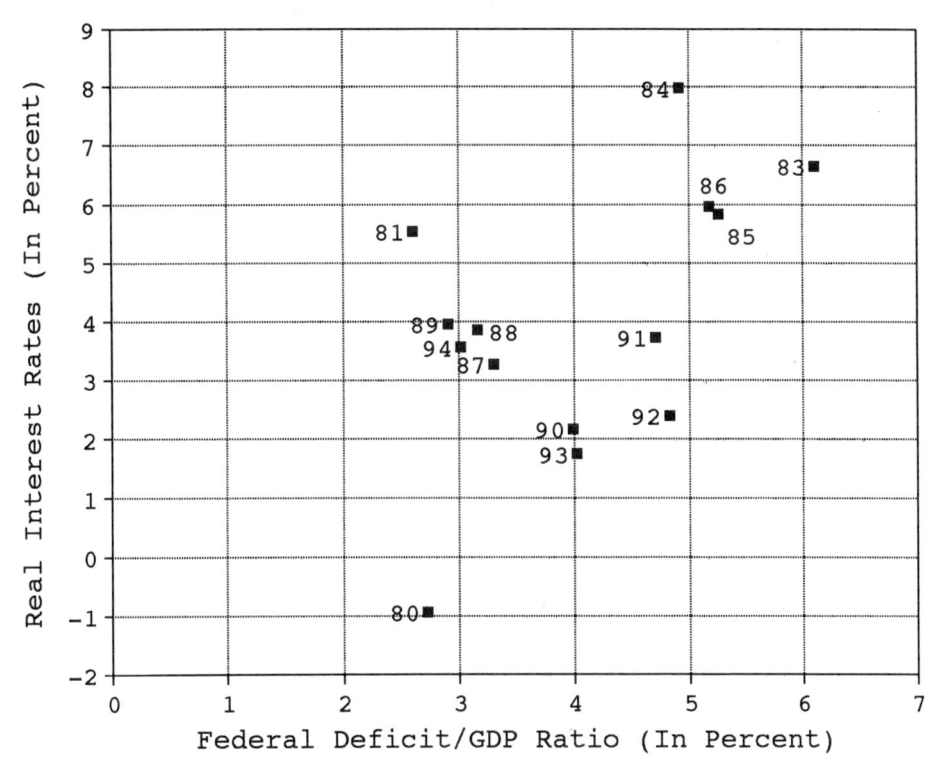

[Scatter plot with Federal Deficit/GDP Ratio (In Percent) on x-axis (0 to 7) and Real Interest Rates (In Percent) on y-axis (-2 to 9), showing data points labeled by year from 80 to 94.]

If the crowding-out hypothesis were correct, what kind of relationship would we expect to see among the data above? **The data should show that real interest rates rise as the deficit/GDP ratio increases. Unfortunately, it is not possible to keep all the other factors that affect real interest rates constant.**

Given the information provided by Figure 23-1, what would you conclude about the crowding-out effect? **It would appear that the crowding-out effect is quite weak. The data do not lend themselves to a clearly defined postive relationship between the two variables. Statistically, there is a weak, positive correlation between real interest rates and federal deficits.**

If a federal deficit of six percent of GDP were projected, what real interest rate would you anticipate on the basis of your graph above? How much confidence would you have in that estimate? **Six percent. Not a great deal of confidence -- there is a lot of variation (statistical noise caused by other factors other than the federal deficit/GDP ratio) contained in the data.**

The Effect of the Balanced Budget Amendment

Time Period	1	2	3	4	5	6	7	8	9	10
Gross Domestic Product	5000	5075	5175	5300	5500	5480	5450	5400	5300	5150
Personal Income	4000	4060	4140	4240	4400	4384	4360	4320	4240	4120
Marginal Tax Rate	0.26	0.26	0.26	0.26	0.26	0.26	0.26	0.26	0.26	0.26
Personal Tax Receipts	890.0	905.6	926.4	952.4	994.0	989.8	983.6	973.2	952.4	921.2
Government Expenditures	1000	1015	1035	1060	1100	1096	1090	1080	1060	1030
Government Deficit/Surplus	-110.0	-109.4	-108.6	-107.6	-106.0	-106.2	-106.4	-106.8	-107.6	-108.8
Government Deficit/Surplus as a Percent of GDP	-2.2%	-2.2%	-2.1%	-2.0%	-1.9%	-1.9%	-2.0%	-2.0%	-2.0%	-2.1%

Explain how the federal budget acts as an automatic stabilizer on the economy. **As nominal income decreases in a period of recession, tax revenues fall, creating a larger deficit. The larger deficit offsets, to some degree, the fall in income. As inflation increases nominal incomes, tax receipts increase, moving the budget towards a surplus position. Since surpluses are a leakage, the inflationary increase in incomes is partially offset.**

Would the automatic stabilizer characteristic of the federal budget be enhanced or dampened if a "flat tax" of 19 % for taxpayers of all income brackets were adopted? **Enhanced. While tax revenues would still rise and fall with changes in nominal incomes, the lack of progressivity in a flat tax scheme means that there is less of a tendency to stabilize the economy.**

Explain how the data contained in Table 23-2 illustrate that concept. **As income rose through time period 5, the budget deficit fell, creating less of an injection into the economy. As income fell from period 6 on, the budget deficit increased, creating more of an injection.**

Explain in general terms what would have to be done in the above scenario if a balanced-budget amendment were passed. **When nominal incomes are increasing, tax revenues are rising, so either tax rates must be decreased or government expenditures increased in order to have the budget balanced. When nominal incomes are decreasing, tax revenues are falling, so either tax rates must be increased or government spending cut so that the budget can be balanced.**

It has been said that if the balanced-budget amendment were passed, the federal budget would change from being counter-cyclical (moving against the business cycle) to pro-cyclical (intensifying the business cycle, magnifying both recessions and inflationary situations). Explain. **The budget changes from being an automatic stabilizer with changes in the deficit automatically offsetting recessions and inflationary conditions to a budget mechanism in which recessions are intensified by required tax increases, or government spending decreases and inflationary situations are fueled by tax cuts and/or government spending increases.**

True/False Statements

1.) **True.** A balanced-budget amendment would change the government budget deficit into a pro-cyclical mechanism instead of a counter-cyclical mechanism. If the economy goes into a recession with the balanced-budget amendment, taxes will decrease and the Congress will have to either raise tax rates or cut government spending in order to balance the budget, either of which will intensify the recession.

2.) **False.** It occurs when the government borrows in the private credit markets to finance its deficit, thus raising the interest rate and crowding-out some private sector interest-sensitive spending.

3.) **True.** As domestic interest rates decrease, there will be less demand for the dollar by international investors, and the value of the dollar will fall. That, in turn, will raise U.S. exports which will enhance domestic GDP -- an additional stimulus associated with an expansionary montetary policy.

4.) **True.** In both cases, borrowing from the public or commercial banks would result in firms and households spending less than they would do otherwise (either a full or partial offset). In contrast, the creation of new bank reserves does not result in less private spending.

5.) **True.** Monetizing the debt increases the money supply, and the Fed risks starting an inflationary wage-price spiral if too much money is created in a particular time period.

6.) **True.** Many monetarists believe in a full crowding-out effect, i.e., the deficit crowds out private spending on a one-to-one basis. If that occurs, the deficit represents merely an increase in public sector spending and a decrease in private sector spending with no net effect.

7.) **It Depends!** Your response depends on whether or not you believe that the Ricardian equivalence holds. The empirical evidence for the U.S. experience seems to indicate that society does not behave in this fashion.

8.) **False.** Whether or not the budget stance is expansionary doesn't depend on the actual or current budget status but rather, what the budget would be if the economy were at full employment. It can be considered to be expansionary only if the budget is at a deficit at full employment.

9.) **True.** Refer #8.

10.) **False.** Although future generations will have to tax themselves to pay off the national debt, they are also the ones that will receive the payments. One has to remember that there are two sides of the debt issue -- an asset and a liability side. Future generations will be the beneficiaries of trillions of dollars worth of assets that will be passed down from this generation. Is that a burden? Hardly. A more likely burden will, that they will not have the standard of living that they might have had if the large deficit hadn't decreased investment, economic growth, and productivity.

Multiple-Choice

1.) c   2.) d   3.) a   4.) d   5.) c   6.) d

7.) a   8.) b

Discussion Questions

1.) Perhaps the best way would be to tell them the federal budget normally goes into a deficit when a recession occurs. The key to whether the government's fiscal stance is expansionary or contractionary revolves around the condition of the budget when the economy is fully employed. For instance, during the 1981-82 recession, one of the worst on record, there was a significant amount of unemployment and at the same time, there was a large budget deficit. Had there been full employment, the budget would have been fairly close to being balanced. If at full employment, there would have been a surplus, it would be difficult to argue that the fiscal stance of the government was in fact expansionary.

2.) When the debt is owned by a country's own citizens, payments on the debt remain in the domestic economy. Such payments are essentially a transfer payment. When payment on the debt is made to foreigners, it constitutes a leakage from the income stream, causing an imbalance between AD and AS, and results in a decline in the flow of income.

Regarding the second part of the question, an inflow of foreign capital can take the place of inadequate domestic savings. If that capital inflow is linked to productive investment projects, the economy will have increased its capital stock and will produce more output in the future than otherwise would have been the case. But there is a foreign claim on ownership that may some day be invoked.

3.) In terms of the future output of the economy, it makes a significant difference. If the deficit enhances the economy's productive capacity, there will be a greater capacity to pay off the debt in the future, as opposed to deficit spending on social programs. That is not to say that spending on social programs is unimportant, but rather there are different economic ramifications of such spending.

4.) Holders of the debt who receive payments and the taxpayers who make such payments are not the same groups of people. Owners of government bonds tend to be more affluent than taxpayers, so payments related to the national debt tend to redistribute money from the middle class to those in the higher income classes. If the debt becomes large enough that could contribute to a deterioration in the income equity that exists in our society.

5.) One could make a case that the constitution should not be involved in such mundane budgetary matters, that it should limit itself to the most important rights of individuals and the appropriate spheres of influence of the different governmental bodies. While Congress could enact a balanced-budget, it appears that members of Congress are unable to do this for fear of alienating constituencies of voters which might undermine their chances for reelection. Thus, if they had a balanced-budget amendment which would force them to make the required spending cuts, they could deal with this difficult issue more effectively. However, it should be noted that some people who are in favor of the amendment do not want the courts to tell Congress what to do if they can not balance the budget. Now that makes for an interesting dilemma!

6.) Monetarists believe that fiscal policy is ineffective, and the crowding-out effect provides a rationale for that belief. If there is a full crowding-out effect, then there would be no net stimulus associated with a government deficit. Keynesians, on the other hand, believe that government deficits will cause the level of equilbrium income to increase and that private investment will not be significantly affected by the deficit. Since changes in interest rates cause changes in interest-sensitive private sector spending, the interest rate becomes the target variable in a Keynesian framework.

7.) When the Fed monetizes the Treasury's debt by buying its bonds directly from the Treasury, the supply of money increases by some multiple of the amount of the securities purchase. Since the Fed is concerned with keeping inflation under control, it is wary about increasing the money supply at too fast a rate. Such purchases would normally make it more difficult for the Fed to attain whatever goal it had set for inflation.

Summary

The questions posed by the levels of public and private debt continue to be among the most controversial facing our society. At the federal level, legislative attempts (Gramm-Rudman-Hollings) to balance the budget have largely failed as have efforts to pass a balanced-budget amendment. Complicating any efforts to achieve a balanced-budget has been the opposition to tax increases. In spite of their commitment to a balanced-budget as spelled out in their "Contract with America", Republicans (as well as Democrats with a somewhat different plan) have continued to press for a sizeable tax cut which would greatly complicate any attempt to balance the budget.

The impact of the large and continued deficits on the private sector is not clear. The crowding-out effect appears to be operative only when the economy is near or at full employment, and even then the effect is ambiguous because of inflows of foreign capital that follow higher interest rates. Of greater concern may be the fact that tax rates have to be higher than they would otherwise because interest payments constitute a significant and increasing proportion of the federal budget (it was the fourth largest spending component in 1993). Federal deficits absorb a substantial proportion of the country's savings, and our lower levels of investment spending (as measured as a percent of GDP) continue to adversely impact economic growth and productivity trends. A significantly lower future standard of living (compared with what we could have achieved based on previous growth and productivity trends) may be the true cost of living beyond our means.

Chapter 24
The Long Run:
Stagflation and Long Term Unemployment

Overview of the Chapter

The relationship that exists between inflation and unemployment is one of the most important for an economy. Economists have long known that increases in spending, once full employment has been achieved, would result in inflation. The Phillips curve relationship (circa late 1950s) seemed to indicate that many modern economies started to inflate well before they reached full employment. This caused a dilemma for economic policy-makers, since they were forced to choose between the goals of full employment and price stability. The original Phillips curve trade-off meant that price stability could be achieved only at the cost of excessive amounts of unemployment and that the attainment of full employment was associated with higher-than-wanted levels of inflation.

Unfortunately, the 1970s ushered in a new problem, stagflation -- simultaneously rising prices and increased unemployment. Had the Phillips curve shifted to the right? If so, what factors had caused it to shift? Was there an alternative conceptual framework that could explain the changing inflation-unemployment relationship?

Stagflation can be easily illustrated within the AD/AS macro model -- a leftward shift in the aggregate supply curve results in an increase in the price level and an increase in the level of unemployment. Supply shocks to the economy, such as an increase in the price of oil or a drought which causes food prices to rise, are recent examples. Policy-makers can reduce the unemployment associated with a decrease in aggregate supply through expansionary fiscal and/or monetary policy. However, such measures intensify inflationary pressures in the economy. If the inflationary asepcts of a decrease in aggregate supply are addressed instead, then there will be an increase in the rate of unemployment and an increased risk of a recession.

Incorporating the concept of the potential level of output into the inflation/unemployment analysis provides some useful perspectives. Whenever the actual level of output is lower than the potential level of output, the rate of unemployment will exceed the natural rate of unemployment. Over the long run, the rate of unemployment will be consistent with the natural rate of unemployment. Through the use of expansionary fiscal and monetary policy, it is possible to decrease the rate of unemployment in the short run, moving along a curve similar to the original Phillips curve. However, levels of unemployment that are below the natural rate of unemployment are not sustainable and will result in increased inflation. With the introduction of more inflation into the economic system, there will be a change in inflationary expectations by both workers and firms, and more inflation will be ratcheted into the economy over time:

The trade-off that exists between inflation and unemployment exists only in a short-run setting. In the long run, a reduction in the rate of unemployment can come about only through a reduction in the natural rate of unemployment. Since the 1970s, the natural rate of unemployment has been increasing as more women entered the labor force. Their tendency to move in and out of the labor force more frequently raised the natural rate as have large numbers of teenagers who change jobs more often than other demographic groups. In addition, greater technological displacement has increased the structural component of unemployment.

As pervasive as these trends have been, recently there has been some discussion about whether or not the natural rate of unemployment has decreased. Labor bottlenecks have not developed in spite of low inflation rates. Wage increases have been moderate, even though the unemployment rates have been below six %. Competitive labor market conditions have moderated wage increases. Demographic changes in the age composition of the labor force have also tended to reduce the unemployment rate. Economic policies which impact unemployment benefits and duration also affect the natural rate of unemployment.

Learning Objectives

After completing this chapter, you should be sure that you are able to:

- understand the short-run Phillips curve and its implications for economic policy-making.

- understand the rationale for the vertical long-run Phillips curve, its relationship to the natural rate of unemployment, and its policy implications.

- understand the role that inflationary expectations play in the inflation/unemployment relationship.

- describe the effect of supply shocks on the economy, how they can lead to stagflation, and how stagflation affects the inflation/unemployment trade-off.

- explain how accomodating fiscal/monetary policy in response to supply shocks can itensify inflationary pressures in the economy.

- explain how contractionary fiscal/monetary policy in response to supply shocks can increase unemployment and the risk of a recession.

- understand the concepts of frictional and structural unemployment and their relationship to the natural rate of unemployment.

- describe the adjustment process that occurs when actual output differs from the potential level of output, particularly in terms of dynamic effects on the rate of inflation and the rate of unemployment.

Self Evaluation

List of Terms

Frictional Unemployment
Hysteresis
Natural Rate of Unemployment
Phillips Curve
Real-Wage Structural Unemployment
Structural Unemployment
Supply Shock
Wage Drift

For the statements below, fill in the term from the list above which provides the best fit.

1.) As initially presented, the _____ suggested a short-run trade-off existed between inflation and unemployment, the two most important macroeconomic goals.

2.) An increase in the cost of an essential imported raw material would result in a _____, causing a decrease in aggregate supply.

3.) _____ provides an explanation of how higher wage agreements in one sector of the economy can be spread throughout the economy.

4.) If members of the labor force start to change jobs more frequently, _____ would increase.

5.) A retail employee who was laid off because computer automation made his or her job redundant would be an example of _____.

6.) _____ refers to a situation in which prolonged unemployment during a recession would lead to greater long-term unemployment.

7.) Over the long run, society finds it difficult to reduce the rate of unemployment below the _____.

8.) _____ can occur if employers decline to hire more workers when wages fall because of high employment-related costs such as unemployment insurance.

Problems

Examining the Phillips Curve Relationship

The Phillips curve plots an economy's performance with respect to its two most important goals -- price stability and full employment. Initially, the empirical data supported the view that the two economic goals were incompatible with each other, i.e., full employment was associated with higher than acceptable rates of inflation, and acceptable rates of inflation were associated with unacceptably high levels of unemployment. The empirical data from the 1950s and 1960s seemed to support that view of the economy.

Data from the 1970s and early 1980s appeared to support the view that the Phillips curve had shifted to the right, away from the origin, resulting in a worse trade-off between inflation and unemployment. Indeed, a new word was coined to describe this dismal situation -- "stagflation" (a stagnant, high unemployment economy with higher than acceptable rates of inflation). While it was possible to explain why the Phillips curve relationship had deteriorated, most of the factors mentioned were of the after-the-fact kind, meaning that they had no predictive power (they could explain the deteriorating relationship, but it was not possible to examine the variables beforehand and use them to predict what changes were likely to occur in the Phillips curve.[1]

The newest conceptualization of the Phillips curve relationship is the one discussed in Chapter 24 of your text, a relationship characterized by a vertical long-run Phillips curve positioned at the natural rate of unemployment. The traditional short-run Phillips curve segment with its negative slope can occur when AD is increased and the inflation rate increases unexpectedly, catching people by surprise. Once everyone takes into account the inflation by increasing their wage demands and their prices, unemployment returns to the natural rate of unemployment, but at a higher rate of inflation than before.

Given the data below, plot the Phillips curve relationship for the three separate time periods: 1958 - 1968, 1969 - 1978, 1979 - 1994. The GDP deflator was used as measure of inflation instead of the CPI; therefore your graphs will look somewhat different from those in your text.

---

[1] Two of the factors thought to be responsible for shifting the Phillips curve were:

(1) increasing welfare expenditures and other kinds of safety net expenditures (such programs maintained the income of the unemployed, thus maintaining AD during periods of recession, preventing downward pressure on prices). Thus, an increase in safety net expenditures results in a worse inflation/unemployment trade-off.

(2) an increase in the services sector of the economy which has historically been more inflation-prone than the goods sector, since productivity increases have been more difficult to achieve in the services sector. Thus, as services have become more significant in our economy, we would expect a worse trade-off between these two macroeconomic goals.

Table 24-1

Year	Rate of Inflation GDP Deflator (in Percent)	Rate of Unemployment Civilian Workers (in Percent)	Year	Rate of Inflation GDP Deflator (in Percent)	Rate of Unemployment Civilian Workers (in Percent)
1958	2.0	6.8	1977	6.9	7.1
1959	2.8	5.5	1978	7.9	6.1
1960	1.6	5.5	1979	8.6	5.8
1961	1.2	6.7	1980	9.5	7.1
1962	2.3	5.5	1981	10.0	7.6
1963	1.1	5.7	1982	6.2	9.7
1964	1.8	5.2	1983	4.1	9.6
1965	2.5	4.5	1984	4.4	7.5
1966	3.5	3.8	1985	3.7	7.2
1967	3.1	3.8	1986	2.6	7.0
1968	5.0	3.6	1987	3.2	6.2
1969	5.0	3.5	1988	3.9	5.5
1970	5.4	4.9	1989	4.4	5.3
1971	5.4	5.9	1990	4.4	5.5
1972	4.6	5.6	1991	3.9	6.7
1973	6.4	4.9	1992	2.9	7.4
1974	8.7	5.6	1993	2.5	6.8
1975	9.6	8.5	1994	2.1	6.1
1976	6.3	7.7			

Source: Economic Report of the President, Transmitted to the Congress, February, 1995.

Figure 24-1

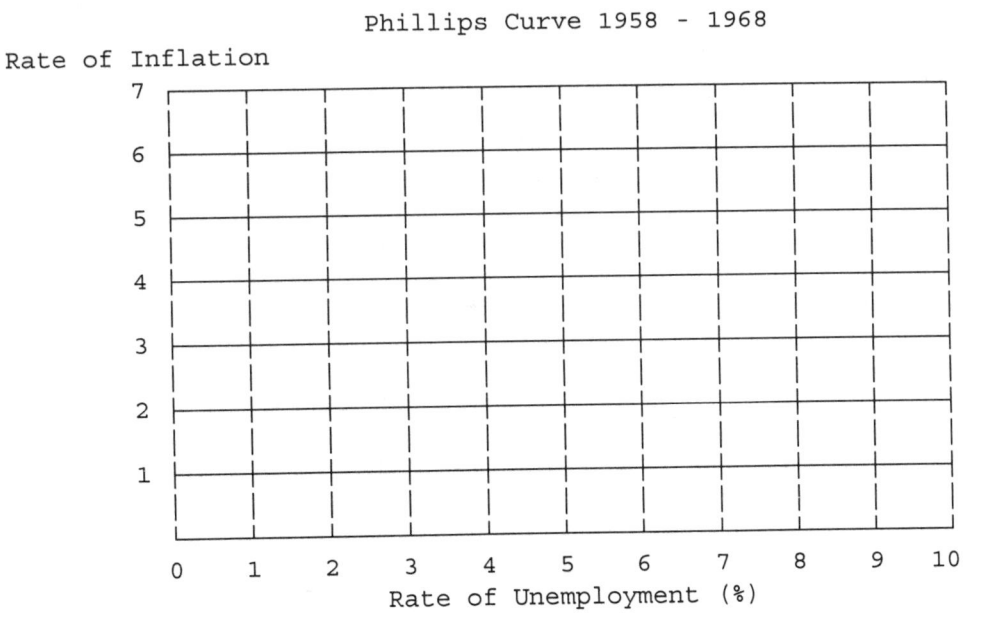

Phillips Curve 1958 - 1968

Rate of Inflation

Rate of Unemployment (%)

As carefully as you can, draw a trend line which represents the relationship between inflation and unemployment (a line which best approximates the data which you have plotted -- one which minimizes the vertical distances between the line and the various points).

On the basis of that trend line, what rate of inflation would you expect if the rate of unemployment decreased to two %? _____

On the basis of that trend line, what rate of unemployment would you expect if the rate of inflation decreased to one %? _____

If your trend line approximates the inflation/unemployment relationship for the economy, what position on the trend line would you recommend the economy try to attain?

_____

_____

Figure 24-2

Phillips Curve 1969 - 1978

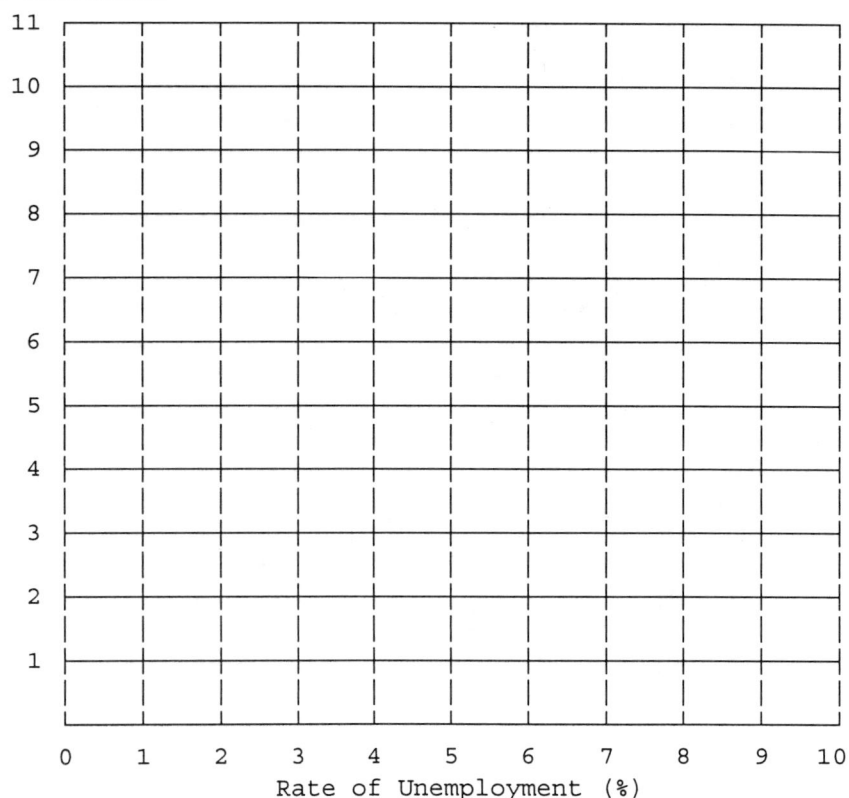

Rate of Inflation

[Blank grid plotted from 0 to 10 on x-axis (Rate of Unemployment (%)) and 1 to 11 on y-axis]

Rate of Unemployment (%)

In the preceding diagram, which sequential sets of points (which years) illustrate stagflation?

_____

In the preceding diagram, which sequential sets of points (which years) illustrate the traditional short-run inflation/unemployment relationship?

_____

Describe the pattern that you obtain when the data observations are connected in a sequential fashion (by year).

_____

_____

The pattern you have observed can be divided into several component parts:

(A) initially there is an unanticipated increase in AD, and employment increases as a result of decreases in the real wage -- the traditional negatively sloped short-run portion of the Phillips curve.

(B) increasing unemployment and rising prices as workers become aware of the reduction in the real wage and attempt to raise prices -- the Phillips curve is upward sloping. Typically there would be some attempt to control the rising rate of inflation somewhere on the B portion of the curve. Inflationary expectations play a role here.

(C) As a result of the policy actions taken against inflation, the inflation rate starts to fall and unemployment rises. Inflationary expectations are still high and fail to reflect the gradually decreasing inflation rate.

(D) Workers begin to accept lower real wages, and unemployment starts to decrease, and inflation continues to fall.

Referring to the diagram for 1969 - 1978, see if you can identify and label the components of the policy cycle shown above.

Draw a vertical line on Figure 24-2 which corresponds to the LRAS. Label it U_n (the natural rate of unemployment). Although there may be exceptions, the LRAS should divide the observations into two groups: one to the left of the LRAS in which the rate of inflation will be increasing and one to the right of the LRAS in which the rate of inflation should be decreasing.

Figure 24-3

Phillips Curve 1979 - 1994

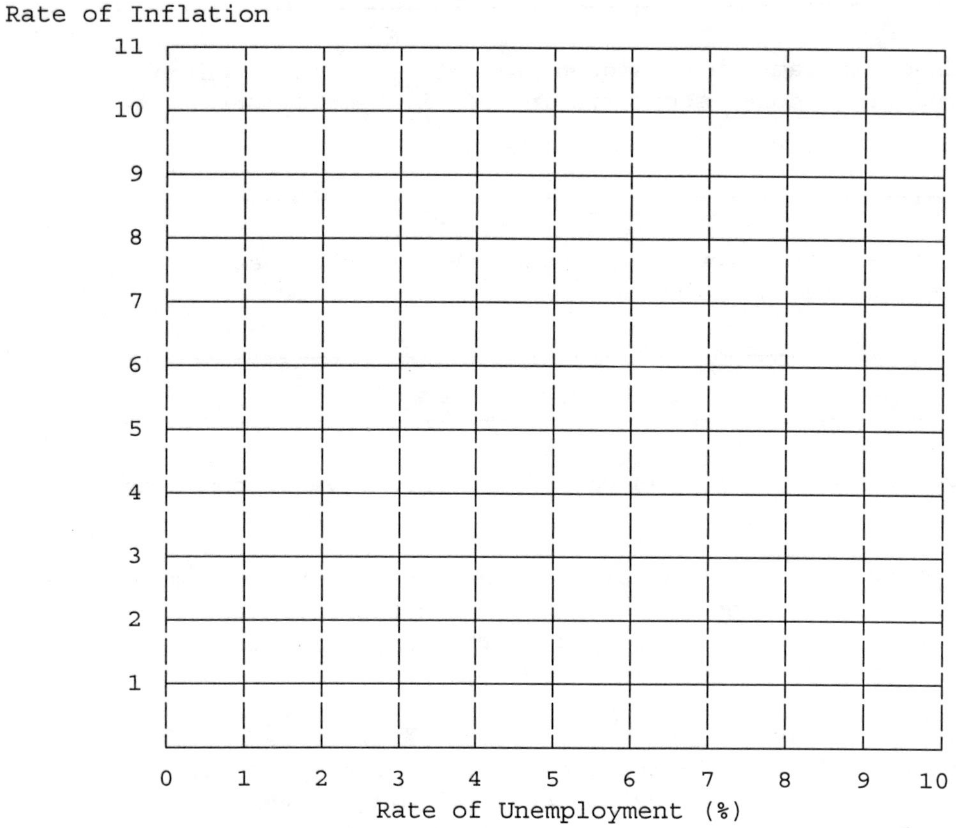

In the diagram above, which sequential sets of points (which years) illustrate stagflation?

____

In the diagram above, which sequential sets of points (which years) illustrate the traditional short-run inflation/unemployment relationship?

____

Describe the pattern that you obtain when the data observations are connected in a sequential fashion (by year).

____

____

Based on the sequential patterns that you have identified in your graphs, what implications might be drawn from the Phillips curve observations about the 1992 elections and Bush being reelected?

____

True/False Statements

Indicate whether you think the statements below are true or false. These questions are designed to make you think about the concepts presented in the text. There may not be any easy clear-cut answers. Some thoughts about the answers are presented at the end of the chapter.

1.) _____ As the economy moves towards full employment, labor bottlenecks and shortages result in an increase in the price level.

2.) _____ The original short-run Phillips curve suggested that less unemployment can be achieved only at the cost of more inflation.

3.) _____ A stable short-run Phillips curve cannot occur in the presence of changes in the aggregate supply (AS) curve.

4.) _____ With an increase in the world price of petroleum, the short-run Phillips curve would be expected to shift left.

5.) _____ An upward shift in aggregate demand (AD) can result in stagflation.

6.) _____ If accommodating monetary/fiscal policies are used in response to a supply shock, both inflation and unemployment can be reduced.

7.) _____ Wage drift could be lessened with annual nationwide labor negotiations in which all major firms and unions participate.

8.) _____ The expectation of additional inflation by both workers and producers can cause inflation to accelerate.

9.) _____ Structural unemployment would tend to be worse if workers were strongly attached to the local area where they lived and worked.

10.) _____ Over the long run, the rate of unemployment cannot be permanently reduced below the natural rate of unemployment.

Multiple-Choice Questions

Select the "best" answer from the alternatives provided.

1.) During a period of stagflation,
   a. appropriate macro policy is to implement expansionary fiscal and monetary policy.
   b. appropriate macro policy is to implement contractionary fiscal and monetary policy.
   c. efforts to address the unemployment problem will intensify the inflationary pressures.
   d. efforts to address the inflation problem will also help with the unemployment problem.

2.) The original short-run Phillips curve
   a. suggested that inflation is not a problem until full employment is reached.
   b. indicated that inflation and unemployment were directly linked together, the higher the inflation, the higher the unemployment.
   c. suggested a constantly changing relationship between inflation and unemployment.
   d. indicated that inflation and unemployment were inversely associated with each other, the higher the inflation, the lower the rate of unemployment.

```
Rate of Inflation
 |        .       .D
 |                 .
 |       A .        .E
 |               .    .
 |            B .
 |                 .   .F
 |                C .     .
 |
 |_____ Rate of Unemployment
```

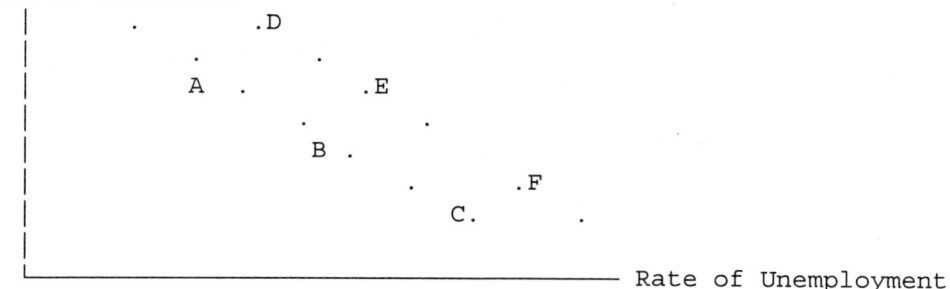

Refer to the diagram above for the next two questions.

3.) If the economy is currently positioned at point B, what will happen if an expansionary fiscal and monetary program is initiated?
   a. The economy will move from point B to point A.
   b. The economy will move from point B to point C.
   c. The economy will move from point B to point E.
   d. The economy will move from point B to point F.

4. Again referring to the above diagram, assume the economy is currently positioned at point B, and a prolonged drought occurs which significantly raises the prices of agricultural products. The most likely movement will be from
   a. point B to point A.   b. point B to point C.
   c. point B to point E.   d. point B to point F.

5.) In terms of the AD/AS theoretical model, stagflation is the result of
   a. an increase in AD.
   b. an increase in both AD and AS.
   c. an increase in AS.
   d. a decrease in AS.
   e. a decrease in both AD and AS.

6.) If the government attempts to accommodate a supply shock to the economy by implementing policies which increase AD, then
   a. the rate of unemployment would decrease, but the rate of inflation would increase.
   b. the rate of unemployment would decrease, and the rate of inflation would decrease.
   c. the rate of unemployment would increase, and the rate of inflation would increase.
   d. the rate of unemployment would increase, but the rate of inflation would decrease.

7.) In comparing the short-run and long-run Phillips curves,
   a. the short-run Phillips curve suggests there is a trade-off between inflation and unemployment, while the long-run curve does not.
   b. according to the short-run Phillips curve, it is possible to reduce the rate of unemployment below the natural rate of unemployment, while the long-run curve indicates that is not possible in the long run.
   c. the short-run Phillips curve gives the illusion that expansionary economic policies are effective in reducing the level of unemployment, while the long-run curve suggests that such policies are ineffective over time.
   d. all of the above.

8.) An increase in frictional unemployment
   a. has no effect on the natural rate of unemployment.
   b. will increase the natural rate of unemployment.
   c. will decrease the natural rate of unemployment.
   d. occurs only when real GDP falls.

9.) Structural unemployment
   a. is associated with increased mobility of the labor force and more frequent job change.
   b. is associated with declines in real GDP.
   c. occurs when the skills of the unemployed don't match the skills required for existing job openings.
   d. occurs when a smaller proportion of each age group enters the labor force.

10.) Which of the following result in a decrease in a natural rate of unemployment?
   a. an increase in unemployment benefits.
   b. a larger proportion of teenagers and young adults in the labor force.
   c. workers gaining greater technical knowledge and computer skills.
   d. less in-migration of unskilled labor.

Discussion Questions

1.) It has been said that Europe has tried to implement a more humane and caring form of capitalism, providing its workers with greater job security by making it more difficult for employers to fire workers and by providing extensive and liberal benefit programs for workers who are laid off. Given the discussion in this chapter, comment on how you think such programs will affect overall economic performance and labor markets.

2.) What are the implications for economic policy-making if the long-run Phillips curve is indeed vertical?

3.) In the last part of 1994 and the first part of 1995, there was considerable discussion about whether or not the natural rate of unemployment had fallen below six %. (1) What evidence would be needed to show that the natural rate had fallen below six % and (2) of what significance is it if it had fallen below six %?

4.) Why is it so difficult to achieve price stability when inflationary expectations exist?

5.) Why did the stagflation of the 70s cause people to question the basic premises of the Keynesian economic model? Why does stagflation make policy-making so difficult?

6.) Briefly discuss the economic effects of the following events on the various types of unemployment and on the natural rate of unemployment. Also indicate what might be done in terms of economic policy to address the events:
   a. an increase in the female labor force participation rate (LFPR) which results in many more women entering the labor force.

   b. a dramatic increase in the world price of petroleum.

   c. an accelerating pace of integrating sophisticated computer processes and programs into the work-place.

Answers and Solutions to Problems and Exercises

Completing Statements from the List of Terms

1.) Phillips Curve
2.) Supply Shock
3.) Wage Drift
4.) Frictional Unemployment
5.) Structural Unemployment
6.) Hysteresis
7.) Natural Rate of Unemployment
8.) Real-Wage Structural Unemployment

Problems

Examining the Phillips Curve Relationship

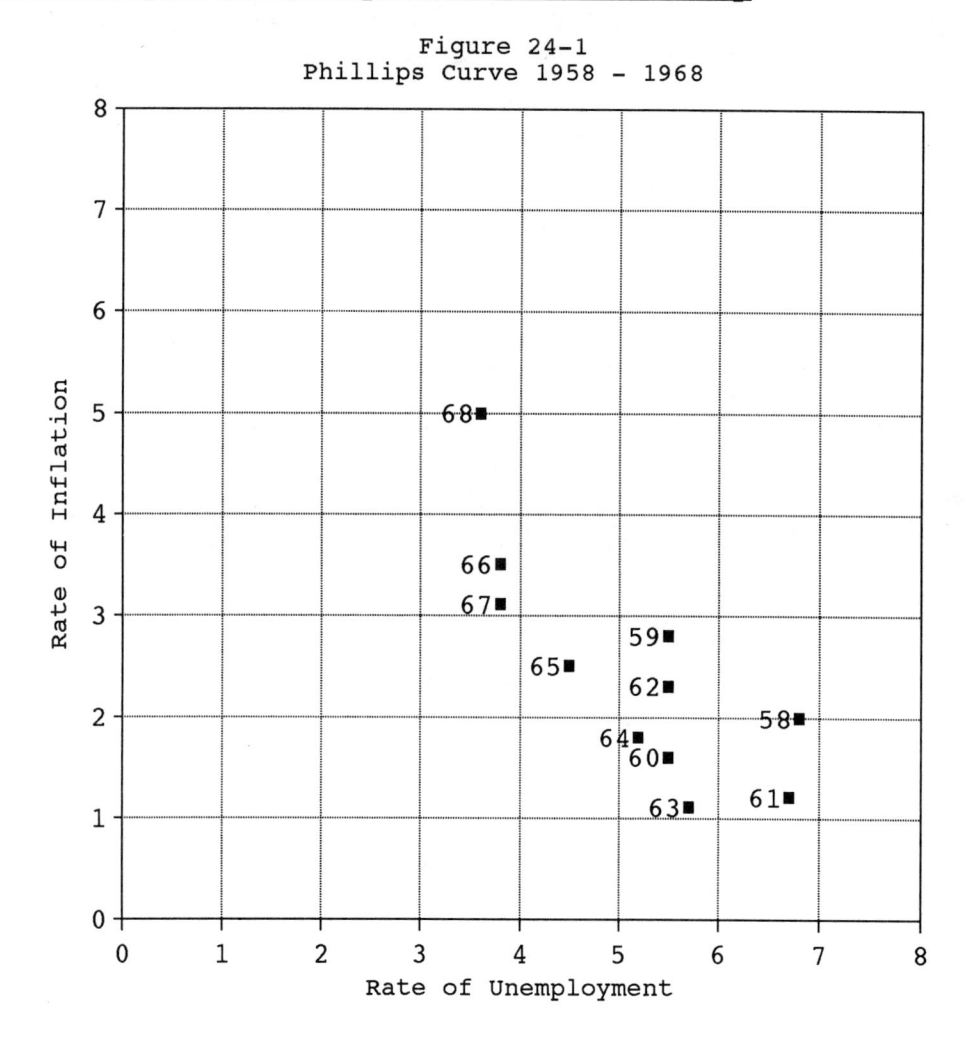

Figure 24-1
Phillips Curve 1958 - 1968

On the basis of that trend line, what rate of inflation would you expect if the rate of unemployment decreased to two %? **6%**

On the basis of that trend line, what rate of unemployment would you expect if the rate of inflation decreased to one %? **about 6%**

If your trend line approximates the inflation/unemployment relationship for the economy, what position on the trend line would you recommend the economy try to attain? **The answer depends upon how a policymaker compares the costs of unemployment to society as opposed to the costs of inflation.** It used to be the case that Democrats favored positions on the lower part of the curve, emphasizing unemployment over inflation, while Republicans were willing to accept greater levels of unemployment in order to obtain lower rates of inflation. There is no set answer; it is value driven.

Figure 24-2
Phillips Curve 1969 - 1978

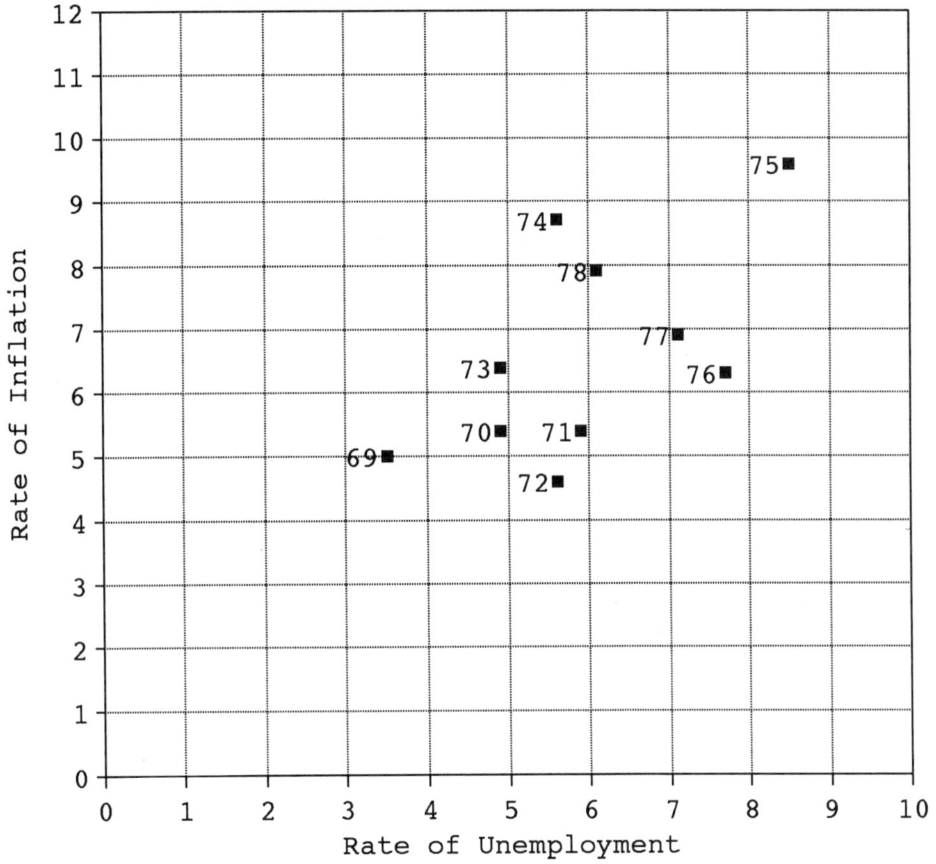

In the diagram above, which sequential sets of points (which years) illustrate stagflation? **1969-1970, 1970-1971, 1973-1974, 1974-1975**

In the diagram above, which sequential sets of points (which years) illustrate the traditional short-run inflation/unemployment relationship? **1972-1973, 1976-1977, 1977-1978**

Describe the pattern that you obtain when the data observations are connected in a sequential fashion (by year.) **There is a cyclical pattern which resembles a series of circles:**

```
           .
        .     .
        .     .
          . .
```

In the diagram, component A: 1972 - 1973;   component B: 1973 - 1975; components C and D: 1975 - 1976

Although not perfect in terms of the diagram, a vertical line located at 5.5% unemployment appears to satisfy the requirements of an LRAS. Prices increased from 1972 to 73 amd 1973 to 74, decreased from 1971 to 72.

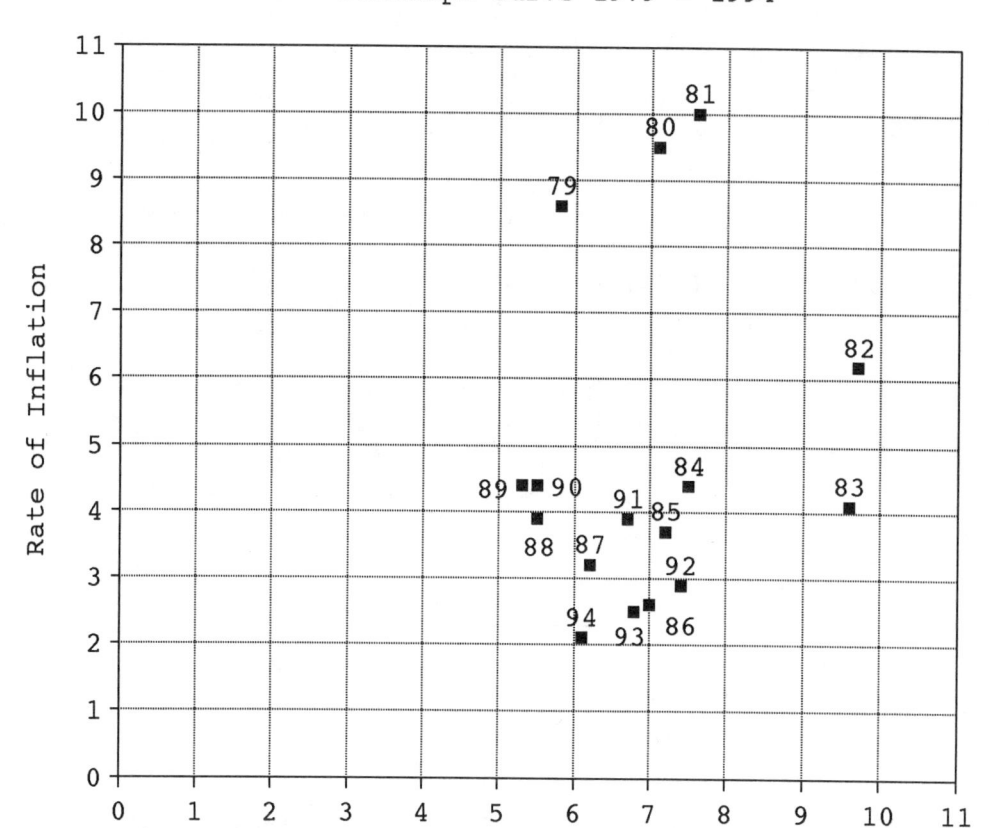

Figure 24-3
Phillips Curve 1979 - 1994

In the diagram above, which sequential sets of points (which years) illustrate stagflation? **1979 - 1980 - 1981, 1989 - 1990**

In the diagram above, which sequential sets of points (which years) illustrate the traditional short-run inflation/unemployment relationship? **1983 - 1984, 1986 - 1987 - 1988 - 1989**

512

Describe the pattern that you obtain when the data observations are connected in a sequential fashion (by year). **Again, the circular pattern is evident, with the 1985 - 1992 spiral representing a much better inflation/unemployment situation than the larger 1979 - 1984 spiral.**

Based on the sequential patterns that you have identified in your graphs, what implications might be drawn from the Phillips curve observations about the 1992 elections and Bush being reelected? **1992 appears to be at the end of a complete spiral with inflation declining, but unemployment increasing. Increases in unemployment have posed difficulties for incumbent administrations in the past.**

True/False Statements

1.) **True.** Inflation begins to accelerate as product and labor shortages start to occur. Wage and price increases in those sectors experiencing shortages and bottlenecks then spread to other sectors of the economy.

2.) **True.** With the stable Phillips curve relationship that existed in the 1950s and early 1960s, it appeared that stimulating the economy to lower the rate of unemployment would also cause the economy to begin to overheat.

3.) **True.** Decreases in aggregate supply result in more inflation and greater unemployment (shifting the Phillips curve to the right), while increases in aggregate supply would yield lower inflation and unemployment (equivalent to the Phillips curve shifting to the left).

4.) **False.** It would cause the Phillips curve to shift to the right, resulting in a deteriorating inflation/unemployment performance.

5.) **False.** Shifts in aggregate demand are consistent with the traditional Phillips curve relationship -- increases in AD result in less unemployment and higher prices (assuming a positively sloped AS curve).

6.) **False.** Accommodating economic policies would reduce the unemployment associated with a supply shock but would intensify inflationary pressures.

7.) **True.** Such negotiations would help eliminate competitive pressures in which each successive wage agreement attempts to surpass the ones previously negotiated.

8.) **True.** Once inflationary expectations are embedded in the economy, both workers and firms will base their future wage demands and prices on what they expect inflation will be. Workers will want to receive a cost of living adjustment (COLA) and an increase based on their productivity. Firms will want to increase their prices at a rate faster than the rate of inflation to obtain a real price increase.

9.) **True.** Workers' lack of mobility will make any adjustment to structural or technological change more difficult, prolonging unemployment. Workers that are displaced by the introduction of new technologies limit their options for new employment by refusing to move.

10.) **True.** Attempts to reduce the rate of unemployment below the natural rate will bring about higher inflation and increases in the short-run aggregate supply curve and eventually lower output. Inflationary expectations will raise wages and unit labor costs, tending to reduce employment.

Multiple- Choice

1.) a   2.) a   3.) a   4.) a   5.) a   6.) a

7.) a   8.) a   9.) a   10.) a

Discussion Questions

1.) A major consequence of the high cost of employing additional workers has been relatively slow growth in employment, with employers hesitant about hiring new workers and substituting capital for labor.

2.) Efforts to permanently reduce the rate of unemployment to a level below the natural rate of unemployment will not be successful. Wage increases and increases in the short-run aggregate supply will cause unemployment to return to its natural rate. Expansionary economic policies will be only temporarily successful.

3.) Empirical evidence which would suggest that the natural rate of unemployment had fallen would consist of non-accelerating inflation rates when unemployment rates are below six %. There was some indication that occurred in late 1994. From a policy standpoint, knowing the natural rate of unemployment would be useful as an future inflation indicator. As your text points out, the theory behind the natural rate of unemployment suggests that inflation will rise whenever the actual rate of unemployment falls below the natural rate.

4.) When inflationary expectations are present, both workers and employers incorporate their estimates of future inflation into their wage demands and pricing policies. Wage increases will typically exceed productivity increases, causing unit labor costs to increase, putting additional pressure on firms to raise prices to keep up with rising labor costs. A wage-price spiral often results and is difficult to break.

5.) Stagflation represents the worst of all possible outcomes -- rising inflation and rising unemployment. If policy-makers attempt to control inflation, unemployment becomes worse, and if they attempt to control unemployment, inflation becomes worse. This puts policy-makers into a "no-win" situation that is distinctly uncomfortable for them. With the traditional Keynesian model, excessive unemployment is resolved by increasing aggregate demand, and excessive inflation is dealt with by decreasing aggregate demand. Stagflation lies outside of the model's parameters.

6.) a. Likely to increase both frictional and structural components of unemployment, thus raising the natural rate of unemployment.

b. Likely to increase structural unemployment as certain energy, intensive sectors of the economy are affected by the increase in the price of petroleum. An increase in structural unemployment will increase the natural rate of unemployment.

c. Very similar to answer above except that technological displacement of labor will take place in a different set of economic sectors.

Summary

Economic theory about the relationship between inflation and unemployment has evolved significantly since the 1950s when the Phillips curve was introduced. Economists, as well as policy-makers, were overly optimistic about the ability to reduce the level of unemployment below its natural rate. The development of inflationary expectations during the Vietnam War, the supply shocks of the 1970s, and the onset of stagflation created enormous challenges for economists to come up with an economic model which could provide a satisfactory explanation of the rapidly changing relationship between inflation and unemployment.

The distinction made between the short-run and long-run Phillips curves is an extremely useful one, focusing attention on the dynamic linkage that exists between the natural and actual rates of unemployment. More extensive and sophisticated usage of computers in every sector of our economy is likely to increase structural unemployment and will put upward pressure on the natural rate. Government policies and societal attitudes towards education, on-the-job training, re-training of displaced workers, and efforts to increase the mobility of unemployed workers will be more important in our increasingly high tech society and will influence the natural rate of unemployment. One of the more interesting proposals being discussed is whether or not the Fed should pursue a zero inflation goal. Since there is general agreement that the consumer price index (CPI) overestimates the actual rate of inflation, the specific inflation goal is unclear. The short-run cost of achieving that goal in terms of lost output and greater unemployment is thought to be significant. Long-term price stability would generate widespread benefits for many groups in society, and those benefits theoretically can be compared against the costs.

As is always the case in periods of rapid technological change, there is a fear that the newly implemented technologies will result in significant displacement and unemployment in the labor force. With the advent of the information age and the widespread implementation of computer-related technology, there will be widespread economic effects, many of which may occur in ways that can't be anticipated very well. For example, will high quality video conferencing result in less air travel? Will interactive telephone-cable systems result in a significant decrease in the labor requirements for providing financial and retail services as people do their shopping and banking at home?

Chapter 25
Macroeconomic Innovation

Overview of the Chapter

The stagflation of 70s illustrated the difficulties of using traditional or orthodox economic policies to control rising prices and increasing levels of unemployment. As a result, a number of alternative "heterodox" policies were either adopted or proposed as a more effective means to address these problems.

Orthodox economic policies emphasize the role of increasing public spending to reduce the rate of unemployment, while heterodox policies tend to concentrate on job training programs which are designed to increase skills and productivity, thus making unemployed workers and new entrants to the labor force more employable. Hopefully such policies would reduce the natural rate of unemployment over the long run. Corporate training policies have been widely implemented in Europe, notably Sweden and the United Kingdom and the consensus is that they have been particularly successful in reducing Sweden's long-term unemployment problem. In contrast, the concept of public service employment and training programs fell out of political favor in the the 1980s in the United States because of philosophical objections from Reagan conservatives.

The mere size of the United States means that it is more difficult to match job openings that occur with job applicants located in different states. This is especially true when the state job service organizations have little incentive to inform out-of-state job seekers about employment opportunities within the state. Recently there has been some renewed discussion about the possibility of providing a public service option for young adults which would provide on-the-job training and funds for later schooling.

The use of wage/price controls by governing bodies has had a long and varied history, with confirmed applications going back as much as three thousand years. Wage/price restraints have tended to be used in situations where there are extraordinary pressures on society's scarce resources, typically war-time situations. It has, on occasion, been used when it simply has been deemed too painful or politically unacceptable to employ traditional anti-inflation measures which reduce aggregate demand and, subsequently, the incomes of some political constituencies.

Although several administrations have tried voluntary controls (such as jawboning or simply voluntary compliance) with varying degrees of success, most programs have utilized specific guidelines or formal legal controls such as the ones Nixon instituted in 1971. Typically, an overall inflation goal is set, and any subsequent wage increases must be less than or equal to the percentage increase in productivity so as to not generate higher per unit labor costs and, thus, create additional cost push inflationary pressures. With wage increases limited in this fashion, prices can be frozen, and supposedly business profits are stabilized because input prices and wages are controlled. Programs like these are difficult and costly to enforce and largely ineffective without a consensus of support from the general population.

Linking incomes and taxes to the rate of inflation is known as indexing, and while it certainly does not cure inflation, it mitigates the distributional aspects of inflation by adjusting incomes and taxes in a proportional fashion as inflation occurs. Private sector cost of living adjustments (COLAs) contained in labor contracts work essentially in the same way, increasing nominal wages whenever the rate of inflation increases. Both indexing and COLAs work to protect real incomes of the groups subject to their provisions, but many of the other societal effects remain unabated, and, as your text notes, indexing provisions and COLAs intensify inflationary pressures by continuing to increase incomes and wages.

Several interesting tax proposals have been devised to help deal with inflation. They include discretionary authority by the president to change taxes, tax-free inventory reserves, and Wallich and Weintraub's tax-based incomes policy (TIP) which would penalize firms that agree to wage increases that exceed national guidelines.

Governments can also address the stagflation problem by doing whatever they can to reduce supply side inefficiencies and bottlenecks which result in higher prices. Supply side reforms would shift the aggregate supply (AS) curve to the right and, *ceteris paribus*, should decrease prices and unemployment. Agricultural price support programs, protectionist policies, and certain labor market policies would fall into this category.

Learning Objectives

After completing this chapter, you should be sure that you are able to:

- define and distinguish between orthodox and heterodox economic policies.

- identify the different types of training programs that have been implemented in the United States, their purpose, and their advantages and disadvantages.

- describe public employment schemes being proposed and how they differ from previous public employment policies.

- recount the history of wage/price controls and their economic effects.

- explain the rationale for indexing wages, incomes, pensions, etc., and the inclusion of COLAs in wage and pension agreements.

- discuss the effectiveness of indexing and COLAs in dealing with inflationary pressures.

- understand how heterdox tax policies can be used to address inflationary problems.

- list supply side reforms that would yield better inflation/unemployment outcomes.

- understand how policies which increase productive capacity reduce inflation and unemployment over the long run.

Self Evaluation

List of Terms

Comprehensive Employment
  and Training Act (CETA)
Cost of Living Adjustments (COLAs)
Heterodox Economic Policies
Incomes Policies
Indexing
Jobs Training Partnership Act (JTPA)

Job Sharing
National Community Service
Supply Side Reforms
Tax-Based Incomes Policy (TIP)
Wage/Price Controls
Workfare

For the statements below, fill in the term from the list above which provides the best fit.

1.) _____ attempts to deal with recessionary pressures and rising unemployment by shortening the work week and sharing existing jobs among members of the labor force.

2.) Comprehensive _____ would allow incomes, taxes, pensions, and interest rates to keep pace with inflation.

3.) After experiencing unanticipated inflation in the late 1960s, many unions included _____ in their labor contracts.

4.) Programs in which a recipient must either agree to be re-trained or accept some kind of public service employment are called _____.

5.) The _____ would allow young adults the opportunity to offer their labor in a wide variety of public service settings, thus enhancing their skills and obtaining financial assistance for more formal training at a later date.

6.) The set of policies designed to reduce inflation without increasing unemployment or decreasing aggregate demand are known collectively as _____.

7.) Employment legislation passed in 1973 which emphasized on-the-job, work experience, and some classroom training: _____.

8.) Eliminating protectionist legislation, restraints on agricultural production, and reducing governmental regulations are all examples of _____ which can potentially reduce both inflation and unemployment.

9.) A _____ attempts to limit inflationary wage increases by increasing the tax rate for firms that authorize wage increases that exceed national inflation guidelines.

10.) The _____ attempted to train workers for specific employment needs in a given area, thus reducing structural unemployment.

11.) Although _____ may at first seem to be a relatively costless way to address inflationary pressures, unfortunately they do nothing to address the basic causes of inflation.

12.) _____ attempt to deal with the economic problems resulting from stagflation by implementing training programs, wage/price controls, and supply side reforms.

Problems

The Problem with Wage and Price Controls

Both gasoline and fuel oil (which require different refining techniques) have significant seasonal variations in their demand patterns, with gasoline demand peaking in the summer travel months and the demand for fuel oil peaking during the colder winter months. Hypothetical demand and supply curves for the two products are shown below:

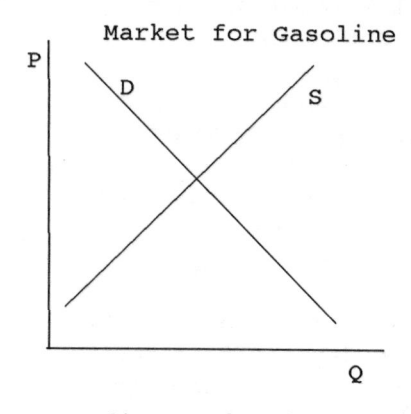

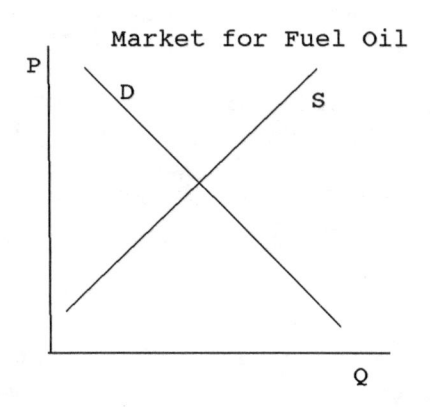

Indicate the changes in demand in the two markets that would occur during the summer months. Label the new demand curves D_1.

Suppose that a wage price freeze is announced by the president in August. Assume that prices in the two markets are frozen at their summer equilibrium prices. Label the frozen prices P_{freeze}.

On that same diagram, indicate the changes in demand that would occur from August to February in the two markets above, keeping in mind that the market prices are frozen at their summer equilibrium levels.

Briefly describe the conditions that will exist in the two markets.

_____

_____

Briefly describe the effects of the price freeze on producers and consumers of gasoline and fuel oil.

_____

_____

_____

Indexing Taxes

Inflation increases nominal incomes, and since taxes are levied on nominal incomes, inflation can result in higher tax liabilities, particularly if a taxpayer's inflated income puts her into a higher marginal tax bracket (a phenomenon sometimes referred to as "bracket creep"). Indexing can offset some or all of the effects of inflation on taxes.

The initial tax situation in year one:

Adjusted gross income:	$30,000
Standard deduction per person:	$ 2,000
Total deduction (4 persons):	$ 8,000
Standard deduction:	$ 5,000
Taxable income:	$17,000
(Adjusted gross income - personal and standard deductions)	
Marginal rate of taxation (MRT):	15 percent (0.15)
Total tax liability:	$2,550
(Total tax liability = taxable income times MRT)	

Now assume that prices rise five percent in year two and that nominal incomes increase by that amount.

The tax situation in year two:

    Adjusted gross income: $ _____

    Standard deduction per person: $ 2,000
    Total deduction (4 persons): $ _____

    Standard deduction: $ 5,000

    Taxable income: $ _____
    (Adjusted gross income - personal and standard deductions)

    Marginal rate of taxation (MRT): 15 percent (0.15)

    Total tax liability: $ _____
    (Total tax liability = taxable income times MRT)

Calculate and compare the following variables for the two years: (base year = year one prices = 100.0)

	Year One	Year Two	Percentage Increase
Total Nominal Income:	_____	_____	_____ %
Total Real Income:	_____	_____	_____ %
Total Nominal Tax Paid:	_____	_____	_____ %
Total Real Tax Paid:	_____	_____	_____ %

If taxes are fully indexed, then both the personal deductions and the standard deductions in year two will be adjusted by the inflation rate. Recalculate the tax liability for year two under an indexing scheme.

Assume again that prices rise five percent in year two and that nominal incomes increase by that amount.

The tax situation in year two:

    Adjusted gross income: $ _____

    Standard deduction per person: $ _____
    Total deduction (4 persons): $ _____

    Standard deduction: $ _____

    Taxable income: $ _____
    (Adjusted gross income - personal and standard deductions)

Marginal rate of taxation (MRT):   15 percent (0.15)

Total tax liability: $_____
(Total tax liability = taxable income times MRT)

Calculate and compare the following variables for the two years:
(base year = year one prices = 100.0)

	Year One	Year Two	Percentage Increase
Total Nominal Income:	_____	_____	_____ %
Total Real Income:	_____	_____	_____ %
Total Nominal Tax Paid:	_____	_____	_____ %
Total Real Tax Paid:	_____	_____	_____ %

What effect did indexing have upon nominal and real tax liability?

_____

_____

True/False Statements

Indicate whether you think the statements below are true or false. These questions are designed to make you think about the concepts presented in the text. There may not be any easy clear-cut answers. Some thoughts about the answers are presented at the end of the chapter.

1.) _____ Wage and price controls can effectively stop inflation, since they make price increases illegal.

2.) _____ Under a full indexing program, workers' real incomes are maintained.

3.) _____ Widespread indexing would effectively control the distibution problems associated with inflation.

4.) _____ Supply side reforms would alleviate inflationary pressures on the economy by increasing the short-run aggregate supply curve (SRAS).

5.) _____ A tax-based incomes program (TIP) would increase taxes on those firms that allowed wages to increase faster than a nationally set standard.

6.) _____ Job sharing is an almost costless way to eliminate unemployment.

Multiple-Choice Questions

Select the "best" answer from the alternatives provided.

1.) Indexing
   a. refers to the practice of linking wage increases with productivity increases.
   b. tends to alleviate inflationary pressures by removing incentives to constantly renegotiate contracts.
   c. completely eliminates the problems associated with inflation so a country can concentrate on more important problems.
   d. tends to build-in inflation into major sectors of the economy, making it difficult to stop.

2.) A tax-based incomes policy (TIP)
   a. penalizes all firms that increase wages.
   b. penalizes all firms that increase wages by more than a government-specified standard.
   c. would penalize those workers with low productivity increases.
   d. would penalize both firms and workers for excessive wage increases.

3.) Supply side reforms help address inflationary problems by
   a. decreasing both AD and SRAS.
   b. decreasing AD and increasing SRAS.
   c. increasing SRAS.
   d. moving down an existing SRAS.

4.) Wage and price controls
   a. effectively eliminate inflation problems by making price increases illegal.
   b. do nothing at all to address the basic causes of inflation.
   c. are more effective if announced well in advance of their implementation.
   d. are more effective if inflation rates are relatively low.

5.) If marginal rates of taxation were decreased in order to effect a supply side reform to fight inflation,
   a. only the SRAS would increase.
   b. only the AD would increase.
   c. the SRAS would increase, then the AD would increase.
   d. the AD would increase, then the SRAS would increase.

6.) Which of the following represents a supply side reform that would lessen inflationary pressures?
   a. decreasing sales taxes and VATs.
   b. increasing levels of tariff protection.
   c. financing Social Security programs through income tax revenues.
   d. reducing regulatory restrictions on professional services.

7.) An administration is attempting to use voluntary wage and price guidelines with price increases not to exceed the target rate of inflation rate of 4% and wage increases not to exceed the target rate of inflation (4%) plus the rate of productivity growth (estimated to be 2%). Under such guidelines,
   a. workers would gain more if their productivity gain exceeded 2%.
   b. firms' could increase their profits if their costs increased by less than the target rate of inflation.
   c. a 6% wage agreement would not increase unit labor costs.
   d. it would not be possible for inflation to exceed the target rate of inflation.

Discussion Questions

1.) Explain how indexing mitigates the redistributional effects of inflation. Your text states "The more indexing solved problems, the more the problems that were created!" Explain.

2.) What would you expect to happen to the rate of inflation after wage/price controls are lifted?

3.) There has been some discussion of adopting a national sales tax or a value-added tax. If revenues from such a tax were used to offset income tax reductions, how would that improve our inflation performance?

4.) Tax legislation is infamous for taking a long time to get through Congress. Why wouldn't everyone be in favor of giving the president discretionary power to temporarily change income tax rates by a small amount, say plus or minus 5%?

5.) How would you respond to the statement "The government itself has implemented a number of programs which effectively frustrate efforts to stabilize the price level."

Since price stability is such an important macroeconomic goal, how could such policies be justified?

Answers and Solutions to Problems and Exercises

Completing Statements from the List of Terms

1.) Job Sharing
2.) Indexing
3.) Cost of Living Adjustments (COLAs)
4.) Workfare
5.) National Community Service
6.) Incomes Policies
7.) Comprehensive Employment and Training Act (CETA)
8.) Supply Side Reforms
9.) Tax-Based Incomes Policy (TIP)
10.) Jobs Training Partnership Act (JTPA)
11.) Wage/Price Controls
12.) Heterodox Economic Policies

Problems

The Problem with Wage and Price Controls

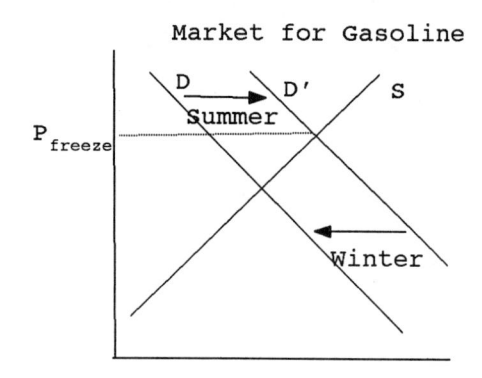

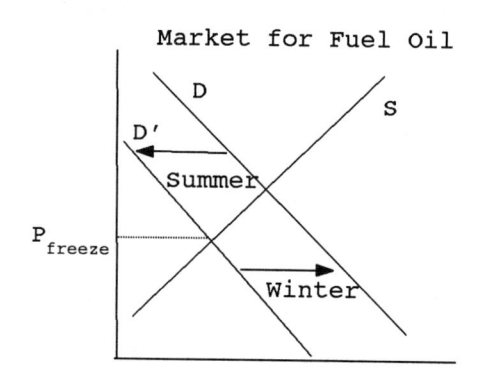

Briefly describe the conditions that will exist in the two markets. **The controlled price of gasoline will be at its seasonal high, while the controlled price of fuel oil will be at or near its seasonal low. In the**

winter, a surplus of gasoline would ensue simultaneously with a shortage of fuel oil.

Briefly describe the effects of the price freeze on producers and consumers of gasoline and fuel oil. **Producers would respond to the controlled prices, producing too much gasoline and too little fuel oil. Consumers of gasoline would enjoy plentiful supplies, while households that heat with fuel oil could have real difficulty in obtaining sufficient fuel oil.**

The important point of this exercise is to reinforce the concept that even if prices are frozen at their equilibrium points, over time with the inevitable changes in demand that occur, the price controls lead to an inefficient allocation of resources.

Indexing Taxes

Now assume that prices rise five percent in year two and that nominal incomes increase by that amount.

The tax situation in year two:

Adjusted gross income:	$31,500
Standard deduction per person:	$ 2,000
Total deduction (4 persons):	$ 8,000
Standard deduction:	$ 5,000
Taxable income:	$18,500

(Adjusted gross income - personal and standard deductions)

Marginal rate of taxation (MRT):	15 percent (0.15)
Total tax liability:	$ 2,775

	Year One	Year Two	Percentage Increase
Total Nominal Income:	$30,000	$31,500	5 %
Total Real Income:	$30,000	$30,000	0%
Total Nominal Tax Paid:	$ 2,550	$ 2,775	8.82 %
Total Real Tax Paid:	$ 2,550	$ 2,643	3.65 %

Assume again that prices rise five percent in year two and that nominal incomes increase by that amount.

The tax situation in year two:

    Adjusted gross income: $31,500

    Standard deduction per person: $ 2,100
    Total deduction (4 persons): $ 8,400

    Standard deduction: $ 5,250

    Taxable income: $17,850
    (Adjusted gross income - personal and standard deductions)

    Marginal rate of taxation (MRT):   15 percent (0.15)
    Total tax liability: $ 2,678

	Year One	Year Two	Percentage Increase
Total Nominal Income:	$30,000	$31,500	5 %
Total Real Income:	$30,000	$30,000	0 %
Total Nominal Tax Paid:	2,550	$ 2,678	5 %
Total Real Tax Paid:	$ 2,550	$ 2,550	0 %

What effect did indexing have upon nominal and real tax liability? **Tax indexing keeps the real tax burden constant. Nominal taxes increase but only by the amount of inflation.**

True/False Statements

1.) **False.** While it may appear that wage-price controls are effective, they do nothing to address the underlying causes of inflation. When the controls are lifted, the inflationary pressures remain. Firms can raise the price implicitly by reducing the quality or quantity of an item, so this type of hidden inflation can occur.

2.) **False.** Theoretically, indexing would increase workers' incomes by a proportional amount based on the previous period's rate of inflation. In a period of rapidly increasing prices, wage adjustment would have to be done quickly, or real incomes would fall. However, in practice it takes some time to determine and publish the offically estimated rate of inflation. There would also be some concern about regional price differences. There is also substantial discussion about whether the CPI overestimates the "actual" rate of inflation, bringing in a whole new set of problems.

3. **False.** How could the self-employed (a fairly large group in the United States) ever be indexed? Every worker (part-time and full-time) would have to be covered by an extensive indexing agreement. It is also difficult to imagine that every aspect of the economy subject to inflation could be covered and indexed.

4.) **True.** The reforms suggested in your text would potentially increase the economy's SRAS, thus decreasing the rate of inflation.

5.) **True.** The purpose of a TIP program is provide a set of incentives for firms to follow the policy guidelines on wage increases. It doesn't prohibit firms from breaking the guidelines but increases the firm's taxes if the guidelines are exceeded.

6.) **False.** There are no free lunches anywhere, every action or policy has a cost associated with it. In this case, job sharing means some workers will have less income than before. There are some jobs where a shorter work week would cause difficulties, perhaps disrupting production shifts.

Multiple-Choice

1.) d   2.) b   3.) c   4.) b   5.) d   6.) a

7.) b

Discussion Questions

1.) Workers, as do other many other income earners, lose out when they do not correctly anticipate inflation. Indexing provides a mechanism for them to keep up with inflation, reducing (or hopefully eliminating) any redistributional effects.

If indexing arrangements become widespread, an increase in the price of a raw material (for example) will cause inflationary repercussions throughout the economy which will, in turn, be reflected in indexing contracts. One price increase will initiate a series of other price increases, which in turn will result in additional price increases. The ability to constrain inflation is impaired.

2.) Once wage and price controls have been imposed, firms and workers (concerned that controls may be used again) will want to raise their prices and wages when they have an opportunity to do so.

3.) Higher marginal rates of taxation affect the incentive to work and invest, so taxes on spending and value-added would be preferred, since they would not cause the SRAS to shift to the left.

4.) The fear of allowing the President the authority to adjust tax rates would be that taxes would be reduced to enhance the incumbent party's chance of retaining the office.

5.) Special interest groups are often able to convince legislators that the positive benefits of legislation which favors their economic sector or group outweigh any negative impacts on overall economic performance. Domestic sugar producers have been effective in limiting cheaper imports of world sugar, thus keeping the domestic price of sugar higher than it otherwise would be. The benefits are a stable supply of sugar and a profitable domestic sugar industry which generates profits and jobs in the selected regions of the country.

Summary

The heterodox policies discussed in this chapter offer a wide range of alternative strategies that can be used to achieve price stability and full employment. They involve structural reforms of the economy in many different areas: increased training and apprenticeship programs, changes in the way that the Social Security program is financed, reduction of marginal rates of taxation and the imposition of sales taxes or value-added taxes, decreased levels of protection, and the removal of minimum wage laws and governmental price supports and subsidies for agricultural products. While most economists oppose wage and price controls, they are yet another option for policy-makers, especially if they feel that orthodox policies are unlikely to be successful and that drastic action is required. Unfortunately, wage and price controls, while dramatic, provide only temporary respite from our inflationary problems and do nothing in addressing long-term solutions to inflation. Not surprisingly, voluntary wage/price guidelines have not been effective.

It seems likely that structural changes and reforms along a broad front as suggested by your text would provide improved macroeconomic performance. Yet, because of the political power and influence of special interest groups (e.g., agriculture, professional organizations, protected industries), significant structural change along the lines suggested in this chapter would undoubtedly prove to be very difficult to achieve. The difference between the perfect world and the practical world is enormous.

Chapter 26
Economic Growth in Market Economies

Overview of the Chapter

The economic growth rate determines the future output and standard of living of a society, and that is why so much attention has been given to it. For some time now, economists have attempted to analyze economic growth in order to identify and understand the factors that contribute the most to the growth process. While economic growth can occur either from increases in the amount of available factor resources or from increases in factor productivity, research has indicated that the growth of factor productivity has been much more important than increases in the factors themselves. Variations in growth rates and productivity can have fairly dramatic impacts on total output and income in relatively short periods because of the multiplicative nature of the growth process.

For a variety of reasons, many developed market economies have experienced declines in the rate of growth of productivity. One reason has been a decline in net saving and investment, and, as a consequence, there has been less capital investment per worker than would otherwise have been the case. The United States, in particular, has also been characterized by declining rates of investment in public infrastructure, and that, in turn, is thought to have decreased the rate of increase in overall productivity. In addition, as societies have become more affluent, consumer preferences have shifted more towards services, and productivity growth in service sectors has been notoriously difficult to measure (teaching and the education sector are excellent examples) and perhaps even more difficult to achieve. Most developed economies now devote considerably more resources to controlling environmental pollution than they once did and while these expenditures certainly provide tangible benefits to society, they do not increase measured output, thus contributing little if any to measured productivity (output per hour).

Some of the factors thought to be responsible for the decline in productivity growth are more easily addressed than others. Public investment in infrastructure projects can be increased, although the size of the federal budget deficit obviously constrains efforts to increase spending. The problem with efforts to upgrade to our infrastructure is that the results are likely to be long-term in nature and difficult to pin down in terms of their specific contribution to the growth process. Economic policies can be put in place to encourage greater national savings and private investment. Some areas, such as education, play an extremely important role in the growth process over the long run and are much more troublesome to deal with and may require major structural changes.

Efforts to increase labor productivity are crucial to any program whose goal is to increase productivity. Devoting more resources towards training and apprenticeships, profit sharing, and increasing worker involvement in management decisions are all options that have been tried with varying degrees of success. One of the more controversial policies is that of a national industrial policy in which the government would provide various kinds of assistance to economic sectors which look to be particularly promising and critical for future economic growth. Subsidizing research and development expenditures (R&D) or providing greater tariff protection would be examples of specific policies that could be implemented under a national industrial policy.

How does the government pick the winners? Can the government select winning economic sectors better than the market mechanism? How much of a subsidy or tariff is necessary? To what degree will the process be politicized? These are some of the questions that detractors raise about a national industrial policy. If the past is to be any guide, it has proven to be very difficult to reduce or terminate such programs once they have become established. To be successful, some sectors which do not look very promising should be downsized or perhaps eliminated entirely, a task not relished by politicians.

Learning Objectives

After completing this chapter, you should be sure that you are able to:

- distinguish between extensive and intensive economic growth.

- briefly describe the sources of economic growth in the United States and how they have changed over time.

- understand the underlying relationship that exists between productivity growth and the growth in incomes.

- list the factors which affect economic growth and productivity in developed market economies.

- understand why the productivity of specific factors is relatively more important than the actual amount of the factor inputs.

- understand and discuss the reasons for the decrease in the rate of productivity growth for the American economy and what can be done to increase the growth rate of productivity.

- discuss the pros and cons of an active industrial strategy for the United States

Self Evaluation

List of Terms

Co-determination
Economic Growth
Extensive Economic Growth
Growth Accounting
Human Capital
Infrastructure
Intensive Economic Growth
Lifetime Employment
National Industrial Strategy
Net National Saving
Profit Sharing

For the statements below, fill in the term from the list above which provides the best fit.

1.) Immigration into the United States and an increasing domestic labor force would be an example of _____.

2.) One explanation for the decline in economic growth and productivity in the United States is the relatively small amount of total _____.

3.) Allowing greater participation by labor in management decisions, _____ has been widely utilized in Europe in an effort to increase labor productivity by giving workers a greater stake in the firm they work for.

4.) Given the success that Japan has had in encouraging newly emerging industries and economic sectors, there has been considerable discussion in the United States about whether or not a _____ should be put in place.

5.) A better trained and educated work force and more productive capital are examples of _____.

6.) Defined as an increase in an economy's productive output and capacity, _____ is one of society's most important goals.

7.) Some economists contend that the downward trend in public investment in _____ has contributed to lower productivity growth.

8.) _____ is one method that has been used at the microeconomic level to enhance labor productivity.

9.) The process of quantifying the contribution of various factor inputs to overall economic growth is known as _____.

10.) Many Japanese firms have made a commitment to _____, a policy which allows them to increase the level of training provided to their employees.

11.) One way to think about the importance of _____ in the overall production process would be to try and imagine what output would be if all existing knowledge and training were completely taken away.

Problems

The Relationship Between Productivity and Real Income

The following table contains productivity and per capita real income data for a thirteen-year period. Plot the productivity index and the index of per capita real Gross Domestic Product for the 1980 - 1993 time period.

Table 26-1

Year	Output per Hour of all Persons Business Sector (1982=100)	Real Per Capita Gross Domestic Product (Billions of 1987 Dollars)	Total Population (in millions)	Real Per Capita Gross Domestic Product (in dollars)	Index of Real Per Capita Gross Domestic Product (1982 = 100)
1980	98.6	3776.3	227.726	16583	102.4
1981	99.9	3843.1	229.966	16712	103.2
1982	100.0	3760.3	232.188	16195	100.0
1983	102.3	3906.6	234.307	16673	103.0
1984	104.8	4148.5	236.348	17553	108.4
1985	106.3	4279.8	238.466	17947	110.8
1986	108.5	4404.5	240.651	18302	113.0
1987	109.6	4539.9	242.804	18698	115.5
1988	110.7	4718.6	245.021	19258	118.9
1989	109.9	4838.0	247.342	19560	120.8
1990	110.7	4897.3	249.911	19596	121.0
1991	112.1	4867.6	252.643	19267	119.0
1992	115.5	4979.3	255.407	19496	120.4
1993	117.2	5134.5	258.120	19892	122.8

Source: *Economic Report of the President*, Transmitted to the Congress, February, 1995.

Figure 26-1

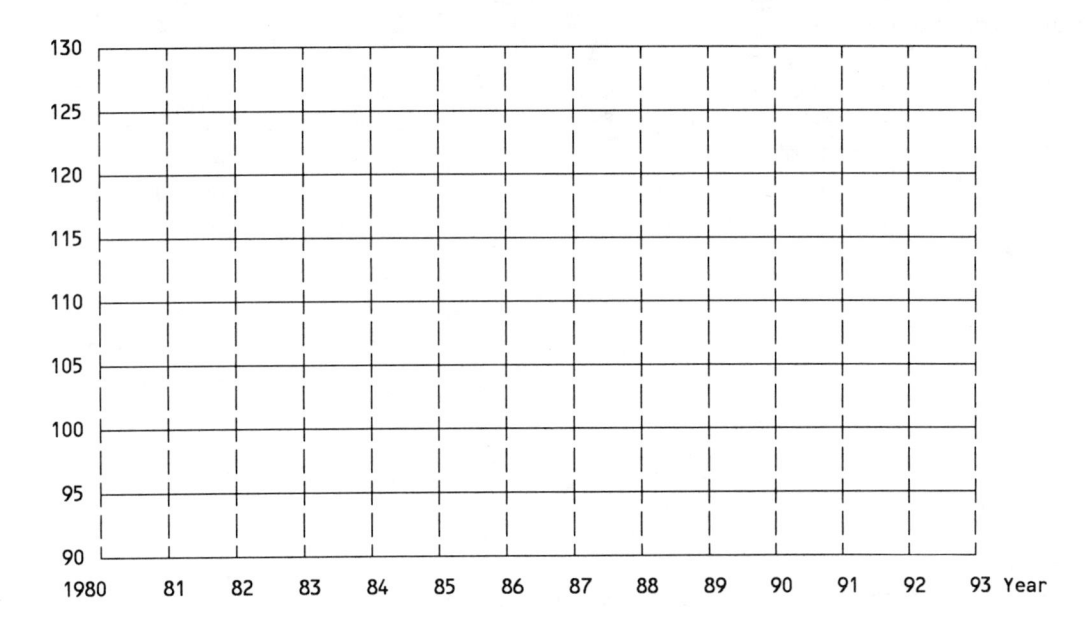

[Graph with y-axis from 90 to 130 in increments of 5, and x-axis showing years from 1980 to 93]

Briefly, how would you define productivity?

_____

_____

Why is productivity important in a macroeconomic context?

_____

_____

Based on the productivity and real income data contained in Table 26-1, what relationship exists between these two variables?

_____

_____

The Effect of Differences in Economic Growth Rates

There have been wide differences in economic growth rates among developed countries. Prevailing wisdom is that it is more difficult for older, more mature economies to grow as rapidly as they once did, and that it is more difficult for larger economies to grow as fast as their smaller counterparts. Japan, for instance, is widely acclaimed for the rapid economic growth that it has been able to achieve, yet most of that country's physical capital was destroyed during World War II as was Germany's, also among the leaders in economic growth. What may not be so apparent is the difference that relatively small differences in growth rates can make over an extended period of time.

Using the long-term economic growth rates contained in Table 26.3 of your text, we can examine the impact of different growth rates on the size of the economy. Setting each of the economy's real GDP equal to 100.0 in the year 1965, we can plot the growth path of the economy through the year 2000, assuming that the growth rates for 1965 - 1990 remained the same for the entire period (1965 - 2000).

Referring to the discussion in Chapter 12 of your text, it is possible to utilize the formula for net present value to obtain the future value of a series that is growing at a constant percentage rate (as we are assuming here).

$$\text{Future Value} = \text{Present Value} (1 + r)^n$$
where r = percentage rate of change (growth rate)
n = number of time periods

Taking the data from Japan as an example, if the Japanese economy is growing at a rate of 4.1% a year and we set the 1965 output level equal to 100, then in 1970 we would expect:

1970 total output = $100.0 (1.041)^5$ = 100 (1.222513455) = 122.3

Similarly, to obtain the estimate of 1975 output:

1975 total output = $100.0 (1.041)^{10}$ = 100 (1.494539) = 149.5

Using the formula, all of the entries in Table 26-2 can be calculated, substituting the different growth rates and number of time periods.

Table 26-2

Year	Index of Real GDP Japan (1965=100)	Index of Real GDP Germany (1965=100)	Index of Real GDP Britain (1965=100)	Index of Real GDP United States (1965=100)
Growth Rate:	4.1%/Yr	2.4%/Yr	2.0%/Yr	1.7%/Yr
1965	100.0	100.0	100.0	100.0
1970	122.3			
1975	149.5			
1980	182.7			
1985	223.4			
1990	273.1			
1995	333.8			
2000	408.1			

Source: Data from Hogendorn, Chapter 26, page 657.

Plot the four countries' output index for the years indicated in the preceding table on the following figure.

More Advanced Analysis

Using the formula above, determine what Japan's level of output would be in the year 2050.

How fast would Japan's economy have to grow per year if it were to double in a period of 15 years?

537

Figure 26-2

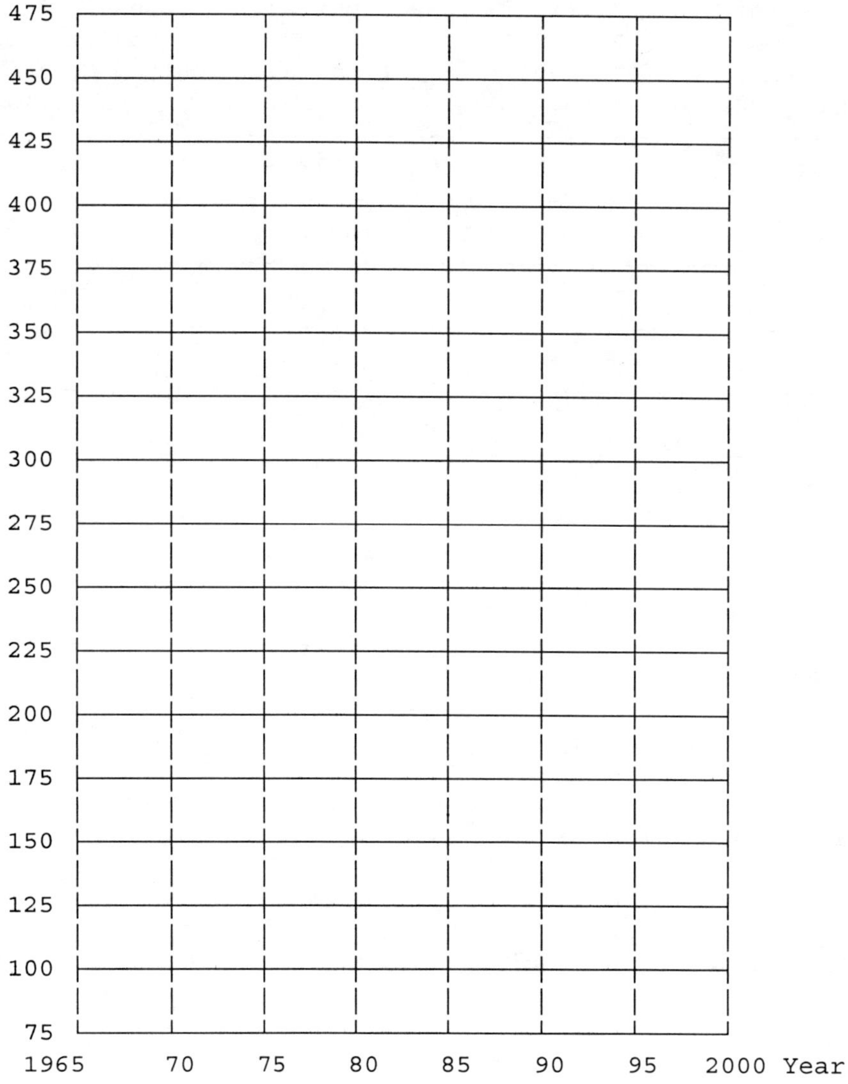

The estimates for the years 1995 and 2000 are dependent upon what crucial assumption about the relationship between the past and the future?

____

____

True/False Statements

Indicate whether you think the statements below are true or false. These questions are designed to make you think about the concepts presented in the text. There may not be any easy clear-cut answers. Some thoughts about the answers are presented at the end of the chapter.

1.) _____ In recent years, economic growth is best characterized by intensive growth rather than extensive growth.

2.) _____ Growth in labor income depends upon productivity growth.

3.) _____ Increasing federal budget deficits have decreased net national saving rates.

4.) _____ One way to increase the net national saving rate is to increase the rate of interest.

5.) _____ Removing the deductibility of interest payments on credit cards and home mortgages should increase the rate of saving.

6.) _____ Although academic test scores (on a variety of assessment measures) have declined in the United States, current research indicates that it has not affected productivity growth, nor is it expected to in the future.

7.) _____ For the most part, public sector investment in infrastructure has little or no effect on productivity in the private sector.

8.) _____ It is easier to increase productivity in the service sector of the economy than in the manufacturing sector.

9.) _____ Hostile corporate takeovers and leveraged buyouts (LBOs) have diverted attention from longer-term investment projects with subsequent declines in the rate of economic growth.

Multiple-Choice Questions

Select the "best" answer from the alternatives provided.

1.) Extensive economic growth would be best characterized by
   a. replacement of older computers with newer, more powerful computers.
   b. a more educated labor force.
   c. substituting computer-aided robots for manual workers.
   d. cultivating previously unproductive land.

2.) Intensive economic growth would be best characterized by
   a. a larger population and labor force.
   b. increases in the capital/labor ratio.
   c. an increase in the start-up rate of new businesses.
   d. greater sharing of information using the Internet.

3.) According to Denison's study on the sources of economic growth in the American economy,
   a. education has never accounted for the largest contributor to total economic growth.
   b. in the most recent period studied, technological change was found to have contributed the most to United States economic growth.
   c. all the factors that Denison studied were shown to have made positive contributions.
   d. increases in the amount of capital have always made the largest contribution to overall economic growth.

4. Concerning total net national savings,
   a. government savings have increased in recent years.
   b. net private savings have remained fairly constant.
   c. large federal deficits have significantly lowered net national savings.
   d. foreign inflows of capital have significantly increased net national savings.

5.) Which of the following statements is an incorrect explanation of the decline in savings in the United States over the last 10 - 15 years?
   a. a significant increase in income taxes.
   b. an increase in the value of housing and other household assets.
   c. demographic changes in the population, with babyboomers saving less.
   d. more extensive government programs for retirement have reduced incentives to save.

6.) Profit sharing plans
   a. introduce greater flexibility in wages and total labor costs.
   b. substantially increase workers' productivity.
   c. substantially increase firms' profits.
   d. are generally favored by labor unions.

7.) Regarding the decline in economic growth and productivity that occurred in the United States in the 1970s and 80s, at least part of the decline is thought be associated with
   a. an inflow of foreign capital and increased foreign ownership of United States assets.
   b. an increase in the manufacturing sector relative to the service sector of the economy.
   c. less public investment in infrastructure.
   d. lower interest rates.

Discussion Questions

1.) A number of retail outlets in the United States emphasize the fact that consumers can make a purchase at their stores with no payments for six or nine months? What effect does their policy have on United States economic growth?

2.) How do United States expenditures on crime and crime prevention affect productivity and the rate of economic growth? What about expenditures on pollution control?

3.) Would it be possible for a country with a large budget deficit to growth faster than a country that had a balanced budget?

4.) Given Denison's most recent results on the factors that contribute to United States economic growth, what types of policies would you suggest the United States pursue to increase the rate of economic growth?

Answers and Solutions to Problems and Exercises

Completing Statements from the List of Terms

1.) Extensive Economic Growth
2.) Net National Saving
3.) Co-determination
4.) National Industrial Policy
5.) Intensive Economic Growth
6.) Economic Growth
7.) Infrastructure
8.) Profit Sharing
9.) Growth Accounting
10.) Lifetime Employment
11.) Human Capital

Problems

The Relationship Between Productivity and Real Income

Productivity and Per Capita Real Income (1980 - 1993)

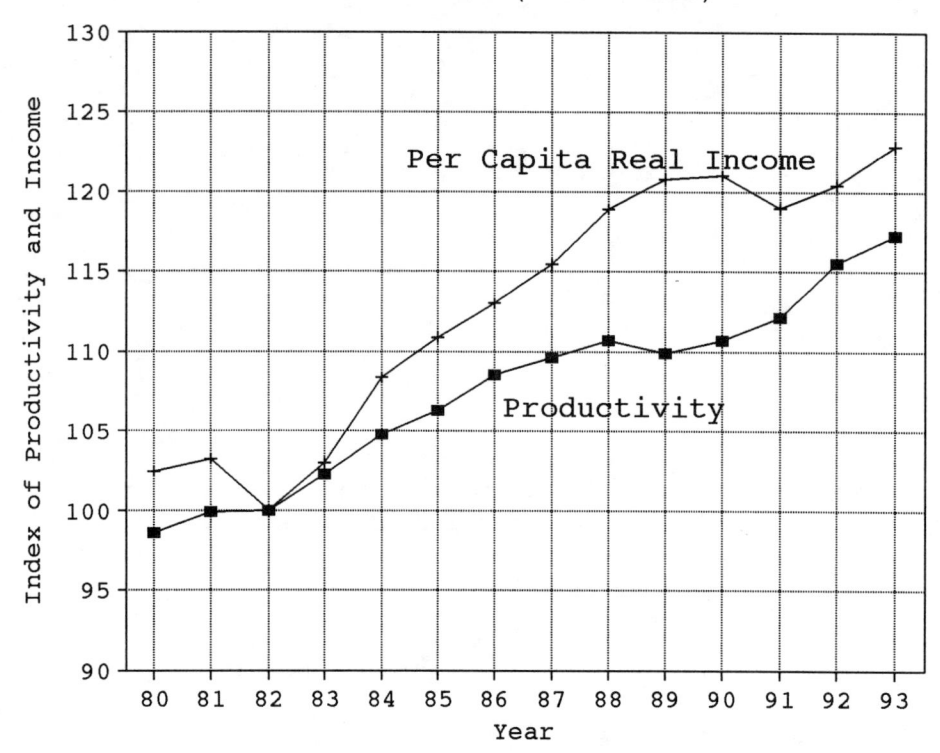

[Graph showing Index of Productivity and Income on y-axis (90 to 130) versus Year on x-axis (80 to 93). Two lines are plotted: "Per Capita Real Income" rising from about 102 in 1980 to about 122 in 1993, and "Productivity" rising from about 98 in 1980 to about 117 in 1993.]

Briefly, how would you define productivity? **Productivity cam be looked at as a measure of how much output is produced per unit of labor -- it tells us how efficient labor is. It can also be defined with respect to other factors of production.**

Why is productivity important in a macroeconomic context? **Productivity is one of the most important macroeconomic variables, since it has such a close relationship with society's real income -- determining in large part the bundle of real goods and services a society is able to consume. The productivity of a society's workers, in conjunction with the other factors of production, largely determines its standard of living. It doesn't come much more important than that!**

Based on the productivity and real income data contained in Table 26-1, what relationship exists between these two variables? **Although it is not a perfect relationship, it is obvious that they are closely related in the positive fashion that we would have expected. Statistically speaking, the two variables exhibited a statistical correlation of +0.95 over this period of time (+1 represents a perfect positive correlation and 0 represents a random relationship).**

The Effect of Differences in Economic Growth Rates

Table 26-2

Year	Index of Real GDP Japan (1965=100)	Index of Real GDP Germany (1965=100)	Index of Real GDP Britain (1965=100)	Index of Real GDP United States (1965=100)
Growth Rate:	4.1%/Yr	2.4%/Yr	2.0%/Yr	1.7%/Yr
1965	100.0	100.0	100.0	100.0
1970	122.3	112.6	110.4	108.8
1975	149.5	126.8	121.9	118.4
1980	182.7	142.7	134.6	128.8
1985	223.4	160.7	148.6	140.1
1990	273.1	180.9	164.1	152.4
1995	333.8	203.7	181.1	165.8
2000	408.1	229.3	200.0	180.4

Figure 26-2
Differences in Growth Rates

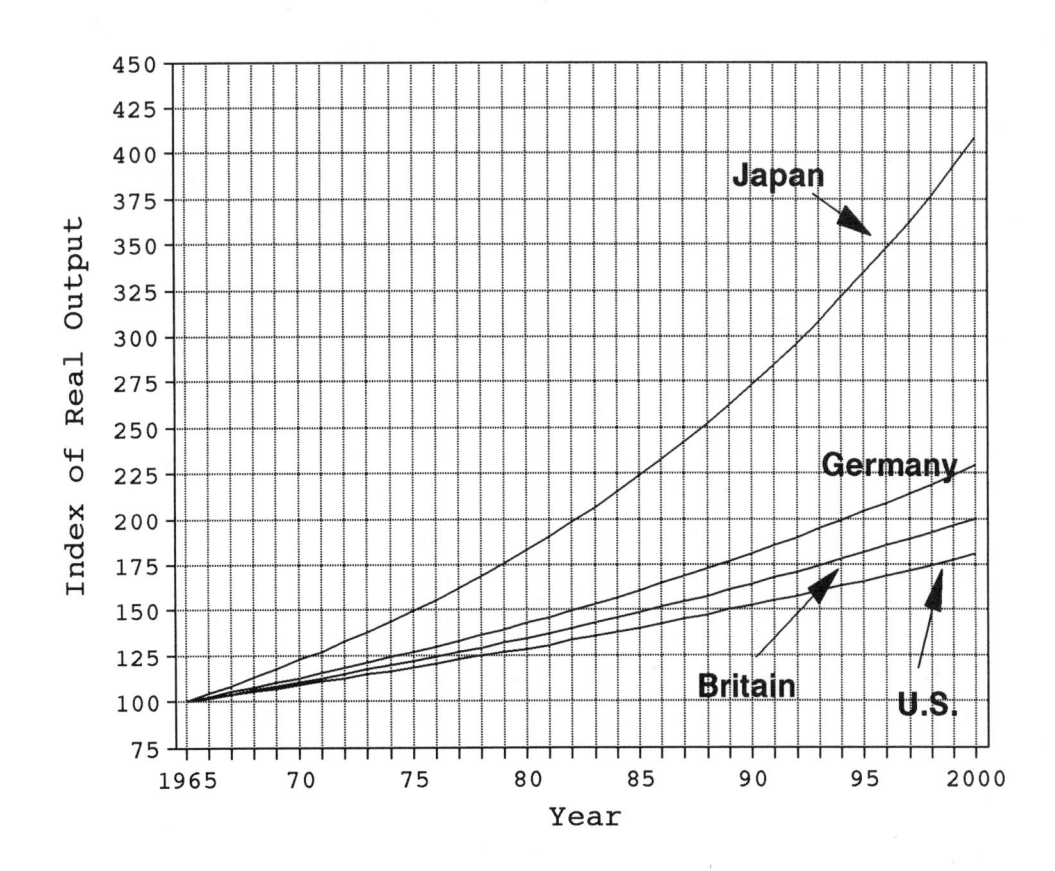

More Advanced Analysis

Using the formula above, determine what Japan's level of output would be in the year 2050. **3043.1!   100 (1.041)^85**

How fast would Japan's economy have to grow per year if it were to double in a period of 15 years? **4.73% per year   200 = 100 (1+r)^15, solve for r by taking the 15th root of each side of the equation.**

The estimates for the years 1995 and 2000 are dependent upon what crucial assumption about the relationship between the past and the future? **The heroic assumption past growth rates will continue unchanged into the future. While what happened in the past can be a good indicator of what will happen in the future, it is by no means a perfect indicator. In a period of change, it is unlikely that the future will exactly mirror the past.**

True/False Statements

1.) **True.** Workers are working fewer hours, while education and technological change are responsible for a significant proportion of total United States growth.

2.) **True.** Wages ultimately depend upon productivity, and, as productivity increases, workers can be paid higher wages.

3.) **True.** Total national net savings are equal to the sum of household savings plus business savings minus the overall government deficit. When the government runs a deficit, it must be financed. It is not a source of funds but rather a user of possible investment funds. It decreases national net savings.

4.) **False.** Private saving is largely dependent upon the level of income and, to a much smaller extent, on the rate of interest. However, it must be kept in mind that higher interest rates tend to lower national income, and lower income is associated with lower saving.

5.) **True.** Having interest rate deductions for any component of consumption spending will provide additional incentives to spend, discouraging saving.

6.) **False.** Although it is difficult to accurately estimate the effect of reduced skills and lower educational attainment, the study refered to in your text estimates a four % reduction in productivity due to lower test scores. Anecdotal evidence and several surveys indicate that firms are encountering increasing difficulty in obtaining employees that are adequately educated.

7.) **False.** While there is considerable disagreement among economists about the nature of the relationship between public investment in infrastructure, private investment, and productivity growth, most economists would agree that public infrastructure projects do have a positive effect on overall productivity.

8.) **False.** The service sector has been somewhat notorious for its lack of productivity growth. Think how difficult it would be to measure productivity growth in college teaching. Are attorneys more productive these days? How about physicians, police, and beauticians? Output is more measurable in the manufacturing sector than in the service sector, and, typically, manufacturing workers have more capital to work with than their counterparts in the service sector.

9.) **True.** The heavy debt burden associated with most of the takeovers and LBOs means that managers must focus primarily on servicing that debt rather than undertaking new investment which will enhance output and productivity.

Multiple Choice

1.) d   2.) d   3.) b   4.) c   5.) a   6.) a

7.) c

Discussion Questions

1.) The policy of allowing buyers to purchase "big ticket" items without having any down payment allows them to consume resources without saving or setting aside any resources and that intensifies the savings problem that has plagued the United States From an economic growth standpoint, it would be preferable for consumers to set aside resources before they consumed goods.

2.) Expenditures on crime and crime prevention use up resources that could be spent in more productive ways, enhancing productivity and economic growth. Pollution control expenditures, while generating real benefits to society, do not show up in traditional productivity measures. Strictly speaking, such expenditures reduce measured economic productivity.

3.) Other factors obviously are of some importance in the economic growth process, and it is possible for those factors to offset the negative influence of a budget deficit on overall economic growth. A country could have a large budget deficit and still achieve good performance by relying more on consumption taxes rather than income taxes, by having a well-educated and well-trained work force, and by investing heavily in its infrastructure.

4.) According to Table 26.1 in your text, technological progress and education appear to make the greatest contribution to the overall growth rate. Policies which encourage companies to engage in research and development activities, provide financing for new technological innovations and innovative start-up firms, and policies which expand human capital would seem to have the most potential for increasing the rate of economic growth.

Summary

One of the most significant economic trends of the 1970s and 80s was the decline in economic growth and productivity. The rise of supply side economics was in large part precipitated by concern over this trend. United States productivity from 1950 - 84 was lower than almost every other developed country, including Great Britain. The United States's poor performance in this important area raised concerns about the its ability to continue in its role as the world's foremost military and economic power.

The decline in net national savings has meant that fewer domestic resources were available for investment purposes. Indeed, the United States ranks among the lowest with respect to net national savings. Regarding possible policy changes, there has been some discussion of imposing a national sales tax or a value-added tax, either of which would tax consumption expenditures, encouraging saving. Possible gains in savings would have to be balanced against the regressive nature of consumption taxes.

The quality of our educational system also plays a role in determining United States performance on productivity and economic growth. The decrease in research and development expenditures may foretell a decline in technological leadership for the United States The low priority given to training/apprenticeship programs suggests that the United States may experience some difficulty in obtaining workers with sufficient skills in a complex, technological society.

Given Japan's apparent success with its National Industrial Strategy (NIS), especially in the area of computer chips and computer-related technologies, there has been some discussion about whether the United States should adopt some kind of NIS to successfully compete abroad. While the political climate in the United States probably precludes very extensive government involvement in the economy, broader programs which supply financing or funding for basic research or which help workers acquire specialized skills may be viable options. A NIS which focuses on specific industries would be very difficult, if not impossible, because of the inherent politicization that would occur.

Chapter 27
International Trade

Overview of the Chapter

The most important goal of Chapter 27 is to provide a better understanding of the basis for trade among countries. David Ricardo's concept of comparative advantage lies at the heart of international trade, stating that in order to maximize overall efficiency and welfare, countries should tend to specialize in and export those commodities in which they have a comparative cost advantage and import those commodities in which they have a comparative cost disadvantage. Interestingly, it can be shown that trade will benefit even a country that could produce all commodities more efficiently than all other countries. The production possibilities model is used to illustrate the comparative advantage principle and to answer questions concerned with the direction and composition of trade, the gains from trade, and how those gains are distributed. The model can show that given different factor endowments among countries, free trade results in the most efficient allocation of resources.

In spite of the theoretical justification of free trade, protectionist measures in the form of tariffs, quotas, so-called voluntary export restraints, and invisible trade barriers are frequently applied to protect specific sectors of the domestic economy from the competitive pressures of foreign producers. Each of the different trade barriers has different economic impacts on the market of the protected commodity, and you need to understand the nature of those differences.

There are a large number of arguments that have been put forth over the years in support of protectionist measures. Many sound quite reasonable, but, on closer examination, you will find that most are based on faulty reasoning or incomplete or incorrect analysis. For example, the "cheap labor" argument is based on the belief that high wage domestic workers cannot compete with workers in low wage countries, seemingly ignoring the fact that wage levels are related to worker productivity. The "national defense" argument maintains that an industry or sector is vital to our national interests, and, in the event of armed conflict, its output would be essential. You would be surprised to see the list of commodities that have been put forth as being essential to our survival as a country.

Many of the protectionist arguments ignore the interests of consumers, instead basing their arguments around employment considerations. Some argue that though Japan provides the United States with many excellent quality, high technology consumer goods, we should limit their importation, since they won't open up their markets to our export goods. Or we have to limit Japanese exports because they are subsidized by their government, and that gives them an unfair advantage. American consumers are helped if foreign countries use part of their own tax revenues to reduce the cost and subsequent price of their exported goods. The producer side of trade issues should not be ignored but, all too often, the consumer side is ignored. Keep in mind that economists are interested in maximizing the overall utility of society, and utility is derived from consumption activities.

Free trade comes under especially heavy fire during times of recession when it is all too easy to reason that imports should be curtailed in order to save the jobs of domestic workers. In fact, the Great Depression resulted in some of the highest tariff barriers that have ever been applied. Those advocating greater import barriers often ignore foreign retaliation. What typically happens is that a trade war breaks out, with the end result being high tariff barriers, reduced trade, and an inefficient allocation of resources as inefficient domestic industries try to replace the output of efficiently-produced imports.

The General Agreement on Trade and Tariffs (GATT) was formed after World War II with the goal of reducing trade barriers through multi-lateral trade agreements, and it has been successful, for the most part, in achieving that goal. Current discussions center around agriculture and the issue of government subsidies and the liberalization of trade in services (the so-called invisibles) and those discussions, as might be expected, have proven to be particularly difficult.

Learning Objectives

After completing this chapter, you should be sure that you are able to:

- distinguish between absolute and comparative advantage.

- explain the theory of comparative advantage and its implications for an efficient allocation of resources.

- understand how the production possibilities model can be used to illustrate the basis for trade between two countries.

- understand the role that the terms of trade (TOT) play in determining the direction and composition of trade and identify the factors which affect the terms of trade.

- explain the rationales for various economic protectionism measures, including the infant industry, the national defense argument, and the cheap labor argument.

- distinguish among the different kinds of trade barriers and explain how they differ from one another in terms of their economic impacts.

- describe the role and purpose of GATT.

Self Evaluation

List of Terms

Absolute Advantage
Ad Valorem Tariff
Comparative Advantage
(General Agreement on Trade & Tariffs) GATT
Infant Industry
Most Favored Nation (MFN)

Protectionism
Quota
Specific Tariff
Tariff
Terms of Trade
Voluntary Export Restraints

For the statements below, fill in the term from the list above which provides the best fit.

1.) The theory of _____ suggests that it is possible for trade to take place even though one country may have an absolute cost advantage in every commodity.

2.) _____ is an economic policy designed to shield domestic industries from competitive pressures of imported goods.

3.) In response to pressures from countries with large trade imbalances (trade deficits) for particular commodities, exporting countries sometimes adopt _____.

4.) If a country can produce a commodity at lower economic cost than another country, that country is said to have an _____ in that commodity.

5.) The argument that protectionist measures should be provided so that newly evolving and emerging domestic industries can develop and mature sufficiently so that they can compete internationally is known as the _____ argument.

6.) _____ has been the mechanism that is most responsible for providing a framework for the mutual reduction of international trade barriers.

7.) A _____ tends to be more restrictive than a tariff, since it restricts the quantity of an imported commodity allowed into a country.

8.) A 12% tariff on automobiles would be an example of an _____.

9.) In an attempt to provide economic protection to domestic producers, a _____ or tax on goods produced abroad is sometimes imposed.

10.) The _____ clause is a provision in trade agreements that requires that any tariff reductions that are given to one country have to be given to all other signatories.

11.) A 12¢ per pound tariff on sugar would be an example of a _____.

12.) The _____ can be thought of as the ratio of the prices of exported commodities to the prices of imported commodities.

Problems

Comparative Advantage and the Basis for Trade

The purpose of this problem is to reinforce the concepts that lie behind the economic basis of trade -- specifically to increase your understanding of the Law of Comparative Advantage and the welfare gains resulting from trade and specialization. Assumptions of the analysis:

(1.) two goods -- Elixir and Ambrosia
(2.) two countries -- Paradise and Shangrila
(3.) two factors -- labor and capital
(4.) fixed resource base -- fixed amounts of labor and capital in both countries
(5.) constant cost production -- both goods can be produced at a specific and constant cost (such an assumption implies that each country's production possibilities curve is a straight line)
(6.) constant technology -- for both goods and both countries
(7.) given preferences -- both goods are economic goods in the sense that more is preferred to less

Assume that if Paradise specialized in the production of Elixir, it could produce 50 units of that wonderful potion, and if it specialized in making Ambrosia, it could produce 20 units, given its current resource base. The corresponding production levels for Shangrila are 40 units of Elixir or 80 units of Ambrosia respectively. Also assume that in the absence of trade (autarky), each country selects a point on its production possibilities curve which represents half of the maximum possible output of each good, i.e., at the midpoint of its production possibilities frontier.

Draw each country's production possibilities frontier on the following graphs and indicate the autarky (no trade) position.

Figure 27-1

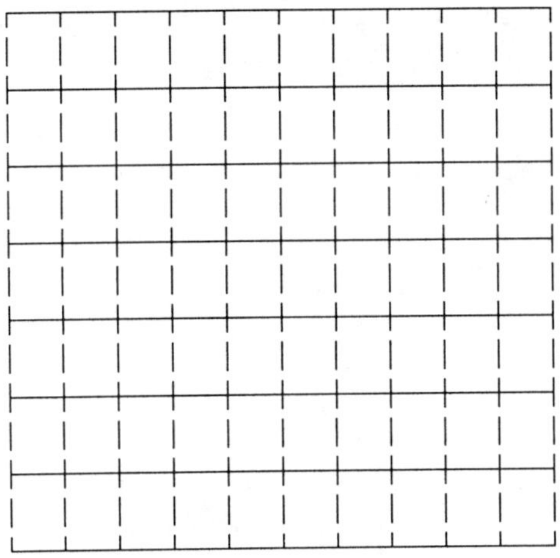

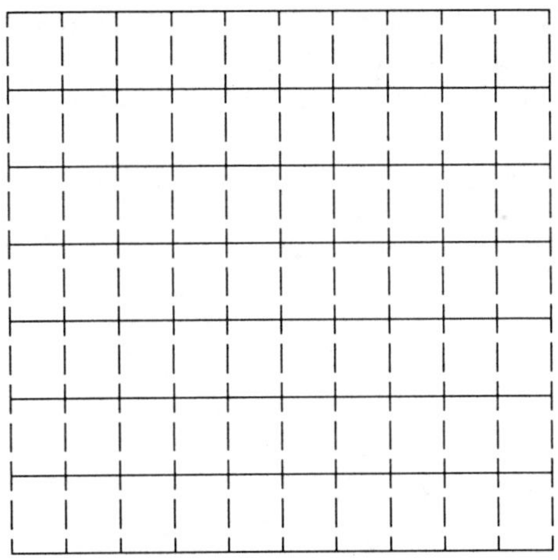

Elixir   Paradise   Elixir   Shangrila

                        Ambrosia   Ambrosia

What are the opportunity costs of each good in the two countries?
_____
_____

Based on the cost data above, what should each country specialize in, and what should they trade for?
_____
_____

State the Law of Comparative Advantage.
_____
_____
_____

Identify the upper and lower terms of trade (TOT) in terms of each of the export goods.
_____
_____

Pick a terms of trade (TOT) that lies somewhere between the two limits stated above, i.e., that is mutually acceptable to both parties. Show on the preceding graphs what would happen if each country specialized in that good in which it held a comparative cost advantage and traded for the other good at the TOT that you selected (the TOT line yielding, in essence, a consumption possibilities curve).

On the basis of the graphs, how could you determine if each country was better off after trade?

_____

_____

Show by means of the table below (showing pre-trade and post-trade production totals for both goods and both countries) and by reference to your graph, that total output of the two goods (and implicitly welfare) has been enhanced by specialization and trade.

Table 27-1

	Pre-Trade Elixir	Pre-Trade Ambroisa	Post-Trade Elixir	Post-Trade Ambrosia
Paradise				
Shangrila				
Totals				

What modifications must be made in the analysis and the conclusions that you reached if the production possibilites frontier reflects increasing costs rather than constant costs (i.e., each country's production possibilities curve is concave-shaped, rather than a straight line)?

_____

_____

Tariffs, Quotas, and Subsidies

Figure 27-2
Tariffs, Quotas, and Subsidies

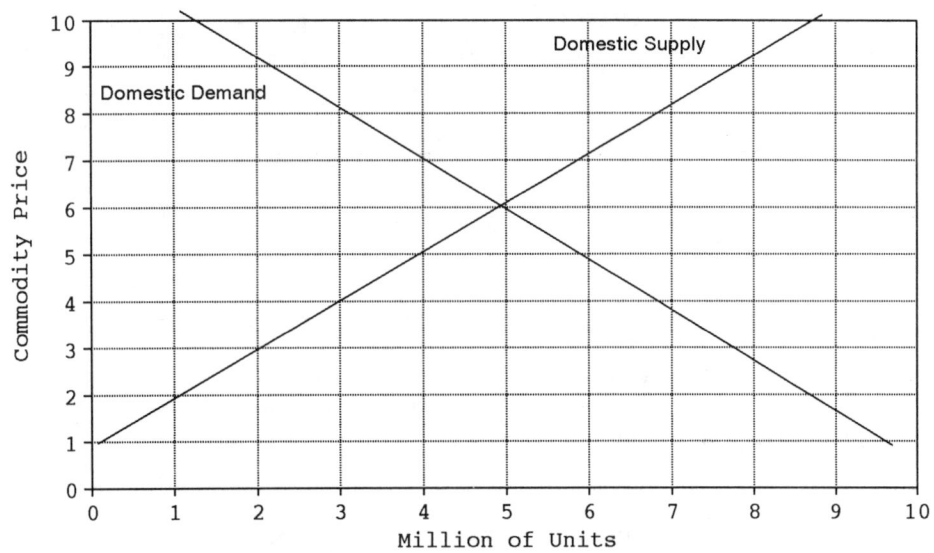

The graph above depicts the market for a particular domestic commodity. Use the graph to answer the questions listed below.

a) **In the absence of world trade:**
the price of the commodity would be? $ _____
the equilibrium quantity would be (in units)? _____
the total amount spent on this commodity would be? $ _____

b) **With completely free world trade:**
the price of this commodity would be? $ _____
the domestic industry would supply how many units? _____
foreign producers would supply how many units? _____
total revenue going to domestic suppliers would be? $ _____
total revenue going to foreign suppliers would be? $ _____

c) Assume that domestic producers exert political pressure and convince legislators that their industry should be protected from "unfair" foreign competition. Suppose a **tariff of $1** is applied to all imports coming into the country. Draw in the new supply curve after the tariff.

The new price after the tariff price will be? $ _____
After the tariff the domestic industry will supply how many units? _____
After the tariff foreign producers will supply how many units? _____
After the tariff, total revenue going to domestic suppliers will be? $ _____
After the tariff, total revenue going to foreign suppliers will be? $ _____
Because of the tariff, domestic producers will able to increase their revenues by how much? $ _____

How much does the government collect in tariff revenues? $ _____
Using the graph squares, estimate (roughly) how much consumers
were harmed by the imposition of the tariff (in dollars): $ _____

d) Assume that domestic producers would like to limit the total amount of imports coming into the country. Why is this not possible with a tariff?

_____

e) Suppose a **quota of 2 million units** is imposed on this commodity. Show the quota amount on your graph.

What is the price of the commodity with the quota? $ _____
After the quota, domestic suppliers will supply how many units? _____
After the quota, total revenues going to domestic suppliers
will be? $ _____
After the quota, total revenues going to foreign suppliers
will be? $ _____

Assuming that the free trade price just covers foreign producer cost, foreign producers will make how much pure profit after the quota? $ _____

How might our government extract that monopoly profit from the foreign producers and importers?

_____

e) One other alternative method of making domestic industries more competitive involves subsidizing domestic firms to reduce their costs. Assume that a **subsidy of $2 per unit** is paid to domestic producers. Show the new domestic supply curve on your graph and label it, **S-1**.

After the subsidy (with free world trade):
the domestic industry would supply how many units? _____
foreign producers would supply how many units? _____
what would the subsidy cost the domestic government? $ _____

f) From society's perspective, which of the three protectionist measures is preferable? Explain.

_____

_____

True/False Statements

Indicate whether you think the statements below are true or false. These questions are designed to make you think about the concepts presented in the text. There may not be any easy clear-cut answers. Some thoughts about the answers are presented at the end of the chapter.

1.) _____ If one country has a relative cost advantage in every good, then there is no basis for trade with other countries.

2.) _____ If the slopes of the production possibilities curves of two different countries are the same (parallel), then there will be no basis for trade between them.

3.) _____ The greater the price range for a good produced in two different countries, the greater the possible gains from trade.

4.) _____ The terms of trade (TOT) that exists for two goods between two countries will be less favorable for the country that has a strong preference for the good it is importing.

5.) _____ Trade allows a country to attain a point outside its production possibilities curve.

6.) _____ Protectionism decreases society's overall welfare.

7.) _____ It is virtually impossible for a country with an average wage level of $15/hour to compete with a country whose wages average $2/hour.

8.) _____ The spread of technology to all areas of the world will make it more difficult for high wage countries to compete internationally.

9.) _____ Unskilled workers in the United States face the prospect of lower wages and greater unemployment because of free trade.

10.) _____ Quotas are more restrictive than tariffs.

11.) _____ Voluntary export restraints (VERs) permit foreign producers to charge higher prices and earn larger profits at the expense of consumers in the protected country.

12.) _____ In a recession or depression, countries raise their tariffs in an attempt to export their unemployment to other countries.

13.) _____ Given the present structure of U.S. employment patterns, it is highly probable that lowering tariffs would cause substantial unemployment among American workers.

14.) _____ Tariffs are a zero sum game (with no net losses) with consumer losses being offset by producer gains.

Multiple-Choice Questions

Select the "best" answer from the alternatives provided.

1.) Barb can paint 100 square feet an hour, or in that same period of time she can change the oil and filter on 4 cars. Julie, on the other hand, can paint 125 square feet an hour and can change the oil and filter on 3 cars. Barb has
   a. an absolute advantage in painting.
   b. an absolute advantage in servicing cars.
   c. a comparative advantage in painting
   d. a comparative advantage in servicing cars.
   e. both (a) and (c) apply.
   f. both (b) and (d) apply.
   g. can't be determined from the information provided.

2.) Kim can wash and groom 10 dogs a day or she can mow 4 lawns during a day. Sean, Kim's brother, can wash and groom 8 dogs a day, or he can complete 2 lawns a day.
   a. Kim has a comparative advantage in both activities and should do as much of each activity as she possibly can.
   b. Kim has a comparative advantage in both activities and should concentrate her efforts on mowing lawns.
   c. Kim has a comparative advantage in both activities and should concentrate her efforts on washing and grooming dogs.
   d. Kim has a comparative advantage in mowing lawns and should concentrate her efforts on mowing lawns.
   e. Kim has a comparative advantage in washing and grooming dogs and should concentrate her efforts on washing and grooming dogs.

3.) You are given the following two production possibilities schedules:

Switzerland:

	A	B	C	D	E
Lederhosen	100	75	50	25	0
Cheese	0	100	200	300	400

Germany:

	A	B	C	D	E
Lederhosen	200	150	100	50	0
Cheese	0	50	100	150	200

For these two countries,
   a. Switzerland should export lederhosen and import cheese.
   b. Switzerland should export cheese and import lederhosen.
   c. Switzerland should export both goods.
   d. Germany should export both goods.
   e. Trade will not be beneficial between these two countries.

4.) Again, referrring to the preceding table, assume that without trade each country produced at point C on its respective production possibilities curves. If both countries specialize in the commodity in which they have a comparative cost advantage, the net gains from trade and specialization will be
a. 200 units of Lederhosen and 400 units of cheese.
b. 50 units of Lederhosen and 100 units of cheese.
c. 150 units of Lederhosen and 300 units of cheese.
d. 100 units of Lederhosen and 100 units of cheese.
e. it is impossible to determine the net gains from trade.

5.) Again, referrring to the preceding table, if Switzerland and Germany decide to trade with one another, which of the following would be an acceptable terms of trade for both parties?
a. 1 Lederhosen = 5 Cheese
b. 1 Cheese = 0.2 Lederhosen
c. 1 Lederhosen = 3 Cheese
d. 1 Lederhosen = 0.5 Cheese

6.) Again, referrring to the preceding table, if the two countries initially agreed to a terms of trade of 1 Lederhosen = 2 Cheese, and then because of an increase in the demand for cheese, the terms of trade changed to 1 Lederhosen = 3 Cheese,
a. Switzerland would not gain as much through trade as it did previously, and Germany would gain more than it did before.
b. Germany would not gain as much through trade as it did previously, and Switzeland would gain more than it did before.
c. each country's gains would remain the same, but the composition of trade would change.
d. the total gains from trade (for both countries) would decrease.
e. the total gains from trade (for both countries) would increase.

7.) The country of Industria can produce 60 units of computers with its resource base, or it can produce 40 units of grain. Lackadasia is not quite so industrious as Industria and with its factors of production, it can produce 40 computers or 30 units of grain.
a. No trade is possible between these two countries.
b. Industria should produce and export both goods, while Lackadasia should import both goods.
c. Lackadasia should produce and export both goods, while Industria should import both goods.
d. Industria should export computers to Lackadasia, and Lackadasia should export grain to Industria.
e. Lackadasia should export computers to Industria, and Industria should export grain to Lackadasia.

8.) If a high wage country like the United States ($16/hour) and a low wage country like Mexico ($4/hour) were both manufacturing the same labor-intensive product and were competing against each other in world markets,
   a. it would be almost impossible for the U.S. to compete with Mexico, since its wages are 4 times as high.
   b. the United States could compete effectively against Mexico as long as worker productivity was higher in the United States.
   c. the United States could compete effectively against Mexico as long as worker productivity was more than four times higher in the United States.
   d. working conditions must be taken into account before comparing wage differences.

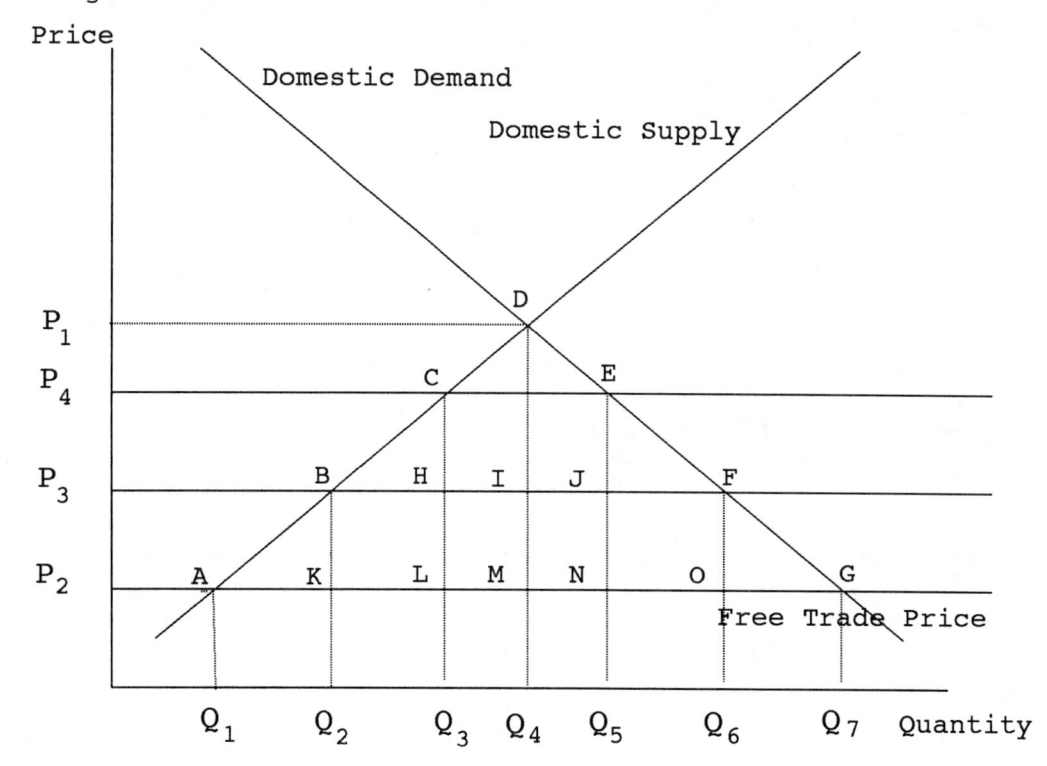

Refer to the graph above for questions 9 -13.

9.) If this country embarked upon a free trade policy, then
   a. domestic price = P_1 and domestic production = Q_4.
   b. domestic price = P_2 and domestic production = Q_1.
   c. domestic price = P_2 and domestic production = Q_7.
   d. domestic price = P_2 and domestic production = Q_4.

10.) If this country embarked upon a free trade policy, then
   a. it will import Q_4.
   b. it will import $Q_4 - Q_1$.
   c. it will import $Q_7 - Q_1$.
   d. it will export $Q_7 - Q_1$.

11.) The amount of tariff revenue the government would raise from imposing a tariff equal to $(P_3 - P_2)$ on the free world price would be
   a. BKFO   b. AGFB   c. BKFO   d. ABK   e. ADG

12.) If the government imposes a tariff of $(P_3 - P_2)$ on the free world price, the increase in domestic producers' surplus would be equal to:
   a. P_3FGP_2 b. P_3BKP_2
   c. P_3BAP_2 d. P_3FOP_2

13.) The total deadweight welfare loss associated with the tariff imposed above would be equal to:
   a. P_3FGP_2 b. P_3BKP_2 c. P_3BAP_2
   d. FOG   e. P_3BAP_2 + FOG

14.) The loss in consumers' surplus associated with the tariff imposed above would be equal to:
   a. FOG   b. P_3BKP_2 c. P_3FOP_2 d. P_3FGP_2

Discussion Questions

1.) One of the points of discussion in the trade talks between the United States and Japan involves Japan's "closed" markets. U.S. firms find it very difficult to gain entry in the domestic Japanese market, even though they feel they have a product with considerable market potential. Based on what you have learned in this chapter, should the United State retaliate against Japan and restrict some or all of their exports to the United States until Japan opens up their markets?

2.) Another source of considerable controversy in international trade concerns dumping. Dumping can be thought of selling goods at prices which are below their cost of production. If it can be proven that another country is dumping one or more products on the U.S. market (which isn't all that easy a task), how should the U.S. respond?

3.) The domestic price of sugar in the United States is about twice to three times as high the world price of sugar. To maintain the higher domestic price, a strict quota is placed on the importation of foreign sugar. The sugar industry is often quoted as saying that its government program doesn't cost the taxpayers one cent.
   a. Draw a diagram which illustrates how such a quota would work.
   b. Is the sugar industry's contention correct? Is it basically a free program?
   c. Briefly discuss what you think the impact of higher sugar prices are on the economy.
   d. What is the impact of the program on consumers and producers?

4.) How would you explain to someone that the theory of comparative advantage indicates that it would be possible for trade to take place between the United States and Malta -- a small country off the "boot" of Italy in the Mediterranean Sea with a population of about 375,000 people and a total land area of 124 square miles)? Wouldn't the United States be more cost efficient in producing any goods that the Maltese could possibly produce?

5.) Now that NAFTA has been approved, what would you expect to happen to wage levels in the United States and Mexico? How will the agreement affect the future location of firms producing labor- and capital-intensive products?

Answers and Solutions to Problems and Exercises

Completing Statements from the List of Terms

1.) Comparative Advantage
2.) Protectionism
3.) Voluntary Export Restraints
4.) Absolute Advantage
5.) Infant Industry
6.) GATT
7.) Quota
8.) Ad Valorem Tariff
9.) Tariff
10.) Most Favored Nation (MFN)
11.) Specific Tariff
12.) Terms of Trade

Problems

Comparative Advantage and The Basis for Trade

Figure 27-1

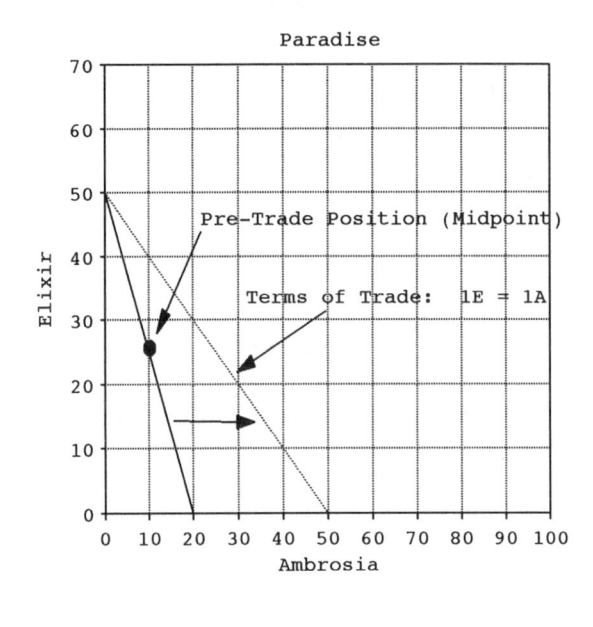

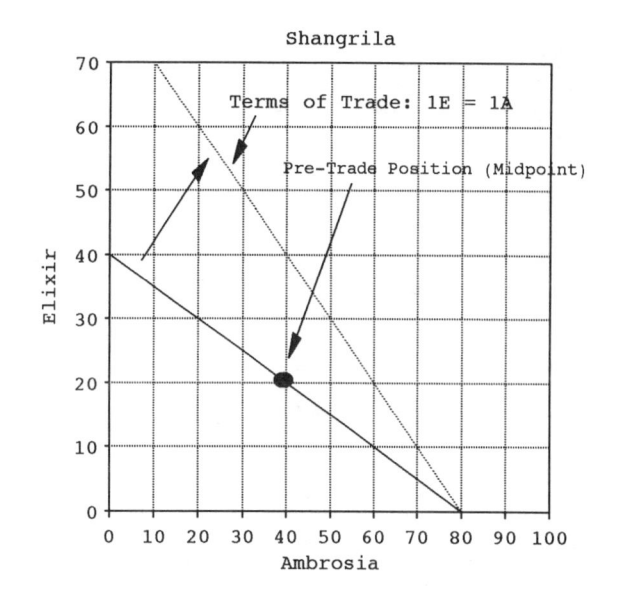

What are the opportunity costs of each good in the two countries?

Based on information provided in the problem:

Paradise: 50 Elixir = 20 Ambrosia =====> 1 Elixir = 2/5 Ambrosia
                                     =====> 5/2 Elixir = 1 Ambrosia

Shangrila: 40 Elixir = 80 Ambrosia =====> 1 Elixir = 2 Ambrosia
                                     =====> 1/2 Elixir = 1 Ambrosia

Based on the cost data above, what should each country specialize in, and what should they trade for? **Paradise has a comparative cost advantage in Elixir, while Shangrila has a comparative cost advantage in Ambrosia. Thus, paradise should export Elixir and import Ambrosia and Shangrila should export Ambrosia and Import elixir.**

State the Law of Comparative Advantage. **Basically, the law states that the world will achieve an efficient allocation of its resources if countries tend to specialize in those commodities in which they have a comparative cost advantage and import those commodities in which they have a comparative cost disadvantage.**

Identify the upper and lower terms of trade (TOT) in terms of each of the export goods.
In terms of Elixir:
    1 Elixir = 2 Ambrosia   (the maximum Shangrila will pay)
    1 Elixir = 0.4 Ambrosia (the minimum Paradise will accept)

In terms of Ambrosia:
    1 Ambrosia = 2.5 Elixir (the maximum Paradise will pay)
    1 Ambrosia = 0.5 Elixir (the minimum Shangrila will accept)

Pick a terms of trade (TOT) that lies somewhere between the two limits stated above. **1 Elixir = 1 Ambrosia is an easy TOT to work with.**

How could you determine, on the basis of the preceding graphs, if each country was better off or not after trade? **If, after trade had taken place, each country was able to attain outside its original production possibilities curve.**

Table 27-1

	Pre-Trade		Post-Trade	
	Elixir	Ambroisa	Elixir	Ambrosia
Paradise	25	10	50	0
Shangrila	20	40	0	80
Totals	45	50	50	80

Post-trade totals for both goods are larger than pre-trade totals; therefore, there is more total output to be distributed between the two countries. By definition, there is more utility associated with the larger output totals.

What modifications must be made in the analysis and the conclusions that you reached if the production possibilites frontier reflects increasing costs rather than constant costs (i.e., each country's production possibilities curve is concave-shaped rather than a straight line)?
A concave-shaped production possibilities curve is associated with increasing costs of production. Thus, as a country moved towards specialization in the commodity that it had a comparative advantage in, the opportunity would rise and eventually eliminate any comparative cost advantage a country might have had. So, the difference is that instead of complete specialization there would only be partial specialization.

Tariffs, Quotas, and Subsidies

Figure 27-2
Tariffs, Quotas, and Subsidies

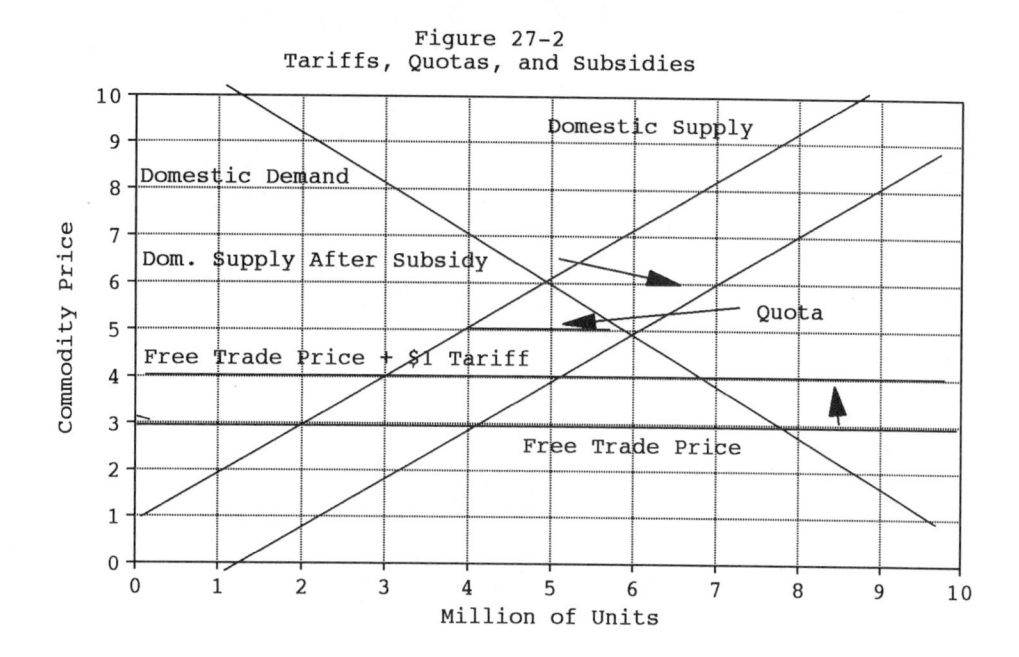

[Graph: Commodity Price (y-axis, 0-10) vs. Million of Units (x-axis, 0-10), showing Domestic Supply, Domestic Demand, Dom. Supply After Subsidy, Free Trade Price + $1 Tariff, Free Trade Price, and Quota lines]

a) **In the absence of world trade:**
   - the price of the commodity would be? $ **6**
   - the equilibrium quantity would be (in units)? **5**
   - the total amount spent on this commodity would be? $ **30**

b) **With completely free world trade:**
   - the price of this commodity would be? $ **3**
   - the domestic industry would supply how many units? **2**
   - foreign producers would supply how many units? **6**
   - total revenue going to domestic suppliers would be? $ **6**
   - total revenue going to foreign suppliers would be? $ **18**

c) Assume that domestic producers exert political pressure and convince legislators that their industry should be protected from "unfair" foreign competition. Suppose a **tariff of $1** is applied to all imports coming into the country. Draw in the new supply curve after the tariff.

   The new price after the tariff price will be? $ **4**
   After the tariff the domestic industry will supply how many units? **3**
   After the tariff foreign producers will supply how many units? **4**
   After the tariff, total revenue going to domestic suppliers will be? $ **12**
   After the tariff, total revenue going to foreign suppliers will be? $ **16**

   Because of the tariff, domestic producers will able to increase their revenues by how much? $ **6**

How much does the government collect in tariff revenues? **$ 4**

Using the graph squares, estimate (roughly) how much consumers were harmed by the imposition of the tariff (in terms of dollars):

Adding up the total loss in consumers' surplus as the price increases from $3 to $4: a total of 30 squaress each worth $0.50 X 500,000 = $250,000 apiece.   **$ 7.5**

d) Assume that domestic producers would like to limit the total amount of imports coming into the country. Why is this not possible with a tariff? **As long as the appropriate tariff is paid for each unit imported, importers can bring in as many units as they desire.**

e) Suppose a **quota of 2 million units** is imposed on this commodity. Show the quota amount on your graph.

What is the price of the commodity with the quota? **$ 5**
After the quota, domestic suppliers will supply how many units? **4**
After the quota, total revenues going to domestic suppliers will be? **$ 20**
After the quota, total revenues going to foreign suppliers will be? **$ 10**

Assuming that the free trade price just covers foreign producer cost, foreign producers will make how much pure profit after the quota? **$ 4**

How might our government extract that monopoly profit from the foreign producers and importers? **Auction off the rights to import the commodity.**

e) One other alternative method of making domestic industries more competitive involves subsidizing domestic firms to reduce their costs. Assume that a **subsidy of $2 per unit** is paid to domestic producers. Show the new domestic supply curve on your graph and label it, **S-1**.

After the subsidy (with free world trade):
the domestic industry would supply how many units? **4**
foreign producers would supply how many units? **4**
what would the subsidy cost the domestic government? **$ 12**

f) From society's perspective, which of the three protectionist measures is preferable? Explain. **The subsidy keeps the price of the commodity at $3 and increases domestic production from 2 to 4 million. It introduces the least amount of distortion; however, it may be the least feasible from a political standpoint. Tariffs are probably the easiest to implement, and quotas introduce the greatest amount of economic distortion.**

True/False Statements

1.) **False.** It would seen that if a country were more efficient at producing everything, then there would be no basis for trade with anyone else. The key point to remember is that no country can be **equally** more efficient at everything. In other words, a country would be better at producing some commodities than others. This difference in efficiencies provides a basis for trade. The country that is more efficient in everything would export the commodity that they were most efficient in producing and would import the commodity that they were least efficient in producing.

2.) **True.** If the slopes were parallel, that would mean that the comparative costs of production for the two commodities are the same and, therefore there is no cost basis for trade.

3.) **True.** The more prices or costs differ between two countries, the more that can be gained through specialization and trade.

4.) **True.** The theory of comparative costs allows us to identify an upper and lower range within which trade will take place. Preferences play a role in determining the actual terms of trade within that range. If the United States has a strong preference for bananas, but the residents of Central America are lukewarm at best about United States wheat, then other things being equal, we would expect the terms of trade to favor Central America (i.e., more wheat would trade for less bananas).

5.) **True.** Only through trade can an economy consume a commodity bundle that is outside its own production limits.

6.) **True.** Protectionism prevents society from achieving the most efficient allocation of scarce resources. Protectionism would prevent the United States from importing cheaper Italian shoes, providing protection and increasing the market for less efficient domestic shoe makers. It is important to keep in mind, that according to the economic point of view, consumption and utility are the end products that we should be pursuing as a society, not jobs.

7.) **False.** What really counts is labor productivity. If the $15/hour worker is eight times more productive than the $2/hour worker, then the higher paid worker will be more competitive than the lower paid worker.

8.) **True.** As workers throughout the world have access to equivalent technology, wages will become more equal, and it will become much more difficult to justify higher wages, because the productivity differences will be much less than they once were.

9.) **True.** With the reduction of trade barriers, unskilled workers in the United States are competing with workers throughout the world that are paid much less than they are. It will be difficult to justify paying American workers higher wages unless they are more productive.

10.) **True.** A quota strictly limits the amount of a commodity that can be imported into a country. There is no such limit on a commodity that has a tariff attached as long as the tariff is paid.

11.) **True.** By restricting the supply of an imported good, a higher price can be charged for that good, and larger profits can be earned.

12.) **True.** If significant unemployment exists, often there is significant pressure to restrict imports coming into the country which are "taking jobs away from domestic workers." It was no coincidence that during the Great Depression, trade barriers reached unprecedented levels. Compounding the problem was retaliation after each tariff increase.

13.) **False.** Just the opposite is true. Almost 80% of total employment is in services which are not threatened very much by imports.

14.) **False.** Tariffs reduce overall welfare and efficiency. There are deadweight losses associated with tariffs that are not offset.

Multiple-Choice

1.) f   2.) d   3.) b   4.) b   5.) c   6.) a

7.) d   8.) c   9.) a   10.) c   11.) a   12.) c

13.) e   14.) d

Discussion Questions

1.) It certainly sounds like an unfair situation when one country opens up its markets to a greater degree than one of its main trading partners. It needs to be kept in mind that if the United States were to retaliate in some way that its own domestic consumers would be the ones that would be harmed by depriving them of the Japanese goods that they had been demanding. With less competition from abroad, domestic producers might raise their prices. This is a frustrating problem when United States producers have so many difficulties selling products for which there would be obvious Japanese demand -- apples and rice are just two of the more visible examples. The Japanese have indicated that they too run into trade barriers when selling to the United States. There is no simple answer to this question, but it is important to realize that the issue is more complex than it appears on the surface.

2.) Whenever a producer sells something at a price which is below its cost of production, it is considered to be predatory in intent, using "unfair" tactics to put fellow competitors out of business. From the consumer standpoint however, dumping increases their welfare, since they will be able to buy more goods and services with their given income restraint. One fear is that the dumping is only a temporary strategic move, designed to put competitors out of business. After that happens, the price of the commodity could be increased to a level which generates significant profits.

A quick theoretical note is useful in understanding this question. It is possible to show that selling in more competitive foreign markets at a price which is below cost is a rational, profit-maximizing strategy when the exporting firm has some excess capacity. By producing more units, the firm can lower its fixed cost per unit (spread the overhead). Since that fixed overhead expense had to be paid no matter what the level of production was, the firm can price its product in the foreign market at a level which merely covers its average variable cost per unit and still increase its overall profitability. This provides a different picture on dumping.

3.) a.

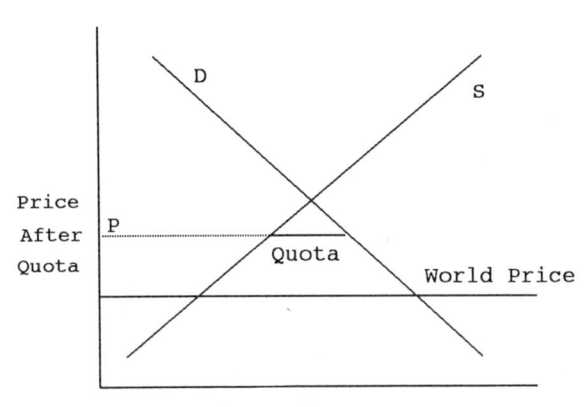

[Graph: Supply and demand diagram with curves D and S intersecting. Horizontal line at "World Price" below intersection, and horizontal line at P (Price After Quota) above world price with "Quota" labeled between the two price lines.]

b. There is no direct outlay by the government other than its costs of administering and monitoring the program. But there is no free lunch here, since the consumers of sugar must pay higher prices for those products containing sugar.

c. Higher costs of production for domestic users of sucrose (derived from beet and cane sugar) and ultimately higher prices for those commodities. Corn syrup (fructose) is making significant inroads into markets previously using sucrose -- higher prices always increase the incentives to find other acceptable substitutes. There would be employment impacts in these two sectors of the economy. The market for artificial sweeteners would also be affected.

d. Domestic sugar producers produce more output and receive higher prices than they otherwise would. Domestic consumers pay higher prices and consume less of products containing sugar.

4.) Even though they are going to be a bit skeptical about this one, I would tell them that the United States is not equally more efficient in the production of goods and services. Trade is indeed possible if the United States concentrates on those commodities in which it has the greatest comparative advantage (perhaps cars, chemicals, land-intensive crops, etc.), while Malta should concentrate its productive talents in those areas in which it has the greatest comparative advantage (hand-made lace is one example).

5.) Since the United States is a high wage country and Mexico a low wage country, economic theory would predict that wages would fall in the United States and rise in Mexico. In fact, labor is not a homogeneous entity but is made of up many different skill levels. From that perspective, firms requiring skilled workers would tend to locate in the United States and those requiring unskilled workers would tend to locate in Mexico. The same holds for firms -- capital-intensive firms locating in the United States and labor-intensive firms locating in Mexico. Other factors also play an important role in the siting decision.

Summary

The issue of free trade has long been a controversial one. From a strictly theoretical point of view, society is best off if production is carried out by the most efficient producers, no matter where they are located. The principle of comparative advantage clearly shows that both parties gain when they tend to specialize in those commodities in which they have a comparative cost advantage.

The effects of protectionism are not limited to those industries that are protected. A highly-protected domestic steel industry will result in higher costs for all the domestic industries using the higher priced, protected domestic steel. To the extent that the domestic automobile industry uses higher priced domestic steel, it will be less efficient than it otherwise could be. Other industries which use domestic automobiles will have higher costs, and so the inefficiencies associated with protectionism spread throughout the economy. The loss of the dynamic gains from trade may be quite significant but are difficult to quantify.

Challenges to free trade materialize when (1) the domestic adjustment costs are large (e.g., the reduction of trade barriers would increase short term unemployment or harm domestic firms); (2) the imposition of trade barriers by trading partners (Japan's relatively closed market is an example); and (3) foreign governments subsidize exporting firms.

Chapter 28
International Finance

Overview of the Chapter

International finance has always been a somewhat mysterious and confusing area of economics. What exactly determines the value of the dollar relative to the value of the British pound or the German Deutschmark? Under flexible exchange rate (ER) systems, the value of a specific currency is determined by demand and supply. When Americans buy French champagne, they are implicitly demanding French francs and supplying dollars on the foreign exchange (FX) markets. As a result of this transaction, the French franc will appreciate (because of an increased demand for its currency), and the United States dollar will depreciate (because of a greater supply of its currency). Given the tremendously large dollar volume that is traded on foreign exchange markets, we are going to have to purchase a fairly large volume of champagne to cause these changes.

The appreciation of the franc and the depreciation of the dollar will, in turn, affect the volume and price of exports and imports for both countries. One of the problems associated with freely fluctuating exchange rate systems is the uncertainty created by constantly changing exchange rates. Fortunately, there are ways in which that exchange rate uncertainty can be dealt with, through what are called "forward" exchange rates.

The forward exchange market facilitates currency transactions at agreed-upon times in the future. If an importer is required to pay on delivery, and delivery will take place in six months, the importer could place an order to purchase the required currency six months forward and would, correspondingly, supply dollars at that time. The forward exchange market allows the importer to pin down the actual exchange rate for the transaction. To not do so would mean waiting until the delivery took place and taking one's chances on the spot (day-to-day) exchange market on that day -- a risky endeavor.

Exchange rates are affected by more than just export and import transactions. Foreign tourism requires substantial amounts of foreign exchange as does investment in foreign stocks and bonds. Direct foreign investment in which foreign firms acquire an interest in domestic firms must eventually work through the foreign exchange markets. When American tourists visit abroad, they demand foreign currencies and supply American dollars, causing the dollar to depreciate. If United States interest rates are higher than German interest rates, then German investors may want to invest in dollar-denominated securities. To do so, they must supply German marks to obtain United States dollars, putting upward pressure on the dollar.

A nation's currency will depreciate against another currency when: (1) its rate of inflation exceeds the other country's; (2) its income grows at a faster rate than the other country's; and (3) its real interest rate exceeds the other country's. Expectations also play a role in determining exchange rates. A currency may be in demand simply because it has been appreciating in value, without any dramatic changes in the underlying economic forces which affect exchange rates.

Exchange rates also have some significant macroeconomic effects -- total spending, the rate of inflation, and the level of unemployment are all directly affected by exchange rate movements. As the dollar appreciates, exports will gradually change, causing total aggregate demand to fall. Imports become cheaper, and the rate of inflation will fall depending upon how important imports are as a percent of total AD. With the decrease in total spending, unemployment will rise.

Although the current international monetary system utilizes floating exchange rates, fixed exchange rate systems have also been used, notably when most of the world was under the gold standard and from 1945 until 1971/73 when the Bretton Woods system was in place. A fixed rate system encourages international trade and financial interactions among countries with its stable exchange rates. When the system is working effectively, participants need not worry about major exchange rate fluctuations which might adversely affect the financial benefits associated with foreign transactions.

Unfortunately, because the exchange rate is fixed within a narrow band and not allowed to adjust to changes in the demand and supply for foreign exchange, serious problems can arise in such monetary systems. As with any commodity, price fixing leads to either shortages or surpluses, depending upon whether the currency is over- or under-valued at its fixed rate. If a currency is under-valued, then there will be a surplus of foreign exchange which will add to the foreign exchange reserves of the central bank. Since most countries view this as a favorable situation, there is little pressure to revalue the currency in an upward direction, since a currency appreciation will decrease a country's exports and increase its imports and destroying jobs.

Real problems can arise when a currency is over-valued. At the fixed par value exchange rate, there will be a shortage of foreign exchange which must resolved by using scarce foreign exchange reserves. Since the exchange rate can't move to its equilibrium level, and since the central bank has only a finite amount of foreign exchange reserves, this situation is not sustainable. When the market, in its wisdom, decides that the central bank does not have sufficient reserves, a monetary crisis develops as market forces put more and more pressure on the central bank. Eventually, as reserves dwindle, the central bank will be forced to devalue its currency to a lower value, nearer the point of equilibrium.

If a trade imbalance exists between two countries, a flexible exchange rate automatically moves in a direction which will eliminate the imbalance. If the exchange rate is fixed, then there is no automatic adjustment, and the imbalance will continue as long as the underlying structural conditions (such as differences in rates of inflation or interest rate) remain unchanged. The effectiveness of domestic fiscal and monetary policy differs significantly between flexible and fixed exchange rates.

Under a fixed exchange rate system, monetary policy is rendered less effective, while it is enhanced under a floating exchange rate system.

Learning Objectives

After completing this chapter, you should be sure that you are able to:

- explain what factors determine the demand for and supply of foreign exchange and how exchange rates are determined in a freely fluctuating exchange rate system.

- identify the factors that cause a country's currency to appreciate/depreciate.

- explain what economic impacts a currency appreciation or depreciation can have on the prices of a country's exports and imports and the subsequent changes on overall exports and imports.

- explain how participants in the foreign exchange market can protect themselves from changes (a process called hedging) in exchange rates.

- explain how the "Dutch Disease" can harm a country's industrial structure and its export sector.

- understand how the gold standard functioned as an international monetary system and how the currencies were valued under that system.

- describe how the Bretton Woods system functioned as an international monetary system, the role of par values and how they were set, the purpose of intervention points, and the role that foreign exchange reserves played in maintaining the par value of currencies.

- discuss the reasons the Bretton Woods monetary system failed.

- understand what arbitrage is and its role in correcting differences among different markets.

- list the advantages and disadvantages of fixed and flexible exchange rate systems.

- specify the goals and rationale of managed exchange rates.

Self Evaluation

List of Terms (includes some terms from the appendix)

Arbitrage
Balance of Payments (BOP)
Balance of Payment Credit
Balance of Payment Debit
Balance of Trade (BOT)
Bretton Woods System
Capital Flight
Currency Appreciation
Currency Depreciation
Current Account
Dutch Disease
Eurodollar Market
European Monetary System (EMS)
Fixed Exchange Rates
Floating Exchange Rates
Foreign Exchange Rate
Foreign Exchange Reserves
Forward Exchange Rate
Gold Standard
Intervention Points
Par Value
Special Drawing Rights (SDRs)
Swap Agreements
Target Zones
Unilateral Transfers

For the statements below, fill in the term from the list above which provides the best fit.

1.) Hard currencies held by a country's central bank are known as _____.

2.) _____ are balance of payments transactions that are associated with gifts to or from non-residents.

3.) An international monetary system in which exchange rates are set and determined by either the gold content of currencies or by the policies of central banks is known as a _____ system.

4.) The problem of _____ has been a signficant problem in countries experiencing significant political or economic instability.

5.) _____ (taking the dollar for example) occurs when there is either a lower demand for dollars or an increased supply of dollars on the foreign exchange market.

6.) _____ are the points above and below the par value of a currency at which central banks agreed to intervene in order to maintain the agreed upon par value.

7.) _____ is dependent upon small discrepancies in a particular market which can be exploited for a profit.

8.) As a first step towards monetary union, European Community (EC) countries have implemented the _____ to provide greater exchange rate stability within the EC.

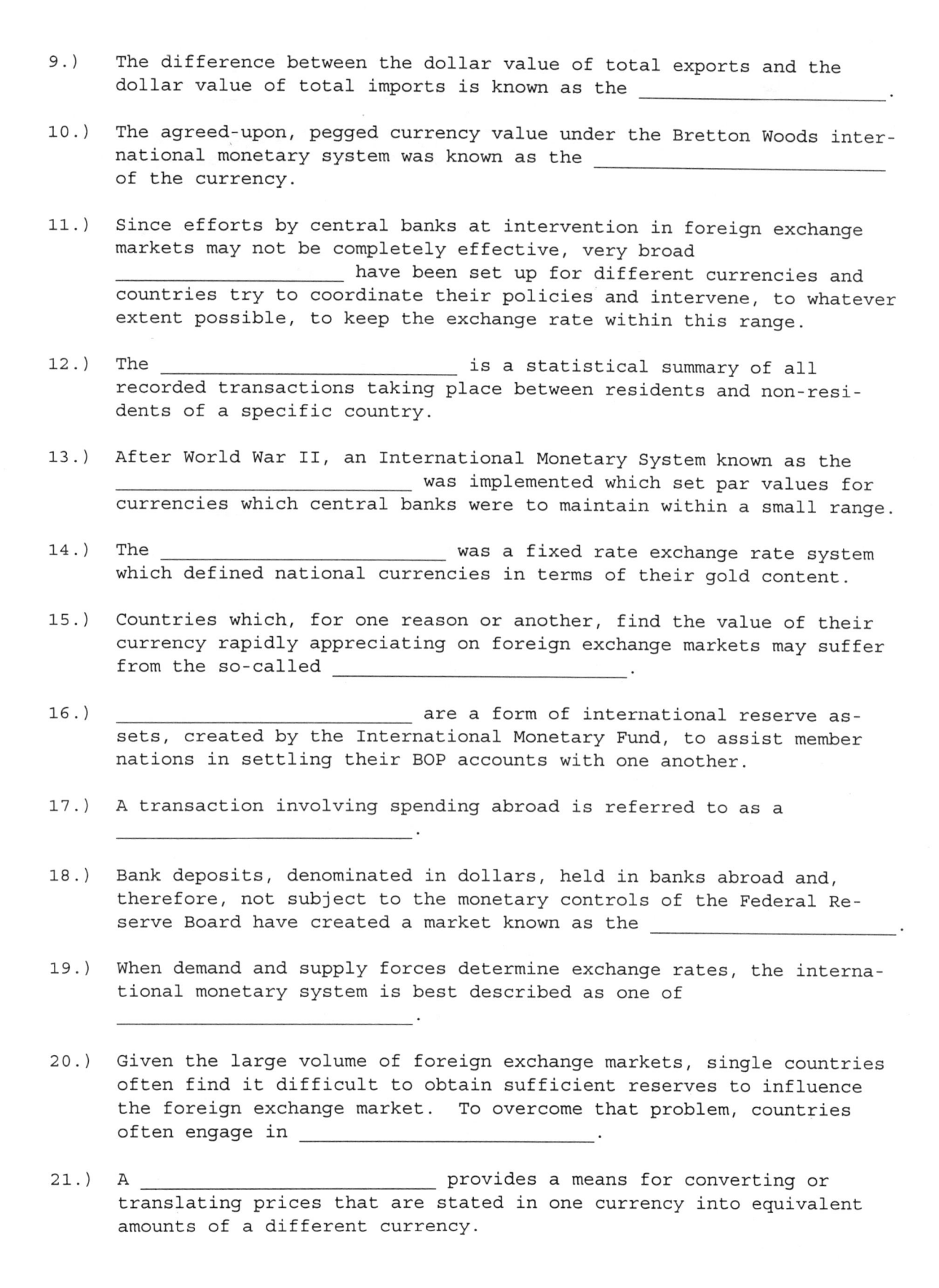

9.) The difference between the dollar value of total exports and the dollar value of total imports is known as the _____.

10.) The agreed-upon, pegged currency value under the Bretton Woods international monetary system was known as the _____ of the currency.

11.) Since efforts by central banks at intervention in foreign exchange markets may not be completely effective, very broad _____ have been set up for different currencies and countries try to coordinate their policies and intervene, to whatever extent possible, to keep the exchange rate within this range.

12.) The _____ is a statistical summary of all recorded transactions taking place between residents and non-residents of a specific country.

13.) After World War II, an International Monetary System known as the _____ was implemented which set par values for currencies which central banks were to maintain within a small range.

14.) The _____ was a fixed rate exchange rate system which defined national currencies in terms of their gold content.

15.) Countries which, for one reason or another, find the value of their currency rapidly appreciating on foreign exchange markets may suffer from the so-called _____.

16.) _____ are a form of international reserve assets, created by the International Monetary Fund, to assist member nations in settling their BOP accounts with one another.

17.) A transaction involving spending abroad is referred to as a _____.

18.) Bank deposits, denominated in dollars, held in banks abroad and, therefore, not subject to the monetary controls of the Federal Reserve Board have created a market known as the _____.

19.) When demand and supply forces determine exchange rates, the international monetary system is best described as one of _____.

20.) Given the large volume of foreign exchange markets, single countries often find it difficult to obtain sufficient reserves to influence the foreign exchange market. To overcome that problem, countries often engage in _____.

21.) A _____ provides a means for converting or translating prices that are stated in one currency into equivalent amounts of a different currency.

22.) A transaction characterized by spending at home carried on by foreigners abroad is referred to as a _____.

23.) The _____ is a balance of payment account which summarizes the net balance of trade, net unilateral transfers, and military transfers and services.

24.) If foreign exchange is demanded or needs to be supplied at a future point in time, the _____ allows firms or individuals to hedge their risk involved in dealing with currencies which are constantly changing in value.

25.) _____ occurs when there is either a higher demand for dollars or an decreased supply of dollars on the foreign exchange market.

Problems

Factor Prices, Comparative Advantage, and Exchange Rates

As is indicated in your text, trade does not typically take place under barter conditions. Production and transactions are usually undertaken in terms of the exporting country's currency units. The exchange rate (ER) provides the basic mechanism to translate one country's prices in terms of another currency. Changes in the ER then determine whether or not trade is feasible and advantageous to the parties involved.

Assume the following:

two goods:	computers and cheese
three factors:	labor, land, and capital
two countries:	United States and Switzerland
two currencies:	United States $ and Swiss Francs CHF

Domestic Factor Costs

	United States	Switzerland
Labor	$5.00/hr	CHF15.00/hr
Capital	$5,000/unit	CHF10,000/unit
Land	$1,000/unit	CHF6,000/unit

Assume that the following factor proportions are used in making each of the two commodities:

1000 units of cheese: 1000 hrs of labor, 3 units of capital, 15 units of land

50 units of computers: 200 hrs of labor, 15 units of capital, 3 units of land

Note: to keep the analysis simple, the same production techniques are assumed to be used in the two countries; in reality the production techniques would differ as well.

Calculate the domestic cost of each good in each currency.

Domestic Costs of Production

	United States		Switzerland	
	Cheese	Computers	Cheese	Computers
Labor				
Capital				
Land				
Total Costs				

Determine the range of exchange rates between the $ and CHF that trade will take place.

Determining an Equilibrium Exchange Rate

The following represents a very simplified version of the process by which exchange rate markets determine an equilibrium exchange rate for two currencies.

Suppose that the following table represents American demand for a French champagne, Chateau LaFete, which sells in France for FF50. Depending on the exchange rate that exists between the United States dollar and the French franc, the American price in dollars will vary.

American Demand for French Champagne (priced at FF50)

Possible Exchange Rates Dollars:Francs	United States Price (in dollars)	Quantity Demanded (Bottles)	Demand for Francs	Dollars Supplied
$1 = FF1	$50	500	FF25,000	$25,000
$1 = FF2	$25	800		
$1 = FF3	$16.67	2000		
$1 = FF4	$12.50	6400		
$1 = FF5	$10	10000		
$1 = FF10	$5	22000		

When Americans purchase French goods they are implicitly demanding French francs as well. And to obtain those French francs, they supply dollars to the foreign exchange (FX) market. The first line of the table above has been completed to assist you. The French champagne is priced at 50 francs. If the exchange rate is $1 = FF1, then the champagne will be priced at $50 in the United States. At that price, 500 bottles of champagne will be demanded, and that translates into a demand for 25,000 francs (50 francs per bottle times 500 bottles). At the $1 = FF1 exchange rate, Americans must supply $25,000 to obtain the FF25,000. You can fill out the remainder of the table in the same fashion.

Suppose that the following table represents French demand for a California wine, from the Upper Sonoma River Winery, which sells for $10. Depending on the exchange rate that exists between the United States dollar and the French franc, the French price for the American wine in francs will vary.

French Demand for American Wine (priced at $10)

Possible Exchange Rates Dollars:Francs	French Price (in francs)	Quantity Demanded (Bottles)	Demand for United States Dollars	French Francs Supplied
$1 = FF1	FF10	20,000	$200,000	FF200,000
$1 = FF2	FF20	15,000		
$1 = FF3	FF30	12.000		
$1 = FF4	FF40	8,000		
$1 = FF5	FF50	6,000		
$1 = FF10	FF100	2,000		

When the French purchase American goods, they are implicitly demanding United States dollars as well. And to obtain those United States dollars, they supply francs to the foreign exchange (FX) market. The first line of the table above has again been completed to assist you. There is one change you should be aware of -- French prices increase with the different exchange rates, because the exchange rates have been kept the same as in the first table. The American wine is priced at $10. If the exchange rate is $1 = FF1, then the American wine will be priced at FF10 in France. At that price, 20,000 bottles of American wine will be demanded, and that translates into a demand for $200,000 ($10 per bottle times 20,000 bottles). At the $1 = FF1 exchange rate, the French must supply FF200,000 to obtain the $200,000. You can fill out the remainder of the table in the same fashion.

To determine the equilibrium exchange between dollars and francs, the demand for dollars (associated with the French demand for American wine) and the supply of dollars (associated with the American demand for French champagne) can be plotted on the following figure. Equilibrium will occur at the point where the quantity of dollars demanded just equals the quantity of dollars supplied on the foreign exchange market.

Francs per Dollar   Figure 28-1

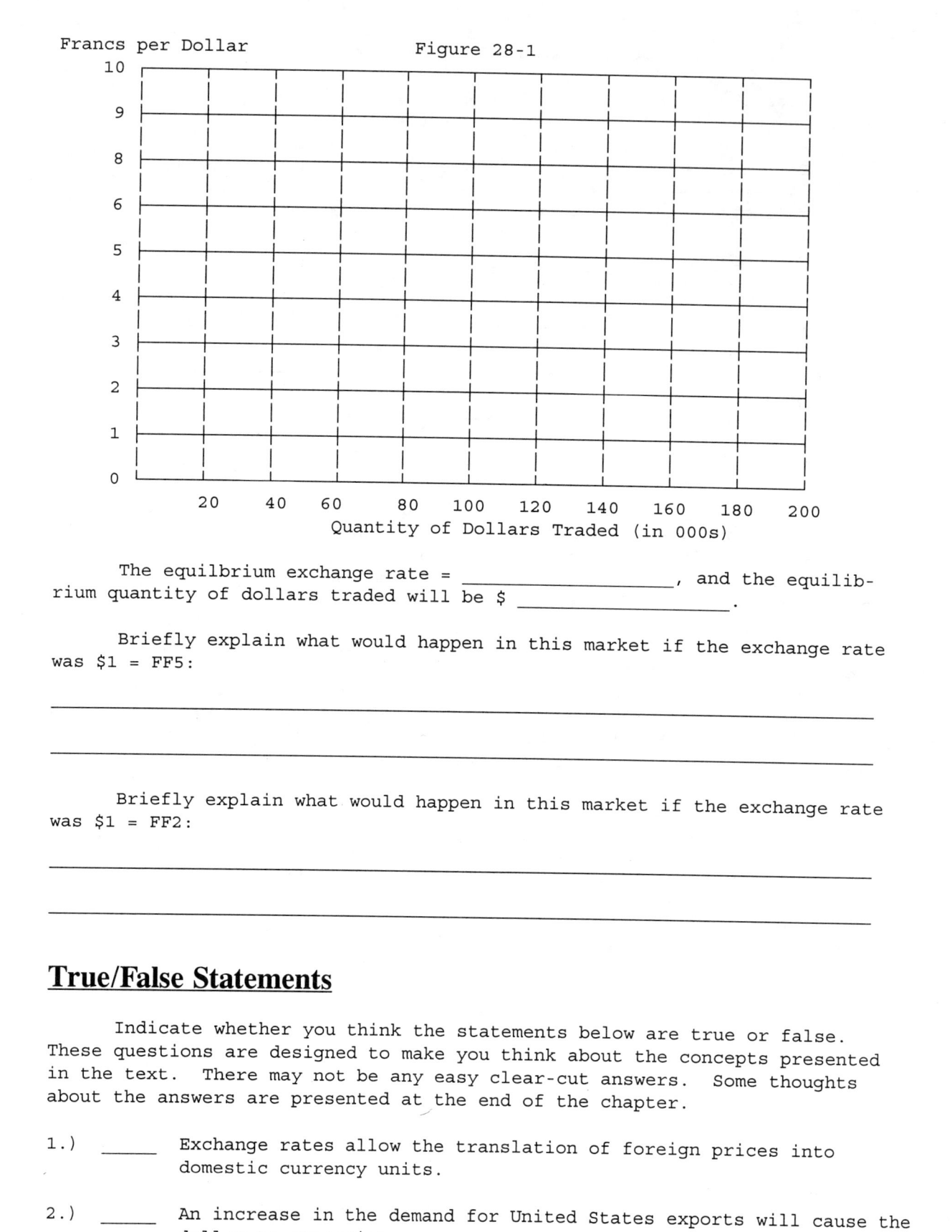

[Blank graph with y-axis labeled 0 to 10 (Francs per Dollar) and x-axis labeled 0 to 200 in increments of 20 (Quantity of Dollars Traded (in 000s))]

The equilbrium exchange rate = _____, and the equilibrium quantity of dollars traded will be $ _____.

Briefly explain what would happen in this market if the exchange rate was $1 = FF5:

_____

_____

Briefly explain what would happen in this market if the exchange rate was $1 = FF2:

_____

_____

True/False Statements

Indicate whether you think the statements below are true or false. These questions are designed to make you think about the concepts presented in the text. There may not be any easy clear-cut answers. Some thoughts about the answers are presented at the end of the chapter.

1.) _____ Exchange rates allow the translation of foreign prices into domestic currency units.

2.) _____ An increase in the demand for United States exports will cause the dollar to appreciate.

3.) _____ An increase in the demand for British goods by Americans will increase the supply of dollars on the foreign exchange market.

4.) _____ It is important from an economic standpoint for a major world power like the United States to have a strong currency.

5.) _____ An appreciation of the Japanese yen will make Japanese exports more expensive in terms of dollars.

6.) _____ If the United States inflation rate is less than the Dutch inflation rate, then the Dutch guilder will appreciate with respect to the dollar.

7.) _____ An economic expansion or recovery would normally be expected to cause a country's currency to appreciate.

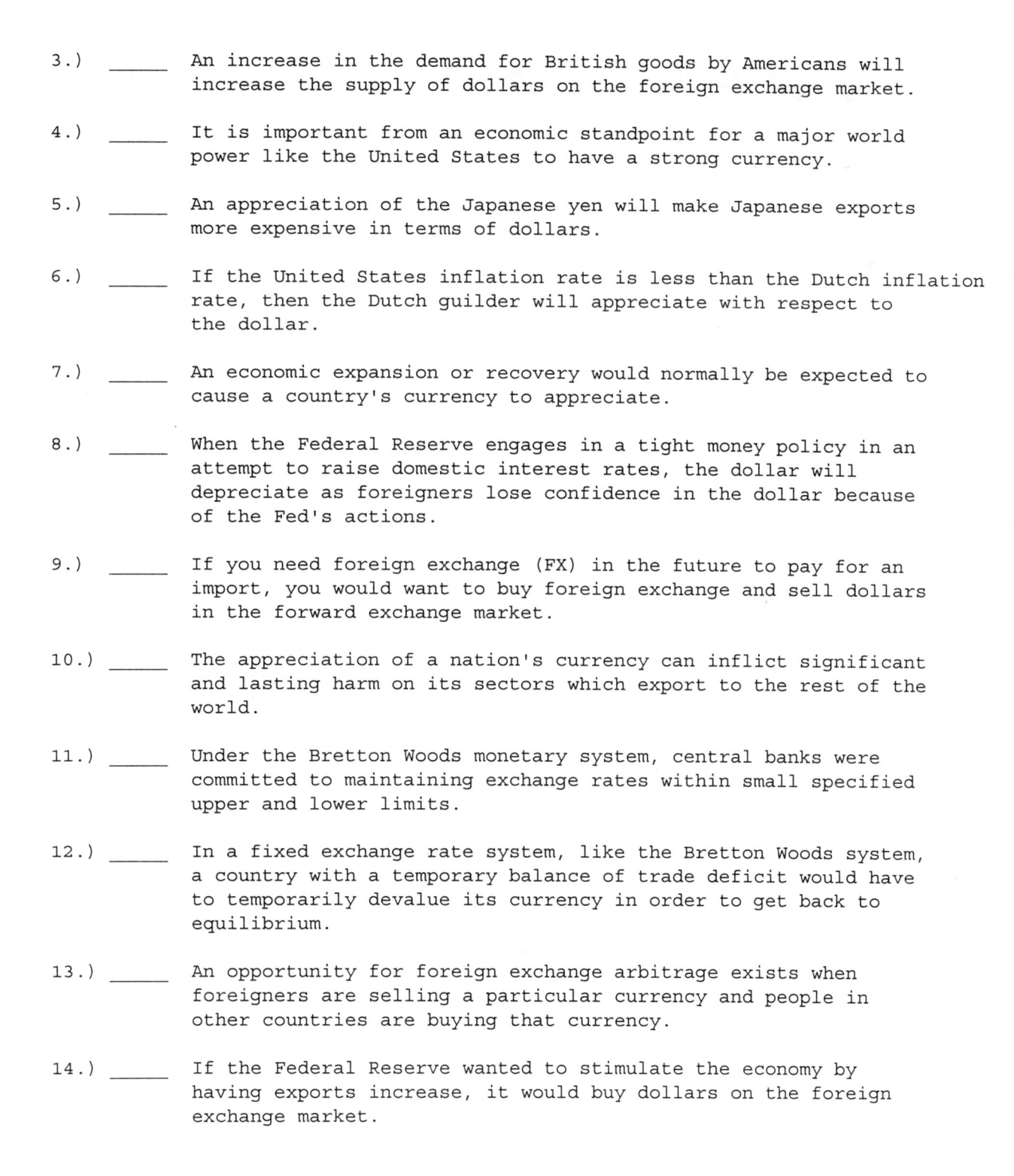

8.) _____ When the Federal Reserve engages in a tight money policy in an attempt to raise domestic interest rates, the dollar will depreciate as foreigners lose confidence in the dollar because of the Fed's actions.

9.) _____ If you need foreign exchange (FX) in the future to pay for an import, you would want to buy foreign exchange and sell dollars in the forward exchange market.

10.) _____ The appreciation of a nation's currency can inflict significant and lasting harm on its sectors which export to the rest of the world.

11.) _____ Under the Bretton Woods monetary system, central banks were committed to maintaining exchange rates within small specified upper and lower limits.

12.) _____ In a fixed exchange rate system, like the Bretton Woods system, a country with a temporary balance of trade deficit would have to temporarily devalue its currency in order to get back to equilibrium.

13.) _____ An opportunity for foreign exchange arbitrage exists when foreigners are selling a particular currency and people in other countries are buying that currency.

14.) _____ If the Federal Reserve wanted to stimulate the economy by having exports increase, it would buy dollars on the foreign exchange market.

Multiple-Choice Questions

Select the "best" answer from the alternatives provided.

1.) Which of the following will result in an appreciation of the Dutch guilder?
    a. An increase in the Dutch GDP.
    b. A decrease in Dutch interest rates.
    c. An increase in Dutch imports.
    d. An increase in Dutch exports.
    e. An increase in the rate of inflation in The Netherlands.

2.) If the United States is running a trade deficit (imports exceeding exports), then
    a. the dollar will appreciate, decreasing exports and increasing imports.
    b. the dollar will appreciate, increasing exports and decreasing imports.
    c. the dollar will depreciate, decreasing exports and increasing imports.
    d. the dollar will depreciate, increasing exports and decreasing imports.
    e. the dollar will depreciate, decreasing both exports and imports.

3.) When an American firm buys a product from a Japanese firm,
    a. the demand for dollars decreases, and the demand for yen increases on the foreign exchange market.
    b. the demand for yen increases, and the supply of dollars increases on the foreign exchange market.
    c. the demand for yen increases as does the supply of yen on the foreign exchange market.
    d. the demand for dollars decreases, and the supply of dollars increases on the foreign exchange market.
    e. the demand for both dollars and yen increases on the foreign exchange market.

4.) Which of the following would contribute to a depreciation of the United States dollar?
    a. An increase in American tourists traveling abroad.
    b. A decline in United States interest rates.
    c. An increase in the growth rate of GDP.
    d. An increase in the rate of inflation.
    e. All of the above.
    f. None of the above.

5.) If a country experiences a trade deficit, we would expect
   a. its currency to depreciate, upward pressure on domestic prices, and increased unemployment in the short run.
   b. its currency to depreciate, downward pressure on domestic prices, and increased unemployment in the short run.
   c. its currency to depreciate, upward pressure on domestic prices, and decreased unemployment in the short run.
   d. its currency to appreciate, downward pressure on domestic prices, and increased unemployment in the short run.

6.) Norway's exports of North Sea oil and natural gas increase significantly. As a result, we would expect
   a. a depreciation of the Norwegian kroner and little if any impact on Norway's other exports.
   b. a depreciation of the Norwegian kroner and an increase in Norway's other exports.
   c. an appreciation of the Norwegian kroner and little if any impact on Norway's other exports.
   d. an appreciation of the Norwegian kroner and a decrease in Norway's other exports.

7.) Assume that your company has just purchased ten large trucks from a Swedish manufacturer, delivery and payment of SEK15 million ($2.5 million) to take place in nine months. If you wanted to minimize the exchange rate risk associated with this transaction, you could
   a. sell dollars and buy Swedish krona in the forward exchange market.
   b. buy and sell dollars in the forward exchange market.
   c. buy and sell krona in the forward exchange market.
   d. sell krona in the forward exchange market.

8.) Foreign exchange arbitrage consists of
   a. charging a small brokerage fee on all foreign exchange transactions.
   b. speculative foreign exchange transactions based on best available estimates of what will happen in the future.
   c. taking advantages of small differences in exchange rates in different foreign exchange markets around the world.
   d. buying currencies when they are overvalued and selling when they are undervalued.

9.) Under the Bretton Woods International Monetary System, a large balance of trade deficit would result in:
   a. a depreciation of that country's currency.
   b. an appreciation of that country's currency.
   c. the country's central bank intervening in the foreign exchange market using its foreign reserves to buy its own currency.
   d. the country's central bank intervening in the foreign exchange market selling its own currency to obtain other currencies.

10.) Under the Bretton Woods System, a country running persistant balance of trade deficits could
   a. repeg its currency value so that its currency appreciated in value.
   b. repeg its currency value so that its currency depreciated in value.
   c. raise the price of gold in terms of its own currency.
   d. lower the price of gold in terms of its own currency.

11.) Under a fixed exchange rate system like the Bretton Woods system, if a country is running a trade deficit,
   a. it must reduce its interest rates.
   b. it must devalue its currency.
   c. it will lose its foreign exchange reserves.
   d. it must impose tariffs and quotas to reduce its imports.

12.) In the absence of capital flows, under a fixed exchange rate system,
   a. domestic monetary policy is reinforced by the exchange rate system.
   b. domestic monetary policy is offset by the exchange rate system.
   c. domestic fiscal policy is reinforced by the exchange rate system.
   d. domestic fiscal policy is offset by the exchange rate system.
   e. both (a) and (c) apply.
   f. both (b) and (d) apply.

13.) In the absence of capital flows, under a floating exchange rate system,
   a. domestic monetary policy is reinforced by the exchange rate system.
   b. domestic monetary policy is offset by the exchange rate system.
   c. domestic fiscal policy is reinforced by the exchange rate system.
   d. domestic fiscal policy is offset by the exchange rate system.
   e. both (a) and (c) apply.
   f. both (b) and (d) apply.

14.) Hot money flows are a potential problem in a fixed rate system, because
   a. they tend to reinforce domestic policies, thus making the final effects stronger than intended.
   b. they tend to offset domestic policies, thus making the final effects weaker than intended.
   c. they tend to make the system unstable when the foreign exchange market believes that a currency is overvalued.
   d. such flows are entirely speculative in nature and not subject to control by monetary authorities.

15.) Central banks engage in managed floats or "dirty floats" as they are sometimes called
   a. when they would like their currency to fall in value in order to make their country's exports more competitive.
   b. when they would like to their currency to maintain its value when heavy selling threatens to drive down a currency's value.
   c. to change the psychological factors in the market, showing resolve on the part of the central bank.
   d. all of the above.

Discussion Questions

1.) How do flexible exchange rates correct a nation's balance of trade deficit? Can you think of any situations in which changes in the exchange rate would not correct a balance of trade deficit?

2.) In a fixed exchange rate monetary system, what kinds of macroeconomic policies could be used by a country having a relatively large balance of trade deficit (i.e., if the exchange rate can't change, what could the country do in the way of economic policy to decrease the trade deficit)?

3.) For a major world power like the United States, it is absolutely essential that it have strong currency (i.e., that it doesn't depreciate over time against other currencies). Comment.

4.) If a fixed rate system were reinstated, briefly describe what speculators should do if they suspect that a currency is overvalued. Does it make it any difference whether a country has large or small foreign exchange reserves?

5.) Central banks can't have a very large impact on foreign exchange, because of the large volume of foreign exchange transactions. Thus, managed floats are largely ineffective. Comment.

6.) Foreign exchange arbitrage is the time-honored art of taking advantage of very small differences in exchange rates among the different financial centers of the world. Does arbitrage help stabilize or destabilize the exchange rate system?

Answers and Solutions to Problems and Exercises

Completing Statements from the List of Terms

1.) Foreign Exchange Reserves
2.) Unilateral Transfers
3.) Fixed Exchange Rates
4.) Capital Flight
5.) Currency Depreciation
6.) Intervention Points
7.) Arbitrage
8.) European Monetary System
9.) Balance of Trade (BOT)
10.) Par Value
11.) Target Zones
12.) Balance of Payments (BOP)
13.) Bretton Woods System
14.) Gold Standard
15.) Dutch Disease
16.) Special Drawing Rights (SDRs)
17.) Balance of Payment Debit
18.) Eurodollar Market
19.) Floating Exchange Rates
20.) Swap Agreements
21.) Foreign Exchange Rate
22.) Balance of Payment Credit
23.) Current Account
24.) Forward Exchange Rate
25.) Currency Appreciation

Problems

Factor Prices, Comparative Advantage, and Exchange Rates

Domestic Costs of Production

	United States		Switzerland	
	Cheese	Computers	Cheese	Computers
Labor	$5,000	$1,000	CHF15,000	CHF3,000
Capital	$15,000	$75,000	CHF30,000	CHF150,000
Land	$15,000	$3,000	CHF90,000	CHF18,000
Total Costs	$35,000	$79,000	CHF135,000	CHF171,000

Determine the range of exchange rates between the $ and CHF that trade will take place. **The exchange rate that would equate the price of cheese is $1 = CHF3.857 (CHF135,000/$35,000), and the exchange rate that equates the price of computers is $1 = CHF2.165 (CHF171,000/$79,000). Thus, exchange rates would be somewhere within the range of $1 to CHF3.857 to CHF 2.165. If the exchange rate were $1 = CHF4, the Swiss would have a cost advantage in both goods. If, on the other hand, the exchange rate were $1 = CHF2, the United States would have a cost advantage in both goods.**

Determining an Equilibrium Exchange Rate

American Demand for French Champagne (priced at FF50)

Possible Exchange Rates Dollars:Francs	United States Price (in dollars)	Quantity Demanded (Bottles)	Demand for Francs	Dollars Supplied
$1 = FF1	$50	500	FF25,000	$25,000
$1 = FF2	$25	800	FF40,000	$20,000
$1 = FF3	$16.67	2000	FF100,000	$33,333
$1 = FF4	$12.50	6400	FF320,000	$80,000
$1 = FF5	$10	10000	FF500,000	$100,000
$1 = FF10	$5	22000	FF1,100,000	$110,000

French Demand for American Wine (priced at $10)

Possible Exchange Rates Dollars:Francs	French Price (in francs)	Quantity Demanded (Bottles)	Demand for United States Dollars	French Francs Supplied
$1 = FF1	FF10	20,000	$200,000	FF200,000
$1 = FF2	FF20	15,000	$150,000	FF300,000
$1 = FF3	FF30	12,000	$120,000	FF360,000
$1 = FF4	FF40	8,000	$80,000	FF320,000
$1 = FF5	FF50	6,000	$60,000	FF300,000
$1 = FF10	FF100	2,000	$20,000	FF200,000

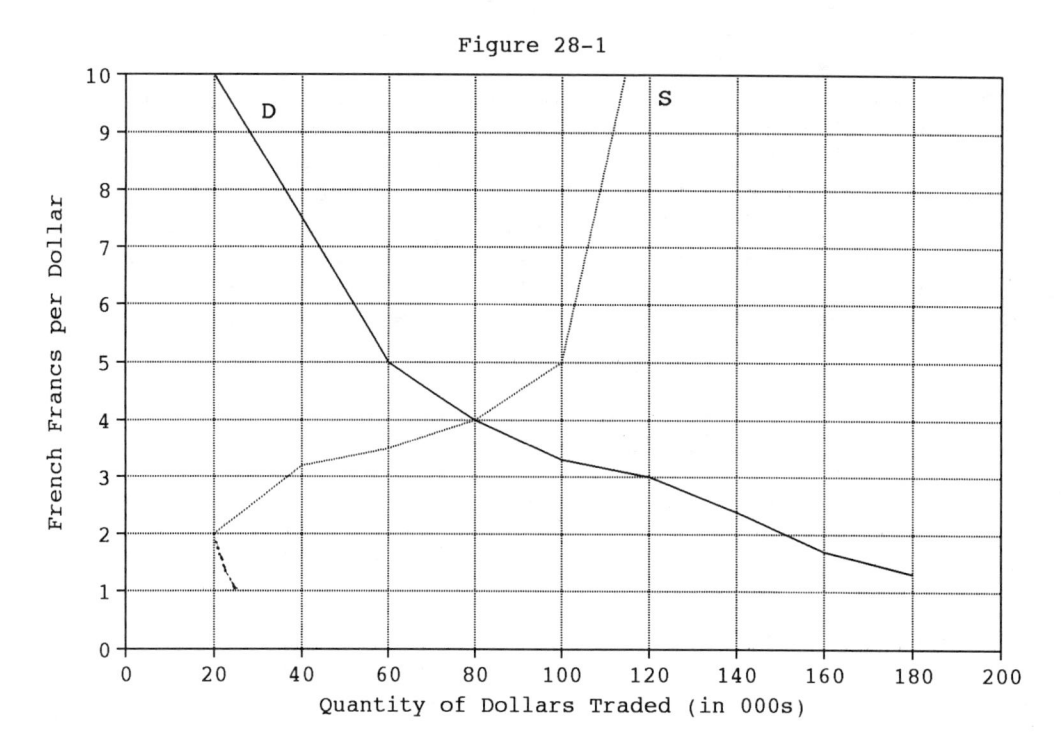

Figure 28-1

The equilibrium exchange rate = **$1 = FF4**, and the equilibrium quantity of dollars traded will be **$80,000**.

Briefly explain what would happen in this market if the exchange rate was $1 = FF5: **At this exchange rate, a surplus of dollars would develop on the FX market. That exchange rate represents an appreciation of the dollar from the equilibrium rate of $1 = FF4, and American consumers respond by wanting to buy more French champagne and French consumers cut back on their consumption of American wine and demand less dollars.**

Briefly explain what would happen in this market if the exchange rate was $1 = FF2: **At this exchange rate, a shortage of dollars would develop on the FX market. That exchange rate represents an depreciation of the dollar from the equilibrium rate of $1 = FF4, and American consumers respond by cutting back on their consumption of French champagne and French** consumers, with their stronger franc, increase their purchases of American wine and demand more dollars.

True/False Statements

1.) **True.** Only by using an exchange rate is it possible to convert foreign prices into the equivalent domestic currency. A London West End theater ticket which costs £18 would be the equivalent of $27.90, if the exchange rate equaled £1 = $1.55.

2.) **True.** If United States exports are in greater demand, then there will be a greater demand for United States dollars by those importing American goods and services and that will cause the value of the dollar to appreciate.

3.) **True.** To obtain British pounds to pay for our British imports, Americans will supply dollars to the foreign exchange market. The increased demand for British pounds will cause the pound to appreciate, and the increased supply of dollars will result in the dollar depreciating.

4.) **It depends!** While a weak currency could possibly make life a bit difficult for a major world power, it would be expected that the foreign exchange markets would be able to handle any problems that might develop. A strong currency, on the other hand, will make a country's exports relatively expensive, making it difficult for domestic firms to compete in global markets. So a strong currency can cause some severe problems in those sectors of the economy which are exporting.

5.) **True.** As the Japanese yen appreciates, it will take more units of other currencies to buy Japanese goods. For example, a VCR priced at ¥20,000 would be equivalent to $200 at an exchange rate of $1 = ¥100, but at an exchange rate of $1 = ¥90, the VCR would cost $222.22.

6.) **False.** The guilder would depreciate against the dollar, since it is losing its value (in terms of real purchasing power) faster than the dollar.

7.) **False.** As economic growth accelerates during an expansion, national income increases, and imports would also be expected to increase. An increase in imports will cause the dollar to depreciate in value.

8.) **False.** A tight money policy will increase domestic interest rates. To take advantage of higher United States interest rates, foreign investors will demand dollars causing its value to increase.

9.) **True.** By buying "forward," a buyer can pin down the exchange rate for the purchase and can determine the price of the purchase. Otherwise, if you waited till the day the contract was due, you would take your chances with whatever the exchange rate happened to be on that day.

10.) **True.** The appreciation of the Swiss franc in the 1970s and 1980s caused major difficulties for its watch-making industry. As the franc appreciated, it became more and more expensive for foreigners to buy the watches. The Swiss were gradually priced out of the market.

11.) **True.** Each currency had a par value which had to be maintained within a plus or minus one % range. If the French franc was on the verge of falling below its defined par value, then the French central bank had to use its scarce foreign reserves to buy its own currency on the foreign exchange market to increase the value of the franc.

12.) **False.** A country might lose reserves because of a deficit, but unless there was persistent and long-term pressure on the currency, a country would not be allowed to change its par value.

13.) **False.** This would be part of the normal workings of the foreign exchange market. Arbitrage refers to making money because of small differences in market prices. Thus, if there was a small discrepancy between the foreign exchange rates in London and Frankfurt, an arbitrageur (what a wonderful term!) would buy a large amount of the currency that was undervalued in one country and sell the currency which was overvalued. In that way, a small profit could be earned.

14.) **False.** To stimulate the export sector of the economy, the dollar should depreciate in value to make export prices more competitive. To do that, the Fed should sell dollars on the foreign exchange market.

Multiple-Choice

1.) d   2.) d   3.) b   4.) e   5.) a   6.) d

7.) a   8.) c   9.) c   10.) c   11.) c   12.) f

13.) e   14.) c   15.) d

Discussion Questions

1.) If a country is running a balance of trade (BOT) deficit (M > X), then the exchange rate (ER) will begin to depreciate. As the ER depreciates, it becomes easier to purchase the country's exports, since foreign currency units will buy more of the country's currency. Alternatively, imports will increase in price, since it will take more of the country's currency to buy foreign goods. These changes in exports and imports will eventually cause the BOT deficit to fade away.

There are situations in which a currency depreciation will not improve a BOT deficit. If the demand for a country's exports is price inelastic (not responsive to price decreases), and if the country's own import demand is inelastic, then a depreciation will not bring about the desired improvement.

2.) Under a fixed rate system, a country can improve its balance of trade position by holding down prices, raising interest rates (both to attract foreign funds and to decrease domestic spending), and it can do what it can to contract the economy. Contractionary economic policies are called for.

3.) It is essential if the United States dollar is to remain a key currency -- a currency which is held as an asset by other foreign central banks. However, from a domestic economic standpoint, a strong currency makes it difficult to compete in export markets and encourages imports from other countries. It all depends on your point of view. If you export to the rest of the world, a strong currency can make it very difficult for you. If you purchase a lot of imported goods, a strong currency increases your purchasing power.

4.) A speculator should sell her holdings of the currency in the expectation that it will be decreasing in value in the future when, and if, it is devalued. If a country has large foreign exchange reserves, it can maintain the value of its currency for an extended period of time, making the actual devaluation a much more uncertain process. Currency swaps among central banks can help maintain a currency's value in the face of heavy speculative pressures.

5.) The volume in foreign exchange transactions involving the dollar make it abundantly clear that even the Fed, with its large resource base, can have no more than a transitory impact on the market. The value of central bank intervention seems to be in showing resolve and in attempting to break the market psychology in a very short-run period of time.

6.) Arbitrage helps stablize the exchange system by bringing exchange rates into equilibrium. By buying low and selling high, market forces are brought to bear to remove any differences.

Summary

The last few years have illustrated how powerful market forces are in determining exchange rate outcomes and the gradual decline in the power of central banks. The problems that major countries have had in staying within the limits of the exchange rate mechanism of the European Monetary System have demonstrated how difficult it is for central banks to maintain exchange rate goals. Once the psychology of the market decides that a country has an overvalued currency, it appears that there is very little that can be done to avoid widescale selloffs of the currency which more or less force a revaluation of the currency.

In spite of the rather large fluctuations that sometimes occur in exchange rates, the forward market functions effectively as a mechanism for dealing with the uncertainty and risk of exchange rate changes. Given the differences in economic growth rates, inflation rates, and interest rates that exist among the world's economies, there does not seem to be any viable plan for returning to any kind of a fixed exchange rate system.

Appendix

Overview of the Appendix

A country's transactions with other countries are recorded in its balance of payments accounts. Within the framework of double entry bookkeeping, every transaction has a credit and debit aspect to it. For example, a merchandise export is recorded as a credit (+), since it gives rise to a claim against a foreigner, and a payment must be made to a domestic resident. If payment is made by crediting the exporter's London bank account, that would be debit (-) entry under private capital payments, since it is equivalent to an outflow of funds from the United States.

The balance of trade indicates the net balance of export and import merchandise transactions, and the balance on current account is determined by the balance of trade and the net balances in the military services account, service and investment account, and the unilateral transfers account. These balances are helpful in determining whether or not a country is running a deficit or surplus in its transactions with other countries.

Learning Objectives

After reading this appendix, you should be sure that you are able to:

- understand the balance of payments accounting framework and its main accounts.

- identify the kinds of international transactions which lead to credit entries on the balance of payments.

- identify the kinds of international transactions which lead to debit entries on the balance of payments.

Problems

For each of the following transactions, indicate the appropriate credit/debit entry. Use the account categories listed below. Remember every transaction results in both a credit and debit entry so that the balance of payments balances out. Remember that most private transactions involve payment through the private capital account (i.e., an export from the United States would be paid for by crediting the exporter's checking account).

a) General Motors builds a $50 million plant in Canada, drawing on its holdings of Canadian dollars in a Toronto bank.

b) Selmer Jones smuggles in $5 million of illegal drugs from Mexico. He is not caught. He paid cash for the drugs and eventually the dollars from the transaction show up at the Mexican central bank. (Think of this as a transaction in which there is no record of goods/services sold but there is a record that indicates that some kind of transaction did in fact take place.)

c) A group of concerned citizens raises $10 million which it gives to Ethiopia to help prevent starvation.

d) Another religious group donates ten large tractors (worth $200,000 each) to a refugee group in Africa.

e) An independently wealthy professor at a small liberal arts college receives dividends of $3 million on her shares of Norsk Data (a Norwegian computer firm.)

f) A small American firm, Hi-Tech Genetics Inc., makes a $7 million sale to a leading Agri-business firm in Scotland. Their account at the Clydesdale Bank in Edinburgh is credited.

g) A leading U.S. retailer buys $1,250,000 of the new French perfume Ooo La La from a perfume company located in Province, France.

h) The NY Federal Reserve Bank sells $12 million of gold in exchange for an increase in their pound-denominated account at the Bank of England.

	Credit	Debit
Exports of merchandise		
Imports of merchandise		
Military transactions		
Services and investment income		
Unilateral transfers		
Private capital payments (increase in U.S. private assets abroad)		
Private capital payments (increase in foreign private assets in the U.S.)		
Gold shipments		
Changes in foreign government holdings of dollar assets		
Changes in U.S. government assets (foreign currency reserves)		
Statistical discrepancy (errors and omissions)		

On the basis of the international transactions listed above, calculate the following balance of payments balances:

Merchandise balance (balance of trade): $_____

Balance on goods and services: $_____

Balance on current Account: $_____

Answers and Solutions to Problems and Exercises

Problems

	Credit	Debit
Exports of Merchandise	$7M(f) $1M(d)	
Imports of Merchandise		$1.25M(g)
Military Transactions		
Services and Investment Income	$3M(e)	
Unilateral Transfers		$10M(c) $1M(d)
Private Capital payments (increase in U.S. private assets abroad)		$50M(a) $7M(f)
Private Capital payments (increase in foreign private assets in the U.S.)	$1.25M(g) $10M(c) $50M(a)	$3M(e)
Gold Shipments	$12M(h)	
Changes in foreign government holdings of dollar assets	$5M(b)	
Changes in U.S. government assets (foreign currency reserves)		$12M(h)
Statistical Discrepancy (errors and omissions)		$5M(b)
Totals:	$89.25M	$89.25M

On the basis of the international transactions listed above, calculate the following balance of payments balances:

Merchandise balance: **+ $6.75M**

Balance on goods and services: **+ $9.75M**

Balance on current account: **− $1.25M**

Chapter 29
Reforming the Command Economies

Overview of the Chapter

The downfall of the Soviet Union, the unification of the two Germanies, and the attempts by former Eastern Bloc countries to reform their economies have focused our interest on the Soviet style economies, their flaws, and the various possibilities for reform. The purpose of this chapter is to provide a brief background on the Soviet style of central planning, the planning process itself, how incentives and bonuses were used within the system, the role of prices, and the chronic problems that have characterized these kinds of economic systems.

As with any economic system, provision must be made for unforeseen contingencies. Firms typically maintained extra raw materials in anticipation of uncertain conditions. Depending on exactly how the output goal was stated, plants modified their products in such a way that they could achieve the target level of output and earn whatever bonuses they could. Thus, if the central planning agency did not specify exactly what it wanted (and that was simply not possible in most instances), the final output might be something no one had intended. This was especially true for consumer goods where product type and quality were easier to change. It is important to note that even though the state was preeminent in the former Soviet Union, managers, farmers, and workers still behaved in a rational, maximizing way within the constraints of the system.

In addition to the raw materials hidden away for whatever crisis might occur, independent sources of supply were often developed by different government ministries, in some instances with little regard for cost. However, in spite of these efforts to minimize supply discontinuities, the rigidity of the Soviet style economies and their inability to respond to rapidly changing conditions contributed to the systems' downfall. With few incentives to invest in new plant and equipment or to modify and improve production techniques, the growth rate of the Soviet economy gradually fell to a fraction of that achieved in the system's better days -- the 1930s. Consumers were frustrated by the lack of quality goods and services, and, as we are finding out today, the centrally planned Soviet style economy was no friend of the environment. The system provided little if any incentive for firms and managers to clean up their industrial effluents -- output goals and quotas being the only game in town.

Chapter 29 outlines many of the major reforms that have been undertaken. Fundamental to any serious effort at reform is the transfer of production decisions from the public sector and the central planning agency to the private sector and the managers of the producing units. In addition, an independent banking system and a stable capital market are needed to provide financing of new ventures and the privatization of state-run enterprises. A stable, convertible currency is especially important for international trade and the inflow of needed foreign capital.

While Poland and Hungary, in particular, have been successful in initiating substantial reforms, the former USSR with its many ethnic constituencies and its very complicated political situation has lagged behind the reforms that have been instituted in its former satellites. Partial changes, while perhaps more acceptable politically, have largely failed to reform and revitalize the economy. A measure allowing firms the right to earn their own profits for reinvestment purposes has failed to help much, since firms were still committed almost entirely to orders from the state. With many final prices still controlled, but intermediate goods free to find their free market level, many firms have incurred large losses rather than earning profits. This, in turn, has put more stress on the central government as it attempted to meet the firms' losses. Thus, the government faced a situation similar to a defeated wartime country with decreasing government revenues and increasing monetary obligations. The temptation to print more money is overwhelming, and there is evidence that large increases in the Russian money supply are occurring, with subsequent inflationary pressures. Many of the firms which were able to generate profits under the reforms initiated new projects which intensified the demand for certain inputs. Because of this and the fact that some firms were shut down because of pollution problems, shortages have become persistent.

Boris Yeltsin proposed a one and a half year plan which would change the former Soviet economy to a market economy. Whatever happens, aid from former cold war enemies will assist in the financing of the changes that are needed. However, as Germany has found out, the costs of revitalizing an eastern bloc economy can be extremely large. It is doubtful that such aid can be of more than marginal assistance.

Learning Objectives

After completing this chapter, you should be sure that you are able to:

- describe in broad terms the central planning process used in command economies.

- understand the role that prices played in the Soviet command type systems.

- describe the incentives that Soviet planners used to meet their output goals.

- understand why the quality of consumer goods was poor in the Soviet command type systems.

- describe the attempts to modify and improve the central planning process.

- discuss the major reform efforts that have been implemented in Russia.

- describe Soviet agricultural policy and the role that state and collective farms and private plots played in the system.

- list the reasons that the Soviet economy deteriorated over time.

3.) Which of the following statements about Soviet agriculture policy is correct?
   a. All agricultural output was required to be sold to the state.
   b. The main purpose of both state farms and collective farms was to keep their workers on the farm, reducing pressure on the cities.
   c. State farms provided more incentives to individual workers than collective farms.
   d. Both state farms and collective farms allowed private plots which could be used by the collective's workers any way they wished.

4.) The privatization of state-owned enterprises
   a. will help consumers in those sectors of the economy formerly controlled by state monopoly firms.
   b. is proceeding at a faster pace in rural areas than in urban areas because of the smaller size of rural firms.
   c. has allowed former communist managers and officials to gain control over former state-run enterprises.
   d. has not succeeded for many of the larger, less efficient state enterprises.

5.) Which of the following measures would assist Russia's efforts at economic reform?
   a. direct foreign investment in the Russian economy.
   b. the reduction of Western trade barriers on Russian goods.
   c. stabilizing the value of the Russian ruble.
   d. Western funding for efforts to provide investment capital for new businesses.
   e. all of the above.

Discussion Questions

1.) Do you think it would be a good idea for the Russian government to set limits on the amount of profits that foreign investors could take out of the country?

2.) Now that you have gained some understanding of central planning in the former Soviet Union and how the five-year economic plans were implemented, can you explain why pollution problems (which we are only just beginning to understand the extent and ecological impact of their environmental problems) were so pervasive?

3.) Briefly explain why it is often easier for centrally planned economies like the former Soviet Union to allocate resources to the investment sector, setting the stage for rapid growth rates.

4.) Given what we now know about the former Soviet Union and its centrally planned economy, what were the main reasons for its declining growth rates in the 1970s and 1980s, coming after a period of relatively rapid growth?

5.) It has been said that part of the demise of the former Soviet Union was due to its military competition with the United States during the cold war. Some have said that the "star wars" program was designed to do exactly that. How could the military competition with the United States have resulted in a collapse of the entire economic system? Do you think that very likely?

6.) Up to the present time, there has been relatively little direct foreign investment in the Russian economy by U.S. investors. Contributing to the lack of investment has been the decline in the value of the Russsian ruble. (1) Why would you expect the ruble to decline in value during a period of rapid economic reform? (2) Why is that so important to foreign investors?

Answers and Solutions to Problems and Exercises

Completing Statements from the List of Terms

1.) Output Targets
2.) State Farms
3.) Perestroika
4.) Storming (Russian slang)
5.) Central Planning
6.) Privatization
7.) Collective Farms
8.) GOSPLAN

True/False Statements

1.) **False.** Until very recently, the Soviet Union heavily allocated its resources to the military and to the investment sector of the economy. Since there was little feedback between consumers and state-run enterprises, consumer goods were characterized by shoddy quality and simultaneous shortages and surpluses of wanted and unwanted consumer goods.

2.) **True.** The premiums or monetary bonuses played a large role in determining what was produced and how it was produced. The bonuses were designed to increase production and efficiency but were subverted by the workers and managers into a system which increased their incomes at the expense of product quality.

3. **False.** Perhaps in a very rare instance were there such penalties, but product quality was so universally poor that it is doubtful that they were used very much.

4.) **True.** Technological innovation was severely curtailed by the Soviet authorities' insistence on tightly controlled borders.

5.) **True.** To guarantee sources of supply, many of the Soviet ministries set up their own factories. Understandable perhaps, but surprising nonetheless.

6.) **True.** Although a portion of their output had to be sold to the state, the remainder could be sold through markets set up in surrounding cities.

7.) **True.** There were fairly large wage differentials within the labor market, with wages being used to attract workers to different areas of the country and to different occupations. Wages were not set by the forces of demand and supply, but the differentials had a market-like effect.

8.) **Somewhat true.** In any market or auction setting, the final outcomes are generally determined by those with the greatest financial resources. To prevent the state-run enterprises from being completely controlled by those who were in power before the market reform, vouchers were issued to the general public and could be used to buy shares of ownership.

Multiple-Choice

1.) c   2.) b   3.) d   4.) d   5.) e

Discussion Questions

1.) While countries understandably want to have profits reinvested into their economies, the reality is that firms will be reticent about investing in any country that limits their ability to repatriate profits. Thus, such measures become self-defeating since investors will tend to stay away from countries which have such measures.

2.) With so many demands on the country's scarce resources, expenditures on pollution controls were given very low priority, even though the costs imposed on society as a whole might be very large. The emphasis was on economic growth, and in that context, expenditures related to pollution are viewed as unproductive, since they do not contribute to measurable output. In addition, the citizens affected by the pollution were not able to generate any pressure on government agencies to clean up any effluents.

3.) The central planning agency finds it relatively easy to allocate resources for investment purposes, since they control the allocation process. In contrast, a market economy is based on meeting consumers' needs and must, by definition, be more responsive to their needs. In a market-oriented economy, if a country is near the subsistence level or at a level not much above subsistence, it is terribly difficult to generate the savings or release the resources needed to finance investment projects.

4.) Initially, the large proportion of resources devoted to the investment sector by the state planning agency resulted in high rates of economic growth. As the Soviet economy matured, however, the economic system's rigidity began to take its toll. The economy began to be characterized by a lack of innovation, and, perhaps worse, the system failed to provide a mechanism which effectively motivated its participants to take actions which furthered both their own interests and the interests of society at large. As your text suggests, the prevailing attitude was to take advantage of the system as best one could and let the results fall where they may.

5.) With the Soviet economic system performing so poorly, the strain put on the system to produce increasingly sophisticated weapons systems must have been considerable. No one knows if there was a point at which the system simply could not support the resources demanded by a "star wars" system. Most people would agree that the military competition played a role in the system's demise. To what degree is debatable.

6.) The pressures on the Russian monetary system after the economic reform effort began in earnest must have been tremendous. As domestic prices began to rise at rates approaching hyperinflation, any attempt to severely curtail monetary growth would have resulted in a catastrophic depression. Tax revenues decreased as a result of the reform, and governments throughout history have used increases in the money supply to alleviate the pressures of declining sources of revenues, especially when faced with ever increasing demands for governmental services.

With regard to the second part of the question, monetary stability is extremely important, since any effort to repatriate profits or invested capital must ultimately be done through foreign exchange markets. Investors will continue to be wary of investing in Russia as long as there is uncertainty about the value of its currency, especially if that uncertainty has no way to be effectively hedged or offset through the financial markets.

Summary

The outcome of economic reform efforts in Russian and other communist bloc countries has important consequences for the United States and other major economies. If Russia fails in its efforts to remake its economy, the consequences for both the Russians and the rest of the world, in terms of political and economic impacts, will be substantial. As more information is obtained about these former command economies, one is struck by the enormity of the task of restructuring them into market economies. Very few analysts outside these systems were fully aware of the extent of their economic problems. The extent and pervasiveness of Russia's environmental problems have astonished Western observers. Because of the need for scarce foreign exchange, there is considerable pressure on the Russian government to allow multi-national companies access to its considerable resource base, and there is evidence that has already occurred in the Siberian forests.

Privatization has already changed the economic landscape in the former Soviet Union. In response to the new market-oriented environment, entrepreneurs have been setting up new businesses at a rapid rate. As your text mentions, price reforms have been pervasive, and the impact of allowing market forces to direct the allocation of goods and services and factor resources such as labor cannot be underestimated. The main problems seem to involve the transformation and privatization of the grossly inefficient larger state enterprises, breaking up those sectors of the economy where monopoly forces are still prevalent, and in achieving a stable currency. Perhaps it is not much of a surprise, but crime is a growing problem in Russia that will have to be controlled if reform efforts are to be successful.

Chapter 30
Economic Development of the LDCs

Overview of the Chapter

This final chapter briefly reviews the factors which are thought to have a major impact on the development process and provides an overview of the most significant problems facing the majority of the world's population.

After exploring the problems of capital formation, efficient resource allocation, institutional structures, demographics and human resources, international trade and tariffs, and export price instability, you should have an appreciation for the dimensions of the problems facing LDCs as well some possible solutions to these problems.

Capital, both public and private, plays an extremely important role in determining a country's overall level of output. Worker productivity is strongly influenced by the amount of capital per worker, and the capital invested in a society's infrastructure affects the efficiency of many sectors of an economy -- transportation, communications, energy, and health care services, to name a few.

Capital is in scarce supply in LDCs for several reasons: low income levels and correspondingly low levels of saving; large foreign debts and the siphoning of real resources away from the economy in order to service that debt; limited ability of LDC governments to collect needed tax revenues which could be used to provide public financing for both public infrastructure projects and private projects; and stable or declining amounts of foreign aid (in real terms).

LDCs face many institutional obstacles as well. Corruption and bureaucratic delays, all too frequently, stifle efforts to initiate new ventures and projects. For a number of reasons, LDCs have instituted price controls of various kinds, and the economic distortion associated with these controls and interferences with markets reduce the economy's overall efficiency and welfare. Given the desperate problems that face LDCs, it is perhaps understandable how these interferences with the market can occur -- subsidizing export markets in order to gain scarce foreign exchange, manipulating exchange rates to more effectively control exports and imports (especially of critically important goods and services). But, inevitably these controls and interferences result in distortions and inefficiencies and a lack of flexibility that ultimately takes its toll on the economy, decreasing economic growth and output.

In spite of the prominent importance of physical capital, economists are gaining more of an appreciation for the role and importance of human capital in the process of economic development. Both Germany and Japan had their physical capital more or less completely destroyed after World War II, but both countries regained their economic status in a comparatively short period of time, whereas far too many LDCs continue their struggle to achieve modest economic goals without much apparent success. The difference is largely attributable to the stock of human capital and the institutional frameworks within the two defeated countries. Many countries continue to emphasize secondary and higher education in spite of major benefits associated with primary level schooling. Here again, cultural and institutional factors play a more dominant role than strictly eocnomic factors.

One route to development has been to have an export sector act as an engine of growth for an economy. As the export sector expanded, its linkages with the other sectors of the economy would increase, generating jobs and incomes through the secondary multiplier effects of foreign spending for the economy's exports. Traditionally, the export sector has been in the primary sector, with export efforts being focused upon some particular primary product. Unfortunately, the export of primary products has a number of problems associated with it, including market price instability, technological substitutions for the product (e.g., synthetic rubber for natural rubber), income inelasticity in developed country markets, and commodity subsidies by developed country governments.

Unfortunately, developed countries have imposed a variety of trade barriers against LDC-manufactured goods, hindering them in their efforts to convert their economies from a primary product emphasis to one of valued added manufacturing.

Learning Objectives

After completing this chapter, you should be sure that you are able to:

- explain why economic growth is important.

- discuss the role that capital formation plays in the development process.

- describe the vicious circle of poverty and several of the ways that it might be interrupted.

- explain why development tends to create inflationary pressures.

- understand the concept of capital flight and the problems it can cause for developing economies.

- understand why taxes are difficult to collect in LDCs.

- describe the debt service problems that have arisen for many LDCs and the difficulties it causes for them.

- list some of the impediments that LDCs have regarding efficient resource allocation.

- discuss the advantages and disadvantages of centralized planning for LDCs.

- understand the impact of population growth on the development process.

- understand the role of LDC exports and imports in the development process.

- identify the major problems associated with exporting primary products.

Self Evaluation

List of Terms

Appropriate Technology
Brain Drain
Burden of Dependency
Debt for Nature Swaps
Debt Service
Green Revolution
Marketing Boards
Population Explosion
Vicious Circle of Poverty

For the statements below, fill in the term from the list above which provides the best fit.

1.) In many LDCs, _____ generate government revenue by paying domestic producers less than the existing world price.

2.) The _____ has made it difficult for LDCs to achieve real per capita growth.

3.) Many LDCs have surpluses of college graduates which, in turn, has resulted in a _____ to DCs where they can earn higher incomes.

4.) For a number of reasons, LDCs may prefer more sophisticated capital-intensive methods of production to ones which utilize _____ based on the LDCs' actual set of factor endowments.

5.) The _____ has made it possible for many LDCs to substantially increase their grain production but has simultaneously increased the need for water, fertilizer, and pesticides which may be in short supply.

6.) The desire by developed countries to preserve critical habitat and the massive foreign debt of LDCs have generated opportunites for _____.

7.) Rapidly increasing populations in LDCs have resulted in a _____ caused by the relatively high proportion of children in the general population.

8.) Heavy borrowing and high floating interest rates combined with lower export earnings have created _____ problems for LDCs.

9.) Low savings and correspondingly low rates of capital formation result in low output levels, low productivity, and, consequently, low income levels. This series of events has been described as the _____.

Problems

Comparison of Differently Structured Economies

Comparing the size of two different economies is a difficult task and in spite of the best efforts of economists, such comparisons should be cautiously interpreted. For disparate economies, such as the United States with a per capita income of $19,870 and Mauritania with an estimated per capita income of $480, it is especially difficult to make a meaningful comparison of the relative size of the two economies. For a low income country such as Mauritania, putting in place a sophisticated data-gathering agency to disseminate economic statistics is probably a luxury that they cannot afford. There certainly would be more in-home production of clothing and food which do not show up in official statistics. The unreported underground economy may be quite large, making it difficult to keep track of income that is earned.

Even if the data about the two economies were accurate, comparisons would be difficult because of the dissimilar structures of the economies. Each economy has a different output structure and a different set of relative prices. When each country's price structure is imposed on the other country's output structure, different estimates of their respective sizes are obtained. Obviously, it would be possible to make a comparison using exchange rates, but those are affected by speculation and a number of economic factors, including differences in interest rates, in growth rates, and inflation rates which may distort the results.

Another method of comparison involves a theoretical concept called purchasing power parity (PPP). Purchasing power parity occurs when the exchange rate equates the cost of similar bundles of goods in two different countries. For example, if a bundle of goods cost $250 in the United States, and a similar bundle of goods cost £100 in the United Kingdom, then an exchange rate of £1 = $2.50 would equate the costs of the two bundles (with the exception of transactions costs) and it make no difference whether the purchase took place in either the United States or the U.K.

In the following table, you are given economic data for two hypothetical economies. Calculate the relative size of the two economies by imposing each country's price structure on the other country's output structure and by using the purchasing power parity exchange rate.

	Great Britain		Sweden	
	Price	Quantity	Price	Quantity
Skis	£ 20	100	SEK 300	200
Cod	£ 3	500	SEK 30	80
Sweaters	£ 12	200	SEK 125	25
Computers	£100	50	SEK 800	20
Wine	£ 3	75	SEK 20	20
Haircuts	£ 4	600	SEK 40	75

(1) Impose Great Britain's price structure on Sweden's output structure, and compare the size of two economies on the basis of £s.

Great Britain's nominal GDP expressed in pounds would be £13,525.
(Calculated by multiplying British prices in £s times the British output structure)

Sweden's nominal GDP expressed in pounds, based on its output structure, would be £6,900.
(Calculated by multiplying British prices in £s times the Swedish output structure)

Based on this method of calculation, the Great Britain economy is about 1.96 times larger than the Swedish economy.

(2) Impose Sweden's price structure on Great Britain's output structure, and compare the size of two economies on the basis of SEKs.

Sweden's nominal GDP expressed in SEK would be SEK 84,925.
(Calculated by multiplying Swedish prices in SEK times the Swedish output structure)

Great Britain's nominal GDP expressed in SEK, based on its output structure, would be SEK 135,500.
(Calculated by multiplying Swedish prices in SEKs times the British output structure)

Based on this method of calculation, the Great Britain economy is about 1.596 times larger than the Swedish economy.

(3.) Compare the size of the two economies using the purchasing power parity exchange rate.

The cost of the two bundles in their respective currencies is £142 and SEK 1315 respectively, implying an exchange rate of £1 = SEK 9.26 would equate the cost of the two bundles. Converting Great Britain's pound GDP of £13,525 into SEK at the £1 = SEK 9.26 rate would yield SEK 125,249.12. That would mean the British economy would be 1.475 times as large as the Swedish economy. That same size ratio could be obtained by converting the Swedish GDP into pounds at that same exchange rate.

You are given the following price and quantity information about two economies. Using the three methods previously discussed, calculate the size ratios for the two economies.

	The Netherlands		Germany	
	Price	Quantity	Price	Quantity
Wheat	NLG16	50	DM10	500
Flowers	NLG10	500	DM10	300
Shoes	NLG50	150	DM30	600
Cheese	NLG30	200	DM25	800

(1) Impose The Netherland's price structure on Germany's output structure, and compare the size of two economies on the basis of NLGs.

(2) Impose Germany's price structure on The Netherland's output structure, and compare the size of two economies on the basis of DMs.

(3) Compare the size of the two economies using the purchasing power parity exchange rate.

An Increasing Absolute Income Gap Between Rich and Poor

For the LDCs catching up with the developed countries is a discouraging task, in large part because of the size of the income gap between high and low income countries. An example will illustrate the point:

The United States has a GDP per capita of $21,100, while Haiti has a GDP per capita of $400. Assume that the United States economy is growing at a rate of 3% per year with a population growth rate of 1% a year, implying a growth in per capita income of 2% a year. For the Haitian economy, assume an economic growth rate of 7% a year, with a population growth rate of 2% a year for a per capita growth rate of 5% a year. On a per capita basis the Haitian economy is growing more than twice as fast as the United States income per person. Note what happens over time:

Year	United States	Haiti	Absolute Gap in Per Capita Incomes	Relative Size of the Two Economies (United States/Haiti)
1990	$21,100	$400	$20,700	52.75 times larger
2000	$25,721	$652	$25,069	39.45 times larger
2010	$31,353	$1,061	$30,292	29.55 times larger

After twenty years of growth in per capita incomes, Haitian per capita incomes have more than doubled, while that of the slower growing United States has increased by a bit less than 50%. While the relative size advantage of the United States decreases, the absolute income gap between the two countries has increased from $20,700 to $30,292, an increase of over 46%! A discouraging process at best. Continuing the process into the future, we obtain the following results:

Year	United States	Haiti	Absolute Gap in Per Capita Incomes	Relative Size of the Two Economies (United States/Haiti)
2030	$46,590	$2,816	$43,774	16.54 times larger
2050	$69,230	$7,472	$61,758	9.27 times larger
2100	$186,338	$85,681	$100,657	2.17 times larger

The absolute income gap is still widening after 110 years, although the relative size of the two economies is down to a factor of two after that period of time. In case you are curious about when the Haitian per capita income will pass that of the United States, the changeover takes place between the 136th and 137th years (between the years 2126 and 2127) when both country's per capita income levels are about $317,000.

There is no assurance whatsoever that either country will ever achieve these levels of per capita income, but this illustration is useful in showing the inevitable effects of differences in compound growth rates and the long-time horizon required for significant differences to be made up.

The Role of Population Growth

To illustrate the effect of different population growth rates on per capita incomes, let's compare two countries with the same amount of total GDP and the same rate of economic growth, but different rates of population growth.

Assume both countries are able to achieve an economic growth rate of 5%. Country One has a population growth rate of 1% while Country Two has a population growth rate of 2.5%. Calculate GDP per capita in the space provided below.

	Country One			Country Two		
Year	Total GDP	Total Population	GDP per Capita	Total GDP	Total Population	GDP per Capita
1	$100B	10 M		$100B	10 M	
5	$127.6	10.5 M		$127.6	11.3 M	
10	$162.8	11.1 M		$162.8	12.8 M	
15	$207.9	11.6 M		$207.9	14.5 M	
20	$265.3	12.2 M		$265.3	16.3 M	
25	$338.6	12.8 M		$338.6	18.5 M	
30	$432.2	13.5 M		$432.2	21.0 M	
50	$1,146.7	16.4 M		$1,146.7	34.4 M	

What conclusions can be drawn from the table above about the role of population growth in the development process?

_____
_____
_____

True/False Statements

Indicate whether you think the statements below are true or false. These questions are designed to make you think about the concepts presented in the text. There may not be any easy clear-cut answers. Some thoughts about the answers are presented at the end of the chapter.

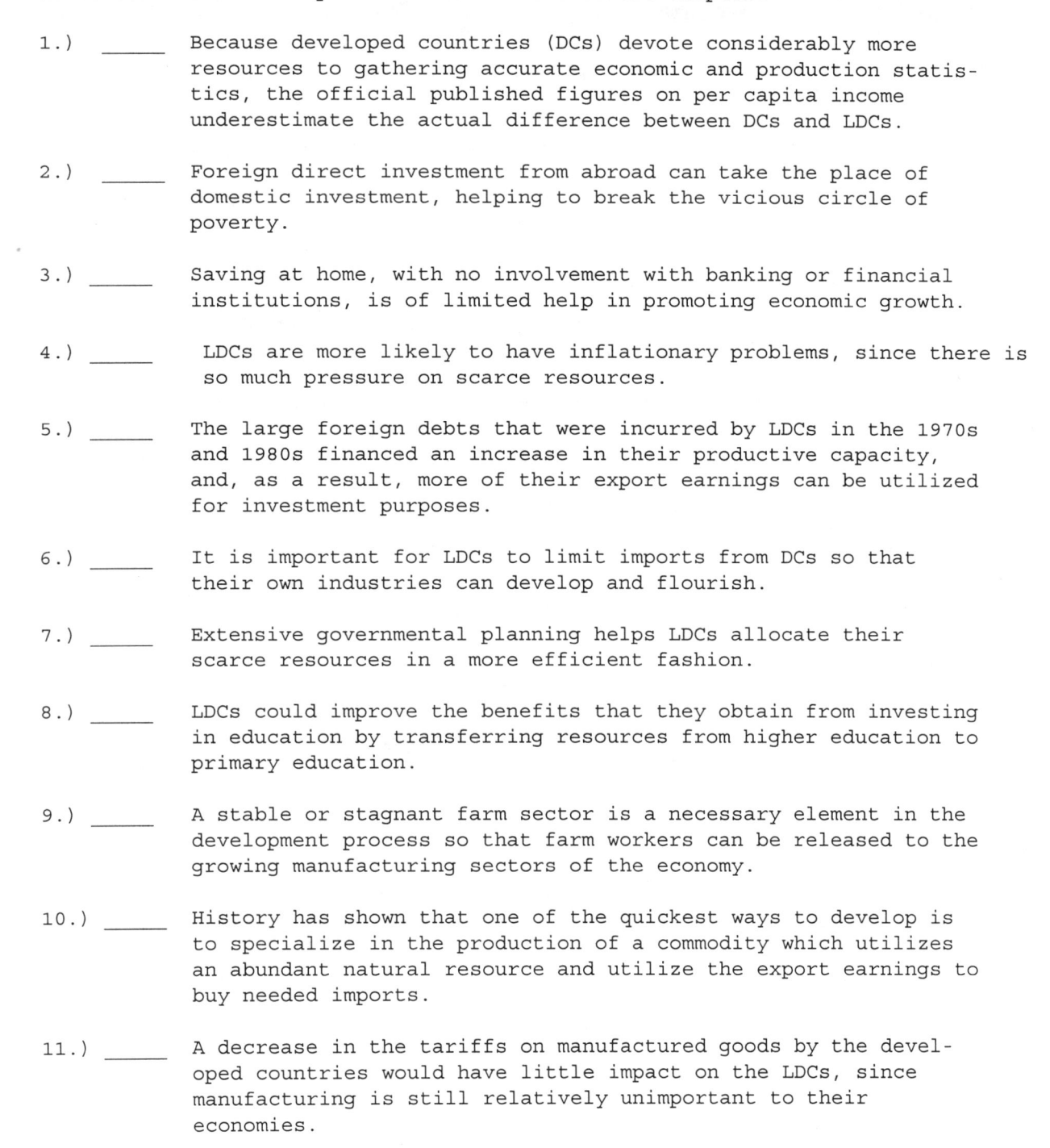

1.) _____ Because developed countries (DCs) devote considerably more resources to gathering accurate economic and production statistics, the official published figures on per capita income underestimate the actual difference between DCs and LDCs.

2.) _____ Foreign direct investment from abroad can take the place of domestic investment, helping to break the vicious circle of poverty.

3.) _____ Saving at home, with no involvement with banking or financial institutions, is of limited help in promoting economic growth.

4.) _____ LDCs are more likely to have inflationary problems, since there is so much pressure on scarce resources.

5.) _____ The large foreign debts that were incurred by LDCs in the 1970s and 1980s financed an increase in their productive capacity, and, as a result, more of their export earnings can be utilized for investment purposes.

6.) _____ It is important for LDCs to limit imports from DCs so that their own industries can develop and flourish.

7.) _____ Extensive governmental planning helps LDCs allocate their scarce resources in a more efficient fashion.

8.) _____ LDCs could improve the benefits that they obtain from investing in education by transferring resources from higher education to primary education.

9.) _____ A stable or stagnant farm sector is a necessary element in the development process so that farm workers can be released to the growing manufacturing sectors of the economy.

10.) _____ History has shown that one of the quickest ways to develop is to specialize in the production of a commodity which utilizes an abundant natural resource and utilize the export earnings to buy needed imports.

11.) _____ A decrease in the tariffs on manufactured goods by the developed countries would have little impact on the LDCs, since manufacturing is still relatively unimportant to their economies.

12.) _____ Worldwide pollution levels are not expected to increase significantly in the future, because increases in pollution associated with the LDCs will be largely offset by decreases in the DCs.

Multiple-Choice Questions

Select the "best" answer from the alternatives provided.

1.) The vicious circle of poverty can be best described as follows:
   a. Low incomes result in subsistence living standards which, in turn, cause low productivity and low incomes.
   b. Rapid rates of population growth tend to dissipate whatever economic gains are made, perpetuating low incomes.
   c. Low technology investment results in relatively small increases in output, thus perpetuating low incomes.
   d. With low incomes come low savings. The lack of savings results in a low level of investment which, in turn, causes low productivity, and with low productivity comes low incomes.

2.) A major reason why it is difficult to accurately compare incomes in developed countries and lesser developed countries is
   a. that many LDCs are unable to gather accurate economic statistics because of cost considerations.
   b. that exchange rates between currencies fail to reflect non-traded goods and services and the larger purchasing power of the the LDC currency.
   c. that exchange rates are biased in favor of the larger, more affluent developed countries' currencies.
   d. that it is virtually impossible to accurately compare such diverse economies.

3.) Concerning the role of savings in financing LDC investment projects
   a. government creation of new money is probably the least costly approach, since it does not involve the sacrifice of other resources.
   b. taxing LDC exports is a popular way of raising revenues, since the taxes are paid by the importing country.
   c. household savings may not be a reliable source of funds, because of a lack of incentives for families to save.
   d. as foreign aid has increased, it has come to be increasingly relied upon by LDCs as a source of funds.

4.) Which of the following is not mentioned by your text as a way of financing new investment in LDCs?
   a. Lowering taxes   b. Foreign aid
   c. The creation of new money d. Capital imports
   e. Lowering interest rates.   f. Domestic savings

5.) Saving would be enhanced in most LDCs with
   a. more extended family units.
   b. lower inflation rates.
   c. more social stratification.
   d. the prohibition of the export of domestic capital.
   e. none of the above.

6.) All of the following are a problem with taxation in the LDCs except
   a. lack of skilled governmental administrators.
   b. political corruption.
   c. widespread tax evasion.
   d. barter transactions.
   e. all of the above.

7.) With respect to the rate of population growth and the development process,
   a. a growing population means a larger labor force and greater economic growth.
   b. a growing population leads to a higher burden of dependency and lower rates of economic growth.
   c. a growing population leads to a lower burden of dependency and lower rates of economic growth.
   d. a growing population means more consumers and spending which stimulates the economy, leading to greater economic growth.

8.) Which of the following is an example of appropriate technology for an LDC?
   a. a nuclear reactor to generate cheap, widely available electricity.
   b. a labor-intensive shoe factory.
   c. a capital-intensive mine which develops a mineral which is abundant in the LDC.
   d. a steel-making complex.

9.) Which of the following is not a problem associated with the LDCs' export of primary products?
   a. Developed countries subsidization of primary products.
   b. Trade barriers on the importation of primary products into developed countries.
   c. Technological substitution for natural primary products.
   d. Income inelastic demand for primary products.

Discussion Questions

1.) Can you think of some primary products that are experiencing decreases in demand because of either changing tastes/preferences or because of the development of technological substitutes for the primary product? How should an LDC exporter respond to such changes?

2.) Why don't developed countries (DCs) do more to encourage exports for LDCs as an effective means of helping them develop?

3.) The inequities in global income patterns are obviously very large. How should the developed countries respond to pleas from the LDCs for a more equitable distribution of the world's income?

4.) Although some disagreement exists, many people believe that current consumption patterns of the world's population are stretching its resources and ecological systems to the limit, with some believing that some systems such as climate are already in the process of changing in ways that may result in large-scale disruptions of human activities and economies. What then, should be done about the future economic development of the large majority of the world's citizens?

Answers and Solutions to Problems and Exercises

Completing Statements from the List of Terms

1.) Marketing Boards
2.) Population Explosion
3.) Brain Drain
4.) Appropriate Technology
5.) Green Revolution
6.) Debt for Nature Swaps
7.) Burden of Dependency
8.) Debt Service
9.) Vicious Circle of Poverty

Problems

Comparison of Differently Structured Economies

	The Netherlands		Germany	
	Price	Quantity	Price	Quantity
Wheat	NLG16	50	DM10	500
Flowers	NLG10	500	DM10	300
Shoes	NLG50	150	DM30	600
Cheese	NLG30	200	DM25	800

(1) Impose The Netherland's price structure on Germany's output structure, and compare the size of two economies on the basis of NLGs. **In Dutch guilders, the Dutch GDP = NLG19,300, while the German economy valued in guilders = NLG65,000. Size ratio = 3.3677**

(2) Impose Germany's price structure on The Netherland's output structure, and compare the size of two economies on the basis of DMs. **In German deutschmarks, the German GDP = DM46,000, while the Dutch economy valued in deutschmarks = DM15,000. Size ratio = 3.07**

(3) Compare the size of the two economies using the purchasing power parity exchange rate. **The bundle of goods valued in Dutch guilders equals NLG106, while the German bundle costs DM75, implying a purchasing power parity exchange rate of NLG1.413 = DM1. At that exchange rate, the size ratio of the two economies would be 3.367**

The Role of Population Growth

	Country One			Country Two		
Year	Total GDP	Total Population	GDP per Capita	Total GDP	Total Population	GDP per Capita
1	$100.0	10.0	$10000	$100.0	10.0	$10000
5	127.6	10.5	12143	127.6	11.3	11280
10	162.9	11.0	14746	162.9	12.8	12725
15	207.9	11.6	17907	207.9	14.5	14354
20	265.3	12.2	21745	265.3	16.4	16192
25	338.6	12.8	26406	338.6	18.5	18266
30	432.2	13.5	32065	432.2	21.0	20605
50	1146.7	16.4	69726	1146.7	34.4	33364

What conclusions can be drawn from the table above about the role of population growth in the development process? **More rapid population growth rates make it more difficult to achieve economic progress on a per capita basis. If the population doubles approximately every generation, that means that economic output will have to double as well just to keep per capita income levels constant.**

True/False Statements

1.) **False.** LDCs have much more non-market production and activity (in proportion to their official measured economy) than do the DCs. With a much larger percentage of people growing their own food and making their own clothing, residents of LDCs have a significantly larger income than the official statistics indicate.

2.) **True.** Since LDCs have difficulty in generating sufficient savings to finance investment projects, attracting foreign investment capital can play a crucial role in breaking the poverty cycle.

3.) **True.** It is important that savings be channeled into investment, and financial institutions are the primary way this is done. If financial institutions have no access to savings, then the savings become a leakage from the income flow with all of the macroeconomic problems associated with leakages.

4.) **True.** Faced with so many different competing projects that should be undertaken and a limited ability to collect taxes, many LDC governments (like some of their DC counterparts) spend beyond their revenue means, and inflation is the inevitable outcome. Although inflation may seem like a relatively costless way to finance government spending, its consequences on the social structure and on investment activity are not conducive to stability and economic growth.

5.) **False.** Well, that probably was the intent of much of the lending that was undertaken in that time period. As it turned out, however, it was often necessary for LDCs to use much of their export earnings to service the loans they had received. Interest rates went up during this period, and anticipated earnings from the LDCs' export markets failed to meet their optimistic expectations.

6.) **False.** This is difficult to answer unequivocally true or false. At one time or another, many LDCs have felt that it would be preferable to promote domestic production of a commodity instead of importing the commodity from DCs. This is basically a policy of import substitution. It is easy to understand both the rationale and the politics of a policy like that; however, over time, many LDCs have found that it is difficult to match the economic efficiency and technological sophistication of the products available from the DCs.

Should an LDC produce its own steel if it can import steel at a lower price (and perhaps of better quality) from other countries? Less efficient and more costly domestic steel will cause other domestic industries to be less efficient as well. On the other side of the debate is the question of whether scarce and hard-earned foreign exchange from a country's export sectors should be used for a commodity like steel or utilized for commodities which they really cannot produce themselves at all. An interesting policy question.

7.) **False.** Another difficult question, since government planning certainly has a role to play in facilitating and coordinating development projects. However, the trend today is towards decentralized economies with markets making decisions rather than government planners. The market is uncontested as an efficient organizer of society's resources; however, there are instances in which planning can provide coordination among different projects which would be lacking in a predominantly market economy.

8.) **True.** A number of studies have shown that reallocating funding from higher education to primary education will yield widespread benefits to the LDCs. Not only is higher education significantly more expensive than primary schooling, but the market for post secondary graduates may result in either unemployment or underemployment. Learning to read, write, and perform basic mathematical operations may result in significantly higher productivity for a person who was previously illiterate. But that kind of education does not have the appeal that higher education has.

9.) **False.** A productive and dynamic farm sector releases much-needed resources for the rest of the economy. At a macroeconomic level, an efficient farm sector reduces the need for using scarce foreign exchange to import food, allowing the purchase of other, non-agricultural commodities.

10.) **True.** Abundant natural resources provide the basis for a comparative advantage which an LDC might find difficult to attain for any other commodities. The exporting sector is expected to function as an "engine of economic growth," with its growth stimulating the growth of other sectors of the economy through its various linkages and interactions. As is noted in your text, however, the export of primary products is not without its difficulties.

11.) **False.** Developed countries place high tariffs on manufactured goods and low tariffs on primary products, making it difficult for LDCs to obtain a market foothold in the area of value-added products. Making it even more difficult is the fact that effective rate of protection provided to DC manufacturing markets is even more than its stated level of tariff protection.

Even countries like the United States face problems in this area. An example: the export of logs from the Pacific Northwest to Japan. Although logging provides some employment and generates some profit, most of the employment, value-added, and profit accrue to those processing the logs, cutting it up into timber and making products from the wood. Is it in our national interest to allow log exports? An interesting and controversial question.

12.) **False.** The development of China and India will pose tremendously large environmental problems for our global society. As their incomes increase, their consumption patterns will start to become more like those in the DCs. Although the DCs are spending large sums of money on environmental problems, the size of the populations of China and India (to name just two examples) will dwarf any efforts on the part of the DCs.

Multiple-Choice

1.) d   2.) b   3.) c   4.) e   5.) b   6.) e

7.) b   8.) b   9.) b

Discussion Questions

1.) Natural rubber has experienced significant displacement by synthetic fibers. The per capita demand for coffee has trended downward as each successive generation shows greater preference for soft drinks. With certain exceptions, raw materials are becoming less and less important in the global economy. One possible strategy is for LDCs to try to broaden their export base to become low cost producers of secondary manufactured products (particularly those which are labor-intensive at some stage of production). DC tariffs then become a problem.

2.) As much as developed countries (DCs) want to assist LDCs, internal economic goals and political agendas must be attended to, and they tend to have more influence when LDC policies are being discussed. Domestic labor groups often oppose any favorable tariff treatment for LDCs because of the fear of domestic displacement by increased imports. Similar pressures to restrict LDC imports come from domestic producers.

3.) Many people would be reluctant to initiate larger income transfers to LDCs, given the widely-held belief that such aid often fails to reach the people who need the aid the most -- internal corruption plagues even the aid process. Aid in kind, such as grain shipments, helps alleviate hunger, but the increased supply of food lowers prices and harms LDC farmers.

Trade and investment flows from DCs probably offer the most promise, but, at the present time, trade barriers on manufacturing goods prevent them from making significant market penetration. Intense competition among LDCs in attracting foreign capital leads them into offering tax advantages and other incentives which diminish their economic effectiveness.

4.) This could present a terrible dilemma for society. If everyone in the world consumed energy at the same per capita levels as Americans, total world energy consumption would increase from about 11,000 million metric tons (mmt) of coal-equivalent energy to about 55,000 mmt (based on 1990 data from the *Statistical Abstract of the United States, 1993*). Given the concerns about global warming and other ecological problems that are occurring at present consumption levels, the dramatically higher consumption amounts are indeed sobering.

The developed countries can certainly assist in the way of providing proven technologies for reducing energy usage and pollution. The DCs are using energy more efficiently but have not committed themselves to reducing their resource use in a significant way. The DCs cannot tell the LDCs to put their development plans on hold because the planet is already at its maximum carrying capacity.

Summary

There is no more important problem facing the world than the achievement of basic economic goals by the large majority of the world's population. Yet, as is so often the case, higher incomes and standards of living for residents of the third world is not without costs -- in this case, environmental costs. With global environmental problems already capturing the world's attention, it is a question of some significance whether the world can support, in a sustainable fashion, billions of third world residents consuming resources at developed country levels.

The medium population projection of the United Nations estimates that by the year 2150, the world will contain almost twelve billion people, with the population of the current developed world almost unchanged at about one billion people. The pressure on resources and ecological systems of such a large world population can only be imagined. In a world with a steadily declining proportion of affluent citizens, the ability of those citizens to remain unaffected by conditions in the third world may be severely tested.

Foreign aid and direct foreign private investment represent the two major ways that developed countries can assist LDCs in breaking the vicious circle of poverty. Unfortunately, not only is the United States among the lowest donors in terms of per capita spending for foreign aid but the real amount of foreign aid granted by the United States has decreased and has been concentrated on a small number of countries. Foreign direct investment has been a factor in helping LDCs, but transnational corporations have been able to extract significant tax advantages as part of a *quid pro quo* agreement for locating in a host country.

Offsetting the efforts of the DCs to provide aid and capital are their trade barriers against LDC-manufactured goods. If LDCs are prevented from effectively competing with DCs in areas where they can add value to raw materials, then they are limited largely to the export of primary raw materials. Primary materials tend to be both price and income inelastic, which means that total revenues from the sale of primary products can vary a great deal from year to year, and, perhaps more importantly, primary producers do not share in the economic growth that occurs in their major developed country markets. Technological change and substitution always remains a threat to raw materials markets.

Tourists from the developed countries can provide an injection of outside income, and tourism has the advantage of being a low technology and labor-intensive sector of the economy. To assist the economy, it is important that the exporting sector (yes, tourism is an export sector) have as many economic linkages and interactions with the domestic economy as possible. Even tourism won't be very helpful if a significant proportion of the inputs required for that sector must be imported (i.e., importing fish from the United States because of greater quality and size control, as happened in one Carribbean country).

The debt crisis has been very troublesome for many LDCs, particularly those who borrowed heavily on the expectation of much improved prices and export markets which, for the most part, never materialized. Although many debts have been renegotiated, considerable sacrifices have been made in order to pay loan payments with hard currency (typically dollars). In more than a few instances, LDCs cut back on programs designed to help children, because that was the most politically expedient means of raising the needed funds. Debt repayment, which is usually considered to be a good thing, takes on a completely different dimension when it comes at the expense of the most dependent members of society.

Greater attention is being paid to the role of human resources and human capital in the devlopment process. Education, particularly at the primary and secondary levels, can yield large benefits in a number of different ways, not the least of which is the impact on females, their participation in the labor force, and the overall birth rate. A recent study, based on data from 93 countries, found a significant relationship between the fertility rate and female literacy.

Structural factors such as corruption are difficult to quantify but obviously play a role in the formation of new firms and in siphoning off needed funds from businesses, funds which could be used to increase productive capacity. Similarly, entrepreneurial spirit and the willingness to invest in long-term projects are important intangibles.